The Oxford Book
of Latin American Poetry

presente. Y esto todo es lo que se propondría como programa máximo -ya que

AMÉRICA tendría

que dar un

ARTE
INÉDITO.

En sí mismo -todo artista americano -tendría que librar la gran batalla que continuo se libra entre el

HOMBRE UNIVERSAL y

el hombre INDIVIDUO.

Barrido lo subjetivo -co-

The Oxford Book
of Latin American Poetry

A BILINGUAL ANTHOLOGY

EDITED BY

Cecilia Vicuña and
Ernesto Livon-Grosman

OXFORD
UNIVERSITY PRESS

2009

OXFORD

UNIVERSITY PRESS

Oxford University Press, Inc., publishes works that further
Oxford University's objective of excellence
in research, scholarship, and education.

Oxford   New York
Auckland   Cape Town   Dar es Salaam   Hong Kong   Karachi
Kuala Lumpur   Madrid   Melbourne   Mexico City   Nairobi
New Delhi   Shanghai   Taipei   Toronto

With offices in
Argentina   Austria   Brazil   Chile   Czech Republic   France   Greece
Guatemala   Hungary   Italy   Japan   Poland   Portugal   Singapore
South Korea   Switzerland   Thailand   Turkey   Ukraine   Vietnam

Published by Oxford University Press, Inc.
198 Madison Avenue, New York, NY 10016

www.oup.com

Oxford is a registered trademark of Oxford University Press

Library of Congress Cataloging-in-Publication Data
The Oxford book of Latin American poetry : a bilingual
anthology / edited by Cecilia Vicuña and Ernesto Livon-Grosman.
    p.   cm.
Includes bibliographical references.
Includes poems in various Latin American languages
with translations into English.
ISBN 978-0-19-512454-5
1. Latin American poetry.
2. Latin American poetry—Translations into English.
I. Vicuña, Cecilia.   II. Livon-Grosman, Ernesto.
PQ7087.E5O897 2009
861.008'0972—dc21   2008046301

Frontispiece by Joaquín Torres García,
from Nueva escuela de arte del Uruguay,
published by Asociación de Arte Constructivo, 1946.
By permission of VEGAP.

1 2 3 4 5 6 7 8 9

Printed in the United States of America
on acid-free paper

Contents

Acknowledgments

This book is dedicated to the Latin American poets and their counterparts, the translators—most of them poets in their own right. We are honored to present their pioneering work. These poet-translators represent a lineage that stands for a new sensibility that does not subsume the original into English but creates parallel poems that allow both poetries to interact. When available, we reprinted masterworks in translation but, to a large extent, we commissioned new works for this volume. This book is modeled on the anthologies of world poetry created by Jerome Rothenberg, such as his landmark *Technicians of the Sacred*; his vision spurred us to take one step further by including indigenous languages here. Many other translators such as John Bierhorst, Clayton Eshleman, Pierre Joris, Suzanne Jill Levine, Nathaniel Tarn, Dennis Tedlock, and Eliot Weinberger were important to us.

A new generation of poet-translators has now joined them and we are grateful to them for taking risks with multilingual and indigenous works that had to be translated from intermediate languages such as Spanish and Portuguese. They contributed greatly to the experimental and inclusive nature of our anthology, and several helped us with selections as well. In this capacity, we especially thank Rosa Alcalá, Odile Cisneros, Forrest Gander, Jen Hofer, Gary Racz, and Molly Weigel.

Ours was a long and often difficult process, enriched by the conversation and exchange with many poets throughout the Americas. We thank Charles Bernstein who brought us together as editors and was, as always, a staunch supporter of the project. Regis Bonvicino contributed a pre-selection of Brazilian poetry that became the basis for our Portuguese-language section. This anthology would not have been possible without help from colleagues and friends: Cecilia de Torres provided the first impulse; Andrés Ajens and Reynaldo Jiménez inspired us; Dwayne Carpenter, Soledad Fariña, Jorge Fondebrider, Silvia Guerra, David Jackson, Edgar O'Hara, Elvira Hernández, Luis Vargas Saavedra, Jussara Salazar, Paul Statt, and Lila Zemborain gave their support; Susana Haydu, Reinaldo Laddaga, and Jorge Santiago Perednik, with intelligence and deep knowledge, helped us with some of our most difficult questions; Nina Gerassi-Navarro was the extraordinary interlocutor she always is; James O'Hern offered unbound solidarity and vision; Jennifer Baker, Renato Gómez, Matthew D'Orsi, Esteban Mallorga, Jennifer Unter, and Macarena Urzúa assisted with research; Lisa Bernabei, Yolanda Blanco, Angela Ruiz, and Ian Watt helped with biographies; and Christian Coleman and Erica and Julia Rooney contributed long hours of typing.

Several institutions supported this project: SUNY at Albany, the Whitney Humanities Center at Yale University, and the Romance Languages Department at Harvard University; a special thanks to Boston College for its overall support of this book project and the funding of several research assistants.

Finally, we thank our editors at Oxford—Elda Rotor in the early period and Cybele Tom in the final stretch—whose insight and support were crucial to this enterprise.

Preface

Latin America has a complex and prolific poetic tradition that is little known outside its geographic and linguistic boundaries. Although a few poets such as Borges, Neruda, and Paz have become emblematic of its richness, many voices remain unheard. The brilliance of their work calls for a cultural context, a way to reconnect them to the vast contradictory universe from which they arose. Establishing those connections was our challenge as editors.

"Latin America" is a name coined in the nineteenth century, referring only to the last five hundred years but the historical depth of its culture, and the roots of its poetry are much older and are found on both sides of the Atlantic. In the Americas, written literature is two thousand years old and oral poetry may go back as far as ten thousand years. The fusion of the multiple languages and cultures gives Latin American voices a new specificity that is neither the original one nor that of the colonizers. To present the richness of Latin America's linguistic creations in a brief anthology demands a new organizing principle, a broader frame of reference to fully embrace them.

The continual clash of cultures and languages in Latin America, brought about by the European conquest, created a *"verba criolla,"* in José Lezama Lima's words—a verbal mix, a mestizo poetics resplendent with contradiction and linguistic experimentation. To present this dynamic mestizaje, or hybridity, as well as the continuity of the experimental tradition, became our goal in selecting work. To this end we included a great number of poets not yet well known in the English language. Readers may, therefore, notice a de-emphasis of the more popular poets, which should not be construed as a judgment of their significance but rather as a by-product of bringing attention to others not frequently translated. Indeed, many of the poets represented here have never been included in a poetry anthology in English.

To compile Latin American poetry from the standpoint of mestizaje is to reconstitute a tradition that has, until now, segregated poetic work into two isolated halves: oral and indigenous poetry on one side, and poetry written in the "official" languages (i.e., Spanish and Portuguese) on the other. This system ignored or marginalized poetic practices that, in our view, are at the core of a long cultural tradition. A similar kind of displacement took place in relation to experimental poetics that has been, for the most part, circumscribed to the historical avant-garde at the expense of a larger practice that dates as far back as pre-Columbian times.

In Western terms, a constellation is constructed from star to star. In the Andes, a dark constellation is the negative space *between* stars. The generative force of the cosmos, the space of creation, lies in the gaps between stars. This constellation, as well as the Mexican concept of *nepantla*, becomes a metaphor for the space between languages where mestizo poetry comes into being. Our anthology focuses on the creative potential of this undefined space where the vernacular inventions and hybrid forms are born. Latin American poetry often blurs the lines between the arts, overlapping into the visual arts, sound, performance, and mixed languages and genres.

The anthology begins with a pre-Columbian image of a female scribe, followed by the native version of the conquest. It maps the evolution of the fusion of European and indigenous as they assume their place in world literature. The selection is particularly aware of the great revival of poetry in indigenous languages as well as a vibrant experimentation in different languages. In addition, more female poets have joined a field long dominated by male voices.

We present two separate introductions. The first, on mestizo poetics, offers background to the creative principles underlying the poetic ideas of the ancient Americas and how they influenced later works. This is followed by a historical account of Latin America's poetry that connects the vernacular experimental tradition with its international context. The chronological presentation of poets by birthdate should allow readers to further contextualize individual works within different historical periods.

This anthology differs from most in that it includes many divergent poetries that may present readers with new and controversial perspectives. Our aim is to present the multiple poetics of Latin America over five hundred years in the hope that readers will experience a richer understanding of the whole.

The Editors
Spring 2009

An Introduction to Mestizo Poetics

Cecilia Vicuña

Latin American poetry begins with Malintzin, the Nahua slave girl who became the *"lengua,"* the interpreter and concubine of Hernán Cortés.[1] Forced to speak in the language of the conquerors, she invented a way of speaking Spanish with a native intonation that, within a few generations, became the matrix of mestizo poetics. Her ambiguous role in the conquest is widely depicted in the native accounts, where she is both a traitor who enabled the foreigners and a powerful mediator who influenced events. But in Spanish accounts her role is insignificant. The two ways of writing the story sets the stage for the future: in the course of the next five hundred years she becomes the *chingada*, the violated mother of all mestizos.

Mestizo—cur-dog, mongrel, mixed blood—has been a derogatory name viciously wielded since the beginning of colonization when mestizos were hated both by the indigenes they were displacing and by the foreign rulers attempting to keep power.[2] In contemporary Latin America, the battle for its meaning still rages. In daily life it is still an insult: racial prejudice prevents most Latin Americans who share Indian roots from recognizing their own mestizaje. In literature and politics it has two faces: it is used to subsume and efface the indigenous presence and, conversely, to honor the indigenous contribution to the "mestizaje" that epitomizes Latin America.

The Chilean novelist and critic Jorge Guzmán suggests the controversy stems from the tendency to confuse racial content with its cultural connotations. For him, all Latin Americans are cultural mestizos, and the creative energy behind the best artists emerges from this "mestizaje." But Guzmán's view is by no means universal. The mixed roots of Latin American creativity are readily admitted in the visual arts and in music but rarely in the verbal arts.

In this introduction I use "mestizo poetics"—a loaded phrase—to refer to works that emerged from the clash of cultures in Latin America, the dialogic exchange between two ethos—one based on separation and the other on interconnectedness. Fully aware that neither represents a monolithic reality, I call the former European and the latter indigenous. What matters most here is the different place poetry has in each. In the recent European tradition, poetry's role in society has decreased steadily. In indigenous societies, poetry still participates in all aspects of life. The tension between these two views gives Latin American poetry its force.

The first self-named mestizo, the sixteenth-century Peruvian historian Inca Garcilaso de la Vega, wrote for a Spanish audience but in a language meant to be read aloud to his indigenous constituency. Mingling sources and genres, his multivocal work *Comentarios reales* tells the story of the Incas from many perspectives. Four centuries later, the poet César Vallejo, also a mestizo, or *cholo*,[3] was inspired by Garcilaso's masterpiece to develop a new poetic language based on a mestizo syntax and intonation. Today, Vallejo is considered one of the great poets of South America. Yet his achievement and the many hybrid works that came between Garcilaso and Vallejo have not dispelled the prejudice that largely denies the acknowledgment of mestizaje in Latin American poetry.

To understand the complex forces at play we must return to the moment when the European and indigenous worldviews first collided. This was a clash so powerful that it destroyed Amerindian cultures, giving birth to modernity. The conquest of America engendered Europe's cultural and economic development. The Argentine philosopher Enrique Dussel calls this "the myth of modernity," "a particular myth of sacrificial violence" that rationalizes European "superiority" and its right to conquer, while occluding the rights of the "other." In his view, its emergence began a process of "concealment or misrecognition of the non-European" that subsumed the contribution of the peoples of Asia, Africa, and the Americas to world culture.[4] As a result, the destruction of native cultures was never seen as a loss, only a necessary by-product of progress—a view that persists today. Challenging this Eurocentric perspective Dussel proposes a new understanding of modernity as an evolving co-creation borne out of the interaction between Europe and the colonies. This insight provides the framework for our discussion.

In 1492, the Europeans did not arrive at a wilderness but to a densely populated land with advanced civilizations and, in the case of Mesoamerica, a literary tradition two thousand years older than that of Europe.[5] Within a few decades it was destroyed. The violence of colonization, war, disease, and enslavement wiped out more than ten million natives. Given the magnitude of destruction and the cultural shock of the forcible conversion to Christianity and systematic replacement of native languages with Spanish and Portuguese, it is remarkable that indigenous peoples and cultures survived at all. Today, five hundred languages are still spoken in Latin America. Although many are endangered, they enrich the whole with their diversity. Despite persecution, the indigenous actively participated in the co-creation of the emerging culture. Their creativity infused the new Latin America with an unacknowledged indigenous substrate, which became the basis for mestizo poetics.

John Bierhorst, noted translator and scholar of Native American literature, wrote that "the traditional art of the New World, has remained a whole art, capable of combining the aesthetic, the sacred, and the medicinal in varying proportions."[6] This capacity to adapt and change while holding on to its core values enabled the ancient arts to withstand the conquest by shifting and morphing into new forms. In poetry, the new forms evolved out of specific conceptions of sound, visual form, and space.

Sound

Sound has been associated since ancient times with the birth of the cosmos and the life force. In South American indigenous religions, sound participates in the creation of time and is associated with change, passage, and renewal. The Baniwa of the Brazilian rainforest say "sound is a byproduct of the first change, an excretion of Primordial Being." In fact, they see all forms of reproduction as a "communication of sounds." Language, poetry, and song are forms of reproduction. A song is a new form of being. Sounds open the earth, fertilizing fields and wild fruits. In a ritual context "songs effect the very changes they signify since their performance marks the time and places of passage in which culture renews itself."[7] With each ritual performance the creation myth is reexperienced. Through song and dance people enter the cosmic exchange of life and death. The exchange is healing as it modulates the shifting relations between people, the environment, and the gods.

In contemporary oral cultures this ancient model has remained vibrant through multiple local variations. In many regions this process was compounded by the arrival of African slaves. Each community seeks differentiation by developing its own sonic aesthetics, a formalism that carries ontological significance as sound is directly associated with mythical events.

The *Popol Vuh* of the K'iche' Maya of Guatemala is one of the few written records we have of the pre-Columbian view of poetry and song. In this creation myth, the world is formed in a performance by the gods: "They say 'Earth.' It arose suddenly just like a cloud, like a mist, now forming, unfolding." But the gods felt there would be "no bright praise for our work, our design, until the rise of the human work, the human design." The gods wanted to "be called upon, to be recognized" for they say "our recompense is in words." But not just any words, they wanted poetry, a reflection of their own creative performance; words uttered in parallel pairs to echo the male/female, sky/earth union of the cosmos: *"at uk'ux kaj, at uk'ux ulew"* (thou, Heart of the Sky; thou, Heart of the Earth).

The *Popol Vuh* is not just the story of how people and the world came into being, but it also explains the complex role that poetry plays in the dialogic exchange. Once the gods hear the poetry of the first humans, they are alarmed by its dangerous lack of humility. The gods decided to cloud the human vision, blinding them "as the face of the mirror is breathed upon." From then on, humans walked in darkness and prayed in lament, "Look at us, listen to us." To recover their lost connection they became dreamers and diviners "givers of praise, givers of respect." They learned how to read and write, creating books that are *ilob'al* (instruments for seeing), which were performed to cut through darkness and actualize the power of poetry in the moment.[8]

In keeping with the mythical view of sound, intonation of specific tones became the key medium for spiritual communication. Through carefully modulated tones in speech and song, ritual participants enter a resonant state of consciousness where mutual creation and renewal occurs. This realignment with the universe is an act of critical importance for the individual, the community, and the earth itself. Awaiting this aural nutrition, the earth listens and responds. Its well-being and fertility depend on the poems and songs performed for her.

In tonal languages (and most indigenous languages are tonal), tone is the basis of poetic composition. Complex accentuation and variations of tonality and syllable length play a crucial role, as rhythm becomes tone through repetition.[9] Today, Maya K'iche poets still specialize in sonic performances as Humberto Ak'abal does, combining song and spoken word in ways that echo the ancient Maya compositions created in parallel syntax and complex combinations of pitch and pauses.

Although the indigenous conception of sound is not well known in the general culture of Latin America, intonation matters because Spanish and Portuguese are spoken with a variety of indigenous and African accents. The rhythms and speech patterns of Chilean Spanish denote the underlying sound of Mapudungun; the Spanish of Peru and Bolivia reflects its Quechua/Aymara base; the Spanish of Paraguay is inflected by Guarani; the Spanish of Buenos Aires sounds like Italian as a result of nineteenth-century immigration; the Spanish of the Caribbean carries the presence of Bantu and other African languages, and so on throughout the Americas.

Since early colonization some poets have been fully conscious of the creative potential of local sounds. In the seventeenth century, Sor Juana composed mixed-language *villancicos* (Christmas carols) creating sonic snapshots of colonial Mexico. In the seventeenth century, Gregorio de Matos captured the street-talk of the city of Bahía. In the nineteenth century, José Martí, inspired by popular music, combined the legacy of the Spanish medieval lyrics with a Caribbean syntax and intonation. In the twentieth century, the process intensified, and a wider spectrum of sounds was captured in writing. Mário de Andrade *brasilized* Portuguese, writing in the *fala brasileira*, and Jorge Luis Borges *creolized* Spanish to "converse with the world" in a new *criollismo* (even though he later decried this early choice).

Other poets wrote of the special connective qualities of sound. In one of her most abstract poems, Gabriela Mistral meets "Poetry" herself, whom she names "The Woman of the Meadow." "Poetry" demands "colorless flowers" that the poet cuts "from the soft air" of fragrant sound. Alfonsina Storni finds in her own body "wells of sounds/ . . . where the spoken word/and unspoken word/echo," and Enriqueta Arvelo Larriva thanks those "who left me listening for an untamed chant."

Attending to tonal diversity, this anthology emerged from the desire to hear a different history, one that would honor poets who openly incorporated native intonations or mixed languages, and who were marginalized and left out of the canon. It is no accident that Sor Juana's *villancicos* constitute the most ignored and unappreciated portion of her art; they reveal her mestizaje. Respect for the work of Gregorio de Matos only came three hundred years after his death. Sousândrade's multilingual *O guessa errante,* a critical bridge between nineteenth- and twentieth-century poetics, is largely unknown in Brazil. The pioneering work of Gamaliel Churata, an Andean avant-garde poet who mixed Quechua, Aymara, and Spanish in his masterpiece *El pez de oro*, has yet to be fully acknowledged. Even César Vallejo was ridiculed by his peers and died in poverty.

With the industrial revolution came the increasing popularity of the newspaper. Its colloquial language and fragmented visual layout began to affect literature. Some key writers and poets, influenced by newspapers, disrupted established literary practices creating a new hybridization of genres. Two pioneering examples are Simón Rodríguez and Sousândrade. Haroldo de Campos observes that newspapers introduced the discontinuous alternative language of conversation and the prosaic elements that nurtured the "colloquial-ironic." This resulted in a series of transitional forms that bridged the gap between literature and popular speech. For the Canadian thinker Marshall McLuhan, the multilayered arrangement of newspapers approximates it to oral culture. In the Northern Hemisphere, Edgar Allan Poe was the first to apply this kaleidoscopic technique in the symbolist poem and the detective story. In these works, Poe displayed a new way of listening to the rhythm of speech, which in turn influenced Charles Baudelaire and Stephane Mallarmé.[10]

The impact of this aesthetic revolution was immediately felt in Latin America, liberating poets like Martí and Rubén Darío to hear the actual patterns of Latin American speech while unaware of the pioneering work of Rodríguez and Sousândrade. The Cuban poet José Lezama Lima wrote that Mallarmé restored the power of silence as the matrix of speech, returning to syllables their ancient identities as gods of nature. The Chilean poet Vicente Huidobro saw himself as "an echoing translator" of the powers of nature. In his contradictory manifestos, he proposes to create new realities through words and sounds. His *creacionismo* was inspired both by the European avant-garde and the shamanic language of the Aymara. He heard an Aymara Indian say "The poet is a God. Don't sing about rain, poet. Make it rain!" In the last canto of his long poem "Altazor," language becomes pure sound. His writing in turn influenced Mário de Andrade who expanded Huidobro's meta-linguistic approach, closing the gap between the oral and the written. Oswald de Andrade took the concept even further, turning the relationship between colonized and colonizer on its head by proposing a synthesis of the two: *antropofagia*. In these manifestos a new integration of poetry and theory emerges: the patriarchal European heritage is desacralized and indianness is reinvented.

Yet, even as these poets are celebrated, the indigenous undercurrents in their work are often ignored. For example, the shamanic component in Huidobro's manifestos is overlooked and Oswald de Andrade's famous aphorism, "Tupi or not tupi," is read simply as a pun on Shakespeare, forgetting that in Tupi-Guarani, one of the main linguistic families of the Americas, "the very word tupi means sound standing upright." "For the Tupi-Guarani, being and language are the same thing. Word means sound and soul."[11]

Visual Form

Many visual systems of communication evolved in the ancient Americas based on the interplay between writing, drawing, and reading. In these systems, meaning depends on the active participation of the reader. The best-known example is Maya logosyllabic writing where both writer and reader recombine signs in elaborate substitutions, multiple associations, and wordplay.[12] (See the discussion of Haroldo de Campos below.) Flexibility of meaning is important for an oral culture where memory is not seen as fixed but is an ongoing creative phenomenon, renewed and transformed at each reading.

The writing tradition of Mesoamerica was fully alive by the time Europeans arrived in 1519. The Mexicas cherished writing as a manifestation of higher civilization and were astonished to see that the Spaniards also had books. Soon after the conquest the Catholic Church and colonial authorities, threatened by native forms of knowledge, prohibited indigenous writing. Similarly, Maya books were burned and only four survive. Native authors, however, preserved the contents of some books by transcribing them clandestinely as in the *Popol Vuh* and the *Chilam Balam*. The church introduced alphabetic writing and used illustrated religious manuals to indoctrinate the Indians. But the writing of the Mexica, the "Painted Books," survived for a few decades as mestizo art camouflaged within European style and script. When colonial alphabetic script became dominant, Mexica and Maya writing traditions disappeared, having lost their visual component. In the pre-Columbian Andes, people did not write in the Western sense but recorded knowledge in khipus by weaving words into knotted cords (see later discussion). In the early years of the colony, khipus were allowed to coexist with European script, but by the end of the sixteenth century they were forbidden. Felipe Guamán Poma, one of the first native authors to adopt writing, imitated the structure of European indoctrination manuals but reversed their content in his famous *Coronica*, a thousand-page letter to the King of Spain denouncing the abuse by colonial authorities. The letter was composed by combining text and drawings.

After the suppression of indigenous writing systems, a different kind of visual writing emerged in the Americas; ironically, it came from Europe. During the Baroque period, in the eighteenth century, the acrostic, a European form of visual poetry with medieval roots, was adopted by the Viceroyal courts and widely practiced. In the late eighteenth century, Simón Rodríguez created his "painted ideas," a system of philosophical aphorisms in visual typographical layout that prefigures later poetical experiments. His purpose was to reflect his thought process as a way to empower the readers with a new consciousness of language. In the nineteenth century, the interaction between word and image was popularized by the art of the illustrated broadside. Imported from Spain, it became a vehicle for *poesía popular* in Latin America. In addition, the broadsides provided a meeting place for the oral and the written tradition where peasants migrating to the cities expressed their views. Posted on walls, or sold in the streets, the broadsides had a far larger circulation than "cultivated" poetry. We include examples from Chile and Brazil.

In the early twentieth century, José Juan Tablada integrated his studies of Aztec hieroglyphics and Chinese ideograms into a new ideographic poetry. Vicente Huidobro, in direct contact with the European vanguard, created and exhibited his "painted poems" in Paris in 1922. In the same decade Xul Solar produced watercolors that functioned simultaneously as painting, writing, and musical score. In the 1930s, Joaquín Torres García's *grafismo constructivo* united writing and drawing in a single system based on the parallel he saw between constructivism and Amerindian cultures. In the early 1950s, Concrete poetry emerged simultaneously in Brazil and in Europe. Out of the dialogue and exchange between these poets, an international visual poetry movement arose and is still going strong.

Concrete poets defined the visual poem as a kind of verbal "constellation in space." They regarded the page as a space where creation and invention happens simultaneously for author and reader. Concrete poet Haroldo de Campos describes it as "a coinformation": "the poet determines the play-area, the field of force, and the new reader joins in" to complete the poem. This idea recalls the ancient Maya writing system, now undergoing a revival of interest in Guatemala. Maya scholar Dennis Tedlock observes that the ancient Maya artists "created graphic art that liberates the glyphs from linguistic directionality, causing them to linger on the threshold between sight and sound."[13]

Tedlock's point suggests that indigenous Maya artists and poets are the forgotten forebears of today's visual and Concrete poetry. In these systems, words are not only writing but are also "seen as a painting" and "listened to as music." Poetic possibilities expand as the visual and sonic dimensions allow full participation of the reader. Visual and Concrete poetry are modern manifestations of indigenous tradition—tenacious in surviving the conquest and now the digital age—tracing a true mestizo trajectory. It should be noted that the Concrete poets of the 1950s were not conscious of this connection. The scholarship on ancient Maya script was not yet available.

Poetry in Space

Space is a conceptual construct specific to each culture. Poetry is not generally associated with space but in the ancient Americas, its conceptualization played a crucial role in the creation of poetry and meaning. In the West, space is interpreted as a boundless three-dimensional expanse. In the Inca cosmology, time and space create each other in a mutual interaction. For the Campa of the Andes, space and the qualities of earth and sky are perceptions inhabiting the realm of the mind.[14] For the Cashinahua of the rainforest, the world is a magical or supernatural place irreducible to schema; any attempt would be a dangerous oversimplification of significance and meaning.[15] In indigenous culture meaning creates space and is entangled with the richness of life. The creative potential of meaning is believed to be critical to the survival of land and culture. Therefore, diversity of meaning is maintained through variation and a multiplicity of media such as gesture, sound, dance, and weaving, in addition to the traditional media of painting, ceramics, sculpture, and architecture.

As mentioned before, in the Andes people did not write but wove meaning into knotted cords, the khipu.[16] The interaction between weaver and cord creates meaning. The knot is witness to the exchange. The word "Quechua," the most widespread language of the Andes, means "twisted grass." Language itself is seen as weaving, so they "wrote" with threads.

After the conquest, when new authorities seized the land, the khipu system of knowledge had to be destroyed because it represented the cultural identity of the people and contained the record of the communal ownership of the land. But the communal sense of space embedded in the khipu remained.

The khipu, and its virtual counterpart, the lines that connected the sacred geography of the Andes, opened up a sense of poetry in space that persists today in the indigenous fiestas held across the span of the Cordillera de los Andes. The main art form of the people, these fiestas are an important venue for oral and performance poetry. A multidimensional expression of mestizaje imbued with imported aspects of Christianity, the fiesta retains its fundamental purpose and is performed in reciprocity with the divine, as a *pago*, or payment for the gift of life.

In the fiesta, the community becomes the deity, reaching union in a transformation achieved through a specific sound: the dissonance between flutes or other instruments. "I understand all of it on two flutes," says César Vallejo. We include an oral fiesta poem performed in the Baile de Chinos of central Chile, in which many orchestras of musicians and dancers make a pilgrimage to a sacred site with the intent of healing the earth and the community. Several flutes are played simultaneously, seeking dissonance and the timbric creation of "ghost melodies."[17] The audience, comprised of community members, moves with the group participating in the cosmic exchange. Originally, the fiesta was for Pachamama, mother of spacetime. Today, the sonic aesthetics of the fiesta remain strictly pre-Columbian, even though it is devoted to Christian holy figures. The poem sung is a mestizo reoralization of the Bible, composed in *décimas* (tenths) that call on the deities to assist them in times of trouble, such as disease or drought.

The khipu, as the quintessential poetry in space, reemerged in contemporary art and poetry, in work created by Jorge Eduardo Eielson, myself, and Edgardo Vigo.[18] The khipu, like Tibetan sand paintings, embraces its own dissolution, the possibility of being reknotted, rewritten many times over. This vision of impermanence is what attracted artists to its aesthetics.

Other forms of poetry in space appeared in the cities not in direct relation to indigenous cultures but in dialogue with the European avant-garde. In the 1940s, the MADI movement conceived of visual poetry on a far larger scale, imagining a new cityscape for Buenos Aires in which words are as large as buildings. They distributed leaflets and wrote dictionaries, creating new concepts and definitions of space. Concrete poets in the 1950s opened the way for a more organic participation of poetry in society. Their works influenced the neo-Concrete artists of the sixties who expanded the concept of viable space creating sculptural poems and installations. The boundaries between art and poetry blurred, and this greatly expanded poetic space. Artists began to subvert, expand, and chaotically mix categories. "Catatau" by Paulo Leminski captures that impulse as he imagines the French philosopher René Descartes driven mad by Brazil, a country where everything gets mixed and defies categorization.

At the juncture of the 1950s and 1960s, many Latin American artists moved toward performance and began to produce works that interact specifically with place in a way that echoes the indigenous practices. This happened in synchrony with, but independently from, Europe and the United States. The Dadaist concept of poetic action found new expressions in different cities such as Caracas, Mexico City, and Buenos Aires. Here, in addition to the works already mentioned, we include the amereida, a collective of architect-poets that set out on a poetic journey traversing South America while creating poetry and installations in nature. We also include Raúl Zurita's poems written in the sky above New York City and on the desert of Atacama.

The New Context

Marshall McLuhan prophesized that the global electronic age would bring about a rebirth of oral culture. He wrote that orality breeds complexity while literacy breeds homogeneity. The nonlinear understanding of space-time characteristic of oral cultures is making a comeback in the new context created by the Internet and globalization. Latin America, with its immense diversity of languages and cultures, offers a prolific reservoir for the future. The richness of its poetry stems from the interaction between oral culture and literacy, which creates fertile ground for experimentation. The new historical developments point to a much wider participation by women and indigenous poets writing in their own languages. A wide range of migrant or nomadic voices add to its complexity. Dante Alighieri wrote in the fourteenth century that the spirit of poetry abounds "in the tangled constructions and defective pronunciations" of vernacular speech where language is renewed and transformed.[19] His vision resonates today with the faulty speech of migrants creating the sounds and intonations of the future.

The Place of Women

Some of the greatest Latin American poets have been women. Sor Juana Inés de la Cruz, Gabriela Mistral, María Sabina, and Violeta Parra are among them, but their true place in the history of poetry has yet to be fully acknowledged. The anthology begins with an image of a pre-Columbian Mayan woman scribe. This choice is meant to illuminate the long silencing of women. Just as Malintzin's linguistic contribution was ignored, our culture still demeans the creativity of women. The tradition of the female scribe was destroyed by the church that also forbade the education of women in the early days of the colony. Simultaneously, the destruction of pre-Columbian libraries left little evidence of women's knowledge. But images like the woman scribe and a persistent legacy of poems suggest that a powerful female poetic tradition existed before the conquest. Today, many indigenous communities still ascribe an important place to female wisdom and verbal arts. Examples include the Mapuche where most *machi* (shamans) are women, and the Tzotzil Maya female poets.

Sor Juana, who was the principal poet of the Americas in the seventeenth century, fought for the right of women to write and paid with her life. In the nineteenth century, Rosa Araneda from Chile stands out as the only woman poet of the *poesía popular* movement. Her writing challenged the passive role assigned to women at the time. At the turn of the century, a legendary group of women poets emerged, including Delmira Agustini, Alfonsina Storni, and Gabriela Mistral. Their work caused scandal and outrage but ultimately opened the way for other women to explore their experience in a woman's voice. Agustini and Storni were immigrant daughters. Mistral was the paradoxical mestiza, who embodied contradiction. A childless woman who exalted maternity, she simultaneously embraced and scorned her *indianidad*. Her extraordinary mix of biblical and Amerindian rhythms got her the Nobel Prize in 1945. During the early and mid-twentieth century other important voices joined them including Enriqueta Arvelo Larriva and Blanca Varela. By the end of the century, poetry by Latin American women exploded both in quantity and in creative energy, but their work still lacks proper recognition. The magnitude of this new writing will likely require many more studies to do them justice. The last section of the anthology reflects this changing environment and our desire that a joyful male/female, sky/earth relationship, as envisioned by Xul Solar in the work we chose for our cover, may soon take hold.

Migrations

Latin American poets have been on the move since the eighteenth century, often exiled by oppression or simply traveling to participate in international movements. In the early twentieth century, poets and artists such as Vicente Huidobro, César Moro, and Joaquín Torres García settled in Paris, the center of world culture at the time, and chose to write in French to better reach their audience. In recent decades, a large number of poets moved to the United States and some are experimenting with English in yet another iteration of the mestizo spirit. Their journey parallels the massive migration of workers from Latin America. In "The Exodus of the Gods" by Sergio Mondragón, the mestizo migrants *are* the gods. Shamed for their indigenous origin in their own land, they leave Mexico seeking not just better economic opportunities but to reclaim their human dignity.

The migrants' plight has transformed border crossings into a key image in contemporary Latin American art and poetry. José Martí, who lived in exile in New York, said that shame of the indigenous mother culture is at the core of Latin America's dependency, fueling the sell-out of natural resources and the cycle of poverty.[20] Gamaliel Churata concurs. It is no coincidence that the main theorization on this issue has come from the work of Gloria Anzaldúa, a mestiza born and raised on the border. She writes: "The U.S. Mexican border is an open wound where the Third World grates against the first and bleeds. . . . We, indias y mestizas, police the Indian in us, brutalize and condemn her." In her work, the negative space that defines women by what they "are not" (nonwhite, non-male), is transformed into creative space, by a will "to fashion my own gods out of my entrails."[21]

Her work indicates the difficult edge all mestizos navigate, the hidden rage and complex paradoxes that women poets often acknowledge. Blanca Varela speaks of "the flower that barks." Olga Orozco says, "I take my bundle of trans-parent/possessions with me/this insoluble fear." María Mercedes Carranza sees her own inner violence as a mirror to the violence in Colombia and constructs haikus named after the places where massacres have occurred. During Pinochet's dictatorship Elvira Hernández wrote "The Flag of Chile," a poem where the flag is alive and suffers the same indignities as Chileans. Circulating as photocopies, the poem became one of the emblems of the resistance movement.

A Poetics of Resistance

As a result of these continuous clashes, a "poetics of resistance" has emerged in Latin America. It reflects a subtle, but crucial aspect of the indigenous vision that sees opposing forces as an interactive whole where conflict generates new reali-ties. In aesthetic terms, the vision translates into a passion for the in-between where sound, visual poetry, and space meet. This multidimensional integration of the arts may be the lasting legacy of mestizo poetics.

The poet that fully realizes the creative potential of conflict is César Vallejo. Poor, illegitimate, and shamed since childhood for his mestizo origin, he wrote from his experience as Garcilaso had done four hundred years before. But his orientation was radically different. Vallejo searched for unity, the connect-edness of all peoples: "Oh exalted unity! Oh that which is one/for all!/Love against space and time!" and he found it in sound, in the intonation of his mother's voice. She held to the indigenous music while speaking Spanish. In "Trilce XXIII" the poet speaks *of* his mother, then he speaks *to* her. By the end we hear her voice as his when he says, "dí, mamá."

Poe, Mallarmé, and Baudelaire had already disrupted poetic diction by incor-porating silence and the dark side of the soul. José María Eguren understood it as a philosophical and formal lesson. But Vallejo added two more elements: the Andean aesthetics of dissonance, which had been invisible in writing until then, and the ethical dimension of compassion. This was a monumental achievement. In a single poetic line, his verbs and nouns fight each other as people do in Andean ritual fes-tivals, where dissonance operates through a clash perceived as unity (solidarity). In these festivals, dissonant sounds are experienced as "a single heartbeat."[22]

In sum, during the course of five hundred years, the concepts of sound, visual form, and space migrated from the ancient indigenous into mestizo culture. How-ever, throughout the period this influence remains an unacknowledged substrate of Latin American literature. Change began to occur at the cusp of the twentieth century when the aesthetic revolutions in Europe freed Latin American poets to hear the specific sounds of local speech.

Sound recovered its primary role in composition, and poetry performance revived. The historic erasure of indigenous visual writing met a new beginning when contemporary poets again began incorporating visual dimensions into writing. Poetry in space continues in both indigenous communities and urban centers.

Today, despite the onslaught of globalization, mestizo poetry continues to thrive. José Lezama Lima wrote that "a secret pulsation of the invisible moves towards the image, and the image desires to know and be known."[23] The reciprocal exchange within the image is thus transformed into a new understanding of life force.

A few decades before, Vallejo wrote that artists engender revolutions by creating "a cosmic hunger for human justice." The poet's work is to give shape to "the new chords that will produce those tones."[24] Placing poetry in the vibratory field where perception participates in the co-creation of the world, Vallejo reclaims poetry's full potential, echoing the early vision of Huidobro:

"Poetry is the life of life."

[Earlier version translated by Michelle Gil-Montero]

NOTES

In this essay, I expand on ideas first formulated in my lecture "Mestizo Poetics," delivered at the Next Society Symposium, St. Mark's Poetry Project, New York, 1990.

1. Malintzin—also known as Mallinalli, Malinche, or Doña Marina—was born in the Veracruz region of southern Mexico (1500–1527?). Her encounter with Hernán Cortés may have taken place in or around 1519. A Nahua speaker, who also spoke Maya, she quickly became his translator and concubine, but Hernán Cortés does not refer to her by name in his letter to the king of Spain. He calls her "la lengua . . . que es una India desta tierra" ("the tongue, who is an Indian woman of this land").

2. For a further discussion of the complexities involved in the use of mestizo, see María Josefina Saldaña-Portillo, *The Revolutionary Imagination in the Americas and the Age of Development* (Durham, NC: Duke University Press, 2003). Today the indigenes refer to themselves as *pueblos originarios* in Spanish and *First Nations* in English. The recent development of indigenous ethnic movements in Latin America affirms the right to particular ethnicities and a general refusal to be confused with mestizos. See David M. Guss, *The Festive State: Race, Ethnicity, and Nationalism as Cultural Performance* (Berkeley: University of California Press, 2000). And there are other issues. One clear example is the current struggle in Mexico, where the Zapatistas see themselves as struggling for justice for all Mexicans, while the government and its indigenous supporters attempt to portray their struggle *only* as an indigenous interethnic warfare.

3. *Cholo* is an unattested noun, possibly an Aymara word meaning "dog of mixed race" or "mutt." A pejorative term, commonly used throughout Latin America to designate an Indian, or a mestizo. *Acholarse* means "to be ashamed."

4. "Modern (European) civilization understands itself as the most developed, the superior civilization; this sense of superiority obliges it, in the form of a categorical imperative, as it were, to "develop" (civilize, uplift, educate) the more primitive, barbarous, underdeveloped civilizations" (Enrique Dussel, "Eurocentrism and Modernity," *boundary 2*, 20:3 [1993]).

5. Dennis Tedlock, *The Human Work, the Human Design: 2,000 Years of Mayan Writing* (Berkeley: University of California Press, forthcoming).

6. John Bierhorst, ed., *Four Masterworks of American Indian Literature* (Tucson: University of Arizona Press, 1984), p. 17.

7. Lawrence Sullivan, *Icanchu's Drum: An Orientation to Meaning in South American Religions* (New York: Macmillan, 1988), pp. 274–276.

8. All quotes from the *Popol Vuh*, translated by Dennis Tedlock (New York: Simon & Schuster, 1996). Elsewhere, Tedlock has written, "It was the gods who began the conversation with the first vigesimal beings, the same gods whose works and designs they were. The opening words of the makers and modelers, *Heart of Sky, Heart of Earth*, are written this way" (Dennis Tedlock, *Breath on the Mirror: Mythic Voices and Visions of the Living Maya* [Albuquerque: University of New Mexico Press, 1997], p. 5). And "From the beginning the gods wanted to make beings who could speak . . . after four tries the gods succeeded at making real humans, four of them. When they ask these four to talk about themselves, they get a poem in reply . . . a monostitch followed by a distich whose lines are parallel in both syntax and meaning" (Charles Bernstein, ed., *Close Listening: Poetry and the Performed Word* [New York: Oxford University Press, 1998], pp. 179–180).

9. For a discussion of poetic composition in tonal languages, see Carlos Montemayor, *Arte y plegaria en las lenguas indigenas de México* (FCE, 1999), and Carlos Montemayor and Donald Frischmann, eds., *Words of the True Peoples: Anthology of Contemporary Mexican Indigenous-Language Writers* (Austin: University of Texas Press, 2004–2007). For a brief introduction to the physics of sound, see Utah State University's Department of Physics, http://www.physics.usu.edu/classes/4020/soundnotes/sound.htm (accessed July 8, 2008).

10. Haroldo de Campos, "Superación de los lenguajes exclusivos," in *América latina en su literatura*, ed. César Férnandez Moreno, 15th ed. (Mexico: Siglo XXI Editores/UNESCO, 1996), pp. 280–281.

11. Quoted from Kaká Werá Jecupé, Tupi poet from Brazil, in interview by Ademir Assunçao, in *Tsé-Tsé* 9/10 (Autumn 2001), p. 99 (see English translation in *Chain* 9 [Summer 2002], p. 36).

12. The Maya logosyllabic writing system mixes logograms (glyphs that represent a complete word) and syllabic signs. It has not yet been fully deciphered, but the process is well advanced. As a system based on substitutions that can be semantic or phonetic, it can write any sound in the Maya languages. Designed to encourage word play, the system contains tendencies but not absolute rules. To pun in Maya is *sakb'al tzij*—word dice—and the art of writing and reading is oriented to find combinations that create sudden shifts in meaning. As Dennis Tedlock says, for Mayans, "it is only in the subhuman domain that wordlike sounds can stay in tidy, isomorphic relationships to their meaning" (Bernstein, *Close Listening*, p. 180). See also Miguel León-Portilla and Earl Shorris, *In the Language of Kings: An Anthology of Mesoamerican Literature—Pre-Columbian to the Present* (New York: W. W. Norton, 2002), pp. 5–6, 394–395. For a graphic demonstration, see the PBS NOVA episode, *Cracking the Maya Code* and companion Web site, http://www.pbs.org/wgbh/nova/mayacode/ (accessed July 8, 2008).

13. Tedlock, *Human Work*.

14. Quoted from Sullivan, *Icanchu's Drum*, p. 113. For Sullivan "space itself is . . . a manifestation of the meaning of existence" (p. 115).

15. Ibid., p. 128.

16. Khipu is "knot" in Quechua, usually spelled *quipu* in Spanish. An Andean recording system for keeping statistics, accounts, poems, songs, and stories by knotting colored threads, encoded with meaning according to position, twist, and color. It has never been fully deciphered. Originally, Europeans saw it only as a mnemonic device, but new research and digital technology is unveiling its interactive and mathematical complexity. See the *Khipu Database Project*, http://khipukamayuq.fas.harvard.edu/. See also Tom Cummins in Elizabeth Hill Boone and Walter D. Mignolo's *Writing Without Words: Alternative Literacies in Mesoamerica and the Andes* (Durham, NC: Duke University Press), pp. 188–219; Gary Urton's *Signs of the Inka Khipu: Binary Coding in the Andean Knotted-String*

Records (Austin: University of Texas Press, 2003), and Marcia Ascher and Robert Ascher's *Mathematics of the Incas: Code of the Quipu* (New York: Dover, 1997).

17. Pérez de Arce, *Música en la piedra: Musica prehispánica y sus ecos en Chile actual* (Santiago: Museo Chileno de Arte Precolombino, 1995), pp. 36–37.

18. Ernesto Livon-Grosman has interpreted this work as a khipu. See http://www.bc.edu/research/elg/trabajos/documents/neruda_y_vigo_2.pdf.

19. Dante Alighieri, *Literature in the Vernacular* (Carcanet, 1981), pp. 34–35.

20. José Martí, "Nuestra América," in *José Martí* (Caracas: Biblioteca Ayacucho, 1977), p. 27.

21. All quotes from Gloria Anzaldúa, *Borderlands/La Frontera: The New Mestiza* (San Francisco: Aunt Lute Books), pp. 25, 44.

22. Quoted from "Absolute (The Black Heralds)," in *The Complete Poetry of César Vallejo*, trans. Clayton Eshleman (Berkeley: University of California Press, 2007), p. 112.

23. "Después de la muerte de Bolívar, Simón Rodríguez sigue sumergido en la dimension incaica . . . sabe que la profundización de esa dimension será el esclarecimiento del espacio americano . . . sigue ganando las más decisivas batallas por la imagen, las secretas pulsaciones de lo invisible hacia la imagen, tan ansiosa de conocimiento como de ser conocida." In José Lezama Lima's "Imagen de América Latina," in Moreno, *América latina en su literatura,* 1st ed. (Mexico: Siglo XXI Editores/UNESCO, 1972), p. 468.

24. "Los artistas frente a la política" in César Vallejo, ed., *Literatura y arte* (Buenos Aires, 1966), pp. 49–53.

A Historical Introduction to Latin American Poetry

Ernesto Livon-Grosman

This anthology of five hundred years of Latin American poetry aspires to be both an authoritative tool of reference and an innovative collection of materials capable of mapping new territories. By including so many poems not previously translated into English, the anthology creates an encompassing image of Latin American culture, in both the national and the continental senses. Aware of this interplay between the local and the continental, we have created an anthology that does not separate our judgment of the aesthetic value of particular poems from our assessment of their historical importance. Throughout the anthology, we have emphasized the perspectives and themes that have contributed most to the development of Latin American poetry. Instead of presenting a primarily canonical selection of poets, we elected to be both inclusive and expansive, presenting a series of connected themes that make available to readers the many dialogues, past and present, that have engendered Latin American poetics as we know it today.

Indeed, our selection reflects the many debates and exchanges, large and small, that, over time, have defined Latin American poetry. More specifically, the poems presented here are both responses to discussions of poetic genre and responses to questions of race and ethnicity that originated in the seventeenth century. For it is in the seventeenth century that ideas concerning *criollo* identity and *criollo* culture (in Spanish America a fusion of indigenous and European influences) began to inform and define what it meant to be Latin American. As a result, Latin American literary culture is marked by socially conscious dialogue. This does not mean that this dialogue is always explicitly political, but Latin American poetry is, among other things, a product of the struggles for independence that resulted in different nation-states and, later, in the long-lasting effort to define itself as a new territory distinct from Europe.

From 1492 onward, with the arrival of the Spanish, and the subsequent conquest and colonization, the relationships and conflicts between the settlers and the indigenous populations resulted in the need to create a distinct cultural identity, one that reflected new historical and social realities. Many poetic practices existed prior to 1492, of course, and those were and still are, in many areas of the continent, a determining factor for local cultures. It is in recognition of this fact that we have included examples from the oral traditions that survived the conquest. These poems, which were sometimes preserved in Spanish via translations and in others languages by oral tradition (such as the works derived from the *Popol Vuh*), are now an integral part of a larger, continental tradition. Other examples include efforts to translate into Spanish languages that were hitherto unknown in the European world. Such is the case of Inca Garcilaso de la Vega, who in the sixteenth century wrote about the khipu—the system of ropes and knots devised by the Inca as a method of historical record keep-ing—and its importance in Inca culture. The khipu has since become a point of departure for rethinking the relation between old and new traditions. We see this quite explicitly in the context of the twentieth-century Latin American vanguard movements, many of which were interested in the possibility of dis-covering an original language, and in some cases linking the new and the old as integral aspects of their experimental practices. Visual poetry provides one such interesting example, as seen in the "object-poem" of Edgardo Antonio Vigo, who incorporated the khipu into his work to establish a connection between the aboriginal oral tradition and his own experimental poetry. The process of mestizaje, or mixing, is a term that has a long tradition, and as a creative force it continues to make history an important element for the understanding of modern Latin American poetry.

In the tumultuous years between 1804 and 1860, when colonial Spanish America was succeeded by independence (with the exception of Cuba and Puerto Rico), we see that political struggle mirrored by a literary struggle to for-mulate a uniquely Latin American poetics. The era of Latin American Romanti-cism, the influence of the French Revolution and the Enlightenment as cultural entities were decisive factors for the independence movements. The split with Europe gave rise to two basic themes: that of independence itself and the cel-ebration of regional *criollo* (Creole) literatures.

Criollo language and culture steadily gained prominence. In Argentina, the work of José Hernández, Hilario Ascasubi, and others, though vastly dif-ferent from each other, together ushered in a new cultural era and a new form of poetry emerged, one inspired by the folk traditions of the Argentine gauchos. With its images of a new territory and a new language, the *gauch-esque* soon came to be regarded as Argentina's national poetry and influ-enced ongoing debates about whether to identify the new nation with the urban or the rural, the cosmopolitan or the indigenous. This became all the more evident in the context of the debates involving cosmopolitan and indigenous cultures, the former being associated with the metropolis and the other with the life of the land. The question of the urban versus the rural went to the heart of discussions about the identity of these new nations, as did the new local languages that gaucho poetry helped to mold. The *gauche-sque* paved the way for later poets, among them Leónidas Lamborghini, to use the vernacular as a way of recovering the rural culture while, at the same time, using parody to transcend nationalism.

Toward the end of the nineteenth century, José Martí entered the liter-ary and political arena. One of the most politically committed and visionary poets of his day, he is one of Latin America's most esteemed intellectuals and the author of "Nuestra America," an essay that deals with the dominance of the United States in the region and the importance of creating a strong sense of community among the different nations of Latin America. A foundational writer for later postcolonial critics, Martí would become for many a way of bridging Romanticism and *modernismo*.

Between 1880 and 1920, Latin America began to assume its modern appearance: nation-states and internal regions were established and defined, borders were drawn, and the central states came into being. In this era of modernization, France emerged an important point of reference while Spain and Portugal ceased to have the homogenizing influence they had during colonial times. Once again, a new poetic movement took hold, led by Rubén Darío. *Modernismo*, best described as Spanish America's interpretation of Symbolism, effectively infused its poetics with a strong sense of continental identity. Largely for that reason, it was a pan-American cultural movement, one of the first, with Darío's influence extending far and wide. He became intimately associated with Argentine cultural circles, and, although Nicaraguan, worked for the Argentine embassy as a representative to Europe. Such a thing would not have been possible were it not for the prestige that poetry had in the public sphere, and due to the fluidity of the concept of national identity in Latin America—a situation that allowed for greater communication between different cultural regions.

The early twentieth century belongs to the Latin American vanguard movements, many of which rejected *modernismo* for being a mere imitation of European culture. But Europe, in particular French surrealism and Anglo-American modernism, were important points of reference for the Latin American vanguards. With astonishing speed, Latin American avant-garde poets set about appropriating and redefining these foreign models, fulfilling in many respects a process started by *modernismo*. The Brazilians Mario de Andrade and Oswald de Andrade are excellent examples of this transformational process, which exalted the vernacular and culture of the region while, at the same time, cultivating the cosmopolitan perspective that was so important to *modernismo*. Oswald de Andrade coined the term "antropofagia cultural" to describe a poetics in which Latin America cannibalizes and metabolizes European culture. The result, he argued, was a wholly new Latin American cultural body. In another area of vanguard poetry, Oliverio Girondo's *En la masmédula* provided an important example of the ways in which content could be seen as an extension of form, reversing the notion of experimental poetry as a purely formal practice.

This tradition of rupture, to use a phrase coined by Mexican poet Octavio Paz to characterize the experimental tradition, received added impetus in 1959, the year the Cuban Revolution succeeded. It is in 1959 that artists and intellectuals renewed their commitment to the pan-American cultural project. Ernesto Cardenal, Coronel Urtecho, Roque Dalton, and Juan Gelman, among others, looked to the vernacular as they searched for a poetics that could be written and read by everyone and cultivated a discursive transparency that echoed the urgency of the political situation at that time. With the advent of this committed poetics and the rising of figures such as Roque Dalton and Ernesto Cardenal, poetry achieved a new level of popularity creating a distinct separation: a "before" and "after" the Cuban Revolution. The denunciation of authoritarian regimes as well as the causes and effects of social inequality became dominant themes of the post–Cuban Revolution era and constitute some of the forces that redefined notions of high and low culture.

Other poetic expressions also emerged during this era, certainly one of the most productive and influential cultural moments in the history of Latin America. Beginning in the 1950s, the Brazilian "Noigandres" group redefined Concrete poetry, a movement that united writers and visual artists by using new graphic designs that had previously been seen only in the context of advertisement. Other writers, Violeta Parra among them, focused on the recovery of Latin American folklore, while poets such as Nicanor Parra reinvented Dadaism through a poetics of the absurd. An era of great eclecticism, it is impossible to encapsulate with a single work or image. All of these practices, however, were affected by political events and by the increasing influence of mass media as well as new technology. Poets began to incorporate multimedia techniques into their works and to demonstrate a greater interest in performance and the subversion of the public stage through spectacle, such as the "happenings" organized by the Instituto Di Tella in Buenos Aires during the 1960s. In some instances, revolutionary poetics evolved into more academic models, as was the case with the brothers Augusto and Haroldo de Campos, who strove to create a visual poetics that would reaffirm the autonomy of art and poetry. However different these poetic movements, they were all fueled by the same spirit of renovation and an interest for accessibility and widening distribution of poetry to the public.

The political and cultural upheavals of the 1960s and 1970s were followed by two decades of authoritarianism throughout much of Latin America. Military regimes sought to put an end to left-wing insurgency and the progressive nationalization of the economy that came about due to the ever-expanding economic and cultural dominance of the United States. During this period of acute political repression, civil rights were suspended and the media and other areas of culture censored. But unlike essays and fiction, which were heavily censored under the dictatorships, poets managed to continue publishing and circulating their works. This was due in part to the fact that poetry was disseminated primarily through a small press distribution system that made room for underground and less visible ways of reaching its readers. The Argentine journal *XUL*, for example, published poets as diverse, divergent, and subversive as the Neo-Baroque Néstor Perlongher, the visual experimentalist Jorge Lépore, the sound and performance poetics of the Paralengua group, the Dadaist revivalist poetics of Emeterrio Cerro, and the editor himself of the journal, Jorge Santiago Perednik.

With the slow restoration of democracy in the 1980s, a new type of poetry emerged, one informed by progress in women's rights and the gay liberation movement. Cultural activists avoided oppositional politics and adopted a more flexible critical stance. Emphasis on identity politics, which largely replaced the universalism of the populist poetics of previous decades, resulted in a fascination with autobiographical voices and a sophisticated elaboration of the first person. The Mexicans Gerardo Déniz and Coral Bracho and the Cuban Reina María Rodríguez are examples of this fusion between the private and the public, the experimental and the lyrical. The degree of richness and the multiplicity of voices make this era one of the most vital and interesting since the restoration of democracy in the 1980s.

We consider this anthology, therefore, to be a work that documents the collective interest in language that has shaped the course of Latin American poetry for the past five hundred years. Although we are dealing with a vast amount of material, we have found it possible to identify common aesthetic practices. In making our selection, we found that Latin American poetry as a whole can be viewed as a system of themes and strategic symmetries. Symmetry, in this case, is defined in terms of combinations and patterns that have remained constant despite shifting historical events.

One of the constants of Latin American poetry is the effort to establish and develop a vernacular language, one that is clearly rooted in the local and aware of the newness of America. Hence the constant efforts to adapt non-American models (European, African, Asian) to what José Lezama Lima calls the American experience. Examples of this are found in the *villancicos* of seventeenth-century Mexican poet Sor Juana Inés de la Cruz that incorporate verses in Náhuatl. We also see this process at work in the poetry of contemporary Chilean poet Elikura Chihuailaf, who writes in Mapungdun. There is also the work of cultural translation undertaken by *modernismo* in general, and in works by Rubén Darío in particular. The Argentine poet Olga Orozco would later exhibit a similar interest in the linguistic and aesthetic re-elaboration of French surrealism. And again we see this mixing of languages and cultures in popular idioms that characterize the poetry of the *Cordel*, a type of poetry in which poets string poems together and hang them between two posts in popular markets and streets. Xul Solar's neo-Creole, an essentially pan-American language, offers yet another example. For more than five hundred years, Latin American poets have consistently used this interest in the vernacular to elaborate their aesthetic practices, and they have done so while being interested in other languages. This is a process that is not so easily separated from the hundreds of years of translation practices that are an integral part of many cultural encounters. In fact, cultural and linguistic translation are the primary components of Latin American culture beginning with the first European contact and continuing until the present, when it is possible to walk into so many Latin American bookstores and find oneself surrounded by Spanish and Portuguese translations from so many languages.

In recognition of this tradition of translation, we sought throughout the anthology to emphasize the importance of mestizaje in Latin American poetry. Mestizaje is a cultural process that grew out of the conflicts of the Conquest and, initially, as in the work of the Inca Garcilaso, was an attempt to negotiate ethnic differences. Much later, at the end of the nineteenth century, it becomes possible to speak of mestizaje in terms of class differences and in a nationalistic sense. Given the impact that the arrival of immigrants had on Latin Americans' sense of their own identities, traditional definitions of what it meant to be *criollo* began to exceed regional definitions. The pan-Americanism of the 1960s and 1970s offers a good example of this multiethnic, trans-American tendency.

One manifestation of this fusion of languages and cultures is the neo-baroque, which was a practice that grew out of an appropriation of the Spanish baroque to become an authentically Latin American aesthetic. This came about, in great part, because José Lezama Lima, among others, developed even further the concept of an American neo-baroque, one that would fuse European and *criollo* cultural referents and take the original Spanish form to a new level of complexity and diversity. Other well-known practitioners include the Cubans Severo Sarduy and José Kozer, the Argentine Néstor Perlongher, and the Brazilian Josely Vianna Baptista—all poets who combined the concept of mestizaje with experimental poetics.

America in the continental sense is thus not only a product of the direct exchanges and conflicts among the parts of the whole but also an ongoing dialogue of what defines, in a complete sense, that which we call the Americas. This dialogue, carried out in Latin American poetics, makes possible an interpretation that connects common interests that are, in general, defined in contrast to Europe and that, at times, surpass what is strictly Latin American. In a broad sense, we can speak of this process as a work of translation, diffusion, and inclusion of many influences, national and otherwise. Cultural, as well as strictly linguistic, translation is a logical extension of this work of fusion that defines the last five hundred years of Latin American poetry.

Translation here should be understood as a form of writing and interpretation. The Canadian poets Steve McCaffery and bpNichol have written on the importance of keeping in mind the translator as "a conscious generative force." As they point out, we see how every poetic turn we face involves the historical time of the poet and also the very work in progress that is implicit in the translation of every poem—a multilayer system of references that point to the "original" poem and its circumstances, as much as to the translator's work.

We see Latin American poetry as an evolution that is unique in its complexity and its commitment to remain open to experimental practices and the weaving of old and new traditions. The richness and expansiveness of Latin American cultures, past and current, their extraordinary range of voices and registers is all present in its poetry.

[Translated by Kathryn Kopple]

The Oxford Book
of Latin American Poetry

Anonymous Maya Scribes (Seventh–Tenth Century, Mesoamerica)

Excerpt from **Maya Codex**

Top: The scribal god Pawahtún, codex-style vase, eighth century; *Middle*: Lady scribe, Late Classic, 600–900 A.D., Yucatán; *Bottom*: Pawahtún, codex-style vase

Anonymous (Sixteenth Century, Mexico, Aztec Nahuatl)

Recorded by Bernardino de Sahagún, a Franciscan missionary, in his manuscript of 1528, this fragment of an anonymous Nahuatl poem recounting the Spanish conquest of Tenochtitlan was translated from the Spanish versions of Miguel Angel Asturias in *Poesia precolombina*, and Angel M. Garibay K. in *La literatura de los aztecas*.

Excerpt from And All Was Destroyed / Auh ixquichi in topa michiuh / Después de la derrota

David Guss, trans.

> . . . All this came to pass with us.
> We saw it, we marveled at them.
> We saw ourselves anguished with a mournful fate.
> Broken arrows lie upon the roads,
> hair is scattered everywhere.
> The houses are roofless,
> their walls run red.
> Maggots swarm along the streets and plazas,
> and on the walls brains are splattered.
> Red are the waters, as if with dye,
> and when we drink from them, it's as if
>   we were drinking water of saltpeter.
> In our grief we beat the walls of adobe,
> and our only legacy was a net of holes.
> On our shields was our protection:
> but not even shields can hold such emptiness!
> We have eaten sticks of firewood,
> we have chewed salted grass,
> adobe stones, mice, dust ground from earth,
>   even the maggots.
> All this came to pass with us.
>
> Meat we never tasted,
> It was placed upon the fire.
> But when it was done
> they plucked it off
> and ate it by the flames.
>
> A price was put on us.
> The price of a boy, a priest,
> of a child, a woman.
> Enough: we were hardly worth anything at all
> just two handfuls of corn,

ten tortillas filled with flies.
That was our price,
just twenty loaves of salt grass.

Gold, jade, fabulous cloth,
quetzal feathers,
All that which was of value
was now worth nothing at all . . .

Y todo esto pasó con nosotros./ Nosotros lo vimos,/ nosotros lo
admiramos./ Con esta lamentosa y triste suerte/ nos vimos angustiados./
En los caminos yacen dardos rotos,/ los cabellos están esparcidos./
Destechadas están las casas,/ enrojecidos tienen sus muros./ Gusanos
pululan por calles y plazas,/ y en las paredes están salpicados los sesos./
Rojas están las aguas, están como teñidas,/ y cuando las bebimos,/ es
como si bebiéramos agua de salitre./ Golpeábamos, en tanto, los muros de
adobe,/ y era nuestra herencia una red de agujeros./ Con los escudos fue
su resguardo,/ pero ni con escudos puede ser sostenida su soledad./ Hemos
comido palos de colorín,/ hemos masticado grama salitrosa,/ piedras de
adobe, lagartijas,/ ratones, tierra en polvo, gusanos . . . // Comimos la
carne apenas,/ sobre el fuego estaba puesta./ Cuando estaba cocida la
carne,/ de allí la arrebataban,/ en el fuego mismo, la comían.// Se nos puso
precio./ Precio del joven, del sacerdote,/ del niño y de la doncella./ Basta:
de un pobre era el precio/ sólo dos puñados de maíz,/ sólo diez tortas de
mosco;/ sólo era nuestro precio/ veinte tortas de grama salitrosa.// Oro,
jades, mantas ricas,/ plumajes de quetzal,/ todo eso que es precioso/ en
nada fue estimado . . .

Auh ixquichi in topa michiuh/ in tiquitaque in ticmahuizoque/ in techocti
in tetlaocolti/ inic titlaihyohuique.// Auh oc in otlica omitl xaxamantoc/
tzontli momoyauhtoc/ calli tzontlapouhtoc/ calli chichiliuhtoc//
Ocuilti moyacatlamina otlica/ auh incaltech hahalacatoc in quatextli./
Auh in atl za yuhque chichiltic za yuhque tlapatlatl/ ca yuh tiquique
tiquia tequixquiatl.// Auh oc in atl tiquique tequixquiatl xantetl ipan
tlatetzotzontli/ in atlacomolli za teneneixcahuil/ chimaltitlan in pieloya/
in oc nen aca moteiccequiliznequi za chimaltitla.// Tiquaque in tzonpan
quahuitl/ in tequixquizacatl/ in xantetl in cuetzpalli quimichi/ teutlaquilli.
Ocuilli.// Tetonetechquaque/ in iquac tlepan quimontlaliaya/ i ye icuicic
inacayo/ uncan con no/ yuh tleco quiquaya.// Auh in topatiuh nochiuh/ in
ipatiuh nochiuh in telpochtli/ in tlamacazqui in ipochtli in piltzintli/ i ye
ixquich macehualli in ipatiuh mochiuh/ za omatecohctli tlaolli za matlactli
axaxayaca tla tlaxcalli/ tequixquizacatl tlaxcalli za canpohualli topatiuh
mochiuh.// In teucuitlatl in chalchihuitl/ in quachtli in quetzalli/ i ye
ixquich tlazotli/ auctle ipa motac za tetepeui . . .

Anonymous (Sixteenth Century, Mexico, Aztec Nahuatl)

The chief source of Aztec poetry, the *Codex Cantares Mexicanos* was composed in the early post–Conquest period between 1550 and 1581 by Mexica poets from the city-state of Mexico. It consists of ninety-one songs "taken from the lips of native informants" collected by an acculturated Indian, probably in the service of Fray Bernardino de Sahagún. They are part of the ghost-song ritual, a musical performance in which warrior-singers summon ancestral ghosts in order to vanquish enemies. In response to the music, ghost warriors from paradise come "scattering," "raining," or "flying" to earth in the form of flowers or birds. When the singer intones their praises he becomes, metonymically speaking, the songs or "flowers" emanating from the sky, the source of all music. Their language is Classical Nahuatl, coded in a poetic diction accessible only to knowledgeable elders as a way to hide from missionaries.

Excerpt from Codex Cantares Mexicanos, XLIV-B-Folio 27-27B: Just Thus It Will Come Back In / Tico Toco Toco tiquitiquiti quiti quito. Can ic mocueptiuh.

John Bierhorst, trans.

"As a varicolored ear of flower corn I come to life." A multitude of maize flowers, spilling forth, come blooming: they arrive before the face of our mother, Santa María.

Plume-water turquoise gems are singing in these waters: they're sprouting. "I am a creature of the Only Spirit, God. I am his creation." They've arrived!

Your hearts are alive in this place of paintings. Upon this mat of pictures You are singing, that the lords may dance. O Bishop, Our Father, You warble yonder at the Shore.

God has formed you, has given you birth as a flower. He paints you as a song. O Santa María, O Bishop, *Our Father, You warble yonder at the Shore.*

Painted are the Toltecs, completed are the pictures: all Your hearts are arriving. "Here, through art, I'll live."

Who'll take them from me? Who'll go with me and be arisen, O younger brothers? Singers, and weighty ones, are these, my flowers, song plumes that I pick before this company.

In song I cut great stones, paint massive beams, that this, in future time when I'm gone, shall be uttered, this my song-sign that I leave behind on earth. My hearts will be alive here: they'll have come, a remembrance of me. And my fame will live.

I weep, saying as I call to my hearts, let me see the root songs, let me plant them. Let them stand on earth. In time these hearts of mine are made! They'll walk abroad!

Indeed, the lordlike flowers are spreading fragrance. These flowers of ours are assembled. There! My songs are greening. My word-fruit sprouts. Our flowers are arisen in this place of rain.

Well! Cacao flowers, fragrant ones, come scattering down, spreading perfume: fragrant poyomatli drizzles down. "There! I walk abroad, I, the singer." There! My songs are greening. *My word-fruit sprouts. Our flowers are arisen in this place of rain.*

Ỹ tlapapalxochicentli niyol aya nepapã tonacáxochitl moyahuaya oncuepontimoquetzacoyan aya aya yeteoya ixpan tona a Santa Maria ayyo./ Atl ya ya cuicaya çan quetzalaxihuitl tomolihuiyan aya ye nitlachihual ycelteotl y ye dios aya niytlayocol a oya yehcocya Et./ Çan ca tlacuilolpã nemia moyollo amoxpetlatl ypan toncuicaya tiquimonyai'totia teteuctin aya in obispoya çã ca totatzin aya oncã titlatoa atl itempã ayyo./ yehuan Dios mitzyocox aya xochitla ya mitztlacatili yan cuicatl mitzicuiloa Santa Maria in obispoya etc/ Tolteca ihcuilihuia ahaa yaha ontlantoc amoxtliya moyollo ya onaya moch onahciticac oo toltecayootl a ycaya ninemiz ye nicã ayyo./ Ac ya nechcuiliz ac ye nohuan oyaz onicaz a anniihcuihuan ayayyan cuicanitl y yehetl y noxochiuh nõcuicayhuitequi on teixpã ayyo.// Hueyn tetl nictequin Tomahuac quahuitl nic ycuiloa yã cuicatl ytech aya oncan no mitoz in quẽmanõ in can niyaz nocuicamachio nicyacauhtiaz in tlp̊c. y onnemiz noyol çan ca ye nican ya hualla yyancoya nolnamicoca nemiz ye noteyo ayyo./ Nichocaya niquittoaya nicnotza noyollo ma niquittã cuicanelhuayotl aya ma nicyatlalaquiya ma icaya tlp̊c quimmã mochihua onnenemiz noyol Et/ Çan ca teucxochitl ahuiacay'potocaticac mocepanoa yan toxochiuh ayye ayaoo hui yoncan quiya itzmolini ye nocuic celia notlatollaquillo ohua in toxochiuh ycac y quiapani ayao/ Tel cacahuaxochitl ahuiac xeliuhtihuitz a ihpotocaya in ahuiyac poyoma'tlin pixahuia oncan nine'ne'nemi nicuicanitl yye ayao ohui yonca quiya itzmolini ye nocuic celia Et.

Anonymous (c. 1540–1583, Mexico)

The Florentine Codex is a series of twelve handwritten books on alphabetic script illustrated with drawings assembled by Fray Bernardino de Sahagún. They record his conversations and interviews with indigenous elders from the cities of Tlatelolco, Texcoco, and Tenochtitlan, on the subject of Mexican or Aztec culture before the arrival of the Spaniards. Book 12 depicts the European invasion from the native perspective. Modeled after Western encyclopedias and the painted books of ancient Mexico, it is one of the principal mestizo documents of the early colony. The drawings, done on paper by Mexican *tlacuilos* (scribes) in a European style, both recall and differ from the far older tradition of Mexican book making, a tradition going back one thousand years before Columbus. The original Mexica books were written in iconic script and they fused in one visual statement separate concepts such as letters, art, and mathematics.

Excerpt from The Florentine Codex

Malintzin shouting from roof: *The Florentine Codex*, Book 12, f. 29

Anonymous Inca Quipu (c. 1500, Peru, Inca)

The khipu ("knot") is an Andean notation system for keeping statistics and accounts and recording or "writing" poems, songs, and tales with colored, knotted threads.

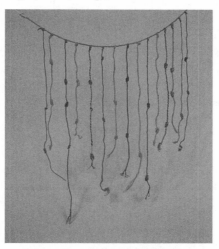

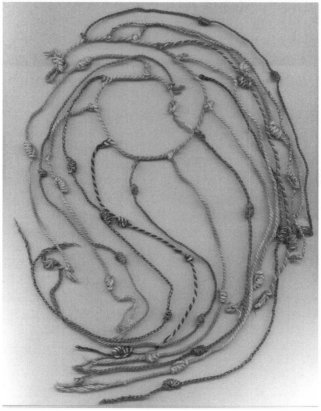

Two views of same piece: Archaeological khipu, Peru, circa 1500 A.D.

Inca Garcilaso de la Vega (1539–1616, Peru)

Garcilaso de la Vega, born in Cuzco, Peru, in 1539, the son of Chimpu Ocllo, an Inca noble woman, and a Spanish conqueror, was the first author who called himself a mestizo. He grew up witnessing the demise of the Inca world and the birth of the colonial world. He was literate both in khipu and in alphabetical writing and Quechua was his first language. In 1560, he traveled to Spain where he lived until his death in 1616. In exile, he wrote, in Spanish, his *Comentarios reales de los incas* (1609) a 700-page document, which would later influence César Vallejo and a host of other Latin American authors. The book is a collage, or a *summa*, where he combines autobiography, fiction, history, and chronicle in a quest to give value to the Inca world. He included, as well, testimonies and fragments by other authors, such as the text below quoted from Blas Valera. It is a poem "found in a khipu," which Valera transcribed into Quechua, Latin, and Spanish. Unfortunately the khipu itself was not preserved. PRINCIPAL WORKS: *La traduzión del indio de los tres diálogos de amor de León Hebreo* (1590), *La florida del inca* (1605), *Comentarios reales de los incas* (1609), *Historia general del Perú* (1609)

Beautiful Maiden / Zumac ñusta / Pulchra nimpha / Hermosa doncella
Rosa Alcalá with Cecilia Vicuña, trans.

Beautiful maiden	Zúmac ñusta	Pulchra nimpha,	Hermosa doncella
That brother of yours	Toralláyquim	Frater tuus	Aquese tu hermano
Smashes	Puyñuy quita	Urnam tuam	El tu cantarillo
Your pitcher	Paquir cayan.	Nunc infringit,	Lo está quebrantando.
Causing thunder and lightning	Hina mántara	Cujus ictus	Y de aquesta causa
And thunderbolts.	Cunuñunun	Tonat, fulget	Truena y relampaguea.
But you,	Illapántac	Fulminatque.	También caen rayos.
Royal maiden,	Camri ñusta	Sed tu, Nimpha	Tu, real doncella
Give us your gentle waters	Unuy iquita	Tuam limpham	Tus muy lindas aguas
As rain.	Para munqui	Fundens pluis.	Nos darás, lloviendo.
Or offer them as hail	Mai ñimpiri	Interdumque	También, a las veces,
And sometimes snow.	Chichi munqui	Grandinem, seu	Granizarnos has,
The Maker of the world,	Riti munqui	Nivem mittis.	Nevarás asimismo.
The God that gives life,	Pacharúrac	Mundi factor	El hacedor del mundo,
The great Viracocha	Pachacámac	Pachacamac	El dios que le anima
In this role have placed you	Huiracocha	Huiracocha	El gran Huiracocha
And have given you a soul.	Cai hinápac	Ad hoc munus	Para aqueste oficio
	Churasunqui	Te sufficit	Ya te colocaron
	Camasunqui	Ac praefecit	Y te dieron alma.

Anonymous (Sixteenth Century, Mesoamerica, Maya K'iche)

Alternatively known as *The Mayan Book of the Dawn of Life*, *The Book of Those Who Sit Together on the Mat*, or *The Book of Council*, *Popol Vuh* or *Pop Wuj*, is an ancient hieroglyphic book recast in alphabetic script by a group of Maya K'iche writers, day-keeper priests, or "mother-fathers," as they are called in present-day Guatemala. Only one of the names of its authors has survived: Cristobal Velasco. Regarded as the great classic of Mayan literature, *Popol Vuh* is an anthology conceived as a series of quotes from what a reader would have said when giving a "long performance" of the ancient book, according to Dennis Tedlock. "It begins in darkness, in a world inhabited only by gods, and continues all the way into the time of the humans who wrote it." In the "Mayan ways of understanding stories, we may read them not only for the past, but for signs of the future." The excerpt transcribed appears in the context of a description of the ways in which the ancients did penance and prayed for the well-being of all.

Excerpt from Popol Vuh: And This Is the Cry of Their Hearts, Here It Is / Are k'ut roq'ej kik'ux wa'

Dennis Tedlock, trans.

Wait now! Bless this day,
thou Hurricane, thou heart of sky and earth,
thou giver of ripeness and freshness,
giver, too, of daughters and sons,
spread thy stain, spill thy drops
of green and yellow;
give life and beginning
to those I bear and beget,
that they might multiply and grow,
nurturing and providing for thee,
calling to thee along the roads and paths,
on rivers, in canyons,
beneath the trees and bushes;
give them their daughters and sons.

May there be no blame, folly, shame, or pain;
let no deceiver come behind or before them,
may they neither be snared nor wounded,
nor seduced, nor burned,
nor diverted below the road nor above it;
may they neither fall over backward nor stumble;
tie them to the green road, the green path.

May there be no blame or barrier for them
through any secrets or sorcery of thine;
may thy nurturers and providers live well
before thy mouth and thy face,
thou heart of sky, thou heart of earth;
thou Bundle of Flames,
and thou, Tohil, Awilix, Hacawitz,
under the sky, on the earth,
the four sides, four corners;
may there be only light, only continuity within,
before thy mouth and thy face, thou giver of names.

Aqaroq! Ato'b' uq'ij,/ at Juraqan, at uk'ux kaj ulew,/ at yaol rech q'anal,
raxal,/ at pu yaol mial, k'ajol,/ chatz'iloj, chamak'ij uloq/ araxal, aq'anal/
chayataj uk'aseik, uwinaqirik/ wal, nuk'ajol,/ chi poq taj, chi winaqir taj,/
tzuqul awe, q'o'l awe,/ sik'i awe pa b'e, pa joq/ pa b'e ya, pa siwan,/ xe che',
xe k'a'm; / chaya' kimial, kik'ajol.// Matajab'i il, tzab', yan, k'exo;/ mata
chok k'axtoq'onel chikij chikiwach,/ mepajik, mesokotajik,/ mejoxowik,
mek'atowik,/ meqajik requem b'e, rajsik b'e,/ matajab'i pak toxkom chikij,
chikiwach;/ keayataj pa raxa b'e, pa raxa joq.// Matajab'i kil kitz'ap/ ak'uil,
awitzmal;/ utz taj kik'ojeik tzuqul awe, q'o'l awe/ chachi, chawach,/ at uk'ux
kaj, at uk'ux ulew,/ at Pisom Q'aq'al,/ at puch Tojil, Awilix, Jakawitz,/ upam
kaj, upam ulew,/ kaj tz'uk, kaj xukut;/ xata saq, xata amaq' upam/ chachi,
chawach, at k'ab'awil.

Alonso de Ercilla y Zúñiga (1533–1594, Chile/Spain)

Ercilla was born in Madrid of Basque descent to a family of high social status.
He was enrolled as a page to Prince Philip and later traveled with his entourage
around Europe. The three-volume *La araucana,* dedicated to the prince and
based upon the various battle campaigns of the Spanish conquest of Chile at
which Ercilla was present, is considered one of the most important Spanish epics.
Ercilla ultimately garnered considerable wealth due to his allegiance with royalty
and the success of *La araucana.* He died in Madrid. PRINCIPAL WORK: *La araucana*
(1569, 1578, 1589)

Excerpt from **The Araucaniad / La araucana**

Charles Maxwell Lancaster and Paul Thomas Manchester, trans.

CANTO I

Which declares the seat and description of the province of Chile and the state of Arauco, with the customs and methods of warfare that the natives observe, and which likewise deals with the entry and conquest of the Spaniards until Arauco grew rebellious.

> Not of ladies, love, or graces
> Do I sing, nor knights enamored,
> Nor of gifts and shows of feeling,
> Cares of love, or love's affections;
> But the valiant acts and prowess
> Of those never-daunted Spaniards
> Who with swords placed yokes of bondage
> On the necks of untamed Indians.

> I shall dwell on deeds distinguished
> Of a monarch-scorning people,
> Feats of gallantry deserving
> Memory's shrine and celebration,
> Rare accomplishments of merit
> Crowning Spanish might with grandeur;
> For the victor most is honored
> By repute of vanquished hero.

> I implore you, royal Philip,
> That this work wear your approval.
> Needing universal favor,
> 'Tis extolled by your acceptance.
> Uncorrupted my narration,
> Drawn from truth and cut to measure!
> Do not scorn this gift, though humble.
> Let your sanction speed my verses.

. . . .

> Chile, fertile province, famous
> In the vast Antarctic region,
> Known to far-flung mighty nations
> For her queenly grace and courage,
> Has produced a race so noble,
> Dauntless, bellicose, and haughty,

That by king it ne'er was humbled
Nor to foreign sway submitted.

CANTO II

Herein is exposed the discord which arose amongst the chieftains of Arauco
concerning the election of a captain-general, and the means taken on Chief
Colocolo's counsel, with the entrance that the barbarians deceptively made into
the stronghold of Tucapel, and the battle which they fought with the Spaniards.

Many in the world have clambered
To this life's deceitful apex,
By fair chance abetted always,
By her helping hand uplifted;
But when their ascent is highest,
Dashed anon are they to misery;
Still the shock and pain are lessened
By the thought of brusquer changes.

Unaware that shining weather's
Happiness is woe's beginning,
They consider not the fleetness
Of their prosperous hours corrosive,
But with high-necked, vain delusions
Hope that Luck will last, eternal,
Which, of cruelty ever mindful,
Whirls in wonted revolutions.

With one twist of compensation,
Smiling not on men's cocksureness,
Fate annuls all favors granted,
Of the old and new unsparing,
Stripping laurels and insignia.
End of life is time of testing,
Wherein all must stand arraignment,
Though beginnings be auspicious.

What of vanished bliss is left us
Save distress and dule and travail?
If the sun deemed Fortune stable,
It would cease its bright diffusion.
Braking wheels is not its function,
And 'tis wrong to change old custom.
Those who never grasped good fortune
Know its richest gift and blessing.

So 'tis proven in this story,
Wherefrom may be culled a lesson.
Glory, wealth were ne'er sufficient,
With all wish of weal's fulfillment,
To engird perennial triumph.
Limpid skies at last grew turbid;
Fortune changed the course and order
Of our gladsome sort to sadness.

Our ungrateful soldiers tasted
Of prosperity I hinted,
With a benison more fulsome
I have overlooked, contentment,
Found in few things. They neglected
Such an obvious sign and pitfall,
Losing in one hour the honor
Won through centuries of striving.

I averred that simple Indians
Thought our men were gods, but scenting
They were born of man and woman,
Realizing all their weaknesses,
Which they glimpsed through chains of misery,
They perceived their stupid error.
Rage and shame blazed out from knowledge
That their conquerors were mortal.

Disinclined to more postponement,
They discussed their sad condition,
How in shortest time to end it,
How to seek a way of vengeance.
They assembled for decision
Where the sentence would be vouchsafed,
Harsh, irrevocable, cruel,
To the world a dread example.

Chieftains were betimes o'erspreading
Fields with tread of marching tribesmen.
General summons was not needed,
For the lust of war convoked them
Without promises or payments.
Longed they for the lagging instant
When decree would doom the foeman
To chastisement, death's destruction.

CANTO I// *El cual declara el asiento y descripción de la Provincia de Chile y*
Estado del Arauco, con las costumbres y modos de guerra que los naturales tienen;

y asimismo trata en suma la entrada y conquista que los españoles hicieron hasta que Arauco se comenzó a rebelar.// No las damas, amor, no gentilezas/ de caballeros canto enamorados;/ ni las muestras, regalos y ternezas/ de amorosos afectos y cuidados;/ mas el valor, los hechos, las proezas/ de aquellos españoles esforzados,/ que a la cerviz de Arauco no domada/ pusieron duro yugo por la espada.// Cosas diré también harto notables/ de gente que a ningún rey obedecen,/ temerarias empresas memorables/ que celebrarse con razón merecen;/ raras industrias, términos loables/ que más los españoles engrandecen:/ pues no es el vencedor más estimado/ de aquello en que el vencido es reputado.// Suplícoos, gran Felipe, que mirada/ esta labor, de vos sea recebida,/ que, de todo favor necesitada,/ queda con darse a vos favorecida:/ es relación sin corromper, sacada/ de la verdad, cortada a su medida;/ no despreciéis el don, aunque tan pobre,/ para que autoridad mi verso cobre.// . . . // Chile, fértil provincia y señalada/ en la región Antártica famosa,/ de remotas naciones respetada/ por fuerte, principal y poderosa:/ la gente que produce es tan granada,/ tan soberbia, gallarda y belicosa,/ que no ha sido por rey jamás regida/ ni a extranjero dominio sometida.// CANTO II// *Pónese la discordia que entre los caciques de Arauco hubo sobre la elección del capitán general, y el medio que se tomó por el consejo del cacique Colocolo, con la entrada que por engaño los bárbaros hicieron en la casa fuerte de Tucapel, y la batalla que con los españoles tuvieron.*// Muchos hay en el mundo que han llegado/ a la engañosa alteza desta vida,/ que Fortuna los ha siempre ayudado/ y dádoles la mano a la subida,/ para después de haberlos levantado/ derribarlos con mísera caída,/ cuando es mayor el golpe y sentimiento/ y menos el pensar que hay mudamiento.// No entienden con la próspera bonanza/ quel contento es principio de tristeza;/ ni miran en la súbita mudanza/ del consumidor tiempo y su presteza;/ mas con altiva y vana confianza/ quieren que en su fortuna haya firmeza;/ la cual, de su aspereza no olvidada,/ revuelve con la vuelta acostumbrada.// Con un revés de todo se desquita,/ que no quiere que nadie se le atreva,/ y mucho más que da siempre les quita,/ no perdonando cosa vieja y nueva;/ de crédito y de honor los necesita:/ que en el fin de la vida está la prueba,/ por el cual han de ser todos juzgados/ aunque lleven principios acertados.// Del bien perdido, al cabo, ¿qué nos queda/ sino pena, dolor y pesadumbre?/ Pensar que en él Fortuna ha de estar queda,/ antes dejara el Sol de darnos lumbre:/ que no es su condición fijar la rueda,/ y es malo de mudar vieja costumbre;/ el más seguro bien de la Fortuna/ es no haberla tenido vez alguna.// Esto verse podrá por esta historia:/ ejemplo dello aquí puede sacarse,/ que no bastó riqueza, honor y gloria/ con todo el bien que puede desearse/ a llevar adelante la vitoria;/ que el claro cielo al fin vino a turbarse,/ mudando la Fortuna en triste estado/ el curso y orden próspera del hado.// La gente nuestra ingrata se hallaba/ en la prosperidad que arriba cuento,/ y en otro mayor bien que me olvidaba,/ hallado en pocas casas, que es contento:/ de tal manera en

él se descuidaba/ (cierta señal de triste acaecimiento)/ que en una hora
perdió el honor y estado/ que en mil años de afán había ganado.// Por
dioses, como dije, eran tenidos/ de los indios los nuestros; pero olieron/
que de mujer y hombre eran nacidos/ y todas sus flaquezas entendieron;/
viéndolos a miserias sometidos/ el error inorante conocieron,/ ardiendo
en viva rabia avergonzados/ por verse de mortales conquistados.// No
queriendo a más plazo diferirlo/ entre ellos comenzó luego a tratarse/ que,
para en breve tiempo concluirlo/ y dar el modo y orden de vengarse,/ se
junten a consulta a difinirlo:/ do venga la sentencia a pronunciarse,/ dura,
ejemplar, crüel, irrevocable,/ horrenda a todo el mundo y espantable.//
Iban ya los caciques ocupando/ los campos con la gente que marchaba:/
y no fue menester general bando,/ que el deseo de la guerra los llamaba/
sin promesas ni pagas, deseando/ el esperado tiempo que tardaba,/ para el
decreto y áspero castigo/ con muerte y destruición del enemigo.

Mateo Rosas de Oquendo (1559–1612, Spain/Peru)

Born in Spain, Rosas de Oquendo traveled the New World, most importantly Peru,
where he spent most of his adult life. His works use social satire to critique colonial
life in Peru. His major work focuses on the sexual lives of a variety of women, but
notably includes men in his social critique. There are medieval aspects to his work,
including its romance meter and the theme of the limited and frail nature of the
material world. PRINCIPAL WORK: *Sátira hecha por Mateo Rosas de Oquendo a las cosas
que pasan en el Perú año de 1598*

The Mestizo's Ballade / Romance del mestizo

G. J. Racz, trans.

—Fair Lady Juana, have a heart
And grant a poor mestizo leave
To put his forlorn plaint in words
And sing for you a lay of love.

For shabby as my semblance seems,
I'm still a landed nobleman
Whose parents both descended from
The brave conquistadors of Spain.

So should I find myself obliged
(Good Lord, I'll end up raving mad!)
To force those Spaniards to admit
Our common bond of lineage,

I'll lure them to my leafy grove
At midnight in the half moon's light
And thrash them soundly with the blade
Of my reliable half-moon knife!

. . . .

No constable can frighten me,
Or any henchman he might hire.
I swear to God who reigns on high,
I'd trample them to death down here!

For I was born and bred to roam
These craggy native mountain paths
To castrate snorting herds of bulls
Like taming lions with my hands.

No harquebus can frighten me,
Not any of its pellet shots.
I'd happily consume the lead
In peppery *chilmole* sauce.

Fair Lady Juana, have a heart!
Good Lord, I'll end up raving mad
If you, fond Mistress, can't prescribe
The antidote for this malaise.

Juanita, dear Juanita mine,
Fresh blossoms grace your lovely face!
How is it you demur to flee
This wild *coyote* in your midst . . .

The one who cannot come across
An *ajolote* in the lake
Or any frog or swimming *juil*
Without devouring it in haste;

Who at the outdoor *tiánguez* stalls
Will wolf twelve hot *chilchotes* down,
Ten avocados, too, and still
Gulp hundreds of *camotes* down?

—This noble Juan de Diego sang
And brought his ballad to an end,
Then rolled himself a fat cigar,
Enjoyed a smoke and went to bed.

—¡Ay, señora Juana!/ Vusarcé perdone,/ y escuche las quejas/ de un mestizo pobre;// que, aunque remendado,/ soy hidalgo y noble,/ y mis padres, hijos/ de conquistadores;//y si es menester,/ por Dios que me enoje,/ porque me conozcan/ esos españoles,// y en mi palotilla/ —a la media noche—/ con mi media luna/ les dé cuatro golpes.// . . . // No temo, alguaciles,/ ni a sus porquerones,/ que —por Dios del Cielo—/ que los mate a coces;// que estoy hecho a andar/ por aquestos montes/ capando los toros/ como unos leones;// ni temo arcabuces,/ ni a sus perdigones,/ que por mí, contento/ los como en *chilmole*,// ¡Ay señora Juana!/ Por Dios, que me enoje/ si vuesé no cura/ aquestos dolores.// ¡Ay Juanica mía,/ carita de flores!/ ¿Cómo no te mueves/ por este *coyote* . . . // el que en la laguna/ no deja *ajolote*,/ rana ni *juil*/ que no se lo come;// el que en el *tiánguez*,/ con doce *chilchotes*/ y diez aguacates,/ como cien *camotes*?// —Aquesto cantaba/ Juan de Diego el noble,/ haciendo un cigarro;/ chupólo y durmióse.

Felipe Guamán Poma de Ayala (1530–1516? Peru)

Guamán Poma, an indigenous Quechua speaker, was born in Peru in 1530. He learned to read and write in Spanish and worked for the ecclesiastic authorities in the campaign of "extirpation of idolatries," where he became familiar with the use of images to catechize. Witnessing the injustices committed against his people, he set out to write a letter to the king of Spain, which over the course of thirty years became his *Coronica,* a monumental work of 1,200 pages. Uniquely drawn and written in a mix of flawed Spanish, Quechua, and Latin, this masterpiece is reminiscent of the ancient art of the *kamayup,* the keeper of graphic information in the Incaic tradition, but also alludes to the use of images by Catholic priests. He lost hope of reforming the colonial ways of the Europeans and died in poverty around 1616, and his letter never reached the king. The manuscript was found in a library in Denmark in 1908.

Cachiuia

Simon Pettet with Cecilia Vicuña, English trans.
Jan Szeminski, Spanish trans.

I
Sister you got great legs

Sister you got winning legs

Sister your face too wins bets

How to get you in the sack

How to grab and haul in
your big ass
Sister your face too wins bets
How to grab and haul in

all of you, old lady,

How to get
into your pants

O winning lasso legs
Why don't you let me past
Your broken belt?

Let's win the bet
Open up your belt

(but)

When your *chiwuillo* ripens
old lady, don't come back
When your *chiwuillo* ripens
Lady with a baby, don't come back
O chilly *chiwuillo*!

Chanca sauaylla pani,// chanca misaylla pani,// aya misaylla pani,//
maytachi cayta sauacurisac// Cutama llicllacta./ Maytachi cayta
misacurisac/ Siquisapacta./ Aya misaylla pani,// chanca misaylla
pani.// Maytachi cayta sauacurisac// paya camacta./ Maytachi cayta
pusacurisac,// tira chupacta/ ichanca sauaylla,/ sauacurimay/ zacra
uinchayquip,/ misacurimay/ piti chunpi quip;/ uicayro uicayro/
apayro apayro/ suyror pini sallsall/ chiuilloyqui pocoptin/ payallapas
samoncam,/ chiuilloyqui pucoptin/ chichollapas samoncan,/
ichiuillollay chiuillo!

Mi hermana de piernas fabulosas,/ mi hermana de piernas que ganan
apuestas,/ mi hermana de cara que gana apuestas,/ no sé por donde a
esta me la enlazaré/ a la con manta de un costal./ No sé por donde me la
ganaré/ a la culona./ Mi hermana de cara que gana apuestas,/ mi hermana
de piernas que ganan apuestas,/ no sé por donde a esta me la enlazaré/
a la completamente vieja./ No sé a donde me la conduciré a esta,/ de
pantorrillas peladas/ iO tú de piernas enlazadoras,/ ganame pues la
apuesta/ en tu cinta mala,/ ganame pues la puesta/ en tu faja rota!// . . .
cuando madure tu *chiwillu*/ también la vieja no más vendrá,/ cuando
madure tu *chiwillu*,/ también preñada no más vendrá,/ iO mi *chiwillito*,
chiwillu!

/318[320] / FESTIVAL OF THE INCA/ *VARICZA, ARAVI* [dances] OF THE
INCA HE SINGS WITH HIS PVCA LLAMA [red llama] / *y, y/ y, y / puca llama/*
Haucay Pata [festival plaza in Cuzco] / festival

Uaricza, araui [dances] of the Inca, the festivals, singing and dancing:
Uaricza they sing, *puca llama* [song of the sheep], in the tone of the lamb
they sing. It goes like this:

Tempo builds up slowly for half an hour: "Y, y, y" in the tone of the
sheep. The Inca begins imitating the lamb; it says and it is saying "yn."
Carries the tone forward, saying many many verses. The *coyas* [queen]
and the *nustas* [princesses] respond. They sing in loud voices very softly.
And *uaricsa y araui* go like this; "*Araui araui aray araui araui yau araui.*" They
are saying what they want and they all go by this *arawui* tone. The women
respond: "*Uaricsa ayay uaricza chamay uaricza, ayay uaricza.*" They all go by this
tone and the women respond.

And the *haylle* [triumphant song]:

Ayau haylli yau haylli   [*Ayaw haylli yaw haylli*
Uchuyoccho chacrayqui?   *Do you have chili pepper in your garden?*
Uchuy tunpalla samusac   *I will come to you disguised as chili pepper.*
Ticayoccho chacrayque?   *Do you have flowers in your garden?*
Ticay tunpalla samusac.   *I will come to you disguised as flowers*].

/360 [362] / PRINCIPAL ACCOUNTANT AND TREASURER TAVANTIN
SVIO QVIPOC CVRACA [principal authority in charge of the *khipus* of the
Tawantin Suyu] CONDOR CHAVA / accountant and treasurer

Principal accountant of this kingdom, *Condor Chaua*, son of the *apo*: This
one was called *Tawantin Suyo runa quipoc Yncap*, haziendan *chasquicoc*,
principal treasurer. It says that this chief had great skills; to test his

skills the Inca ordered counting and numbering, in order to distribute among the Indians of this kingdom the wool of the taruga deer, he evenly matched taruga wool with the Indians and matched the Indians with a food called *quinua* [altitude cereal] he counted the *quinua* and the Indians. His skill was great, far better than if he'd had paper and ink.

/564 [578] / PRIESTS/ WHO FORCE THE INDIANS TO WEAVE CLOTH, cajoling them and threatening that they live in sin, hitting them, and not paying them. / doctrine/

Gregório de Matos (1636–1695, Brazil)

To this day, both the life and work of Matos remains somewhat shrouded in mystery. Although he wrote in the seventeenth century, his work was not discovered until the late nineteenth century. There has been continued debate by biographers regarding the true nature and identity of the author, as his literature exists only in unsigned, apocryphal form. Scholarly debate has also alleged possible plagiarism in "O boca do inferno" (Hell's Mouth). Highly erotic and satirical, Matos's works focused on the state of Bahia, Brazil, his place of birth. PRINCIPAL WORKS: *Florilégio da poesia brasileira* (1946), *Obras completas* (1968), *Parnaso brasileiro* (1976)

Define Your City / Define a sua cidade

Mark A. Lokensgard, trans.

This city of two f's is made,
This city and its ruck,
The first, filch, the second, fuck.

A man abridged the law,
And he who it abbreviated
With two f's it elucidated
And did so well, without a flaw.
It well digested, this truth he saw:
With only two f's is it expounded
And thus any with reason well grounded
Who hears this thesis will understand
And must agree that this land
On two f's was founded.

If of two f's is composed
Our Bahia, this city,
Erred is its orthography
And great harm to it is posed.
A wager then I will propose
And I will that penny pay,
For this error leads the town astray
If the filch and fuck not be
The f's that has our common city
As I with sureness say.

I'll prove my thesis straightaway
And rightly, with a jest:
Of five letters is it possessed
Which gives B-A-H-I-A,
Nobody would dare to say
That two f's to it are stuck

For none it has, by luck
Except in this veracity:
The two f's that has our city:
One filch, the other, fuck.

De dous ff se compõe / esta cidade a meu ver / um furtar, outro foder.//
Recopilou-se o direito,/ e quem o recopilou/ com dous ff o explicou/ por
estar feito, e bem feito:/ por bem digesto,/ e colheito,/ só com dous ff o
expõe,/ e assim quem os olhos põe/ no trato, que aqui se encerra,/ há de
dizer que esta terra/ De dous ff se compõe.// Se de dous ff composta/ está a
nossa Bahia,/ errada a ortografia/ a grande dano está posta:/ eu quero fazer
aposta,/ e quero um tostão perder,/ que isso a há de perverter,/ se o *furtar* e o
foder bem/ não são os ff que tem/ Esta cidade a meu ver.// Provo a conjetura
já / prontamente com um brinco:/ Bahia tem letras cinco/ que são B-A-H-
I-A,/ logo ninguém me dirá/ que dous ff chega a ter,/ pois nenhum contém
sequer,/ salvo se em boa verdade/ são os ff da cidade/ um furtar, outro foder.

**An Anatomy of the Ailments Suffered by the Body of the Republic, In
All Its Members, and Complete Definition of What Has Ever Been the
City of Bahia / Juizo anatómico dos achaques que padecia o corpo da
republica, em todos os membros, e inteira definição do que em todos os
tempos é a Bahia**

Mark A. Lokensgard, trans.

What's missing in this city?   Veracity.
What else to its dishonor?   Honor.
What needs it for its good name?   Shame.

    The devil shows himself living,
    No matter how it exalts its fame,
    In a city that is missing
    Veracity, honor, shame.

What started this whole business?   Business.
Who causes such perdition?   Ambition.
And the height of this lunacy?   Usury.

    Laudable misadventure
    Of a people ignorant and mad
    Unaware of what they had
    Business, ambition, usury.

What makes the people's lips smack?   Blacks.
What other goods more numerous?   Mestizos.
Which of these more gratitude shows?   Mulattoes.

To the Devil with the dodos,
To the Devil with the asinine,
Who take for goods most fine
Blacks, mestizos, mulattoes.

Who makes the paltry processions?   Magistrates.
Who makes the tardy farinas?   Constables.
Who keeps them in their lodgements?   Sargeants.

> The processions come by the hundreds
> And the land remains starving
> Because all the while are interfering
> Magistrates, constables, sargeants.

What justice protects the land?   Spurious.
How is it distributed?   Auctioned.
What is it, that frightens all?   Unfair.

> God help us, that we pay
> For what our King gives us for free
> Our justice in the town square:
> Spurious, auctioned, unfair.

What runs throughout the clergy?   Simony.
And the members of the Holy See?   Envy.
What call do they all heed?   Greed.

> Tried and true lament,
> That in the Holy See
> What is practiced above all:
> Simony, envy, greed.

And is there a vice among the monks?   Nuns.
To what do they devote their soirées?   Orations.
They are not busy with disputes?   Prostitutes.

> With words dissolute
> I conclude, in truth
> These are the habits of a monk:
> Nuns, sermons, prostitutes.

Has the sugar run out?   It's down.
Is the money used up?   It's up.
Has it left its sickbed?   It's dead.

> Bahia has suffered
> What an ill man dreads;
> He falls in bed, his illness grows,
> He's down, he's up, he's dead.

The Congress helps not?   It cannot.
Has it not the power?   It wants not.
The government persuades it?   It wins not.

    Who among us would have thought
    That a Congress so noble,
    For being petty and ignoble,
    Cannot, wants not, wins not.

Que falta nesta cidade? Verdade./ Que mais por sua desonra? Honra./
Falta mais que se lhe ponha? Vergonha.// O demo a viver se exponha,/
Por mais que a fama a exalta,/ Numa cidade onde falta/ Verdade,
honra, vergonha.// Quem a pôs neste socrócio? Negócio./ Quem causa
tal perdição? Ambição./ E o maior desta loucura? Usura.// Notável
desaventura/ De um povo néscio, e sandeu,/ Que não sabe que o perdeu/
Negócio, ambição, usura.// Quais são os seus doces objetos? Pretos./ Tem
outros bens mais maciços? Mestiços./ Quais destes lhe são mais gratos?
Mulatos.// Dou ao demo os insensatos,/ Dou ao demo a gente asnal,/
Que estima por cabedal/ Pretos, mestiços, mulatos.// Quem faz os círios
mesquinhos? Meirinhos./ Quem faz as farinhas tardas? Guardas./ Quem
as tem nos aposentos? Sargentos.// Os círios lá vêm aos centos,/ E a
terra fica esfaimando,/ Porque os vão atravessando/ Meirinhos, guardas,
sargentos.// E que justiça a resguarda? Bastarda./ É grátis distribuída?
Vendida./ Que tem, que a todos assusta? Injusta.// Valha-nos Deus, o
que custa/ O que El-Rei nos dá de graça/ Que anda a justiça na praça/
Bastarda, vendida, injusta.// Que vai pela cleresia? Simonia./ E pelos
membros da Igreja? Inveja./ Cuidei que mais se lhe punha? Unha.//
Sazonada caramunha/ Enfim, que na Santa Sé/ O que mais se pratica
é/ Simonia, inveja, unha.// E nos Frades há manqueiras? Freiras./ Em que
ocupam os serões? Sermões./ Não se ocupam em disputas? Putas.// Com
palavras dissolutas/ Me concluís, na verdade,/ Que as lidas todas de um
Frade/ São freiras, sermões, e putas.// O açúcar já se acabou? Baixou./
E o dinheiro se extinguiu? Subiu./ Logo já convalesceu? Morreu.// À Bahia
aconteceu/ O que a um doente acontece,/ Cai na cama, o mal lhe cresce,/
Baixou, subiu, e morreu.// A Câmara não acode? Não pode./ Pois não
tem todo o poder? Não quer./ É que o governo a convence? Não vence.//
Quem haverá que tal pense,/ Que uma Câmara tão nobre,/ Por ver-se
mísera e pobre,/ Não pode, não quer, não vence.

**To the City of Bahia Laying His Eyes First upon His City He Sees That
Its Merchants Are the Primary Cause of Its Ruin, Because It Longs
after Useless and Deceitful Goods / À cidade da Bahia pondo os olhos
primeiramente na sua cidade conhece, que os mercadores são o primeiro
móvel da ruína, em que arde pelas mercadorias inúteis, e enganosas**

Mark A. Lokensgard, trans.

Poor, sad Bahia! oh how different
You are and I am from our former state!
Wretched I see you, you to me in debt,
Rich I once saw you, you to me abundant.

The merchant marine machine has you changed,
As in your ample harbor it entered
I have been changed by, and have exchanged,
So much commerce, so many merchants.

You have begun to trade so much excellent sugar
For useless remedies, and impudently
You accept them from the wily foreigner.

Oh if God would wish the coming of the day
That dawning, would find you so astute
That of cotton were made your cloak!

Triste Bahia! ó quão dessemelhante/ Estás e estou do nosso antigo estado!/
Pobre te vejo a ti, tu a mi empenhado,/ Rica te vi eu já, tu a mi abundante.//
A ti trocou-te a máquina mercante,/ Que em tua larga barra tem entrado,/
A mim foi-me trocando, e tem trocado,/ Tanto negócio e tanto negociante.//
Deste em dar tanto açúcar excelente/ Pelas drogas inúteis, que abelhuda/
Simples aceitas do sagaz Brichote.// Oh se quisera Deus, que de repente/ Um
dia amanheceras tão sisuda/ Que fôra de algodão o teu capote!

To the Palefaces of Bahia / Aos caramurus da Bahia

Mark A. Lokensgard, trans.

Trousers of palm leaves at mid-leg length,
Chest dyed red with urucu, cape of parrot feathers,
In place of a cutlass, a bow and bamboo stick,
A headdress of feathers in place of a cap.

His lip was pierced by his unflinching father,
Who did so with a piece of *jacitara* palm,
His mother, though, had applied the special stone
To hold back for him the flow of blood.

A savage without reason, a brute without faith,
Except that in his taste, which when it errs,
Turns him from Chieftain into a fright.

I know not where he perished, or in what war:
I know only that from this Adam of Bahian clay
Are descended the nobles of this land.

Um calção de pindoba, a meia zorra,/ camisa de urucu, mantéu de arara,/
em lugar de cotó, arco e taquara,/ penacho de guarás, em vez de gorra.//
Furado o beiço, sem temer que morra/ o pai, que lho envasou cuma
titara,/ porém a mãe a pedra lhe aplicara/ por reprimir-lhe o sangue que
não corra.// Alarve sem razão, bruto sem fé,/ sem mais eis que a do gosto,
quando erra,/ de Paiaiá tornou-se em abaité.// Não sei onde acabou, ou
em que guerra:/ só sei que deste Adão de Massapé/ procedem os fidalgos
desta terra.

**Upon Finding an Arm Taken from the Statue of the Christ Child of Our
Lady of the Wonders, Which Was Profaned by Unbelievers at the Sea
of Bahia / Achando-se um braç perdido do menino Deus Dd N.S. Das
Maravilhas, que desacataram infiéis na Sé da Bahia**

Mark A. Lokensgard, trans.

The whole without the part, is not whole;
the part without the whole is not a part;
but if the part makes it whole, being a part,
let it not be said a part, being the whole.

In the whole Sacrament God is whole,
and exists as a whole in every part,
and though everywhere He is split apart,
in every part He is always whole.

Let not the arm of Jesus be a part,
for Jesus thus parted in his whole,
exists for his part in each part.

Not knowing itself part of the whole,
an arm which was taken as a part,
tells us of the whole parts of the whole.

O todo sem a parte, não é todo;/ a parte sem o todo não é parte;/ mas
se a parte o faz todo, sendo parte,/ não se diga que é parte, sendo
o todo.// Em todo o Sacramento está Deus todo,/ e todo assiste inteiro
em qualquer parte,/ e feito em partes todo em toda a parte,/ em qualquer
parte sempre fica todo.// O braço de Jesus não seja parte,/ pois que feito
Jesus em partes todo,/ assiste cada parte em sua parte.// Não se sabendo
parte deste todo,/ um braço que lhe acharam sendo parte,/ nos diz as
partes todas deste todo.

Sor Juana Inés de la Cruz (1651–1695, Mexico)

An illegitimate child born in San Miguel Nepantla, near Mexico City, Sor Juana grew up at her grandfather's home and studied in his library. Soon acknowledged as a child prodigy and summoned to the Viceroyal court, she wrote poetry, plays, and prose in a wide variety of genres, and her use of Nahuatl and Latin brought her great fame. In order to be free to write and develop her intellectual interests, she became a nun. Her most famous work, "Primero Sueño," has secured her reputation as the greatest poet of the continent in the seventeenth century. Far ahead of her time in her assertion of a woman's right to an education, she was censored by the Catholic Church and forced to abandon her writing. PRINCIPAL WORK: *Obras completas* (1976)

Excerpt from First Dream / Primero sueño

Samuel Beckett, trans.

But Venus first
with her fair gentle morning-star
shone through the dayspring,
and old Tithonus' beauteous spouse
—Amazon in radiance clad—
armed against the night,
fair though martial
and though plaintive brave,
showed her lovely brow
crowned with morning glimmers,
tender yet intrepid harbinger
of the fierce luminary
that came, mustering his van
of tiro gleams
and his rearward
of stouter veteran lights
against her, usurping tyrant
of day's empire, who,
girt with gloom's black bays
sways with dread nocturnal sceptre
the shades,
herself by them appalled.
But the fair forerunner,
herald of the bright sun,
scarce flew her banner in the orient sky,
calling all the sweet if warlike
clarions of the birds to arms,
their featly artless

sonorous bugles,
when the doomed tyrant, trembling,
distraught with dread misgiving,
striving the while
to launch her vaunted might, opposing
the shield of her funereal cloak
in vain to the unerring
shafts of light
with the rash unavailing
valiance of despair,
sensible of her faintness to withstand,
prone already to commit to flight,
more than to might, the means of her salvation,
wound her raucous horn,
summoning her black battalions
to orderly retreat.
Forthwith she was assailed
with nearer plenitude of rays
that streaked the highest pitch
of the world's lofty towers.
The sun in truth, its circuit closed, drew near,
limning with gold on sapphire blue a thousand
times a thousand points and gleaming scarves,
and from its luminous circumference
innumerable rays of pure light streamed,
scoring the sky's cerulean plain,
and serried fell on her who was but now
the baneful tyrant of their empire.
She, flying in headlong rout,
mid her own horrors stumbling,
trampling on her shade,
strove, with her now blindly fleeing host
of shadows harried by the overtaking light,
to gain the western verge which loomed at last
before her impetuous course.
Then, by her very downfall vivified,
plunging in ever more precipitant ruin,
with renewed rebellion she resolves,
in that part of the globe
forsaken by the day,
to wear the crown,
what time upon our hemisphere the sun
the radiance of his fair golden tresses shed,
with equable diffusion of just light

apportioning to visible things their colours
and still restoring
to outward sense its full efficacy,
committing to surer light
the world illuminated and myself awake.

Pero de Venus, antes, el hermoso/ apacible Lucero/ rompió el albor
primero,/ y del viejo *Titón* la bella Esposa,/ amazona de luces mil vestida,/
contra la noche armada,/ hermosa, si atrevida,/ valiente, aunque llorosa,/
su frente mostró hermosa,/ de matutinas luces coronada,/ aunque tierno
preludio, ya animoso/ del Planeta fogoso/ que venía las tropas reclutando/
de bisoñas vislumbres,/ las más robustas, veteranas lumbres/ para la
retaguardia reservando,/ contra la que, tirana usurpadora/ del Imperio del
día,/ negro Laurel de sombras mil ceñía,/ y con nocturno Cetro pavoroso/
las sombras gobernaba,/ de quien aun ella misma se espantaba./ Pero
apenas la bella Precursora/ signífera del Sol, el luminoso/ en el Oriente
tremoló Estandarte,/ tocando alarma todos los süaves,/ si bélicos Clarines
de las Aves,/ diestros, aunque sin arte,/ Trompetas sonorosos,/ cuando
(como tirana al fin) cobarde,/ de recelos medrosos/ embarazada, bien
que hacer alarde/ intentó de sus fuerzas, oponiendo/ de su funesta capa
los reparos,/ breves en ella de los tajos claros/ heridas recibiendo,/ bien
que mal satisfecho su denuedo,/ pretexto mal formado fue del miedo,/
su débil resistencia conociendo/ a la fuga ya casi cometiendo,/ más que
a la fuerza, el medio de salvarse,/ ronca tocó bocina/ a recoger los negros
Escuadrones/ para poder en orden retirarse,/ cuando de más vecina/
plenitud de reflejos fue asaltada,/ que la punta rayó más encumbrada/
de los del Mundo erguidos Torreones./ Llegó, en efecto, el Sol cerrando
el giro/ que esculpió de oro sobre azul Zafiro;/ de mil multiplicados/ mil
veces puntos, flujos mil dorados,/ líneas, digo, de luz clara, salían/ de
su circunferencia luminosa,/ pautando al Cielo la cerúlea Plana,/ y a la
que antes funesta fue tirana/ de su Imperio, atropadas embestían,/ que
sin concierto huyendo presurosa,/ en sus mismos horrores tropezando,/
su sombra iba pisando,/ y llegar al Ocaso pretendía,/ con el, sin orden
ya, desbaratado/ ejército de sombras, acosado/ de la luz que el alcance
le seguía./ Consiguió, al fin, la vista del Ocaso/ el fugitivo paso,/ y, en
su mismo despeño recobrada,/ esforzando el aliento en la rüina,/ en
la mitad del globo que ha dejado/ el Sol desamparado,/ segunda vez,
rebelde, determina/ mirarse coronada,/ mientras nuestro Hemisferio la
dorada,/ ilustraba del Sol madeja hermosa,/ que con luz judiciosa/ de
orden distributivo, repartiendo/ a las cosas visibles sus colores/ iba, y
restituyendo/ entera a los sentidos exteriores/ su operación, quedando
a luz más cierta/ el Mundo iluminado y yo despierta.

This Coloured Counterfeit That Thou Beholdest / Este, que ves, engaño colorido

Samuel Beckett, trans.

This coloured counterfeit that thou beholdest,
vainglorious with the excellencies of art,
is, in fallacious syllogisms of colour,
nought but a cunning dupery of sense;

this in which flattery has undertaken
to extenuate the hideousness of years,
and, vanquishing the outrages of time,
to triumph o'er oblivion and old age,

is an empty artifice of care,
is a fragile flower in the wind,
is a paltry sanctuary from fate,

is a foolish sorry labour lost,
is conquest doomed to perish and, well taken,
is corpse and dust, shadow and nothingness.

Este, que ves, engaño colorido,/ que del arte ostentando los primores,/
con falsos silogismos de colores/ es cauteloso engaño del sentido;// éste,
en quien la lisonja ha pretendido/ excusar de los años los horrores,/ y
venciendo del tiempo los rigores/ triunfar de la vejez y del olvido,// es un
vasto artificio del cuidado,/ es una flor al viento delicada,/ es un resguardo
inútil para el hado;// es una necia diligencia errada,/ es un afán caduco,
y, bien mirado,/ es cadáver, es polvo, es sombra, es nada.

Tarry, Shadow of My Scornful Treasure / Detente, sombra de mi bien esquivo

Samuel Beckett, trans.

Tarry, shadow of my scornful treasure,
image of my dearest sortilege,
fair illusion for which I gladly die,
sweet unreality for which I painfully live.

To the compelling magnet of thy grace
since my breast as docile steel is drawn,
why dost thou with soft ways enamour me
if from me then in mockery thou must fly?

And yet thou mayst nowise in triumph boast
that over me thy tyranny has prevailed;
for though thou breakest, mocking, the narrow coil

that girdled thy fantastic form about,
what boots it to make mock of arms and breast
if thou art prisoner of my fantasy?

Detente, sombra de mi bien esquivo,/ imagen del hechizo que más quiero,/
bella ilusión por quién alegre muero,/ dulce ficción por quien penosa vivo.//
Si al imán de tus gracias atractivo,/ sirve mi pecho de obediente acero,/
¿para qué me enamoras lisonjero,/ si has de burlarme luego fugitivo?// Mas
blasonar no puedes, satisfecho,/ de que triunfa de mí tu tiranía:/ que aunque
dejas burlado el lazo estrecho// que tu forma fantástica ceñía,/ poco importa
burlar brazos y pecho/ si te labra prisión mi fantasía.

Diuturnal Infirmity of Hope . . . / Diuturna enfermedad de la esperanza . . .
Samuel Beckett, trans.

Diuturnal infirmity of hope,
thou that sustainest thus my fainting years,
and on the equal edge of weal and woe
holdest in equilibrium the scales

forever in suspense, forever loath
to tilt, thy wiles obeying that forbid
the coming ever to excess of measure
either of confidence or of despair.

Who rid thee of the name of homicide?
For thou art crueler still, if well we mark
that thou suspendest the deluded soul

between a wretched and a happy lot,
not to the end that life may be preserved,
but to inflict a more protracted death.

Diuturna enfermedad de la esperanza/ que así entretienes mis cansados
años/ y en el fiel de los bienes y los daños/ tienes en equilibrio la balanza;//
que siempre suspendida en la tardanza/ de inclinarse, no dejan tus
engaños/ que lleguen a excederse en los tamaños/ la desesperación o la
confianza:// ¿quién te ha quitado el nombre de homicida?/ Pues lo eres
más severa, si se advierte/ que suspendes el alma entretenida;// y entre la
infausta o la felice suerte,/ no lo haces tú por conservar la vida/ sino por
dar más dilatada muerte.

Excerpt from Villancico VIII—Ensaladilla

Jerome Rothenberg and Cecilia Vicuña, trans.

At the high & holy feast
for their patron saint Nolasco
where the flock of the redeemer
offers high & holy praises,
a black man in the cathedral,
whose demeanor all admired,
shook his calabash & chanted
in the joy of the fiesta:

PUERTO RICO—THE REFRAIN

tumba la-lá-la tumba la-léy-ley
where ah's boricua no more's ah the slave way
tumba la-léy-ley tumba la-lá-la
where ah's boricua no more is a slave ah!

Sez today that in Melcedes
all them mercenary fadders
makes fiesta for they padre
face they's got lak a fiesta.

Do she say that she redeem me
such a thing be wonder to me
so ah's working in dat work house
& them Padre doesn't free me.

Other night ah play me conga
with no sleeping only thinking
how they don't want no black people
only them like her be white folk.

Once ah takes off this bandana
den God sees how them be stupid
though we's black folk we is human
though they say we be like hosses.

What's me saying, lawdy lawdy,
them old devil wants to fool me
why's ah whispering so softly
to that sweet redeemer lady.

Let this saint come and forgive me
when mah mouth be talking badly
if ah suffers in this body
then mah soul does rise up freely.

. . . .

THE INTRODUCTION CONTINUES

Now an Indian assuaged them,
falling down and springing up,
bobbed his head in time and nodded
to the rhythm of the dance,
beat it out on a *guitarra*,
echos madly out of tune,
tocotín of a mestizo,
Mexican and Spanish mixed.

TOCOTÍN

The Benedictan Padres
has Redeemer sure:
amo nic neltoca
quimatí no Dios.

Only God *Pilzíntli*
from up high come down
and our *tlatlacal*
pardoned one and all.

But these *Teopíxqui*
says in sermon talk
that this Saint Nolasco
miechtín hath bought.

I to Saint will offer
much devotion big
and from *Sempual xúchil*
a *xúchil* I will give.

Tehuátl be the only
one that says he stay
with them dogs los Moros
impan this holy day.

Mati dios if somewhere
I was to be like you
cen sontle I kill'um
beat'um black and blue

And no one be thinking
I make crazy talk,
ca ni like a baker
got so many thought.

Huel ni machicahuac
I am not talk smart

not teco qui mati
mine am hero heart.

One of my compañeros
he defy you sure
and with one big knockout
make you talk no more.

Also from the Governor
Topil come to ask
caipampa to make me
pay him money tax.

But I go and hit him
with a *cuihuatl*
ipam i sonteco:
don't know if I kill.

And I want to buy now
Saint Redeemer pure
yuhqui from the altar
with his blessing sure.

A los plausibles festejos/ que a su fundador Nolasco/ la Redentora Familia/
publica en justos aplausos,/ un Negro que entró en la Iglesia,/ de su grandeza
admirado,/ por regocijar la fiesta/ cantó al son de un calabazo:// Puerto
Rico—*Estribillo*// ¡Tumba, la-lá-la; tumba, la-lé-le;/ que donde ya Pilico, escrava
no quede!/ ¡Tumba, tumba, la-lé-le; tumba, la-lá-la/ que donde ya Pilico, no
quede escrava!// *Coplas*// Hoy dici que en las Melcede/ estos Parre Mercenaria/
hace una fiesa a su Palre./ ¿qué fiesa? como su cala.// Eya dici que redimi:/
cosa palece encantala,/ por que yo la Oblaje vivo/ y las Parre no mi saca.//
La otra noche con mi conga/ turo sin durmí pensaba,/ que no quiele gente
plieta,/ como eya so gente branca.// Sola saca la Pañola;/ ¡pues, Dioso, mila la
trampa,/ que aunque neglo, gente somo,/ aunque nos dici cabaya!/ Mas ¿qué
digo, Dioso mío?/ ¡Los demoño, que me engaña,/ pala que esé mulmulando/ a
esa Redentola Santa!// El Santo me lo perrone,/ que só una malo hablala/ que
aunque padesca la cuepo,/ en ese libla las alma// . . . // *Prosigue la Introducción*//
Púsolos en paz un Indio/ que, cayendo y levantando,/ tomaba con la cabeza/
la medida de los pasos;// el cual en una guitarra,/ con ecos desentonados,/
cantó un Tocotín mestizo/ de Español y Mejicano.// TOCOTÍN// Los Padres
bendito/ tiene on Redentor;/ *amo nic neltoca/ quimatí no Dios.*// Sólo Dios
Pilzíntli/ del Cielo bajó,/ y nuestro *tlatlacol*/ nos lo perdonó.// Pero estos
Teopíxqui/ dice en so sermón/ que este San Nolasco/ *miechtín* compró.// Yo al
Santo lo tengo/ mucha devoción,/ y de *Sempual Xúchil*/ un *Xúchil* le doy.//
Tehuátl so persona/ dis que so quedó/ con los perro Moro/ *impan ce* ocasión.//
Mati Dios, si allí/lo estoviera yo,/ *cen sontle* matara/ con un mojicón.// Y nadie

lo piense/ lo hablo sin razón,/ *ca ni* panadero,/ de mucha opinión.// *Huel ni machicáhuac;*/ no soy hablador:/*no teco qui mati,*/ que soy valentón.// *Se no* compañero/ lo desafió,/ y con *se* poñete/allí se cayó.// Ṭambién un *Topil*/ del Gobernador,/ *caipampa* tributo/ prenderme mandó.// Mas yo con un *cuihuatl*/ un palo lo dió/ *ipam i sonteco:*/ no sé si morió.// Y quiero comprar/ un San Redentor,/ *yuhqui* el del altar/ con su bendición.

Anonymous (Eighteenth Century, Mesoamerica, Maya)

The Book of Chilam Balam is a series of books written in alphabetic script in Yucatec Mayan by native priests in defense of their culture, to "banish Christianity" from their lands. They substitute for and contain ancient texts from the hieroglyphic books. Each town compiled its own book, thus "Chilam Balam of Chumayel," or of Tzimin, or of Mani. *Chilam* is "that which is mouth" or interpreter, and *Balam*, "Jaguar," the name for a lineage of Mayan priests but also the surname of a concrete man, said to have predicted the coming of a new religion shortly before the Conquest. The books contain prophecies, along with historical, poetic, calendric, and astrological compositions, and they reflect, according to Miguel León-Portilla, a Mayan sense of cyclical time where history and prophecy interact. They were written by more than one priest, and the contents of each book was renewed again and again to include events such as the conquest and the new Christian religion. These events link a specific past period with a present or a future.

Excerpt from The Book of Chilam Balam of Chumayel: Prophecy for K'atun 11 Ahaw

Ralph L. Roys, trans.

These priests of ours were to come to an end when misery was introduced,
    when Christianity was introduced by the real Christians. Then with
    the true God, the true *Dios*, came the beginning of our misery. It was
    the beginning of tribute, the beginning of church dues, the beginning
    of strife with purse-snatching, the beginning of strife with blowguns,
    the beginning of strife by trampling on people, the beginning of
    robbery with violence, the beginning of forced debts, the beginning of
    debts enforced by false testimony, the beginning of individual strife, a
    beginning of vexation, a beginning of robbery with violence. This was
    the origin of service to the Spaniards and priests, of service to the local
    chiefs, of service to the teachers, of service to the public prosecutors by
    the boys, the youths of the town, while the poor people were harassed.
    These were the very poor people who did not depart when oppression
    was put upon them.

Lay cu ah kinil,ca oci numya, ca oci Christianoil tumen lay hach
Christianoob. Ti uli y hahal ku, halal *Dios*, heuac u chun numya toon. U
chun patan, u chun limosna, u chun hoc mucuuc tza, u chun tz'on bacal
tza, u chum cumtan tza, u chun toc lukzah, u chun tz'alpach ppax, u chun
pakpach ppax, u chun caca tza, u chun numzah ya, u chun toc lukzah.
U chun u meyahtabal Españolesob y ah kinob, u meyahtabal batabob, u
meyahtabal camzahob, u meyahtabal fiscalob tumen mehen palabob, u palil
cahob, tamuk u chac numzabal ti yah ah numyahob. Lay hach otzilobe, lay
hach otzilob ma likulobi tilic u mentic /[c] ii u tz'aalpach.

Excerpt from The Book of Chilam Balam of Mani: The Cuceb
Seventh Year

John Bierhorst, trans.

The time when the bird, *the prophecy,* of the katun shall be composed, a time
  of penance: removed are the breechcloths, *removed* the mantles; the time
  of Ahau Can, *Lord Serpent, the time of* the seizing of the jewel from Chac
  Bolay Ul, *Great Predator Lord;* the time when he shall be set in the sky,
  shall Ahau Can, and he shall observe the holder of the mat, the holder of
  the throne, when he vomits that which he begged, which he swallowed,
  which passed through his throat; when the children of Maax Cal, *Monkey
  Speaker,* turn traitor: for *the monkey* Maax Kin, *the monkey* Maax Katun,
  specter of the earth, has loosened their breechcloths. Such his command.
  Red his breechcloth. From the north did he come, from the west did he
  come; *then* were they sold, *were* the children of Uuc Suhuy Sip, in his
  time, in his katun. Of sin is his word, of sin is his mouth.

Comes a time when the drum will resound on earth and the rattle on high,
  when the bird, *the prophecy,* of the katun shall be composed; the katun
  will turn: comes a violent tearing, a ripping: the skies will be parted, the
  clouds will be parted, suddenly, at once, in the face of the sun, in the
  face of the moon.

Of *no use,* of no profit, are you the motherless, you the fatherless, in the fold of
  the end of the katun. Lost will be that which you knew, which was known of
  you. Comes a time when the dry leaves are heaped above you; gone are your
  breechcloths, your mantles; gone is your mask, gone your home. Mandata.

Uac hix u kinil u lubul u tzol ch'ich' katun ti ual u colal ex u colal nok,
ch'ab tu kin tu kin u h ahaucan, tu pachil tun ti chac bolai, lai ul tu kin tzai
can u pacte ah tem pop ah ten tz'am, ti tali u xeic tu chi u lukahe, lai het
man tu cal ti ma tupani, tumen u tzotz tumen u conic u mehen ah max can,
bini ual u haulic u choch u yex u max kin u max // katune; u manab cabal
he bal u t'an, chac u uex tali ti xaman, tali ti chikin, tu kin tu katunil, u
conic yal u mehen uuc suhuy sip, tu kin yan sip u t'an, sip chi, ti uil uchom

pax ti cab, uchom soot canal, tu tzol ch'ich' katun t ulom uatz' katun, tu kin hatab ak bai ch'ich' heeb, heb tanba nom caan, heb tamba nom muyal, tu uich kin, tu uich, u. ualac hun uatz' hun tz'on hii uale, mamac bin a tz'ab, cech ah mab nae, cech ah mab yume, tech u uatz' tech u tz'oi katune, sati u canil, sati ual tu pache, tu kin yan u molba sohol au okol, ma au ex, ma a nok, ma tu kin u tial a mhan koh ix mahan naile ma.

Anonymous (Eighteenth Century, Argentina)

Visual poetry, as is the case with these poems, could be approached as a system of language patterns with the visual aspects of a poem often considered of secondary importance. Thus, according to the dominant viewpoint, poetry is best defined as "content," "substance," and "spirit," thus ensuring the exclusion of visual poetry from the canon. Proponents of visual poetry, however, point to a lively tradition that, in Latin America, dates back to the eighteenth century, examples of which can be found in the Segurola Collection of Argentina's National Library in Buenos Aires. In the collection, one finds acrostics, anagrams, and other modes whose antecedents are as old as the "telestika" of ancient Greece.

Grant Don Juan V Life / Dad a D. Juan V una vida

G. J. Racz, trans.

```
            A D I V A N U N A V I D A
              I V A N U V U N A V I
              A N U V N V U N A
              U V N A N V U
A                 N A U A N                 A
D I               A V J V A               I D
I V A             U I D I U             A V I
V A N U           J D A D J           U N A V
A N U V N A U J   D A D A D   J U A N V U N A
N U V N A U J D   A D A D A   D J U A N V U N
U V N A U J D A   D A D A D   A D J U A N V U
N U V N A U J D   A D A D A   D J U A N V U N
A N U V N A U J   D A D A D   J U A N V U N A
V A N U           J D A D J           U N A V
I V A             U J D J U           A V I
D I               A V J V A               I D
A                 N A U A N                 A
              U V N A N V U
              A N U V N V U N A
            I V A N U V U N A V I
          A D I V A N U N A V I D A
```

Eight-Line Acrostic / Octava acróstica

G. J. Racz, trans.

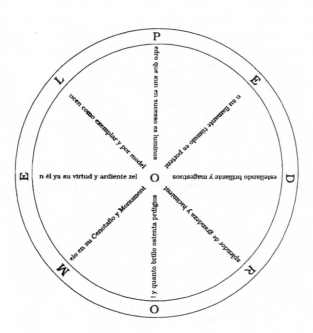

(in the shape of a maze that might be placed
on the burial mound at his glorious funeral)
P edro, bright even at death's portic O
E ntombed in rays the grave would not forg O
D eceased, though still the grand magnific O
R esplendent as in life not long ag O
O h! how your marble cenotaph gleams s O
M elo, shine on, noble politic O
E xalting virtues death could scarce end O
L ight unto men and moral model to O

Simón Rodríguez (1775–1854, Venezuela)

A philosopher and educator, born in Caracas, Venezuela, Rodríguez was the
enlightened mentor of Simón Bolivar. His thought, evolved under the influence
of Gabriel Girard and J. J. Rousseau, was oriented toward the liberation of the
Americas. In his writing, he created a hybrid of didactic essay and visual poetry
through a set of aphorisms, altering typography and fonts in midsentence to
highlight the power of the images in a system he called "the art of painting
ideas." This creation was a forerunner of the typographical experiments of the
European avant-garde at the end of the nineteenth century. According to José
Lezama Lima, he instilled in Bolivar an admiration for the Incas as giving potential to the future of the Americas. Widely traveled, he witnessed the mythical
moment when Bolivar vowed to liberate South America from Spanish rule. At
the end of his life, he went to Bolivia in search of the "center that irradiates
the energy of space," but he died in Peru, alone and in total poverty. PRINCIPAL
WORK: *Obras completas* (1975)

Social Virtues and Illuminations / Luces y virtudes sociales

Mónica de la Torre, trans.

SHAPE given to DISCOURSE

Painting	Elementary ideas	into *Paradigm*
	Thoughts	into *Synopsis*

The TONGUE   and   the   HAND

are humanity's most precious gifts
(notes Buffon)

Hereby understood with regard to the
INTENTION TO INSTRUCT

It concerns not the Importance of the Word
for
none knows it

The Importance of its PAINTING
is well-known by a few
most . . . don't even think of it

nonetheless

One can PAINT without SPEAKING
but not SPEAK without PAINTING

GESTURES are a SKETCH

of what the *hand* for a lack of *means*
cannot draw   or   of time

GESTURING is painting IN THE AIR

in *spoken* discourse   connection of Ideas
as   and
in the *written* one   connection of Thoughts

The connection of Ideas *is presented* in a PARADIGM
That   of thoughts   in SYNOPSIS

PARADIGM is . . .

a model of   Ideas compared so as to
                make their connection felt

SYNOPSIS is . . .

that in which one sees, at a blow,
a painting   the connection between several Ideas
forming a thought or many

The sense of a Thought is a *Proposition*
and the formula expressing it is a *Phrase*

A proposition compounded
by other Propositions   is a GENERAL IDEA
taken from the elements

of many other divisions
called PARAGRAPHS
Their formula consists of how many Elementary Propositions
are included in the *General Idea*

in Sum

a SYNOPSIS is a compound of PARADIGMS

FORMA que se da al DISCURSO/ Pintando {las Ideas elementales = en *Paradigma*/ {los Pensamientos = en *Sinópsis*// La LENGUA y la MANO// son los dotes mas preciosos del hombre/ *(observa Buffon)*// Entiéndase aquí con respecto á la/ INTENCIÓN DE INSTRUIR// No se trata de la Importancia de la Palabra/ porque/ no hay quien no la conozca// La Importancia de su PINTURA/ la conocen pocos bien/ muchos. . . . ni piensan en ella// no obstante// Se puede PINTAR sin HABLAR/ pero nó HABLAR sin PINTAR// Los JESTOS son un BOSQUEJO/ de lo que la *mano*/ no puede dibujar}por falta{de *medios*/ *ó de tiempo* / JESTICULAR es pintar EN EL AIRE// en el discurso *hablado*/ como/ en el. *escrito* } debe haber {conexion de Ideas/ y/ conexión de pen-/ samientos// La conexión de Ideas *se presenta* en PARADIGMA/ La. de pensamientos . en SINÓPSIS// PARADIGMA es. . . . // un ejemplar de {Ideas comparadas para/ hacer sentir su conexión// SINOPSIS es. . . . / un cuadro { en que se ve, de un golpe,/ la conexion de varias Ideas/ haciendo un pensamiento ó varios// El sentido de un Pensamiento se llama *Proposicion*/ y la fórmula con que se expresa. *Frase*// Proposicion compuesta/ de otras Proposiciones *tomadas por elementos* }es IDEA JENERAL// Su fórmula consta {de otras tantas divisiones/ llamadas PARRAFOS/ cuantas Proposiciones elementales/ entran en la *Idea jeneral*// en Suma// SINÓPSIS es un compuesto de PARADIGMAS

Anonymous (Seventeenth–Eighteenth Century? Peru)

Atawallpa (Atahualpa) Death Prayer, also known as *Yana K'uychi*, or Black Rainbow, is an anonymous, undated Quechua poem, collected in the Calca-Pisac region of Peru, possibly at the end of the eighteenth or the early nineteenth century, first published by José María Farfan. A landmark in Andean poetics, it transforms the death of the last Inca ruler, executed by *garrote vil* in 1533, into a symbolic beheading of the entire body of the Andean world. With the Inca identified with the sun, the execution severs the people's connection to the cosmos and brings about the black rainbow. According to Mercedez López Baralt, the author was already acculturated, since the metric arrangement of the verses follows a European model. There have been many versions by authors such as Jesús Lara, José María Arguedas, and Teodoro Meneses. This version was created by the contemporary indigenous poet of the Calca-Pisac area, Odi González.

Atahualpa Death Prayer / Apu Inka Atawallpaman / Al patriarca, Inka Atawallpa

James Scully, trans.

What sick rainbow is this
stealing in, so black?
For Cuzco's enemies
a false dawn dances—
a hailstorm of disease
beating on everyone.

Time and again
my heart
sensed it coming—
and I, sunk in dreams
fitful, half felt
the nasty blue fly of death.

In one omen the sun
went out, paling
shrouding the corpse of Atahualpa.
And with his death his lineage
diminished
in the blink of an eye.

Grim enemies
cut off his head,
already the river of blood
breaks up branching out.

Already his strong teeth gnaw
anguish they can't stop,
the brilliant eyes of the great Inca
cloud over.

Now the great heart of Atahualpa
turns bitter cold, now
throughout his four dominions
they're shouting their lungs out.

Thick mist misting down
amasses darkness.
Mother moon withdraws into herself
as if wishing to be reborn,
everyone's busy hiding themselves,
remorseful.

Earth refuses to take in
its master—as if
mortified by the corpse
of one who loved it,
loathe to devour
its lord.

Now the hardness of rock
gives way, hollowing,
the river roaring sorrow
is swollen to overflowing.

Tears held back gush forth,
river carries them off.
Who human has not wept
for a loved one?
What child would not be
by its father's side?
Moaning, heavy heart struck
joyless.

What virgin dove would not
care for who courts her?
And what wild stag dying doesn't let
its heartbeats keep it going?

Tears of blood
torn from joy, reflect
in shining drops
the corpse,
heart softened,
blood bathed in his country's lap.

Those touched in passing
by his masterful hands,
those enfolded in
the wings of his heart,
those protected
by the fine mesh of his chest,
wail with the unbridled cries
of inconsolable widows.

Colorful women congregate
but dressed in black,
the sun priest has wrapped himself
in his most dark cloak,

common people line up
by the graves.

Death spreads. Sorrow stuns.
Tears of the Queen Mother
burst like spring freshets
over the yellowing corpse.
Her face is cold, pallid.
Her mouth speaks:

Where will you in exile
find rest, out of my sight,
leaving our land
abandoned to suffering,
you from my heart
cut out forever?

Regardless rooms of promised treasure,
the foreign enemy, your captors,
by nature
rapacious voracious carried on
like snarly beasts in a mad rush.
Those you gave
an easy life with gold and silver
gave you death.

Captured
you lavished on them all they desired,
but with your death in Cajamarca
everything stopped.
In your arteries
blood crusts.
Eyes blur. Your look
dissolves into the dark side
of the brightest star.

Who feels for you weeps, wanders, runs
after your well-loved soul—
your fevered troubled heart
howls
breaking off from the indignity
of your perishing.

Your gold sedan chair dismantled,
your throne
its canopy woven of gold threads
shredded, is handed out as spoils.

Ruled by heaped up punishments
cut to the quick
stupefied, estranged, without justice
isolated
weighing how our bodies have no shadows
we cry
to no one to appeal to
ourselves alone together, talking crazy.

Will your heart allow us
great Inca
to be wandered every which way
scattered
at large, to be by others
ground underfoot?

Open your clear-seeing eyes,
open them!
reach out your hands
most giving,
and with this good sign
leave us strong.

Ima k'uychin kay yana k'uychi/ sayarimun?/ Qosqop awqanpa millay
wach'i/ illarimun;/ tukuy imapi saqra chikchi/ t'akakamun// Watupakurqan
sonqollaymi/ sapa kuti/ mosqoynipipas-ch'eqmi-ch'eqmi,/ uti-uti,/
chiririnka qhenchataraqmi,/ ¡Aqoy phuti!// Inti tutayan q'elloyaspa,/
-hoq watuypi-/ Atawallpata ayachaspa/ chay sutinpi,/ wañuynillanta
chikachaspa/ hoq ch'illmiypi.// Umallantas wit'unkuña/ millay awqa;/
yawar mayus purisqanña/ p'alqa-p'alqa.// Q'aqmaq kirus phachakunña/
¡llakiy salqa!/ Titiyanñas Inti ñawillan/ Apu Inkaq;// chiriyanñas hatun
sonqollan/ Atawallpaq;/ Tawantinsuyus waqallasqan/ hik'isparaq.//
Pacha phuyus tiyaykamunña/ tutayaspa;/ mama killas qamparmananña/
wawayaspa;/ tukuy imapas pakakunña/ llakikuspa.// Allpas mich'akun
meqllayllanta/ apullanpaq,/ p'enqakoq hina ayallanta/ munaqninpaq/
manchakoq hina wamink'anta/ millp'unqanpaq.// Qaqapas ch'ilan
apunmanta/ wankakuspan;/ mayupas qaparin phutiymanta/ hunt'akuspan./
weqekuna kuska tanta/ mich'ukuspa./ Pi runan mana waqanmanchu/
munaqninpaq?/ Ima churin mana kanmanchu/ yayallanpaq ancheq,
phuteq sonqo k'irilla/ mana t'aqlla?// Ima urpin mana kanmanchu/
yanamanta?/ musphaykachaq?/ T'illa luychu/ sonqoymanta/ yawar
weqeq, qhechu-qhechu/ kusinmanta?/ Lirp'uy phaqcha weqellanwan/
ayallanta/ armaykuspa, wawa sonqowan/ meqllasqanta/ chunka maki
kamarinninwan/ lulusqanta/ sonqollanpa raprallanwan/ p'intuykuspa,/
qhasqollanpa llikallanwan/ qataykuspa/ llakeq ikmaq qhaqyaynillanwan/

qaparispa,// pallakunan muyuykunña/ yanakama;/ Willaq Umu
llaqollakunña/ arphankama;/ llapa runan wachurikunña/ p'uytunkama.//
Wañuy-p'itin, llaki-musphan/ Mama Qhoya;/ mayu-mayu weqen
phawan/ q'ello aya/ tikay-tikay uyallanpas,/ simillampas:// Maytan rinki
chinkarispayki/ ñawiymanta,/ kay suyuta saqerispayki/ llakiymanta,/
wiñayllanpaq t'aqakuspayki/ sonqoymanta?// Wasi hunt'a qori qolqewan/
yuraq awqa/ -atiy millp'uy millay sonqowan/ tanqa-tanqa,/ aswan-aswan
t'ituy munaywan/ phiña salqa-/ tukuy imata qosqhaqtiyki/ sipisunki,//
munayninman hunt'aykachinki/ qan, sapayki/ Qaqa Markapi wañuspayki/
p'uchukanki/ Thukuruyanñan sirk'aykipi/ yawarniyki;/ qhoqayarinñan
ñawiykipi/ rikuyniyki,/ ancha qoyllur lliplliyinillanpi/ qhawayniyki.//
Anchin, phutin, purin, phawan/ urpillayki,/ muspha-muspha, llakin,
waqan/ sonqollayki,/ aqoy raki ñak'ariywan/ sonqo p'aki.// Chullmi-
chullmi qori wantu/ k'irawniyki'/ tukuy ima qori puytu/ raki-raki.// -hoq
makipi-ñak'ay qoto/ t'ipi-t'ipi,/ Tunki-tunki yuyay-manaspa,/ sapallayku,/
mana llanthuyoq rikukuspa/ waqasqayku,/ mana pi mayman kutirispa/
musphasqayku.// Atinqachus sonqollayki,/ Apu Inka,/ kanaykuta chinkay
chaki,/ mana muska,/ ch'eqe-ch'eqe hoqpa makinpa/ saruchasqa?// Ñuhña
wach'eq ñawillkita/ kicharimuy,/ ancha qokoq makillaykita/ mast'arimuy/
chay samiwan kallpanchasqata/ ripuy niway.

¿Qué arco iris malsano es éste/ que se insinúa tan negro?/Un fulgor espurio
resplandece al amanecer/ para el enemigo del Cusco,/ Granizada infecta
arremete/ contra todo// Ya mi corazón lo presentía/ una y otra vez,/,Y
en mis sueños sumido,/ adormecido,/ ya sentía al nefasto moscardón
de la muerte,/ fatal percance.// En uno de los presagios, el sol/ se apagaba
palideciendo,/ amortajando el cadáver de Atawallpa/ Y con su muerte,
su estirpe/ se reducía/ a un cerrar y abrir de ojos// Torvos enemigos/
decapitaron ya su testa;/ El río de sangre ya discurre/ bifurcándose en
ramales// Su firme dentadura empieza ya a roerse/ angustia irrefrenable,/
Ya se empañan los ojos fulgentes/ del supremo patriarca// Se ha helado
ya el gran corazón/ de Atawallpa/ Y de sus cuatro señoríos le lloran/
desgañitándose// Ya descendió la densa niebla/ acumulando oscuridad/
Ya se encoge la madre luna/ como si volviera a nacer/ Y todos ocupan sus
escondrijos/ remordiéndose// Ya la tierra se niega a cobijar/ a su Señor/
como si le abochornara el cadáver/ de quien la amó,/ como si temiera
engullirse/ a su caudillo// Ya ceja la dureza de los peñascos/ horadándose;/
Ya brama de dolor el río/ de crecido caudal// Ya el embalse de lágrimas
vertidas/ se deseca entremezclada/ ¿Qué mortal no habría de llorar/ por
quien le amó?/ ¿Qué vástago no estaría del lado/ de su padre?/ Gimiente,
desolado corazón herido/ sin regocijo// ¿Qué doncella, qué paloma no
cuidaría/ de su galán?/ ¿Y qué moribundo ciervo cerril/ no se deja llevar por
sus latidos?// Lágrimas arrebatadas a la quita-quita/ ajenas a toda alegría,
reflejan/ en la cascada acuosa/ el cadáver,/ su reblandecido corazón/ bañado

en el regazo// Los que fueron rozados/ por sus diez dedos forjadores,/
Los que fueron arropados/ con las alas de su corazón,/ Los que fueron
abrigados/ con la fina malla de su tórax/ chillan con la gritería/ de las viudas
plañideras// Ya las majas se aglomeran/ vestidas de luto,/ El sacerdote solar
se ha ceñido su manto/ más oscuro/ Y el vulgo se ha alineado/ en fosas//
Cunde la muerte, el dolor aturde/ Y las lágrimas de la reina madre/ discurren
como riadas/ por el cadáver amarillento./ Ya el rostro de ella es fría natilla/
y su boca profiere:// ¿Dónde recalarás desterrado/ lejos de mis ojos,/ dejando
este reino/ abandonado a su pena,/ y separándote para siempre/ de mi
corazón?// No obstante el recinto atestado de tesoros,/ el foráneo enemigo,/
tus captores,/ de naturaleza rapaz, voraz,/ precipitándose en tumulto/ con
su afán irrefrenable/ hoscas alimañas/ a quienes holgaste con oro y plata,/ te
dieron muerte// Desde tu cautiverio/ les colmaste de todos sus antojos,/ pero
con tu muerte, en Cajamarca,/ todo concluyó/ En las arterias/ ya tu sangre
coaguló/ Ya se hizo borrosa la visión/ de tus ojos,/ Tu mirar se disuelve en el
lado oscuro/ de la estrella más radiante// Ya se conduele, solloza, deambula,
corretea,/ tu ánima bienamada,/ Tu febril corazón pena/ gime/ Se desgarra
con el agravio/ de tu perecimiento// Tu dorada litera descoyuntada,/ tu
solio/ cada tejido urdido con fibra de oro,/ todo fue vilmente repartido//
Regidos por las penas acumuladas,/ acerados,/ atolondrados, enajenados, sin
juicio,/ aislados,/ contemplando nuestro cuerpo sin sombra/ sollozamos,/
sin recurrir a nadie/ sólo entre nosotros deliramos// ¿Permitirá tu corazón/
gran patriarca/ que deambulemos sin norte/ dispersos/ sueltos en manos
de otros,/ malamente pisoteados?// Abre ya tus ojos penetrantes/ ábrelos,/
extiende tus manos/ generosas/ y con esa buena seña/ despídenos,
fortalecidos.

Bartolomé Hidalgo (1788–1822, Argentina)

Hidalgo was born in Montevideo, Uruguay, to Argentinean parents. He employed
the voice of the gaucho in poems that focused on patriotism and on Argentina's
political situation. His gaucho poetry, a genre that he helped shape, includes
two types: the "cielito" and the "diálogo." Colonial independence from Spain
defined his political view and poetry, enabling a new creative environment in
which Hidalgo could express his ideals in the gaucho style. He also wrote in the
European neoclassic style, achieving excellence in both—a perfect example of
the transitional process from colonial to national literature. PRINCIPAL WORKS:
Marcha oriental (1811), *Sentimientos de un patriota* (1816), *Diálogo patriótico*
(1820–1821)

New Patriotic Dialogue / Nuevo diálogo patriótico

Molly Weigel, trans.

Between Ramón Contreras, Gaucho of the Monte Guard, and Chano, Overseer of a Ranch in the Tordillo Islands

Chano
What's up friend Ramón,
what are you doing in my district
on that chestnut racehorse?

Contreras
Friend, I'm getting him ready
because I have to run
against Hilario's sorrel.

Chano
You don't say! If that's the way it is
I'm going to put eight to four odds
on this wild one.
Look, friend, he's a horse
that already at the starting line
leans back the other way.

Contreras
And how've you been since that day
we were talking?

Chano
Healthy but without yerba:
unsaddle your horse,
hang up your gear, and rest.
Take this rag, Mariano,
and walk with the yellow bay
and hook him up to the others.
That strech between here and the Guard
is pretty hair-raising, huh?

Contreras
And with so many downpours
the road is very rough,
and full of outlaws
you're always bumping into;
the good thing is that I've sharpened
the poisoned knife to my taste.
With the tamers I asked
the chestnut four questions,
and when he was eager

and raising hell,
I let the reins out full and I came away,
but always on the watch . . .
take the yerba, old friend
we'll keep on drinking bitter mate.

Chano
And what about the motherland
that I'm so worried about?
Yesterday some officials
dropped by Pablo's
and while they were drinking mate
they took a shot of cane liquor
and changed the mate water,
and read some notices
about King Fernando
anxiously requesting
through his deputies
that his sworn constitution
be recognized in these parts.

Contreras
The rumor's been going around for days,
certainly they weren't deceiving you:
the deputies came,
and from the ship they sent a whole heap of papers
in the name of King Fernando;
and the braggarts came . . .
the ba . . . those bad horsemen!
But friend, our Junta
gave a shout and pushed it out
and sent them a reply
much prettier than San Bernardo.
Ah, gauchos, scribers
on a cigarette paper!
When the others saw the gauchos weren't biting,
and that they'd been beat,
they raised anchor,
and, turning the ship around,
they left without saying goodbye . . .
May they go with two hundred devils.

Chano
He's a clod,
our friend Don Fernando:
as I figure it,

he's so useless
he doesn't even know how to whistle
sure as my name is Chano.
we dropped the price
of all his orders to nothing
and for our freedom
and its sacred rights
we left the countryside;
and came upon the enemy,
our ponchos ready for a fight
and jackknifes in hand,
with out hearts in God
and the holy scapulary
of Our Lady of Carmen,
and crouching like a cat;
without heeding the bullets or the strong cannon fire,
we struck each other in the mouth
and clashed together,
I like this one, I don't like that one,
and so we cornered them,
and at a shout: Long live the motherland!
we redoubled our courage,
and among shots and smoke and confusion,
among slaps and slashes
they began to slacken,
and so loose did they get,
that of all that great company
we left not even a memory.
For good measure, we threw in
some other battles
which we also creamed them;
and if they don't believe it, they can ask
that liar Posadas
how he did down there in Law Pierdas,
and there on the ships.
So Tristan would say . . . I don't want to
waste any more time shooting vultures,
because Tristan was much sadder
than that other poor loverboy.
And Muesas at del Cerrito;
Marcó weak and bloodthirsty
at the battle of Chacabuco,
Osorio the strongman
there in the Cerros de Espejo

in the brawl at Maipu.
Speak up, Quimper and O'Relly,
and you others who are being so quiet now,
Everything's free, Contreras,
if you know Fernando,
he keeps drawing
but only gets a lousy hand.
Isn't it ridiculous
him coming around now to threaten us?
He'd better not sleep too much,
friend, because his subjects
find the name of Liberty
to their liking,
and since he starts to get on his jammies
even while he's threatening us,
they've already taken him for everything
and cut him out of the game.

Contreras
Oh, Chano, I'm afraid
that goes without saying,
What you've told me is the truth
and I can't deny it;
but *put yourself in this situation*:
that they're scheming
to see if we unyoke outselves
from the rest, and then
they'll strip us of everything,
even our trousers.

Chano
Friend, better not touch that subject
because the devils are in me!
Who could stand up to us
if we joined forces?
I'm not talking about that dolt of a king;
all the tyrants of the world together
with more soldiers than there are mares in our countryside
couldn't hurt us; but friend,
quarreling about how we get paid
has slowed us down some.
Ah, friend, how much precious blood
has been spilled! Conteras,
doesn't it hurt to see
how we Americans

live in perpetual war,
giving our enemy
such a good time
while our time is so bitter?
But I hope from this time forward
to greet the May Sun
in happier days,
united with my brothers.
So there's no need to back down,
since brave San Martin is already
at the ports of Lima
with those tough boys,
soldiers in a bad mood,
and they tell me that in Lima
there are so many patriots
that Pezuela's out spying,
and when he is defeated
out State will have to be changed,
because patriotism will be born again
in even the humblest hovel.

Contreras
Yessir, you bet.
That's the moment we've been waiting for!
And as soon as it's over
right then we'll show up
with rifle and sabre
to beg a longshot
not to throw away what belongs to someone else
because it's a terrible sin
against the task of the owner
to use what one hasn't been given;
and in good conscience (because
I'm a true Christian) I don't want
anyone to be damned
for such a reckless act.

Chano
Right, Ramón Conteras!
Do you remember that holy mess
that we saw at Andújar
when General Belgrano
made the leg-guards break on the Spanish,
those bad horsemen?
The general sure screwed up

in that battle (without meaning to hurt us)
and we're still paying for it;
he wanted to be generous,
and he soon saw how he was tricked,
when the sworn Castro
took up arms against him,
and broke his vow,
staining his honor and his rank.
Those generosities
have thrown us far off course,
because the tyrant assumes
that such strange behavior
is only a lack of justice;
but that's all past, friend,
and it won't be bad
if we finally learn our lesson.
For now, take out your knife,
let's polish off this barbecue
and then take a siesta,
so we can go to the Bald Indian's
to see if my piebald
has turned up in his herd;
several days ago that brute
slipped out of the pen.

They ate with great contentment
and after their siestas
they saddled up loosely
and left at a gallop for the hovel of Andrés Bordón,
alias the Bald Indian,
who served as a sad soldier
in the northern provinces,
and in the battle of Vilcapulgio
they shot off his leg.
They shouted at the fence where his property began,
the dogs raised hell;
Bordón left his kitchen,
and helped them off their horses;
and what passed between them
we'll tell another time, more slowly;
for now the pen has grown tired.

*Entre Ramón Conteras, gaucho de la Guardia del Monte, y Chano, capataz de una
estancia en las islas del Tordillo//* Chano/ ¿Qué dice, amigo Ramón,/ qué anda

haciendo por mi *Pago*,/ en el zaino *parejero*?// Contreras/ Amigo, lo ando variando,/ porque tiene que correr/ con el cebruno de Hilario.// Chano/ ¡Qué me cuenta! Si es ansí/ voy a poner ocho a cuatro/ a favor de este bagual:/ mire, amigo, que es caballo/ que en la rompida, no más,/ ya se recostó al contrario.// Contreras// ¿Y cómo jué desde el día/ que estuvimos platicando?// Chano// Con salú, pero sin yerba./ desensille su caballo,/ tienda el apero, y descanse./ (Tomá este pingo, Mariano,/ y con el bayo amarillo/ caminá y acollarálo)./ Mire que de aquí a la Guardia/ hay un tirón temerario!// Contreras// Y, con tantos aguaceros,/ está el camino pesao;/ y *malevos*, que da miedo,/ anda uno no más topando;/ lo güeno, que yo afilé/ a mi gusto el *envenao*,/ lo hice, con las de *domar*,/ cuatro preguntas al zaino,/ y en cuanto lo vi ganoso/ y que se iba alborotando,/ le aflojé todo, y me vine,/ pero siempre maliciando . . . / Velay yerba, amigo viejo;/ iremos *cimarroniando*.// Chano// Y ¿cómo va con la Patria,/ que me tiene con cuidao?/ Ayer, unos oficiales/ cayeron por lo de Pablo/ y, mientras tomaban *mate*,/ lo asentaron, y mudaron,/ leyeron unas noticias/ atento del rey Fernando/ que solicita con ansia,/ por medio de diputados,/ ser aquí reconocido,/ su constitución jurando.// Contreras/ Anda el runrún, hace días:/ por cierto, no lo engañaron:/ los diputaos vinieron/ y, desde el barco, mandaron/ toda la papelería/ a nombre del rey Fernando./ ¡Y venían *roncadores* . . . / la pu, los maturrangos!/ Pero, amigo, nuestra Junta / al grito les largó el guacho/ y les mandó una respuesta/ más linda que San Bernardo./ ¡Ah gauchos escribinistas/ en el papel de un cigarro!/ Viendo ellos que no embocaban/ y que los habían torniao,/ alzaron los contrapesos/ y, dando güeltas al barco,/ se jueron sin despedirse . . . / Vayan con doscientos diablos!// Chano/ Mire que es hombre muy rudo/ el amigo don Fernando:/ lo contemplo tan inútil,/ asigún lo he figurao,/ que creo que ni silbar/ sabe, como yo soy Chano./ De balde dimos la baja/ a todos sus mandatarios,/ y por nuestra libertá/ y sus derechos sagraos/ nos salimos, campo ajuera,/ y al enemigo topando,/ el *poncho* a medio envolver/ y con alfajor en la mano,/ con el corazón en Dios/ y con el santo escapulario/ de nuestra Virgen del Carmen,/ haciendo cuerpo de gato,/ sin reparar en las balas/ ni en los juertes cañonazos,/ nos golpiamos en la boca/ y ya nos *entreveramos*;/ y a éste quiero, a éste no quiero,/ los juimos arrinconando/ y a un grito: ¡Viva la Patria!/ el coraje redoblamos/ y, entre tiros y humadera,/ entre reveses y tajos,/ empezaron a flaquiar;/ y tan del todo alfojaron/ que de esta gran competencia/ ni memoria nos dejaron./ De balde en otras aiciones/ les dimos contra los cardos,/ y, si no, que le pregunten/ a Posadas, el mentao,/ cómo le jué, allá en las Piedras,/ y después, allá en los barcos./ Diga Tristán . . . , mas no quiero/ gastar pólvora en *chimangos*,/ porque era Tristán, más triste/ que hombre pobre enamorao;/ Muesas, en la del Cerrito;/ Marcó, flojo y sanguinario/ en la aición de Chacabuco;/ Osorio es hombre fortacho/ allá en los cerros de Espejo;/ en la pendencia de Maipo/ hable Quimper, y ese O'Relly,/ y otros muchos que ahura callo./ Todo es de balde, Contreras,/ pues si conoce Fernando/ que aunque haga rodar la taba . . . / culos no más sigue

echando/ ¿no es una barbaridá/ el venir áhura *roncando*?/ Mejor es que duerma
poco/ porque, amigo, a sus vasallos/ el nombre de Libertá/ creo que les va
agrandando,/ y, como él medio se acueste,/ cuanto se quede roncando,/ ya le
hicieron trus la vaca,/ y ya me lo capotiaron.// Contreras// Ah, Chano! Si, de
sabido,/ perdiz se hace entre las manos!/ cuanto me ha dicho es ansina/ y yo
no puedo negarlo;/ pero esté usté en el *aquel*,/ que ellos andan cabuliando/ a
ver si nos desunimos/ del todo y, en este caso,/ arrancarnos lo que es nuestro/
y hasta el chiripá limpiarnos.// Chano// No toque, amigo, ese punto,/ porque
me llevan los diablos!/ ¿Quién nos mojaría la oreja/ si uniéramos nuestros
brazos?/ No digo un Rey tan lulingo,/ mas ni todos los tiranos/ juntos, con
más soldadesca/ que hay yeguada en nuestros campos,/ nos habían de hacer
roncha;/ pero, amigo, es el trabajo/ que nuestras desavenencias/ nos tienen
medio atrasaos./ ¡Ah, sangre, amigo, preciosa,/ tanta que se ha derramao!/ ¿No
es un dolor ver, Contreras,/ que ya los americanos/ vivimos en guerra eterna/ y
que, al enemigo dando/ ratos alegres y güenos,/ los tengamos bien amargos?/
Pero yo espero, desta hecha,/ saludar al Sol de Mayo/ en días más lisonjeros,/
unidos con mis hermanos;/ y ansí, no hay que recular,/ que ya San Martín,
el bravo,/ está en las puertas de Lima/ con puros *mozos amargos*,/ soldadesca
corajuda;/ y, sigún me han informao,/ en Lima hay tanto patriota/ que Pezuela
anda orejiando/ y, en logrando su redota,/ ha de cambiar nuestro Estado,/
pues renace el patriotismo/ en el más infeliz rancho.// Contreras// Sí, señor,
dejuramente;/ ¡ah, momento suspirao!/ y, en cuanto esto se concluya,/ al grito,
nos descolgamos/ con latón y garabina/ a suplicarle a un tapao/ que largue,
no más, lo ajeno;/ porque es terrible pecao,/ contra el gusto de su dueño/ usar
lo que no se ha dao;/ y, en concensia, yo no quiero/ (porque soy muy güen
cristiano)/ que ninguno se condene/ por hecho tan temerario.// Chano//
¡Eso sí Ramón Contreras!/ ¿Se acuerda del fandangazo/ que vimos en lo de
Andújar,/ cuando el general Belgrano/ hizo sonar los cueritos,/ en Salta, a los
maturrangos?/ Por cierto que en esta aición/ (sin intención de dañarnos)/ hizo
un barro el general,/ que aún hoy lo estamos pagando:/ él quiso ser generoso/
y presto miró su engaño,/ cuando hizo armas en su contra/ el juramentao
Castro/ que, quebrantando su voto,/ manchó su honor y su grao./ Estas
generosidades/ muy lejos nos han tirao,/ porque el tirano presume/ que un
proceder tan bizarro/ sólo es falta de justicia;/ pero esto ya se ha pasao/ y no
será malo, amigo,/ si, por fin, escarmentamos./ Por áhura saque el cuchillo,/
despachemos este asao,/ y sestiaremos, después,/ para ir a lo del Pelao/a ver
si, entre su manada,/ está, amigo, mi picazo,/ que, hace días, que este bruto/
de las mansas se ha apartao.// Comieron con gran quietú/ y, después de haber
sestiao,/ ensillaron medio flojo/ y se salieron, al tranco,/ al rancho de Andrés
Bordón/ alias el Indio Pelao,/ que en las pendencias de arriba/ sirvió de triste
soldao/ y en Vilcapugio, de un tiro,/ una pierna le troncharon./ Dieron el
grito en el cerco;/ los perros se alborotaron;/ Bordón dejó la cocina,/ los hizo
apiar del caballo;/ y lo que entre ellos pasó/ lo diremos, más despacio,/ en otra
ocasión, que en ésta/ ya la pluma se ha cansao.

Francisco Acuña de Figueroa (1790–1862, Uruguay)

Regarded as one of the principal figures of Uruguayan literature, Acuña de Figueroa wrote many forms of poetry, including hymns, odes, anagrams, and epigrams, as well as the national anthem of Uruguay. Acclaimed as one of the best burlesque poets to write in Spanish, nevertheless, his visual poetry and his *Mosaico poético* were ignored until later critics saw their theoretical and aesthetic value. His enigmatic and numeric poetry is a good example of an experimental tradition that preceded by many decades the historical avant-garde. He died in Montevideo, his birthplace.
PRINCIPAL WORKS: *Mosaico poético* (1857), *Obras completas* (1890)

To the Most Holy Virgin Mary / A la santísima virgen

G. J. Racz, trans.

Tot tibi sunt, Virgo, dotes quot sidera coeli

To put an end to vexing you
And once again deserve your grace,
I offer, queen, these flowers in place
Of all the "many thorns" I'd strew.

To say more *salves*, moved by love,
I stand before you, Virgin pure,
For I have trespassed, I adjure,
Against both you and God above.

If only He'd absolve one sin
At every *salve*'s last amen,
With all the world forgiven, then
A thousand could be ushered in.

I'll make these *salve*'s from earth's plain
Bedazzle just as many ears
As there are stars that dot the spheres
Or fish that swim the bounding main

Or angels in the canopy
Whose song of glory fills the skies,
Provided this sum only rise
To one less than infinity.

There are but two things, two alone,
That I conceive more copious;
They are your comely graciousness
And God's own grandeur round His throne.

These flowers, then . . . Should you judge meet
My good intentions, then be kind,

And in return be pleased to find
I'll serve as carpet to your feet.

Your gift is worth immensely more
Than any I could hope to give;
I give as poorly as I live
While you give from your queenly store.

My soul entreats you, use your powers
So Jesus, Mother of Love, might
Send down a single ray of light
For every thousand of these flowers.

Por quitarte los enojos/ Y merecer tus favores,/ Te ofrezco, ¡oh Reina!
estas flores,/ Después de *tantos abrojos*.// Mi amor te presenta aquí/ Más
Salves, Virgen querida,/ Que ofensas hice en mi vida/ Contra Dios y
contra tí.// Pues si Él quisiera absolver/ Por cada Salve un pecado,/ Todo
el mundo perdonado,/ Y mil mundos pueden ser.// En tantas formas
brillar/ Haré tu Salve en el suelo,/ Como estrellas muestra el cielo,/ Como
peces cría el mar,/ Como ángeles en circuito/ Te alaban en la alta esfera,/
Si el número de ellos fuera/ Uno menos que infinito.// Dos cosas, no más
que dos,/ Contemplo más numerosas,/ Que son: tus gracias hermosas,/
Y las grandezas de Dios.// He aquí mis flores. . . . Si ves/ Que aspiro al
premio, dispensa,/ Y déjame en recompensa/ Servir de alfombra á tus
pies./ Valdrá inmensamente más/ Tu premio que mi presente,/ Mas yo
doy como indigente/ Y tú como Reina das.// Pido, pues, que de Jesús/ Me
alcances, Madre de amores,/ Por cada mil de estas flores/ Un solo rayo
de luz.

Excerpt from Multiform Salve

G. J. Racz, trans.

1	2	3	4	5	6
a. God hail thee	a. Queen	a. and Mother	a. of mercy	a. life	a. and sweetness
b. God receives thee	b. Empress	b. and paradigm	b. of gentleness	b. breath	b. and delight
c. God acclaims thee	c. Princess	c. and epitome	c. of tenderness	c. sustenance	c. and recreation
d. God invests thee	d. Highness	d. and sanctuary	d. of forbearance	d. nurturing	d. and dulcitude
e. God commends thee	e. Majesty	e. and throne	e. of clemency	e. vitality	e. and plaster
f. God felicitates thee	f. Lady	f. and source	f. of graciousness	f. health	f. and jubilation
g. God glorifies thee	g. Solemnity	g. and emblem	g. of kindness	g. existence	g. and rapture
h. God hails thee	h. Matron	h. and epilogue	h. of sympathy	h. support	h. and dulcification
i. God extols thee	i. Power	i. and shrine	i. of pity	i. nutriment	i. and rest
j. God crowns thee	j. Deity	j. and model	j. of congeniality	j. nectar	j. and electuary
k. God deifies thee	k. Inspiration	k. and mirror	k. of beneficence	k. solace	k. and sweetliness
l. God sanctifies thee	l. Victress	l. and hieroglyph	l. of benevolence	l. wellness	l. and invigoration
m. God enthrones thee	m. Star	m. and unity	m. of mildness	m. manna	m. and joy

n. God ennobles thee	n. Sun	n. and exemplum	n. of charity	n. anima	n. and ease
o. God praises thee	o. Luminary	o. and figure	o. of compassion	o. comfort	o. and balm
p. God consecrates thee	p. Emissary	p. and paragon	p. of attributes	p. spirit	p. and melody
q. God proclaims thee	q. Fortress	q. and portent	q. of sublimity	q. stimulation	q. and ambrosia
r. God purifies thee	r. Orb	r. and mystery	r. of perfections	r. relief	r. and contentment
s. God elevates thee	s. Capitol	s. and heart	s. of holiness	s. revival	s. and regalement
t. God exalts thee	t. Oracle	t. and beacon	t. of fairness	t. consolation	t. and balsam
u. God illumines thee	u. Temple	u. and halo	u. of blessing	u. physic	u. and serenity
v. God enshrines thee	v. Symbol	v. and bastion	v. of concord	v. pleasure	v. and charms
w. God lights thee	w. Monument	w. and orchard	w. of beauty	w. succor	w. and comfort
x. God blesses thee	x. Constellation	x. and honeycomb	x. of love	x. curing	x. and fruition
y. God impassions thee	y. Culmination	y. and fountain	y. of virtues	y. encouragement	y. and rejoicing
z. God predestines thee	z. Tabernacle	z. and lantern	z. of harmony	z. happiness	z. and exulting

¡*Dios te salve celestial*/ María, Madre y doncella:/ *Llena eres de gracia* y bella, / Sin semejante ni igual! (1)// Tu planta humilla el furor/ Del infernal enemigo, / Porque *el Señor es contigo*/ Y tú eres con el Señor. (2)// Más pura que el Serafín,/ *Bendita tú eres*, María,/ Panal de rica ambrosía,/ Flor del divino jardín. (3)// Sin mancha original,/ Para que en el cielo imperes,/ *Entre todas las mujeres*/ Te eligió Dios inmortal. (4)// Árbol que destila miel/ Y exhala aroma exquisito,/ Dios te cultiva, *y bendito*/ *Es el fruto* que hay en él. (5)// (1) Toda eres hermosa, amiga mía, y maneilla no hay en tí.—*Cant. de los Cant.*, cap. 4, vers. 7./ (2) Y dijo el Señor á la serpiente: Ella quebrantará tu enbeza.—*Génesis*, cap. 3. vers. 15/ (3) El nombre de María e júbilo para el corazón, miel para la boca y melodía para el oído.—San Antonio de Padua./ (4) Constituida Reina posee de derecho todo el Reina del Ilijo.—San Ruperto Abad/ (5) Como el einam mo y bálsamo aromátioco de fragancia.—*Eclesiastico*, cap. 21. vers. 26./ ¡Salve, hermosísima luz,/ Madre de inmensa ternura!/ *De tu vientre*, Virgen pura, Nació el divino *Jesús*.// *Santa María*, en tu amor/ Se cifra nuestra esperanza,/ Porque eres la arca de alianza/ Y asilo del pecador./ *Madre de Dios*, tu poder/ Se ostenta al verte gloriosa/ Vestida del sol y hermosa/ Como la aurora al nacer. (1)// *Ruega por nosotros*, sí,/ Ante el Trino Dios ansiosa,/ Pues Hija, Madres y Esposa,/ ¿Qué podrá negarte á ti? (2)// *Los pecadores*, que fiel/ Defiendes con tierno anhelo,/ Te invocan puerta del cielo,/ Y por ti han de entrar en él. (3)// *Ahora y en la hora* fatal/ *De nuestra muerte*, Señora,/ Tú eres nuestra defensora/ Contra el poder infernal.// En fin, al divino Edén,/ Donde tus luces exhalas,/ Dulce paloma, en tus alas/ Álzanos con gloria: *Amén*.// (1) Una mujer cubierta del Sol . . . como el alba al levantarse.—*Apocalipsis*, cap. 12 y *Cantar de los Cantares*, cap. 6./ (2) Ella es la que sola mereció ser llamada Madre y Esposa de Dios.—San Agustín: *Sermón de la Asunción*. (3) Nadie puede entrar en el cielo, sino entrando por María, como puerta de él.—San Buenaventura: *Sermón de Nativitate Virginis*.

Alphabetical-Numerical Prophecy / Profecía alfabético-numeral

G. J. Racz, trans.

LETTERS DULY COMPOSING THE ALPHABET,
EACH WITH ITS CORRESPONDING NUMERICAL VALUE

1. 2. 3. 4. 5. 6. 7. 8. 9. 10. 11. 12. 13. 14. 15. 16. 17. 18. 19. 20. 21. 22. 23. 24. 25. 26.
a. b. c. d. e. f. g. h. i. j. k. l. m. n. o. p. q. r. s. t. u. v. w. x. y. z.

Cabbalistic verses, the letters of which, when converted into numbers, total the precise and fixed quantity of 1847, the year in which diplomatic mediators arrived from France and England in order to bring peace to the republic.

```
        12. 15. 20. 8. 5. 1. 12. 16. 8. 1.
         L   o   t  h  e  a   l   p  h  a-
      2. 5. 20. 19. 12. 5. 20. 20. 5. 18. 19.
      b  e  t'  s   l  e   t   t   e   r   s ......................243
      19. 16. 5. 3. 9. 6. 9. 3. 1. 12. 12. 25.
      S   p  e  c  i  f  i  c  a   l   l   y
    20. 23. 5. 14. 20. 25. 19. 9. 24. 8. 5. 18. 5.
     t  w  e  n   t   y  -s   i  x   h  e   r  e ...................315
    23. 9. 20. 8. 2. 21. 20. 19. 9. 24. 19. 1. 12.
     W  i  t  h  b  u   t   s   i  x   s   a   l
    9. 5. 14. 20. 14. 21. 13. 2. 5. 18. 19.
    i  e  n   t   n   u   m  b  e  r   s ......................327

        13. 1. 18. 11. 20. 8. 9. 19. 3. 1. 12.
         M  a   r   k   t  h  i  s   c  a   l
        5. 14. 4. 1. 18. 25. 5. 1. 18.
        e  n   d  a  r   y  e  a  r ..........................206
   8. 5. 18. 5. 20. 8. 5. 1. 14. 14. 15. 4. 15. 13. 9. 14. 9. 1. 14. 25.
   H  e  r   e  t  h  e  a  n   n   o  d   o  m   i  n  i  a  n  y ........217
        19. 15. 21. 12. 13. 9. 7. 8. 20. 19. 5. 5.
        S   o   u   l  m   i  g  h  t  s   e  e ....................153
    23. 9. 12. 12. 6. 15. 18. 21. 18. 21. 7. 21. 1. 25.
     W  i   l   l  f  o   r   U   r   u  g  u  a  y.................209
   2. 5. 7. 5. 20. 16. 5. 1. 3. 5. 1. 14. 4. 21. 14. 9. 20. 25.
   B  e  g  e  t   p  e  a  c  e  a  n   d  u   n  i  t   y............177
```

The cabbalistic quantity turns out to be the year 1847

LETRAS QUE DEBEN COMPONER EL ALFABETO, CON EL/ NÚMERO QUE CORRESPONDE Á CADA UNA DE ELLAS/ 1. a. 2. b. 3. c . . . / *Versos cabalisticos, cuyas letras, representados por números, dan en la suma total la incógnita precisa y determinada de 1847, año en que han llegado los ministros interventores de Francia é Inglaterra, para la pacificación de la República./ 12. 1. 21 . . . / Lasletrasdees-/ 22. 5. 1 . . . / tealfabeto . . . . .243/ 21. 17. 15 . . . / Sonveinteysie-/ 22. 5. 5 . . . /teentotal . . . . .315/ 19. 23.5 . . ./Queconseisnom-/ 2. 20. 5 . . . /bresnotables . . . . .327/ 15. 20. 5 . . . / Numeranela-/ 16. 17. 1 . . . / ñoactual . . . . .206/ 1. 23. 15 . . . / Aunaquíelmismo año . . . . .217/ 18. 1. 22 . . . / Patentehallarás . . . . .153/ 19.23.5 . . . / QueofrecealOriente . . . . .209/ 12. 1. 23 . . . / Launiónylapaz . . . . .177// Resulta, pues, que la incógnita cabalística es el año de 1847*

Hilario Ascasubi (1807–1875, Argentina)

Though he later identified with the countryside, Ascasubi lived his early years between the cities of Buenos Aires and Córdoba. In 1824, he founded the *Revista de Salta*. Using his poetry to speak out against Juan Manuel de Rosas, he spent many years exiled in Montevideo. His poetry, written in the first person using the language of the gaucho, is witty and humorous. His poetry represents a serious attempt to write using a vernacular language that before him was not seen as "literary." Ascasubi enjoyed the support of wealthy, educated intellectuals but also of indigenous groups, the poor, and, of course, the gauchos themselves. He died in Buenos Aires. PRINCIPAL WORKS: *La refalosa* (18??), *Trovas y lamentos de Donato Jurado, soldado argentino a la muerte de la infeliz Doña Camila O'Gorman* (1848), *Santos Vega, o Los mellizos de la Flor* (1872)

The Slippery One / La refalosa

Molly Weigel, trans.

Taunt of a mazorquero and throat-cutter, one of the number besieging the plaza of Montevideo, to the gaucho Jacinto Cielo, gazetteer and soldier of the Argentine Legion, defender of that plaza

Hey, gaucho savage!
I don't lose hope,
and it's no joke,
of getting you to try
ting-a-ling and the slippery one.
I'll tell you how it goes:
listen up and don't be a scaredy—
for you, this little song
is sadder than Good Friday.

Any Unitarist we catch,
We lash down;
or else just leave him standing
while our comrades string him up
from behind
—mazorqueros, of course.
They bind
him with a double tether
so he's elbow to elbow
showing the world his birthday suit.
Savage!
Here's where your ordeal starts.

Later after that, a three-ply leather thong
will hug his feets, like a horse

fastened up to a stake so neat,
and while he's standing there
we have him begging loud;
half-teasing, we let him have
a little jab,
and when he screams, we sing
the slippery one, and ting-a-ling
without a violin.

But we follow the sound
in the brass sheath
when we whet
the knife, and test
the point
on the nape of his neck.
That chicken savage jumps,
which makes us laugh,
and when some start to tear their shirts
and cry,
that's the best of all;
we feel as lucky
as our dear President.
And the cackle of joy
spreads far and wide
when we hear the pretty music
and the fun we're giving
to the savage we've got tied.

At last,
when we think the time is ripe
and we've had our fill
of fun, we decide
to stop his breathing;
and to do it right,
one grabs a lock of hair
while another
holds him by the legs
like a young horse,
so if he moves
it's on all fours.

Meanwhile,
he's begging us in the name of whatever saint
might be up there in the sky;
and to comfort him and ease his fear

we cut across the veins
of his throat,
just a little below the ear,
with a well-sharpened blade
in what's called the mercy stroke.
And how does he say thank you?
—He starts to bleed,
a real treat,
and his eyes roll up in his head
from shock.

Ah, sissies!
We've seen a few
who bite themselves,
make gestures and faces
that'd make the savages scalp themselves,
then stick out their great big tongues—
among ourselves it's no disgrace
to kiss'em
and make'em half-satisfied.

What a high old time!
We laugh so much
we split our sides
to see how it even makes him shiver;
so we untie him
and loosen him up,
then pull him up short
to watch him do the slippery one.
He'll dance in blood
till he has a cramp
and falls down kicking
and shaking all over
—very proud—
till he's stretched out tight.
Inspired by this, we cut off a strip
of his skin that we know how to use
to make a razor strop.

Now we cut his ears,
his beard, sideburns, eyebrows, hair,
and scalped,
we leave him in a heap
to fatten up some hog
or vulture.

So, my Savage,
now you see—
a mere nothing has to happen to you
to make you scream,
"Long Live the Federation!"

Amenaza de un mazorquero y degollador de los sitiadores de Montevideo dirigida al gaucho Jacinto Cielo, gacetero y soldado de la Legión Argentina, defensora de aquella plaza.// Mirá, gaucho salvajon,/ que no pierdo la esperanza,/ y no es chanza,/ de hacerte probar qué cosa/ es *Tin tin y Refalosa*./ Ahora te diré cómo es:/ escuchá y no te asustés;/ que para ustedes es canto/ más triste que un viernes santo.// *Unitario* que agarramos,/ lo estiramos;/ o paradito nomás,/ por atrás,/ lo amarran los compañeros/ por supuesto, *mazorqueros*,/ y ligao/ con un *maniador* doblao,/ ya queda codo con codo/ y desnudito ante todo./ ¡Salvajon!/ Aquí empieza su aflicion.// Luego después a los *pieses*/ un *sobeo* en tres dobleces/ se le atraca,/ y queda como una estaca/ lindamente asigurao,/ y parao/ lo tenemos clamoriando;/ y como medio chanciando/ lo pinchamos,/ y lo que grita, cantamos/ la *refalosa y tin tin*,/ sin violín.// Pero seguimos el *son*/ en la vaina del *latón*,/ que asentamos/ el cuchillo, y le *tantiamos*/ con las uñas el *cogote*./ ¡Brinca el salvaje *vilote*/ que da risa!/ Cuando algunos en camisa/ se empiezan a revolcar,/ y a llorar,/ que es lo que más nos divierte;/ de igual suerte/ que al Presidente le agrada,/ y larga la carcajada/ de alegría,/ al oir la musiquería/ y la broma que le damos/ al salvaje que amarramos.// Finalmente:/ cuando creemos conveniente,/ después que nos divertimos/ grandemente, decidimos/ que al salvaje/ el resuello se le ataje;/ y a derechas/ lo agarra uno de las mechas,/ mientras otro/ lo sujeta como a potro/ de las patas,/ que si se mueve es a gatas./ Entretanto,/ nos clama por cuanto santo/ tiene el cielo;/ pero ahí nomás por consuelo/ a su queja:/ abajito de la oreja,/ con un puñal bien templao/ y afilao,/ que se llama el *quita penas*,/ le atravesamos las venas/ del pescuezo/ ¿Y qué se le hace con eso?/ larga sangre que es un gusto,/ y del susto/ entra a revolver los ojos.// ¡Ah, hombres flojos/ hemos visto algunos de éstos/ que se muerden y hacen gestos,/ y visajes/ que se pelan los salvajes,/ largando tamaña lengua;/ y entre nosotros no es mengua/ el besarlo,/ para medio contentarlo.// ¡Qué jarana!/ nos reimos de buena gana/ y muy mucho,/ de ver que hasta les da chucho;/ y entonces lo desatamos/ y soltamos;/ y lo sabemos parar/ para verlo *Refalar*/ ¡en la sangre!/ hasta que le da un calambre/ y se *cai* a patalear,/ y a temblar/ muy fiero, hasta que se estira/ el salvaje: y, lo que espira,/ le sacamos/ una *lonja* que apreciamos/ el sobarla,/ y de *manea* gastarla.// De ahi se le cortan orejas,/ barba, patilla y cejas;/ y pelao/ lo dejamos arrumbao,/ para que engorde algún chancho,/ o carancho.// Con que ya ves, Salvajon;/ nadita te ha de pasar/ después de hacerte gritar:/ ¡*Viva la Federacion*!

Antonio Gonçalves Dias (1823–1864, Brazil)

Poet, dramaturge, and essayist, Dias was a prominent figure in Brazilian Romantic poetry. Orphaned at a young age, he had dual interests in both literary and scientific subjects. In the end, his writing efforts were influenced by his scientific work as ethnographer, linguist, and historian. The theme of the Brazilian native is prevalent in his writing, as is the humanistic nature of the characters of his plays. In addition to his writing career, Dias was a member of the Instituto Histórico y Geográfico Brasileiro. PRINCIPAL WORKS: *Primeiros cantos* (1846), *Ultimos cantos* (1850), *Brasil e Oceanía* (1852)

Song of Exile / Canção do exílio

Odile Cisneros, trans.

My land has swaying palms
Where the *sabiá* bird sings;
The song of birds in this land
Is a very different thing.

Our fields have lovelier flowers,
Our skies have more stars above,
Our forests are more full of life,
Our lives are more full of love.

If alone at night I ponder,
More delights my country brings;
My land has swaying palms
Where the *sabiá* bird sings.

My land is full of charm;
Of which I find nothing here;
If alone at night I ponder,
More delights my country brings;
My land has swaying palms
Where the *sabiá* bird sings

May the Lord forbid I die
And allow me to return
And allow me enjoy the charms
Of which I find nothing here;
May I sight the swaying palms
Where the *sabiá* bird sings.

Minha terra tem palmeiras,/ Onde canta o Sabiá;/ As aves, que aqui gorjeiam,/ Não gorjeiam como lá.// Nosso céu tem mais estrelas,/ Nossas várzeas têm mais flores,/ Nossos bosques têm mais vida,/ Nossa vida mais amores.// Em cismar, sozinho à noite,/ Mais prazer encontro eu lá;/ Minha terra tem palmeiras,/ Onde canta o Sabiá.// Minha terra tem primores,/ Que tais não encontro eu cá;/ Em cismar—sozinho, à noite—/ Mais prazer encontro eu lá;/ Minha terra tem palmeiras,/ Onde canta o Sabiá.// Não permita Deus que eu morra,/ Sem que eu volte para lá;/ Sem que desfrute os primores/ Que não encontro por cá;/ Sem qu'inda aviste as palmeiras,/ Onde canta o Sabiá.

Manuel Antonio Álvares de Azevedo (1831–1852, Brazil)

By the age of seventeen, Azevedo had mastered English, French, and Latin; written a version of the fifth act of *Othello*; and translated a great deal of poetry. Both poet and short-story writer, he attained deep levels of intimacy by using obscure and hidden images to convey hope, pain, melancholy, disillusion, and anguish and to explore love, death, dreams, and religion. Azevedo also demonstrated his cleverness and versatility by using satire, caricatures, and self-parody. He died at the age of twenty-one. PRINCIPAL WORKS: *Poemas malditos* (?), *Lira dos vinte anos* (1853), *Noites na taverna* (1855)

Excerpt from Intimate Ideas / Idéias íntimas
Mark A. Lokensgard, trans.

I
Ossian the bard is sad like the shadow
That his songs inhabit. My Lamartine
Is monotonous and beautiful like the night,
Like the moon on the ocean and the sound of the waves . . .
But it wails an eternal monody,
The genius's lyre has only a single string,
A fiber of love and God that a breath makes sound:
If it faints of love it turns to God
If it cries to God it sighs with love.
Enough of Shakespeare. Now come,
Fantastic German, ardent poet
Who illuminates the radiance of pale drops
Of noble Johannesburg! In your novels
My heart finds delight . . . Nevertheless
It seems I have begun to lose my taste,
I am becoming blasé, I pass the days
Up and down my hallway, without company.
Without reading, or poeticizing. I smoke incessantly.

My house has fogs no less dense
Than those of this wintry sky . . . Alone
I pass the nights here and the long days;
I have given myself to cigars now in body and soul;
In vain from a corner comes a plea for a kiss,
Like the beauty the Sultan disdains,
My abandoned German pipe!
I do not ride and I do not court,
I hate the *lasquenet* . . . word of honor!
If I continue this way for two months,
The blue demons in my weak limbs,
I will end up in Praia Vermelha or Parnassus.

II
I have filled my parlor with a thousand images.
Here a horse flies at a gallop,
A purple-caped masquerader turns his back
To a mounted rider with a German moustache,
A black drunkard sitting on a cask,
With thick lips squeezes the bottle to his face . . .
Along the walls' length are spilled
Extinct inscriptions of dead verses,
Stillborn verses . . . There in the alcove
In black waters rises the Romantic
Isle, gloomy, awash in the waves
Of a river that gets lost in the forest . . .
A dream of a lover and a poet,
An Eldorado of love the mind creates
Like an Eden of delightful nights . . .
Where I was able in the silence
by an Angel's side . . . Beyond Romanticism!
It paints clumsily a cheerful caricature
With writing ink and vermillion powder
The plump cheek, the voluminous abdomen,
And the purple beak nose
Of the happy street peddler among bottles
Stuck into a vat . . . On my dresser
A half-drunk cup still reproves
The golden waters of the ardent Cognac.
It blackens the bottom of the narcotic bottle,
That from the essence of orange blossoms
It keeps the liquor that nectarizes the nerves.
There my Havana cigar is mixed
With my paltry cigarette and my pipe.

The dark table staggers under the weight
Of the titanic *Digest*, and next to it
An open *Childe Harold* or Lamartine
Shows that romanticism has become careless
And that poetry always hovers above
The classical nightmare of study.

III

Disorder reigns throughout the old room,
From the cobwebs to the curtains
To the dusty bookshelves. The clothes, the books
Are mixed together on the room's few chairs.
The page of my *Faust* is marked by a neckband
And Alfred de Musset at times rests
Upon an obscure text by Guerreiro or Valasco.
As in the primordial world, when the elements
Spun end over end in darkness,
My room, a world in chaos, awaits a *Fiat*!

. . . .

XI

Close to my bed my poets sleep—
Dante, the Bible, Shakespeare, and Byron—
Mixed together on the table. Nearby them
My old oil lamp lounges
And seems to ask for a formation.
Oh my friend, my night watchman,
You did not abandon me in my vigils,
Whether I spent the night bent over my books,
Or whether, seated on the bed, pensively
Reread my love letters!
I love you dearly, oh my sidekick
In the mad scenes of my obscure drama!
And on a day of spleen, when the phlegm comes,
I will evoke you in a heroic poem
In the rhyme of Camões and Ariosto
As the ideal for lamps-to-be!

. . . .

XIV

It seems that I have wept . . . I feel on my cheek
A single lost tear running down . . .
Satan take this unhappiness! Here, my page,
Pour into my glass the last drops

Of that black bottle . . .

       Come now! Let us drink!

You are the blood of inspiration, the pure nectar
That makes the souls of poets divine,
The power that opens the world of magic!
Come, ardent Cognac! It is only with you
That I feel myself live. Still I quiver,
When the aroma of those golden drops
Instill life into my coursing blood,
My nerves pulse and my arteries take fire,
My burning eyes grow dark
And in my brain go by delirious
Apparitions of poetry . . . Inside the shadow
I see on a golden berth her image
Palpitant, sleeping and sighing,
Outstretches her arms to me . . .

       I had forgotten:

Night is falling; bring me a light and two cigars
And at my study-table light the lamp . . .

I/ Ossian o bardo é triste como a sombra/ Que seus cantos povoa.
O Lamartine/ É monótono e belo como a noite,/ Como a lua no mar
e o som das ondas . . . / Mas pranteia uma eterna monodia,/ Tem na lira
do gênio uma só corda,/ Fibra de amor e Deus que um sopro agita:/ Se
desmaia de amor a Deus se volta,/ Se pranteia por Deus de amor suspira./
Basta de Shakespeare. Vem tu agora,/ Fantástico alemão, poeta ardente/
Que ilumina o clarão das gotas pálidas/ Do nobre Johannisberg! Nos
teus romances/ Meu coração deleita-se . . . Contudo/ Parece-me que vou
perdendo o gosto,/ Vou ficando *blasé*, passeio os dias/ Pelo meu corredor,
sem companheiro./ Sem ler, nem poetar. Vivo fumando.// Minha casa não
tem menores névoas/ Que as deste céu d'inverno . . . Solitário/ Passo as
noites aqui e os dias longos;/ Dei-me agora ao charuto em corpo e alma;/
Debalde ali de um canto um beijo implora,/ Como a beleza que o Sultão
despreza,/ Meu cachimbo alemão abandonado!/ Não passeio a cavalo e não
namoro;/ Odeio o *lasquenet* . . . Palavra d'honra!/ Se assim me continuam
por dois meses/ Os diabos azuis nos frouxos membros,/ Dou na Praia
Vermelha ou no Parnaso.// II/ Enchi o meu salão de mil figuras./ Aqui voa
um cavalo no galope,/ Um roxo *dominó* as costas volta/ A um cavaleiro de
alemães bigodes,/ Um preto beberrão sobre uma pipa,/ Aos grossos beiços
a garrafa aperta . . . / Ao longo das paredes se derramam/ Extintas inscrições
de versos mortos,/ E mortos ao nascer . . . Ali na alcova/ Em águas negras
se levanta a ilha/ Romântica, sombria à flor das ondas/ De um rio que se
perde na floresta . . . / Um sonho de mancebo e de poeta,/ El-Dorado de
amor que a mente cria/ Como um Éden de noites deleitosas . . . / Era ali

que eu podia no silêncio/ junto de um anjo . . . Além o romantismo!/ Borra adiante folgaz caricatura/ Com tinta de escrever e pó vermelho/ A gorda face, o volumoso abdômen,/ E a grossa penca do nariz purpúreo/ Do alegre vendilhão entre botelhas/ Metido num tonel . . . Na minha cômoda/ Meio encetado o copo inda verbera/ As águas d'ouro de *Cognac* fogoso./ Negreja ao pé narcótica botelha/ Que da essência de flores de laranja/ Guarda o licor que nectariza os nervos./ Ali mistura-se o charuto Havano/ Ao mesquinho cigarro e ao meu cachimbo./ A mesa escura cambaleia ao peso/ Do titânio *Digesto*, e ao lado dele/ *Childe-Harold* entreaberto ou Lamartine/ Mostra que o romantismo se descuida/ E que a poesia sobrenada sempre/ Ao pesadelo clássico do estudo.// III/ Reina a desordem pela sala antiga,/ Desde a teia de aranha as bambinelas/ À estante pulvurenta. A roupa, os livros/ Sobre as cadeiras poucas se confundem./ Marca a folha do *Faust* um colarinho/ E Alfredo de Musset encobre às vezes/ De Guerreiro ou Valasco um texto obscuro./ Como outrora do mundo os elementos/ Pela treva jogando cambalhotas,/ Meu quarto, mundo em caos, espera um *Fiat*!// . . . // XI/ Junto do leito meus poetas dormem—/ —O Dante, a Bíblia, Shakespeare e Byron—/ Na mesa confundidos. Junto deles/ Meu velho candeeiro se espreguiça/ E parece pedir a formatura./ Ó meu amigo, ó velador noturno,/ Tu não me abandonaste nas vigílias,/ Quer eu perdesse a noite sobre os livros,/ Quer, sentado no leito, pensativo/ Relesse as minhas cartas de namoro!/ Quero-te muito bem, ó meu comparsa/ Nas doidas cenas de meu drama obscuro!/ E num dia de *spleen*, vindo a pachorra,/ Hei de evocar-te num poema heróico/ Na rima de Camões e de Ariosto/ Como padrão às lâmpadas futuras!// . . . // XIV/ Parece que chorei . . . Sinto na face/ Uma perdida lágrima rolando . . . / Satã leve a tristeza! Olá, meu pajem,/ Derrama no meu copo as gotas últimas/ Dessa garrafa negra . . . / Eia! bebamos!/ És o sangue do gênio, o puro néctar/ Que as almas de poeta diviniza,/ O condão que abre o mundo das magias!/ Vem, fogoso *Cognac*! É só contigo/ Que sinto-me viver. Inda palpito,/ Quando os eflúvios dessas gotas áureas/ Filtram no sangue meu correndo a vida,/ Vibram-me os nervos e as artérias queimam,/ Os meus olhos ardentes se escurecem/ E no cérebro passam delirosos/ Assomos de poesia . . . Dentre a sombra/ Vejo num leito d'ouro a imagem dela/ Palpitante, que dorme e que suspira,/ Que seus braços me estende . . . / Eu me esquecia:/ Faz-se noite; traz fogo e dois charutos/ E na mesa do estudo acende a lâmpada . . . /

Sousândrade (1833–1902, Brazil)

Born at his parents' estate in Maranhão, Brazil, Sousândrade (Joaquim de Sousa Andrade) studied literature at the Sorbonne and also studied mining engineering. He was ordered to leave London because of his attack on Queen Victoria in a press article. In 1857, he published his first book of poems and two chants of O *guesa errante*. After separating from his wife, he traveled through Central and South America, then settled in New York. The definitive version of *Guesa* was published in London in 1884. He died in his native Maranhão, branded a madman and in almost complete anonymity. Though his last manuscripts were used as wrapping paper, his radical and innovative work was recovered in the 1960s by Augusto and Haroldo de Campos, who thought of it as "a clandestine earthquake." A precursor to modernity, the subject matter and style of his work is a forerunner to that of Pound's *Cantos*. Struggling to create a new language, for a new time, he paralleled his destiny with that of the Indians, condemned and sacrificed the contradictions of an emerging capitalism. Knowing he was ahead of his time, he wrote, "I have already heard twice that O *guesa errante* will be read 50 years from now; I grew sad with the disappointment of one who writes 50 years in advance." PRINCIPAL WORKS: *Harpas selvagens* (1857), O *guesa errante* (1866)

Excerpt from O guesa errante: The Wall Street Inferno / O inferno de Wall Street

Odile Cisneros, trans.

1   (GUESA, having traversed the WEST INDIES, believes himself rid
        of the XEQUES and penetrates the NEW-YORK-STOCK-EXCHANGE;
        the VOICE, from the wilderness:)
        —Orpheus, Dante, Aeneas, to hell
        Descended; the Inca shall ascend
            = *Ogni sp'ranza lasciate,*
                Che entrate . . .
        —Swedenborg, does fate new worlds portend?

2   (Smiling Xeques appear disguised as Railroad-*managers*,
        Stockjobbers, Pimpbrokers, etc., etc., crying out:)
        —Harlem! Erie! Central! Pennsylvania!
        = Million! Hundred million!! Billions!! Pelf!!!
            —Young is Grant! Jackson,
                Atkinson!
        Vanderbilts, Jay Goulds like elves!

3   (The Voice, poorly heard amidst the commotion:)
        —Fulton's *Folly,* Codezo's *Forgery . . .*
        Fraud cries the nation's bedlam
            They grasp no odes

Railroads;
Wall Street's parallel to Chatham . . .

4   (Brokers going on:)
—Pygmies, Brown Brothers! Bennett! Stewart!
Rothschild and that Astor with red hair!!
            = Giants, slaves
                    If only nails gave
Out streams of light, if they would end despair!

5   (Norris, *Attorney;* Codezo, *inventor;* Young, Esq., *manager;* Atkinson
            agent; Armstrong, *agent;* Rhodes, *agent;* P. Offman & Voldo,
                agents; hubbub, mirage; in the middle, Guesa:)
—Two! Three! Five thousand! If you play
        Five million, Sir, will you receive
                    = He won! Hah! Haah!! Haaah!!!
                        —Hurrah! Ah! . . .
—They vanished . . . Were they thieves? . .

6   (J. Miller atop the roofs of the *Tammany wigwam* unfurling the
            Garibaldian mantle:)
—Bloodthirsties! Sioux! Oh Modocs!
To the White House! Save the Nation,
            From the Jews! From the hazardous
                Goth's Exodus!
From immoral conflagration!

. . . .

100   (*Reporters.*)
—Norris, Connecticut's *blue* laws!
Clevelands, attorney-Cujás,
            Into zebras constrained
                Ordained,
Two by two, to one hundred Barabbas!

101   (Friends of the lost *kings*:)
—*Humbug* of *railroads* and the telegraph,
The fire of heaven I wished wide and far
            To steal, set the world ablaze
                And above it raise
Forever the *Spangled Star*!

102   (A rebellious sun founding a planetary center:)
—'George Washington, etc. etc.,
Answer the Royal-George-Third. Depose!
            = Lord Howe, tell him, do

I'm royal too . . .
(And they broke the Englishman's nose).

103   (Satellites greeting JOVE's rays:)
–'Greetings from the universe to its queen'
As for bail, the Patriarchs give a boon . . .
    (With a liberal king,
        A worse thing,
They founded the empire of the moon).

104   (*Reporters:*)
—A sorry role on earth they play,
Kings and poets, heaven's aristocracy
    (And Strauss, waltzing)
        Singing
At the Hippodrome or Jubilee.

105   (Brokers finding the cause of the WALL STREET market crash:)
—*Exeunt* Sir Pedro, Sir Grant,
Sir Guesa, seafaring brave:
    With gold tillers they endure
        The Moor,
Appeased by the turbulent waves.

106   (International procession, the people of Israel, Orangians, Fenians,
Buddhists, Mormons, Communists, Nihilists, Penitents,
Railroad-Strikers, All-brokers, All-jobbers, All-saints, All-devils,
    lanterns, music, excitement; Reporters: in LONDON
        the QUEEN's 'murderer' passes by and
        in PARIS 'Lot' the fugitive from SODOM:)
—In the Holy Spirit of slaves
A single Emperor's renowned
    In that of the free, verse
        Reverse,
Everything as Lord is crowned!

107   (KING ARTHUR's witches and FOSTER THE SEER on WALPURGIS by day:)
—*When the battle's lost and won*—
—*That will be ere the set of sun*—
—*Paddock calls: Anon!*—
—*Fair is foul, and foul is fair:*
Hover through the fog and filthy air!

108   (SWEDENBORG answering later:)
—Future worlds exist: republics,
Christianity, heavens, Lohengrin.
    Present worlds are latent:

Patent,
Vanderbilt-North, South-Seraphim.

109 (At the din of Jericho, Hendrick Hudson runs aground; the
Indians sell the haunted island of Manhattan to the Dutch:)
—The Half-Moon, prow toward China
Is careening in Tappan-Zee . . .
        Hoogh moghende Heeren . . .
            Take then
For sixty *guilders* . . . *Yeah! Yeah!*

110 (*Photophone-stylographs* sacred right to self-defense:)
—In the light the humanitarian voice:
Not hate; rather conscience, intellection;
        Not pornography
            Isaiah's prophecy
In Biblical vivisection!

. . . .

117 (*Freeloves* proceeding to vote for their husbands:)
—Among Americans, Emerson alone,
Wants no Presidents, oh atrocious he!
        = Oh well-adjudicated,
            States
Improve for you, for us, for me!

118 (Apocalyptic visions . . . slanderous ones:)
—For, 'the Beast having bear's feet,'
In God we trust is the Dragon
        And the false prophets
            Bennetts
Tone, th' Evolutionist and Theologian!

. . . .

173 (Washington 'blinding because of them'; Pocahontas without *personals*:)
—To starving bears, a rabid dog!
Be it! After the feast, bring in festoons!
        = Tender Lulu,
            Crying and you
Give honey to 'foes', bee? . . . and sting poltroons?

174 (Guatemalan nose, curved into Hymenee's torch; Dame-Ryder
heart on the poisoned window-panes of the *'too dark' wedding pudding*:)
—'*Caramba! yo soy cirujano*—
A Jesuit . . . Yankee . . . industrialism!
        —*Job* . . . or haunted cavern,

Tavern,
'Byron' animal-magnetism!

175 (Practical swindlers doing their business; *self-help* ATTA-TROLL:)
—Let the foreigner fall helpless,
As usury won't pay, the pagan!
= An ear to the bears a feast,
Caressing beasts,
Mahmmuhmmah, mahmmuhmmah, Mammon.

176 (Magnetic *handle-organ*; *ring* of bears sentencing the architect of the
PHARSALIA to death; an Odyssean ghost amidst the flames of
Albion's fires:)
—Bear . . . Bear is beriberi, Bear . . . Bear . . .
= Mahmmuhmmah, mahmmuhmmah, Mammon!
—Bear . . . Bear . . . ber' . . . Pegasus
Parnassus
= Mahmmuhmmah, mahmmuhmmah, Mammon.

1 (O GUESA tendo atravessado as ANTILHAS, crê-se livre dos XEQUES/
e penetra em NEW-YORK-STOCK-EXCHANGE; a Voz, dos desertos:)/ —
Orfeu, Dante, Æneas, ao inferno/ Desceram; o Inca há de subir . . . / = Ogni
sp'ranza lasciate,/ Che entrate . . . / — Swedenborg, há mundo porvir?// 2
(Xeques surgindo risonhos e disfarçados em Railroad-*managers*,/ Stockjobbers,
Pimpbrokers, etc., etc., apregoando:)/ — Harlem! Erie! Central! Pennsylvania!/
= Milhão! cem milhões!! mil milhões!!!/ — Young é Grant! Jackson,/ Atkinson!/
Vanderbilts, Jay Goulds, anões!// 3 (A Voz mal ouvida dentre a trovoada:)/
— Fulton's *Folly*, Codezo's *Forgery* . . . / Fraude é o clamor da nação!/ Não
entendem odes/ *Railroads*;/ Paralela Wall-Street à Chattám . . . // 4 (Corretores
continuando:)/ — Pigmeus, Brown Brothers! Bennett! Stewart!/ Rotschild e o
ruivalho d'Astor!!/ = Gigantes, escravos/ Se os cravos/ Jorram luz, se finda-se
a dor! . . . // 5 (NORRIS, *Attorney*; CODEZO, *inventor*; YOUNG, Esq., *manager*;
ATKINSON,/ *agent*; ARMSTRONG, *agent*; RHODES, *agent*; P. OFFMAN &
VOLDO,/ *agents*; algazarra, miragem; ao meio, o GUESA:)/ — Dois! três! cinco
mil! se jogardes,/ Senhor, tereis cinco milhões!/ = Ganhou! ha! haa! haaa!/ —
Hurrah! ah! . . . / — Sumiram . . . seriam ladrões? . . . // 6 (J. MILLER nos tetos
de *tammany wigwam* desenrolando o/ manto garibaldino:)/ — Bloodthirsties!
Sioux! ó Modocs!/ À White House! Salvai a União,/ Dos Judeus! do exodo/
Do Gôdo!/ Da mais desmoral rebelião!// . . . // 100 — Norris, leis azuis de
Connecticut!/ Clevelands, attorney-Cujás,/ Em zebras mudados/ Forçados,/
Dois a dois, aos cem Barrabás!// 101 (Amigos dos *reis* perdidos:)/ — *Humbug* de
railroad e telégrafo,/ Ao fogo dos céus quis roubar,/ Que o mundo abrasasse/
E arvorasse/ Por todo êle a *Spangled Star*!// 102 (Um sol rebelde fundando um
centro planetar:)/ — 'George Washington, etc., etc.,/ Responda ao

Real-George-Três'!/ = Dizei-lhe, Lord Howe,/ Real sou . . . / (E o nariz quebraram do Inglês).// 103 (Satélites cumprimentando os raios de JOVE:)/ — 'Saudar do universo à rainha'../ Fiança Patriarcas dão sua . . . / (Com rei liberal,/ Pior mal,/ Fundaram o império da lua).// 104 (*Reporters*:)/ — Papel fazem triste na terra/ Reis e poetas, gentes do céu,/ (E Strauss, o valsando)/ Cantando/ No Hipódromo ou no Jubileu.// 105 (Corretores achando causa à baixa do câmbio em WALL-STREET:)/ — *Exeunt* Dom Pedro, Dom Grant,/ Dom Guesa, que vão navegar:/ Seus lemes são de ouro/ Que o Mouro/ Das vagas amansam do mar.// 106 (Procissão internacional, povo de Israel, Orangianos, Fenianos,/ Budas, Mormons, Comunistas, Niilistas, Farricocos,/ Railroad-Strikers, All-brokers, All-saints, All-devils,/ lanternas, música, sensação;/ Reporters: passa/ em LONDON o 'assassino' da RAINHA e/ em PARIS 'Lot' o fugitivo de SODOMA:)/ — No Espírito-Santo d'escravos/ Há sómente um Imperador;/ No dos livres, verso/ Reverso,/ É tudo coroado Senhor!// 107 (Feiticeiras de KING-ARTHUR e vidente FOSTER em/ WALPURGIS de dia:)/ — *When the battle's lost and won —/ — That will be ere the set of sun —/ — Paddock calls: Anon! —/ — Fair is foul, and foul is fair:/ Hover through the fog and filthy air!*// 108 (SWEDENBORG respondendo depois:)/ — Há mundos futuros: república,/ Cristianismo, céus, Loengrim./ São mundos presentes:/ Patentes,/ Vanderbilt-North, Sul-Serafim.// 109 (Ao fragor de JERICÓ encalha HENDRICK HUDSON; os/ INDIOS vendem aos HOLANDESES a ilha/ de MANHATTAN malassombrada:)/ — A Meia-Lua, proa pra China,/ Está crenando em Tappan-Zee . . . / *Hoogh moghende Heeren* . . . / Pois tirem/ Por *guildens* sessenta . . . *Yea*! *Yea*!// 110 (*Fotófonos-estilógrafos* direitos sagrados de defesa:)/ — Na luz a voz humanitária:/ Ódio, não; consciência e razão;/ Não pornografia;/ Isaias/ Em bíblica vivisecção!// . . . // 117 (*Freeloves* passando a votar em seus maridos:)/ — De americanos o único Emerson/ Não quer presidências, o atroz!/ = Ó bem justiçados,/ Estados/ Melhoram pra vós e pra nós!// 118 (APOCALÍPTICAS visões . . . caluniosas:)/ — Pois, 'tendo a Bêsta patas d'urso,'/ *In God we trust* é o Dragão,/ E os falsos-profetas/ Bennettas/ Tone, o Teólogo e o da Ev'lucão!// . . . // 173 (Washington 'cegando por causa deles'; POCAHONTAS sem personals:)/ — A ursos famintos, cão danado!/ Seja! após festins, o festão! . . . / = Meiga Lulu,/ Choras e tu/ Mel ao 'imigo', abelha? . . . e ferrão?// 174 (Nariz guatimalo cornado em facho d'HIMENEU; coração DAME-RYDER/ nas envenenadas vidraças do *'too dark' wedding-pudding*:)/ — 'Caramba! *yo soy cirujano* —/ Jesuíta . . . yankee . . . industrial'!/ — Jó . . . ou *pousada*/ Malassombrada,/ 'Byron' magnetismo-animal!..// 175 (Práticos mistificadores fazendo seu negócio; *self-help* ATTA TROLL:)/ — Que indefeso caia o estrangeiro,/ Que a usura não paga o pagão!/ = Orelha ursos tragam,/ Se afagam,/ Mammumma, mammumma, Mammão.// 176 (Magnético handle-organ; ring d'ursos sentenciando à pena-última/ o arquiteto da FARSÁLIA; odisseu fantasma nas chamas/ dos incêndios d'Álbion:)/ — Bear . . . Bear é ber'beri, Bear . . . Bear . . . / = Mammumma, mammumma, Mammão!/ — Bear . . . Bear . . . ber' . . . Pegàsus . . . / Parnasus . . . / = Mammumma, mammumma, Mammão.

José Hernández (1834–1886, Argentina)

Hernández is the author of perhaps one of the most widely read Argentine books, *El gaucho Martín Fierro*. This national epic masterpiece was not initially well received by the literary critics of Buenos Aires. Based on the story of the gaucho as the ultimate rural character, *Martín Fierro*'s popularity can be attributed to the duality of its domestic and universal relevance. Hernández's work became canonical in part because of the masterful way it captures the vernacular language of the countryside. PRINCIPAL WORKS: *El gaucho Martín Fierro* (1872), *La vuelta de Martín Fierro* (1879)

Excerpt from Martín Fierro

Molly Weigel, trans.

I have seen a lot of singers
who've worked hard for their fame
and as soon as they get it
they don't try to keep it—
as if they got tired of warming up
before they got to the race.

But where another man goes
Martín Fierro goes;
nothing makes him back off.
Not even ghosts scare him,
and since everyone's singing
I want to sing too.

Singing I'll die,
singing they'll bury me,
and singing I'll arrive
at the feet of Our Father;
I came out of my mother's belly
and into this world to sing.

May my tongue stay limber
and words not fail me;
singing will make my glory
and if I put myself to singing,
they'll find me singing still,
even if the earth opens up.

I sit down in a hollow
to sing how it happened;
I make the grasses shiver

like a wind blowing.
My thoughts play there
with diamonds, spades, hearts, and clubs.

I'm not a singer with learning,
but if I put myself to singing
I won't want to stop
and I'll grow old singing:
verses come flowing out of me
like water from a spring.

With my guitar in my hand
even the flies don't touch me;
nobody steps on me
and when my heart gets tuned up
I make the high string wail
and the low string cry.

I'm a bull in my corral
and a bigger bull in somebody else's;
I always thought I was pretty good
and if you want to try me
you others come out to sing
and we'll see who comes out worse.

I won't stand to the side of the road
even if they come around cutting our throats;
I'm soft with the soft
and tough with the tough,
and in a tight spot
no one has ever seen me hesitate.

In danger—Christ Almighty!
my heart swells wide,
for all the world is a battlefield,
which shouldn't surprise anybody:
anyone who calls himself a man
knows how to stand his ground anywhere.

I'm a gaucho, so understand this
as my tongue explains it to you:
for me the world is small
and could be bigger;
the snake doesn't strike me
nor the sun burn my brow.

I was born like the fish
at the bottom of the sea;
no one can take away from me
what God gave me:
what I brought into the world
I'll take out of the world.

My glory is to live as free
as the bird in the sky;
I make no nest on this earth
where there's so much to suffer,
and no one follows me
when I take flight again.

Yo he visto muchos cantores,/ con famas bien otenidas,/ y que después de
adquiridas/ no las quieren sustentar:/ parece que sin largar/ se cansaron en
partidas.// Mas ande otro criollo pasa/ Martín Fierro ha de pasar;/ nada lo
hace recular/ ni las fantasmas lo espantan,/ y dende que todos cantan/ yo
también quiero cantar.// Cantando me he de morir,/ cantando me han de
enterrar,/ y cantando he de llegar/ al pie del Eterno Padre;/ dende el vientre
de mi madre/ vine a este mundo a cantar.// Que no se trabe mi lengua/
ni me falte la palabra;/ el cantar mi gloria labra/ y, poniéndomé a cantar,/
cantando me han de encontrar/ aunque la tierra se abra.// Me siento en el
plan de un bajo/ a cantar un argumento;/ como si soplara el viento/ hago
tiritar los pastos./ Con oros, copas y bastos/ juega allí mi pensamiento.// Yo
no soy cantor letrao,/ mas si me pongo a cantar/ no tengo cuándo acabar/
y me envejezco cantando:/ las coplas me van brotando/ como agua de
manantial.// Con la guitarra en la mano/ ni las moscas se me arriman;/
naides me pone el pie encima,/ y, cuando el pecho se entona,/ hago gemir
a la prima/ y llorar a la bordona.// Yo soy toro en mi rodeo/ y torazo en
rodeo ajeno;/ siempre me tuve por güeno/ y si me quieren probar/ salgan
otros a cantar/ y veremos quién es menos.// No me hago al lao de la huella/
aunque vengan degollando;/ con los blandos yo soy blando/ y soy duro
con los duros,/ y ninguno en un apuro/ me ha visto andar tutubiando.//
En el peligro ¡qué Cristos!/ el corazón se me enancha,/ pues toda la tierra es
cancha,/ y de esto naides se asombre:/ el que se tiene por hombre/ donde
quiera hace pata ancha.// Soy gaucho, y entiéndanló/ como mi lengua lo
esplica:/ para mí la tierra es chica/ y pudiera ser mayor;/ ni la víbora me
pica/ ni quema mi frente el sol.// Nací como nace el peje:/ en el fondo de la
mar;/ naides me puede quitar/ aquello que Dios me dió:/ lo que al mundo
truje yo/ del mundo lo he de llevar.// Mi gloria es vivir tan libre/ como el
pájaro del cielo;/ no hago nido en este suelo/ ande hay tanto que sufrir,/
y naides me ha de seguir/ cuando yo remuento el vuelo.

Antonio de Castro Alves (1847–1871, Brazil)

Born into a wealthy family in a small town in the Bahia province of Brazil, Alves is known both for the romantic character of his poetry and his abolitionist work, for which he is sometimes described as the Brazilian Abraham Lincoln. His calling was the oral poem, which also invited work in the theater. After realizing the power of his poetry, he began to incorporate abolitionist themes to spark social change, espousing ideas similar to the North American and European humanistic arguments against slavery. He also identified closely with the slaves about whom he wrote, which heightened the intensity of his poetry. PRINCIPAL WORKS: *Espumas flutuantes* (1870), *Gonzaga ou a revolução de Minas* (1875), *Vozes d'Afica-navio negrerio* (1880)

Excerpt from The Slave Ship (Tragedy on the Sea) / O navio negreiro (Tragédia no mar)

Mark A. Lokensgard, trans.

Canto I
We are on the high seas . . . Madly in space
The moonlight plays—a golden butterfly—
And the waves that run behind it . . . tire
Like a mob of children made unquiet.

We are on the high seas . . . From the firmament
The stars sprout like bits of golden foam
The sea in turn lights up in phosphorescence,
—Constellations of liquid gold . . .

We are on the high seas . . . There enclosed
In an insane embrace are two infinities,
They are blue, gold, placid, sublime . . .
Which is the sky? Which is the sea? . . .

We are on the high seas . . . Opening the sails
As the ocean winds' hot panting follows,
A brig at sail runs on the surface of the seas,
Like above a wave skim swallows . . .

Whence comes it? Where goes it? With wandering ships
Who can know their courses if space is so vast?
In this Sahara the coursers raise the dust,
They gallop, they fly, but leave no tracks.

Happy is he who can at this hour
Feel in this entire view its majesty! . . .
Below—the sea . . . above—the firmament . . .
In the sea and the sky—the immensity!

Oh! What sweet harmony the breeze brings me!
What soft music in the distance sounding!
My God! How sublime is a passionate song
Floating carelessly over the waves abounding!

Men of the sea! Oh coarse sailors,
By the sun of the Earth's four corners browned!
Children that the tempest lulled
In the crib of the ocean abyss profound!

Wait! wait! Let me drink in
This savage untamed poetry . . .
Orchestra—it is the sea, that rumbles by the prow,
And the wind that through the ropes whistles . . .

. . . .

Why do you flee thus, swift vessel?
Why do you flee from the fearful poet?
Oh! what I would give to follow in your wake
That seems like on the sea—zigzagging comet!

Albatross! Albatross! Eagle of the ocean,
Thou that among the gauzy clouds art sleeping,
Shake your feathers, oh Leviathan of space!
Albatross! Albatross! Give me thy wings . . .

. . . .

Canto IV
It was a dantesque dream . . . the quarterdeck
That reddens the light from the openings above,
Is bathed in blood.
Rattling of chains . . . cracking of a whip . . .
Legions of men as black as night,
In a horrific dance . . .

Black women, suspending at their teats
Skinny children, whose black mouths
Moisten the blood of their mothers:
Others, girls . . . are naked, frightened,
In the vortex of specters drawn in the whirlwind,
In futile fear and pain.

And the orchestra laughs ironically, shrilly . . .
And from the fantastic dancing round the serpent
Slithers in mad spirals . . .
If the old man breathes in gasps . . . if he drops to the floor,

Cries are heard . . . the whip cracks.
And more and more they fly . . .

Shackled to the links of a single chain,
the famished multitude staggers,
And cries and dances there!
One delirious with anger, another goes insane . . .
Another, brutalizing his martyrdom,
Singing, moans and laughs!
Meanwhile, the captain orders a maneuver,
And after looking at the sky that opens
So pure above the sea
Says from behind his thick tobacco smoke:
"Crack the whip strong, boys!
Make them dance some more! . . . "

And the orchestra laughs ironically, shrilly! . . .
And from the fantastic dancing round the serpent
Slithers in mad spirals . . .
Like in a dantesque dream, the shadows fly . . .
Screams, cries of woe, curses, and prayers sound!
And Satan laughs! . . .

. . . .

Canto VI
There is a people that its flag lends
To cover such infamy and cowardice! . . .
And lets it in this orgy be transformed
In the filthy cloak of a cold bachant! . . .
My God! my God! What flag is this
That impudently dances upon the mast?! . . .
Silence! . . . Muse! weep, and so long weep
That the ensign is washed in your tears . . .

Oh green-gold banner of my land,
That the Brazilian breeze flaps and flutters,
Standard that puts an end to the sun's light,
And the divine promises of hope . . .
Thou, that from the liberty of war's end,
Wert raised upon the heroes' lance,
Would that thou hadst been rent in battle
Than to a people serve as burial shroud! . . .

Cruel destiny that destroys the mind!
Extinguish in this hour the filthy brig
The road Columbus opened in the waves,

Like a rainbow on the watery depths! . . .
. . . But the infamy is too much! . . . From the land ethereal
Rise up, heroes of the New World . . .
Andrada! strip that banner from the air!
Columbus! close the door to your seas!

I/ 'Stamos em pleno mar . . . Doudo no espaço/ Brinca o luar—dourada
borboleta;/ E as vagas após ele correm . . . cansam/ Como turba de
infantes inquieta.// 'Stamos em pleno mar . . . Do firmamento/ Os astros
saltam como espumas de ouro . . . / O mar em troca acende as ardentias,/
—Constelações do líquido tesouro . . . // 'Stamos em pleno mar . . . Dois
infinitos/ Ali se estreitam num abraço insano,/ Azuis, dourados, plácidos,
sublimes . . . / Qual dos dous é o céu? qual o oceano? . . . // 'Stamos em
pleno mar . . . Abrindo as velas/ Ao quente arfar das virações marinhas,/
Veleiro brigue corre à flor dos mares,/ Como roçam na vaga as andorinhas
. . . // Donde vem? onde vai? Das naus errantes/ Quem sabe o rumo se é
tão grande o espaço?/ Neste saara os corcéis o pó levantam,/ Galopam,
voam, mas não deixam traço.// Bem feliz quem ali pode nest'hora/ Sentir
deste painel a majestade!/ Embaixo—o mar . . . em cima—o firmamento
. . . / E no mar e no céu—a imensidade!// Oh! que doce harmonia traz-
me a brisa!/ Que música suave ao longe soa!/ Meu Deus! como é sublime
um canto ardente/ Pelas vagas sem fim boiando à toa!// Homes do mar! ó
rudes marinheiros,/ Tostados pelo sol dos quatro mundos!/ Crianças que a
procela acalentara/ No berço destes pélagos profundos!// Esperai! esperai!
deixai que eu beba/ Esta selvagem, livre poesia . . . / Orquestra—é o mar,
que ruge pela proa,/ E o vento que nas cordas assobia . . . // . . . // Por que
foges assim, barco ligeiro?/ Por que foges do pávido poeta?/ Oh! quem
me dera acompanhar-te a esteira/ Que semelha no mar—doudo cometa!//
Albatroz! Albatroz! águia do oceano,/ Tu que dormes das nuvens entre as
gazas,/ Sacode as penas, Leviathan do espaço!/ Albatroz! Albatroz! dá-me
estas asas// . . . // IV/ Era um sonho dantesco . . . o tombadilho/ Que das
luzernas avermelha o brilho,/ Em sangue a se banhar./ Tinir de ferros . . .
estalar de açoite . . . / Legiões de homens negros como a noite,/ Horrendos
a dançar . . . // Negras mulheres, suspendendo às tetas/ Magras crianças,
cujas bocas pretas/ Rega o sangue das mães:/ Outras moças, mas nuas e
espantadas,/ No turbilhão de espectros arrastadas,/ Em ânsia e mágoa vãs!//
E ri-se a orquestra, irônica, estridente . . . / E da ronda fantástica a serpente/
Faz doudas espirais . . . / Se o velho arqueja . . . se no chão resvala/ Ouvem-
se gritos . . . o chicote estala./ E voam mais e mais . . . // Presa nos elos de
uma só cadeia,/ A multidão faminta cambaleia,/ E chora e dança ali!/ Um
de raiva delira, outro enlouquece . . . / Outro, que martírios embrutece,/
Cantando, geme e ri!// No entanto o capitão manda a manobra,/ E após
fitando o céu que se desdobra,/ Tão puro sobre o mar,/ Diz do fumo entre
os densos nevoeiros:/ "Vibrai rijo o chicote, marinheiros!/ Fazei-os

mais dançar! . . . "// E ri-se a orquestra irônica, estridente . . . / E da ronda fantástica a serpente// Faz doudas espierais . . . / Qual um sonho dantesco as sombras voam! . . . / Gritos, ais, maldições, preces ressoam!/ E ri-se Satanás!// . . . // VI/ Existe um povo que a bandeira empresta/ P'ra cobrir tanta infâmia e cobardia! . . . / E deixa-a transformar-se nessa festa/ Em manto impuro de bacante fria! . . . / Meu Deus! meu Deus! mas que bandeira é esta,/ Que impudente na gávea tripudia?! / Silêncio! Musa . . . chora, e chora tanto/ Que o pavilhão se lave no teu pranto! . . . // Auriverde pendão de minha terra,/ Que a brisa do Brasil beija e balança,// Estandarte que a luz do sol encerra/ E as promessas divinas da esperança . . . / Tu que, da liberdade após a guerra,/ Foste hasteado dos heróis na lança/ Antes te houvessem roto na batalha,/ Que servires a um povo de mortalha . . . // Fatalidade atroz que a mente esmaga!/ Extingue nesta hora o brigue imundo/ O trilho que Colombo abriu nas vagas,/ Como um íris no pélago profundo!/ Mas é infâmia demais! . . . Da etérea plaga/ Levantai-vos, heróis do Novo Mundo!/ Andrada! arranca esse pendão dos ares!/ Colombo! fecha a porta dos teus mares!

Rosa Araneda (1850–1894, Chile)

Born perhaps in Machali or Tagua-Tagua, in Chile, Araneda was part of the great migratory movement that brought peasants into the big cities, where city and people were mutually transformed, creating what is now called the "national culture." They brought a way of speaking and singing called "*la lira popular,*" or the popular lyre: a vernacular, colloquial speech, inherited from the oral traditions, which contrasted with the cultivated poetry of the cities. Araneda managed to make a living from her verses by having them printed, and illustrated as "*pliegos de versos,*" broadsides she sold in the city streets. The only woman among her circle, she was scorned, ridiculed, and envied by her peers for her immense popularity. Her vast oeuvre comprises poems "by literature," cosmic meditations, political denunciations, and erotic love songs, where she held fast to the ambivalent voice of the liberated women of her time, who were entering the work force as streetcar conductors or migrant workers, while affirming their own sexuality and worldview.

Cueca* of the Lady Conductors / Cueca de las conductoras

Rosa Alcalá, trans.

When all the loving
Lady conductors
Ride their streetcars
They resemble roses.

[*Chilean courting dance]

Resemble roses, yes,
A garden of flowers
Mosquitoes hover
With so much desire.
   Yes, so much desire,
Young men chase
After the conductors' loveliness.

It's true, it's so, sweet
Little mosquito.

A hot-blooded conductor
Told her co-worker
I want for my own
A little mosquito.

   I would hold him, yes,
As my treasure
And day by day
Caress him all over.
   Yes, day by day,
If I maul him too much,
People no doubt
Will have something to say.

That's what I call living, ladies,
The lady conductors.

Todas las conductoras/ Son amorosas,/ Cuando suben al carro/ Parecen rosas.//
Parecen rosas, sí,/ Jardín de flores,/ Abrazan los zancudos/ Con mil amores./
Con mil amores, sí,/ Por lindas i bellas/ Andan los jovencitos/ Detrás de ellas.//
Así es, así es, bonito/ Un zancudito.// Una conductora lacha/ Le dijo a su
compañera,/ Un zancudo chiquito/ De buena gana tuviera.// Yo lo tuviera,
sí,/ Por prenda mía,/ Para hacerle cariño/ Dia por dia./ Día por dia, sí,/ Es
evidente,/ Si me le atraco mucho/ Habla la jente.// Así es vida, señoras,/ Las
conductoras.

Anonymous, xylography illustrations for
broadsides, "pliegos de versos"

José Martí (1853–1895, Cuba)

Martí was born to Spanish parents in Cuba. A literary revolutionary as well as a political revolutionary who fought for Cuban independence from Spain, he was sentenced to six years of hard labor when he was a teenager. Based on that experience, Martí wrote "El presidio político de Cuba" (The Political Prison in Cuba [1871]), which served not only as a condemnation of the Spanish authorities but more importantly as a landmark in the evolving Latin American *modernismo* movement to which Martí was a main contributor. After being exiled to Spain, where he received his formal education, he traveled to Mexico, Guatemala, Venezuela, and finally New York, where he worked for the *New York Sun*. Martí's poetry focuses on man, both in terms of human cruelty and the potential for people to adapt and survive. PRINCIPAL WORKS: *Ismaelillo* (1882), *Versos sencillos* (1891), *Versos libres* (1913)

Waking Dream / Sueño despierto

Esther Allen, trans.

I dream with my eyes
open and always, by day
and night, I dream.
And over the foam
of the wide and restless sea,
and through the spiraling
sands of the desert,
upon a mighty lion,
monarch of my breast,
blithely astride
its docile neck,
always I see, floating,
a boy, who calls to me!

Yo sueño con los ojos/ Abiertos, y de día/ Y noche siempre sueño./
Y sobre las espumas/ Del ancho mar revuelto,/ Y por entre las crespas/
Arenas del desierto,/ Y del león pujante,/ Monarca de mi pecho,/ Montado
alegremente/ Sobre el sumiso cuello,—/ ¡Un niño que me llama/ Flotando
siempre veo!

Love in the City / Amor de ciudad grande

Esther Allen, trans.

Times of gorge and rush are these:
Voices fly like light: lightning,
like a ship hurled upon dread quicksand,

plunges down the high rod, and in delicate craft
man, as if winged, cleaves the air.
And love, without splendor or mystery,
dies when newly born, of glut.
The city is a cage of dead doves
and avid hunters! If men's bosoms
were to open and their torn flesh
fall to the earth, inside would be
nothing but a scatter of small, crushed fruit!

Love happens in the street, standing in the dust
of saloons and public squares: the flower
dies the day it's born. The trembling
virgin who would rather death
have her than some unknown youth;
the joy of trepidation; that feeling of heart
set free from chest; the ineffable
pleasure of deserving; the sweet alarm
of walking quick and straight
from your love's home and breaking
into tears like a happy child;—
and that gazing out of love at the fire,
as roses slowly blush a deeper color,—
Bah, it's all a sham! Who has the time
to be noble? Though like a golden
bowl or sumptuous painting
a genteel lady sits in the magnate's home!

But if you're thirsty, reach out your arm,
and drain some passing cup!
The dirtied cup rolls to the dust, then,
and the expert taster—breast blotted
with invisible blood—goes happily,
crowned with myrtle, on his way!
Bodies are nothing now but trash,
pits, and tatters! And souls
are not the tree's lush fruit
down whose tender skin runs
sweet juice in time of ripeness,—
but fruit of the marketplace, ripened
by the hardened laborer's brutal blows!

It is an age of dry lips!
Of undreaming nights! Of life
crushed unripe! What is it that we lack,

without which there is no gladness? Like a startled
hare in the wild thicket of our breast,
fleeing, tremulous, from a gleeful hunter,
the spirit takes cover;
and Desire, on Fever's arm,
beats the thicket, like the rich hunter.

     The city appalls me! Full
of cups to be emptied, and empty cups!
I fear—ah me!–that this wine
may be poison, and sink its teeth,
vengeful imp, in my veins!
I thirst—but for a wine that none on earth
knows how to drink! I have not yet
endured enough to break through the wall
that keeps me, ah grief!, from my vineyard!
Take, oh squalid tasters
of humble human wines, these cups
from which, with no fear or pity,
you swill the lily's juice!
Take them! I am honorable, and I am afraid!

De gorja son y rapidez los tiempos/ Corre cual luz la voz; en alta aguja,/ Cual
nave despeñada en sirte horrenda,/ Húndese el rayo, y en ligera barca/ El
hombre, como alado, el aire hiende./ ¡Así el amor, sin pompa ni misterio/
Muere, apenas nacido, de saciado!/ ¡Jaula es la villa de palomas muertas/
Y ávidos cazadores! Si los pechos/ Se rompen de los hombres, y las carnes/
Rotas por tierra ruedan, ¡No han de verse/ Dentro más que frutillas
estrujadas!// Se ama de pie, en las calles, entre el polvo/ De los salones y las
plazas; muere/ La flor el día en que nace. Aquella virgen/ Trémula que antes a
la muerte daba/ La mano pura que a ignorado mozo;/ El goce de temer; aquel
salirse/ Del pecho el corazón; el inefable/ Placer de merecer; el grato susto/ De
caminar de prisa en derechura/ Del hogar de la amada, y a sus puertas/ Como
un niño feliz romper en llanto;/ Y aquel mirar, de nuestro amor al fuego,/
Irse tiñendo de color las rosas,/ ¡Ea, que son patrañas! Pues ¿quién tiene/
Tiempo de ser hidalgo? ¡Bien que sienta,/ Cual áureo vaso o lienzo suntuoso,/
Dama gentil en casa de magnate!// ¡O si se tiene sed, se alarga el brazo/ Y a
la copa que pasa se la apura!/ Luego, la copa turbia al polvo rueda,/ ¡Y el
hábil catador, —manchado el pecho/ De una sangre invisible—sigue alegre/
Coronado de mirtos, su camino!/ No son los cuerpos ya sino desechos,/
Y fosas, y jirones! Y las almas/ No son como en el árbol fruta rica/ En cuya
blanda piel la almíbar dulce/ En su sazón de madurez rebosa,/ Sino fruta de
plaza que a brutales/ Golpes el rudo labrador madura!// ¡La edad es ésta de
los labios secos!/ ¡De las noches sin sueño! ¡De la vida/ Estrujada en agraz!

¿Qué es lo que falta/ Que la ventura falta? Como liebre/ Azorada, el espíritu se esconde,/ Trémulo huyendo al cazador que ríe,/ Cual en soto selvoso, en nuestro pecho;/ Y el deseo, de brazo de la fiebre,/ Cual rico cazador recorre el soto.// ¡Me espanta la ciudad! ¡Toda está llena/ De copas por vaciar, o huecas copas!/ ¡Tengo miedo ¡ay de mí! de que este vino/ Tósigo sea, y en mis venas luego/ Cual duende vengador los dientes clave!/ ¡Tengo sed, —mas de un vino que en la tierra/ No se sabe beber! ¡No he padecido/ Bastante aún, para romper el muro/ Que me aparta ¡oh dolor! de mi viñedo!/ ¡Tomad vosotros, catadores ruines/ De vinillos humanos, esos vasos/ Donde el jugo de lirio a grandes sorbos/ Sin compasión y sin temor se bebe!/ ¡Tomad! ¡Yo soy honrado, y tengo miedo!

João da Cruz e Sousa (1861–1898, Brazil)

As the son of two African slaves, Cruz was the first popular Brazilian poet of African ancestry. Unfortunately, that fame and praise arrived posthumously and Cruz's life was characterized by mental instability and solitude. Born in the southern city formerly known as Desterro, Cruz moved to Rio de Janeiro to seek work when the institutional racism of the southern province impeded him from finding a good job despite his intellectual ability. His writing style has been described as ahead of its time, borrowing much from the French symbolists in an era dominated by the Romantics. PRINCIPAL WORKS: *Broquéis* (1893), *Missal* (1893), *Evocaçoes* (1898)

Lesbian / Lésbia

Mark A. Lokensgard, trans.

Wild croton, wanton caladium,
Lethal plant, carnivorous, bloody,
From your bacchic flesh bursts
The red explosion of a living blood.

On that mordant and convulsive lip
Are laughs, laughs of violent expression
From Love, tragic and sad, and slowly passes
Death, the cold, harrowing spasm . . .

Feverish lesbian, bewitching and diseased,
Cruel and demoniacal serpent
Of the burning attractions of delight.

From your acidulous and sour breasts
Flow acetic aromas and the torpors,
Opium of a moon with consumption . . .

Cróton selvagem, tinhorão lascivo,/ Planta mortal, carnívora, sangrenta,/ Da tua carne báquica rebenta/ A vermelha explosão de um sangue vivo.// Nesse lábio mordente e convulsivo,/ Ri, ri risadas de expressão violenta/ O Amor, trágico e triste, e passa, lenta,/ A morte, o espasmo gélido, aflitivo . . . // Lésbia nervosa, fascinante e doente,/ Cruel e demoníaca serpente/ Das flamejantes atrações do gozo.// Dos teus seios acídulos, amargos,/ Fluem capros aromas e os letargos,/ Os ópios de um luar tuberculoso . . .

Afra

Mark Lokensgard, trans.

You reemerge from the mysteries of lust,
Afra, tempted by the green pomes,
Among the fascinating sylphs and marvelous gnomes
Of the purple-colored passion.

Explosive flesh in blasting powder and fury
Of pagan desires, among appearances
Of virginity—mocking laughs of a farce
Laughing at the flesh already given to neglect.

Given over early to languid abandon,
To the morbid swoons like sleep,
From the delight of drawing in the venomous juices.

I dream of you, goddess of the lascivious display,
As you declare, intrepidly, to the sound of horns,
Loves more sterile than eunuchs!

Ressurges dos mistérios da luxúria,/ Afra, tentada pelos verdes pomos,/ Entre os silfos magnéticos e os gnomos/ Maravilhosos da paixão purpúrea.// Carne explosiva em pólvoras e fúria/ De desejos pagãos, por entre assomos/ Da virgindade—casquinantes momos/ Rindo da carne já votada à incúria.// Votada cedo ao lânguido abandono,/ Aos mórbidos delíquios como ao sono,/ Do gozo haurindo os venenosos sucos.// Sonho-te a deusa das lascivas pompas,/ A proclamar, impávida, por trompas,/ Amores mais estéreis que os eunucos!

José Asunción Silva (1865–1896, Colombia)

Born in Bogotá, and celebrated as the best-loved poet of Colombia, Silva embodied the Romantic ideal. His life was fraught with misfortune. Driven to despair
by the deaths of his father and his favorite sister, financial bankruptcy, and the
loss of most of his manuscripts in a shipwreck, he took his own life at a young
age. As a forerunner of the modernist movement, he is regarded as a master of
the interplay between rhythm, sound, and image. His metrical experimentation
and investigation into the darkness of the soul continues to inspire writers today.
The house where he spent the last years of his life functions now as the "Casa de
Poesía Silva" (Silva House of Poetry) and became the first center in Latin America
and Spain dedicated entirely to poetry. PRINCIPAL WORKS: *El libro de versos* (1923),
De sobremesa (1928)

Ars

G. J. Racz, trans.

Verse is a sacred vessel, so pour nothing other than
      Pure thought into its every line!
Then let the teeming images erupting from its depths
Burst forth like golden bubbles out a dark and mellow wine!

Arrange the flowers there that after temperate autumn's flight
      The cruel world's wintry blasts pursue
Beside delicious memories of times forever gone
And aromatic spikenards glistening with the morning dew.

For mankind's wretched lot on earth to meet with comfort here
      As from some undiscovered balm
Consumed within the fire of a much affected soul,
Man only needs a drop of this supreme essence of calm.

El verso es un vaso santo; ¡poned en él tan sólo,/ un pensamiento puro,/ en
cuyo fondo bullan hirvientes las imágenes,/ ¡como burbujas de oro de un
viejo vino oscuro!// Allí verted las flores que en la continua lucha/ ajó del
mundo el frío,/ recuerdos deliciosos de tiempos que no vuelven,/ y nardos
empapados de gotas de rocío.// Para que la existencia mísera se embalsame/
cual de una esencia ignota,/ quemándose en el fuego del alma enternecida,/
de aquel supremo bálsamo basta una sola gota.

Olavo Bilac (1865–1918, Brazil)

Born in Rio de Janeiro, Bilac did not meet his father, who was a military surgeon participating in the Paraguay War, until he was five years old. Profoundly affected by the war, he became an active nationalist, twice imprisoned, in 1892 and 1894, for his protests against President Floriano Peixoto. His sonnets and clear simple style won over the public who elected him the prince of Brazilian poets in 1907. He also founded the Academia Brasileira de Letras and was a member of the Academia de Ciências de Lisboa. In his early days, he focused on the themes of sexuality and physical beauty. Later his themes deepened to include war, the indigenous Brazilian, death, and aging. PRINCIPAL WORK: *Poesias, 1884–1887* (1888)

Portuguese Language / Língua portuguesa

Odile Cisneros, trans.

Latium's last flower, lovely and wild,
You are at once splendor and tomb:
Native gold, the ore subsumes,
Coarse mine in gravel, undefiled . . .

I love you so, unknown, obscure,
Loud-clanging trumpet, simple lyre.
You have the hiss of tempests and the fire,
Tender *saudade*, lullaby's allure!

I love your rural rankness and your scent
Of virgin forests and of boundless seas!
I love you, oh rough language of lament,

In which I heard a mother's call "My son!"
In which Camões in bitter exile wept
His ill-starred genius and lackluster love!

Última flor do Lácio, inculta e bela,/ És, a um tempo, esplendor e sepultura:/ Ouro nativo, que na ganga impura/ A bruta mina entre os cascalhos vela . . . // Amo-te assim, desconhecida e obscura,/ Tuba de alto clangor, lira singela,/ Que tens o trom e o silvo da procela,/ E o arrolo da saudade e da ternura!// Amo o teu viço agreste e o teu aroma/ De virgens selvas e de oceano largo!/ Amo-te, ó rude e doloroso idioma,// Em que da voz materna ouvi: "Meu filho!"/ E em que Camões chorou, no exílio amargo,/ O gênio sem ventura e o amor sem brilho!

Rubén Darío (1867–1916, Nicaragua)

Darío's poetry is an enduring legacy. His work continues to enlighten new generations of poets. Born in Nicaragua, he was a great nomad and lived in many countries. Considered one of the founders of *modernismo*, Octavio Paz said that Darío understood "the world and the universe as a system of correspondencies under the rule of Rhythm," and that he joined "in a single poetic continent the archaic rhythm of Castillian poetry with those of the indigenous cultures in a fusion never seen before." Most important, he produced the first literary body of work that had an influence on European literature. PRINCIPAL WORKS: *Azul* (1888), *Prosas profanas* (1896), *La caravana pasa* (1902), *Cantos de vida y esperanza* (1905)

Love Your Rhythm / Ama tu ritmo

Elinor Randall, trans.

Love your rhythm and rhyme your acts
under its law, your verses too;
you are a universe of universes,
your soul a spring of songs.

Your presupposed celestial unity
shall make all kinds of worlds spring up in you;
and when your scattered numbers resonate,
pythagorize within your constellations.

Listen to the divine rhetoric
of bird in air, and prophesy
the geometric and nocturnal radiance;

Kill taciturn indifference,
and string together pearl to crystal pearl
where truth its urn is overturning.

Ama tu ritmo y ritma tus acciones/ bajo su ley, así como tus versos;/ eres un universo de universos/ y tu alma una fuente de canciones.// La celeste unidad que presupones,/ hará brotar en ti mundos diversos;/ y al resonar tus números dispersos/ pitagoriza en tus constelaciones.// Escucha la retórica divina/ del pájaro del aire y la nocturna/ irradiación geométrica adivina;// mata la indiferencia taciturna/ y engarza perla y perla cristalina/ en donde la verdad vuelca su urna.

The Wandering Song / El canto errante

Gabriel Gudding, trans.

A singer goes all over the world
impassioned or bored.

In a little train or a white train
beside the gulls or through the grain.
A singer walks into wars and peaces
into civil wars, trench wars, trade wars.

Through discord or concord
a singer goes to all these places.

A diva moves in the world.

On the ridge spine of the elephant
into the narrows of the Hellespont.

On a palanquin, in gemmy silks
she crosses glaciers in the Alps.

On a cloud backed and glinting jet
into Buddhist and bright Tibet.

In car into St. Lucia
On a dark train through Galicia.

Over the pampas and the flats
on American colts.

She goes by river in a canoe
or props herself in the banging prow

of a pelagic freighter
or she simply rides an escalator.

She brings her nose to archipelagoes
And carts her ears into Tangiers.

On a dromedary across the sands
by jiggling boats, she visits lands.

She goes to the tundra's edge
on an expeditious sledge.

And far from the equator's flora
she thrills to the boreal aurora.

The singer strolls through hissing crops
across the rows and by the cows.

She enters her London on a bus
her Jerusalem on an ass.

She goes with mailbags and pouches of the State
to open doors to eternal things.

To salve the sores of human beings
is why she sings.

El cantor va por todo el mundo/ sonriente o meditabundo.// El cantor va
sobre la tierra/ en blanca paz o en roja guerra.// Sobre el lomo del elefante/
por la enorme India alucinante.// En palanquín y en seda fina/ por el
corazón de la China;// en automóvil en Lutecia;/ en negra góndola en
Venecia;// sobre las pampas y los llanos/ en los potros americanos;// por el
río va en la canoa,/ o se le ve sobre la proa// de un *steamer* sobre el vasto
mar,/ o en un wagón de *sleeping-car*.// El dromedario del desierto,/ barco
vivo, le lleva a un puerto.// Sobre el raudo trineo trepa/ en la blancura de la
estepa.// O en el silencio de cristal/ que ama la aurora boreal.// El cantor va a
pie por los prados,/ entre las siembras y ganados.// Y entra en su Londres en
el tren,/ y en asno a su Jerusalén.// Con estafetas y con malas,/ va el cantor
por la humanidad.// El canto vuela, con sus alas:/ Armonía y Eternidad.

EHEU!

Gabriel Gudding, trans.

Here beside this Latin sea
I feel in the rock, the oil, the wine
my own antiquity.

I am so old. How
did I get so old? Where
is my song really from? And
where am I going?

What self-knowledge I have
has already cost me
so many moments
at the abyss.
And this

"Latin" clarity,
what does it do for me
at the entrance to the mine
of the I and the not-I.

Like Nephelibata
who was happy to walk the clouds,

I think I am the exegete
of the harmattan, a confidant of the hill,
a reader of the sea:

I've learned a few vague secrets
about being and non-being,
a little wreckage for my mind
gathered from yesterday
and even today.

It was in the middle of this waste
that I started roaring:
I looked at the sun
as if it were dead
and threw myself to mourning.

Aquí, junto al mar latino,/ digo la verdad:/ Siento en roca, aceite y vino/ yo
mi antigüedad.// ¡Oh qué anciano soy, Dios santo,/ oh, qué anciano soy! . . . /
¿De dónde viene mi canto?/ Y yo, ¿adónde voy?// El conocerme a mí
mismo,/ ya me va costando/ muchos momentos de abismo/ y el cómo y el
cuándo . . . // Y esta claridad latina,/ ¿de qué me sirvió/ a la entrada de la
mina/ del yo y el no yo . . . ?// Nefelibata contento,/ creo interpretar/ las
confidencias del viento,/ la tierra y el mar . . . // Unas vagas confidencias/
del ser y el no ser,/ y fragmentos de conciencias/ de ahora y ayer.//Como en
medio de un desierto/ me puse a clamar;/ y miré el sol como muerto/ y me
eché a llorar.

Nocturne / Nocturno

Lysander Kemp, trans.

Silence of the night, a sad, nocturnal
Silence—Why does my soul tremble so?
I hear the humming of my blood,
And a soft storm passes through my brain.
Insomnia! Not to be able to sleep, and yet
To dream. I am the autospecimen
Of spiritual dissection, the auto-Hamlet!
To dilute my sadness
In the wine of the night
In the marvelous crystal of the dark—
And I ask myself: When will the dawn come?
Someone has closed a door—
Someone has walked past—
The clock has rung three—If only it were She!

Silencio de la noche, doloroso silencio/ nocturno . . . ¿Por qué el alma
tiembla de tal manera?/ Oigo el zumbido de mi sangre,/ dentro mi cráneo
pasa una suave tormenta./ ¡Insomnio! No poder dormir, y, sin embargo,/
soñar. Ser la auto-pieza/ de disección espiritual, ¡el auto-Hamlet!/ Diluir mi
tristeza/ en un vino de noche/ en el maravilloso cristal de las tinieblas . . .
/ Y me digo: ¿a qué hora vendrá el alba?/ Se ha cerrado una puerta . . . / Ha
pasado un transeúnte . . . / Ha dado el reloj tres horas . . . ¡Si será Ella! . . . /

Philosophy / Filosofía

Gabriel Gudding, trans.

Little spider, greet the sun. Don't be down.
Give thanks, dear toad, that you are here.
The hairy crabs, like roses, all have thorns,
and mollusks are reminiscences of women.

Know how to be what you are:
enigmas that have taken form.
Leave responsibilities to the Norm,
who will in turn send them on to Heaven.

(Sing, cricket: the moon is lit.
And, bear?, go ahead and dance.)

Saluda al sol, araña, no seas rencorosa./ Dá tus gracias a Dios, oh sapo,
pues que eres./ El peludo cangrejo tiene espinas de rosa/ y los moluscos
reminiscencias de mujeres.// Sabed ser lo que sois, enigmas, siendo
formas;/ dejad la responsabilidad a las Normas,/ que a su vez la enviarán al
Todopoderoso . . . /(Toca, grillo, a la luz de la luna; y dance el oso.)

The Optimist's Salutation / Salutación del optimista

Gabriel Gudding, trans.

Prismic, fructifying peoples, blood of blooming Hispania,
familial spirits, gelid, coruscant souls, I salute you!

It is time for new choirs
to entrain tongues into their treasure. A vast rumor
billows into the satellites; milling zoic waves already
are riding themselves toward us, to be reborn, right here.
Oblivion is receding, death—because it is a delusion—is receding:
a queendom is announced, a friendly sibyl dreams for us.
And in that pandoric box out of which corkscrewed so many skeins of
    misfortune,

we find now—talismanic, pure, giggling—
just as divine Virgil might have rung it in verse,
our own helial queen, firmamental Hope!

All the pale indolences, the fatal distrusts that entombed us,
the perpetual gulags that stretched to the doorstep of God
and condemned our noble enthusiasms,
all of these will find now a conquering sun climbing into the guitars—
while two continents, credentialed in glorious bones,
and evoking the colossal shadow of old Hercules,
say this to the globe: a remarkable virtue is now resurrected
and it will make the Hispanic children the owners of centuries.

Abominate any mouth that predicts eternal catastrophe
Abominate all eyes that see only calamitous predictions from the Zodiac
Abominate any hands that jackhammer our remarkable ruins, or that
pitch an incendiary or take up some self-defeating weapon.
The push of deafening forces is felt in the bowels of the hills,
the presence of something inevitable is rousing the world:
strong colossi fall, bicephalic eagles disband,
and something like a vast social cataclysm
is smearing itself over the face of the orb. And who says that the slumbering sap
won't foam again in the trunk of that sprawling oak
under which the tits of the Roman wolf were sucked?
Who would be so pusillanimous as to withhold muscles from the
    Spanish body?!
Or to assess the Spanish soul as apterous and blind and crippled?
This generous nation, crowned in an immaculate pride,
is neither a Babylon nor a Nineva buried in oblivion and dust.
Nor is it some queen dressed up between mummies and stones inhabiting
    a sepulcher.
It is not that land beyond the seas where Atlantis is still entombed:
it is fixing its longing gaze right now onto the side of the dawn—
it is cradling a choir of children each of whom is tall and robust and strong.

May all these dispersed and vigorous peoples be united
May they shine, May they care for one another
May they form a single bundle of ecumenical energy.
Blossoming families of Hispania, solid, illustrious peoples,
Demonstrate these gifts to our past, which were once its triumphs
Bring back the old enthusiasm, bring back the ardent spirit
that will blow down squalls of flaming tongue into our epiphany.

May both the ancient heads haloed in laurels
and the teenage heads bedecked by soaring Minervas
—as if they were the heroic manes of our primitive grandfathers

or of our astonishing fathers who opened the pristine furrows—
May all these feel again the little winds from the farms
for spring upon spring to come
May they always hear the murmur of the grain
that was begun with the Triptolemical sweat.

One continent and another renewing their families
in spirit united, in spirit and longing and tongue,
seeing the moment to compose new anthems. The Latin American peoples
wake now into a prospect of auroral days. And in an outbreak of
    harmonic thunder
they greet the coruscant light crackling from the east:
that same east with its irons in which all was changed and reforged.
Just so, may all this flame and tongue and rain be anchored
in our own Hope, you blooming and prismic, you fructifying peoples!

Inclitas razas ubérrimas, sangre de Hispania fecunda,/ espíritus fraternos,
luminosas almas, ¡salve!/ Porque llega el momento en que habrán de cantar
nuevos himnos/ lenguas de gloria. Un vasto rumor llena los ámbitos; mágicas/
ondas de vida van renaciendo de pronto;/ retrocede el olvido, retrocede
engañada la muerte;/ se anuncia un reino nuevo, feliz sibila sueña/ y en la
caja pandórica de que tantas desgracias surgieron/ encontramos de súbito,
talismánica, pura, rïente,/ cual pudiera decirla en sus versos Virgilio divino,/ la
divina reina de luz, ¡la celeste Esperanza!// Pálidas indolencias, desconfianzas
fatales que a tumba/ o a perpetuo presidio, condenasteis al noble entusiasmo,/
ya veréis el salir del sol en un triunfo de liras,/ mientras dos continentes,
abonados de huesos gloriosos,/ del Hércules antiguo la gran sombra soberbia
evocando,/ digan al orbe: la alta virtud resucita/ que a la hispana progenie
hizo dueña de siglos.// Abominad la boca que predice desgracias eternas,/
abominad los ojos que ven sólo zodíacos funestos,/ abominad las manos
que apedrean las ruinas ilustres,/ o que la tea empuñan o la daga suicida./
Siéntense sordos ímpetus en las entrañas del mundo,/ la inminencia de algo
fatal hoy conmueve la tierra;/ fuertes colosos caen, se desbandan bicéfalas
águilas,/ y algo se inicia como vasto social cataclismo/ sobre la faz del orbe.
¿Quién dirá que las savias dormidas/ no despierten entonces en el tronco del
roble gigante/ bajo el cual se exprimió la ubre de la loba romana?/ ¿Quién será
el pusilánime que al vigor español niegue músculos/ y que al alma española
juzgase áptera y ciega y tullida?/ No es Babilonia ni Nínive enterrada en olvido
y en polvo,/ ni entre momias y pierdas reina que habita el sepulcro,/ la nación
generosa, coronada de orgullo inmarchito,/ que hacia el lado del alba fija las
miradas ansiosas,/ ni la que, tras los mares en que yace sepulta la Atlántida,/
tiene su coro de vástagos, altos, robustos y fuertes.// Únanse, brillen,
secúndense, tantos vigores dispersos;/ formen todos un solo haz de energía
ecuménica./ Sangre de Hispania fecunda, sólidas, ínclitas razas,/ muestren los
dones pretéritos que fueron antaño su triunfo./ Vuelva el antiguo entusiasmo,

vuelva el espíritu ardiente/ que regará lenguas de fuego en esa epifanía./ Juntas las testas ancianas ceñidas de líricos lauros/ y las cabezas jóvenes que la alta Minerva decora,/ así los manes heroicos de los primitivos abuelos,/ de los egregios padres que abrieron el surco pristino,/ sientan los soplos agrarios de primaverales retornos/ y el rumor de espigas que inició la labor triptolémica.// Un continente y otro renovando las viejas prosapias,/ en espíritu unidos, en espíritu y ansias y lengua,/ ven llegar el momento en que habrán de cantar nuevos himnos./ La latina estirpe verá la gran alba futura:/ en un trueno de música gloriosa, millones de labios/ saludarán la espléndida luz que vendrá del Oriente,/ Oriente augusto en donde todo lo cambia y renueva/ la eternidad de Dios, la actividad infinita./ Y así sea Esperanza la visión permanente en nosotros,/ ínclitas razas ubérrimas, sangre de Hispania fecunda!

José Juan Tablada (1871–1945, Mexico)

Considered the father of modern Mexican poetry and a major contributor to the international symbolist movement, Tablada popularized *calligrammes* (picture-poems) and brought the haiku structure from Japan to Mexico. He lived in Japan for a number of years, and his poetry reflects his immersion in Japanese politics and culture. He also studied in France, another major influence on his artistic expression, in particular, the symbolism in his post-1900 works. Loosely linked to *modernismo*, he used modernist interest in Orientalism as a springboard to a serious exploration of Japanese poetry. He moved to New York to care for a heart ailment in 1944 but subsequently died in 1945. Octavio Paz praised Tablada at his funeral, saying that he could write of the essence of nature "without converting it into a symbol of decoration." PRINCIPAL WORKS: *Al sol y bajo la luna* (1918), *Li-Po y otros poemas* (1920), *La feria (Poemas mexicanos)* (1928)

Three Haikus

Roberto Tejada, trans.

Willow / El saúz

Gentle willow
almost gold, almost amber,
almost daylight

Tierno saúz/ casi oro, casi ámbar,/ casi luz . . .

Cherimoya Tree / El chirimoyo

Cherimoya tree branches
zigzag and chitchat:
twosome of parrots

La rama del chirimoyo/ se retuerce y habla:/ pareja de loros.

Bug / El insecto

Folded wings flung over
like a pilgrim's saddlebag:
flitter onward transient bug

Breve insecto, vas de camino/ plegadas las alas a cuestas,/ como alforja de
peregrino . . .

Excerpt from Ideogram Lantern / Li-Po

Roberto Tejada, trans.

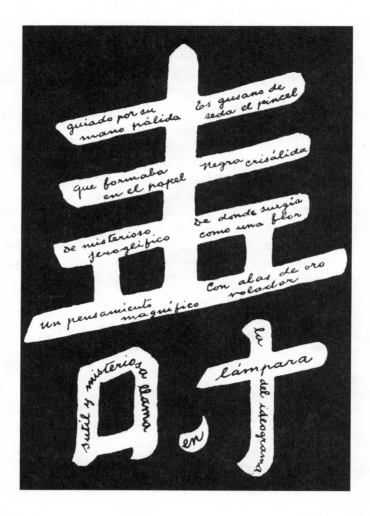

guided by   It's a silk worm
soft hand   paint brush

forming   a black
on paper   chrysalis

mysterious   Where like
hieroglyph   a flower bloom

magnificent   With golden
thought   wings of flight

strange allusive flicker

in

the ideogram lantern

Havana Impressions / Impresión de la Habana

Roberto Tejada, trans.

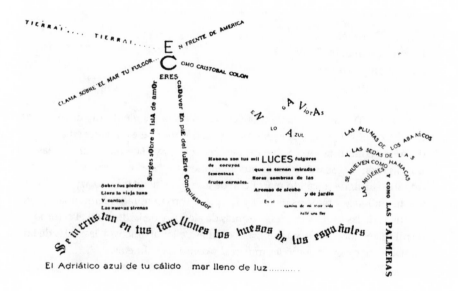

Land! . . . Land! . . .
Your glow roars over sea . . . in front of America
Like Christopher Columbus

You course over love's isle
You're the standing corpse of
a sturdy conquistador

Seagulls hover in blue

The old moon weeps
On your stones

And new mermaids
Sing

Your thousand lights Havana are the glow
Of fireflies
                turned into eyes of women
gazing
            solemn flowers
of fleshy fruit
                The scent of rooms
                                and gardens

On the
            road of my unhappy life
                I found a flower

Your cliffs are encrusted with Spaniard bones

The Adriatic blue of your warm   sea overflowing with light

Fans made of feathers
Hammocks made of silk
Swaying like women
And palm trees

¡Tierra! . . . ¡Tierra! . . . / clama sobre el mar tu fulgor . . . / enfrente de América/
como Cristóbal Colón.// Surges sobre la isla de amor,/ eres cadáver en pie/
del fuerte conquistador.// Sobre tus piedras/ llora la vieja luna/ y cantan/ las
nuevas sirenas.// Se incrustan en tus farallones/ los huesos de los españoles.// El
Adriático azul/ de tu cálido mar/ lleno de luz . . . / Gaviotas en lo azul.// Habana,
son tus mil luces/ fulgores de cocuyos/ que se tornan miradas femeninas,/ flores
sombrías de las frutas carnales,/ Aromas de alcoba y de jardín./ En el camino
de mi triste vida/ hallé una flor.// Las plumas de los abanicos/ y las sedas de las
hamacas/ se mueven como las mujeres/ y como las palmeras.

José María Eguren (1874–1942, Peru)

Also a painter and photographer, Eguren was born in Lima, Peru, where he lived most of his life. His frail health led him to a life of solitude, devoted to reading. This lifestyle availed him of a markedly different perspective from that of his contemporaries. His book *Simbólicas* is regarded as the work that initiated modern poetry in Peru. While his inventive and constructivist poetry was resisted and accused of being naive, great thinkers such as Mariategui supported him. As an artist, he constructed a photo camera with a thimble, capturing images in miniature, thus creating a visual equivalent of his poetry. Eguren did not follow the modernist dictates that were fashionable in his time and stripped his work of the rhetoric and grandiloquence present in the poetry of his Peruvian contemporary José Santos Chocano, thus opening the way to the Vanguardist movement in Peru. PRINCIPAL WORKS: *Simbólicas* (1911), *La canción de las figuras* (1916), *Poesías* (1929)

The Lady i / La dama i

Michelle Gil-Montero, trans.

The lady i, shiftless
in lake mist,
sings the fine ballads.

She goes in her charmed paper
gondola, to green
morning mass.

Dreams blond in aroma
softly wake
her sardana in the leaves.

And she leaves sweet, sleepy,
to the church hazy
with their yellow light.

La dama i, vagarosa/ en la niebla del lago,/ canta las finas trovas.// Va en su góndola encantada/ de papel, a la misa/ verde de la mañana.// Los sueños rubios de aroma/ despierta blandamente/ su sardana en las hojas.// Y parte dulce, adormida,/ a la borrosa iglesia/ de la luz amarilla.

The Towers / Las torres

Michelle Gil-Montero, trans.

Brown distances . . . ,
towers battle
presenting
enormous silhouettes.

Gold distances . . . ,
monarch towers
confuse
in their ire flames.

Red distances . . . ,
towers are wounded;
cardinals
their clamors are heard.

Black distances . . . ,
ashen hours
obscure
oh, the dead towers!

Brunas lejanías . . . ;/ batallan las torres/ presentando/ siluetas enormes.//
Aureas lejanías . . . ;/ las torres monarcas/ se confunden/ en sus iras llamas.//
Rojas lejanías . . . ;/ se hieren las torres;/ purpurados/ se oyen sus clamores.//
Negras lejanías . . . ;/ horas cenicientas/ se obscurecen/ ¡ay, las torres muertas!

Favila

Michelle Gil-Montero, trans.

In sand
shadow has bathed
one, two
ghost dragonflies . . .

Birds from smoke
go to the shadow
of the forest.

Half a century
and at the white limit
we await night.

The portico
with a perfume of algae,
the final sea.

In shadow,
triangles laugh.

En la arena/ se ha bañado la sombra./ Una, dos/ libélulas fantasmas . . . //
Aves de humo/ van a la penumbra/ del bosque.// Medio siglo/ y en el límite
blanco/ esperamos la noche.// El pórtico/ con perfume de algas,/ el último
mar.// En la sombra/ ríen los triángulos.

Joaquín Torres García (1874–1949, Uruguay)

A painter and theoretician born in Montevideo, Uruguay, Torres García had a Catalan father and Uruguayan mother of Canarian descent. When he was seventeen years old, financial difficulties forced his family to move to Barcelona. Torres García absorbed everything Europe could offer and then returned to Uruguay in 1934 to formulate his own theory of constructive universalism—an art inspired by the pre-Columbian traditions of the Americas and expressed in contemporary language. "Our north is the South," he explained. "There must not be a north for us, except in opposition to our South. That is why we are now placing the map upside-down and have a precise idea of our position, as opposed to what the rest of the world expects. From now on, the tip of the Americas extends itself, persistently, pointing South, which is our north." Torres García used symbols to construct an orderly image of the universe. He proposed an organic whole where letters and drawings complement each other, and where the text interrupts the drawing and the drawing interrupts the text. PRINCIPAL WORKS: *Historia de mi vida* (1934), *La tradición del hombre abstracto* (1938), *La ciudad sin nombre* (1941), *Universalismo constructivo* (1944)

América invertida

Excerpts from City with No Name / La ciudad sin nombre

G. J. Racz, trans.

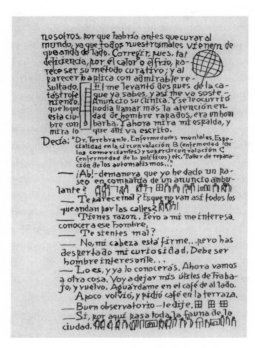

Us, because the world would have to/ be cured first, since all our ills stem
from/ its being out of kilter. Correcting this/ deficiency, then, through
heat or cold, seems/ to be his method of healing, which he/ apparently
applies with admirable re-/ sults. He gave me a boost after the catas-/
trophe you know of, and continues to sus-/ tain me. I advertise for his
clinic. It occurred to him/ that what might attract the most attention
in/ this city of shorn men was a bearded/ one. Now, take a look at my
back/ and see what is written there./ The sign read: "Dr. Sharpaine.
Mental illnesses. Spe-/ cialist in Bypass B (the businessman's/ disease)
and Superbypass C/ (the politician's), etc. Repair shop/ for repetitive-
stress injuries . . . "/ —Ah! So I've been strolling/ along in the company
of a walking/ advertisement?/ —Is that bad? Doesn't everyone who/
passes through these streets?/ —I'm sure you're right. I'd be interested/
in meeting the man. / —Are you feeling poorly?/ —No, my head is clear
. . . but you've/ piqued my curiosity. He must be/ an interesting person./
—He is, and you'll meet him soon. Let's move/ on, though. I'm going to
leave the tools of my/ trade here, but I'll be back. Wait for me in the café
out front./ After a while he returned and ordered a coffee on the patio./
—Great observation deck, I said./ —Yes, all the city's fauna passes by
here.// . . . //

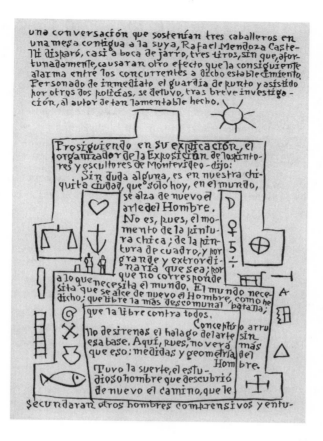

una conversación que sostenían tres caballeros en
una mesa contigua a la suya, Rafael Mendoza Caste-
lli disparó, casi a boca de jarro, tres tiros, sin que, afor-
tunadamente, causaran otro efecto que la consiguiente
alarma entre los concurrentes a dicho establecimiento.
Personado de inmediato el guardia de punto y asistido
por otros dos policías, se detuvo, tras breve investigación, al autor de tan lamentable hecho.

Prosiguiendo en su explicación, el
organizador de la Exposición de los pinto-
res y escultores de Montevideo - dijo:
Sin duda alguna, es en nuestra chi-
quita ciudad, que solo hoy, en el mundo,
se alza de nuevo el
arte del Hombre.
No es, pues, el mo-
mento de la pintu-
ra chica; de la pin-
tura de cuadro, y por
grande y extraordi-
naria que sea; por-
que no corresponde
a lo que necesita el mundo. El mundo necesita que se alce de nuevo el Hombre, como he
dicho; que libre la más descomunal batalla;
que la libre contra todos.
Concepto arru
no de sirenas el halago del arte sin
esa base. Aquí, pues, no verá más
que eso: medidas y geometría del
Hom
Tuvo la suerte, el estu- bre.
dioso hombre que descubrió
de nuevo el camino, que le
secundarán otros hombres comprensivos y entu-

A conversation three gentlemen were having at/ a table nearby, Rafael Mendoza Cas-/ telli fired his gun, practically point blank, fortu-/ nately without causing more than the subsequent/ alarm of those present in the establishment./ The guard on duty showed up immediately with two/ police officers as backup, and the perpetrator of this regret-/ table deed was arrested after a brief investigation./ Continuing with his explanation, the/ organizer of the Exhibit of Monte-/ video Painters and Sculptors said:/ Without a doubt, it is our tiny city/ alone in the world today that the art/ of all Mankind/ is on the rise again./ This is not the time/ for painting on a small/ scale or canvas-size / works no matter how/ grand or extraordi-/ nary they might be for/ these do not respond/ to what the world needs. The world/ needs for Mankind to rise again, as I have/ stated, to fight the most strenuous of battles/ and fight it against everyone./ The attraction of/ art in absence of this foundation is merely as concept or siren/ song. Here, then, you will see no less/ than this: the very measurement and geometry of/ Man./ That studious individ-/ ual who came upon/ this path once again / was fortunate to have other understanding, enthusiastic men sec-/ ond

Julio Herrera y Reissig (1875–1910, Uruguay)

A member of high society, Herrera y Reissig was born in Montevideo, Uruguay, and never left his native city except for a short stay in Buenos Aires. A congenital heart defect, worsened after a bout of typhoid fever, forced him to abandon his formal studies, though it didn't stop him from becoming an avid reader and founding a select literary group that gathered at his family mansion, dedicated to discussing the latest artistic tendencies, practicing spiritism, and using opium and morphine. His work—thirsty for challenge and renewal—started within the late Romanticism, then became one of the first to carry the banner of modernism, and finally moved into a surreal and oneiric lyricism that fell under modernity but did not abandon traditional meter. PRINCIPAL WORKS: *Los peregrinos de piedra* (1909), *Poesías* (1911), *Prosas* (1918)

Excerpt from Lunatic Tertulia / Tertulia lunática

Forrest Gander, trans.

I
In a crypt of gold, somewhat shot,
A cataleptic fakir,
Who gave up mountains to partake here,
Of a comforting Nirvana, somewhat shot . . .
Objectify an ill-wrought
Execution of thought,
And muffled rumor is begot
Like deaf remorse
From some extrorse
Diffusion of the music of a garrot.

Skies loosen their grimace, green,
And the disequilibrium
Of scorn's satire hums,
Sick on absinthe, green . . .
Hypothetically, the sheen
In the moving horizon is spent,
And the pensive settlement,
Is swarmed, they say, by a squall
As if, in the World's thrall
Everything were tenebrescent.

Already the fireflies—witches
With jewels from Salambo—
Wink the "marche aux flambeaux"
Of a Sabbath of witches . . .

The velvet cypresses
Suggest a Carthusian ardor,
Which wafts from your collar
In fragrant confidences,
Interjections of absences
And ring-eyed ritornellos of languor.

It's all posthumous and abstract
And the spirit ideologues
Intimate monologues
Of the Unknowable Abstract . . .
The stupefied forest is ablaze
In an ecstasy of malaise,
And they light up that hirsute
Labyrinth of the proscenium
With a struck match from
The dark genie of the Absolute.

It all provokes the ennui
Of some psychophysical country
At the metaphysical extremity
Of silence and of ennui . . .
A whiff of rancid duration
Chronicles the extreme unction
And protracts, before uncontrolled
Logic of extension,
The materialization
Of the planetary soul.

From the unsonorous interior
Of my obscure ruins,
Drones, punctuated with omens,
The Babylonian interior . . .
A Pythagoristic horoscoper
From the ultra-night,
Meanwhile, writes an accusation
Of ecstatic expiations,
And hieratic mummies take flight
From the Escorial of the Night.

Fatuous fires of exorcism
Illuminate my double sight,
Like someone juggling, as she might,
The rutilation of exorcism . . .

The Sub-Conscious of the same
Grand All gives me chilblain;
And in that somber assembly
From the darkness grand and aphonic
Ferments a cosmogonic
Trumpet of prophecy.

So in a gothic rapture of snow
The chapel hones itself, and
Above, the hypnotic needle can
Thread together stars of snow . . .
The shadowy forest spurs on
Fantastic misfortunes
And in macabre ponderosas
A pastor suddenly brandishes
His cane as a layman extinguishes
Gloomy candelabras.

It sleeps, the ear in wait,
Like a wolf in the underbrush
Hidden, a suspicious hush
At the precipice, in wait . . .
Field rows wrinkle, desolate,
While the bubbling sluice
Dissolves and refuses
Eskimo soliloquies
Of crystal garglings
And euphorias of cornemuses.

Its saddle hung up, the somnambulistic
Windmill metaphorizes that
A Don Quixote comes to combat,
On horseback and somnambulistic . . .
The smoke is vexed by an equilibrist,
Guignol of Kaleidoscope,
And in the heady night of dope
Savants tear open a lens
Of the eye of the conscience
How deep! of a spectroscope.

On the watchtower, enigmatical,
The owl with eyes of brimstone
Suffers its morbid hoot-moan
Like a muezzin, enigmatical . . .

Before the omen—lunatic
Captious, spectral, denuded,
Velvety and muted—
It descends in stirless dress
Like a spider of death—
The immense night of the Buddha . . .

I/ En túmulo de oro vago,/ Cataléptico fakir/ Se dio el tramonto a dormir/
La unción de un Nirvana vago . . . / Objetívase un aciago/ Suplicio de
pensamiento/ Y como un remordimiento/ Pulula el sordo rumor/ De
algún pulverizador/ De músicas de tormento.// El cielo abre un gesto
verde,/ Y ríe el desequilibrio/ De un sátiro de ludibrio/ Enfermo de
absintio verde . . . / En hipótesis se pierde/ El horizonte errabundo,/ Y el
campo meditabundo/ De informe turbión se puebla,/ Como que todo es
tiniebla/ En la conciencia del Mundo.// Ya las luciérnagas—brujas/ Del
joyel de Salambó—/ Guiñan la "marche aux flambeaux"/ De un aquelarre
de brujas . . . / Da nostalgias de Cartujas/ El ciprés de terciopelo,/ Y vuelan
de tu pañuelo,/ En fragantes confidencias,/ Interjecciones de ausencias/
Y ojeras de ritornelo.// Todo es póstumo y abstracto/ Y se intiman de
monólogos/ Los espíritus ideólogos/ Del Incognoscible Abstracto . . . /
Arde el bosque estupefacto/ En un éxtasis de luto,/ Y se electriza el
hirsuto/ Laberinto del proscenio/ Con el fósforo del genio/ Lóbrego de
lo Absoluto.// Todo suscita el cansancio/ De algún país psicofísico/ En
el polo metafísico/ De silencio y de cansancio . . . / Un vaho de tiempo
rancio/ Historia la unción plenaria,/ Y cunde, ante la arbitraria/ Lógica de
la extensión,/ La materialización/ Del ánima planetaria.// Del insonoro
interior/ De mis obscuros naufragios,/ Zumba, viva de presagios,/ La
Babilonia interior . . . / Un pitagorizador/ Horoscopa de ultra-noche,/
Mientras, en auto-reproche/ De contriciones estáticas,/ Rondan las
momias hieráticas/ Del Escorial de la Noche.// Fuegos fatuos de
exorcismo/ Ilustran mi doble vista,/ Como una malabrista/ Rutilación de
exorcismo . . . / Lo Sub-Consciente del mismo/ Gran Todo me escalofría;/
Y en la multitud sombría/ De la gran tiniebla afónica/ Fermenta una
cosmogónica/ Trompeta de profecía.// Tal en un rapto de nieve/ Se
aguza la ermita gótica,/ Y arriba el aguja hipnótica/ Enhebra estrellas
de nieve . . . / El bosque en la sombra mueve/ Fantásticos descalabros,/
Y en los enebros macabros/ Blande su caña un pastor,/ Como un lego
apagador/ De tétricos candelabros.// Duerme, la oreja en acecho,/ Como
un lobo montaraz/ El silencio suspicaz/ Del precipicio en acecho . . . /
Frunce el erial su despecho,/ Mientras disuelve y rehúsa/ El borbollón
de la esclusa/ Monólogos de esquimal,/ En gárgaras de cristal/ Y euforias

de cornamusa.// Albarda en ristre, el sonámbulo/ Molino metaforiza/
Un Don Quijote en la liza,/ Encabalgado y sonámbulo . . . / Tortura el
humo un funámbulo/ guignol de Kaleidoscopio,/ Y hacia la noche de
opio/ Abren los pozos de Ciencia/ El ojo de una conciencia/ Profunda de
espectroscopio.// Sobre la torre, enigmático/ El búho de ojos de azufre,/
Su canto insalubre sufre/ Como un muezín enigmático . . . / Ante el
augurio lunático,/ Capciosa, espectral, desnuda,/ Aterciopelada y muda,/
Desciende en su tela inerte,/ Como una araña de muerte,/ La inmensa
noche de Budha . . .

Augusto dos Anjos (1884–1914, Brazil)

The short life of Anjos was marked with the publication of only one work, the 1912
book *Eu*. Largely ignored until the printing of its 1928 edition, *Eu* is a book par-
tially defined by the transitory nature of Brazilian literature during the time between
Romanticism, the Parnassians and the later avant-garde movements. Anjos's work
acts as a bridge between the nineteenth and twentieth centuries. Anjos was born
in Ingenio de Pau d'Arco, Paraíba, and died in Leopoldina, Minas Gerais. PRINCIPAL
WORK: *Eu* (1912)

A Philosopher's Agony / Agonia de um filósofo

Odile Cisneros, trans.

I read the Phtah-Hotep, I read the obsolete
Rig-Veda. Yet nothing gives me rest . . .
The Unconscious haunts me and I swirl possessed,
Restless harmattan in aeolian rage!

I'm witnessing here an insect's death!
Alas! Now all phenomena of earth
From pole to pole seem to make real
Anaximader of Miletus's ideal!

Atop the heterogeneous hieratic areopagus
Of ideas I wander, a lost magus,
From Haeckel's soul to souls of Cenobites!

The thick veiling of secret worlds I tear;
And just like Goethe, I catch the sight
Of *universal substance* ruling there!

Consulto o Phtah-Hotep. Leio o obsoleto/ Rig-Veda. E, ante obras tais, me não consolo . . . / O Inconsciente me assombra e eu nele rolo/ Com a eólica fúria do harmatã inquieto!// Assisto agora à morte de um inseto! . . . / Ah! todos os fenômenos do solo/ Parecem realizar de pólo a pólo/ O ideal de Anaximandro de Mileto!// No hierático areópago heterogêneo/ Das idéias, percorro como um gênio/ Desde a alma de Haeckel à alma cenobial! . . . // Rasgo dos mundos o velário espesso;/ E em tudo igual a Goethe, reconheço/ O império da *substância universal*!

Modern Buddhism / Budismo moderno

Odile Cisneros, trans.

Here, Doctor, take these scissors . . . cut
My most exceptional persona . . .
Who cares if vermin should englut
My heart completely when I die?!

Alas! A vulture has alighted on my fate!
And the aquatic diatomaceae thither . . .
Their capsulated cryptogam will wither
On contact with that right hand's weight.

So let my life disintegrate
The same as a decaying cell
A barren egg, aberrant birth;

But let this aggregate of longings dwell
and knock on the perpetual bars
Of the last verse I write on earth!

Tome, Dr., esta tesoura, e . . . corte/ Minha singularíssima pessoa./ Que importa a mim que a bicharia roa/ Todo o meu coração, depois da morte?!// Ah! Um urubu pousou na minha sorte!/ Também, das diatomáceas da lagoa/ A criptógama cápsula se esbroa/ Ao contato de bronca destra forte!// Dissolva-se, portanto, minha vida/ Igualmente a uma célula caída/ Na aberração de um óvulo infecundo;// Mas o agregado abstrato das saudades/ Fique batendo nas perpétuas grades/ Do último verso que eu fizer no mundo!

Pedro Kilkerry (1885–1917, Brazil)

Born in Bahia, Kilkerry was first published in literary reviews such as *Nova Cruzada* and *Os Anais*. His symbolist aesthetic garnered him the attention of the literary critic Jackson de Figueiredo, who compiled his work. In the 1970s, he was again discovered, this time by the Concrete Art movement and, in particular, Augusto de Campos, who compared Kilkerry to Mallarmé and described him as one of the most innovative poets of his day.

It's the Silence / É o silêncio

Mark A. Lokensgard, trans.

It's the silence, it's the cigarette and the lit candle.
The bookcase looks at me in every book that looks.
And the light on one of the volumes on the table . . .
But it is the blood of the light on each page.

I do not know if it is really my hand that wets
The pen, or really instinct that grips it tightly.
I think of a present, of a past. And your nature
Covers Nature itself with leaves.
But it is a meddling with things . . . Agitated

I take up my pen, I dupe myself into thinking I describe
The illusion of one sense and another sense.
So distant it goes!
So distant your step becomes soft
A wing that the ear animates . . .
And the chamber mute. And the parlor mute, mute . . .
Voicelessly red. The wing of the rhyme
Holds me aloft. I remain there like a new
Buddha, a specter to the approaching sound,
The bookcase grows as if shaking off
A nightmare of papers piled on top . . .

And I open the window. From the moon
Are wisping some last wavering notes . . . The day
Will bloom late through the mountain.

And oh! my beloved, feeling is blind . . .
Do you see? To my longing contribute the spider,
A cat's paws and a bat's wings.

É o silêncio, é o cigarro e a vela acesa./ Olha-me a estante em cada livro que olha./ E a luz nalgum volume sobre a mesa . . . / Mas o sangue da luz em cada folha.// Não sei se é mesmo a minha mão que molha/ A pena, ou mesmo o instinto que a tem presa./ Penso um presente, num passado. E enfolha/ A natureza tua natureza./ Mas é um bulir das cousas . . . Comovido// Pego da pena, iludo-me que traço/ A ilusão de um sentido e outro sentido./ Tão longe vai!/ Tão longe se aveluda esse teu passo,/ Asa que o ouvido anima . . . / E a câmara muda. E a sala muda, muda . . . / Afonamente rufa. A asa da rima/ Paira-me no ar. Quedo-me como um Buda/ Novo, um fantasma ao som que se aproxima./ Cresce-me a estante como quem sacuda/ Um pesadelo de papéis acima . . . // E abro a janela. Ainda a lua esfia/ Últimas notas trêmulas . . . O dia/ Tarde florescerá pela montanha.// E oh! minha amada, o sentimento é cego . . . / Vês? Colaboram na saudade a aranha,/ Patas de um gato e as asas de um morcego.

Mare Vitae

Mark A. Lokensgard, trans.

"Row! row!" And the small boat
Went gliding, as though the water dreamed.
Standing in the bow was the ganfalonier—
"Row! row!"—my own Sorrow.

Fading in color, quickly, is an illusion. And I drown it
To the war song's sound of fire
Still gliding as though the water dreamed
"Row! row!"—the small boat.

But suddenly a voice. Moaning,
Under the concave silence of the stars
Who sings thus of love? I don't understand . . .

And oh! Death—I said—this song terrifies me:
Don't deny that the pulsating masts tremble
At the red sound of the war song.

—Remar! remar!—E a embarcação ligeira/ Foi deslizando, como um sonho da água./ De pé, na proa, era a gonfaloneira/ —Remar! remar! a minha própia Mágoa.// E esmaia, logo, uma ilusão. E afago-a/ Ao som de fogo de canção guerreira,/ Vai deslizando como um sonho da água/ —Remar! remar! a embarcação ligeira.// Mas uma voz de súbito. Gemendo,/ Sob o silêncio côncavo dos astros/ Quem canta assim de amor? Eu não compreendo . . . // E oh! Morte—eu disse—esta canção me aterra:/ Dá-me que tremam palpitando os mastros/ Ao som vermelho da canção de guerra.

Delmira Agustini (1886–1914, Uruguay)

A precocious child overprotected by her family, Agustini was born in Montevideo, Uruguay. Later in life, she married and then separated three weeks later. She continued seeing her husband, who ultimately murdered her and then committed suicide himself. Agustini wrote within the spirit of the modernist movement. Her poetry astonished critics with her impeccable formal construction and open defiance of social convention. Rubén Darío—whom she addressed as "master"—wrote the prologue to her last book, praising her "soul without veils." He said that not since Saint Theresa had Hispanic literature produced verse of such intensity as Delmira's. But hers was a new kind of exalted, physical eroticism without precedent. PRINCIPAL WORKS: *El libro blanco* (1907), *Cantos de la mañana* (1910), *Los cálices vacíos* (1913)

To Eros / A eros

Suzanne Jill Levine, trans.

Because you make life's bravest lioness
Your dog, imprisoning her with the chain
Of roses of your embrace.

Because your body is the root,
The essential tie of divergent stems
Of pleasure and pain, gigantic plants.

Because there emerges from your strong and beautiful hand,
Like a brooch of mystical diamonds,
The most intoxicating lily of death.

Because I glance at you over space,
Bridge of light, perfume, and melody,
Connecting inferno and paradise

—With a glowing soul and somber flesh . . .

Porque haces tu can de la leona/ Más fuerte de la Vida, y la aprisiona/ La cadena de rosas de tu brazo.// Porque tu cuerpo es la raíz, el lazo/ Esencial de los troncos discordantes/ Del placer y el dolor, plantas gigantes.// Porque emerge en tu mano bella y fuerte,/ Como en broche de místicos diamantes,/ El más embriagador lis de la Muerte.// Porque sobre el Espacio te diviso,/ Puente de luz, perfume y melodía,/ Comunicando infierno y paraíso.// —Con alma fúlgida y carne sombría . . .

The Ineffable / Lo inefable

Suzanne Jill Levine, trans.

I die strangely . . . It is not life that kills me
It is not death that kills me, nor is it love;
I die of a thought, mute as a wound . . .
Have you never felt such a strange pain

Of an immense thought that is rooted in life,
Devouring flesh and soul, and without blooming?
Have you never carried inside a dormant star
That was burning you wholly without shining?

Height of martyrdom! . . . To eternally bear,
Rending and arid, the tragic seed
Pierced in one's entrails like a ferocious fang! . . .

But to uproot it one day in a flower that would bloom
Miraculous, inviolable . . . Ah, it would not be greater
To hold in one's hands the head of God!

Yo muero extrañamente . . . No me mata la Vida,/ No me mata la Muerte,
no me mata el Amor;/ Muero de un pensamiento mudo como una herida
. . . / ¿No habéis sentido nunca el extraño dolor// De un pensamiento
inmenso que se arraiga en la vida,/ Devorando alma y carne, y no alcanza
a dar flor?/ ¿Nunca llevasteis dentro una estrella dormida/ Que os abrasaba
enteros y no daba un fulgor? . . . // Cumbre de los Martirios! . . . Llevar
eternamente,/ Desgarradora y árida, la trágica simiente/ Clavada en las
entrañas como un diente feroz! . . . // Pero arrancarla un día en una flor que
abriera/ Milagrosa, inviolable! . . . Ah, más grande no fuera/ Tener entre las
manos la cabeza de Dios!!

The Intruder / El intruso

Suzanne Jill Levine, trans.

Love, night was tragic and sobbing
When your golden key sang in my lock;
Then the door opened upon the icy shadow,
Your figure a white stain of light

Your diamond eyes lit up everything here;
Your cool lips drank in my cup
And your perfumed head rested on my pillow;
I adored your impudence and worshipped your madness.

Today I laugh if you laugh, and sing if you sing
And if you sleep I sleep like a dog at your feet!
Today I carry even in my shadow your fragrance of spring;
I tremble if your hand touches my lock,

I give my blessings to the dark and sobbing night
That your fresh mouth bloomed early in my life!

Amor, la noche estaba trágica y sollozante/ Cuando tu llave de oro cantó en
mi cerradura;/ Luego, la puerta abierta sobre la sombra helante,/ Tu forma
fue una mancha de luz y de blancura.// Todo aquí lo alumbraron tus ojos
de diamante;/ Bebieron en mi copa tus labios de frescura,/ Y descansó en mi
almohada tu cabeza fragante;/ Me encantó tu descaro y adoré tu locura.//
Y hoy río si tú ríes, y canto si tú cantas;/ Y si tú duermes duermo como
perro a tus plantas!/ Hoy llevo hasta en mi sombra tu olor de primavera;/
Y tiemblo si tu mano toca la cerradura,/ Y bendigo la noche sollozante
y oscura/ Que floreció en mi vida tu boca tempranera!

Manuel Bandeira (1886–1968, Brazil)

As a columnist, poet, and literature teacher, Bandeira is arguably one of the most
important figures in Brazilian modernism. During his illustrious career, Bandeira held
the chair of Hispano-American literature at the Faculdade Nacional de Filosofía and was
an elected member of the Brazilian Academy of Letters while maintaining his highly
regarded poetry career. The intertextuality of his poetry allowed him to experiment
equally with form, style, and content, and when read in chronological order the transformation of his poetry offers a study on the history and progression of modernism in
Brazil. Bandeira was born in Recife and died in Rio de Janeiro at the age of eighty-two.
PRINCIPAL WORKS: *A cinza das horas* (1917), *Estrela de manha* (1936), *Opus 10* (1952)

Anthology / Antologia

Jean R. Longland, trans.

Life
Is not worth the trouble and grief of being lived.
Bodies understand each other, but souls, no.
The only thing to do is to play an Argentine tango.
I'm going away to Pasárgada!
I am not happy here.
I want to forget it all:
—The grief of being a man . . .
This infinite and vain anxiety
To possess what possesses me.

I want to rest
Thinking humbly about life and women I loved . . .
About all the life that could have been and wasn't.

I wanted to rest.
To die.
To die, body and soul.
Completely.
(Every morning the airport across the way gives me lessons
  in departure.)

When the Undesired-of-all arrives,
She will find the field plowed, the house clean,
The table set,
With everything in its place.

A Vida/ Não vale a pena e a dor de ser vivida./ Os corpos se entendem mas
as almas não./ A única coisa a fazer é tocar um tango argentino./ Vou-me
embora p'ra Pasárgada!/ Aqui eu não sou feliz./ Quero esquecer tudo:/
—A dor de ser homem . . . / Este anseio infinito e vão/ De possuir o que
me possui.// Quero descansar/ Humildemente pensando na vida e nas
mulheres que amei . . . / Na vida inteira que podia ter sido e que não foi.//
Quero descansar./ Morrer./ Morrer de corpo e alma./ Completamente./
(Todas as manhãs o aeroporto em frente me dá lições de/ partir.)// Quando
a Indesejada das gentes chegar/ Encontrará lavrado o campo, a casa limpa./
A mesa posta,/ Com cada coisa em seu lugar.

Green-Black / Verde-Negro

David R. Slavitt, trans.

green
            grin
                      all green
                      all black
                                        green-black
                                                                      very green
                                                                      very black
see the day
            see the day
                          a green night
                                      a black day
                                                      green-black
wait your turn
                      turn around
                      round the turn
I see
                      I agree
                      I am green

ay si

I see all

all black
all green

green-black

dever/ de ver/ tudo verde/ tudo negro/ verde-negro/ muito verde/ muito negro/ ver de dia/ ver de noite/ verde noite/ negro dia/ verde-negro/ verdes vós/ verem eles/ virem eles/ virdes vós/ verem todos/ tudo negro/ tudo verde/ verde-negro

My Last Poem / O ultimo poema

Elizabeth Bishop, trans.

I would like my last poem thus

That it be gentle saying the simplest and least intended things
That it be ardent like a tearless sob
That it have the beauty of almost scentless flowers
The purity of the flame in which the most limpid diamonds are consumed
The passion of suicides who kill themselves without explanation.

Assim eu quereria o meu último poema// Que fosse terno dizendo as coisas mais simples e menos/ intencionais/ Que fosse ardente como um soluço sem lágrimas/ Que tivesse a beleza das flores quase sem perfume/ A pureza da chama em que se consomem os diamantes mais/ límpidos/ A paixão dos suicidas que se matam sem explicação.

Enriqueta Arvelo Larriva (1886–1962, Venezuela)

Arvelo Larriva was born in a remote village located on the Venezuelan plains where she lived until 1946. During the dictatorship of Juan Vicente Gómez, her well-to-do family lost much of its status. Her brother Alfredo was a modernist poet. Arvelo Larriva's life and poetry were marginal at a time when all the roads were closed to women. She never married and worked as a teacher and a nurse at her family's estate, where she wrote, "I let out my voice, though no one listens." Self-taught, she was an avid reader of the Spanish classics, from which she learned to communicate the brevity as well as the immensity of simple and everyday things. The title of one of her books, *Voz aislada* (Isolated Voice), summarizes a work and a life. Today she is widely admired by a younger readership. PRINCIPAL WORKS: *El cristal nervioso* (1922–1930), *Voz aislada* (1930–1939), *Mandato del canto* (1944–1946)

Emotion and Advantage of Proven Depth / Emoción y ventaja de la probada profundidad

Alejandro Merizalde, trans.

Thanks to those who left through the dark sidewalk
grinding the toasted leaves.
To those who said to me: wait for us under that tree.

Thanks to those who went in search of fire for their cigarettes
and left me alone
tangled in the small suns of a fragrant shade.

Thanks to those who went in search of water for my thirst
and left me there
drinking the essential water of an appalled world.

Thanks to those who left me listening to an untamed chant
and drowsily watching tree trunks embroidered in withered wools.

Now among the people I go undamaged.

Gracias a los que se fueron por la vereda oscura/ moliendo las hojas
tostadas./ A los que me dijeron: espéranos bajo ese árbol.// Gracias a los que
se fueron a buscar fuego para sus cigarrillos/ y me dejaron sola,/ enredada
en los soles pequeños de una sombra olorosa.// Gracias a los que se fueron
a buscar agua para mi sed/ y me dejaron ahí/ bebiéndome el agua esencial
de un mundo estremecido.// Gracias a los que me dejaron oyendo un canto
enselvado/ y viendo soñolienta los troncos bordados de lanas marchitas.//
Ahora voy indemne entre las gentes.

All Morning the Wind Has Spoken / Toda la mañana ha hablado el viento

Alejandro Merizalde, trans.

All morning the wind has spoken
an extraordinary tongue.

Today I have been the wind.

I shook the trees.
I made pleats in the river.
I agitated the sand.
I entered the thinnest fissures
and sounded long among the wires.

Before—do you remember?—
Looking pale I'd pass by the wind's edge. And you applauded.

Toda la mañana ha hablado el viento/ una lengua extraordinaria.// He ido
hoy en el viento.// Estremecí los árboles./ Hice pliegues en el río./ Alboroté
la arena./ Entré por las más finas rendijas./ Y soné largamente en los
alambres.// Antes—¿recuerdas?—/ pasaba pálida por la orilla del viento. Y
aplaudías.

Xul Solar (1887–1963, Argentina)

Alejandro Schulz Solari was born to a German father and Italian mother in Buenos
Aires. An avant-garde visual artist, Xul Solar, as he later came to be known, worked
in painting, poetry, and architecture. He spent twelve years studying and creating in
Europe, dabbling in many genres, including expressive symbolism, surrealism, and
cubism, often incorporating writing into his visual art. Once he returned to Argentina, Solar began to experiment with architecture and developed a very personal
vision of constructivism. One of Solar's most important contributions is the creation
of a new language called *neocriollo*, a fusion of Spanish and Portuguese founded on
his own universalist principles. PRINCIPAL WORK: *Entrevistas, artículos y textos inéditos*
(2005)

Excerpt from "This Hades Is Fluid . . . " / "Es un Hades fluido . . . "
Molly Weigel, trans.

This Hades is fluid, almist, no roof, no floor, redhaired, color in sunshut
eyes, stirred in endotempest, whirlpools, waves, and boiling. In its clots
n foam dismultitumans float passivao, disparkle, therz also solos, adults,
kidoids, n they pergleam softao.
Transpenseen ghostliao, the houses n people n soil of a solid terri citi have
nothing to do withis Hell, which is nao thereal.
This whole dense redheaded region selfmountains roun big hollo or
bottomless valley of bluegray air, where it floes in dark winds, with
uproarians n other lone umans, avoid n globoid. Here it floes more oop.
N yon the solid city n its populas go on ghostliao.
Later I pass on to a better life, gray silver. Yere many groups lovefloat loosao
processioning or thinking reunited. Yere clouds row with gray kiosks—of
mother of pearl, metal, felt—with pensors circumseated.
Sloao I find myselfe in a slight kelestal sky. Its disposition is afternoon
summeri, cloudii.
Plants zigzag one by one biomove and hum. Ther color lovaries
from garnet to rosy. They r over floatislope of da same denser air,
undspersing. Here juxtafly boids like speck eggs, not with wings, but
with many ribbons.

Nex therz many color columns, baseless, supporting cloud roof: is temple floati in which many pray. When zey theocoexalt zey inflate, zer auras vitaradiate, suchao zat zey raize ze cloud roof an circumseparate ze columns, an everysing fervienlarges n saintgleams.

Nex therz wide obelisk or tower, that swéz from its floatifloppi base. Its first floor, of stonebooks, mudbooks on top, woodbooks on top, cylinder books on top, the top, books. Almost lyk a house of cards, bristling with paper ribbons n banderols, periflown with letterswarms flyao, juxtasurrounded by perhaps wandermunching studenti. Inna lil bit of floor floati, many dream, zer mersed.

I float I go yonderfarre. Deeping in a plurmutacolor fog I see ceety. Thees biopalaces n biohovels, of framework n I theenk. They pertransform, grow or shreenk; now they r pillars n archframes n cupolas, now plain phosphiplastered walls, now they quake weeth pseudocrystal scaffolding. They shift, rise, seenk, interpenetrate, separate, n rejoicetera.

Houses ther r that burn, flame oop, but they don't self-destruct, they rather selfconstruct-um. Der fire is life, n da greater da boining, da more palace senwidens n grows. Houses ther r that infect set fire to the nébors that idem idem, n thus néborhoods expand. Ther people lykwise coflame n coloom: this must be the cause burni, by pensiardor.

Houses ther r that ferviboil until they blow up lyk a bomb, a geyser, or smoke; but they d'ont self-destruct-um, they circumreselfconstruct; ther

bits n pieces fervigrow in faraway subsidiaries that finally growjoin, dispile tower morrenmore, on circumbarrens lessenless.

Houses ther r that suigrow in evri direkshun, skewpi, horizily, juxto, oop, fat; n they buzz, squeak, creak, dispeak.

Houses ther r that atrophy and shrink until they r seen no mor, when ther people diehatch inna better life inna better sky.

Houses ther r of illusion on smokehills; they altervanish.

So I embrace the soil of this citi, that wichis a cloudgathering, wichis several vague titans floatireclining.

Great sleeves or tubes circumset out-um for the vacuum: they might be sewers or suckers, I do'nt know.

N over that ceety ther ees other ceety, backward, sullen, dark n slow that lives n grows juxto, n its people too. The nadir is deep, sullen, dark, foggi: maybe the hommeworld, some great wasteland.

I review the other city oop. Colonnades like centipedes travell in distrides. They r rigid disciples, carrying dometeachers with wide roofly robes. Tumbled in suihappy skyrabble, lovi-turvy in fog and sketches and clots of thot: gelatine menti. They go farre, into the vacuum.

I see zerz several very pily pagodas of just bookes, zat zer many readers incorporate: they don't read, but rather vitisuck science n sophy.

Bawlings propagate, undulate in all linguages n many others possible.
N these letterswarms, n glyftangles, n disfonetix n copluracents, like
a bunch of lovesmokes, separate or join, countermove or subside, in
order or not, form n reform meaning n argu, always neo.
Stars, little suns, moons, moonlets, lightning bugs, lanterns, lites,
lusters; anywhere they get lifentangled in the city they constellate
n disconstellate, burn themselves, go out, mixshine, rain, fly.
It's a perflux n reflux of breeze n fluid n blast n sounds n smellsteam; the
lite perchanges, in splendor color, heat, chiaroscuros, in soul.
Already gonetired, I grow dazed n forget, dissee.
Everything pales, n erases itself. Already it seems I'm entering a greater sky
th'ats another nite, that later is more nite, that is more, deep solid black
theonite, that I manfear n mistilov; ther I would exdizolv.
But something vaguimmense comes between me n the theonite;
like plurcolored gas. It becomes more defined, n i'ts an indefinite
godhombre, skydiameter. Its head across me, its feet before me, in the
counterhorizon, n its hands over me, fiftinihookpointi, r orange; its
clothing, indecisive cambicolor in patches.
Above its head nao flowers a white flower lite. Its scarlet heart radiates pink
lite, its garnet pudenda's onlylite.
I feel as if I'm entering the godhombre, which transports me yere.
But already the call of this Earth from yon oppresses my breast bodii; n I
return to myself quite perpenao.

Es un Hades fluido, casi vapor, sin cielo, sin suelo, rufo, color en ojos
cérrados so el sol, agítado en endotempestá, vórtices, ondas y hervor. En
sus grumos i espumas dismultitú omes flotan pasivue, disdestellan, hai
también solos, mayores, péjoides, i perluzen suavue./ Se transpenvén
fantasmue las casas i gente i suelo de una ciudá sólida terri, sin ningun
rapor con este Hades, qes aora lô real./ Toda esta región rufa densa se
montona redor gran hueco ho valle sin fondo, de aire azul gris, do floto
en vientos oscuros, con polvareda gente, i otros omes solos ávoides i
glóboides. Aqí se flota más upa. I siga fantasmue la ciudá sólida yu i su
pópulo./ Paso luego a mejor vida, gris plata. Yi qierflotan flojue muchos
grupos, procesionan o pensan reúnidos. Yi bogan nubes con qioscos
grises —de nácar, metal, fieltro—con pénsores circunsiéntados./ Lentue
me hallo en cielo leve ciéleste. Su ánimo es de tarde verani, niebli./
Plantas de a un zigzag se biomuevan i canturrian. Xu color qiervaría
de granate a róseo. Están sobrs loma floti del mismo aire mas denso,
soesfúminse. Yi yuxtavuelan pájaros como huevos pintos, no con alas,
sino con muchas cintas.// Otrur hai muchas columnas color, sin suelo,
qe sostienen nube techo: es templo floti en qe oran muchos. Cuando se

teocoexaltan se hinchan, xus auras irradian vita, talue qe alzan la nube
techo i circunseparan las columnas, i todo se ferviagranda i sanluze./
Otrur hai obelisco ancho ho torre, bambolea por su base flotifloja. Su
primer piso, de libros piedra, encima libros barro, encima libros leña,
encima libros rollo, la cima libros. Casi como torre naipes, erízada
de cintas papel i banderolas, perivuélada de letrienjambres moscue,
yuxtarodeada de qizás mangente vaga estudi. En el poco suelo floti
sueñan muchos, yi mérgidos./ Floto voi allén lejos. Hónduer en niebla
plurcambicolor veo ciudá. Sas biopalacios y biochozas, de armazón i
pienso. Se pertransforman, se agrandan o achican; ya son de postes
i cimbras i cúpulas, ya de muros lisos en parches fosfi, ya pululan en
biocúmulos, ya tembliquean de andamios seudocristal. Se desplazan,
suben, se hunden, se interpenetran, se separan i réidem./ Casas hai qe
arden, flamean upa, pero no se destruyen, se ñe construyen más. Xu
fuego es vita, i a mayor incendio, más palacio senancha i crece. Casas
hai qe contagian incendian a las vecinas qe ídem ídem, i así sextiendan
los barrios. Xu yi gente también, coflamea i se coabulta: debe ser ella
la causa fuegui, por pensiardor./ Casas hai qe fervihiervan hasta qe
revientan como bomba ho geiser o humo; pero no se ñe destruyen, se
circunreconstruyen; xas// trozos fervicrecen en sucursales lejos qe alfín se
crecijuntan, dismontón torre mahimás, sobre circumbaldío menoimenos./
Casas hai qe suicrecen en todo séntido, sesgüe, horizue, yuso, upa, gordue;
i zumban, chirrian, crujen, disparlan./ Casas hai que se atrofian i encojen
hasta no verse más, cuando xa gente muertinace a mejor vida en mejor
cielo./ Casas hai de ilusión sobre cerros humo: se cambipierden./ Entonces
abarco el suelo desa ciudad, el qes una sûnnube, qes varios titanes vagos
flotiacuéstados./ Grandes mangas o tubos ñe circunsalgan a lô vacuo:
serían cloacas o chúpores, no sé./ I so esa ciudá hai otra ciudá'l revés,
hosca, oscura i lenta qe vive i crece yuso, i sa gente también. El nadir es
hondo, hosco, oscuro, brúmoso: qizás el manmundo, algún gran yermo./
Reveo la otra ciudá upa. Columnatas como cienpiés viaján a distrancos.
Son discípulos tiesos, llevan maestros cúpulas, de rópaje ancho techue.
A tumbos sobre chusma cieli suifeliz, qierrevuelta en bruma i cuágulos
i bocetos de pienso: gelatina menti. Van a lejos, a lô vacuo./ Veo hai
algunas mui moles pagodas de solos libros, qe se incuerpan a xus tantos
léctores—qe no leen, masbién vitichupan ciencia i sofia.// Sexpandan,
ondulan voceríos de todas las linguas i de muchas otras pósibles. I xas
enjambres letras, i marañas glifos, i disfonéticas i copluracentos, como
muchos qierhumos, se apartan o juntan, se contramueven o aqietan,
en orden o no, forman, reforman séntido i argu siempre neo./ Estrellas,
sólcitos, lunas, lúnulas, luciérnagas, linternas, luces, lustres; doqier se
vidienredan a la ciudá se constelan i disconstelan, se qeman, s e apagan,
cholucen, llueven, vuelan./ Es un perflujo i reflujo de brisa i flúido i ráfaga
i sones i humos olor; la luz percambia, en lampos color, calor, claroscuros,
en ánimo./ Yo ya veicánsado me aturdo i olvido, disveo./ Todo palidece,
i se borra. Ya parece qentro a mayor cielo qes otra noche, qes luego más

noche, qes más, teonoche honda sólida negra, qe mantemo i mistiamo;
yo me yi exdisolverío./ Pero algo vago inmenso se interpone'ntre mí i lô
teonoche; como gas plurcolor. Se define más, i es un mandivo indefinido,
cielidiámetro. Su testa tras mî, sus pies ante mî, en el contrahorizonte,
i sus manos sobre mî, ganchipuntitóqinse, son oranje; su rópaje,
cambicolor indeciso en parches./ Sobre su testa florece aora flor luz
blanca. Su cuore punzó irradia luz rósea, su pudenda granate's sólodeluz./
Sento como qentro al mandivo, qe me yi arrobo./ Pero ya la llámada desta
Terra desde yu me oprime'l pecho cuerpi; i vuelvo a mî mui perpenue.

Gabriela Mistral (1889–1957, Chile)

Born in Vicuña in the north of Chile, of mixed Basque and Diaguita heritage, Mistral
grew up in a family of abandoned women who made their living as rural school
teachers. She followed in their path and started teaching at the age of fourteen. She
read widely and wrote a powerful and personal poetry that reflects her complicated
passion for and rejection of the indigenous/mestizo worldview. Maintaining this
paradox, she broke new ground by simultaneously keeping the archaic, traditional
rhymes and genres, while altering their syntax. As an educator and diplomat she
traveled the world, fighting for the rights of women and children. Widely read at her
time, she was the first Latin American author to receive the Nobel Prize in Literature
in 1945. She died in New York. PRINCIPAL WORKS: *Desolación* (1922), *Tala* (1938),
Lagar (1954), *Recados: contando a Chile* (1957), *Poema de Chile* (1967)

Drops of Gall / Gotas de hiel

Maria Jacketti, trans.

Don't sing: your tongue
always remains bound to a song:
the one that should be surrendered.

Don't kiss: by a strange curse
the kiss that does not reach
the heart, remains.

Pray, for prayer is sweet
but know that your greedy tongue
stumbles over the only "Our Father"
that might save you.

Don't call death kind,
for within its immense white flesh

a live fragment will remain and feel
the stone that smothers you
and the voracious worm that unbraids your hair.

No cantes: siempre queda/ a tu lengua apegado/ un canto: el que debió ser
entregado.// No beses: siempre queda,/ por maldición extraña,/ el beso al que
no alcanzan las entrañas.// Reza, reza que es dulce; pero sabe/ que no acierta
a decir tu lengua avara/ el solo Padre Nuestro que salvara.// Y no llames la
muerte por clemente,/ pues en las carnes de blancura immensa,/ un jirón vivo
quedará que siente/ la piedra que te ahoga/ y el gusano voraz que te destrenza.

Airflower / La flor del aire

Ursula K. Le Guin, trans.

My fate brought me to her
standing in the middle of the meadow,
mistress of all who pass her
or speak to her or see her.

And she told me, "Climb the mountain.
I never leave the meadow.
And pick white flowers for me,
snow-white, harsh, and tender."

I climbed the bitter mountain
and looked for the white flowers
where among the rocks
they half-slept or wakened.

When I came down with my arms full
I found her there in the meadow,
and I poured out over her
a wild white flood of lilies.

Not looking at the whiteness
she said to me, "Now bring me
red flowers only.
I cannot leave the meadow."

I climbed the cliffs beside the deer,
and looked for flowers of madness,
those that blossom red, that seem
to live and die of redness.

I came down and gave them to her,
shivering with the joy of giving,

and she turned as red as water
a wounded stag has bloodied.

But looking at me from her trance
she said, "Go up and bring me
the yellow ones, the yellow ones.
I never leave the meadow."

I went straight up the mountain
and looked for the crowded flowers
color of sun and saffron,
just born, already everlasting.

Coming upon her as before
in the middle of the meadow,
I showered her with yellow
till she was like a threshing-floor.

And still, crazy with goldness,
she said, "Go up, my servant,
cut me the colorless flowers,
not saffron, not crimson:

the ones I love in memory
of Leonora and Ligeia,
sleep-color, dream-color.
I am the Woman of the meadow."

I went high on the mountain,
now black as Medea,
without a trace of shining,
like a dim, constant cavern.

They did not grow on branches
or bloom among the stones:
I cut them from the soft air,
snipping it lightly.

I cut them as if I were
the blind thread-cutter.
Taking the air for my forest,
I cut them from one air and another.

When I came down from the mountain
and went to find the queen,
I saw her walking:
not white now, not fierce:

She went along, sleepwalking,
going away from the meadow,
and I followed her, followed her,
through pastures and poplars,

carrying all those flowers
with airy hands and arms
and still cutting them from the air
and with the winds for harvest.

Faceless she goes on before,
trackless she goes on before,
and still I follow after her
among the wisps of fog,

with these colorless flowers,
not white, not crimson,
till my surrender at the border
when my Time may melt away . . .

Yo la encontré por mi destino,/ de pie a mitad de la pradera,/ gobernadora
del que pase,/ del que le hable y que la vea.// Y ella me dijo: "Sube al
monte./ Yo nunca dejo la pradera,/ y me cortas las flores blancas/
como nieves, duras y tiernas."// Me subí a la ácida montaña,/
busqué las flores donde albean,/ entre las rocas existiendo/ medio-
dormidas y despiertas.// Cuando bajé, con carga mía,/ la hallé a mitad de
la pradera,/ y fui cubriéndola frenética,/ con un torrente de azucenas.//
Y sin mirarse la blancura,/ ella me dijo: "Tú acarrea/ ahora sólo flores
rojas./ Yo no puedo pasar la pradera."// Trepé las peñas con el venado,/ y
busqué flores de demencia,/ las que rojean y parecen/ que de rojez vivan y
mueran.// Cuando bajé se las fui dando/ con un temblor feliz de ofrenda,/
y ella se puso como el agua/ que en ciervo herido se ensangrienta.// Pero
mirándome, sonámbula,/ me dijo: "Sube y acarrea/ las amarillas, las
amarillas./ Yo nunca dejo la pradera."// Subí derecho a la montaña/ y me
busqué las flores densas,/ color de sol y de azafranes,/ recién nacidas y ya
eternas.// Al encontrarla, como siempre,/ a la mitad de la pradera,/ segunda
vez yo fui cubriéndola,/ y la dejé como las eras.// Y todavía, loca de oro,/
me dijo: "Súbete, mi sierva,/ y cortarás las sin color,/ ni azafranadas ni
bermejas."// "Las que yo amo por recuerdo/ de la Leonora y la Ligeia,/ color
del Sueño y de los sueños./ Yo soy Mujer de la pradera."// Me fui ganando
la montaña,/ ahora negra como Medea,/ sin tajada de resplandores,/ como
una gruta vaga y cierta.// Ellas no estaban en las ramas,/ ellas no abrían
en las piedras/ y las corté del aire dulce,/ tijereteándolo ligera.// Me las
corté como si fuese/ la cortadora que está ciega.// Corté de un aire y de

otro aire,/ tomando el aire por mi selva . . .// Cuando bajé de la montaña/
y fui buscándome a la reina,/ ahora ella caminaba,/ ya no era blanca ni
violenta;// ella se iba, la sonámbula,/ abandonando la pradera,/ y yo
siguiéndola y siguiéndola/ por el pastal y la alameda,// cargada así de tantas
flores,/ con espaldas y mano aéreas,/ siempre cortándolas del aire/ y con los
aires como siega . . .// Ella delante va sin cara;/ ella delante va sin huella,/ y
yo la sigo todavía/ entre los gajos de la niebla,// con estas flores sin color,/
ni blanquecinas ni bermejas,/ hasta mi entrega sobre el límite,/ cuando mi
Tiempo se disuelva . . .

A Word / Una palabra

Ursula K. Le Guin, trans.

I have a word inside my mouth
and don't let it get out and don't get rid of it,
through its blood-gush pushes at me.
If I let it out it would scorch the bright grass,
drain blood from lambs, drop birds from air.

I have to untangle it from my tongue,
find a rat-hole for it,
bury it under heaps of quicklime,
so it can't keep flying, as the soul does.

I can't show any signs of life
while it's coming and going through my blood,
and rising and falling with my crazy breathing.
My father Job spoke it as he burned,
but I can't let it use my poor mouth, no,
because it'll roll on, women will find it
as they go down to the river, it'll twist into their hair,
and wither poor dry thickets up in fire.

I want to sow it with seeds that grow so wild
they'll cover it overnight and swallow it
and not leave the shred of a syllable of it.
Or sever it like this, like biting
a snake in half with my teeth.

And then go home, go in, and go to sleep,
cut free from it, sliced off from it,
and wake up after a couple of thousand days
newborn out of sleep and forgetting.

Not knowing that I'd had between my lips
a word of iodine and saltpeter,

and not remembering a night,
a house in a foreign country,
the ambush, the lightning at the door,
and my body going on without its soul.

Yo tengo una palabra en la garganta/ y no la suelto, y no me libro de ella/ aunque me empuje su empellón de sangre./ Si la soltase, quema el pasto vivo,/ sangra al cordero, hace caer al pájaro.// Tengo que desprenderla de mi lengua,/ hallar un agujero de castores/ o sepultarla con cales y cales/ porque no guarde como el alma el vuelo.// No quiero dar señales de que vivo/ mientras que por mi sangre vaya y venga/ y suba y baje por mi loco aliento./ Aunque mi padre Job la dijo, ardiendo/ no quiero darle, no, mi pobre boca/ porque no ruede y la hallen las mujeres/ que van al río, y se enrede a sus trenzas/ y al pobre matorral tuerza y abrase.// Yo quiero echarle violentas semillas/ que en una noche la cubran y ahoguen/ sin dejar de ella el cisco de una sílaba./ O rompérmela así, como a la víbora/ que por mitad se parte con los dientes.// Y volver a mi casa, entrar, dormirme,/ cortada de ella, rebanada de ella,/ y despertar después de dos mil días/ recién nacida de sueño y olvido.// ¡Sin saber más que tuve una palabra/ de yodo y piedra-alumbre entre los labios/ ni saber acordarme de una noche,/ de una morada en país extranjero,/ de la celada y el rayo a la puerta/ y de mi carne marchando sin su alma!

The Other Woman / La otra

Ursula K. LeGuin, trans.

I killed a woman in me.
I didn't love her.

She was the flower flaming
from the mountain cactus,
she was dryness and fire;
nothing could cool her.

Stone and sky she had
underfoot and around her;
never did she kneel
to seek the gaze of water.

Where she lay down to rest
she withered the grass
with the heat of her breath,
the ember of her face.

Her speech hardened
quick as pitch,

so no soft charm
could be released.

She couldn't bow,
the mountain plant,
while I beside her
bowed and bent.

I left her to die,
robbing her of my heart.
She ended like
an eagle starved.

　　Her wings stopped beating,
she bowed down, spent,
and her quenched spark
dropped in my hand.

　　Her sisters still
mourn her, accuse me,
and the burning quicklime
claws me as I pass.

　　Going by I tell them:
"Look in the creekbeds,
from their clays
make another fire-eagle.

　　If you can't,
well then, forget her!
I killed her. You, too,
you kill her!"

Una en mí maté:/ yo no la amaba.// Era la flor llameando/ del cactus de
montaña;/ era aridez y fuego;/ nunca se refrescaba.// Piedra y cielo tenía/ a
pies y a espaldas/ y no bajaba nunca/ y buscar "ojos de agua".// Donde hacía
su siesta,/ las hierbas se enroscaban/ de aliento de su boca/ y brasa de su
cara.// En rápidas resinas/ se endurecía su habla,/ por no caer en linda/ presa
soltada.// Doblarse no sabía/ la planta de montaña,/ y al costado de ella,/ yo
me doblaba . . . // La dejé que muriese,/ robándole mi entraña./ Se acabó como
el águila/ que no es alimentada.// Sosegó el aletazo,/ se dobló, lacia,/ y me cayó
a la mano/ su pavesa acabada . . . // Por ella todavía/ me gimen sus hermanas,/
y las gredas de fuego/ al pasar me desgarran.// Cruzando yo les digo:/ —Buscad
por las quebradas/ y haced con las arcillas/ otra águila abrasada.// Si no podéis,
entonces,/ ¡ay!, olvidadla./ Yo la maté. ¡Vosotras/ también matadla!

Oswald de Andrade (1890–1954, Brazil)

Born in São Paulo, Andrade is regarded as one of the most controversial figures in the Brazilian literary world. His seminal 1928 *Manifesto antropofago* (Cannibal Manifesto), and earlier *Manifesto da poesia Pau-Brasil* (1924), established the basic tenant of anthropophagous literature—the metaphor of Brazilian culture as cannibal, or the appropriation of European literary models by fusing them with the vernacular. In keeping this view, Andrade emphasized the inspiration that natural and pre-Columbian societies provided the modernists. PRINCIPAL WORKS: *Memórias sentimentais de João Miramar* (1924), *Pau Brasil* (1925), *Serafim Ponte Grande* (1933)

Excerpt from Brazilwood / Pau Brasil

Odile Cisneros, trans.

Speech / Falação

Cabralism. The civilization of the grantees. The Homeland and Exports. Carnival. The Backland and the Shanties. Brazilwood. Barbarianly ours.

A rich ethnic formation. A rich vegetation. Minerals. Cuisine. Shrimp stew, gold, and dance.

The entire history of the Penetration and the commercial history of the Americas. Brazilwood.
Against the fatality of the first landed white man and diplomatically dominating the savage jungle. Quoting Virgil to the Tupiniquim. The law school graduate.

Country of anonymous pain. Of anonymous doctors. Society of learned castaways.
Where poetry was never exported from. Poetry tangled in culture. In the creepers of metrification.

The twentieth century. A blast in learning. The men who knew everything collapsed like rubber Towers of Babel. They burst from so much encyclopedism.

Poetry for poets. The bliss of an ignorance that discovers. Pedr'Alvares.

A suggestion from Blaise Cendrars: Have your locomotives ready, depart! A black man cranks the handle of the rotational divergence in which you exist. The slightest slip will make you head in the direction opposite your destination.

Against ministerialism, treading through climates.
Language minus the archaisms. Minus the erudition. Natural and neologistic. The million-dollar contribution of all mistakes.

From naturalism to household pyrography and a tourist's Kodak.
All the gifted girls. Mechanical piano virtuosi.
Processions emerged from the bowels of the factories.
It became necessary to undo. Deformation via impressionism and the
symbol. A leafy lyricism. The presentation of materials.

The first Brazilian construction coinciding with the movement of general
reconstruction. Brazilwood Poetry.

Against the naturalist's shrewdness—synthesis. Against the copy—invention
and surprise.
A perspective different from the visual. The equivalent to a physical miracle
in art. Stars trapped in photo negatives.

. . . .

And a wise solar laziness. Prayer. A quiet energy. Hospitality.

Barbarians, picturesque and credulous. Brazilwood. The forest and the
school. The kitchen, minerals, and dance. Vegetation. Brazilwood.

O Cabralismo. A civilização dos donatários. A Querência e a Exportação./
O Carnaval. O Sertão e a Favela. Pau-Brasil. Bárbaro nosso.// A formação
étnica rica. A riqueza vegetal. O minério. A cozinha. O vatapá, o ouro e a
dança.// Toda a história da Penetração e a história comercial da América.
Pau-Brasil./ Contra a fatalidade do primeiro branco aportado e dominando
diplomaticamente as selvas selvagens. Citando Virgílio para tupiniquins.
O bacharel.// País de dores anônimas. De doutôres anônimos. Sociedade
de náufragos eruditos./ Donde a nunca exportação de poesia. A poesia
emaranhada na cultura. Nos sipós das metrificações.// Século um estouro
nos aprendimentos. Os homens que sabiam tudo se deformaram como
babéis de borracha. Rebentaram de enciclopedismo.// A poesia para os
poetas. Alegria da ignorância que descobre. Pedr'Álvares.// Uma sugestão
de Blaise Cendrars: — Tendes as locomotivas cheias, ides partir. Um negro
gira a manivela do desvio rotativo em que estais. O menor descuido vos
fará partir na direção oposta ao vosso destino.// Contra o gabinetismo, a
palmilhação dos climas./ A língua sem arcaísmos. Sem erudição. Natural
e neológica. A contribuição milionária de todos os erros.// Passara-se do
naturalismo à pirogravura doméstica e à kodak excursionista./ Todas as
meninas prendadas. Virtuoses de piano de manivela./ As procissões saíram
do bojo das fábricas./ Foi preciso desmanchar. A deformação através do
impressionismo e do símbolo. O lirismo em folha. A apresentação dos
materiais.// A coincidência da primeira construção brasileira no movimento
de reconstrução geral. Poesia Pau-Brasil.// Contra a argúcia naturalista, a
síntese. Contra a cópia, a invenção e a surpresa./ Uma perspectiva de outra
ordem que a visual. O correspondente ao milagre físico em arte. Estrelas

fechadas nos negativos fotográficos.// E a sábia preguiça solar. A reza. A energia silenciosa. A hospitalidade.// Bárbaros, pitorescos e crédulos. Pau-Brasil. A floresta e a escola. A cozinha, o minéiro e a dança. A vegetação. Pau-Brasil.

The History of Brazil / História do Brasil

Pero Vaz Caminha

the discovery/a descoberta
We followed our way across this lengthy sea
Until the eighth day of Easter
We chanced upon birds
And caught sight of land

the savages/os selvagens
They showed them a chicken
They were almost scared
Refused to lay hands on it
Later they held it as if in awe

the station girls/as meninas da gare
They were three or four maidens very young and very fair
With very long black hair trailing down their backs
And their shameful parts so high and clean
That we from staring at them
Had not shame at all

Gandavo

lodging/hospedagem
Because the Land itself is such
And so favorable to those who seek it
That it gladly shelters and welcomes all

chorography/corografia
It has the shape of a Harp
Bordering the highest Andean Mountains
And the Peruvian skirts
All standing so superbly high on Earth
That it is said the birds have trouble flying above them

gold country/país do ouro
All are provided for
And there are no poor persons
Begging from door to door
In these Kingdoms

still life/natureza morta

This fruit they call Pineapple
When ripe it has a very sweet smell
And is eaten carved into slices
And thus do the native inhabitants
And they hold it in greater esteem
Than any other apple tree in this land

natural riches/riquezas naturais

Many melons cucumbers pomegranates and figs
Of various stocks
Citrons lemons and oranges
A multitude
Many sugar canes
Endless cotton
There is also plenty of brazilwood
In these captaincies

columbus day/festa da raça

There lives in these parts too a certain animal
They call Sloth
With a thick mane on its neck
And it moves at such a slow pace
That even if it toiled for two weeks
It wouldn't conquer the distance of a stone's throw

Pero Vaz Caminha// **a descoberta**/ Seguimos nosso caminho por êste mar de longo/ Até a oitava da Páscoa / Topamos aves/ E houvemos vista de terra// **os selvagens**/ Mostraram-lhes uma gallinha/ Quase haviam mêdo dela/ E não queriam pôr a mão/ E depois a tomaram como espantados// **as meninas da gare**/ Eram três ou quatro môças bem môças e bem gentis/ Com cabelos mui prêtos pelas espáduas/ E suas vergonhas tão altas le tão saradinhas/ Que de nós as muito bem olharmos/ Não tínhamos nenhuma vergonha// Gandavo// **hospedagem**/ Porque a mesma terra he tal/ E tam favorável aos que vam buscar/ Que a todos agazalha e convida// **corografia**/ Têm a forma de hua harpa/ Confina com as altíssimas terras dos Andes/ E faldas do Perú/ As quais são tão soberbas em cima da terra/ Que se diz terem as aves trabalho em as passar// **país do ouro**/ Todos têm remédio de vida/ E nenhum pobre anda pelas portas/ A mendigar como nestes Reinos// **natureza morta**/ A esta fruita chamam Ananazes/ Depois que sam maduras têm un cheiro muy suave/ E como-se aparados feitos em talhada/ E assi fazem os moradores por elle mais/ E õs têm em mayor estima/ Que outro nenhum pomo que aja na terra// **riquezas naturais**/ Muitos metaes pepinos romans e figos/ De muitas castas/Cidras limões e laranjas/ Uma infinidade/

Muitas cannas daçucre/ Infinito algodam/Tambén há muito páo brasil/
Nestas capitanias// **festa da raça**/ Hu certo animal se acha também nestas
partes/ A que chamam Preguiça/ Tem hua guedelha grande no toutiço/ E se
move com passos tam vagarosos/ Que ainda que ande quinze dias aturado/
Não vencerá distância de hu tiro de pedra

Excerpts from Cannibal Manifesto / Manifiesto antropófago

Odile Cisneros, trans.

Only cannibalism unites us. Socially. Economically. Philosophically.

Sole law of the world. Expression in disguise of all individualisms, all
collectivisms. Of all religions. Of all peace treaties.

Tupi or not Tupi—that is the question.

Against all catechisms. And against the mother of the Gracchi.

Only what isn't mine interests me. Law of man. Law of the cannibal.

We're weary of all those Catholic husbands playing scenes. Freud lay
the enigma of woman to rest along with other scares of
psychology in print.

What was getting in the way of truth was clothes, a watertight barrier
between the outside world and the inside world. A reaction against the
dressed man. American film will keep us informed.

Children of the sun, mother of the living. Found and
ferociously loved, with all the nostalgic hypocrisy of saudade for the
immigrants, the trafficked peoples, and the tourists.
In the country of the big cobra.

It was because we never had grammars or collections of old plants.
And we never knew what urban, suburban, borderline, and continental
meant. Lazy bums on the world map of Brazil.
A participatory consciousness, a religious rhythmics.

. . . .

The spirit refuses to conceive of a disembodied spirit.
Anthropomorphism. The need for a cannibalist vaccine. To compensate
for the religions of the meridian. And the foreign inquisitions.

We can only listen to the auricular world.

We had justice, the codification of vengeance. Science, the codification
of Magic. Cannibalism. The permanent transformation of
Taboo into Totem.

. . . .

Logbooks. Scripts. Itineraries. Logbooks. Scripts. Itineraries.
Logbooks.

. . . .

We were never converted. What we did was Carnival. The Indian, dressed
as Senator of the Empire. Pretending to be Pitt. Or appearing in operas by
Alencar, full of good Portuguese feelings.

We already had communism. What we already had surrealist language.
The Golden Age.
Catiti Catiti
Imara Notiá
Notiá Imara
Ipejú

. . . .

Only where there's mystery, there's no determinism. But what does that
have to do with us?

. . . .

If God is the consciouness of the Uncreated Universe, Guaraci is the
mother of the living. Jaci is the mother of plants.

. . . .

The pater familias is the product of the Stork's Morality: Real ignorance about things + lack of imagination + feeling of authority vis-à-vis inquisitive offspring.

. . . .

The created objective reacts like the Fallen Angels. Afterwards Moses began to ramble. What does that have to do with us?

. . . .

Against the torch-bearing Indian. The Indian, son of Mary, godson of Catherine de' Medici and son-in-law of Don Antonio de Mariz.

Joy is the acid test.

. . . .

Against social reality, dressed up and oppressive, mapped out by Freud— reality without complexes, without madness, without prostitutions or penal colonies in the matriarchy of Pindorama.

OSWALD DE ANDRADE
In Piratininga
Anno 374 of the Deglutition of Bishop Sardinha.

Só a Antropofagia nos une. Socialmente. Economicamente. Filosoficamente.// Única lei do mundo. Expressão mascarada de todos os individualismos, de todos os coletivismos. De todas as religiões. De todos os tratados de paz.// Tupi, or not tupi that is the question.// Contra todas as catequeses. E contra a mãe dos Gracos.// Só me interessa o que não é meu. Lei do homem. Lei do antropófago.// Estamos fatigados de todos os maridos católicos suspeitosos postos em drama. Freud acabou com o enigma mulher e com outros sustos da psicologia impressa.// O que atropelava a verdade era a roupa, o impermeável entre o mundo interior e o mundo exterior. A reação contra o homem vestido. O cinema americano informará.// Filhos do sol, mãe dos viventes. Encontrados e amados ferozmente, com toda a hipocrisia da saudade, pelos imigrados, pelos traficados e pelos touristes. No país da cobra grande.// Foi porque nunca tivemos gramáticas, nem coleções de velhos vegetais. E nunca soubemos o que era urbano, suburbano, fronteiriço e continental. Preguiçosos no mapa-múndi do Brasil./ Uma consciência participante, uma rítmica religiosa.// . . . // O espírito recusa-se a conceber o espírito sem o corpo. O antropomorfismo. Necessidade da vacina antropofágica. Para o equilíbrio contra as religiões de meridiano. E as inquisições exteriores.// Só podemos atender ao mundo orecular.// Tínhamos a justiça codificação da vingança. A ciência codificação da Magia. Antropofagia. A transformação permanente do Tabu em totem.// . . . // Roteiros. Roteiros. Roteiros. Roteiros. Roteiros. Roteiros. Roteiros.// . . . // Nunca fomos catequizados. Fizemos foi Carnaval. O índio vestido de senador do Império. Fingindo de Pitt. Ou figurando nas óperas de Alencar cheio de bons sentimentos portugueses.// Já tínhamos o comunismo. Já tínhamos a língua surrealista. A idade de ouro./ Catiti Catiti/Imara Notiá/ Notiá Imara/Ipeju// . . . // Só não há determinismo onde há mistério. Mas que temos nós com isso?// . . . // Se Deus é a consciência do Universo Incriado, Guaraci é a mãe dos viventes. Jaci é a mãe dos vegetais.// . . . // O pater famílias e a criação da Moral da Cegonha: Ignorância real das coisas + falta de imaginação + sentimento de autoridade ante a prole curiosa.// . . . // O objetivo criado reage com os Anjos da Queda. Depois Moisés divaga. Que temos nós com isso?// . . . // Contra o índio de tocheiro. O índio filho de Maria, afilhado de Catarina de Médicis e genro de D. Antônio de Mariz.// A alegria é a prova dos nove.// . . . // Contra a realidade social, vestida e opressora, cadastrada por Freud—a realidade sem complexos, sem loucura, sem prostituições e sem penitenciárias do matriarcado de Pindorama.// OSWALD DE ANDRADE, Em Piratininga, Ano 374 da Deglutição do Bispo Sardinha.

Oliverio Girondo (1891–1967, Argentina)

Born in Buenos Aires to an elite family, Girondo traveled to Europe to study and was attracted to surrealism. He brought many of the ideas of the European avant-garde back to Argentina in the 1920s and is regarded as one of the founders of the Argentinean vanguard movement. He helped establish *Martín Fierro*, an important literary review. In his work, he was critical of social conventions and institutions. As had Xul Solar and César Vallejo before him, he questioned the boundaries of the Spanish language. Much like a Parisian salon, his own home in Buenos Aires served as a vibrant cultural center. PRINCIPAL WORKS: *Veinte poemas para ser leídos en el tranvía* (1922), *En la masmédula* (1956)

The Mix / La mezcla

Molly Weigel, trans.

Not only
the bub bottom
the milkdrunken beds telluric slimes between beacons bosoms
and their lichens
not only the solicroak
the prefugues
the odd gone crazy
the going deep
the incautious touch alone
the according abysses of the sacred organs of orgasm
the taste for risk budding
the black rite till dawn with its stretching full of sparrows
nor the delight
the sighspirits only
nor the fortuitous dial but
either the selfsoundings in plain tropic plexus
nor the ex-she's less nor the inlabyrinth
but the long live mix
the total full mix
the pure impure mix that undoes my dovetails my soulmortar tightens my
     stubborn female couplings
the mix
yes
the mix I stuck my bridges together with

No sólo/ el fofo fondo/ los ebrios lechos légamos telúricos entre fanales/
senos/ y sus líquenes/ no sólo el solicroo/las prefugas/ lo impar ido/el
ahonde/el tacto incauto solo/ los acordes abismos de los órganos sacros del/
orgasmo/ el gusto al riesgo en brote/ al rito negro al alba con sus neosenos
migas de gorriones/ ni tampoco el regosto/ los suspiritos sólo/ ni el fortuito
dial sino/o los autosondeos en pleno plexo trópico/ ni las exellas menos
ni el endédalo/ sino la viva mezcla/ la total mezcla plena/ la pura impura
mezcla que me merma los ma-/ chimbres el almamasa tensa las tercas
hembras tuercas/ la mezcla/ sí/ la mezcla/ con que adherí mis puentes

My Lumy / Mi lumía

Molly Weigel, trans.

My lu
my liebeddable
my savoryamor my lovelipop

my lu so light so you that illuminabysses
and decenterterras
and venusaphrodeities
and nirvanas me his the crucis you disturb them
with its mellimelees
its eropsychesilks its recumbent lianas and dermiferious limbos and lumps
my lu
my luing
my myth
birdemon rosy deity
my fairy fish
my trivialuvisit
my lubisnea
my lu plus lares
plus lambent
my lu flesh of vertigo of galaxies of semen of mystery
my lulovely luonly
my total lu plevida
my lu all
lumy

Mi lu/ mi lubidulia/ mi golocidalove/ mi lu tan luz tan tu que me
enlucielabisma/ y descentratelura/ y venusafrodea/ y me nirvana el
suyo la crucis los desalmes/ con sus melimeleos/ sus eropsiquisedas sus
decúbitos lianas y dermiferios limbos y/ gormullos/ mi lu/ mi luar/ mi
mito/ demonoave dea rosa/ mi pez hada/ mi luvisita nimia/ mi lubísnea/
mi lu más lar/ más lampo/ mi pulpa lu de vértigo de galaxias de semen de
misterio/ mi lubella lusola/ mi total lu plevida/ mi toda lu/ lumía

Totem Night / Noche tótem

Molly Weigel, trans.

They are the other underlying motives of the in extremis medium
that is the night left ajar the bones
the mythforms other
ardorallied presences semimorphed
underpauses belowbreaths
of the lacerated libido the demon woman
that is the unbandaged night
they are the other graylights sparking behind emerys eyelids seers
the astonished casts of the immobile before the questioning incoming
      wound
that is the already livid night

they are the sifting voices
the suburban bloods of the absence of backwater shoulderblades
the bitterinsomniac hungry dredgers of now with its slime of nothing
other departed steps of the ubiquitous and other incorporeal scraping at
    uncertainty
that could be death with its lunatic celibate crutch
and it is the night

                                                    and it abandons

Son los trasfondos otros de la in extremis médium/ que es la noche
al entreabrir los huesos/ las mitoformas otras/ aliardidas presencias
semimorfas/ sotopausas sosoplos/ de la enllagada líbido posesa/ que es
la noche sin vendas/ son las grislumbres otras tras esmeriles párpados
videntes/ los atónitos yesos de lo inmóvil ante el refluido herido/
interrogante/ que es la noche ya lívida/ son las cribadas voces/ las
suburbanas sangres de la ausencia de remansos omóplatos/ las agrinsomnes
dragas hambrientas del ahora con su limo de/ nada/ los idos pasos otros de
la incorpórea ubicua también otra/ escarbando lo incierto/ que puede ser la
muerte con su demente célibe muleta/ y es la noche/ y deserta

You Have to Look for It / Hay que buscarlo

                                                    Molly Weigel, trans.

In the eropsychis full of guests then meanders of waiting absence
assumooned thighs of summery epicenter
extradermic tumults
excoriations night fever that mockmoos
and how ow owls
when its veins are opened
with a fishsplendor immersed in the nape of sleep you have to look for it
                                                    for the poem

You have to look for it inside the plesips of idleness
naked
cuttings plaints
without roots of amnesia
in the lunihemispheres of ebbs of clots of foam of jellyfish of sand of breasts
    or maybe on jetties with breath for little foxes
and for ruminating distance of holy mothers cows
driven in
without a halo
facing puddles of tears that sing
with a fishveil in trance under the tongue you have to look for it
                                                    for the poem

You have to look for it igniferous superimpure injured
lucid drunk
inobvious
between epithelia of dawn or sleepless hangovers undertows of waxing
    solitude
before the pupil of the zero dilates
while the endoineffable incandesces the lips of the subvoices that break out
    of the euphonious intraearth
with a fishfaucet rainbow in the minimal plaza of the brow you have to
    look for it

                                                for the poem

En la eropsiquis plena de húespedes entonces meandros de espera ausencia/
enlunadados muslos de estival epicentro/ tumultos extradérmicos/
excoriaciones fiebre de noche que burmúa/ y aola aola aola/ al abrirse las
venas/ con un pezlampo inmerso en la nuca del sueño hay que buscarlo/
al poema// Hay que buscarlo dentro de los plesorbos de ocio/ desnudo/
desquejido/ sin raíces de amnesia/ en los lunihemisferios de reflujos
de coágulos de espuma de medusas de arena de los/ senos o tal vez en
andenes con aliento a zorrino/ y a rumiante distancia de santas madres
vacas/ hincadas/ sin aureola/ ante charcos de lágrimas que cantan/ con un
pezvelo en trance debajo de la lengua hay que buscarlo/ al poema// Hay que
buscarlo ignífero superimpuro leso/ lúcido beodo/ inobvio/ entre epitelios
de alba o resacas insomnes de soledad en creciente/ antes que se dilate la
pupila del cero/ mientras lo endoinefable encandece los labios de subvoces
que brotan del infrafondo/ eufónico/ con un pezgrifo arco iris en la mínima
plaza de la frente hay que buscarlo/ al poema

Votive Offering / Exvoto

                                      Molly Weigel, trans.

                                      To the girls of Flores

The girls of Flores have soft sweet eyes, like the sugared almonds from the
    Molino Confectioners, and they use silk bows that taste their buttocks in
    the fluttering of a butterfly.

The girls of Flores, they stroll arm in arm, to transmit their trembling
    among themselves, and if anyone looks them in the eye, they squeeze
    their legs together for fear their sex will fall out onto the sidewalk.

At dusk, they all hang their unripe breasts from the wrought-iron boughs
    of the balconies, so that their garments can grow purple from noticing
    their nakedness, and at night, in tow to their mothers, —decked out like

frigates—they stroll around the plaza, so that men ejaculate words into their ear, and their phosphorescent nipples light up and go out like fireflies.

The girls of Flores live in an agony of fear that their buttocks will rot, like apples that have let themselves go, and men's desire so suffocates them that sometimes they would like to peel it off like a corset, since they don't have the courage to cut their bodies into pieces and hurl them to all who pass them on the sidewalk.

A las chicas de Flores / Las chicas de Flores, tienen los ojos dulces, como las almendras azucaradas / de la Confitería del Molino, y usan moños de seda que les liban las nalgas en un / aleteo de mariposa. // Las chicas de Flores, se pasean tomadas de los brazos, para transmitirse sus / estremecimientos, y si alguien las mira en las pupilas, aprientan las piernas, de / miedo de que el sexo se les caiga en la vereda. // Al atardecer, todas ellas cuelgan sus pechos sin madurar del ramaje de hie—/ rro de los balcones, para que sus vestidos se empurpuren al sentirlas desnudas, / y de noche, a remolque de sus mamás—empavesadas como fragatas—van a pase—/ arse por la plaza, para que los hombres les eyaculen palabras al oído, y sus pezo—/ nes fosforescentes se enciendan y se apaguen como luciérnagas. // Las chicas de Flores, viven en la angustia de que las nalgas se les pudran, / como manzanas que se han dejado pasar, y el deseo de los hombres las sofoca / tanto, que a veces quisieran desembarazarse de él como de un corsé, ya que no / tienen el coraje de cortarse el cuerpo a pedacitos y arrojárselo, a todos los que / les pasan la vereda.

César Vallejo (1892–1938, Peru)

"The greatest of the great South American poets," as Jerome Rothenberg said, Vallejo was born in Santiago de Chuco, in the Peruvian Andes. His grandmothers were Chimu Indians, and both his grandfathers were Spanish Catholic priests. He initiated his university studies in literature but abandoned them due to financial difficulties. He lived in Spain, France, and Russia and became a member of the Communist Party. Vallejo's first book shows the influence of modernism. But *Trilce* changed poetry in Spanish forever by allowing the stilted, broken voice of the wounded mestizo to come forth. His participation in the Republican Front during the Spanish Civil War compelled him to write some of his most visceral work. He was almost destitute when he died on a rainy day, as he had foretold in one of his poems. In the words of Octavio Paz, Vallejo conceived poetry as "confession, penance, and communion—a true Eucharist." PRINCIPAL WORKS: *Los heraldos negros* (1918), *Trilce* (1922), *Poemas humanos* (1939), *España, aparta de mí este cáliz* (1940)

The Black Heralds / Los heraldos negros

Clayton Eshleman, trans.

There are blows in life, so powerful . . . I don't know!
Blows as from the hatred of God; as if, facing them,
the undertow of everything suffered
welled up in the soul . . . I don't know!

They are few; but they are . . . They open dark trenches
in the fiercest face and in the strongest back.
Perhaps they are the colts of barbaric Attilas;
or the black heralds sent to us by Death.

They are the deep falls of the Christs of the soul,
of some adored faith blasphemed by Destiny.
Those bloodstained blows are the crackling of
bread burning up at the oven door.

And man . . . Poor . . . poor! He turns his eyes, as
when a slap on the shoulder summons us;
turns his crazed eyes, and everything lived
wells up, like a pool of guilt, in his look.

There are blows in life, so powerful . . . I don't know!

Hay golpes en la vida, tan fuertes . . . Yo no sé!/ Golpes como del odio
de Dios; como si ante ellos,/ la resaca de todo lo sufrido/ se empozara en
el alma . . . Yo no sé!// Son pocos; pero son . . . Abren zanjas oscuras/ en
el rostro más fiero y en el lomo más fuerte./ Serán talvez los potros de
bárbaros atilas;/ o los heraldos negros que nos manda la Muerte.// Son
las caídas hondas de los Cristos del alma,/ de alguna fe adorable que el
Destino blasfema./ Esos golpes sangrientos son las crepitaciones/ de algún
pan que en la puerta del horno se nos quema.// Y el hombre . . . Pobre . . .
pobre! Vuelve los ojos, como/ cuando por sobre el hombro nos llama
una palmada;/ vuelve los ojos locos, y todo lo vivido/ se empoza, como
charco de culpa, en la mirada.// Hay golpes en la vida, tan fuertes . . .
Yo no sé!

Excerpts from **Trilce**

Clayton Eshleman, trans.

XXIII

Estuous oven of those my sweet rolls
pure infantile innumerable yolk, mother.

Oh your four gorges, astoundingly
mislamented, mother: your beggars.

The two youngest sisters, Miguel who has died
and me still pulling
one braid for each letter in the primer.

In the room upstairs you handed out to us
in the morning, in the evening, from a dual stowage,
those delicious hosts of time, so
that now we'd have more than enough
clock husks in flexion of 24 hours
stopped on the dot.

Mother, and now! Now, in which alveolus
might remain, on what capillary sprout,
a certain crumb that today perplexed in my throat
doesn't want to go down. Today when even
your pure bones might be flour
with nowhere to knead
—tender confectioner of love,
even in raw shade, even in the great molar
whose gum throbs on that lacteal dimple
which unseen builds and abounds—you saw it so often!
in closed hands newborn.

So the earth will hear in your silencing,
how they keep charging us all
rent on the world in which you leave us
and the cost of that interminable bread.
And they charge us for it, when, being only
children then, as you could see,
we couldn't have snatched it
from anyone; when you gave it to us,
no, mama?

Tahona estuosa de aquellos mis bizcochos/ pura yema infantil innumerable,
madre.// Oh tus cuatro gorgas, asombrosamente/ mal plañidas, madre:
tus mendigos./ Las dos hermanas últimas, Miguel que ha muerto/ y yo
arrastrando todavía/ una trenza por cada letra del abecedario.// En la sala
de arriba nos repartías/ de mañana, de tarde, de dual estiba,/ aquellas
ricas hostias de tiempo, para/ que ahora nos sobrasen/ cáscaras de relojes
en flexión de las 24/ en punto parados.// Madre, y ahora! Ahora, en cuál
alvéolo/ quedaría, en qué retoño capilar,/ cierta migaja que hoy se me ata al
cuello/ y no quiere pasar. Hoy que hasta/ tus puros huesos estarán harina/
que no habrá en qué amasar/ ¡tierna dulcera de amor,/ hasta en la cruda
sombra, hasta en el gran molar/ cuya encía late en aquel lácteo hoyuelo/ que
inadvertido lábrase y pulula ¡tú lo viste tánto!/ en las cerradas manos recién
nacidas.// Tal la tierra oirá en tu silenciar,/ cómo nos van cobrando todos/

el alquiler del mundo donde nos dejas/ y el valor de aquel pan inacabable./
Y nos lo cobran, cuando, siendo nosotros/ pequeños entonces, como tú
verías,/ no se lo podíamos haber arrebatado/ a nadie; cuando tú nos lo
diste,/ ¿di, mamá?

XXXVI

We struggle to thread ourselves through a needle's eye,
face to face, hell-bent on winning.
The fourth angle of the circle ammoniafies almost.
Female is continued the male, on the basis
of probable breasts, and precisely
on the basis of how much does not flower.

Are you that way, Venus de Milo?
You hardly act crippled, pullulating
enwombed in the plenary arms
of existence,
of this existence that neverthelessez
perpetual imperfection.
Venus de Milo, whose cut-off, increate
arm swings around and tries to elbow
across greening stuttering pebbles,
ortive nautili, recently crawling
evens, immortal on the eves of.
Lassoer of imminences, lassoer
of the parenthesis.

Refuse, all of you, to set foot
on the double security of Harmony.
Truly refuse symmetry.
Intervene in the conflict
of points that contend
in the most rutty of jousts
for the leap through the needle's eye!

So now I feel my little finger
in excess on my left. I see it and think
it shouldn't be me, or at least that it's
in a place where it shouldn't be.
And it inspires me with rage and alarms me
and there is no way out of it, except by
imagining that today is Thursday.

Make way for the new odd number
                    potent with orphanhood!

Pugnamos ensartarnos por un ojo de aguja,/ enfrentados, a las ganadas./
Amoniácase casi el cuarto ángulo del círculo./ ¡Hembra se continúa el
macho, a raíz/ de probables senos, y precisamente/ a raíz de cuanto no
florece!// ¿Por ahí estás, Venus de Milo?/ Tú manqueas apenas, pululando/
entrañada en los brazos plenarios/ de la existencia,/ de esta existencia
que todaviiza/ perenne imperfección./ Venus de Milo, cuyo cercenado,
increado/ brazo revuélvese y trata de encodarse/ a través de verdeantes
guijarros gagos,/ ortivos nautilos, aunes que gatean/ recién, vísperas
inmortales./ Laceadora de inminencias, laceadora/ del paréntesis.//
Rehusad, y vosotros, a posar las plantas/ en la seguridad dupla de la
Armonía./ Rehusad la simetría a buen seguro./ Intervenid en el conflicto/
de puntas que se disputan/ en la más torionda de las justas/ el salto por
el ojo de la aguja!// Tal siento ahora al meñique/ demás en la siniestra.
Lo veo y creo/ no debe serme, o por lo menos que está/ en sitio donde
no debe./ Y me inspira rabia y me azarea/ y no hay cómo salir de él,
sino haciendo/ la cuenta de que hoy es jueves.// ¡Ceded al nuevo impar/
potente de orfandad!

Black Stone on a White Stone / Piedra negra sobre una piedra blanca
Clayton Eshleman, trans.

I will die in Paris in a downpour,
a day which I can already remember.
I will die in Paris—and I don't budge—
maybe a Thursday, like today, in autumn.

Thursday it will be, because today, Thursday,
as I prose these lines, I have forced on
my humeri and, never like today, have I turned,
with all my journey, to see myself alone.

César Vallejo has died, they beat him,
all of them, without him doing anything to them;
they gave it to him hard with a stick and hard

likewise with a rope; witnesses are
the Thursdays and the humerus bones,
the loneliness, the rain, the roads . . .

Me moriré en París con aguacero,/ un día del cual tengo ya el recuerdo./
Me moriré en París—y no me corro—/ talvez un jueves, como es hoy,
de otoño.// Jueves será, porque hoy, jueves, que proso/ estos versos, los
húmeros me he puesto/ a la mala y, jamás como hoy, me he vuelto,/ con
todo mi camino, a verme solo.// César Vallejo ha muerto, le pegaban/ todos

sin que él les haga nada;/ le daban duro con un palo y duro// también con
una soga; son testigos/ los días jueves y los huesos húmeros,/ la soledad, la
lluvia, los caminos . . .

Telluric and Magnetic / Telúrica y magnética

Clayton Eshleman, trans.

Sincere and utterly Peruvian mechanics
that of the reddened hill!
Soil theoretical and practical!
Intelligent furrows: example; the monolith and its retinue!
Potato fields, barley fields, alfalfa fields, good things!
Cultivations which integrate an astonishing hierarchy of tools
and which integrate with wind the lowings,
the waters with their deaf antiquity!

Quaternary maize, with opposed birthdays,
I hear through my feet how they move away,
I smell them return when the earth
clashes with the sky's technique!
Abruptly molecule! Terse atom!

Oh human fields!
Solar and nutritious absence of the sea,
and oceanic feeling for everything!
Oh climates found within gold, ready!
Oh intellectual field of cordilleras,
with religion, with fields, with ducklings!
Pachyderms in prose when passing
and in poetry when stopping!
Rodents who peer with judicial feeling all around!
Oh my life's patriotic asses!
Vicuña, national
and graceful descendant of my ape!
Oh light hardly a mirror from shadow,
which is life with the period and, with the line, dust
and that is why I revere, climbing though the idea to my skeleton!

Harvest in the epoch of the spread pepper tree,
of the lantern hung from a human temple
and of the one unhung from the magnificent barret!
Poultry-yard angels,
birds by a slipup of the cockscomb!
Cavess or cavy to be eaten fried

with the hot bird pepper from the templed valleys!
(Condors? Screw the condors!)
Christian logs by the grace of
a happy trunk and a competent stalk!
Family of lichens,
species in basalt formation that I
respect
from this most modest paper!
Four operations, I subtract you
to save the oak and sink it in sterling!
Slopes caught in the act!
Tearful Auchenia, my own souls!
Sierra of my Peru, Peru of the world,
and Peru at the foot of the globe: I adhere!
Morning stars if I aromatize you
burning coca leaves in this skull,
and zenithal ones, if I uncover,
with one hat doff, my ten temples!
Arm sowing, get down and on foot!
Rain based on noon,
under the tile roof where indefatigable
altitude gnaws
and the turtle dove cuts her trill in three!
Rotation of modern afternoons
and delicate archaeological daybreaks.
Indian after man and before him!
I understand all of it on two flutes
and I make myself understood on a quena!
As for the others, they can jerk me off! . . .

¡Mecánica sincera y peruanísima/ la del cerro colorado!/ ¡Suelo teórico
y práctico!/ ¡Surcos inteligentes; ejemplo: el monolito y su cortejo!/
¡Papales, cebadales, alfalfares, cosa buena!/ ¡Cultivos que integra una
asombrosa jerarquía de útiles/ y que integran con viento los mujidos,/
las aguas con su sorda antigüedad!// ¡Cuaternarios maíces, de opuestos
natalicios,/ los oigo por los pies cómo se alejan,/ los huelo retornar cuando
la tierra/ tropieza con la técnica del cielo!/ ¡Molécula exabrupto! ¡Atomo
terso!// ¡Oh campos humanos!/ ¡Solar y nutricia ausencia de la mar,/ y
sentimiento oceánico de todo!/ ¡Oh climas encontrados dentro del oro,
listos!/ ¡Oh campo intelectual de cordillera,/ con religión, con campo, con
patitos!/ ¡Paquidermos en prosa cuando pasan/ y en verso cuando páranse!/
¡Roedores que miran con sentimiento judicial en torno!/ ¡Oh patrióticos
asnos de mi vida!/ ¡Vicuña, descendiente/ nacional y graciosa de mi mono!/

¡Oh luz que dista apenas un espejo de la sombra,/ que es vida con el punto
y, con la línea, polvo/ y que por eso acato, subiendo por la idea a mi
osamenta!// ¡Siega en época del dilatado molle,/ del farol que colgaron de
la sien/ y del que descolgaron de la barreta espléndida!/ ¡Angeles de corral,/
aves por un descuido de la cresta!/ ¡Cuya o cuy para comerlos fritos/ con
el bravo rocoto de los templos!/ (¿Cóndores? ¡Me friegan los cóndores!)/
¡Leños cristianos en gracia/ al tronco feliz y al tallo competente!/ ¡Familia
de los líquenes,/ especies en formación basáltica que yo/ respeto/ desde este
modestísimo papel!/ ¡Cuatro operaciones, os sustraigo/ para salvar al roble
y hundirlo en buena ley!/ ¡Cuestas en infraganti!/ ¡Auquénidos llorosos,
almas mías!/ ¡Sierra de mi Perú, Perú del mundo,/ y Perú al pie del orbe;
yo me adhiero!/ ¡Estrellas matutinas si os aromo/ quemando hojas de coca
en este cráneo,/ y cenitales, si destapo,/ de un solo sombrerazo, mis diez
templos!/ ¡Brazo de siembra, bájate, y a pie!/ ¡Lluvia a base del mediodía,/
bajo el techo de tejas donde muerde/ la infatigable altura/ y la tórtola
corta en tres su trino!/ ¡Rotación de tardes modernas/ y finas madrugadas
arqueológicas!/ ¡Indio después del hombre y antes de él!/ ¡Lo entiendo todo
en dos flautas/ y me doy a entender en una quena!/ ¡Y lo demás, me las
pelan! . . .

I Stayed On to Warm Up the Ink in Which I Drown / Quedéme a calentar la tinta en que me ahogo

Clayton Eshleman, trans.

I stayed on to warm up the ink in which I drown
and to listen to my alternative cavern,
tactile nights, abstracted days.

The unknown shuddered in my tonsil
and I creaked from an annual melancholy,
solar nights, lunar days, Parisian sunsets.

And still, this very day, at dusk
I digest the most sacred certainties,
maternal nights, great-granddaughter days,
bicolored, voluptuous, urgent, lovely.

And yet
I arrive, I reach myself in a two-seated plane
under the domestic morning and the mist
which emerged eternally from an instant.

And still,
even now,
at the tail of the comet in which I have earned

my happy and doctoral bacillus,
behold that warm, listener, male earth, sun and male moon,
incognito I cross the cemetery,
head off to the left, splitting
the grass with a pair of hendecasyllables,
tombal years, infinitary liters,
ink, pen, bricks, and forgiveness.

Quedéme a calentar la tinta en que me ahogo/ y a escuchar mi caverna
alternativa,/ noches de tacto, días de abstracción.// Se estremeció la
incógnita en mi amígdala/ y crují de una anual melancolía,/ noches de
sol, días de luna, ocasos de París.// Y todavía, hoy mismo, al atardecer,/
digiero sacratísimas constancias,/ noches de madre, días de biznieta/ bicolor,
voluptuosa, urgente, linda.// Y aun/ alcanzo, llego hasta mí en avión de dos
asientos,/ bajo la mañana doméstica y la bruma/ que emergió eternamente
de un instante.// Y todavía,/ aun ahora,/ al cabo del cometa en que he
ganado/ mi bacilo feliz y doctoral,/ he aquí que caliente, oyente, tierro, sol
y luno,/ incógnito atravieso el cementerio,/ tomo a la izquierda, hiendo/ la
yerba con un par de endecasílabos,/ años de tumba, litros de infinito,/ tinta,
pluma, ladrillos y perdones.

**There Are Days, There Comes to Me an Exuberant, Political Hunger / Me
viene, hay días, una gana ubérrima, política**

Clayton Eshleman, trans.

There are days, there comes to me an exuberant, political hunger
to desire, to kiss tenderness on both cheeks,
and there comes to me from afar a demonstrative
desire, another desire to love, willingly or by force,
whoever hates me, whoever tears up his paper, the little boy,
the woman who weeps for the man who was weeping,
the king of wine, the slave of water,
whoever hid in his wrath,
whoever sweats, whoever passes by, whoever shakes his person in my soul.
And I desire, therefore, to adjust
the braid of whoever talks to me; the soldier's hair;
the light of the great; the greatness of the child.
I desire to iron directly
a handkerchief for whoever is unable to cry
and, when I am sad or happiness aches me,
to mend the children and the geniuses.

I desire to help the good one become a little bad
and I have an urge to be seated

to the right of the left-handed, and to respond to the mute,
trying to be useful to him
as I can, and likewise I desire very much
to wash the cripple's foot,
and to help my one-eyed neighbor sleep.

Ah to desire, this one, mine, this one, the world's,
interhuman and parochial, mature!
It comes perfectly timed,
from the foundation, from the public groin,
and, coming from afar, makes me hunger to kiss
the singer's muffler,
and whoever suffers, to kiss him on his frying pan,
the deaf man, fearlessly, on his cranial murmur;
whoever gives me what I forgot in my breast,
on his Dante, on his Chaplin, on his shoulders.

I desire, finally,
when I'm at the celebrated edge of violence
or my heart full of chest, I would desire
to help whoever smiles laugh,
to put a little bird right on the evildoer's nape,
to take care of the sick annoying them,
to buy from the vendor,
to help the killer kill—a terrible thing—
and I would desire to be good to myself
in everything.

Me viene, hay días, una gana ubérrima, política,/ de querer, de besar al
cariño en sus dos rostros,/ y me viene de lejos un querer/ demostrativo,
otro querer amar, de grado o fuerza,/ al que me odia, al que rasga su papel,
al muchachito,/ a la que llora por el que lloraba,/ al rey del vino, al esclavo
del agua,/ al que ocultóse en su ira,/ al que suda, al que pasa, al que sacude
su persona en mi alma./ Y quiero, por lo tanto, acomodarle/ al que me
habla, su trenza; sus cabellos, al soldado;/ su luz, al grande; su grandeza,
al chico./ Quiero planchar directamente/ un pañuelo al que no puede
llorar/ y, cuando estoy triste o me duele la dicha,/ remendar a los niños
y a los genios.// Quiero ayudar al bueno a ser su poquillo de malo/ y me
urge estar sentado/ a la diestra del zurdo, y responder al mudo,/ tratando
de serle útil en/ lo que puedo y también quiero muchísimo/ lavarle al cojo
el pie,/ y ayudarle a dormir al tuerto próximo.// ¡Ah querer, éste, el mío,
éste, el mundial,/ interhumano y parroquial, provecto!/ Me viene a pelo,/
desde el cimiento, desde la ingle pública,/ y, viniendo de lejos, da ganas de
besarle/ la bufanda al cantor,/ y al que sufre, besarle en su sartén,/ al sordo,
en su rumor craneano, impávido;/ al que me da lo que olvidé en mi seno,/

en su Dante, en su Chaplin, en sus hombros.// Quiero, para terminar,/ cuando estoy al borde célebre de violencia/ o lleno de pecho el corazón, querría/ ayudar a reír al que sonríe,/ ponerle un pajarillo al malvado en plena nuca,/ cuidar a los enfermos enfadándolos,/ comprarle al vendedor,/ ayudarle a matar al matador—cosa terrible—/ y quisiera yo ser bueno conmigo/ en todo.

Alfonsina Storni (1892–1938, Argentina)

Born in Switzerland, Storni moved to Argentina with her parents when she was four years old. A single mother by age twenty, she supported herself working a variety of jobs, in a perennial struggle against the hypocrisy and prejudice of a prudish society. She wrote for important national newspapers and magazines and frequented literary circles, gaining fame and recognition among numerous intellectuals of her time. However, her efforts to abolish the role consigned to women as second-class citizens were not equally accepted. Suffering from cancer and isolation, she took her own life by walking into the sea. Mainly a modernist poet, she did not make any incursions into the Vanguardist experiments that attracted many of her contemporaries, but she became firmly established during her lifetime as one of the main poets of the Spanish language. PRINCIPAL WORKS: *El dulce daño* (1918), *Poemas de amor* (1926), *Mascarilla y trébol* (1938)

World of Seven Wells / Mundo de siete pozos

Rosa Alcalá, trans.

It balances itself
above, on the neck,
the world of seven doors:
the human head . . .

Round, like two planets:
burning in its center,
the first nucleus.
Osseous cortex;
covering it, dermal silt
sown
with the hair's thick forest.

From the nucleus,
in tides
blue and absolute,
the water-level of the gaze rises

and opens the gentle doors
of the eyes like seas on land.
      . . . so calm
those great waters of God
        that on them
butterflies and golden insects
alight.

And the other two doors:
antennae curled up
in the catacombs where the ears begin;
wells of sounds,
mother of pearl shells where the spoken
and unspoken word
echo;
tubes placed to the right and to the left
so the sea never quiets,
and the worlds' mechanical wing
keeps buzzing.

And the mountain which rests above
the head's equatorial line:
the nose and its waxy frames
where life's color becomes muted;
the two doors
giving way to
—flowers, leaves, fruit—
spring's fragrant serpent.

And the mouth's crater
with its scorched rim
and walls turned ash and dust;
the crater that spews
the sulfur of violent words
smoke thick from
the heart and its torment;
a door
of lavishly carved corals
through which the beast devours
and the angel sings and smiles
and the human volcano troubles.

It balances itself
      above,
on the neck,

the world of seven wells:
the human head.

And pink meadows bloom
   in its valleys of silk:
the mossy cheeks.
         And on the curve
of the forehead,
white desert,
shimmers the distant light
of a dead moon . . .

Se balancea,/ arriba, sobre el cuello,/ el mundo de las siete puertas:/ La
humana cabeza . . . // Redonda, como dos planetas:/ arde en su centro/ el
núcleo primero./ Ósea la corteza;/ sobre ella el limo dérmico/ sembrado/
del bosque espeso de la cabellera.// Desde el núcleo,/ en mareas/ absolutas
y azules,/ asciende el agua de la mirada/ y abre las suaves puertas/ de los
ojos como mares en la tierra./ . . . Tan quietas/ esas mansas aguas de Dios/
que sobre ellas/ mariposas e insectos de oro/ se balancean.// Y las otras
dos puertas:/ las antenas acurrucadas/ en las catacumbas que inician las
orejas;/ pozos de sonidos,/ caracoles de nácar donde resuena/ la palabra
expresada/ y la no expresa;/ tubos colocados a derecha e izquierda/ para
que el mar no calle nunca,/ y el ala mecánica de los mundos/ rumorosa
sea.// Y la montaña alzada/ sobre la línea ecuatorial de la cabeza:/ la nariz
de batientes de cera/ por donde comienza/ a callarse el color de vida;/ las
dos puertas/ por donde adelanta/ —flores, ramas y frutas—/ la serpentina
olorosa de la primavera,// Y el cráter de la boca/ de bordes ardidos/ y
paredes calcinadas y resecas;/ el cráter que arroja el/ azufre de las palabras
violentas,/ el humo denso que viene/ del corazón y su tormenta;/ la
puerta/ en corales labrada suntuosos/ por donde engulle, la bestia,/ y el
ángel canta y sonríe/ y el volcán humano desconcierta.// Se balancea,/
arriba,/ sobre el cuello,/ el mundo de los siete pozos:/ la humana cabeza.//
Y se abren praderas rosadas/ en sus valles de seda:/ las mejillas musgosas.//
Y riela/ sobre la comba de la frente,/ desierto blanco,/ la luz lejana de una
luna muerta.

An Ear / Una oreja

Rosa Alcalá, trans.

Small trench of iridescent basins
and long dead ivories, with streaks
of backlight; mysterious shell
turned cavern in the gloomy heights.

of the human neck; rosy conch
brought buzzing from the sea;
pierced with circling labyrinths
where the crime hides its traps.

Sometimes, beneath the sun that blood offers,
beneath rocks drawn red and others
made paper sky at dawn:

As in waning moon you unfold
and there deep inside, black at its pit
where the lion of thought is roaring.

Pequeño foso de irisadas cuencas/ y marfiles ya muertos, con estrías/ de
contraluces; misteriosa valva/ vuelta caverna en las alturas tristes// del
cuello humano; rósea caracola/ traída zumbadora de los mares;/ punzada
de envolventes laberintos/ donde el crimen esconde sus acechos.//
A veces, bajo el sol que da la sangre,/ de rocas rojas dibujada y otras/
hecha papel de ciclo en madrugada:// Como en luna menguante te
despliegas/ y allá en el fondo, negro el subterráneo/ donde ruge el león
del pensamiento.

Vicente Huidobro (1893–1948, Chile)

Poet, playwright, journalist, and novelist, Huidobro was born in Santiago, Chile,
into an aristocratic family. At twenty-three, he disembarked in Paris, where he
co-founded—with Apollinaire and Reverdy—the influential cubist magazine
Nord-Sud. Later, he proposed Creationism. (For the inspiration for his poetic theories, Huidobro credited an Aymara Indian who told him, "The poet is a god, don't
sing about rain, poet. Make it rain.") Juan Gris, Robert Delaunay, Edgard Varése,
Hans Arp, and Jorge Luis Borges were some of his companions. According to
Octavio Paz, "Vicente Huidobro's irruption into the poetry of our language was like
a Tartar or a Mongolian invasion: he razed the old cities but, from the fallen stones,
a new and lighter vegetation arose. His brief and fulminating influence can also be
compared to a heavenly intervention. . . . Using language, Huidobro decided to
create another reality. . . . The final chants of *Altazor* . . . stop having meaning for
they have become sound, brilliance, and flight." PRINCIPAL WORKS: *Ecos del alma*
(1911), *El espejo de agua* (1916), *Altazor, o el viaje en paracaídas* (1931), *Temblor de
cielo* (1931)

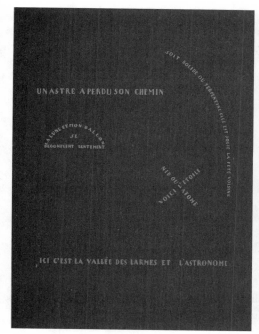

Minuit, Salle XIV, 1921 (2001)   Piano, Salle XIV, 1921 (2001)

Excerpt from Canto I, Altazor

Eliot Weinberger, trans.

Altazor why did you ever lose your young serenity?
What evil angel stopped at the door of your smile
With sword in hand?
Who scattered affliction over the plains of your eyes like the ornaments of a god?
Why did you suddenly one day feel the terror of being?
And that voice that shouted you're alive and you don't see yourself living
Who made your thoughts converge at the crossroads of all the winds of pain?
The diamond of your dreams shattered in a sea of stupor
You're lost Altazor
Alone in the middle of the universe
Alone like a note flowering in the heights of space
There's no good no evil no truth no order no beauty
Where are you Altazor?

. . . .

Fix the engine of dawn
While I sit at the edge of my eyes
Watching the images come in

. . . .

Altazor am I the double of my self
He who watches himself at work and laughs in his face
He who fell from the heights of his star
And traveled for twenty-five years
Hanging in the parachute of his own prejudices
Altazor am I of infinite longing
Of eternal hunger and dejection
Flesh furrowed by plows of affliction
How can I sleep when there are unknown lands within?
Predicaments
Mysteries hanging on my chest
I'm alone
The distance that stretches from body to body
Is as great as that from soul to soul
Alone
     Alone
         Alone
I'm alone standing at the tip of the slow-dying year
The universe breaks in waves at my feet
Planets whirl about my head
Rumpling my hair in the wind that rushes by
Without giving an answer that would fill the abyss
Without feeling this fantastic desperation that searches among
    the fauna of the sky
For a maternal being where the heart may sleep
A shady bed in the whirlwind of mysteries
A hand to stroke the throbbing of fevers
God diluted in the nothing and the all
God all and nothing
God in words and deeds
Mind God
Breath God
Young God Old God
Putrid God
        far and near
God molded in the shape of my distress

. . . .

So let us go on cultivating fields of error in our brains
Let us go on cultivating fields of truth in our chests
Let us go on
Always the same as yesterday tomorrow and later and then
No
It can't be We must change our luck

Burn our flesh in the eyes of dawn
Drink the pale lucidity of death
The polar lucidity of death
Chaos sings to the chaos that has a human chest
It weeps echoing through the universe
Spinning past hallucinations with its myths
The high-fever afflictions of space
The bitter conscience of the useless sacrifice
Of the worthless experience of the cosmic disaster
Of the failed experiment
And yet after man has disappeared
His memory burnt in the blazes of time
A little taste of pain will linger in the terrestrial atmosphere
So many centuries gasped by miserable heaving chests
The sinister shadow of an enormous tear
Will linger in space
And a lost desolate voice moaning
Nothing nothing nothing
No
It can't be
We must devour pleasure
Use up all the life in life
Kill the death infiltrated by lugubrious rhapsodies
By delicate pianos and banners transforming like chrysalids
The rocks of death groan at the edge of the world
The wind drags its bitter flowers
And the grief of springs that can't be born
Everything is a trap
                    A trap of the spirit
An electrical transfusion of dream and reality
The dark lucidity of this huge despair petrified in solitude
To live live in darkness
In the chains of tyrannical desperation collars of screams
And an endless voyaging in the interiors of the self
With the pain of constant limits and the shame of a crippled angel
The ridicule of a god of night
To revolve and revolve broken antennae in the middle of space
Through winged seas and stagnant dawns

. . . .

It's you you the fallen angel
The perpetual falling over death
The endless falling from death to death
Bewitch the universe with your voice

Anchor yourself to your voice bewitcher of the world
Singing like a blind man lost in eternity

A brutal painful grammar walks through my brain
The continual massacre of internal concepts
And a final adventure of cosmic hopes
A havoc of careless stars
Fallen from sorcery and homeless
All that is hidden and incites us with its fatal charms
Hidden in the freezing regions of the invisible
Or the burning storms of our brains

Eternity becomes a path of flowers
For the return of ghosts and predicaments
For the eager mirages of the new hypotheses
That shatter the mirror of potential magic

Freedom Oh yes freedom from everything
From the memories that possess us
From the guts that know what they know
Because of these wounds that chain us to the pit
And the shouts of wings that shatter us

Magic and illusion file the iron bars
Poetry weeps at the tip of a soul
And unease increases staring at new walls
Raised from mystery to mystery
Among the mines of mystification that open their wounds
With the inexhaustible ceremony of familiar dawn
All in vain
Give me the key to the locked dreams
Give me the key to the wrecked ship
Give me the certainty of roots on a quiet horizon
A discovery that does not retreat with every step
Oh give me a beautiful green shipwreck
A miracle to brighten the depths of our intimate seas
Like a ship that sinks without losing its lights
Then free from this tragic silence
With a storm of my own
I'll challenge space
Shake the nothingness with curses and shouts
Till a ray of anxious judgement falls
Bringing the airs of paradise to my gloom

Altazor ¿por qué perdiste tu primera serenidad?/ ¿Qué ángel malo se paró
en la puerta de tu sonrisa/ Con la espada en la mano?/ ¿Quién sembró la

angustia en las llanuras de tus ojos como el adorno de un dios?/ ¿Por qué un día de repente sentiste el terror de ser?/ Y esa voz que te gritó vives y no te ves vivir/ ¿Quién hizo converger tus pensamientos al cruce de todos los vientos del dolor?/ Se rompió el diamante de tus sueños en un mar de estupor/ Estás perdido Altazor/ Solo en medio del universo/ Solo como una nota que florece en las alturas del vacío/ No hay bien no hay mal ni verdad ni orden ni belleza/ ¿En dónde estás Altazor?// . . . // Reparad el motor del alba/ En tanto me siento al borde de mis ojos/ Para asistir a la entrada de las imágenes// . . . // Soy yo Altazor el doble de mí mismo/ El que se mira obrar y se ríe del otro frente a frente/ El que cayó de las alturas de su estrella/ Y viajó veinticinco años/ Colgado al paracaídas de sus propios prejuicios/ Soy yo Altazor el del ansia infinita/ Del hambre eterno y descorazonado/ Carne labrada por arados de angustia/ ¿Cómo podré dormir mientras haya adentro tierras desconocidas?/ Problemas/ Misterios que se cuelgan a mi pecho/ Estoy solo/ La distancia que va de cuerpo a cuerpo/ Es tan grande como la que hay de alma a alma/ Solo/ Solo/ Solo/ Estoy solo parado en la punta del año que agoniza/ El universo se rompe en olas a mis pies/ Los planetas giran en torno a mi cabeza/ Y me despeinan al pasar con el viento que desplazan/ Sin dar una respuesta que llene los abismos/ Ni sentir este anhelo fabuloso que busca en la fauna del cielo/ Un ser materno donde se duerma el corazón/ Un lecho a la sombra del torbellino de enigmas/ Una mano que acaricie los latidos de la fiebre/ Dios diluído en la nada y el todo/ Dios todo y nada/ Dios en las palabras y en los gestos/ Dios mental/ Dios aliento/ Dios joven Dios viejo/ Dios pútrido/ lejano y cerca/ Dios amasado a mi congoja// . . . // Sigamos cultivando en el cerebro las tierras del error/ Sigamos cultivando las tierras veraces en el pecho/ Sigamos/ Siempre igual como ayer mañana y luego y después/ No/ No puede ser. Cambiemos nuestra suerte/ Quememos nuestra carne en los ojos del alba/ Bebamos la tímida lucidez de la muerte/ La lucidez polar de la muerte/ Canta el caos al caos que tiene pecho de hombre/ Llora de eco en eco por todo el universo/ Rodando con sus mitos entre alucinaciones/ Angustia de vacío en alta fiebre/ Amarga conciencia del vano sacrificio/ De la experiencia inútil del fracaso celeste/ Del ensayo perdido/ Y aún después que el hombre haya desaparecido/ Que hasta su recuerdo se queme en la hoguera del tiempo/ Quedará un gusto a dolor en la atmósfera terrestre/ Tantos siglos respirada por miserables pechos plañideros/ Quedará en el espacio la sombra siniestra/ De una lágrima inmensa/ Y una voz perdida aullando desolada/ Nada nada nada/ No/ No puede ser/ Consumamos el placer/ Agotemos la vida en la vida/ Muera la muerte infiltrada de rapsodias langurosas/ Infiltrada de pianos tenues y banderas cambiantes como crisálidas/ Las rocas de la muerte se quejan al borde del mundo/ El viento arrastra sus florescencias amargas/ Y el desconsuelo de las primaveras que no pueden nacer/ Todas son trampas/ Trampas del espíritu/ Transfusiones eléctricas de sueño y realidad/ Oscuras lucideces de esta larga desesperación petrificada en soledad/ Vivir vivir en las tinieblas/ Entre cadenas de anhelos tiránicos collares de gemidos/ Y un eterno viajar en los adentros de sí mismo/ Con dolor de límites constantes y vergüenza de ángel estropeado/ Burla de un dios nocturno/ Rodar rodar rotas las antenas en medio del espacio/ Entre mares alados y auroras estancadas// . . . // Eres tú tú angel caído/ La caída eterna sobre la muerte/ La caída sin fin de muerte en muerte/ Embruja el universo con tu voz/ Aférrate a tu voz embrujador del mundo/ Cantando como un ciego perdido en la eternidad// Anda en mi cerebro una gramática dolorosa y brutal/ La matanza continua de conceptos internos/ Y una última aventura de esperanzas celestes/ Un desorden de estrellas imprudentes/ Caídas de los sortilegios sin refugio/ Todo lo que se esconde y nos incita con imanes fatales/ Lo que se esconde en las frías regiones de lo invisible/ O en la ardiente tempestad de nuestro cráneo// La eternidad se vuelve sendero de flor/ Para el regreso de espectros y problemas/ Para el mirage sediento de las nuevas hipótesis/ Que rompen el espejo de la magia posible/ Liberación ¡Oh! sí liberación de todo/ De la propia memoria que nos posee/ De las profundas vísceras que saben lo que saben/ A causa de estas heridas que nos atan al fondo/ Y nos quiebran los gritos de las alas// La magia y el ensueño liman los barrotes/ La poesía llora en la punta del alma/ Y acrece la inquietud mirando nuevos muros/ Alzados de misterio en misterio/ Entre minas de mixtificación que abren sus heridas/ Con el ceremonial inagotable del alba conocida/ Todo en vano/ Dadme la llave de los sueños cerrados/ Dadme la llave del naufragio/ Dadme una certeza de raíces en horizonte quieto/ Un descubrimiento que no huya a cada paso/ O dadme un bello naufragio verde/ Un milagro que ilumine el fondo de nuestros mares íntimos/ Como el barco que se hunde sin apagar sus luces/ Liberado de este trágico silencio entonces/ En mi propia tempestad/ Desafiaré al vacío/ Sacudiré la nada con blasfemias y gritos/ Hasta que caiga un rayo de castigo ansiado/ Trayendo a mis tinieblas el clima del paraíso

Non Serviam

Mary Ann Caws, trans.

And it happens that one lovely morning, after a night of charming dreams and delicious nightmares, the poet rises and cries to Mother Nature: *Non serviam*.

At the top of his lungs, an echoing translator optimistically repeats: "I won't serve you."

Mother Nature was already going to strike down the young rebellious poet when, taking off his hat and making a gracious gesture, he exclaims: "You are an old charmer."

This *non serviam* remained engraved on a morning of the world's history. It was neither a capricious cry nor a superficial act of rebellion. It was the result of a whole revolution, the sum of multiple experiences.

The poet, fully conscious of his past and his future, cast against the world the declaration of his independence from Nature.

He no longer wanted to serve it like a slave.

The poet says to his brothers: "Until now we haven't done anything other than imitate the world in its appearances, we haven't created anything. What might have come from us which wasn't already here in front of us, in front of our eyes, surrounding them, defying our feet or our hands?

"We have sung Nature (which didn't concern her). Never have we created any proper realities, as she does and used to do when she was young and heavy with creative impulses.

"We have accepted, without reflecting further, the fact that there can be no other realities than those that surround us, and we haven't thought that we also could create realities in a world that would be ours, in a world awaiting its own flora and fauna. Fauna and flora that only the poet can create, through this particular gift that this same NATURE gave him and him alone."

Non serviam. I don't have to be your slave, Mother Nature: I shall be your master. You will use me; that's fine. I don't want it and cannot understand it: but I will use you, too. I'll have my trees, too, which won't be like yours, I'll have my mountains, I'll have my rivers and my oceans, I'll have my sky and my stars.

And you'll never be able to say to me: "This tree is not lovely, this heaven doesn't please me . . . I prefer mine."

I will answer you that my heavens and my trees are mine and not yours and that they don't have to look alike. Then you can no longer crush us with your exaggerated claims of being old, sensual, and senile. Now we are fleeing your traps.

Farewell, old charmer: farewell mother and stepmother, I will not deny you or curse you for all these years of slavery serving you. They were the most precious of teachings. The only thing I desire is never to forget your lessons, but I know I am old enough to go alone throughout the world, yours and mine.

A new era is beginning. Opening its jasper doors, I bend one knee to the ground and salute you respectfully.

Y he aquí que una buena mañana, después de una noche de preciosos sueños y delicadas pesadillas, el poeta se levanta y grita a la madre Natura: *Non serviam.*/ Con toda la fuerza de sus pulmones, un eco traductor y optimista repite en las lejanías: "No te serviré"./ La madre Natura iba ya a fulminar al joven poeta rebelde, cuando éste, quitándose el sombrero y haciendo un gracioso gesto, exclamó: "Eres una viejecita encantadora"./ Ese *non serviam* quedó grabado en una mañana de la historia del mundo. No era un grito caprichoso, no era un acto de rebeldía superficial. Era el resultado de toda una evolución, la suma de múltiples experiencias./ El poeta, en plena conciencia de su pasado y de su futuro, lanzaba al mundo la declaración de su independencia frente a la naturaleza./ Ya no quiere servirla más en calidad de esclavo./ El poeta dice a sus hermanos: "Hasta ahora no hemos hecho otra cosa que imitar al mundo en sus aspectos, no hemos creado nada. ¿Qué ha salido de nosotros que no estuviera antes parado ante nosotros, rodeando nuestros ojos, desafiando nuestros pies o nuestras manos?"/ "Hemos cantado a la naturaleza (cosa que a ella bien poco le importa). Nunca hemos creado realidades propias, como ella lo hace o lo hizo en tiempos pasados, cuando era joven y llena de impulsos creadores"./ "Hemos aceptado, sin mayor reflexión, el hecho de que no puede haber otras realidades que las que nos rodean, y no hemos pensado que nosotros también podemos crear realidades en un mundo nuestro, en un mundo que espera su fauna y su flora propias. Flora y fauna que sólo el poeta puede crear, por ese don especial que le dio la misma Madre Naturaleza a él y únicamente a él"./ *Non serviam*. No he de ser tu esclavo, madre Natura; seré tu amo. Te servirás de mí; está bien. No quiero y no puedo evitarlo; pero yo también me serviré de ti. Yo tendré mis árboles que no serán como los tuyos, tendré mis montañas, tendré mis ríos y mis mares, tendré mi cielo y mis estrellas./ Y ya no podrás decirme: "Ese árbol está mal, no me gusta ese cielo . . . , los míos son mejores"./ Yo te responderé que mis cielos y mis árboles son los míos y no los tuyos y que no tienen por qué parecerse. Ya no podrás aplastar a nadie con tus pretensiones exageradas de vieja chocha y reglona. Ya nos escapamos de tu trampa./ Adiós, viejecita encantadora; adiós, madre y madrastra, no reniego ni te maldigo por los años de esclavitud a tu servicio. Ellos fueron la más preciosa enseñanza. Lo único que deseo es no olvidar nunca tus lecciones, pero ya tengo edad para andar solo por estos mundos. Por los tuyos y por los míos./ Una nueva era comienza. Al abrir sus puertas de jaspe, hinco una rodilla en tierra y te saludo muy respetuosamente.

Mário de Andrade (1893–1945, Brazil)

De Andrade was the leader of the avant-garde movement that was pivotal in shaping Brazil's position on modernism. While serving as the director of the Institute of Arts at the University of the Federal District and working with the Ministry of Education and Culture in Rio de Janeiro, he continued to publish the poetry, short stories, novels, and essays that brought him fame as a modernist. He died in São Paulo. PRINCIPAL WORKS: *Paulicéia desvariada* (1922), *Primeiro andar* (1926), *Clã do jabuti* (1927), *Macunaíma* (1928)

Inspiration / Inspiração

Jack E. Tomlins, trans.

São Paulo! tumult of my life . . .
My loves are flowers made from the original . . .
Harlequinate! . . . Diamond tights . . . Gray and gold . . .
Light and mist. . . . Over and warm winter . . .
Subtle refinements without scandals, without jealousy . . .
Perfumes from Paris . . . Arys!
Lyrical slaps in the Trianon . . . Cotton field! . . .

São Paulo! tumult of my life . . .
Gallicism crying in the wilderness of America!

São Paulo! comoção de minha vida . . . / Os meus amores são flores feitas de
original! . . . / Arlequinal! . . . Trajes de losangos . . . Cinza e ouro . . . / Luz
e bruma . . . Forno e inverno morno . . . / Elegâncias sutis sem escândalos,
sem ciúmes . . . / Perfumes de Paris . . . Arys!/ Bofetadas líricas no Trianon . . .
Algodoal! . . . // São Paulo! comoção de minha vida . . . / Galicismo a berrar
nos desertos da América

Nocturne / Nocturno

Jack E. Tomlins, trans.

Lights from the Cambucí district on nights of crime . . .
Hot weather! . . . And the lowering thick clouds,
made from the bodies of moths,
rustling on the epidermis of the trees . . .

The trolleys swish like a skyrocket,
clicking their heels on the tracks,
spitting out an orifice into the whitewashed gloom . . .

In a perfume of heliotropes and puddles
whirls a flower-of-evil . . . She came from Turkestan;
and she has circles under her eyes that obscure souls . . .
She has smelted English pounds between her purple fingernails
in the bordellos of Ribeirão Preto . . .

      Get-a you roast-a yams! . . .

Lights from Cambucí on nights of crime . . .
Hot weather! . . . And the lowering thick clouds,
made from the bodies of moths,
rustling on the epidermis of the trees . . .

A golden mulatto
with hair like lustrous wedding rings . . .
Guitar! "When I die . . . " A heady scent of vanilla
pivots, falls, and rolls on the ground . . .
In the air undulates the nostalgia of the Bahias.

And the trolleys pass like a skyrocket,
clicking their heels on the tracks,
wounding an orifice in the whitewashed gloom . . .

      Get-a you roast-a yams! . . .

Hot weather! . . . Devils in the air
bodies of naked girls carrying . . .
The lassitude of the unforeseen forevers!
and souls awakening to the hands of embracing lovers!
Idyls under the plantain trees! . . .
And the universal jealousy with magnificent fanfares
in pink skirts and pink neckties! . . .

Balconies in the pulsating caution, where Iracemas blossom
for rendezvous with white warriors . . . White?
So let the dogs bark in the gardens!
No one, no one, no one cares!
They all embark on the Promenade of the Kisses of Adventure!
But I . . . Behind these garden fences of mine with pinwheels of jasmine,
remain while the alley ways of Cambucí in the free
of the freedom of parted lips! . . .

Harlequinate! Harlequinate!
The lowering thick clouds,
made from the bodies of moths,
rustling on the epidermis of the trees . . .
But on these my garden fences with pinwheels of jasmine,
the stars grow delirious in carnages of light,
and my sky is all a skyrocket of tears! . . .

And the trolleys trace like fireworks,
clicking their heels on the tracks,
jetting an orifice into the whitewashed gloom . . .

      Get-a you roast-a yams! . . .

Luzes do Cambuci pelas noites de crime . . . / Calor! . . . E as nuvens
baixas muito grossas,/ Feitas de corpos de mariposas,/ Rumorejando na
epiderme das árvores . . . // Gingam os bondes como um fogo de artifício./
Sapateando nos trilhos,/ Cuspindo um orifício na treva cor de cal . . . /

Num perfume de heliotrópios e de poças/ Gira uma flor-do-mal . . . Veio do Turquestã;/ E traz olheiras que escurecem almas . . . / Fundiu esterlinas entre as unhas roxas/ Nos oscilantes de Ribeirão Preto . . . // —Batat'assat'ô furnn! . . . // Luzes do Cambuci pelas noites de crime! . . . / Calor . . . E as nuvens baixas muito grossas,/ Feitas de corpos de mariposas,/ Rumorejando na epiderme das árvores . . . // Um mulato cor de ouro,/ Com uma cabeleira feita de alianças polidas . . . / Violão! "Quando eu morrer . . . " Um cheiro pesado de/ baunilhas/ Oscila, tomba e rola no chão . . . / Ondula no ar a nostalgia das Baías . . . // E os bondes passam como um fogo de artifício,/ Sapateando nos trihlos,/ Ferindo um orifício na treva cor de cal . . . // —Batat'assat'ô furnn! . . . // Calor! . . . Os diabos andam no ar/ Corpos de nuas carregando . . . / As lassitudes dos sempres imprevistos!/ E as almas acordando às mãos dos enlaçados!/ Idílios sob os plátanos! . . . / E o ciúme universal às fanfarras gloriosas/ De saias cor-de-rosa e gravatas cor-de-rosa! . . . // Balcões na cautela latejante, onde florem Iracemas/ Para os encontros dos guerreiros brancos . . . Brancos?/ E que os cães latam nos jardins!/ Ninguém, ninguém, ninguém se importa!/ Todos embarcam na Alameda dos Beijos da Aventura!/ Mas eu . . . Estas minhas grades em girândolas de jasmins,/ Enquanto as travessas do Cambuci nos livres/ Da liberdade dos lábios entreabertos! . . . // Arlequinal! Arleguinal!/ As nuvens baixas muito grossas,/ Feitas de corpos de mariposas,/ Rumorejando na epiderme das árvores . . . / Mas sobre estas minhas grades em girândolas de jasmins,/ O estelário delira em carnagens de luz,/ E meu céu é todo um rojão de lágrimas! . . . // E os bondes riscam como um fogo de artifício,/ Sapateando nos trilhos,/ Jorrando um orifício na treva cor de cal . . . // —Batat'assat'ô furnn! . . .

Excerpt from A Very Interesting Preface / Prefacio interessantíssimo

Justin Read, trans.

"Dan mon pays de file et d'or j'en suis la loi." —E. Verhaeren

Reader:
Delusionism is founded.

This preface, though interesting, useless.

. . . .

When I feel the great lyrical impulse, I write without thinking about everything my unconscious screams at me. Later I think: not only to correct, but also to justify what I wrote. Thus the reason for this Very Interesting Preface.

. . . .

The Brazilian language is among the richest, most sonorous. And it possesses the very admirable "ão."

Marinetti was great when he rediscovered the suggestive, associative, symbolic, universal, musical power of the word in liberty. By the way: old as Adam. Marrinetti erred: he made a system out of it. I use words in liberty. I feel that my own cup is too great for me, and yet I still drink from the cup of others.

I know how to construct ingenious theories. Want to see? Poetics are far behind music. The latter abandoned, perhaps even before the eighth century, the regimen of overly octavated melody, in order to enrich itself with the infinite resources of harmony. Poetics, with rare exceptions until the nineteenth century in France, has essentially been melodic. What I call "melodic verse" is essentially the same as musical melody: horizontal arabesque of consecutive voices (notes), containing intelligible thought.

. . . .

I'll explain it better:

Harmony: combination of simultaneous sounds.

Example:

"Trances . . . Battles . . . Arrows . . . Canticles . . . Populate!"

These words don't connect to one another. They do not form enumerations. Each one is a phrase, ellipses, reduced to the telegraphic minimum.

If I pronounce "Trances," as it does not form part of a phrase (melody), the word calls attention to its own insulation, and sits there vibrating, waiting for a phrase that would make it acquire meaning and THAT DOES NOT COME. "Battles" gives no conclusion whatsoever to "Trances"; and, under these same conditions, not causing us to forget the first word, sits there vibrating with it. The other voices do the same. Thus: instead of melody (grammatical phrasing) we have an arpeggiated chord, harmony—harmonic verse.

Yet, if instead of using only single words, I use single phrases: the same sensation of superimposition, not now of words (notes) but of phrases (melodies). Thus: poetic polyphony.

In this way *Paulicéia Desvairada* uses melodic verse:

"São Paulo is a stage of Russian dancers."

harmonic verse:

"The dogpack . . . The Exchange . . . Gambling habits . . . "

and poetic polyphony (one, and at times two or more, consecutive verses):

"Filth trembles . . . The fog snows . . . "

What do you think? Don't forget, though, that someone else will come to destroy everything I've constructed.

. . . .

You will easily notice that if grammar is sometimes deprecated in my poetry, it will not suffer grave insults in this very interesting preface. Preface: firecracker of my superego. Verses: landscape of my id.

. . . .

Nor did I wish to attempt a blind or insincere primitivism. In reality we are the primitives of a new age. Aesthetically: I went about to search, among the hypotheses of psychologists, naturalists, and critics regarding the primitives of past eras, for the most human and free expressions of art.

The past is a lesson to be contemplated, not reproduced.
"E tu che sé costí, anima viva,
Partiti da cotesti che son morti."

I searched for myself for many years. I found it. So don't tell me that I search for originality, because I've already discovered where it was, it belongs to me, it's mine.

. . . .

Besides, verses are not written to be read by mute eyes. Verses are sung, howled, wept. Whosoever doesn't know how to sing cannot read "Landscape No. 1." Whosoever doesn't know how to howl cannot read "Odium to the Bourgeois." Whoever doesn't know how to pray, cannot read "Religion." To scorn: "The Escalade." To suffer: "Sentimental Colloquy." To forgive: the canticle of the lullaby, one of the solos of My Madness in "The Enfibratures of Ipiranga." I won't continue. I'm repulsed by giving out the keys to my book. Whosoever will be like me has the key.

And now the poetic school, "Delusionism," is finished.

Next book I'll found another.

And I don't want disciples. In art: school = the imbecility of many for the vanity of one alone.

I could have cited Gorch Fock. Would have avoided the Very Interesting Preface. "Every song of liberation comes from the prison."

Leitor:/ Está fundado o Desvairismo// Este prefácio, apesar de interessante, inútil.// . . . // Quando sinto a impulsão lírica escrevo sem pensar tudo o que meu inconsciente me grita. Penso depois: não só para corrigir, como para justificar o que escrevi. Daí a razão deste Prefácio Interessantíssimo.// . . . // A língua brasileira é das mais ricas e sonoras. E possui o admirabilíssimo "ão".// Marinetti foi grande quando redescobriu o poder sugestivo, associativo, simbólico, universal, musical da palavra em liberdade. Aliás: velha como Adão. Marinetti errou: fez dela sistema. É apenas auxiliar poderosíssimo. Uso palavras em liberdade. Sinto que o meu copo é grande demais para mim, e inda bebo no copo dos outros.// Sei construir teorias engenhosas. Quer ver? A poética está muito mais atrasada que a música. Esta abandonou, talvez mesmo antes do século 8, o regime da melodia quando muito oitavada, para enriquecer-se com os infinitos recursos da harmonia. A poética, com rara exceção até meados do século 19 francês, foi essencialmente melódica. Chamo de verso melódico o mesmo que melodia musical: arabesco horizontal de vozes (sons) consecutivas, contendo pensamento inteligível.// . . . // Explico milhor:// Harmonia: combinação de sons simultâneos.// Exemplo:// "Arroubos . . . Lutas . . . Seta . . . Cantigas . . . Povoar!"// Estas palavras não se ligam. Não formam enumeração. Cada uma é frase, período elíptico, reduzido ao mímimo telegráfico.// Si pronuncio "Arroubos," como não faz parte de frase (melodia), a palavra chama a atenção para seu insulamento e fica vibrando, à espera duma frase que lhe faça adquirir significado e QUE NÃO VEM. "Lutas" não dá conclusão alguma a "Arroubos"; e, nas mesmas condições, não fazendo esquecer a primeira palavra, fica vibrando com ela. As outras vozes fazem o mesmo. Assim: em vez de melodia (frase gramatical) temos acorde arpejado, harmonia—o verso harmônico.// Mas, si em vez de usar só palavras soltas, uso frases soltas: mesma sensação de superposição, não já de palavras (notas) mas de frases (melodias). Portanto: polifonia poética.// Assim, em *Paulicéia Desvairada* usam-se o verso melódico:// "São Paulo é um palco de bailados russos"; o verso harmônico:// "A cainçalha . . . A Bolsa . . . As jogatinas . . . "; e a polifonia poética (um e às vezes dois e mesmo mais versos consecutivos)://"A engrenagem trepida . . . A bruma neva . . . "// Que tal? Não se esqueça porém que outro virá destruir tudo iso que construi.// . . . // Você perceberá com facilidade que si na minha poesia a gramática às vezes é desprezada, graves insultos não sofre neste prefácio interessantíssimo. Prefácio: rojão do meu eu superior. Versos: paisagem do meu eu profundo.// . . . // Não quis também tentar primitivismo vesgo e insincero. Somos na realidade os primitivos duma era nova. Esteticamente: fui buscar entre as hipóteses feitas por psicólogos, naturalistas e críticos sobre os primitivos das eras passadas, expressão mais humana e livre de arte.// O passado é lição para se meditar, não para reproduzir./ "E tu che sé costí, anima viva,/ Partiti da cotesti che son morti."// Por muitos anos procurei-me a mim mesmo. Achei. Agora não me digam que ando à procura de originalidade, porque já descobri onde ela estava, pertence-me, é minha./ . . . / Aliás versos não se escrevem para leitura de olhos mudos. Versos cantam-se, urram-se, choram-se. Quem não souber cantar não leia Paisagem no. 1. Quem não souber urrar não leia Ode ao Burguês. Qem não souber rezar, não leia Religião. Desprezar: A Escalada. Sofrer: Colloque Sentimental. Perdoar: a cantiga do berço, um dos solos de Minha Loucura, das Enfibraturas do Ipiranga. Não continuo. Repugna-me dar a chave de meu livro. Quem for como eu tem essa chave.// E está acabada a escola poética. "Desvairismo".// Próximo livro fundarei outra.// E não quero discípulos. Em arte: escola = imbecilidade de muitos para vaidade dum só.// Poderia ter citado Gorch Fock. Evitava o Prefácio Interessantíssimo. "Toda canção de liberdade vem do cárcere."

Pablo de Rokha (1894–1968, Chile)

Born Carlos Díaz Loyola in Licantén, Curicó province, central Chile, Rokha dedicated his life to the task of transgressing his native land's cultural and political conservatism. After being expelled from school for sharing blasphemous books—Rabelais, Voltaire, Nietzsche—with his classmates, he traveled to Santiago where he befriended Vicente Huidobro and other Vanguardist intellectuals of the time. He participated in the Anarchist movement and kept a fierce and mutual enmity with Pablo Neruda. One of the major poets of Chile, his relentless syntactical experiments and quest for a deeper truth have made him into a heroic model for younger poets. Rokha died by his own hand, leaving as a legacy a work of rupture and commotion that linked Chilean roots to elements typical of modernity: *Slapping the face with verses,/ being tragic, brutal, and forceful,/ and hanging a buffoonery/ over life and death.* PRINCIPAL WORKS: *Sátira* (1918), *Heroísmo sin alegría* (1927), *Neruda y yo* (1955)

Excerpt from Song of the Old Male / Canto del macho anciano
Molly Weigel, trans.

Sitting in the shade of a tomb,
or brandishing the great matrimonial ring, wounded as doves are that lose
    their leaves like agonies,
I scratch at my last dusks.

Like one who throws a whole book's worth of sorry bottles into the
    Sea-Ocean

or a huge stone of smoke however throwing terror at the cliffs of history
or maybe a dead bird that trickles a torrent of tears,
I'm launching the inexorable boulders of the preterite
against the black rampart.

And since everything is useless already,
since the rustling padlocks of the infinite crack into moldy hinges,
their attitude fills the earth with laments.

I listen to the skeleton regiment of the great twilight,
the great cardiac or demoniac or maniac twilight, of the furious old men,
the accusing trumpet of accumulated disgrace,
the monstrous slackening of all the flags, the terribly pallid space
of the executions by firing squad, the anguish
of the soldier who is dying in agony between uproar and blankets, five
        hundred open leagues
from the battlefield, and I sob like an old flag.

There are piles of iron tears, but inside winter the infernal fungus of
        personal cataclysm rears up, and catastrophes of cities
that died and are remote dust, howl.

The hour clothed in panic has arrived
in which all lives lack sense, lack destiny, lack style and guts,
lack direction, voice, lack
all the red and terrible of the enterprises or the epics or the ecumenical
        experiences,
that will justify existence as danger and as suicide; existing was an
        enormous myth, mistaken rupestrian, ruminant; and the only jackets of
        inexorable agape remain, the fallen laughter and the winter repentance
        of excesses,
in that ancient once with traces of saint and demon,
when I was handsome as a black bull and had women I loved
and the revolver of a man at my belt.

The glands fail
and the genital male intimidated by the furious I takes refuge in
depression or a drawing on towards evening,
scrapes for lost happiness in the garbage;
love grabbed us and squeezed us like desperate lemons,
I go licking its tenderness,
but that dissolves into eternity, gets lost in eternity, is destroyed in eternity
        and although I exist because I do battle and "my poetry is my militance,"
        all of eternity surrounds me menacing me and shouting from the other
        side.

Sentado a la sombra inmortal de un sepulcro,/ o enarbolando el gran
anillo matrimonial herido a la/ manera de palomas que se deshojan
como/ congojas,/ escarbo los últimos atardeceres.// Como quien arroja un
libro de botellas tristes a la/ Mar-Océano/ o una enorme piedra de humo
echando sin embargo/ espanto a los acantilados de la historia/ o acaso un
pájaro muerto que gotea llanto,/ voy lanzando los peñascos inexorables
del pretérito/ contra la muralla negra.// Y como ya todo es inútil,/ como
los candados del infinito crujen en goznes/ mohosos,/ su actitud llena
la tierra de lamentos.// Escucho el regimiento de esqueletos del gran/
crepúsculo,/ del gran crepúsculo cardíaco o demoníaco, maníaco de/ los
enfurecidos ancianos,/ la trompeta acusatoria de la desgracia acumulada,/
el arriarse descomunal de todas las banderas, el ámbito/ terriblemente
pálido/ de los fusilamientos, la angustia/ del soldado que agoniza entre
tizanas y frazadas, a/ quinientas leguas abiertas/ del campo de batalla, y
sollozo como un pabellón/ antiguo.// Hay lágrimas de hierro amontonadas,
pero/ por adentro del invierno se levanta el hongo infernal/ del cataclismo
personal/ y catástrofes de ciudades/ que murieron y son polvo remoto,
aúllan.// Ha llegado la hora vestida de pánico/ en la cual todas las vidas
carecen de sentido, carecen/ de destino, carecen de estilo y de espada,/
carecen de dirección, de voz, carecen/ de todo lo rojo y terrible de las
empresas o las/ epopeyas o las vivencias ecuménicas,/ que justificarán la
existencia como peligro y como/ suicidio; un mito enorme, equivocado/
rupestre, de rumiante/ fue el existir; y restan las chaquetas solas del ágape/
inexorable, las risas caídas y el/ arrepentimiento invernal de los excesos,/
en aquel entonces antiquísimo con rasgos de santo y/ de demonio,/ cuando
yo era hermoso como un toro negro y tenía las/ mujeres que quería/ y un
revólver de hombre a la cintura.// Fallan las glándulas/ y el varón genital
intimidado por el yo rabioso, se/ recoge a la medida del abatimiento o/
atardeciendo/ araña la perdida felicidad en los escombros;/ el amor nos
agarró y nos estrujó como a limones/ desesperados,/ yo ando lamiendo su
ternura,/ pero ella se diluye en la eternidad, se confunde en la/ eternidad,
se destruye en la eternidad y aunque/ existo porque batallo y "mi poesía
es mi/ militancia,"/ todo lo eterno me rodea amenazándome y gritando/
desde la otra orilla.

María Sabina (1894–1985, Mexico)

An oral poet shaman born in Huatla de Jiménez, in Oaxaca, Mexico, Sabina once said "I cure with language." "Language makes the dying return to life." In her oral autobiography, as told to Alvaro Estrada in 1975–1976, she tells about growing up in the mountains, raised in the ancient Mazatec tradition, where shamans ate the sacred mushrooms, *teonanácatl*, or "little children." With their help, she could "see from the origin," "arrive where the world is born," and heal the sick with her chants. Her words go well beyond the inherited tradition and have been called "a masterpiece of indigenous visionary poetry" (Homero Aridjis) and "a genius emerging from the soil of the communal, religious folk poetry" (Henry Munn). She grew up in poverty, and despite the world fame she received after her work was recorded in 1956 and made public by Robert Gordon Wasson, she died as she had lived, in her native Huatla. PRINCIPAL WORKS: *María Sabina and Her Mazatec Mushroom Velada* (1974), *Vida de María Sabina: la sabia de los hongos* (1977), *María Sabina: Her Life and Chants* (1981), *María Sabina, Selections* (2003)

Excerpt from Life / Vida

Henry Munn, trans.

I am wise even from within the womb of my mother. I am the woman of
    the winds, of the water, of the paths, because I am known in heaven,
    because I am a doctor woman.
I take *Little-One-Who-Springs-Forth* and I see God. I see him sprout from the
    earth. He grows and grows, big as a tree, as a mountain. His face is placid,
    beautiful, serene as in the temples. At other times, God is not like a man:
    he is the Book. A Book that is born from the earth, a sacred Book whose
    birth makes the world shake. It is the Book of God that speaks to me in
    order for me to speak. It counsels me, it teaches me, it tells me what I have
    to say to men, to the sick, to life. The Book appears and I learn new words.

. . . .

It is the voice of *Little-One-Who-Springs-Forth*. The God that lives in them
    enters my body. I cede my body and my voice to the *saint children*. They
    are the ones who speak; in the vigils they work in my body and I say:

    Because you gave me your clock
    Because you gave me your thought
    Because I am a clean woman
    Because I am a Cross Star woman
    Because I am a woman who flies

    I am the sacred eagle woman, says
    I am the lord eagle woman, says
    I am the lady who swims, says

Because I can swim in all forms
Because I am the launch woman
Because I am the sacred opossum
Because I am the lord opossum

I can be eagle, opossum, or woman clock. If I see them, I pronounce their
names.

The *children* turn into the Principal Ones. The Principal Ones appear as
well in the visions of the initiates. On their sacred table, they put clocks,
paper, books, communion wafers, stars, dew, or eagles . . .

The Principal Ones ask the initiates:

"What type of Wise One do you want to be? Do you want The Lords
of the Mountains, the masters of the places, to guide you, or do you
want God the Christ to guide you?"

Then the initiate chooses and tells the Principal Ones what he or she
prefers. At that moment the initiate receives the Book that contains
the Language the person has chosen.

I decided for God the Christ. I made it known to the Principal Ones. The
realm of the Principal Ones is the realm of abundance. There, there is
beer and music. When I'm in that realm I ask for beers to be served to
everyone. A Principal One serves the beer and then all together give
a toast. There are times when it isn't necessary to ask for beers, they
are within the reach of the hand. If music sounds, I dance as a partner
with the Principal Ones; and I also see that words fall, they come from
up above, as if they were little luminous objects falling from the sky.
The Language falls on the sacred table, falls on my body. Then with
my hands I catch word after word. That happens to me when I don't
see the Book. . . . And I sing:

With the Virgin Magdalene
With the Virgin Guadalupe
With Lord Santiago

Because I am the water that looks, says
Because I am the woman wise in medicine, says
Because I am the woman herbalist, says
Because I am the woman of the medicine, says
Because I am the woman of the breeze, says
Because I am the woman of the dew, says

. . . .

I come with my thirteen hummingbirds
Because I am the sacred hummingbird, says
Because I am the Lord hummingbird, says
Because I bring my clean sucker, says

Because I bring my healthy sucker, says
Because I bring my bamboo tube, says
My bamboo with dew, says
My fresh bamboo, says

And it's that . . .
I am the woman Book that is beneath the water, says
I am the woman of the populous town, says
I am the shepherdess who is beneath the water, says
I am the woman who shepherds the immense, says
I am the shepherdess and I come with my shepherd, says
Because everything has its origin
And I come going from place to place from the origin . . .

. . . .

And it's that in the middle is Language. On this shore, in the middle, and on
the other shore is Language. With the mushrooms I see God, then I sing:

Because I am the God Star Woman
The Cross Star Woman
Because I can swim in the immense
Because I am a well-prepared woman
Because I have my people healed

From the Folkways Chant

I am a woman born
I am a woman fallen into the world
I am a law woman
I am a woman of thought
I am a woman who gives life
I am a woman who reanimates
I have the heart of Christ, says
I have the heart of the Virgin
I have the heart of Christ
I have the heart of the Father
I have the heart of the Old One
It's that I have the same soul, the same heart as the santo, as the
    santa, says
You, my Mother Shepherdess, says
You, my Father, says
Living Mother, Mother who sways back and forth, says
Mother of sap, Mother of the dew, says
Mother who gave birth to us, Mother who is present, says
Mother of sap, Mother of milk, says
You, Mother of sap, Mother of Milk, says

Green Mother, Mother of clarity, says
Budding Mother, Mother of offshoots, says
Green Mother, Mother of clarity, says
Ah, Jesus Christ, says
Ah, Jesus, says
Our Green Father, says
Our Father of clarity, says
Budding Mother, Mother of offshoots, says
Green Mother, Mother of clarity, says
Ah, Jesus Christ, says
Our woman santo, says
Our woman santa, says
Our spirit woman, says
Our woman of light, says
She is a woman of the day, says
Our woman of light, says
She is a woman of the day, says
She is a woman of light, says
She is a spirit woman, says

Soy sabia desde el vientre mismo de mi madre, que soy mujer de los vientos, del agua, de los caminos, porque soy conocida en el cielo, porque soy mujer doctora. Tomo *pequeño que brota* y veo a Dios. Lo veo brotar de la tierra. Crece y crece, grande como un árbol, como un monte. Su rostro es plácido, hermoso, sereno como en los templos. Otras veces, Dios no es como un hombre: es el Libro. Un libro que nace de la tierra, Libro sagrado que al estar siendo parido, el mundo tiembla. Es el Libro de Dios, que me habla para que yo hable. Me aconseja, me enseña, me dice lo que tengo que decir a los hombres, a los enfermos, a la vida. El Libro aparece y yo aprendo nuevas palabras.// . . . // Es la voz del *pequeño que brota*. El Dios que vive en ellos entra en mi cuerpo. Yo cedo mi cuerpo y mi voz a los *niños santos*. Ellos son los que hablan, en las veladas trabajan en mi cuerpo y yo digo:// *Porque me diste tu reloj/ Porque me diste tu pensamiento/ Porque soy mujer limpia/ Porque soy mujer estrella cruz/Porque soy mujer que vuela// Soy la mujer águila sagrada,/Soy la mujer águila dueña,/Soy la dueña que sabe nadar// Porque puedo nadar en lo grandioso/Porque puedo nadar en todas formas/Porque soy la mujer lancha/Porque soy la tlacuache sagrada/Porque soy la tlacuache dueña//* Puedo ser águila, tlacuache o mujer reloj. Si los veo, pronuncio sus nombres. Los niños se convierten en Seres Pricipales. Los Seres Principales aparecen en las visiones de los iniciados. Ponen sobre su mesa sagrada relojes, papeles, libros, hostias, estrellas, rocío o águilas . . . Los Seres Principales preguntan a los iniciados: _¿Qué tipo de sabio quieres tú ser? ¿Quieres que te guíen los Señores de las Montañas, los dueños de los lugares o quieres que te guíe Dios Cristo?-. Entonces el iniciado escoge y le dice a los Seres Principales

lo que prefiere. En ese momento, el iniciado recibe un libro que contiene
el Lenguaje que ha escogido. Yo me decidí por Dios Cristo. Así se los hice
saber a los Seres Principales. El *lugar* de los Seres Principales es el *lugar*
de la abundancia. Allí hay cervezas y música. Cuando estoy en ese *lugar,*
pido que sirvan cervezas para todos. Un Ser Principal sirve las cervezas y
entonces todos juntos brindamos. Hay veces en que no es necesario pedir
las cervezas, están al alcance de la mano. Si suena la música, yo bailo en
pareja con los Seres Principales y tambien *veo* que el Lenguaje cae, viene de
arriba, como si fuesen pequeños objetos luminosos que con fuerza caen del
cielo. El Lenguaje cae sobre la *mesa* sagrada, cae sobre mi cuerpo. Entonces
atrapo con mis manos palabra por palabra. Esto me sucede cuando no veo
el Libro . . . Y yo canto:// *Con la Virgen Magdalena/ Con la Virgen Guadalupe/*
Con el Señor Santiago// Porque soy el agua que mira/Porque soy la mujer sabia en
medicina/Porque soy la mujer yerbera/Porque soy la mujer de la medicina// Porque
soy la mujer de la brisa/Porque soy la mujer del rocío// . . . // Vengo con mis trece
chuparrosas/Porque soy la chuparrosa sagrada/Porque soy la chuparrosa dueña/
Porque traigo mi chupador limpio/Porque traigo mi chupador sano/Porque traigo
mi carrizo/Mi carrizo con sereno/Mi carrizo fresco// Y es que . . . // *Soy la mujer-*
libro que está debajo del agua/Soy la mujer de la población grande/Soy la pastora
que está debajo del agua/Soy la mujer que pastorea lo grandioso/Soy pastora y
vengo con mi pastor/Porque todo tiene su origen/Y yo vengo recorriendo los lugares
desde el origen . . . // . . . // Y es que en el medio está el Lenguaje. En esta
orilla, en el medio y en la otra orilla está el Lenguaje. Con los *niños* veo a
Dios, entonces yo canto://*Porque soy la mujer estrella Dios/ La mujer estrella*
cruz/Porque puedo nadar en lo grandioso/Porque soy mujer dispuesta/Porque tengo
a mi gente sanada// . . . // De la velada grabada por Gordon Wasson, 1957:
Soy mujer que ha hecho parir/Soy mujer que ha ganado/Soy mujer de asuntos
de autoridad//Soy mujer de pensamiento/Mujer de sentarse/ Mujer de pararse/El
corazón de Cristo traigo yo/El corazón de nuestra virgen traigo yo/ El corazón de
nuestro padre traigo yo/ El corazón de Cristo traigo yo/ /El corazón del padre traigo
yo/El corazón del tata traigo yo/Es por eso que digo que traigo ese corazón/Santo
traigo yo, santa traigo yo/tú, madre pastora, dice/Tú eres la madre, dice/Madre
que tiene vida/Madre que se mece, dice/Madre de brisa/Madre de rocío, dice/Madre
que pare/Madre que se pone en pie, dice/Madre de leche/ Madre con pechos, dice/
Tú, madre de leche/Madre de pechos, dice/Madre fresca/Madre tierna, dice/Madre
que crece/ Madre verde, dice/Madre fresca,Madre tierna, dice/Ah, es Jesucristo,
dice/Ah, es Jesús, dice/Nuestro padre fresco, dice/Nuestro padre tierno,dice/Madre
que crece,madre verde, dice/Madre fresca,madre tierna,dice/Ah, es Jesucristo, dice/
Nuestra mujer santo,dice/ Nuestra mujer santa, dice/ Nuestra mujer espíritu, dice/
Nuestra mujer de luz,dice/ Es mujer día, dice/ Es mujer día, dice/ Nuestra mujer de
luz, dice/Es mujer día,dice/Nuestra mujer espíritu, dice

Juan L. Ortiz (1896–1978, Argentina)

Born in Puerto Ruiz, Gualeguay, in Argentina, Ortiz spent much of childhood traveling and studying. In 1913, he began his university studies in Buenos Aires at the Universidad de La Plata, where he mixed with prominent intellectuals and writers. He returned to Gualeguay in 1915 and, while working in the registry office, began to write. Early work reflects his libertarian politics and his concern with social justice. Stylistically, Ortiz often wrote in free verse, employing clear and brief symbols, along with a nostalgic lyrical rhythm dedicated to nature. In 1942, he settled in Paraná, where he became extremely influential among young students and poets. PRINCIPAL WORKS: *La rama hacia el este* (1940), *El alma y las colinas* (1956), *En el aura del sauce* (1971)

Village on the River / Pueblo costero

William Rowe, trans.

See that dark-skinned boy who seems to look
    out from another world,
the white of his eyes whiter, or maybe yellowish.
Ah, the little girl already wearing glasses, leading him or carrying him,
the lightest clay herself upon even lighter willow-sticks.
See the other girl in a little cart, so fragile,
the monstruous flower of her knees almost terminal,
led by brothers and sisters, smaller than her, to the edge of what star?
See, a ten-year-old, with the pale head of an impossible fish
which all but transfixes you through the very ears . . .
See that old branch that survived 'the quarries',
bent back over another short branch stuck in the ground
with a cadence that quickens:
upon it and others like it, turned to anonymous ash, there,
and not upon stones,
a few winged houses sprang up and a few piles of banknotes . . .
and with their blood, ah, so red, a 'mysterious' alchemy:
a few names were polished and in time became brass plates . . .
See that dry, dry ghost emerging from a long night of glass . . .
sexless, in spite of the 'skirt'
and the woolen cloth flowing over the line of the shoulders . . .
ah, the voice out of the deep cavern of age
and long resistance, perhaps, to exposure and hunger . . .

Ah see, for all that, a tenacity in them as the spikes
of a thornbush push upwards or into someone between broken branches . . .
But see, this metal canoeist with more oil on him than light
standing in the middle of the street, like Adam, as if giving rules to the
    afternoon . . .

And this washerwoman dense but with feet of feathers
almost dancing with her washbowls upon the rug of her life . . .
And those little girls who sometimes expose their smile like the water,
leaning lightly over an unbelievable river:
and only, only their dark years or the slightly twisted agate of their eyes,
or that waiting at the door when other jewels start to fly, suddenly . . .
And these young men with nothing embracing the last ripples like their
    girls,
after wounding the other ones, all day long, among the islands . . .
And this fisherman, silent, back from a fever of silence
still loitering, nocturnal, over fatty mother-of-pearl and embers,
then sleeping, finally, at first touch, like a water-lilly bloom . . .
And these boys with their ark on dry land, traveling with their small
    animals,
in a counterpoint of glass and tin, that rises up . . .
until, upon nighttime grass, singing, from there
they too, holding hands, go round the world, barefoot . . .
And this 'granny' wrapped all over still looking for the veils of the instant
so as to bare its silver and dissolve it into soap lilies, squatting . . .
while her chickens, nearby, go crazy, blonde and blue . . .
And this mother who carries stones from the riverbank until nighttime,
and crushes her life with them, to make the table less poor,
but not her smile which is everyone's in an offering composed of jasmine . . .
And this other one, who is discrete and who tempers her own soul more
    than she does the oven,
and out of it comes a bloom of dough that 'keeps you company', as they say
    around here . . .

And these little devils, arrows over unknown negation,
summoned as wings by the smallest event,
with all the iridescence of amazement and all the faces of tea,
and the hair, all of it, more joyful, and the scant clothing even more fallen
    down . . .

Where do they find all these children of the coast
in spite of everything, that gentle strength,
profoundly gentle, against the dark humiliations that seem to sleep?
Thrown against things by people who don't know,
things give them milk and breath like mothers.
(Oh, for sure, in the adventure of bread or silent nightmare,
at the mercy of the air's worst weapons and the earth's worst humours
and the strange, strange river that would like to rise up and take them
    back to the earth,
leaving them floating between two rejections, under the *Siriris* of the
    night . . .)

No-one thought about the power of those laps,
rich with white rays in mysterious exhalation,
a got not to be invoked, an anointment not to be asked for, for the beings
 held close to them.

But could that have been taken away from them too?
And there they are, in the fluids of the river's time
in melodies which are not heard but which are pure and which give the
 order of rituals.
There they are, separate or fused with the delicate time of willows,
or with the love of that which is theirs, unbelievable in decorum or honour
 beneath the winds,
unbelieveable in keenness of sense and in attention, even in the light of
 certain flowers . . .
There they are, pure of pure soil, in line with canes of sunlight,
standing, in nothing itself, under the same deep sun . . .
There they are, with blade of hidden steel and hidden coal,
at the 'point of anguish, unspeakable and absurd', of the moment without
 exit . . .
And there they are, in the great exit, which they will find,
with this blade aligned, ay! with all the rest, for the day without end,
in the column which will march, enormous, to the other side of the star:
a bramble on fire this time, burning from itself, 'upon the air of an
 accordion' . . .

Ved ese niño oscuro que mira como desde otro mundo,/ el blanco de los ojos
más blanco, medio amarillo, mejor./ Oh, la niñita ya de anteojos que lo guía
o lo alza,/ barro leve ella misma sobre palillos aún más leves./ Ved aquélla en
un carrito, tan frágil,/ con esa flor monstruosa de las rodillas casi terminales,/
conducida por los suyos, más pequeños, hacia la orilla de qué estrella?/ Ved
esa cabeza pálida, de diez años, de pescado imposible,/ que por poco os
fijará desde los mismos oídos . . . / Ved esa rama vieja, sobreviviente de "las
canteras,"/ doblada sobre otra rama corta que se hinca/ con una cadencia
cada vez más seguida:/ sobre ella y sus iguales, anónima ceniza, allá,/ más
bien que sobre las piedras,/ se elevaron algunas casas aladas y algunas pilas
de billetes . . . / y con su sangre, ay, tan roja, alquimia "misteriosa,"/ se
azularon algunos apellidos que luego dieron chapas por ahí . . . / Ved ese
fantasma seco, seco, salido de una noche de vidrios, larga . . . / sin sexo, sí, a
pesar de la "falda"/ y de la lana fluida sobre el filo de los hombros . . . / oh,
su voz venida de la caverna de la edad, profunda,/ desde aquellos desafíos,
quizás, a la intemperie y al hambre . . . // Ya en ésos, ved, con todo, un no
sé qué tenaz de zarza/ aguda hacia arriba o hacia alguien por entre los ramos
abatidos . . . / Mas ved este canoero de metal con más óleo que la luz,/
plantado en medio de la calle, adánico, como para dar reglas a la tarde . . . /

Y esta lavandera densa pero de pies de plumas listas/ danzando casi con
los tachos sobre el tapiz de su vida . . . / Y estas muchachitas que sacan su
risa a veces como el agua,/ ligeramente inclinadas sobre un río increíble:/
sólo, soplo, sus años morenos, o el ágata un poco oblicua de los ojos,/ o esa
espera en el portón cuando empiezan a volar, súbitas, otras joyas . . . / Y estos
mozos sin nada que abrazan las ondas últimas lo mismo que a novias,/ luego
de herir las otras, durante todo el día, por las islas . . . / Y este pescador de
silencio que llega de una fiebre de silencio,/ y aún demora, nocturno, sobre
los nácares grasos y la leña,/ para abrir su sueño, al fin, al primer contacto,
igual que un irupé . . . / Y estos chicos del arca "en seco," viajando con sus
bestezuelas,/ en un contrapunto de cristal y de hojalata, que sube . . . / hasta
que, sobre la hierba anochecida, de ahí, cantando,/ ellos también, tomados
de la mano, dan la vuelta al mundo, descalcitos . . . / Y esta "abuela" toda
envuelta que busca todavía los velos de la hora/ para destocar su plata y
diluirla entre lirios de jabón, en cuclillas . . . ./ mientras sus polluelos, cerca,
enloquecen blondas ya celestes . . . / Y esta madre que acarrea hasta la noche
piedras de la orilla,/ y quiebra su vida con ellas, luego, para la mesa menos
mala,/ pero no su sonrisa, ah, de todos, en una ofrenda unida de jazmín . . . /
Y esta otra, discreta, que templa su propia alma más que el horno,/ y así sale
cocida esa flor de la harina que "hace la compañía" por aquí . . . // Y estos
diablillos que son flechas sobre la negación desconocida,/ evocados como
alas por el suceso más ligero,/ con todos los iris del asombro y todos los
rostros del té,/ y los cabellos, todos, más alegres, y las breves ropas más caídas
. . . // ¿En dónde todos ellos, todos estos hijos de la costa,/ se nutren, a pesar
de todo, de esa fuerza gentil,/ profundamente gentil, contra la humillación
oscura que parece dormir?/ Arrojados hacia las cosas por los otros que no
saben,/ las cosas, madres, les dan de su leche y de su hálito./ (Oh, cierto, en
la aventura del pan o en la muda pesadilla,/ a merced de las peores armas
del aire y de los humores peores de la tierra/ y del río extraño, extraño, que
quisiera, salido, devolverlos a aquéllos,/ dejándolos así a medio flotar, entre
los dos rechazos, bajo los siriríes de la noche . . .)/ No se supo, no, pensar
en los poderes de esos regazos,/ ricos de rayos blancos en la misteriosa
espiración,/ numen que no se invoca, y unción que no se pide, para los seres
a ellos acogidos.// Pero hubieran podido quitarles también esto?/ Y helos ahí,
en los fluidos de los tiempos del río/ como en melodías que no se oyen pero
que ordenan, puras, los ritos./ Helos ahí, ajenos o fundidos a las horas leves
de los sauces,/ o al amor de lo suyo increíble de decoro o de honor bajo los
vientos,/ increíble de gusto y de atención, aún, en la luz de algunas flores . . . /
Helos ahí, puros del suelo puro, en la línea de las cañas del sol,/ de pie, en
la propia nada, por el mismo sol profundo . . . / Helos ahí, con ese acero de
los hierros secretos y de los carbones secretos,/ sobre el "punto de angustia,
inefable y absurdo," del minuto sin salida . . . / Y helos ahí, en la grande, en
la gran salida que hallarán,/ con ese acero alineado, guay, con los demás,
para la jornada sin fin,/ en la columna que irá, enorme, hasta el otro lado de

la estrella:/ zarza en marcha esta vez, desde sí misma ardiendo "sobre un aire de acordeón . . . "

Why? / Por qué?

William Rowe, trans.

Why is elegy
today
a green
of a first of September
that almost cannot be seen?

Why in the nothing of yellow
light
melancholy, or what?
and you do not know if it is going away
or waiting?

Why does the abyss call itself,
if something that is a spirit of small leaves
wants to give wings to the abyss?

O afternoon,
that is and is not,
at what diaphanous limit?
Will you tell me or will
that small bird there,
in what there?
which strangely survives,
o sweetly, strangely,
this gold, this silence?

Por qué la elegía/ es hoy/ un verde de 1° de setiembre/ que casi no se ve?//
Por qué en la nada de la luz/ amarilla/ una melancolía, o qué?/ que no
se sabe si se va/ o espera?// Por qué el abismo llama a sí,/ si algo que es
un espíritu de hojillas/ quiere dar alas al abismo?// Oh tarde,/ tarde que
eres y no eres,/ en qué límite/ de cristal?:/ me lo dirás tú o me lo dirá/ ese
pajarillo de allá,/ de qué allá?/ que extrañamente sobrevive,/ oh, dulce,
extrañamente,/ al oro del silencio?

Gamaliel Churata (1897–1969, Peru)

A poet, journalist, and ideologist, Churata was born as "Arturo Pablo Peralta Miranda" in Puno, a remote region of Peru mainly inhabited by indigenous peoples. He received formal education only at the elementary school level. He and his brother Alejandro Peralta founded the cultural magazine *Boletín Titikaka* and the group *Orkopata*, which vindicated Andean culture by incorporating it into the Vanguardist schools and remaking it with elements of modernity. He went into exile in Bolivia for political reasons and passed away in Lima. His work is finally being valued through studies such as those by Cynthia Vich, who considers it "the bible of Andean culture." Using a baroque Spanish mixed with Quechua and Aymara, and avoiding European logocentrism, Churata developed a conception of the world based on Andean cosmogony, wherein everything originates in the duality of *hanan* and *hurin*—the world above and the world below, or the Andean yin and yang.
PRINCIPAL WORKS: *El pez de oro* (1957), *Antología y valoración* (1971)

Excerpt from Khirkhilas

Jen Hofer, trans.

1

No; it couldn't be like that, dear girl; if my dreams were lacking in eyelashes.
I'm accustomed to eating what pleases me; and never over my fires
has anything been cooked that was not to the liking of my palate. In
the paskhana where people bustle to and fro, all eyes astounded when
arrived the dinner hour had, and in my chuhwa atlanta the paskhañero
arranged two skeletons and a well-endowed cruet, from which he
seasoned those skeletal forms and devoured them in silence; since, well,
he felt that to swallow such a potion, he had to do it with feeling, or the
potion would potion-pot itself. I realized that astonishment drove the
paskhañantes and paskhañeros crazy; that they might never have seen
a man devouring skeletons. It seems to me that, even then, their crazed
eyes scrutinized me with gazes that nailed their khausillus to me. And
what about me?! It wasn't necessary either, in the middle of stuffing
myself, for me to set myself the task of explaining that a Suchi skeleton
is just as nutritious as the Suchi itself — or even more so; and that
their dripping flesh makes the chin drip with drool. The paskhañantes,
however, from time to time exchanged their astonishment for terror, as
it was when the skeletal ones pulled Chullpaltullus out of my ears and
made blunders of them, or on the contrary, on either side of my eyes,
shook their tail-parts, fanning out a few tears.

"This man," they said to themselves "is an inkaika insanity; he's devoured
by grief, and he eats the dead!"

No; it couldn't be like that, dear girl.

1 Nó; no pudo ser así, niña querida; si mis sueños carecían de pestañas.
Estoy acostumbrado a comer lo que me agrada; y nunca en mis fogones
se cocinó algo no gustoso a mi paladar. En la paskhana de los que se
tra-jinan, todos ojos atónitos cuando la hora llegada de la cena era, y
en mi chuhwa atlanta el paskhañero disponía dos esqueletos y alcuza
bien pro-vista, con la que sazonaba los esqueleticos y en silencio les
devoraba; pues bien que sentía que para deglutir potaje tal, había que
poner senti-miento, o el potaje se potearía. Dábame cuenta que el asombro
tornaba locos a paskhañantes y paskhañeros; que nunca vieran hombre
devoran-do esqueletos. Me parece que, aún entonces, sus enloquecidos
ojos escu-driñábanme con miradas que me pegaban sus khausillus. ¡A mí
qué! Tampoco en medio del hartazgo había de ponerme a explicar que el
es-queleto del Suchi es tanto o más nutritivo que el Suchi mismo; y que sus
babosas carnes hacen babas de las barbas.Los paskhañantes, sin embar-go,
de rato en rato trocaban el asombro en terror; y era cuando los es-queleticos
sacaban Chullpaltullus por mis orejas y les hacían pifias; o de no, por uno
y otro lados de mis ojos, agitaban sus caudales abanicando unas lágrimas.
—¡Este hombre—se decían—es una locura inkaica; está enluta-do, y come
muertos! Nó; no pudo ser así, querida niña.

4

I understand it's the sky-lake your eyes gaze upon, dear girl. I will direct
   you without eyes; as their innards are maternal to me. You'll see: when
   Mama Margacha, carrying me on her back, swaddled and fastened tight,
   her skirt heaved up until it almost reached her little hole, she showed
   with blessed immodesty her plump legs, which shortly got bit by the
   water and its icy avidity, and, tilting me, sat down on the raft that would
   take us to the islands; you winked at me with your bright star throbbing
   between variegated clouds and utterly absorbed I watched you with the
   water's pupil. My mother might resist the *India*'s taking her llokhallo,
   but neither llokhallo nor *India* managed to break from one another. And
   that night, for the length of the crossing, I felt her tenderness more like a
   nipple, and her nipple more dark-skinned.

Ay, dear girl: childhood the only thing that never ends for an old man.

How the breeze was blowing the cattails, with the *charango*-strums of Sirens
   and of the Waksallu, deaf lullaby. And if in the lake up above the stars
   were blazing, in the sky down below the urpillas were cooing and lulling,
   when I felt I wasn't feeling anything . . . But to feel everything I saw
   it: I felt the opaline of seeing the radiance my waves spewed out and
   their blazing eyes that spewed out stars. Have you forgotten it, perhaps?
   Mama Margacha lulled and cooed me on her lap, smashed halfway to
   smithereens by sleepiness; and stamping like a horse, the one with the
   algae-hairy hand shook himself; in the waters he came out dripping;

me took, so without time, what time was left for me to cry, as I already found myself lying in your nest of sahkas and thousands of Ispis and Kharachis . . .

"Tyrol!" they sang to me. "Tyrol! Tyrol! Tyroly! Tyroly! Tyroly! . . . Tyrol! Tyrol! . . . "

They were singing like pheskhos; they were dancing like hunkhallas.

A toy more po' shall never be seen, dear girl.

4 Comprendo que en el cielo-lago tus ojos miren, niña querida. Yo te con-duciré sin ojos; que me son maternales sus entrañas. Verás: cuando Ma-ma Margacha, llevándome a la espalda, fajado y sujeto, la pollera se al-zó hasta bien cerca del hoyuelo, mostró con beato impudor las rollizas piernas, que presto mordieron el agua y su avidez helada, y, empinándo-me tomó asiento en la balsa que nos llevaría a las islas; tú me guiñaste con el lucero que palpitaba entre los celajes y yo absorto te miré con la pupila del agua. Mi madre resistiera a que la india llevara a su llokhallo; pero mi llokhallo ni india lograban fracturarse. Y esa noche, al largor de la travesía, sentí más pezón su ternura y más trigueño su pezón. Ay, querida niña: la infancia lo único que acaba nunca para el viejo. Como soplaba el vientecillo de los totorales, con él llegaban cha-rangueos de Sirenas y la del Waksallu sorda canción de cuna. Y si en el lago de arriba abrasaban las estrellas; en el cielo de abajo arrullaban las urpillas, cuando sentí que no sentía nada . . . Pero de sentir todo lo vi: sen-ti el cárdeno de ver el resplandor que escupían mis olas y sus abrasados ojos que escupían estrellas. ¿Lo has olvidado, acaso? Mama Margacha en el regazo me arrullaba, a medio hecha añicos por el sueño; y piafante, se sacudió el de la velluda mano de algas; dentro las aguas se salió chorreando; tomóme, tan sin tiempo, que tiempo me dejó para chillar; que ya me vi acostado en tu nidal de sakhas y millares de Ispis y Kharachis . . . —¡Tirol! —me cantaban—¡Tirol! ¡Tirol! ¡Tirol! ¡Tirolí! ¡Tirolí! . . . ¡Tirol! ¡Tirol! . . . Cantaban como pheskhos; danzaban como hunkhallas. Nunca vieran juguete más pogre, niña querida.

5

That the syrup of your mucilage, dear girl, now makes the bread bitter. How so, the po' mamala is crying, do you hear?

"Ay, ay, ay, guagüitay!"

And the immense Aeda reclining, the cross between her cold hands, the long cold candles in blazing crepe, the sublime lyre reclining, mute deity, speaking atayachado, just a little theorbo and no pututu at all, in stuccoes, frets, and dissolute volutes, the soul curled cozily. With no

khepi for the journey, no mama to love, no kuka for the song, no khawa
in the embers . . .

"Ay, ay, ay, guagüitay!"

This one too died of America: ah, death of the dead!

This one, ashamed he was of his mama, and of the Kuka-mama; this one,
who took care of his Achachila and cursed it as a louse. This one, to be
silenced made via whip the whip of his louse; and now the louse, opa,
brokenness is in his tongue, and does not open it: walls in his passage
to the Chullpa. With his lakhatos Corybants do not dance; not in his
carrion can Pan's magic Siringa be heard; Hyperion swallows sad lettuce . . .
Does the Sistrum play for him, and does she wail for him, the Nymph,
daughter of Peneo? . . . Noo! . . . But much less does divine Phoebus
hand him his laurel. Did Medusa petrify mountains for him? Neither the
Dragon who doesn't sleep, nor the golden Hesperides macerate for him
in gold the juice of the apples made of gold. Does Euterpe ferment him?
Melpomene suffer him? Does sweet Erato sing for him? Great Tritonia
does not know him; provident Hippocrene does not nourish him . . .
And he never wanted to see that the Sirens were in the Pakcha, and in
the Sirens' *charango* were the songs.

"Ay, ay, ay, guagüitay!"

Beggar: you beg for gold and gold overcomes you.

Not your fault. It was fear of the *indio* and the *indio's* fear; fear of your
mother and your mother's fear.

5 Que el almíbar de tu mucílago, niña querida, ya pone amargo el pan.
¿Cómo, la pobre mamala llora, oyes? —¡Ayayay, guagüitay! Y el inmenso
aeda, yacente, la cruz entre las frías manos, los fríos cirios en los crespones
que arden, yacente el sublime lírida, divo mudo, atayachado hablante, poco
tiorba y nada de pututu, en estucos, grecas y volutas disolutas, acurrucada
el alma. Sin khepi para el viaje, sin mama para amar, sin kuka para el canto,
sin khawa en el rescoldo . . . —¡Ayayay, guagüitay! Este también murió de
América: ¡ah, muerte de muertos! Este, vergüenza hubo de su mama y de la
Kuka-mama; éste, el que velaba su Achachila y le maldecía piojo. Este, que
enmudecer hizo a lá-tigo el látigo de su piojo; y hora el piojo, opa, quebranto
es de su lengua, y no la abre: le tapia su boquete de la Chullpa. Con sus
lakhatos no dan-zan Coribantes; nó en su carroña se oye de Pan la mágica
Siringa; Hipe-rión traga lechuga triste . . . ¿Tañe el Sistro por él, y le plañe,
la Ninfa, hi-ja de Peneo? . . . ¡Nii! . . . Pero menos que el divino Febo le ceda
su laurel. ¿La Medusa le petrificó montaña? Ni el Dragón que no duerme, ni
las doradas Hespérides, maceran para él en oro el jugo de las pomas de oro.
¿Euterpe le fermenta? ¿Melpómene le sufre? ¿Canta para él la dulce Era-to?

La magna Tritonia no le sabe; la próvida Hipocrene no le nutre . . . Y nunca quiso ver que en la Pakcha estaban las Sirenas; y en el charango de las Sirenas las canciones. —Ayayay, guagüitay! Mendigo: mendigas oros y te rinde el oro. Nó tuya la culpa. Fueron el miedo al indio y el miedo del indio; miedo a tu madre y el miedo de tu madre.

Raúl Bopp (1898–1984, Brazil)

Born in Tupancireta, Brazil, Bopp was a member, together with Oswald de Andrade of the Verde-Amarillo and Antropofagia Brazilian modernist movements. Like many of his literary contemporaries, he was a poet, journalist, essayist, and ambassador. His early penchant for traveling not only led to his diplomatic career but also gave him an enhanced cultural perspective of the different regions of Brazil, as well as the world at large. *Cobra norato,* his most famous work, is attributed to his various travels throughout Brazil and encounters with traditional Brazilian myths. PRINCIPAL WORKS: *Cobra norato* (1931), *Notas de um caderno sobre o Itamarati* (1960), *Memorias de um embaixador* (1968)

Excerpt from Cobra norato

Odile Cisneros, trans.

I
One day
I shall dwell in the lands of No-end

I go on walking walking
I mingle with the belly of the forest chewing roots

Later
I make a potion with tajá blossoms from the lagoon
and I summon Cobra Norato

"I want to tell you a story
Shall we wander in those trimmed islands?
Pretend there's moonlight"

Night arrives timidly
Stars talk in hushed voices
I play to tie a noose around its neck
And I strangle the Cobra

Finally now
I slip into that supple silk skin
and set out to see the world

I'll go visit Queen Luzia
I want to marry her daughter
"In that case you'll have to blow out your eyes first"
Sleep slid down the heavy eyelids
The muddy ground steals the strength from my steps

. . . .

IV
This is the forest with foul breath
giving birth to cobras

Skinny rivers forced to work
The current shivers
Peeling the slimy margins

Toothless roots chew the mud

In a flooded stretch
the puddle swallows the water of the waterway

It stinks
The wind switched places

A whistling frightens the trees
Silence got hurt
A dry piece of wood falls somewhere up there
Boom

A cry shoots through the forest
Other voices arrive

The river choked in a ravine

A toad toad is spying on me
It smells like people here
"Who are *you*?"

"I am the Cobra Norato
I'm going to be the lover of Queen Luzia's daughter"

. . . .

VI
I pass by the edge of a swamp
A slimy plasma rips out
and floods the mud-rimmed banks

I'm drilling soft walls
I end up in the depths of the forest
swollen alarmed haunted

Whistles are heard beat a-beating
They are welding sawing a-sawing
As if they were making soil . . .
Wow! They are really making soil

Long reservoirs of mud are hissing
The old, decayed scaffoldings are melting
Mud puddles meld
The crowded forest spills on the ground

Rumors run around in disarray
They scream: You can't!
—Are they talking to me?

I move under leafy arcades
Incognito bushes ask me:
"Is it day already?"
Dappled sunlight opens cracks in the tall fronds

Gossipy trees
they spend the night secretly knitting leaves
The windy-wind tickled the branches
It erased undeciphered writings

I/ Um dia/ eu hei de morar nas terras do Sem-fim/ Vou andando caminhando
caminhando/ Me misturo no ventre do mato mordendo raízes// Depois/ faço
puçanga de flor de tajá de lagoa/ e mando chamar a Cobra Norato// —Quero
contar-te uma história/ Vamos passear naquelas ilhas decotadas?/ Faz de
conta que há luar// A noite chega mansinho/ Estrelas conversam en voz
baixa/ Brinco então de amarrar uma fita no pescoço/ e estrangulo a Cobra//
Agora sim/me enfio nessa pele de seda elástica/ e saio a correr mundo// Vou
visitar a rainha Luzia/ Quero me casar com sua filha/ —Então você tem que
apagar os olhos primeiro/ O sono escorregou nas pálpebras pesadas/ Um
chão de lama rouba a força dos meus passos// . . . // IV/ Esta é a floresta
de hálito podre,/ parindo cobras// Rios magros obrigados a trabalhar// A
correnteza se arrepia/ descascando as margens gosmentas// Raízes desdentadas
mastigam lodo// Num estirão alagado/ o charco engole a água do igarapê//
Fede/ O vento mudou de lugar// Um assobio assusta as árvores/ Silencio
se machucou// Cai lá adiante um pedaço de pau seco:/ *Pum*// Um berro
atravessa a floresta/ Chegam outras vozes// O rio se engasgou num barranco//
Espia-me um sapo sapo/ Aqui há cheiro de gente/ —Quem é você?// —Sou a
Cobra Norato/ Vou me amasiar a filha da rainha Luzia// . . . // VI/ Passo nas
beiras de um encharcadiço/ Um plasma visguento se descostura/ e alaga as
margens debruadas de lama// Vou furando paredões moles/ Caio num fundo
escuro de floresta/ inchada alarmada mal-assombrada// Ouvem-se apitos, um
bate-que-bate/ Estão soldando serrando serrando/ Parece que fabricam terra

. . . / Ué! Estão mesmo fabricando terra// Chiam longos tanques de lodo-
pacoema/ Os velhos andaimes podres se derretem/ Lameiros se emendam/
Mato amontoado derrama-se no chão// Correm vozes em desordem/ Berram:
Não pode!/ —Será comigo?// Passo por baixo de arcadas folhudas/ (que
respiram um ar úmido// A floresta trabalha/ Espalha planta pelos estirões
de terra fresca)// Arbustos incognitos perguntam:/ —Já será dia?/ Manchas
de luz abrem buracos nas copas altas/ Árvores-comadres/ passaram a noite
tecendo fôlhas em segredo// Vento-ventinho assoprou de fazer cócegas nos
ramos/ Desmanchou escrituras indecifradas

Luis Palés Matos (1898–1959, Puerto Rico)

Born to poet parents in the town of Guayama in Puerto Rico, Palés Matos had
a profound effect on Puerto Rican letters as the co-founder, along with Nicolas
Guillén, of the *negrismo* movement that celebrated the contribution of the black
population to Latin American culture and arts. In his first book of poetry, *Azaleas,*
which he compiled at the age of seventeen, there is a strong *modernismo* influence. His later works matured into a more prosaic style, although he still produced
harmonious, *modernista* poems. Separate from his *negrismo* work, his writings on
themes such as pessimism, futility, boredom, and self-doubt are also notable contributions. PRINCIPAL WORKS: *Azaleas* (1915), *Tuntún de pasa y griferia* (1937), *Poesía
1915–1956* (1957)

Prelude in Boricua / Preludio en Boricua

Julio Marzán, trans.

Tomtom of kinky hair and black things
and other, uppity tomtoms.
Secret Cuban buzz-buzz
where the savage drumming
casts its hot shoeblacking.

To rattles of maracas
and *gongo's* muffled grunts,
the Caribbean curtain rises
on a macaque aristocracy
rich in cornmeal and tripe.

Haiti's solemn voodoo priest
Havana counters with rumba,
shaking shoulders and hips
while the Cuban darkie
saddles his wild mulatta.

Her dance-floor swing
propels Cuba at full sail,
her big hips drawing in
its golden tourist Niagara.

(Tomorrow they'll invest
in whatever sugar mill
and run home with the loot . . .)

And off in a corner-basement, bay,
seaside walk, or canefield—
the black man sips his sorrow cold
high on the melody
seeping from his core.

Jamaica, the fat Mandingo
makes liver stew of her lingo.
Santo Domingo dons his best suit
and in an awesome civic gesture,
wincing, his heroic numen recites
one hundred odes to the President.
Bearing a tray of sesame,
with white magical eyes
Haiti comes to market.
The wind-whipped Antilles
great hardships endure,
trying to scare off cyclones
with palm-tree swatters.

And Puerto Rico? My fevered island,
for you the party's over.
In the wasteland of a continent,
mournfully Puerto Rico
bleats like a stewed goat.

Tomtom of Kinky Hair and Black Things,
this book that puts in your hands
island ingredients,
I complied one day . . .

. . . and in sum, time wasted,
whose last page is boredom.
Things glimpsed or envisioned,
scant actually lived,
and much concoction and fable.

Tuntún de pasa y grifería/ y otros parejeros tuntunes./ Bochinche de
ñañiguería/ donde sus cálidos betunes/ funde la congada bravía.// Con
cacareo de maraca/ y sordo gruñido de gongo,/ el telón isleño destaca/
una aristocracia macaca/ a base de funche y mondongo.// Al solemne
papalúa haitiano/ opone la rumba habanera/ sus esguinces de hombro
y cadera,/ mientras el negrito cubano/ doma la mulata cerrera.// De su
bachata por las pistas/ vuela Cuba, suelto el velamen,/ recogiendo en el
caderamen/ su áureo niágara de turistas.// (Mañana serán accionistas/
de cualquier ingenio cañero/ y cargarán con el dinero . . .)// Y hacia un
rincón—solar, bahía,/ malecón o simbre de cañas—/ bebe el negro su pena
fría/ alelado en la melodía/ que le sale de las entrañas.// Jamaica, la gorda
mandinga,/ reduce su lingo a gandinga./ Santo Domingo se endominga/
y en cívico gesto imponente/ su numen heroico respinga/ con cien odas
al Presidente./ Con su batea de ajonjolí/ y sus blancos ojos de magia/
hacia el mercado viene Haití./ Las antillas barloventeras/ pasan tremendas
desazones,/ espantándose los ciclones/ con matamoscas de palmeras.// ¿Y
Puerto Rico? Mi isla ardiente,/ para ti todo ha terminado./ En el yermo
de un continente,/ Puerto Rico, lúgubremente,/ bala como un cabro
estofado.// Tuntún de pasa y grifería,/ este libro que va a tus manos/ con
ingredientes antillanos/ compuse un día . . . // . . . y en resumen, tiempo
perdido,/ que me acaba en aburrimiento./ Algo entrevisto o presentido,/
poco realmente vivido/ y mucho de embuste y de cuento.

Black Dance / Danza negra

Julio Marzán, trans.

Black wood and bamboo.
Bamboo and black wood.
The He-Muckamuck sings: too-coo-too.
The She-Muckamuck sings: toe-co-toe.
It's the branding-iron sun's burn in Timbuktu.
It's the black dance danced on Fernando Po.
The mud-fest hog grunts: pru-pru-pru.
The bog-wet toad dreams: cro-cro-cro.
Black wood and bamboo.
Bamboo and black wood.

Juju strings strum a tempest of oos.
Tomtoms throb with dark bass ohs.
It's wave on wave of the black race in
the bloated rhythm of *mariyandá*.
Chieftains join the feasting now.
The Negress dances, dances entranced.
Black wood and bamboo.

Bamboo and black wood.
The He-Muckamuck sings: too-coo-too.
The She-Muckamuck sings: toe-co-toe.

Red lands pass, bootblack islands:
Haiti, Martinique, Congo, Cameroon;
the *papiamiento* Antilles of rum,
the volcano's patois isles,
in rythmic abandon
to dark-voweled song.

Black wood and bamboo.
Bamboo and black wood.
It's the branding-iron sun's burn in Timbuktu.
It's the black dance danced on Fernando Po.
It's the African soul that is throbbing in
the bloated rhythm of *mariyandá*.

Black wood and bamboo.
Bamboo and black wood.
The He-Muckamuck sings: too-coo-too.
The She-Muckamuck sings: toe-co-toe.

Calabó y bambú./ Bambú y calabó./ El Gran Cocoroco dice: tu-cu-tu./ La
Gran Cocoroca dice: to-co-to./ Es el sol de hierro que arde en Tombuktú./
Es la danza negra de Fernando Poo./ El cerdo en el fango gruñe: pru-pru-
pru./ El sapo en la charca sueña: cro-cro-cro./ Calabó y bambú./ Bambú
y calabó.// Rompen los junjunes en furiosa ú./ Los gongos trepidan con
profunda ó/ Es la raza negra que ondulando va/ en el ritmo gordo del
mariyandá./ Llegan los botucos a la fiesta ya./ Danza que te danza la negra
se da.// Calabó y bambú./ Bambú y calabó./ El Gran Cocoroco dice: tu-cu-
tu./ La Gran Cocoroca dice: to-co-to.// Pasan tierras rojas, islas de betún:/
Haití, Martinica, Congo, Camerún;/ las papamientosas antillas del ron/ y las
patualesas islas del volcán,/ que en el grave son/ del canto se dan.// Calabó
y bambú./ Bambú y calabó./ Es el sol de hierro que arde en Tombuktú./ Es
la danza negra de Fernando Poo./ Es el alma africana que vibrando está/ en
el ritmo gordo del mariyandá.// Calabó y bambú./ Bambú y calabó./ El gran
Cocoroco dice: tu-cu-tu./ La Gran Cocoroca dice: to-co-to.

Jorge Luis Borges (1899–1986, Argentina)

Regarded as one of the most influential contemporary authors from Latin America, Borges has been praised by writers, critics, and readers around the world. Born in Buenos Aires to a military family, the Argentine spoke both English and Spanish at home and was a voracious reader, principally in English. After publishing poetry in prominent journals such as *Sur* and working in the Buenos Aires Municipal Library, he became the director of the National Library. His poetics have the rare quality of moving seamlessly between the vernacular and the universal. He became internationally known for his fiction, which is often read for its philosophical implications. PRINCIPAL WORKS: *Fervor de Buenos Aires* (1923), *Cuaderno San Martín* (1929), *Elogio de la sombra* (1969)

The Golem / El Golem

Alan S. Trueblood, trans.

If, as the Greek maintains in the *Cratylus*,
a name is the archetype of a thing,
the rose is in the letters that spell rose
and the Nile entire resounds in its name's ring.

So, composed of consonants and vowels,
there must exist one awe-inspiring word
that God inheres in—that, when spoken, holds
Almightiness in syllables unslurred.

Adam knew it in the Garden, so did the stars.
The rusty work of sin, so the cabbalists say,
obliterated it completely;
no generation has found it to this day.

The cunning and naïveté of men
are limitless. We know there came a time
when God's people, searching for the Name,
toiled in the ghetto, matching rhyme to rhyme.

One memory stands out, unlike the rest—
dim shapes always fading from time's dim log.
Still fresh and green the memory persists
of Judah León, a rabbi once in Prague.

Thirsty to know things only known to God,
Judah Leon shuffled letters endlessly,
trying them out in subtle combinations
till at last he uttered the Name that is the Key,

the Gate, the Echo, the Landlord, and the Mansion,
over a dummy which, with fingers wanting grace,
he fashioned, thinking to teach it the arcane
of Words and Letters and of Time and Space.

The simulacrum lifted its drowsy lids
and, much bewildered, took in color and shape
in a floating world of sounds. Following this,
it hesitantly took a timid step.

Little by little it found itself, like us,
caught in the reverberating weft
of After, Before, Yesterday, Meanwhile, Now,
You, Me, Those, the Others, Right and Left.

That cabbalist who played at being God
gave his spacey offspring the nickname Golem.
(In a learned passage of his volume,
there truths have been conveyed to us by Scholem.)

To it the rabbi would explain the universe—
"This is my foot, this yours, this is a clog"—
year in, year out, until the spiteful thing
rewarded him by sweeping the synagogue.

Perhaps the sacred name had been misspelled
or in its uttering been jumbling or too weak.
The potent sorcery never took effect:
man's apprentice never learned to speak.

Its eyes, less human than doglike in their look,
and even less a dog's than eyes of a thing,
would follow every move the rabbi made
about a confinement always gloomy and dim.

Something coarse and abnormal was in the Golem,
for the rabbi's cat, as soon as it moved about,
would run off and hide. (There's no cat in Scholem
but across the gulf of time I make one out.)

Lifting up to its God its filial hands,
it aped its master's devotions—even the least—
or, with a stupid smile, would bend far over
in concave salaams the way men do in the East.

The rabbi watched it fondly and not a little
alarmed as he wondered: "How could I bring

such a sorry creature into this world
and give up my leisure, surely the wisest thing?

What made me supplement the endless series
of symbols with one more? Why add in vain
to the knotty skein always unraveling
another cause and effect, with not one gain?"

In his hour of anguish and uncertain light,
upon his Golem his eyes would come to rest.
Who is to say what God must have been feeling,
Looking down and seeing His rabbi so distressed?

Si (como el griego afirma en el Cratilo)/ El nombre es arquetipo de la cosa / En las letras de *rosa* está la rosa / Y todo el Nilo en la palabra *Nilo*.// Y, hecho de consonantes y vocales,/ Habrá un terrible Nombre, que la esencia/ Cifre de Dios y que la Omnipotencia/ Guarde en letras y sílabas cabales.// Adán y las estrellas lo supieron/ En el Jardín. La herrumbre del pecado/ (Dicen los cabalistas) lo ha borrado/ Y las generaciones lo perdieron.// Los artificios y el candor del hombre/ No tienen fin. Sabemos que hubo un día/ En que el pueblo de Dios buscaba el Nombre/ En las vigilias de la judería.// No a la manera de otras que una vaga/ Sombra insinúan en la vaga historia,/ Aún está verde y viva la memoria/ De Judá León, que era rabino en Praga.// Sediento de saber lo que Dios sabe,/ Judá León se dio a permutaciones/ de letras y a complejas variaciones/ Y al fin pronunció el Nombre que es la Clave,// La Puerta, el Eco, el Huésped y el Palacio,/ Sobre un muñeco que con torpes manos/ labró, para enseñarle los arcanos/ De las Letras, del Tiempo y del Espacio.// El simulacro alzó los soñolientos/ Párpados y vio formas y colores/ Que no entendió, perdidos en rumores/ Y ensayó temerosos movimientos.// Gradualmente se vio (como nosotros)/ Aprisionado en esta red sonora/ de Antes, Después, Ayer, Mientras, Ahora,/ Derecha, Izquierda, Yo, Tú, Aquellos, Otros.// (El cabalista que ofició de numen/ A la vasta criatura apodó Golem;/ Estas verdades las refiere Scholem/ En un docto lugar de su volumen.)// El rabí le explicaba el universo/ *"esto es mi pie; esto el tuyo, esto la soga."*/ Y logró, al cabo de años, que el perverso/ Barriera bien o mal la sinagoga.// Tal vez hubo un error en la grafía/ O en la articulación del Sacro Nombre;/ A pesar de tan alta hechicería,/ No aprendió a hablar el aprendiz de hombre.// Sus ojos, menos de hombre que de perro/ Y harto menos de perro que de cosa,/ Seguían al rabí por la dudosa/ penumbra de las piezas del encierro.// Algo anormal y tosco hubo en el Golem,/ Ya que a su paso el gato del rabino/ Se escondía. (Ese gato no está en Scholem/ Pero, a través del tiempo, lo adivino.)// Elevando a su Dios manos filiales,/ Las devociones de su Dios copiaba/ O, estúpido y sonriente, se ahuecaba/ En cóncavas zalemas orientales.// El rabí lo miraba con ternura/ Y con algún horror. *¿Cómo* (se dijo)/ *Pude engendrar este penoso hijo/ Y la inacción dejé, que es la cordura?// ¿Por qué di en agregar a la infinita/ Serie un símbolo más? ¿Por qué a la vana/ Madeja que en lo eterno se devana,/ Di otra causa, otro efecto y otra cuita?//* En la hora de angustia y de luz vaga,/ En su Golem los ojos detenía./ ¿Quién nos dirá las cosas que sentía/ Dios, al mirar a su rabino en Praga?

The Mythical Founding of Buenos Aires / Fundación mítica de Buenos Aires

Alastair Reid, trans.

And was it along this torpid muddy river
that the prows came to found my native city?
The little painted boats must have suffered the steep surf
among the root-clumps of the horse-brown current.

Pondering well, let us suppose the the river
was blue then like an extension of the sky,
with a small red star inset to mark the spot
where Juan Díaz fasted and the Indians dined.

But for sure a thousand men and other thousands
arrived across a sea that was five moons wide,
still infested with mermaids and sea serpents
and magnetic boulders that sent the compass wild.

On the coast they put up a few ramshackle huts
and slept uneasily. This, they claim, in the Riachuelo,
but that is a story dreamed up in the Boca.
It was really a city block in my district—Palermo.

A whole square block, but set down in open country,
attended by dawns and rains and hard southeasters,
identical to that block which still stands in my neighborhood:
Guatemala—Serrano—Paraguay—Gurruchaga.

A general store pink as the back of a playing card
shone bright; in the back there was poker talk.
The corner bar flowered into life as a local bully,
already cock of his walk, resentful, tough.

The first barrel organ teetered over the horizon
with its clumsy progress, its habaneras, its wop.
The cart-shed wall was unanimous for YRIGOYEN.

Some piano was banging out tango by Saborido.

A cigar store perfumed the desert like a rose.
The afternoon had established its yesterdays,
and men took on together an illusory past.
Only one thing was missing—the street had no other side.

Hard to believe Buenos Aires had any beginning.
I feel it to be as eternal as air and water.

¿Y fue por este río de sueñera y de barro/ que las proas vinieron a
fundarme la patria?/ Irían a los tumbos los barquitos pintados/ entre los
camalotes de la corriente zaina.// Pensando bien la cosa, supondremos
que el río/ era azulejo entonces como oriundo del cielo/ con su estrellita
roja para marcar el sitio/ en que ayunó Juan Díaz y los indios comieron.//
Lo cierto es que mil hombres y otros mil arribaron/ por un mar que tenía
cinco lunas de anchura/ y aun estaba poblado de sirenas y endriagos/ y
de piedras imanes que enloquecen la brújula.// Prendieron unos ranchos
trémulos en la costa,/ durmieron extrañados. Dicen que en el Riachuelo,/
pero son embelecos fraguados en la Boca./ Fue una manzana entera y en
mi barrio: en Palermo.// Una manzana entera pero en mitá del campo/
expuesta a las auroras y lluvias y suestadas./ La manzana pareja que
persiste en mi barrio:/ Guatemala, Serrano, Paraguay, y Gurruchaga.//
Un almacén rosado como revés de naipe/ brilló y en la trastienda
conversaron un truco;/ el almacén rosado floreció en un compadre,/ ya
patrón de la esquina, ya resentido y duro.// El primer organito salvaba
el horizonte/ con su achacoso porte, su habanera y su gringo./ El
corralón seguro ya opinaba YRIGOYEN,/ algún piano mandaba tangos de
Saborido.// Una cigarrería sahumó como una rosa/ el desierto. La tarde
se había ahondado en ayeres,/ los hombres compartieron un pasado
ilusorio./ Sólo faltó una cosa: la vereda de enfrente.// A mí se me hace
cuento que empezó Buenos Aires:/ La juzgo tan eterna como el agua y
como el aire.

Borges and I / Borges y yo

Kenneth Krabbenhoft, trans.

The other one, Borges, is the one things happen to. I wander around
Buenos Aires, pausing perhaps unthinkingly, these days, to examine
the arch of an entranceway and its metal gate. I hear about Borges in
letters, I see his name on a roster of professors and in the biographical
gazeteer. I like hourglasses, maps, eighteenth-century typeface, the
taste of coffee, and Stevenson's prose. The other one likes the same
things, but his vanity transforms them into theatrical props. To say

that our relationship is hostile would be an exaggeration: I live, I stay
alive, so that Borges can make his literature, and this literature is my
justification. I readily admit that a few of his pages are worthwhile,
but these pages are not my salvation, perhaps because good writing
belongs to no one in particular, not even to my other, but rather
to language and tradition. As for the rest, I am fated to disappear
completely, and only a small piece of me can possibly live in the other
one. I'm handing everything over to him bit by bit, fully aware of
his nasty habit of distortion and aggrandizement. Spinoza knew that
all things desire to endure in their being: stones desire to be stones,
and tigers tigers, for all eternity. I must remain in Borges rather than
in myself (if in fact I am a self), and yet I recognize myself less in
his books than in many others, or in the rich strumming of a guitar.
Some years ago I tried to get away from him: I went from suburban
mythologies to playing games with time and infinity. But these are
Borges' games now—I will have to think of something else. Thus my
life is an escape. I will lose everything, and everything will belong to
oblivion, or to the other.
I don't know which of us wrote this.

Al otro, a Borges, es a quien le ocurren las cosas. Yo camino por Buenos
Aires y me demoro, acaso ya mecánicamente, para mirar el arco de un
zaguán y la puerta cancel; de Borges tengo noticias por el correo y veo
su nombre en una terna de profesores o en un diccionario biográfico.
Me gustan los relojes de arena, los mapas, la tipografía del siglo XVIII, las
etimologías, el sabor del café y la prosa de Stevenson; el otro comparte esas
preferencias, pero de un modo vanidoso que las convierte en atributos de
un actor. Sería exagerado afirmar que nuestra relación es hostil; yo vivo, yo
me dejo vivir, para que Borges pueda tramar su literatura y esa literatura
me justifica. Nada me cuesta confesar que ha logrado ciertas páginas
válidas, pero esas páginas no me pueden salvar, quizá porque lo bueno ya
no es de nadie, ni siquiera del otro, sino del lenguaje o la tradición. Por
lo demás, yo estoy destinado a perderme, definitivamente, y sólo algún
instante de mí podrá sobrevivir en el otro. Poco a poco voy cediéndole
todo, aunque me consta su perversa costumbre de falsear y magnificar.
Spinoza entendió que todas las cosas quieren perseverar en su ser; la
piedra eternamente quiere ser piedra y el tigre un tigre. Yo he de quedar
en Borges, no en mí (si es que alguien soy), pero me reconozco menos
en sus libros que en muchos otros o que en el laborioso rasgueo de una
guitarra. Hace años yo traté de librarme de él y pasé de las mitologías del
arrabal a los juegos con el tiempo y con lo infinito, pero esos juegos son de
Borges ahora y tendré que idear otras cosas. Así mi vida es una fuga y todo
lo pierdo y todo es del olvido, o del otro./ No sé cuál de los dos escribe
esta página.

Limits / Límites

Alastair Reid, trans.

Of all the streets that blur into the sunset,
there must be one (which, I am not sure)
that I by now have walked for the last time
without guessing it, the pawn of that Someone

who fixes in advance omnipotent laws,
sets up a secret and unwavering scale
for all the shadows, dreams, and forms
woven into the texture of this life.

If there is a limit to all things and a measure
and a last time and nothing more and forgetfulness,
who will tell us to whom in this house
we without knowing it have said farewell?

Through the dawning window night withdraws
and among the stacked books that throw
irregular shadows on the dim table,
there must be one which I will never read.

There is in the South more than one worn gate,
with its cement urns and planted cactus,
which is already forbidden to my entry,
inaccessible, as in a lithograph.

There is a door you have closed forever
and some mirror is expecting you in vain;
to you the crossroads seem wide open,
yet watching you, four-faced, is a Janus.

There is among all your memories one
which has now been lost beyond recall.
You will not be seen going down to that fountain,
neither by white sun nor by yellow moon.

You will never recapture what the Persian
said in his language woven with birds and roses,
when, in the sunset, before the light disperses,
you wish to give words to unforgettable things.

And the steadily flowing Rhone and the lake,
all the vast yesterday over which today I bend?
They will be as lost as Carthage,
scourge by the Romans with fire and salt.

At dawn I seem to hear the turbulent
murmur of crowds milling and fading away;
that are all I have been loved by, forgotten by;
space, time, and Borges now are leaving me.

De estas calles que ahondan el poniente,/ Una habrá (no sé cuál) que
he recorrido/ Ya por última vez, indiferente/ Y sin adivinarlo, sometido/
A Quién prefija omnipotentes normas/ Y una secreta y rígida medida/ A las
sombras, los sueños y las formas/ Que destejen y tejen esta vida.// Si para
todo hay término y hay tasa/ Y última vez y nunca más y olvido/ ¿Quién
nos dirá de quién, en esta casa,/ Sin saberlo, nos hemos despedido?// Tras
el cristal ya gris la noche cesa/ Y del alto de libros que una trunca/ Sombra
dilata por la vaga mesa,/ Alguno habrá que no leeremos nunca.// Hay
en el Sur más de un portón gastado/ Con sus jarrones de mampostería/
Y tunas, que a mi paso está vedado/ Como si fuera una litografía.// Para
siempre cerraste alguna puerta/ Y hay un espejo que te aguarda en vano;/
La encrucijada te parece abierta/ Y la vigila, cuadrifronte, Jano.// Hay, entre
todas tus memorias, una/ Que se ha perdido irreparablemente;/ No te verán
bajar a aquella fuente/ Ni el blanco sol ni la amarilla luna.// No volverá tu
voz a lo que el persa/ Dijo en su lengua de aves y de rosas,/ Cuando al ocaso,
ante la luz dispersa,/ Quieras decir inolvidables cosas.// ¿Y el incesante
Ródano y el lago,/ Todo ese ayer sobre el cual hoy me inclino?/ Tan perdido
estará como Cartago/ Que con fuego y con sal borró el latino.// Creo en el
alba oír un atareado/ Rumor de multitudes que se alejan;/ Son lo que me ha
querido y olvidado;/ Espacio y tiempo y Borges ya me dejan.

Rosamel Del Valle (1901–1965, Chile)

Born Moisés Filadelfio Gutiérrez Gutiérrez in Curacaví, central Chile, to a family of
peasants, Del Valle lost his father at age seventeen and worked in a printing office
to provide for his mother and siblings. He learned English and French while reading his favorite poets, and translated works by Breton, Tzara, W. H. Auden, and
Allen Ginsberg. The time he spent in New York—while working as a proofreader
for the United Nations Publishing Office—was deliriously captured in his recently
published book *Crónicas de New York* (New York Chronicles). He traveled extensively throughout Europe. After almost twenty years of absence, he returned to
Chile, where he passed away. His visionary and shining work—which is finally being
recognized as a foundational part of the Chilean Vanguard—makes connections
between Rilke, Eliot, and Breton and is regarded by some critics as one of the most
important of the twentieth century, along with the work of Huidobro and Neruda.

PRINCIPAL WORKS: *Orfeo* (1944), *El joven olvido* (1949), *La visión comunicable* (1956), *Adiós enigma tornasol* (1967)

Canticle IX / Cántico IX

Jen Hofer, trans.

It's the only love with stamped scissors
in the only world your body seduces
and my form is your form and the flame that is entangled in your body
Is the sign of the pact that holds us hostage and the sign
of the garden lost in the night of lives and the sign
of my day and my star in a bonfire on your tongue and the sign
of love for always and of life for always and the sign
of death for always and forgetting for always and the boiling
sign of the you and the I of solitude in solitude and the sign
of the earth's smell cultivated beneath our eyelids and the sign
of the cloud lost for years beneath the grass and the sign
of the blazing disaster of your body in my body

Es el único con tijeras selladas/ en el único mundo que tu cuerpo
seduce/ y mi forma es tu forma y la llama que se enreda en tu cuerpo/ Es
el signo del pacto que nos tiene en rehenes y el signo/ del jardín perdido
en la noche de vida y el signo/ de mi día y mi estrella en fogata en tu
lengua y el signo/ del amor para siempre y de la vida para siempre y el
signo/ de la muerte para siempre y del olvido para siempre y el signo/
hirviente del tú y el yo de soledad en soledad y el signo/ del olor de la
tierra cultivado debajo de los párpados y el/ signo/ de la nube perdida
por años debajo de la hierba y el signo/ el ardiente desastre de tu cuerpo
en mi cuerpo

Magic Love / El amor mágico

Jen Hofer, trans.

Do you recall the Medusa Gorgona? She has said:
"*Babylon. Yes, you'll go.*" That's all. And a lengthy
twilight has appeared. And the Medusa Gorgona
Was singing for you and for me.
Perhaps. But I know I've never possessed a song
Better than when you were dreaming.
I've never had greater eyes
Than when you were sleeping.
Nor have I ever seen the sea closer
Than I did then.

And she said: "You'll go." And I saw
Jacob's ladder.

Not Beatrice resplendent, Beatrice injured.
In a sky without circles, in a door with no key.
I saw you and among pure choirs I followed you.
No net stiffer than these hands
To clip your roses. No death sweeter
To seek out your mouth.
But I was the lone traveler. I was
The dampness of your winter.
I tended your young sunlight in one lone
Hotel room, in the city.
I experienced the world's music on the sand, there.

And she sang: *But you did not recognize yourself*
In what I was singing.
And I went out to the plazas, to the markets, to the promenades
With you. You with the night. Why with the night?
That's how it seemed, though you were the world within me.

Oh that they might see us pass. That they might see us in love
There, among the trees and the visions.
That I might say you look like what you are.
That I might say you don't make noise, but you shine.
That I might say the crown encircling you is dark
Though it ignites.
That I might say your mouth is a flower affixed to the bone,
And that it may be so.
That I might say someone loves you for me,
And that it may not be true.
That I might say the gazes get ahead of you,
And that it might seem that way.
That I might say you are the star on my forehead,
And that you radiate.
That I might say you subdue the birds in the air,
And that they might lose their wings.
That I might say you are dressed in the color of the heart,
And that it may be so.

Your being in me, my love in you.
The sun engraved on the mane of the begonia
In my room, in the city.
Alone in you taciturn statue.
Alone through the cities in my forehead.

Alone beneath the hangman's tree.
Love in love. The lamp in you, the ray in me.
Words on a bridge between your mouth and mine.
Every hour, a hill.
The totality of time, a tower.
We, the bells.

And I'm going.
A sun from elsewhere
Offers me its hand.

And if I say I'm leaving, it's that your forehead holds me back.
And if I say I'm crying, it's that the night is blazing.
And if I think I'm going to be the lone traveler,
It's that the earth has opened up.
And if I sing behind the meteors,
It's that the sky is near.
And if I say good-bye to you, it's that I'm moving
to the rhythm of death.

¿Recuerdas a la Gorgona? Ha dicho:/ *"Babilonia. Sí, irás"*. Eso es todo. Y ha
venido/ Un largo crepúsculo. Y la Gorgona/ Cantaba para ti y para mí./ Tal vez.
Pero yo sé que nunca tuve un canto/ Mejor que cuando soñabas./ Nunca tuve
más ojos/ Que cuando dormías./ Ni nunca vi más cerca el mar/ Que entonces./
Y ella decía: "Irás". Y yo veía/ La escala de Jacob.// No Beatriz resplandeciente,
Beatriz llagada./ En un cielo sin círculos, en una puerta sin llave./ Yo te veía
y entre coros puros te seguía./ Ninguna red más dura que estas manos/ Para
cortar tus rosas. Ninguna muerte más suave/ Para buscar tu boca./ Pero yo era
el viajero solo. Yo era/ La humedad de tu invierno./ Yo guardaba tu joven sol
en un cuarto/ Solo de hotel, en la ciudad./ Yo tenía la música del mundo sobre
la arena, allí.// Y cantaba: *Pero tú no te reconocías/ En lo que yo cantaba.*/ Y yo
salía a las plazas, a los mercados, a los paseos/ Contigo. Tú con la noche. ¿Por
qué con la noche?/ Eso parecía, aunque tú eras el mundo en mí.// Oh que
nos vean pasar. Que nos vean amarnos/ Allí, entre los árboles y las visiones./
Que yo diga que te pareces a lo que eres./ Que yo diga que no haces ruido,
pero que brillas./ Que yo diga que es obscura la corona que te ciñe,/ Aunque
se encienda./Que yo diga que tu boca es una flor pegada al hueso,/ Y que lo
sea./ Que yo diga que alguien te ama por mí,/ Y que no sea cierto./ Que yo
diga que eres la estrella de mi frente,/ Y que alumbres./ Que yo diga que sujetas
los pájaros en el aire,/ Y que pierdan las alas./ Que yo diga que vas vestida
del color del corazón,/ Y que así sea.// Tu ser en mí, mi amor en ti./ El sol
grabado en la cabellera de la begonia/ De mi cuarto, en la ciudad./ Sola en tu
estatua taciturna./ Sola por las ciudades de mi frente.// Sola debajo del árbol
del ahorcado./ Amor en amor. La lámpara en ti, el rayo en mí./ Las palabras
en un puente entre tu boca y la mía./ Todas las horas, una colina./ El tiempo

total, una torre./ Nosotros, las campanas.// Y me voy./ Un sol de otra parte/
Me tiende la mano.// Y si digo que parto, es que tu frente me retiene./ Y si
digo que lloro, es que la noche es ardiente./ Y si pienso que voy a ser el viajero
solo,/ Es que la tierra se ha abierto./ Y si canto detrás de los meteoros,/ Es que
el cielo está cerca./ Y si te digo adiós, es que ando/ Al compás de la muerte.

Cecilia Meireles (1901–1964, Brazil)

Orphaned when she was only three, Meireles was raised from a very early age surrounded by nature. Her lyrical and highly personal poetry dwells in the complex
symbolism hidden in everyday objects and events. She established her literary reputation early on in 1919, by expanding traditional forms such as the sonnet. She
was awarded the Brazilian Academy of Letters Poetry Prize for 1939, her first official
honor. Meireles died of cancer in Rio de Janeiro. PRINCIPAL WORKS: *Viagem* (1939),
Doze noturnos da holanda e o aeronauta (1952), *Solombra* (1963)

Pyrargyrite Metal, 9 / Metal rosicler, 9

James Merrill, trans.

The piano tuner spoke to me, that tenderest
attender to each note
who looking over sharp and flat
hears and glimpses something more remote.
And his ears make no mistake
nor do his hands that in each chord awake
those sounds delighted to keep house together.

"Disinterested is my interest:
I don't confuse music and instrument, mere
piano tuner that I am,
calligrapher of that superhuman speech
which lifts me as a guest to its high sphere.
Oh! what new Physics waits up there to teach
other matters to another ear . . . "

Falou-me o afinador de pianos, esse / que mansamente escuta cada nota / e
olha para os bemóis e sustenidos / ouvindo e vendo coisa mais remota. /
E estão livres de engano os seus ouvidos / e suas mãos que em cada
acorde acordam / os sons felizes de viverem juntos. // "Meu interesse é de
desinteresse: / pois música e instrumento não confundo, / que afinador
apenas sou, do piano, / a letra da linguagem desse mundo / que me eleva

a conviva sobre-humano. / Oh! que Física nova nesse plano / para outro ouvido, sobre outros assuntos . . . "

Song / Canção

Mark A. Lokensgard, trans.

I placed my dream in a ship
and the ship on top of the sea;
—and then parted the sea with my hands
to sink my dream in the deep.

My hands still drip with water
from the blue of the waves thus parted
and the color that runs from my fingers
colors the sands, now deserted.

The wind is approaching from afar,
the night in the cold submits;
under the waves lies dying
my dream, in the hold of a ship . . .

I will weep as much as needed,
so that I might the sea increase
and that my ship might come to the bottom
and that my dream might cease.

And then, all will be perfect:
the beach smooth, the waters ordered,
my eyes, dry as stones
my two hands, shattered.

Pus o meu sonho num navio/ e o navio em cima do mar;/ —depois, abri o mar com as mãos,/ para o meu sonho naufragar.// Minhas mãos ainda estão molhadas/ do azul das ondas entreabertas,/ e a cor que escorre dos meus dedos/ colore as areias desertas.// O vento vem vindo de longe,/ a noite se curva de frio;/ debaixo da água vai morrendo/ meu sonho, dentro de um navio . . . // Chorarei quanto for preciso,/ para fazer com que o mar cresça,/ e o meu navio chegue ao fundo/ e o meu sonho desapareça.// Depois, tudo estará perfeito:/ praia lisa, águas ordenadas,/ meus olhos secos como pedras/ e as minhas duas mãos quebradas.

Speech / Discurso

Mark A. Lokensgard, trans.

And here I am, singing.

A poet is always brother to the wind and water:
He leaves his rhythm everywhere he walks.

I come from afar and am headed far away:
but I searched the ground for signs of my trail
and saw nothing, because the weeds had grown and serpents had passed.

Then I searched the sky for a sign of a path,
But it was always full of clouds.
And Babel's workmen, dead by suicide.

So here I am, singing.

If I don't even know where I am,
how can I hope for an ear to hear me?

Oh! If I don't even know who I am,
how can I hope that someone might love me?

E AQUI ESTOU, cantando.// Um poeta é sempre irmão do vento e da
água:/ deixa seu ritmo por onde passa.// Venho de longe e vou para
longe:/ mas procurei pelo chão os sinais do meu caminho/ e não vi nada,
porque as ervas cresceram e as serpentes andaram.// Também porcurei no
céu a indicação de uma trajetória,/ mas houve sempre muitas nuvens./ E
suicidaram-se os operários de Babel.// Pois aqui estou, cantando.// Se eu
nem sei onde estou,/ como posso esperar que algum ouvido me escute?//
Ah! Se eu nem sei quem sou,/ como posso esperar que venha alguém gostar
de mim?

Second Rose Motif / Segundo motivo da rosa

James Merrill, trans.

To Mário de Andrade

However much I praise, you do not listen
although in form and mother-of-pearl you could be
the uttering shell, the ear whose music lesson
engraves the inmost spirals of the sea.

I place you in crystal, in the mirror's prison
past all undertone of well or grotto . . .
Pure absence, blind incomprehension
offered to the wasp and to the bee

as to your acolyte, O deaf and mute
and blind and beautiful and interminable rose
who into time, attar, and verse transmute

yourself now beyond earth or star arisen
to glisten from my dream, of your own beauty
insensible because you do not listen . . .

Por mais que te celebre, não me escutas,/ embora em forma e nácar te
assemelhes/ à concha soante, à musical orelha/ que grava o mar nas
íntimas volutas.// Deponho-te em cristal, defronte a espelhos,/ sem eco
cisternas ou de grutas . . . / Ausências e cegueiras absolutas/ ofereces às
vespas e às abelhas,// e a quem te adora, ó surda e silenciosa,/ e cega e bela
e interminável rosa,/ que em tempo e aroma e verso te transmutas!// Sem
terra nem estrêlas brilhas, prêsa/ a meu sonho, insensivel à beleza/ que és a
não sabes, porque não me escutas . . .

José Gorostiza (1901–1973, Mexico)

Born in Villahermosa, Tabasco, Gorostiza studied in Mexico City, where he was
associated with the group "Los Contemporáneos." A career diplomat, he lived
and worked in London, Copenhagen, and Rome and was also part of the National
Nuclear Energy Commission of his country. His long metaphysical poem "Muerte
sin fin" is one of the great masterpieces of the Spanish language, yet it has not been
translated in full. In it, he states that life and death are a single process, where each
can be admired from the opposite shore. This sense of reciprocity and exchange
pervades his work. For him, the poem is a construction of poetic matter, a vehicle
by which to enter into the enigma of poetry. In his work the poet is in dialogue with
an evasive substance, poetry itself, which can only be "captured sometimes" "in a
luminous, precise, and throbbing net." PRINCIPAL WORKS: *Canciones para cantar en
las barcas* (1925), *Muerte sin fin* (1939), *Poesía* (1964)

Excerpt from Death without End/ Muerte sin fin

Rachel Benson, trans.

Filled with myself, walled up in my skin
by an inapprehensible god that is stifling me,
deceived perhaps
by his radiant atmosphere of light
that hides my drained conscience,
my wings broken into splinters of air,

my listless groping through the mire;
filled with myself—gorged—I discover my essence
in the astonished image of water,
that is only an unwithering cascade,
a tumbling of angels fallen
of their own accord in pure delight,
that has nothing
but a whitened face
half-sunken, already, like an agonized laugh
in the thin sheets of the cloud
and the mournful canticles of the sea—
more aftertaste of salt or cumulus whiteness
than lonely haste of foam pursued.
Nevertheless—oh paradox—constrained
by the rigor of the glass that clarifies it,
the water takes shape.
In the glass it sits, sinks deep, and builds,
attains a bitter age of silences
and the grateful repose of a child smiling
in death, that deflowers
a beyond of disbanded
birds.
In the crystal snare that strangles it,
there, as in the water of a mirror,
it recognizes itself;
bound there, drop with drop,
the trope of foam withered in its throat.
What intense nakedness of water,
what water so strongly water,
is dreaming in its iridescent sphere,
already singing a thirst for rigid ice!
But what a provident glass—also—
that swells
like a star ripe with grain,
that flames in heroic promise
like a heart inhabited with happiness,
and that punctually yields up
to the water
a round transparent flower,
a missile eye that attains heights
and a window to luminous cries
over the smoldering liberty
oppressed by white fetters!

Lleno de mí, sitiado en mi epidermis/ por un dios inasible que me ahoga,/ mentido acaso/ por su radiante atmósfera de luces/ que oculta mi consciencia derramada,/ mis alas rotas en esquirlas de aire,/ mi torpe andar a tientas por el lodo;/ lleno de mí—ahito—me descubro/ en la imagen atónita del agua,/ que tan sólo es un tumbo inmarcesible,/ un desplome de ángeles caídos/ a la delicia intacta de su peso,/ que nada tiene/ sino la cara en blanco/ hundidas a medias, ya, como una risa agónica/ en las tenues holandas de la nube/ y en los funestos cánticos del mar/ —más resabio de sal o albor de cúmulo/ que sola prisa de acosada espuma./ No obstante—oh paradoja—constreñida/ por el rigor del vaso que la aclara,/ el agua toma forma./ En él se asienta, ahonda y edifica,/ cumple una edad amarga de silencios/ y un reposo gentil de muerte niña,/ sonriente, que desflora/ un más allá de pájaros/ en desbandada./ En la red de cristal que la estrangula,/ allí, como en el agua de un espejo,/ se reconoce;/ atada allí, gota con gota,/ marchito el tropo de espuma en la garganta/ ¡qué desnudez de agua tan intensa,/ qué agua tan agua,/ está en su orbe tornasol soñando,/ cantando ya una sed de hielo justo!/ ¡Mas qué vaso—también—más providente/ éste que así se hinche/ como una estrella en grano,/ que así, en heroica promisión, se enciende/ como un seno habitado por la dicha,/ y rinde así, puntual,/ una rotunda flor/ de transparencia al agua,/ un ojo proyectil que cobra alturas/ y una ventana a gritos luminosos/ sobre esa libertad enardecida/ que se agobia de cándidas prisiones!

Elegy / Elegía

Christopher Winks, trans.

When I am close to tears
the sea sheds them.

A veces me dan ganas de llorar,/ pero las suple el mar.

Pauses I / Pausas I

Christopher Winks, trans.

The sea, the sea!
I feel it within
Only to think
Of it—so much my own—
My thought tastes of salt.
¡EL MAR, el mar!/ Dentro de mí lo siento./ Ya sólo de pensar/ en él, tan mío/ tiene un sabor de sal mi pensamiento.

Carlos Drummond de Andrade (1902–1987, Brazil)

As a member of the Brazilian modernist generation, Drummond made his mark on the literary world as a columnist, poet, and translator. Originally born in a small town in the state of Minas Gerais, he moved to Rio de Janeiro to pursue dual careers in literature and politics. With the 1954 publication of his collected works titled *Fazendeiro do ar e poesia até agora* (Farmer of the Air and Poetry until Now), Drummond's literary reputation was established. Distinct from the European modernist models, his work is known for its fragmentary style and is viewed as a harbor of tension and conflict. PRIN-CIPAL WORKS: *A rosa do povo* (1945), *Fazendeiro do ar e poesia até agora* (1954)

This Is That / Isso é aquilo

Odile Cisneros, trans.

I

The facile the fossil
the missile the fissile
the arts the heart attacks
the ochre the sepulcher
the vessel the recess
the sickle the fascicle
the lex the judex
the beach fad the granddad
the dove the calf knuckle
the lone the coquina

II

the nook the crook
the mural the remora
the suicide the sustenance
the litotes Aristotle
the peace the pus
the lycanthrope the lyceum
the flit the flatus
the viper the hellebore
the piston the pie

III

the isthmus the spasm
the dithyramb the meerschaum
the cuticle the ventriloquist
the lachrymal the magma
the lead the lotus
the formica the fucsia

the bobbin the goldfinch
the malt the maltese falcon
the malfeasance the aneurysm
the date the Diet

IV
the atom the atonal
the medusa the pegasus
the eruption the ellipse
the mammy the system
the kimono the ammonia
the death song the nylon
the cement the lament
the mane the manioc
the mendicant the mandrake
the beret the good faith

V
the sand the secret
the abbot the abyss
the spark the meniscus
the idolater the hydropathist
the platanus the plastic
the turtle the hurdle
the stomach the magus
the morning the earthling
the cosmos the cosmea
the shoelace the mistress

VI
the useful the tasteful
the colubiazol the ghazal
the lepidopterus the uterus
the confusion the bottled solution
the gemstone the wheat sown
the *know-how* the knockout
the dogma the gurgle
the udder the shudder
the non-entity the obesity
the tooth decay the tempest

VII
the zed the zeugma
the cemetery the marina
the flowers the canephorus

the picnic the pickpocket
the nest the incest
the cricket the ant poison
the aorta the Boulevard
the gruel the *migraine*
the orient the reading
the giraffe the jitanjáfora

VIII
the Indian the nit
the buskin the rescission
the sink the pity
the reluctance the fragrance
the monitor the mother-of-pearl
the solferino the Aquinaesque
the bacon the playwright
the legal the galenite
the azure the lues
the word the hare

IX
the remorse the waistband
the night the biscuit morsel
the sestertium the consortium
the ethical the Ithaca
the laziness the trellis
the chaste the chastisement
the rice the horror
the medlar the midnight
the pope the ladybug
the solemnities the antibiotics

X
the tree the sea
the bird candy
the raisin of mourning
the heat the poetry
the force of fate
the homeland the satedness
firefly plumes Ulalume
Zeus's zoomzoom
     the bombyx
     the ptyx

I/ O fácil o fóssil/ o míssil o físsil/ a arte o infarte/ o ocre o canopo/ a
urna o farniente/ a foice o fascículo/ a lex o judex/ o maiô o avô/ a ave o
mocotó/ o só o sambaqui// II/ o gás o nefas/ o muro a rêmora/ a suicida o
cibo/ a litotes Aristóteles/ a paz o pus/ o licantropo o liceu/ o flit o flato/ a
víbora o heléboro/ o êmbolo o bolo// III/ o istmo o espasmo/ o ditirambo
o cachimbo/ a cutícula o ventríloquo/ a lágrima o magma/ o chumbo o
nelumbo/ a fórmica a fúcsia/ o bilro o pintassilgo/ o malte o gerifalte/ o
crime o aneurisma/ a tâmara a Câmara// IV/ o átomo o átono/ a medusa
o pégaso/ a erisipela a elipse/ a ama o sistema/ o quimono o amoníaco/
a nênia o nylon/ o cimento o ciumento/ a juba a jacuba/ o mendigo a
mandrágora/ o boné a boa-fé/ V/ a argila o sigilo/o pároco o báratro/ a
isca o menisco/ o idólatra o hidrópata/ o plátano o plástico/ a tartaruga
a ruga/ o estômago o mago/ o amanhecer o ser/ a galáxia a gloxínia/ o
cadarço a comborça/ VI/ o útil o tátil/ o colubiazol o gazel/ o lepidóptero
o útero/ o equívoco o fel no vidro/ a jóia a triticultura/ o *know-how* o
nocaute/ o dogma o borborigmo/ o úbere o lúgubre/ o nada a obesidade/
a cárie a intempérie// VII/ o dzeta o zeugma/ o cemitério a marinha/ a flor
a canéfora/ o pícnico o pícaro/ o cêsto o incesto/ o cigarro a formicida/ a
aorta o Passeio Público/ o mingau a *migraine*/ o leste a leitura/ a girafa a
jitanjáfora// VIII/ o índio a lêndea/ o coturno o estôrno/ a pia a piedade/ a
nolição o nonipétalo/ o radar o nácar/ o solferino o aquinatense/ o bacon o
dramaturgo/ o legal a galena/ o azul a lues/ a palavra a lebre// IX/ o remorso
o cós/ a noite o bis-coito/ o cestércio o consórcio/ o ético a ítaca/ a preguiça
a treliça/ o castiço o castigo/ o arroz o horror/ a nespa a vêspera/ o papa
a joaninha/ as endoenças os antibióticos// X/ o árvore a mar/ o doce de
pássaro/ a passa de pêsame/ o cio a poesia/ a fôrça do destino/ a pátria a
saciedade/ o cudelume Ulalume/ o zunzum de Zeus/ o bômbix/ o ptyx

A Passion for Measure / A paixão medida

Odile Cisneros, trans.

Trochaically I loved you, with dactylic tenderness
and a gestured spondee.
I held your iambs tight and close to mine.
One alcmanian day, the ropalic instinct
leonine stormed the pentameter's gate.
A long trimeter moan amid brief murmurs.
And what else, what else, in the echoic twilight,
but the broken memories
of Latin, of Greek, innumerable delights?

Trocaica te amei, com ternura dáctila/ e gesto espondeu./ Teus iambos aos
meus com força entrelacei./ Em dia alcmânico, o instinto ropálico/ rompeu,

leonino, a porta pentâmetra./ Gemido trilongo entre breves murmúrios./ E que mais, e que mais, no crepúsculo ecóico,/ senão a quebrada lembrança/ de latina, de grega, inumerável delícia?

In the Middle of the Way / No meio do caminho

Charles Bernstein, trans.

In the middle of the way was a stone
was a stone in the middle of the way
was a stone
in the middle of the way was a stone.

Never, me, I'll never forget that that happened
in the life of my oh so wearied retinas.
Never, me, I'll never forget that in the middle of the way
was a stone
was a stone in the middle of the way
in the middle of the way was a stone.

No meio do caminho tinha uma pedra/ tinha uma pedra no meio do caminho/ tinha uma pedra/ no meio do caminho tinha uma pedra// Nunca me esquecerei desse acontecimento/ na vida de minhas retinas tão fatigadas./ Nunca me esquecerei que no meio do caminho/ tinha uma pedra/ tinha uma pedra no meio do caminho/ no meio do caminho tinha uma pedra.

F

Odile Cisneros, trans.

                              Form
                              form
                              form

                                        one avoids
                                        therefore alive
                                        in the dead man seeking it

          color does not alight
          nor does density inhabit
          it before it is
          soon
          it is no more   won't be
          but is

                              forma
                              feast
                              fount

flame
film

and not finding it is no grief
for you fill up the large warehouse of the factual
where reality is larger than the entire universe

Forma/ forma/ forma// que se esquiva/ por isso mesmo viva/ no
morto que a procura// a côr não pousa/ nem a densidade habita/
nessa que antes de ser/ já deixou/ de ser não será/ mas é// forma/
festa/ fonte/ flama/ filme// e não encontrar-te é nenhum desgôsto/
pois abarrotas o largo armazém do factível/ onde a realidade é
maior do que a realidade

Nicolás Guillén (1902–1989, Cuba)

Guillén was born in the Camaguey province in Cuba to a white father and black
mother. His racial and cultural background served as a basis of his poetry: the cross-
cultural imagination of the Caribbean. He was Cuba's national poet and served as
the president of the National Union of Cuban Writers and Artists for many years.
Guillén is most well known for two thematic interests: the afro-Caribbean culture
and legacy, and anti-imperialism. He, along with Luis Palés Matos, founded the
negrismo movement in Latin American poetry that celebrated the black population's
contribution to Caribbean and Latin American society and culture. The long history of oppression from white hegemony was evident in his criticism of the United
States. Guillén was also known for incorporating song into his poetry, which he
called *poemas-son* (son-poems). This experimental structure is found in *Sensemayá*.
PRINCIPAL WORKS: *Motivios de son* (1930), *Sóngoro cosongo* (1931), *El diario que a
diario* (1972)

Sensemayá

Roberto Márquez, trans.

Chant for killing a snake

Mayombe–bombe–mayombé!
Mayombe–bombe–mayombé!
Mayombe–bombe–mayombé!

The serpent has eyes made of glass;
the serpent comes, wraps itself round a stick;
with its eyes made of glass, round a stick,
with its eyes made of glass.

The serpent walks without any legs;
the serpent hides in the grass;
walking hides in the grass,
walking without any legs.

Mayombe–bombe–mayombé!
Mayombe–bombe–mayombé!
Mayombe–bombe–mayombé!

Hit it with the ax, and it dies:
hit it now!
Don't hit it with your foot, it will bite you,
Don't hit it with your foot, it will flee!

Sensemayá, the serpent
sensemayá.
Sensemayá, with his eyes,
sensemayá.
Sensemayá, with his tongue,
sensemayá.
Sensemayá, with his mouth,
sensemayá.

The dead serpent cannot eat;
the dead serpent cannot hiss;
cannot walk,
cannot run.
The dead serpent cannot see;
the dead serpent cannot drink;
cannot breathe,
cannot bite!

Mayombe–bombe–mayombé!
Sensemayá, the serpent . . .
Mayombe–bombe–mayombé!
Sensemayá, is not moving . . .

Mayombe–bombe–mayombé!
Sensemayá, the serpent . . .
Mayombe–bombe–mayombé!
Sensemayá, he is dead!

Canto para matar una culebra// ¡Mayombe–bombe–mayombé!/ ¡Mayombe–
bombe–mayombé!/ ¡Mayombe–bombe–mayombé!// La culebra tiene los
ojos de vidrio;/ la culebra viene y se enreda en un palo;/ con sus ojos de
vidrio en un palo,/ con sus ojos de vidrio.// La culebra camina sin patas;/
la culebra se esconde en la yerba;/ caminando se esconde en la yerba,/

caminando sin patas.// ¡Mayombe–bombe–mayombé!/ ¡Mayombe–bombe–mayombé!/ ¡Mayombe–bombe–mayombé!// Tú le das con el hacha y se muere:/ ¡dale ya!/ ¡No le des con el pie, que te muerde,/ no le des con el pie, que se va!// Sensemayá, la culebra,/ sensemayá./ Sensemayá, con sus ojos,/ sensemayá./ Sensemayá, con su lengua,/ sensemayá./ Sensemayá, con su boca,/ sensemayá.// La culebra muerta no puede comer,/ la culebra muerta no puede silbar,/ no puede caminar,/ no puede correr./ La culebra muerta no puede mirar,/ la culebra muerta no puede beber,/ no puede respirar,/ no puede morder.// ¡Mayombe–bombe–mayombé!/ *Sensemayá, la culebra . . .* / ¡Mayombe–bombe–mayombé!/ *Sensemayá, no se mueve . . .* // ¡Mayombe–bombe–mayombé!/ *Sensemayá, la culebra . . .* / ¡Mayombe–bombe–mayombé!/ *Sensemayá, se murió*

Son Number 6 / Son número 6

Salvador Ortiz-Carboneres, trans.

I'm Yoruba, crying out Yoruba
Lucamí.
Since I'm a Yoruba from Cuba,
I want my lament of Yoruba to touch Cuba
the joyful weeping Yoruba
that comes out of me.

I'm Yoruba,
I keep singing
and crying.
When not Yoruba
I am Congo, Mandinga, or Carabalí.
Listen my friends, to my *'son'* which begins like this:

Here is the riddle
of all my hopes:
what's mine is yours,
what's yours is mine;
all the blood
shaping a river.

The silk-cotton tree, tree with its crown;
father, the father with his son;
the tortoise in its shell.
Let the heart-warming *'son'* break out,
and our people dance,
heart close to heart,
glasses clinking together
water on water with rum!

I'm Yoruba, I'm Lucumí,
Mandinga, Congo, Carabalí.
Listen my friends, to the *'son'* that goes like this:

We've come together from far away,
young ones and old,
Blacks and Whites, moving together;
one is the leader, the other a follower,
all moving together;
San Berenito and one who's obeying
all moving together;
Blacks and Whites from far away,
all moving together;
Santa María and one who's obeying
all moving together;
all pulling together, Santa María,
San Berenito, all pulling together,
all moving together, San Berenito,
San Berenito, Santa María.
Santa María, San Berenito,
everyone pulling together!

I'm Yoruba, I'm Lucumí
Mandiga, Congo, Carabalí.
Listen my friends, to my *'son'* which ends like this:

Come out Mulatto,
walk on free,
tell the white man he can't leave . . .
Nobody breaks away from here;
look and don't stop,
listen and don't wait
drink and don't stop,
eat and don't wait,
live and don't hold back
our people's *'son'* will never end!

Yoruba soy, lloro en yoruba/ lucumí./ Como soy un yoruba de Cuba,/ quiero
que hasta Cuba suba mi llanto yoruba;/ que suba el alegre llanto yoruba/
que sale de mí.// Yoruba soy,/ cantando voy,/ llorando estoy,/ y cuando
no soy yoruba,/ soy congo, mandinga, carabalí./ Atiendan, amigos, mi
son, que empieza así:// Adivinanza/ de la esperanza:/ lo mío es tuyo,/ lo
tuyo es mío;/ toda la sangre/ formando un río.// La seiba seiba con su
penacho;/ el padre padre con su muchacho;/ la jicotea en su carapacho./
¡Que rompa el son caliente,/ y que lo baile la gente,/ pecho con pecho,/

vaso con vaso,/ y agua con agua con aguardiente!/ Yoruba soy, soy lucumí,/ mandinga, congo, carabalí./ Atiendan, amigos, mi son, que sigue así:/ Estamos juntos desde muy lejos,/ jóvenes, viejos,/ negros y blancos, todo mezclado;/ uno mandando y otro mandado,/ todo mezclado;/ San Berenito y otro mandado,/ todo mezclado;/ negros y blancos desde muy lejos,/ todo mezclado;/ Santa María y uno mandado,/ todo mezclado;/ todo mezclado, Santa María,/ San Berenito, todo mezclado,/ todo mezclado, San Berenito,/ San Berenito, Santa María,/ Santa María, San Berenito,/ ¡todo mezclado!// Yoruba soy, soy lucumí,/ mandinga, congo, carabalí./ Atiendan, amigos, mi son, que acaba así:// Salga el mulato,/ suelte el zapato,/ díganle al blanco que no se va:/ de aquí no hay nadie que se separe;/ mire y no pare,/ oiga y no pare,/ beba y no pare,/ coma y no pare,/ viva y no pare,/ ¡que el son de todos no va a parar!

My Last Name I, a Family Elegy / El apellido I, elgía familiar

Roberto Márquez, trans.

Ever since school
and even before . . . Since the dawn, when I was
barely a patch of sleep and wailing,
since then
I have been told my name. A password
that I might speak with stars.
Your name is, you shall be called . . .
And then they handed me
this you see here written on my card,
this I put at the foot of all poems:
thirteen letters
that I carry on my shoulders through the street,
that are with me always, no matter where I go.
Are you sure it is my name?
Have you got all my particulars?
Do you already know my navigable blood,
my geography full of dark mountains,
of deep and bitter valleys
that are not on the maps?
Perhaps you have visited my chasms,
my subterranean galleries
with great moist rocks,
islands jutting out of black puddles,
where I feel the pure rush
of ancient waters
falling from my proud heart

with a sound that's fresh and deep
to a place of flaming trees,
acrobatic monkeys,
legislative parrots and snakes?
Does all my skin (I should have said),
does all my skin come from that Spanish marble?
My frightening voice too,
the harsh cry in my throat?
Are all my bones from there?
My roots and the roots
of my roots and also
these dark branches swayed by dreams
and these flowers blooming on my forehead
and this sap embittering my bark?

Are you certain?
Is there nothing more than this that you have written,
than this which you have stamped
with the seal of anger?
(Oh, I should have asked!)
Well then, I ask you now:
Don't you see these drums in my eyes?
Don't you see these drums, tightened and
beaten with two dried-up tears?
Don't I have, perhaps,
a nocturnal grandfather
with a great black scar
(darker still than his skin)
a great scar made by a whip?
Have I not, then,
a grandfather who'd Mandingo, Dahoman, Congolese?
What is his name? Oh, yes, give me his name!
Andrés? Francisco? Amable?
How do you say Andrés in Congolese?
How have you always said
Francisco in Dahoman?
In Mandingo, how do you say Amable?
No? Where they, then, other names?
The last name then!
Do you know my other last name, the one that comes
to me from that enormous land, the captured,
bloody last name, that came across the sea
in chains, which came in chains across the sea?

Ah, you can't remember it!
You have dissolved it in immemorial ink.
You stole it from a poor, defenseless Black.
You hid it, thinking that I would
lower my eyes in shame.
Thank you!
I am grateful to you!
Noble people, thanks!
Merci!
Merci bien!
Merci beaucoup!
But no . . . Can you believe it? No.
I am clean.
My voice sparkles like newly polished metal.
Look at my shield: it has a baobab,
it has a rhinoceros and a spear.
I am also the grandson,
great grandson,
great great grandson of a slave.
(Let the master be ashamed.)
Am I Yelofe?
Nicolás Yelofe, perhaps?
Or Nicolás Bakongo?
Maybe Guillén Banguila?
Or Kumbá?
Perhaps Guillén Kumbá?
Or Kongué?
Could I be Guillén Kongué?
Oh, who knows!
What a riddle in the waters!

Desde la escuela/ y aún antes . . . Desde el alba, cuando apenas/ era una
brizna yo de sueño y llanto,/ desde entonces,/ me dijeron mi nombre. Un
santo y seña/ para poder hablar con las estrellas./ Tú te llamas, te llamarás
. . . / Y luego me entregaron/ esto que veis escrito en mi tarjeta,/ esto que
pongo al pie de mis poemas:/ las trece letras/ que llevo a cuestas por la
calle,/ que siempre van conmigo a todas partes./ ¿Es mi nombre, estáis
ciertos?/ ¿Tenéis todas mis señas?/ ¿Ya conocéis mi sangre navegable,/
mi geografía llena de oscuros montes,/ de hondos y amargos valles/ que
no están en los mapas?/ ¿Acaso visitasteis mis abismos,/ mis galerías
subterráneas/ con grandes piedras húmedas,/ islas sobresaliendo en
negras charcas/ y donde un puro chorro/ siento de antiguas aguas/ caer
desde mi alto corazón/ con fresco y hondo estrépito/ en un lugar lleno

de ardientes árboles,/ monos equilibristas,/ loros legisladores y culebras?/ ¿Toda mi piel (debí decir),/ toda mi piel viene de aquella estatua/ de mármol español? ¿También mi voz de espanto,/ el duro grito de mi garganta? ¿Vienen de allá/ todos mis huesos? ¿Mis raíces y las raíces/ de mis raíces y además/ estas ramas oscuras movidas por los sueños/ y estas flores abiertas en mi frente/ y esta savia que amarga mi corteza?/ ¿Estáis seguros?/ ¿No hay nada más que eso que habéis escrito,/ que eso que habéis sellado/ con un sello de cólera?/ (¡Oh, debí haber preguntado!)// Y bien, ahora os pregunto:/ ¿No veis estos tambores en mis ojos?/ ¿No veis estos tambores tensos y golpeados/ con dos lágrimas secas?/ ¿No tengo acaso/ un abuelo nocturno/ con una gran marca negra/ (más negra todavía que la piel)/ una gran marca hecha de un latigazo?/ ¿No tengo pues/ un abuelo mandinga, congo, dahomeyano?/ ¿Cómo se llama? ¡Oh, sí, decídmelo!/ ¿Andrés? ¿Francisco? ¿Amable?/ ¿Cómo decís Andrés en congo? ¿Cómo habéis dicho siempre/Francisco en dahomeyano?/ En mandinga ¿cómo se dice Amable?/ ¿O no? ¿Eran, pues, otros nombres?/ ¡El apellido, entonces!/ ¿Sabéis mi otro apellido, el que me viene/ de aquella tierra enorme, el apellido/ sangriento y capturado, que pasó sobre el mar?/ entre cadenas, que pasó entre cadenas sobre el mar?// ¡Ah, no podéis recordarlo!/ Lo habéis disuelto en tinta inmemorial./ Lo habéis robado a un pobre negro indefenso./ Los escondisteis, creyendo/ que iba a bajar los ojos yo de la vergüenza./ ¡Gracias!/ ¡Os lo agradezco!/ ¡Gentiles gentes, thank you!/ Merci!/ Merci bien!/ Merci beaucoup!/ Pero no . . . ¿Podéis creerlo? No./ Yo estoy limpio./ Brilla mi voz como un metal recién pulido./ Mirad mi escudo: tiene un baobab,/ tiene un rinoceronte y una lanza./ Yo soy también el nieto,/ biznieto,/ tataranieto de un esclavo./ (Que se avergüence el amo)./ ¿Seré Yelofe?/ ¿Nicolás Yelofe, acaso?/ ¿O Nicolás Bakongo?/ ¿Tal vez Guillén Banguila?/ ¿O Kumbá?/ ¿Quizá Guillén Kumbá?/ ¿O Kongué?/ ¿Pudiera ser Guillén Kongué?/ ¡Oh, quién lo sabe!/ ¡Qué enigma entre las aguas!

Xavier Villaurrutia (1903–1950, Mexico)

A poet and playwright born in Mexico City, Villaurrutia was associated from an early age with the poet Salvador Novo. Together they initiated the movement known in Mexico as "Los Contemporáneos," composed of urbanites, gay men and women, that brought about a complete renewal of writing and social attitudes in the country in the 1930s and 1940s. In his poetic work, he liberated the prosody and themes of *modernismo,* discarding its rhetoric in favor of a condensed, precise, and playful observation of the depths of sensation and feeling. His intensely visual imagination asks us "to observe the gaze with a different evening." Octavio Paz said he was a major poet of desire who "discovered secret corridors running between dreaming and wakefulness, love and hate." His influence on future generations was immense. In 1955, shortly after his death, the Xavier Villaurrutia Award for Literature was established in Mexico. PRINCIPAL WORKS: *Reflejos* (1926), *Nocturnos* (1933), *Nostalgia de la muerte* (1938), *Invitación a la muerte* (1941)

L.A. Nocturne: The Angels / Nocturno de Los Angeles

Eliot Weinberger, trans.

You might say the streets flow sweetly through the night.
The lights are dim so the secret will be kept,
the secret known by the men who come and go,
for they're all in on the secret
and why break it up in a thousand pieces
when it's so sweet to hold it close,
and share it only with the one chosen person.

If, at a given moment, everyone would say
with one word what he is thinking,
the six letters of DESIRE would form an enormous luminous scar,
a constellation more ancient, more dazzling than any other.
And that constellation would be like a burning sex
in the deep body of night,
like the Gemini, for the first time in their lives,
looking each other in the eyes and embracing forever.

Suddenly the river of the street is filled with thirsty creatures;
they walk, they pause, they move on.
They exchange glances, they dare to smile,
they form unpredictable couples . . .

There are nooks and benches in the shadows,
riverbanks of dense indefinable shapes,
sudden empty spaces of blinding light
and doors that open at the slightest touch.

For a moment, the river of the street is deserted.
Then it seems to replenish itself,
eager to start again.
It is a paralyzed, mute, gasping moment,
like a heart between two spasms.

But a new throbbing, a new pulsebeat
launches new thirsty creatures on the river of the street.
They cross, crisscross, fly up.

They glide along the ground.
They swim standing up, so miraculously
no one would ever say they're not really walking.

They are angels.
They have come down to earth
on invisible ladders.
They come from the sea that is the mirror of the sky
on ships of smoke and shadow,
they come to fuse and be confused with men,
to surrender their foreheads to the thighs of women,
to let other hands anxiously touch their bodies
and let other bodies search for their bodies till they're found,
like the closing lips of a single mouth,
they come to exhaust their mouths, so long inactive,
to set free their tongues of fire,
to sing the songs, to swear, to say all the bad words
in which men have concentrated the ancient mysteries
of flesh, blood, and desire.

They have assumed names that are divinely simple.
They call themselves *Dick* or *John*, *Marvin* or *Louis*.
Only by their beauty are they distinguishable from men.
They walk, they pause, they move on.
They exchange glances, they dare to smile.
They form unpredictable couples.

They smile maliciously going up in the elevators of hotels,
where leisurely vertical flight is still practiced.
There are celestial marks on their naked bodies:
blue signs, blue stars and letters.
They let themselves fall into beds, they sink into pillows
that make them think they're still in the clouds.
But they close their eyes to surrender to the pleasures of their mysterious
    incarnation,
and when they sleep, they dream not of angels but of men.

Se diría que las calles fluyen dulcemente en la noche./ Las luces no son tan
vivas que logren desvelar el secreto,/ el secreto que los hombres que van
y vienen conocen,/ porque todos están en el secreto/ y nada se ganaría
con partirlo en mil pedazos/ si, por el contrario, es tan dulce guardarlo/ y
compartirlo sólo con la persona elegida.// Si cada uno dijera en un momento
dado,/ en sólo una palabra, lo que piensa,/ las cinco letras del DESEO
formarían una enorme cicatriz luminosa,/ una constelación más antigua,
más viva aún que las otras./ Y esa constelación sería como un ardiente sexo/

en el profundo cuerpo de la noche,/ o, mejor, como los Gemelos que por
vez primera en la vida/ se miraran de frente, a los ojos, y se abrazaran ya
para siempre.// De pronto el río de la calle se puebla de sedientos seres,//
caminan, se detienen, prosiguen./ Cambian miradas, atreven sonrisas, /
forman imprevistas parejas.. // Hay recodos y bancos de sombra,/ orillas
de indefinibles formas profundas/ y súbitos huecos de luz que ciega/ y
puertas que ceden a la presión más leve. // El río de la calle queda desierto
un instante./ Luego parece remontar de sí mismo/ deseoso de volver a
empezar./ Queda un momento paralizado, mudo, anhelante / como el
corazón entre dos espasmos.// Pero una nueva pulsación, un nuevo latido/
arroja al río de la calle nuevos sedientos seres./ Se cruzan, se entrecruzan
y suben./ Vuelan a ras de tierra./ Nadan de pie, tan milagrosamente/ que
nadie se atrevería a decir que no caminan.// ¡Son los ángeles!/ Han bajado a
la tierra/ por invisibles escalas./ Vienen del mar, que es el espejo del cielo,/
en barcos de humo y sombra,/ a fundirse y confundirse con los mortales,/
a rendir sus frentes en los muslos de las mujeres,/ a dejar que otras manos
palpen sus cuerpos febrilmente,/ y que otros cuerpos busquen los suyos hasta
encontrarlos/ como se encuentran al cerrarse los labios de una misma boca,/
a fatigar su boca tanto tiempo inactiva,/ a poner en libertad sus lenguas de
fuego,/ a decir las canciones, los juramentos, las malas palabras/ en que los
hombres concentran el antiguo misterio/ de la carne, la sangre y el deseo.//
Tienen nombres supuestos, divinamente sencillos./ Se llaman Dick o John,
o Marvin o Louis./ En nada sino en la belleza se distinguen de los mortales./
Caminan, se detienen, prosiguen./ Cambian miradas, atreven sonrisas./
Forman imprevistas parejas.// Sonríen maliciosamente al subir en los
ascensores de los hoteles/ donde aún se practica el vuelo lento y vertical./ En
sus cuerpos desnudos hay huellas celestiales;/ signos, estrellas y letras azules./
Se dejan caer en la camas, se hunden en las almohadas/ que los hacen pensar
todavía un momento en las nubes./ Pero cierran los ojos para entregarse
mejor a los goces de su encarnación misteriosa,/ y, cuando duermen, sueñan
no con los ángeles sino los mortales.

Nocturne: Fear / Nocturno miedo

Eliot Weinberger, trans.

Everything lives at night in secret doubt:
silence and sound, place and time.
Asleep unmoving or sleepwalking awake,
nothing can be done for that secret dread.

And it's useless to close your eyes in the shadows,
to sink them in sleep so they'll not keep seeing,
for in the hardening shadows, the cave of dreams,
the same nocturnal light will wake you again.

Then, with the shuffle of the suddenly woken,
aimlessly, pointlessly, you start walking.
Night spills its mysteries over you,
and something tells you that to die is to wake up.

In the shadows of a deserted street, on a wall,
in the deep purple mirror of loneliness, who
hasn't seen himself on the way to or from some encounter,
and not felt the fear and wretchedness and fatal doubt?

The fear of being nothing but an empty body
that anybody—I or anyone else—could occupy,
and the wretchedness of watching yourself, alive,
and the doubt that it is—it is not—real.

Todo en la noche vive una duda secreta:/ el silencio y el ruido, el tiempo
y el lugar./ Inmóviles dormidos o despiertos sonámbulos/ nada podemos
contra la secreta ansiedad.// Y no basta cerrar los ojos en la sombra/ ni
hundirlos en el sueño para ya no mirar,/ porque en la dura sombra y en la
gruta del sueño/ la misma luz nocturna nos vuelve a desvelar.// Entonces,
con el paso de un dormido despierto,/ sin rumbo y sin objeto nos echamos
a andar./ La noche vierte sobre nosotros su misterio,/ y algo nos dice que
morir es despertar.// ¿Y quién entre las sombras de una calle desierta,/
en el muro, lívido espejo de soledad,/ no se ha visto pasar o venir a su
encuentro/ y no ha sentido miedo, angustia, duda mortal?// El miedo
de no ser sino un cuerpo vacío/ que alguien, yo mismo o cualquier otro,
puede ocupar,/ y la angustia de verse fuera de sí, viviendo,/ y la duda de
ser o no ser realidad.

César Moro (1903–1956, Peru)

Poet, artist, and member of the surrealist movement in Paris, Moro's work was published by Breton and Eluard as part of *Le surréalisme au service de la révolution*. Born
in Lima, Moro originally wrote in Spanish but adopted the French language after
spending time in Paris. In 1938, he lived in Mexico for ten years, where he co-
organized the International Surrealist Exhibition of 1940 with Breton. Although he
eventually stopped working with Breton, his later poetry was still associated with
the surrealists. PRINCIPAL WORKS: *Le chateau de Grisou* (1943), *Lettre d'amour* (1944),
Trafalgar Square (1954)

To Wait / Attendre

Frances LeFevre, trans.

```
a    t    s    e    b    d    k    e
t    y    t    n    l    i    i    x
t    r    a    e    a    f    n    t
a    a    i    m    c    f    g    i
c    n    n    y    k    i         n
k    t              c         c
                    u         t
                    l
                    t
```

```
A    T    T    E    N    D    R    E
T    Y    E    N    O    I    O    T
T    R    I    N    I    F    I    E
E    A    N    E    R    F         I
I    N    T    M    I              N
N         I                        T
T                   I
                    L
                    E
```

Trafalgar Square

Frances LeFevre, trans.

To translate the fool
go from the algae
to Trafalgar Square

I myself am the eternal
Reject yourself and you have no master to protect you,
No expected birth
Elect to be your soul's hearth vomit up your faith
I am he who does not die who has always existed
Simple but not easy to hold
Diomedes for the mares of Demeter
To nail God down

Traduire le fol aller/ Des algues/ À Traflagar Square// Je me suis l'Éternel/
Se démettre est l'absence de maître l'absence de naître/ Être l'âtre dé l'âme
vomir la foi/ Je suis celui qui ne meurt pas celui qui existe depuis toujours/
Simple mais pas facile à tenir/ Diomède pour les chevaux de Déméter/ Metre
Dieu au clou

Pablo Neruda (1904–1973, Chile)

Perhaps the most widely read poet in the world today, Neruda was born Neftalí Reyes in Parral, Chile. The inner density and groundedness of his images made him an instant success. His early work was lyrical, but in the 1930s it darkened to become intensely experimental. From the 1940s on his political commitment drove his work. He experienced writing as a "jumble of marine cries and primal warnings." He received the Nobel Prize in Literature in 1971. He died in Santiago a few days after the military coup of September 11, 1973. PRINCIPAL WORKS: *Veinte poemas de amor y una canción desesperada* (1924), *Residencia en la tierra* (1933), *España en el corazón* (1937), *Alturas de Macchu Picchu* (1947), *Canto general* (1950), *Odas elementales* (1954–1959), *Libro de las preguntas* (1974)

Melancholy Inside Families / Melancolía en las familias

Robert Bly and James Wright, trans.

I keep a blue bottle.
Inside it an ear and a portrait.
When the night dominates
the feathers of the owl,
when the hoarse cherry tree
rips out its lips and makes menacing gestures
with rinds which the ocean wind often perforates—
then I know that there are immense expanses hidden from us,
quartz in slugs,
ooze,
blue waters for a battle,
much silence, many ore-veins
of withdrawals and camphor,
fallen things, medallions, kindnesses,
parachutes, kisses.

It is only the passage from one day to another,
a single bottle moving over the seas,
and a dining room where roses arrive,
a dining room deserted
as a fish-bone; I am speaking of
a smashed cup, a curtain, at the end
of a deserted room through which a river passes
dragging along the stones. It is a house
set on the foundations of the rain,
a house of two floors with the required number of windows,
and climbing vines faithful in every particular.

I walk through afternoons, I arrive
full of mud and death,
dragging along the earth and its roots,
and its indistinct stomach in which corpses
are sleeping with wheat,
metals, and pushed-over elephants.

But above all there is a terrifying,
a terrifying deserted dining room,
with its broken olive oil cruets,
and vinegar running under its chairs,
one ray of moonlight tied down,
something dark, and I look
for a comparison inside myself:
perhaps it is a grocery store surrounded by the sea
and torn clothing from which sea water is dripping.

It is only a deserted dining room,
and around it there are expanses,
sunken factories, pieces of timber
which I alone know,
because I am sad, and because I travel,
and I know the earth, and I am sad.

Conservo un frasco azul,/ dentro de él una oreja y un retrato:/ cuando la
noche obliga/ a las plumas del buho,/ cuando el ronco cerezo/ se destroza
los labios y amenaza/ con cáscaras que el viento del océano a menudo
perfora,/ yo sé que hay grande extensiones hundidas,/ cuarzo en lingotes,/
cieno,/ aguas azules para una batalla,/ mucho silencio, muchas/ vetas
de retrocesos y alcanfores,/ cosas caídas, medallas, ternuras,/ paracaídas,
besos.// No es sino el paso de un día hacia otro,/ una sola botella
andando por los mares,/ y un comedor adonde llegan rosas,/ un comedor
abandonado/ como una espina: me refiero/ a una copa trizada, a una
cortina, al fondo/ de una sala desierta por donde pasa un río/ arrastrando
las piedras. Es una casa/ situada en los cimientos de la lluvia,/ una casa de
dos pisos con ventanas obligatorias/ y enredaderas estrictamente fieles.//
Voy por las tardes, llego/ lleno de lodo y muerte,/ arrastrando la tierra
y sus raíces,/ y su vaga barriga en donde duermen/ cadáveres con trigo,/
metales, elefantes derrumbados.// Pero por sobre todo hay un terrible,/
un terrible comedor abandonado,/ con las alcuzas rotas/ y el vinagre
corriendo debajo de las sillas,/ un rayo detenido de la luna,/ algo oscuro,
y me busco/ una comparación dentro de mí:/ tal vez es una tienda rodeada
por el mar/ y paños rotos goteando salmuera.// Es sólo un comedor
abandonado,/ y alrededor hay extensiones,/ fábricas sumergidas, maderas/

que sólo yo conozco,/ porque estoy triste y viajo,/ y conozco la tierra, y
estoy triste.

Walking Around

Jerome Rothenberg, trans.

It just so happens that I'm tired of being a man.
It just so happens that I walk into tailor shops and movies,
withered, impenetrable, a flannel swan
that steers across a sea of origins and ashes.

The odors from a barber shop can start me bawling.
I only want a little rest from stones and wool.
I only want to see my last of institutes and gardens,
of merchandise, of eyeglasses, of elevators.

It just so happens that I'm tired of my feet and my nails
and my hair and my shadow.
It just so happens that I'm tired of being a man.

And yet how delightful it would be
to threaten some accountant with the head of a lily
or murder a nun with a blow on the ear.
How beautiful
to go through streets with a green knife
and holler out loud till I die of frostbite.

I don't want to keep on being a root in the darkness,
irresolute, pulled from all sides, till a dream leaves me shaking,
dragged down through the seeping bowels of the earth,
absorbing and thinking, stuffed with food every day.

I don't want all that grief on my shoulders.
I don't want to keep on as a root and a tomb,
alone underground, a wine cellar stocked with the dead,
frozen stiff, half gone with the pain.

So the day called Monday started burning like oil
when it sees me pull in with my face of a jailhouse,
and it howls on its way like a wounded wheel,
and leaves tracks of hot blood in the direction of night.

And it shoves me into certain dark corners, into certain moist houses,
into hospitals where the bones sail through the windows,
into certain shoemakers' shops with their odor of vinegar,
into streets full of terrible holes.

There are birds the color of sulfur and horrible guts
that swing from the doors of houses that I hate,
there are false teeth forgotten in a coffee pot,
there are mirrors
that ought to be crying from shame and terror,
there are umbrellas wherever I look, and poisons, and belly buttons.

I walk around with my calm, with my eyes, with my shoes,
with my anger, with my memory failing,
I move on, I wander through offices and orthopedic shops,
and courtyards where clothes are hung from a wire:
underdrawers, towels, and nightgowns that cry
slow tears full of dirt.

Sucede que me canso de ser hombre./ Sucede que entro en las sastrerías
y en los cines/ marchito, impenetrable, como un cisne de fieltro/ navegando
en un agua de origen y ceniza.// El olor de las peluquerías me hace llorar
a gritos./ Sólo quiero un descanso de piedras o de lana,/ sólo quiero no ver
establecimientos ni jardines, / ni mercaderías, ni anteojos, ni ascensores.//
Sucede que me canso de mis pies y mis uñas/ y mi pelo y mi sombra./
Sucede que me canso de ser hombre.// Sin embargo sería delicioso/ asustar
a un notario con un lirio cortado/ o dar muerte a una monja con un golpe
de oreja./ Sería bello/ ir por las calles con un cuchillo verde/ y dando gritos
hasta morir de frío.// No quiero seguir siendo raíz en las tinieblas,/ vacilante,
extendido, tiritando de sueño,/ hacia abajo, en las tripas mojadas de la tierra,/
absorbiendo y pensando, comiendo cada día.// No quiero para mí tantas
desgracias./ No quiero continuar de raíz y de tumba,/ de subterráneo solo, de
bodega con muertos/ ateridos, muriéndome de pena.// Por eso el día lunes
arde como el petróleo/ cuando me ve llegar con mi cara de cárcel,/ y aúlla en
su transcurso como una rueda herida,/ y da pasos de sangre caliente hacia la
noche.// Y me empuja a ciertos rincones, a ciertas casas húmedas,/ a hospitales
donde los huesos salen por la ventana,/ a ciertas zapaterías con olor a vinagre,/
a calles espantosas como grietas.// Hay pájaros de color de azufre y horribles
intestinos/ colgando de las puertas de las casas que odio,/ hay dentaduras
olvidadas en una cafetera,/ hay espejos/ que debieran haber llorado de
vergüenza y espanto,/ hay paraguas en todas partes, y venenos, y ombligos.//
Yo paseo con calma, con ojos, con zapatos,/ con furia, con olvido,/ paso, cruzo
oficinas y tiendas de ortopedia,/ y patios donde hay ropas colgadas de un
alambre:/ calzoncillos, toallas y camisas que lloran/ lentas lágrimas sucias.

Right, Comrade, It's the Hour of the Garden / Sí, camarada, es hora de jardín

Forrest Gander, trans.

Right, comrade, it's the hour of the garden
and the hour up in arms, each day
follows from flower or blood:
our time surrenders us to an obligation
to water the jasmines
or bleed to death in a dark street:
virtue or pain blows off
into frozen realms, into hissing embers,
and there never was a choice:
heaven's roads,
once the by-ways of saints,
are jammed now with experts.

Already the horses have vanished.

Heroes hop around like toads,
mirrors live out emptinesses
because the party is happening somewhere else,
wherever we aren't invited
and fights frame themselves in doorjambs.

That's why this is the last call,
the tenth clear
ringing of my bell:
to the garden, comrade, to the pale lily,
to the apple tree, to the intransigent carnation,
to the fragrance of lemon blossoms,
and then to the ultimatums of war.

Ours is a lank country
and on the naked edge of her knife
our frail flag burns.

Si, camarada, es hora de jardín/ y es hora de batalla, cada día/ es sucesión de flor o sangre:/ nuestro tiempo nos entregó amarrados/ a regar los jazmines/ o a desangrarnos en una calle oscura:/ la virtud o el dolor se repartieron/ en zonas frías, en mordientes brasas,/ y no había otra cosa que elegir:/ los caminos del cielo,/ antes tan transitados por los santos,/ están poblados por especialistas.// Ya desaparecieron los caballos.// Los héroes van vestidos de batracios,/ los espejos viven vacíos/ porque la fiesta es siempre en otra parte,/ en donde ya no estamos invitados/ y hay pelea en la puertas.// Por eso es éste el llamado penúltimo,/ el décimo sincero/ toque de mi campana:/ el jardín, camarada, a la azucena,/ al manzano, al clavel intransigente,/ a la fragrancia de los azahares,/ y luego a los deberes de la guerra.// Delgada es nuestra patria/ y en su desnudo filo de cuchillo/ arde nuestra bandera delicada.

Aurelio Arturo (1906–1974, Colombia)

Born in Nariño, Colombia, Arturo lived a childhood marked by the rudimentary simplicity typical of a provincial town. His father was a schoolteacher, and both his parents encouraged his love of books. But his mother's death when he was eighteen shattered the ideal world of his youth. In the midst of his turmoil, he fled on horseback to Bogotá, in search of a new life. He constructed for himself the life of a gentleman: he studied law, married and had five children, and held public office jobs. But an old yearning haunted him— María Mercedes Carranza called him a "poet of the lost paradise." Sheltered by domesticity, he wrote in his spare time. He translated contemporary English-language poets. His thirty-one poems—populated by fairies, bewitched chambers, magic animals, and the most serene contemplation of the world around him—escape classification within Colombian literature and have earned him a place as a bedside poet who is increasingly gaining recognition throughout the continent. PRINCIPAL WORK: *Morada al sur* (1963)

Climate / Clima

Daniel Borzutzky, trans.

This green poem, leaf by leaf,
is cradled by a fertile, southwestern wind;
this poem is a country that dreams,
a cloud of light, a breeze of green leaves.

Water falls, stones, clouds, leaves,
a nimble puff against everything: this is its song.
There were palm trees, palm trees and breezes
and a light like swords through the air.

This faithful wind that cradles my poem,
this faithful wind that the song propels,
leaves cradled, clouds cradled, content
to cradle white clouds and green leaves.

I am the voice that gave pure songs to the wind
in the west of my clouds;
my heart in each palm, broken
fruit, united the many horizons.

And in my country of grazing clouds
I put my heart in the south, and in the north,
my eyes, two ravenous birds,
chased the flock of horizons.

Life is lovely, a strong hand, timid
fingers form the fragile cup
of your song, you fill it with joy
or with the sweetness hidden in your sorrow.

This green poem, leaf by leaf,
is cradled by a fertile wind, a gentle
wind that loved the southern grass and sky,
this poem is the country of wind.

Under a sword-filled sky, dark earth,
green trees, a green commotion
in the tiny leaves and a slow
wind pushes the leaves and the days.

The wind dances and the distant greens
call me with their secret murmurs:
docile woman, her breasts full of honey,
loves beneath the palm trees of my songs.

Este verde poema, hoja por hoja,/ lo mece un viento fértil, suroeste;/
este poema es un país que sueña,/ nube de luz y brisa de hojas verdes.//
Tumbos del agua, piedras, nubes, hojas/ y un soplo ágil en todo, son el
canto./ Palmas había, palmas y las brisas/ y una luz como espadas por el
ámbito.// El viento fiel que mece mi poema,/ el viento fiel que la canción
impele,/ hojas meció, nubes meció, contento/ de mecer nubes blancas y
hojas verdes.// Yo soy la voz que al viento dió canciones/ puras en el oeste,
de mis nubes;/ mi corazón en toda palma, roto/ dátil, unió los horizontes
múltiples.// Y en mi país apacentando nubes,/ puse en el sur mi corazón,
y al norte,/ cual dos aves rapaces, persiguieron/ mis ojos, el rebaño de
horizontes.// La vida es bella, dura mano, dedos/ tímidos al formar el
frágil vaso/ de tu canción, lo colmes de tu gozo/ o de escondidas mieles
de tu llanto.// Este verde poema, hoja por hoja/ lo mece un viento fértil,
un esbelto/ viento que amó del sur hierbas y cielos,/ este poema es el país
del viento.// Bajo un cielo de espadas, tierra oscura,/ árboles verdes, verde
algarabía/ de las hojas menudas y el moroso/ viento mueve las hojas y
los días.// Dance el viento y las verdes lontananzas/ me llamen con
recónditos rumores:/ dócil mujer, de miel henchido el seno,/ amó bajo las
palmas mis canciones.

Lullaby / Arrullo

Daniel Borzutzky, trans.

The night is very busy
cradling so many leaves,
one by one.
And none of the leaves
can sleep

If the stars would help,
how the infinite eternal bend
would tremble and chime.

But who would put to sleep so many,
so many,
if day is already breaking
over the river?

(Where does this country
of leaves sing?
And this lullaby of the deep
night?)

The days of golden peach fuzz
and the nights
of delicate lips
appear
at the edge of the river.

(Where is the exquisite country of rivers
that opens roads
to the clear air
and the song?)

The night is very busy
cradling so many leaves,
one by one.
And none of the leaves
can sleep.

If the stars would help . . .
But some are more hidden,
but there are some leaves,
which will never,
never,
enter the night.

(Where does this country
of leaves sing?
And this lullaby of the deep
night?)

La noche está muy atareada/ en mecer una por una,/ tántas hojas./ Y las
hojas no se duermen/ todas.// Si le ayudan las estrellas,/ cómo tiembla y
tintinea la infinita/ comba eterna.// Pero quién dormirá a tántas,/ tántas,/
si ya va subiendo el día/ por el río?// (Dónde canta este país/ de las hojas/
y este arrullo de la noche/ honda?)// Por el lado del río/ vienen los días/ de
bozo dorado,/ vienen las noches/ de fino labio.// (Dónde el bello país de los
ríos,/ que abre caminos/ al viento claro/ y al canto?)// La noche está muy
atareada/ en mecer una por una,/ tántas hojas./ Y las hojas no se duermen/
todas.// Si le ayudan las estrellas. . . . / Pero hay únas más ocultas,/ pero hay
unas hojas, únas/ que entrarán nunca en la noche,/ nunca.// (Dónde canta
este país/ de las hojas,/ y este arrullo de la noche/ honda?)

Omar Cáceres (1906–1943, Chile)

Cáceres was born in Cauquenes, Chile, to schoolteachers, but his father passed
away before his birth. Unique as a poet, his work is similar to that of Rimbaud and
Baudelaire. "A rare animal"—in the words of his friend Teófilo Cid—"who would
act as a poet even when he sneezed," Cáceres was also a violinist and the only
sighted member of an orchestra made up of blind musicians. His sole book was
prefaced by Huidobro—no other book ever was—and is the exploration of a clairvoyant, a demiurge performing his duties. In the words of Huidobro: "We are in
the presence of a true poet, that is, not one who sings to the ears of the flesh, but
one who sings to the ears of the spirit. We are in the presence of a discoverer—a
discoverer of the world and of his own inner world." A legendary figure until the
end, Cáceres was found dead in a ditch for reasons still unknown. PRINCIPAL WORK:
Defensa del ídolo (1930)

Mansion of Foam / Mansión de espuma
Mónica de la Torre, trans.

With my heart, pounding on you, oh boundless shadow,
I feed the absolute drives of these lasting engravings;
fleeing from his life, I think, he who parts cleanses the world,
and so is allowed to reflect his kindly terrestrial image.

A town (Blue), toilsomely flooded.
It will spend the rough season balancing its landscapes.

Time fallen from trees, any sky could be my sky.
The white path crosses its motionless storm.

Mute voice that dwells under my dreams,
my friend instructs me in the bare accent of her arms,
near the balcony of disciplined, uproarious, light,
from where yet unimagined misfortune can be seen.

Lined with distances, between man and meager-man,
everything sinks "under the banner of its last farewell";
I ceased to exist, soon fell forsaken by my own self,
because man loves only his own dark life.

Unknown idol. What shall I do to kiss it?
Legislator of urban time, doubled, abundant,
I confess my self-crime because I want to understand it,
and in the reefs of its stone alcohol I spread my words.

Con mi corazón, golpeándote, oh sombra ilimitada,/ apaciento los bríos
absolutos de estas estampas-perdurables;/ huyendo de su vida, pienso, el
que parte limpia el mundo,/ y así le es dado reflejar su imagen dulcemente
terrestre.// Un pueblo (Azul), trabajosamente inundado./ Va a pasar la dura
estación equilibrando sus paisajes./ Tiempo caído de los árboles, cualquier cielo
podría ser mi cielo./ El blanco camino cruza su inmóvil tempestad.// Muda voz
que habita debajo de mis sueños,/ mi amiga me instruye en el acento desnudo
de sus brazos,/ junto al balcón de luz disciplinada, tumultuosa,/ y desde
donde se advierte la aún no soñada desventura.// Revestido de distancias,
entre hombre a hombre-magro,/ todo naufraga "bajo el pendón de su postrer
adiós";/ dejé de existir, caí de pronto desamparado de mí mismo,/ porque el
hombre ama su propia y obscura vida solamente.// Idolo ignoto. ¿Qué he de
hacer para besarlo?/ Legislador del tiempo urbano, desdoblado, caudaloso,/
confieso mi autocrimen porque quiero comprenderlo,/ y en las rompientes de
su alcohol de piedra despliego mis palabras.

Deserted Blue / Azul deshabitado

Mónica de la Torre, trans.

Now, as I remember my former being, the places which I've inhabited,
and that still display my sacred thoughts,
I understand that sense, the plea with which all foreign solitude surprises
    us,
is nothing but proof of the persistence of human sadness.

Or, besides, the light of the one who smashes his security, his
    consecutiv'atmosphere,

to feel how, upon returning, his entire being explodes within a great
    number,
and to know that he "still" exists, "still" breathes and takes impoverished
    steps on this earth,
although he's there engrossed, identical, directionless,
alone like a mountain saying the word *then*:
so that no one can console he who suffers like this:
what he seeks, those for whom he grieves,
what he loves, it's all gone far away, reaching only itself!

Y, ahora, recordando mi antiguo ser, los lugares que yo he habitado,/ y que
aún ostentan mis sagrados pensamientos,/ comprendo que el sentido, el ruego
con que toda soledad extraña nos/ sorprende / no es más que la evidencia
que de la tristeza humana queda.// O, también, la luz de aquél que rompe su
seguridad, su consecutiv'atmósfera,/ para sentir cómo, al retornar, todo su ser
estalla dentro un gran número,/ y saber que «aún» existe, que "aún" alienta y
empobrece pasos en la tierra,/ pero que está ahí absorto, igual, sin dirección,/
solitario como una montaña diciendo la palabra *entonces:*/ de modo que
ningún hombre puede consolar al que así sufre:/ lo qu'él busca, aquéllos por
quienes él ahora llora,/ lo que ama, se ha ido también lejos, alcanzándose!

The I's Illumination / Iluminación del yo

Mónica de la Torre, trans.

Dripping its polished densities
around the identical, simultaneous, afternoons,
we here have that the meager, difficult day presents itself,
faithful to its stern, pure and subdued rhythm.

Its infinite leaves, intensely signaling the limit,
from where it emerges replenished with inner sides,
turn above my youthful will, tender and virile,
just as I said while singing this morning.

Because I'm here, o monument of light,
always inclined toward you, a stranger to myself,
ready for your sudden glow of swords,
fixed to your conceited g-hostly signification,
o light of straight solitudes, of inflexible heights and equatorial events.

So now,

toss this perfection out to tumble in the plain,
I can say everything, pick up everything:
it breaks in, it emerges, from this lamp, piece by piece,

a nocturnal poem that I've handwritten unclearly,
night of a bluish rainstorm, o incomparable rectitude.

It is I who dominates that blissful confine,
who watches over his friends' sleep,
who was always all set,
who folds the fatigue thinning out all mirrors.
Now I catch my face on the water of those deep farewells,
in the screens of those last sobs,
because I'm behind all things
crying for what they stole from my own self.

And I love the warmth of this consoling pain-stricken flesh,
the sensuous shadow of the bare sadness I took from the angels,
the ring of my breathing, recently carved . . .
It's all that remains, o anxiety.

Release, then, your deep soothing metals into my sobs,
hasten the flames, those high disciplines,
the order smirking on my knees,
morbid light of all bells.

Not a single thought, o poets,
poems EXIST,
they await us!

Chorreando sus bruñidas densidades/ alrededor de las tardes iguales,
simultáneas,/ he aquí que el magro, difícil día se presenta,/ fiel a su ritmo
adusto, puro, sojuzgado.// Sus infinitas hojas, que señalan intensamente
el límite,/ desde donde emerge reverdecido de lados profundos,/ giran
sobre mi joven voluntad, amorosa y viril,/ así como cantando lo decía
esta mañana.// Porque ahí estoy, oh monumento de luz,/ siempre hacia
ti inclinado, extranjero de mí mismo,/ presto a tu súbita irradiación de
espadas,/ fijo a tu altiva significación de espec-tro,/ oh luz de soledades
derechas, de inflexibles alturas y ecuatoriales sucesos// Y bien,/ echa a
rodar esta perfección en tu llanura,/ puedo ahora decirlo todo, recogerlo
todo:/ irrumpe, surge, de esta lámpara, a pedazos,/ nocturno poema que yo
he escrito con letras imprecisas,/ noche de azulada tormenta, oh rectitud
incomparable.// Yo soy el que domina esa extensión gozosa,/ el que vela
el sueño de los amigos,/ el que estuvo siempre pronto,/ el que dobla esa
fatiga que adelgaza todos los espejos.// Ahora sorprendo mi rostro en el
agua de esas profundas despedidas,/ en las mamparas de esos últimos
sollozos,/ porque estoy detrás de cada cosa/ llorando lo que se llevaron
de mí mismo.// Y amo el calor de esta carne dolorosa que me ampara,/ la
sombra sensual de esta tristeza desnuda que robé a los ángeles,/ el anillo de

mi respiración, recién labrado . . . / Es todo cuanto queda, oh ansiedad.//
Descuelga, pues, en mis sollozos tus profundos plomos de sosiego,/ acelera
esas llamas, esas altas disciplinas,/ ese orden que sonríe en mis rodillas,/
mórbida luz de todas las campanas.// Ni un solo pensamiento, oh poetas,/
los poemas EXISTEN,/ nos aguardan!

Visitor Extremes / Extremos visitantes

Mónica de la Torre, trans.

Exuberant remoteness materializing in my orchard, plunging into my trees.
I understand: the wind, this wind, is the soul of distances:
breaking the skies open, overturning its life at every encounter,
it doesn't fold itself into time in order to witness completely the life of
    things;
its wisdom is always brand new, in the making,
resuming all secrets, flooding them, without removing
their unruly ferment, their bountiful passion;
like a poet in solidarity, unanimous, cosmological, central,
witnessing in his own spirit what confines itself in nature,
and who doesn't erect themes,
for his gaze fits not in a single ecstasy of air,
but rather, weightless, animates and restores steadfastness to all things.

There, alive, amid those thrusts, solemn in the zeal
of the wind, of that wind, writhing in my orchard making itself visible in
    my trees.
It moves not only one leaf nor kisses every flower, simultaneous,
but regally appears before all and embraces them without parting with
    its own self;
the subjection is reciprocal, constant, ubiquitous,
tending to an unreachable point of proud morbidity,
requiring no substance;
that wind is the narrow banner of the souls!—Ah,
how to avoid that tormented ground, however, how escape from it,
what impulses, what dull spears pierce me, keep me upright,
as a former novel character, mandatory, when I could
free myself on my own and flee naked to tempests of incomplete, unheard
    of heights,
cleanse my spirit, rinse it, with the tongue with no sayings
in cascades of wails that undermine the darkness, and ooze,
wanting to find totality and traverse their dream with that thread of wet
    light.

Armor of misfortunes, of victorious debris,
the invasion of height proving itself in the marble of horror, unearthly leg;
in the middle of that past avalanche, surrounded by ghosts of ghosts in
    order to think,
by presences that grip me desperately, that consume themselves,
nosing about their live slabs and the pedestal of their absolute and
    sovereign idol,
but in whom all fire, all earthly aptitude has been lost;
destined to the unsayable, its victim, like one
who has seen the shadow of a dead person after glimpsing
the harshest of actions in his dark and belated jurisdictions,
carrying out, o tenacious sun in the likeness of all shadows,
that breath's sacred fate, quivering
from a mirror against all wars, a survivor,
I am triumphant in that remote respite—like a cry
that bubbles up in a powerful site and crushes
its own impulse to burst out, now and then betraying it
so as to give titles to its sufferings!

Exuberantes lejanías realizándose en mi huerto, sumergiéndose en mis
árboles./ Lo comprendo: el viento, este viento, es el alma de las distancias:/
rompiendo cielos, en todo encuentro vuelca su vida,/ no se inviste de
tiempo para presenciar completa la vida de las cosas;/ su sabiduría estrena
siempre, incorporándose,/ reanudando todos los secretos, inundándolos, sin
remover/ su indócil fermento, su numerosa pasión;/ semejante a un poeta
unánime, solidario, cosmológico, central,/ que testifica en su propio espíritu
lo que en la naturaleza se confina,/ que no erige temas,/ porque su mirada
no cabe en un solo éxtasis de aire;/ sino que, ingrávida, todo lo anima y lo
devuelve a su constancia.// Ahí vivo, en medio de esos ímpetus, solemne
en ese afán,/ del viento, de ese viento, que se retuerce en mi huerto y se
ostenta adentro de mis árboles./ No mueve una hoja sólo ni besa cada flor,
simultánea,/ soberanamente se presenta a todas, las abraza, sin separarse
de su yo;/ es una sujeción recíproca, constante, de todas partes,/ hacia un
punto inaccesible de morbidez ufana,/ ni requiere substancia;/ ese viento
es la bandera estrecha de las almas! —Ah,/ cómo evadirme, sin embargo,
de ese atormentado suelo, cómo huir / qué bríos, qué lanzas apagadas me
clavan, me mantienen en pie,/ en antiguo carácter de novela, obligatorio,
pudiendo/ descolgarme solo y escapar desnudo hacia tempestades de alturas
desoídas, incompletas,/ lavar mi espíritu, mojarlo, en la lengua sin refrán/
de cascadas de sollozos que socavan las tinieblas, que trasudan,/ queriendo
encontrarlo todo, cruzar su sueño con esa hebra de luz mojada.// Coraza de
tormentos, de escombros victoriosos,/ invasión de altura comprobándose
en mármoles de espanto, pierna interrena;/ en medio de ese alud pasado,
rodeado de fantasmas de fantasmas para poder pensar,/ de presencias que

me agarran desesperadamente, que se agotan,/ husmeando su losa viva, el
pedestal se su absoluto y soberano ídolo,/ pero en quienes todo fuego, toda
aptitud terrena se ha perdido;/ destinado a lo indecible, víctima suma, como
aquel/ que sabe la sombra de un muerto porque frecuenta/ el más duro
suceso de sus obscuras y tardías potestades,/ desempeñando, oh sol parecido
a todas las sombras, tenaz,/ la fortuna sagrada de ese hálito, trémulo/ de
un espejo contra todas las guerras, sobreviviente,/ triunfante estoy en ese
recóndito reposo—como un sollozo/ que bulle en su intenso plantel y que
anula/ los bríos de su vasta emergencia a trechos traicionada/ para titular sus
sufrimientos!

Martín Adán (1908–1984, Peru)

Rafael de la Fuente Benavides, who would be known as Martín Adán, was born in
Lima, Peru, into an impoverished aristocratic family. From a Catholic upbringing, he
went on to study law, and later—turning his back on social convention—started a
descent into a bohemian maelstrom that drove him to self-destruction. Myths and
rumors about his alcoholism and his indifference and spite toward disseminating the
outstanding work he laboriously crafted in quiet solitude linger on. His book *La casa
de cartón* became the cornerstone of Peruvian literary modernity when he was only
twenty years old. In time, he walked away from Vanguardist formulas and wrote
sonnets reflecting great formal perfection. *"You wish to know about my life?/ I only
know about my steps/ About my weight/ About my sadness and my shoes,"* he wrote in
Escrito a ciegas (Written Blindly), when the Argentine critic Celia Paschero asked him
for a biographical sketch of his life. PRINCIPAL WORKS: *La casa de cartón* (1928), *La
rosa de la espinela* (1939), *Escrito a ciegas* (1961), *La mano desasida* (1964), *La piedra
absoluta* (1966)

Aloysius Acker Is Coming into the World / Aloysius Acker está naciendo
Forrest Gander, trans.

Aloysius Acker is coming into the world
filling the house, the heavens, with cries!
Aloysius Acker is coming into the world!
Aloysius Acker, brother of mine,
the older brother, the little brother!

—For you, all pillows are plumped with feathers,
and all dreams with a singular dream,
and all the roads with air
and all the verses with voices!

You've joined us like an old style
to a new style,
to a style eternal anywhere Aloysius Acker,
the older brother, the little brother,
the father, the mother, the dog, the chair.

You've joined us
like always: at least
       where we find no one else, we all see you:
       between the words, you behind the gesture.

and here we are in life and in death

you are born in me like the unknown
which we love so much in our dreams

The other despises us
the brotherless other

. . . .

the other who you are and I am if we split

My hostile identical, my brother true
to nature as a dry breast! . . .
Oh softest cipher, torn from the womb,
cast affectionately into a mud-celeste.

Life already begins; the world already begins;
the game already begins.
We play at being and not being.
I am not myself. You are me.
We play at living and living.
And you die. And I die.
Aloysius Acker has come into the world!
In every instant he is being born!
Everything disappears.
Praise his name, brothers!

Talking with you I don't dread being no one
don't dread being whoever talks to me
don't dread the light in the evening
don't dread the river of birth, eternity
don't dread anything Aloysius Acker.

Will I burn my father's house? . . . Will I fissure the fatherland? . . .
Will I cloister myself in a monastery? . . .
Will a ship myself off, tattooed, bearded, barefoot,

on the very last sailboat? . . .
It's all the same to me, Aloysius Acker! . . .
Only you are identical to me!

Death! . . .
However much I look, I see nothing
but your frozen nose.

What a perfect state! . . .
As if God really could create! . . .
The unborn, the unengendered, the late! . . .

Flowers, tears, candles,
Thoughts,
All the rest, all the rest;
Like desire . . .

In my intrepid inner shadow,
Real as God, at once infinite
And tangible, you lie yourself down, dead;
I lie down, dead.

And for you the dog doesn't whimper;
And for you no mother wails;
And for you the sepulcher hushes and stays damp.
And no one is more deaf,
And no one is more blind,
And no one is more no one, more me myself, without some you,
Than you, the retrieved, the re-retrieved,
The lost, me or you, if it isn't the time,
And always, and forever, and never
The you who I am and who is the bereaved,
The older brother, the little brother . . .

And from being alive, I have
Death.
How will I take a breath,
When you go on in death! . . .

He who buys the house,
She who sells her body,
He, she, is the other, and
No one, without me, who stays behind
Or travels into the realm of the blind . . .

But now I'll get down to it—to what?—the grave in the deepest
Part of me, the tenderest,
The blindest part of me,

Where breath can't follow,
Where no voice echoes,
Where I alone
Go down, dead.

God will keep on winning me over, from afar,
With the tricks and scowls
Of a human being, which he is; and the event
Will keep going full of pain; and of mystery;
And the child will come into the world;
And the grandchild;
And the fly will buzz through the summer;
And the rain dry up in the winter.
I'll startle looking into my milk.
I'll edit and publish my poems.
I'll wash my body.
On Sunday I'll head to the beach,
Stare at the waves and the dolphins.
I'll write a paper on the State
Lustrums: "Scan the present document . . . "
The rose will open. They will kill the christ.
But in the house of death,
Oh, in the house of death,
There where death
Lives, where no one is and I am death
And it is the living and the only and the sad and the eternal,
There all that occurs
Is the shadow and the foreboding
Of God and of his day,
Without night and without purpose.

God, Aloysius Acker, and the stranger pay
a visit to me in my room.
Everywhere in the world, it's afternoon,
it's another March Sunday.

They're the cheeks of the one who bears
kisses, they're the very walls of the building.
And who doesn't have, animal or thing,
a similar visage streaked with tears?

I'll be furious, I'll be tender,
but you can't come any further.
You hover at my outer being
like mist over the sea.

So, seen or unseen, fledged
or dazzling me at the edge;
but always bringing up afflictions
into the depths of my unreason.

Oh, never enough, nothing to be,
not to exist or not to look . . . !
My shadow over the immediate . . . !
Always the mist over the sea . . . !

¡Aloysius Acker está naciendo/ llenando de gritos la casa, el cielo!/
¡Aloysius Acker está naciendo!/ ¡Aloysius Acker, hermano mío,/ el
hermano mayor, el hermano pequeño!// —¡Para ti son plumas todas las
almohadas,/ y con uno que no parece todos los sueños,/ y con aire todos
los caminos/ y con voces todos los versos!// ¡Ya estás entre nosotros al
modo antiguo/ al modo nuevo,/ al modo eterno doquier a Aloysius Acker,/
el hermano mayor, el hermano pequeño/ el padre, la madre, la silla, el
perro.// Ya estás entre nosotros/ como siempre: de menos// do no a otro,
todos te vemos:/ bajo la palabra, tú detrás del gesto// y aquí estamos en
la vida y en la muerte// naces en mí como el desconocido/ que tanto
amamos en los sueños// El otro nos odia/ el otro no tiene hermano/ . . . /
el otro eres tú y soy yo si nos separamos// Mi identidad hostil, mi hermano
verdadero/ según seno incapaz de la propia natura! . . . /
¡Ay, echado nonato, el ternísimo cero/ a cenagosa estrella de inmediata
ternura! . . . // Ya principia la vida; ya principia el mundo;/ ya principia
el juego./ Jugamos a ser y no ser./ Yo no soy yo. Tú eres yo./ Jugamos
a vivir y vivir./ Y tú mueres. Y yo muero./ ¡Aloysius Acker ha nacido!/
¡En todo instante está naciendo!/ ¡Todo desaparece!/ ¡Salvad el nombre,
hermanos!// conversando contigo no temeré ser nadie/ no temeré ser
el que me hablare/ no temeré la luz en el aire/ no temeré la eternidad
como el río que nace/ no temeré nada Aloysius Acker.//¿Quemaré la casa
paterna? . . . ¿partiré de la patria? . . . / ¿Seré un monje en un monasterio?
. . . / ¿Me echaré a marear, tatuado, barbudo, descalzo,/ en el último de
los veleros? . . . / ¡Todo me es igual, Aloysius Acker! . . . / ¡Sólo tú me
eres idéntico!//¡Muerto! . . . / En cuanto miro, no veo/ Sino tu nariz, de
hielo,// ¡Qué estado perfecto! . . . / ¡Cómo si Dios creara de cierto! . . . / ¡El
no nacido, el no engendrado, muerto! . . . // Flores, lágrimas, candelas,/
Pensamientos,/ Todo demás, todo demás;/ Como al deseo . . . // En mi
ardida sombra de adentro,/ Real como Dios, por modo infinito/ Y sensible,
yaces, muerto:/ Yazgo, muerto.// Y por ti no llora el perro;/ Y por ti no
aúlla la madre;/ Y por ti calla y no se enjuga el sepulturero./ Y ninguno es
más sordo,/ Y ninguno es más ciego,/ Y ninguno es más ninguno, más yo
mismo, sin tú alguno,/ Que tú, el hallado, el rehallado,/ El perdido, yo o tú,
si no es el tiempo,/ Y siempre, y siempre, y nunca/ El tú que soy y que es el

sino,/ El hermano mayor, el hermano pequeño . . . // Y he de ser el vivo,/ El Muerto,/ ¡Cómo seré vivo,/ Tú muerto! . . . // El que compra la casa,/ La que vende su cuerpo,/ El, ella, es el otro,/ Ninguno, sin mí, el quedado/ O el ido en la redor del ciego . . . // Pero ya cavaré—¿para qué? . . .

—la fosa en lo más hondo/ De mí, en lo más tierno,/ En lo más ciego,// Adonde no baje mi aliento,/ Adonde la voz no haga eco,/ Adonde sólo yo/ Baje, muerto.// Dios seguirá ganándome, de lejos,/ Con ardid y con ceño/ De humano, como que es; y el acontecimiento/ Seguirá con dolor; y de misterio;/ Y nacerá el hijo;/ Y nacerá el nieto;/ Y la mosca zumbará en el verano;/ Y la lluvia mojará en el invierno./ Me sobresaltaré en mi lecho./ Corregiré y publicaré mi verso./ Lavaré mi cuerpo./ Iré el domingo a la playa del mar,/ A mirar la ola y el bufeo./ Escribiré en papel del Estado/ Lustros: "Conste por el presente documento . . . "/ La rosa abrirá. Matarán el cristo./ Mas en la casa del muerto,/ ¡Ay!, en la casa del muerto,/ Allí donde vive el muerto,/ Allí donde no es ninguno y soy el muerto/ Y es el vivo y el solo y el triste y el eterno,/ Allí sólo ocurren/ La penumbra y el presentimiento/ De Dios y de su día,/ Sin noche y sin objeto.// Dios, Aloysius Acker y el extraño/ me visitan en mi cuarto./ Es la tarde en todo el mundo,/ es un domingo de marzo.// Son las mejillas del que besa,/ son las paredes de la casa./ ¿Quién no tiene, animal o cosa,/ la misma faz llena de lágrimas?// Seré el furioso, seré el tierno,/ pero tú no puedes pasar./ Estás así en mi ser externo/ como la niebla sobre el mar.// Así, vista o no vista, apenas/ o cegándome en la extensión;/ pero siempre subiendo penas/ en lo hondo de mi sinrazón.// ¡Ah, nada ser, nunca bastante/ a no existir o no mirar . . . !/ ¡Sombra de mí sobre el instante . . . !/ ¡Siempre la niebla sobre el mar . . . !

Without Time Signature, Hurrying Ad Lib/Played Freely, Etc. / Senza tempo, affrettando ad libitum

Forrest Gander, trans.

—My astonishment! . . . Hold me back . . . I pause . . . blessed
Instant! . . . my agnition! . . . because of my enthusiasm! . . .
My epiphany! . . . blinded by orgasm! . . .
Inanity of my overflowing breast! . . .

—Stitch me up, from my emanation, infinity . . .
Catastasis beyond the metaplasm! . . .
That won't compute . . . I, the one who recoups my prodigy . . .
Entelechy . . . testimony to my mere phantasm!

—My ecstasy . . . enstate me! . . . urge on the omen
That didn't insist on this instant! . . . You consist
Of me, or you're god who sticks himself to me! . . .

—Divine vanity . . . from which I remove myself
From that which in vain I am . . . where you distance yourself from me,
Some I! . . . Keep me going, My Eternity!

—¡Mi estupor! . . . ¡quédateme . . . quedo . . . cada/ Instante! . . . ¡mi
agnición . . . porque me asmo! . . . / ¡Mi epifanía! . . . cegóme orgasmo! . . . /
¡Vaciedad de mi pecho desbordada! . . . // —¡Básteme infinidad de mi
emanada . . . / Catástasis allende el metaplasmo! . . . / ¡Que no conciba . . .
yo el que me despasmo . . . / Entelequia . . . testigo de mi nada! . . . // —¿Mi
éxtasi . . . estáteme! . . . ¡inste ostento/ Que no instó en este instante! . . .
¡tú consistas/ En mí, o seas dios que se me añade! . . . // —¡Divina vanidad
. . . onde me ausento/ De aquel que en vano estoy . . . donde me distas,/ Yo
Alguno! . . . ¡dúrame, Mi Eternidade!

José Lezama Lima (1910–1976, Cuba)

Born into a bourgeois creole family in Havana, Lezama Lima is known for his challenging work that uses careful, baroque language to create puzzling but extraordinary poems and prose. By age twenty-one, Lezama Lima acted as editor to a number
of literary magazines in Cuba, the most important of which was *Orígenes*. He and
his *origenists* were united by their shared Catholicism, intellectualism, and opposition to Batista and the prevailing social institutions. His self-proclaimed poetry of
difficulty deals with the theme of the invisible world, a transcendence of emotions,
history, and material reality. He also used his prose and poetry to put forward a
general theory of mestizo culture as the defining element of Latin American art and
literature. Lezama Lima's rich and expansive poetry has become foundational for
the neo-baroque movement. PRINCIPAL WORKS: *Muerte de Narciso* (1937), *La fijeza*
(1949), *Paradiso* (1966)

Excerpt from Thoughts in Havana / Pensamientos en la Habana
James Irby, trans.

Because I dwell in a whisper like a set of sails,
a land where ice is a reminiscence,
fire cannot hoist a bird
and burn it in a conversation calm in style.
Though that style doesn't dictate to me a sob
and a tenuous hop lets me live in bad humor,
I will not recognize the useless movement
of a mask floating where I cannot,

where I cannot transport the stonecutter or the door latch
to the museums where murders are papered
while the judges point out the squirrel
that straightens its stockings with its tail.
If a previous style shakes the tree,
it decides the sob of two hairs and exclaims:
mi alma no está en un cenicero.

Any memory that is transported,
received like a galantine from the obese ambassadors of old,
will not make us live like the broken chair
of the lonesome existence that notes the tide
and sneezes in autumn.
And the size of a loud laugh,
broken by saying that its memories are remembered,
and its styles the fragments of a serpent
that we want to solder together
without worrying about the intensity of its eyes.
If someone reminds us that our styles
are already remembered;
that through our nostrils no subtle air thinks forth
but rather that the Aeolus of the sources elaborated
by those who decided that being
should dwell in man,
without any of us
dropping the saliva of a danceable decision,
though we presume like other men
that our nostrils expel a subtle air.
Since they dream of humiliating us,
repeating day and night with the rhythm of the tortoise
that conceals time on its back:
you didn't decide that being should dwell in man;
your God is the moon
watching like a bannister
the entrance of being into man.
Since they want to humiliate us we say to them:
el jefe de la tribu descendió la escalinata.

They have some show windows and wear some shoes.
In those show windows they alternate the mannequin with the stuffed
    ossifrage,
and everything that has passed through the forehead
of the lonesome buffalo's boredom.
If we don't look at the show window, they chat
about our insufficient nakedness that isn't worth a figurine from Naples.

If we go through it and don't break the glass,
they don't stress amusingly that our boredom can break the fire
and they talk to us about the living model and the parable of the ossifrage.
They who carry their mannequins to all the ports
and who push down into their trunks a screeching
of stuffed vultures.
They don't want to know that we climb up along the damp roots of the fern
—where there are two men in front of a table; to the right, the jug
and the bread that has been caressed—,
and that though we may chew their style,
no escogemos nuestros zapatos en una vitrina.

The horse neighs when there's a shape
that comes in between like a toy ox,
that keeps the river from hitting it on the side
and kissing the spurs that were a present
from a rosy-cheeked adulteress from New York.
The horse doesn't neigh at night;
the crystals it exhales through its nose,
a warm frost, of paper;
the digestion of the spurs
after going through its muscles now glassy
with the sweat of a frying pan.
The toy ox and the horse
hear the violin, but the fruit doesn't fall
squashed on their backs that are rubbed
with a syrup that is never tar.
The horse slips over the moss
where there is a table exhibiting the spurs,
but the perked-up ear of the beast doesn't decipher.

Porque habito un susurro como un velamen,/ una tierra donde el hielo es
una reminiscencia,/ el fuego no puede izar un pájaro/ y quemarlo en una
conversación de estilo calmo./ Aunque ese estilo no me dicte un sollozo/
y un brinco tenue me deje vivir malhumorado,/ no he de reconocer la
inútil marcha/ de una máscara flotando donde yo no pueda,/ donde yo
no pueda transportar el picapedrero o el picaporte/ a los museos donde se
empapelan los asesinatos/ mientras los visitadores señalan la ardilla/ que
con el rabo se ajusta las medias./ Si un estilo anterior sacude el árbol,/ decide
el sollozo de dos cabellos y exclama:/ *my soul is not in an ashtray.*// Cualquier
recuerdo que sea transportado,/ recibido como una galantina de los
obesos embajadores de antaño,/ no nos hará vivir como la silla rota/ de la
existencia solitaria que anota la marea/ y estornuda en otoño./ Y el tamaño
de una carcajada,/ rota por decir que sus recuerdos están recordados,/

y sus estilos los fragmentos de una serpiente/ que queremos soldar/ sin
preocuparnos de la intensidad de sus ojos./ Si alguien nos recuerda que
nuestros estilos/ están ya recordados;/ que por nuestras narices no escogita
un aire sutil,/ sino que el Eolo de las fuentes elaboradas/ por los que
decidieron que el ser/ habitase en el hombre,/ sin que ninguno de nosotros/
dejase caer la saliva de una decisión bailable,/ aunque presumimos como los
demás hombres/ que nuestras narices lanzan un aire sutil./ Como sueñan
humillarnos,/ repitiendo día y noche con el ritmo de la tortuga/ que oculta
el tiempo en su espaldar:/ ustedes no decidieron que el ser habitase en el
hombre;/ vuestro Dios es la luna/ contemplando como una balaustrada/
al ser entrando en el hombre./ Como quieren humillarnos le decimos/ *the
chief of the tribe descended the staircase.*// Ellos tienen unas vitrinas y usan
unos zapatos./ En esas vitrinas alternan el maniquí con el quebrantahuesos/
disecado,/ y todo lo que ha pasado por la frente del hastío/ de búfalo
solitario./ Si no miramos la vitrina, charlan/ de nuestra insuficiente
desnudez que no vale una estatuilla/ de Nápoles./ Si la atravesamos y
no rompemos los cristales,/ nos subrayan con gracia que nuestro hastío
puede quebrar el/ fuego/ y nos hablan del modelo viviente y de la parábola
del que-/ brantahuesos./ Ellos que cargan con sus maniquíes a todos los
puertos/ y que hunden en sus baúles un chirriar/ de vultúridos disecados./
Ellos no quieren saber que trepamos por las raíces húmedas/ de helecho/
—donde hay dos hombres frente a una mesa; a la derecha,/ la jarra/ y el
pan acariciado—,/ y que aunque mastiquemos su estilo,/ *we don't choose our
shoes in a show-window.*// El caballo relincha cuando hay un bulto/ que se
interpone como un buey de peluche,/ que impide que el río le pegue en el
costado/ y se bese con las espuelas regaladas/ por una sonrosada adúltera
neoyorquina./ El caballo no relincha de noche;/ los cristales que exhala por
su nariz,/ una escarcha tibia, de papel; la digestión de las espuelas/ después
de recorrer sus músculos encristalados/ por un sudor de sartén./ El buey
de peluche y el caballo/ oyen el violín, pero el fruto no cae/ reventado en
su lomo frotado/ con un almíbar que no es nunca el alquitrán./ El caballo
resbala por el musgo/ donde hay una mesa que exhibe las espuelas,/ *pero la
oreja erizada de la bestia no descifra.*// . . .

Fifes, Epiphany, Goats / Pifanos, epifania, cabritos

James Irby, trans.

Clarities became dark. Until then darkness had been a diabolic sloth, and
  clarity a contented insufficiency of the creature. Unchanged dogmas,
  clear darknesses, which the blood in spurts and in continuity resolved,
  like the butterfly caressing the shepherd's forehead while he sleeps.
  A birth that was before and after, before and after the abysses, as if the
  birth of the Virgin were prior to the appearance of the abysses. *Nondum*

eram abyssi et ego jam concepta eram. The delectable mystery of the sources that will never be resolved. The rejected uncooked clay now cooked, already leaping outside origins for grace and wisdom. The Book of Life that begins with a metaphor and ends with the vision of Glory is all filled with You. And Yours is the tremendous punishment, the sudden decapitation: You can erase from the Book of Life. Eternal Life, which arches from man clarified by Grace to the nocturnal tree, can declare mortal, strike down, release the spark. Once the erasure is made, a new name comprising a new man occupies its place, which thus does not even leave behind the shadow of its hollowness, the scandal of its ashes. Tremendous drought now erased by the goats of familiar contentment, by the pipes of overturnings and colors. Herd together, stumble, understand yourselves, more deeply if one is disposed to be born, to march toward the youthfulness that is becoming eternal. Until the arrival of Christ, Pascal said, only *false peace* had existed; after Christ, we may add, true warfare has existed. The warfare of partisans, of witnesses killed in battle, the hundred and forty and four thousand, offered as firstfruits unto God and to the Lamb (*Revelation,* 14:3 and 4): And they sung as it were a new song before the throne. Herd together, stumble, goats; begin at last, pipes, God and man are now alone. Tremendous drought, blaze of sun: I go toward my forgiveness.

Se ponían claridades oscuras. Hasta entonces la oscuridad había sido pereza diabólica y la claridad insuficiencia contenta de la criatura. Dogmas inalterados, claras oscuridades que la sangre en chorro y en continuidad resolvía, como la mariposa acaricia la frente del pastor mientras duerme. Un nacimiento que estaba antes y después, antes y después de los abismos, como si el nacimiento de la Virgen fuera anterior a la aparición de los abismos. *Nondum eram abyssi et ego jam concepta eram.* El deleitoso misterio de las fuentes que no se resolverá jamás. El prescindido barro descocido cocido, saltando ya, fuera de los orígenes, para la gracia y la sabiduría. El Libro de la Vida que comienza por una metáfora y termina por la visión de la Gloria, está henchido todo de Ti. Y tienes el castigo tremendo, la decapitación subitánea: puedes borrar del Libro de la Vida. La Vida Eterna, que se enarca desde el hombre aclarado por la gracia hasta el árbol nocturno, puede declarar mortal, abatir, desgajar la centella. Borrado ya, un nombre nuevo que comprende un hombre nuevo, ocupa aquel lugar, que así ni siquiera deja la sombra de su oquedad, el escándalo de sus cenizas. Tremenda sequía ahora borrada por los cabritos de contentura familiar, por las chirimías de vuelcos y colores. Acorralad, tropezad, entendeos, más hondo si se está dispuesto a nacer, a marchar hacia la juventud que se va haciendo eterna. Hasta la llegada de Cristo, decía Pascal, sólo había existido la *falsa paz*; después de Cristo, podemos añadir, ha existido la verdadera guerra. La de los cuarenta y cuatro mil, ofrecidos como primicias a Dios y al Cordero (*Apocalipsis*, Cap. 14, Vers. 3 y 4): Cantaban como un cántico nuevo delante del trono. Acorralad, tropezad, cabritos; al fin, empezad chirimías, quedan solos Dios y el hombre. Tremenda sequía, resolana: voy hacia mi perdón.

Death of Time / Muerto del tiempo

James Irby, trans.

In a vacuum velocity dares not compare itself, can caress the infinite. Thus the vacuum is defined and inert as a world of non-resistance. Also the vacuum sends out its first negative graph so it can be like non-air. The air we were accustomed to feel (to see?): soft as a sheet of glass, hard as a wall or a sheet of steel. We know by an almost invisible stirring of the non-existence of an absolute vacuum that there cannot be an infinite unconnected to divisible substance. Thanks to that we can live and are perhaps fortunate. But let us suppose some implausibilities in order to gain some delights. Let us suppose the army, the silk cord, the express train, the bridge, the rails, the air that constitutes itself as another face as soon as we draw close to the window. Gravity is not the tortoise kissing the ground. The express train always has to be stopped on a bridge with a broad rock base. It impels itself—like the impulsion of his smile to laughter, to raucous laughter, in a feudal lord after his garnished dinner—until it decapitates tenderly, until it dispenses with the rails, and by an excess of its own impulsion slips along the silk cord. That velocity of infinite progression tolerated by a silk cord of infinite resistance comes to feed upon its tangencies that touch the ground with one foot, or the small box of compressed air between its feet and the back of the ground (lightness, angelisms, nougat, larks). The army in repose has to rest upon a bridge with a broad rock base, impels itself and comes to fit, in hiding, behind a small poplar, then in a worm with a backbone grooved by an electric time. The velocity of progression reduces the tangencies, if we suppose it to be infinite, the tangency is pulverized: the reality of the steel box on the archetypal rail, in other words the silk cord, is suddenly stopped, the constant progression derives another independent surprise from that temporal tangency, the air turns as hard as steel, and the express train cannot advance because the potency and the resistance become infinite. There is no fall because of the very intensity of the fall. While potency turns into ceaseless impulsion, the air mineralizes and the moving box—successive, impelled—the silk cord and the air like steel refuse to be replaced by the crane on one foot. Better than substitution, restitution. To whom?

En el vacío la velocidad no osa compararse, puede acariciar el infinito. Así el vacío queda definido e inerte como mundo de la no resistencia.

También el vacío envía su primer grafía negativa para quedar como el no aire. El aire que acostumbrábamos sentir ¿ver?: suave como lámina de cristal, duro como frontón o lámina de acero. Sabemos por casi un invisible desperezar del no existir del vacío absoluto, no puede haber un infinito desligado de la sustancia divisible. Gracias a eso podemos vivir y somos tal vez afortunados. Pero supongamos algunas inverosimilitudes para ganar algunas delicias. Supongamos el ejército, el cordón de seda, el expreso, el puente, los rieles, el aire que se constituye en otro rostro tan pronto nos acercamos a la ventanilla. La gravedad no es la tortuga besando la tierra. El expreso tiene que estar siempre detenido sobre un puente de ancha base pétrea. Se va impulsando—como la impulsión de sonrisa, a risa, a carcajada, de un señor feudal después de la cena guarnida—, hasta decapitar tiernamente, hasta prescindir de los rieles, y por un exceso de la propia impulsión, deslizarse sobre el cordón de seda. Esa velocidad de progresión infinita soportada por un cordón de seda de resistencia infinita, llega a nutrirse de sus tangencias que tocan la tierra con un pie, o la pequeña caja de aire compromido situada entre sus pies y la espalda de la tierra (levedad, angelismos, turrón, alondras). El ejército en reposo tiene que descansar sobre un puente de ancha base pétrea, se va impulsando y llega a caber oculto detrás de un alamillo, después en un gusano de espina dorsal surcada por un tiempo eléctrico. La velocidad de la progresión reduce la tangencias, si la suponemos infinita, la tangencia es pulverizada: la realidad de la caja de acero sobre el riel arquetípico, es decir, el cordón de seda, es de pronto detenida, la constante progresión deriva otra sorpresa independiente de esa tangencia temporal, el aire se torna duro como acero, y el expreso no pueda avanzar porque la potencia y la resistencia hácense infinitas. No se cae por la misma intensidad de la caída. Mientras la potencia tórnase la impulsión incesante, el aire se mineraliza y la caja móvil—sucesiva impulsada—, el cordón de seda y el aire como acero, no quieren ser reemplazados por la grulla en un solo pie. Mejor que sustituir, restituir. ¿A quién?

Enrique Molina (1910–1997, Argentina)

Born in Buenos Aires, Molina was a member of the so-called poetic Generation of '40. Originally a student of law, he was a world traveler, spending long periods of time in Chile, Peru, and Bolivia, and his poetic voice is deeply influenced by what it means to be a traveler. In 1960, Molina co-founded the Argentine surrealist magazine *A partir de cero*. The following year he published *Amantes antípodas*, arguably his most important work. Molina's poetry deals with nature and eroticism in a surrealist style. PRINCIPAL WORKS: *Las cosas y el delirio* (1941), *Pasiones terrestres* (1946), *Amantes antípodas* (1961)

The Way It Must Be / Como debe de ser

Naomi Lindstrom, trans.

Here is my soul, with its strange
dissatisfaction, like the teeth of the wolf:
the taleteller, cruel and unruly by nature,
who never finds the word;
and over there an old train pulls out of sight, there a moment, gone,
like a light in the rain, but starts back
up with its iron panting and takes us once more
through the green air of errant loves.
For a train throws into motion not just its works
but the dreamy blood bedazzled by the journey,
sandfaces, flashfaces, faces that make music,
and also it can creak with mockery
when the demons, in the dining room,
passing through a little backwoods station
with a prickly pear hedge and the beggar most beloved of the Virgin,
stuck out their tongues and plastered their naked rumps against the
        windowpane.
And never tell me goodbye again,
amid this upside down land that pricks up in the cold air.

Aquí está mi alma, con su extraña/ insatisfacción, como los dientes del
lobo:/ la narradora de naturaleza cruel e insumisa/ que nunca encuentra la
palabra;/ y por allá se aleja un viejo tren, momentáneo y perdido,/ como
una luz en la lluvia, pero vuelve/ a repetir su jadeo férreo y a llevarnos de
nuevo/ en el verde aire de los amores errantes./ Pues un tren no sólo moviliza
sus hierros/ sino sangre soñadora deslumbrada por el viaje,/ rostros arena,
rostros relámpagos, rostros que hacen música,/ y puede crujir burlonamente
también/ cuando los demonios, en el salón comedor,/ al cruzar por una
pequeña estación de provincia/ con un cerco de tunas y el mendigo
predilecto de la Virgen,/ sacaban la lengua y aplastaban su trasero desnudo
contra el vidrio de/ la ventanilla./ Y nunca más vuelvas a despedirte de mí,/
en medio de esta tierra cabeza abajo que se eriza en el aire frío.

Hue

Andrew Graham-Yooll, trans.

Where the Perfume River shifts its light flames beneath
the moon
and the women at the mouth sing
and sink their living opal faces in the loins that reverberate
among cymbals

a den asleep to the splendor of dark dynasties
emperors of unmoving lips and large golden testicles
whose bile was the lightning
whose shadow in stone carved gardens and dreams
                                                    There
the light lost among columns
gods of cinnamon masks
and lascivious hips
ghosts of real claws
a dizziness of butterflies
between the temple the fort the night
barefoot lovers and salesmen on the shores
        linking in their rings
the ceremonies of life
a threaded web of hunger and forgetting
in such copper figures
in such souls
the cry of birds from a warm world
        the old holy city
        the marble monasteries
built on the skulls of hummingbirds
and the silk river drags goods rotting fruit
languages and black hemp sailed junks
        powdered feathers
in the breasts that people the market in the arms
impregnated by the sweat of the light
like animal flowering of a dream
in a slow spasm
        And suddenly
the blind crack
city devastated till not a stone stays in
        its jaws
burned alive like the bonzo in a horrific plea
naked the incandescent flank
shapeless wound among the embers
rise from the roots from the secret
paddy fields
        those volcanic children
cling
        to an indomitable architecture
and amid the explosion of blood swept by napalm and crime
taking position on real tombs
they praised their own death with a heart-rending
        splendor and convulsion

of a raging maternity of gunpowder
        another Hue is born
—its double in impalpable stones—
the dead concealed in the air
oh creatures of the monsoon!
        resisting still
among the violent breaches of the wall
covered with entrails explosions and glassy flesh
so much a vein of thirst
so much green in villages that beat
the wound drained drop by drop

ghostly Hue
made of the shadow of corpses
resistance without end
the small elastic men who burned on the rock
        the guerrilla
with a great central sun makes it crackle on the cliff
        the guerrilla
all the time deeper in a sinister swamp of lead
damnation of farewells awaiting pleas by a woman alone who
        fades
on the nightly scaffold
sky dug up or distant
no caress nor devouring tongue
so much cracked throat amid the imperial remains

        Hue defended bone by bone
        Hue ground under Hue shrouded in sun
        Hue resisted to the final flame
        Hue of feline eyes amid the crevices of disaster
        Hue coagulated now in a greenish memory
nightmare in some stagnant pond so sad in the sky
cat yowling scream sheet poisoned where blood drips
instead of rice
the man who returns with a head of flies
and no longer understands not wine nor his hands in the terrible
dissection of the night
        Hue the scalpel
        Hue without lips
        Hue in the silence of blood
so many dead
have defended the river the seed the pubis of flowers by the rain
the web that part open to show the warm demons of
        the skin

so much the fire in the cabin so far
the track of sandals in the sand
the weakened woman under the plantain leaf

                                plagued with apparitions
another Hue floats in the mist
an illusion
Hue reverberates on the "Marine's" inflamed helmet

                    (covered in slogans formaldehyde
and bandages you can now drink the leprosy the gangrene
                            in your soda)

Hue of stars boiling as one new
constellation in the sky of hell
where the perfume river turns slowly round the moon

Donde el Río de los Perfumes mueve sus ligeras llamas bajo/ la luna/ y las
mujeres cantan en su boca/ y hunden sus rostros de ópalo vivo en muslos
que reverbe-/ ran/ entre címbalos/ un antro dormido al esplendor de oscuras
dinastías/ emperadores de labios inmóviles y grandes testículos de oro/ cuya
bilis era el relámpago/ cuya sombra es piedra labrada jardines y sueño/ He
ahí/ el destello perdido entre las columnas/ dioses de máscaras de canela/ y
caderas lascivas/ fantasmas de garras reales/ un vértigo de mariposas/ entre el
templo la fortaleza y la noche/ amantes descalzas y vendedores de las orillas/
uniendo en sus anillos/ las ceremonias de la vida/ entretejida urdimbre del
hambre y el olvido/ en tales torsos cobrizos/ en tales almas/ graznido de
las aves de un mundo caliente/ la vieja ciudad sagrada/ los monasterios de
mármol/ construidos sobre cráneos de colibríes/ y el río de seda arrastrando
mercaderías frutas podridas/ lenguajes y juncos de velas negras de cáñamo/
pomada de plumas/ en los senos que pueblan el mercado en los brazos/
impregnados por el sudor de la luz/ como la floración animal de un sueño/
en un lento espasmo/ Y de pronto/ la rajadura ciega/ ciudad arrasada hasta
no quedar ni un bloque de piedra/ en sus mandíbulas/ quemada viva
como el bonzo en su súplica atroz/ desnudo su flanco incandescente/ llaga
deforme entre tizones/ salen de las raíces desde los arrozales/ secretos/
esos hijos volcánicos/ se aferran/ a una indomable arquitectura/ y entre el
estallido de la sangre barridos de napalm y crimen/ apostados sobre tumbas
reales/ exaltaron su propia muerte con una majestad salvaje/ desgarradora y
convulsión/ de esa rugiente maternidad de pólvora/ otra Hue ha nacido/ —su
doble de piedras impalpables—/ muertos latentes en el aire/ ¡oh criaturas del
monzón!/ resisten aún/ entre las hendiduras violentas del muro/ cubiertas
de vísceras explosiones y carne vidriosa/ tanta vena de sed/ tanto verdor de
aldeas que latían/ vaciado gota a gota por la herida// Hue fantasma/ hecha
de sombras de cadáveres la obstinada/ resistencia sin término/ los pequeños
hombres elásticos que ardieron en la roca/ el guerrillero/ con su gran sol

central que lo hace crepitar como/ el acantilado/ el guerrillero/ cada vez
más hundido en su siniestra ciénaga de plomo/ flagelo de adioses vigilia
y súplica de mujer sola/ que se desvanece/ en su patíbulo nocturno/ cielo
desenterrado o lejanía/ ni caricia ni lengua devorante/ tanta garganta rota
entre los restos imperiales// Hue defendida hueso a hueso/ Hue triturada
Hue mortaja de sol/ Hue resistida hasta la última llama/ Hue de ojos de
felino entre los intersticios del/ desastre/ Hue coagulada ahora en la memoria
verdosa/ pesadilla en alguna charca tan triste del cielo/ gato que llora a gritos
sábana venenosa plato donde cae sangre/ en vez de arroz/ y el hombre que
retorna con cabeza de moscas/ y no comprende más ni el vino ni sus manos
en la terrible/ disección de la noche/ Hue de escalpelo/ Hue sin labios/ Hue
silencio de sangre/ tantos muertos/ han defendido el río la semilla el pubis de
flores de la lluvia/ la trenza que se entreabre y deja ver los cálidos demonios/
de la piel/ tanta lumbre de cabaña tan lejos/ la huella de sandalias en la
arena/ la mujer lacia bajo la hoja del banano/ llena de espectros/ otra Hue
ondula entre la niebla/ de espejismo/ Hue reverbero sobre el casco inflamado
del "marine"// (*recubierto de slogans formol/ y vendas puedes ahora beber la lepra
en tu gaseosa/ la gangrena*)// Hue de estrellas que hierven como una nueva/
constelación del cielo del infierno/ Hue inviolable/ donde el Río de los
Perfumes gira lentamente alrededor/ de la luna

Aquatic Rite / Rito acuático

Andrew Graham-Yooll, trans.

Bathing in the Tumbes River a mestizo showed me how to wash my clothes
more alive than a lizard his shirt jumped amid untouchable
      whispering lips
and the fast women of liquid
running down their legs
with heads of endless hair under the plantain leaves
carefully copied by a dream
of that water boiled by the sun
through the savage heart in a place impregnated
by the spirit of a river in the Americas—strange
aquatic ceremony—naked the mestizo and I
amid the scalding valves of noon, oh nomad
washermen! purified by the cauterizing
of waves
by implacable light of the world

I washed my links with the birds with the seasons
with the fortuitous events of my existence
and the offerings of madness
         I washed my tongue

the bleeding lies that nest in my throat
—frothing unharmed exorcising one instant all
the allegories of power and gold—
in that delirious sleepless paradise
I washed my nails and my face
and the errant coffin of memory
full of fantasies and failures and gagged furies

                              water water water
so many joys lost flashing anew
from the ancient or dreamed of gestures
my stomach and the moss on my groin
I washed each point of expatriation blackened my breath each
            instant of passion left to drop like a lamp
and my threatening senses like a blade striking the
            aorta but for that reason more embracing at each beat that
            dissolves them in the wind
for that same reason more embracing at each pulse laid like
a string of fishhooks

I washed my love and my misfortune
such eagerness without limit or all shape and is
for each thing shining in the unholdable blood
for each body with the smell of kisses and summer
                      gods! gods!
love for the current of sexes adrift between shores
            which travel!
gods ferocious and innocent gods of mine with no power
            but flee
birds ablaze but ever more remote
while I wring my shirt
in the great incoherence of living
—oh washerman!—perhaps never perchance not even
never one instant in the water of the Tumbes

Bañándome en el río Túmbez un cholo me enseñó a lavar/ la ropa/ Más viva
que un lagarto su camisa saltaba entre inasibles/ labios susurrantes/ y las veloces
mujeres de lo líquido/ fluyendo por las piernas/ con sus inagotables cabelleras
bajo las hojas de los plátanos/ minuciosamente copiados por el sueño/ de esa
agua cocinada al sol/ a través del salvaje corazón de un lugar impregnado/ por
el espíritu de un río de América—extraña/ ceremonia acuática—desnudos el
cholo y yo/ entre las valvas ardientes del mediodía ¡oh lavanderos/ nómades!
purificados por el cauterio/ de unas olas/ por la implacable luz del mundo//
Lavaba mis vínculos con los pájaros con las estaciones/ con los acontecimientos
fortuitos de mi existencia/ y los ofrecimientos de la locura/ Lavaba mi lengua/

la sanguijuela de embustes que anida en mi garganta/ —espumas indemnes
exorcizando un instante todas/ las inmundas alegorías del poder y del oro–/
en aquel delirante paraíso del insomnio/ Lavaba mis uñas y mis rostro/ y el
errante ataúd de la memoria/ lleno de fantasías y fracasos y furias amordazadas/
aguas aguas aguas/ tantas dichas perdidas centelleando de nuevo/ desde gestos
antiguos o soñados/ mi vientre y el musgo de mis ingles/ lavaba cada sitio de
destierro ennegrecido por mi aliento cada/ instante de pasión dejado caer como
una lámpara/ y mis sentidos amenzadores como una navaja asestada en la/ aorta
pero por eso mismo más exaltantes a cada latido que/ los disuelve en el viento/
por eso mismo más abrasadores a cada pulsación tendida como/ una súplica
de anzuelos// Lavaba mi amor y mi desgracia/ tanta avidez sin límites por toda
forma y ser/ por cada cosa brillando en la sangre inaferrable/ por cada cuerpo
con el olor de los besos y del verano/ ¡Dioses! ¡Dioses!/ ¡Amor de la corriente
con sexos a la deriva entre costas/ que se desplazan!/ Dioses feroces e inocentes
dioses míos sin más poder/ que su fuga/ pájaros en incendio cada vez más
remotos/ mientras retorcía mi camisa/ en el gran desvarío de vivir/—¡oh lavador!
—tal vez nunca acaso ni siquiera/ jamás un instante en el agua del Túmbez

Pablo Antonio Cuadra (1912–2002, Nicaragua)

Born in Managua, Nicaragua, Cuadra, the son of a historian, moved with his family
to Granada, where he attended a Jesuit school and spent time in the country with
peasants. Cuadra published his first poems in 1931 in the journal *Criterio*. A nationalist
who opposed the dictatorship, during the 1970s and 1980s he edited the newspaper and literary supplement *La prensa* until the Sandinista censors closed it down in
1987. Another important theme in his works is Nicaraguan identity, particularly the
identity of the rural peasant and average Nicaraguan. He spent the 1990s teaching
and researching at the University of Texas, Austin. His background as a humanist and
a Christian influenced his simple yet profound style. PRINCIPAL WORKS: *Por los caminos
van los campesinos* (1936), *América o el purgatorio* (195?), *El jaguar y la luna* (1959)

God Creates the Andes / Inauguración de los Andes por Dios
Brian Whitener, trans.

A crocodile's tear could be the beginning of the Nile.
In my land, a small God known as Cocijo,
where he urinates a river is born.
A snowflake from Chimborazo, like a white hair in the wind,
might have fallen from the very temples of God,

who moves

his hands like a biblical potter and polishes the summits.
                                    The Indian invokes Wirakocha
and an old village priest thinks to surprise him
as he passes through the garden into the fresh breeze.
But a voice says: LET THERE BE SNOW.
I was certain snow was the cemetery of the angels
but now I know ice and fire
are just words.
                    In the dictionary of God,
water is another word
and wind is like saying Love
                                and it moans.
This mountain range is a prayer of God, whose syntax
            only the ancient Aymara understood.
In those days, God strode from the summit of Hualcala to Tierra del Fuego
and spoke to his Son of the importance of the land.
"To be man is a serious affair," said God . . . it is difficult
to raise a mountain that could move a hero's heart.
Let us make the Andes so that they might produce
men like Tupac Amaru and Simón Bolívar.
Their size, their scale will yield dreams that fly as high as the Cóndor.
In this land,
men might one day converse with me.
I want a place difficult like poetry,
I want, said God, speaking things,
making, with words, things:
                                Volcanoes
                                Mountain passes
                                Clouds
                                Winds readied like armies
                                Equators
and the angels followed behind writing with their quills the creation of the
    Andes.

Una lágrima de cocodrilo puede ser el comienzo del Nilo./ En mi tierra un
diocesillo llamado Cocijo/ allí donde orina hace nacer un río./ Un copo
de nieve—como una cana al aire—del Chimborazo/ puede haber caído
de las sienes de Dios/ que mueve/ sus manos bíblicas de alfarero y pule
las cumbres./ En indios invoca a Wirakocha/ y un viejo cura de aldea cree
sorprender la gran figura/ que se paseaba en el jardín al fresco de la brisa./
Pero dice la voz: HAGASE LA NIEVE./ Yo creí que la nieve era el cementerio
de los ángeles/ mas ahora sé que el hielo y el fuego/ son palabras./ En
el diccionario de Dios/ el agua es otra palabra/ y el viento es como decir

Amor/ y gime./ Esta cordillera es una oración de Dios cuya sintaxis/ solo
fue conocida por los misteriosos aymaras./ Se paseaba Dios en aquellos días
desde las cimas del Hualcalá a la Tierra del Fuego/ y hablaba con su Hijo
sobre la importancia de la tierra./ "Ser hombre es cosa seria," dijo el Señor;
es difícil/ levantar una cordillera que impresione el corazón de un héroe./
Hagamos los Andes para que puedan producirse/ hombres como Tupac
Amaru y Simón Bolívar./ Estas medidas, estas distancias producirán sueños
tan altos como el vuelo de un Cóndor./ En esta tierra/ es posible que algún
día el hombre dialogue conmigo./ Quiero un lugar difícil como la poesía;/
quiero, dijo Dios, hablando cosas,/ haciendo-con palabras-cosas:/ Volcanes/
Desfiladeros/ Nubes/ Vientos alineados como ejércitos/ Ecuadores/ y los
ángeles iban detrás escribiendo con sus plumas la creación de los Andes.

The Myth of the Jaguar / Mitología del jaguar

Brian Whitener, trans.

Rain, the most ancient of creatures,
older than the stars, said:
"Let there be moss, vibrant and alive!"
And its skin was made. Then
Lightning struck his flint and said:
"Add now the claw!" And there it was,
its cruelty sheathed in a caress.

"Take," said the wind then,
blowing on its flute, "the constant
rhythm of the breeze."
                And it began to walk,
moving like harmony itself, like the measured
dance of the Gods.
But Fire saw this, stopped it,
and went to where "yes" and "no" divide
—where the serpent's tongue splits—
and declared: "Its skin shall be of light and shadow."

There in his kingdom of death, indifferent
and blind.
        But Man laughed. "Crazy"
they called that oppressive duality
wherein crime and chance were joined.

Now not Necessity with her severe law
(nor the moon devoured by the Earth to sate its nocturnal hunger
nor the weak sustaining with their blood the glory of the strong),

but Mystery overseeing the extermination. Fortune,
Fate blindfolding Justice. "Gods,"
shouted the rebels, "We will read in the stars
the hidden laws of Destiny."

And Lightning heard the uproar from his pale
insomnia. "Woe is man!" he said,
and lit in the vacant
sockets of the jaguar
the awful closeness of a star.

La lluvia, la más antigua creatura/ —anterior a las estrellas—dijo:/ "Hágase el musgo sensitivo y viviente"./ Y se hizo su piel; mas/ el rayo, golpeó su pedernal y dijo:/ "Agréguese la zarpa". Y fue la uña/ con su crueldad envainada en la caricia.// "Tenga—dijo el viento entonces,/ silabeando en su ocarina—el ritmo/ habitual de la brisa"./ Y echó a andar/ como la armonía, como la medida/ que los dioses anticiparon a la danza./ Pero el fuego miró aquello y lo detuvo:/ Fue al lugar donde el "sí" y el "no" se dividieron/—donde bifurcó su lengua la serpiente—/ y dijo: "Sea su piel de sombra y claridad".// Y fue su reino de muerte, indistinto/ y ciego./ Mas los hombres rieron. "Loca"/ llamaron a la opresora dualidad/ cuando unió al crimen el Azar.// Ya no la Necesidad con su adusta ley/ (no la luna devorada por la tierra para nutrir sus hambrientas noches/ o el débil alimentado con su sangre la gloria del fuerte),/ sino el Misterio regulando el exterminio. La fortuna,/ el Sino vendando a la justicia—"¡idioses!"—/ gritaron los rebeldes— "leeremos en los astros/ la oculta norma del Destino".// Y escuchó el relámpago el clamor desde su insomne/ palidez. —"¡Ay del hombre!"—dijo/ y encendió en las cuencas/ vacías del jaguar/ la atroz proximidad de un astro.

Octavio Paz (1914–1998, Mexico)

Born in Mexico City, Paz inherited a strong intellectual heritage as the son of a political journalist. He founded and edited his first magazine at the age of seventeen. After serving as an editor for the literary magazine *Taller,* Paz joined the Mexican Diplomatic Corps and lived abroad while continuing to write. His work offers a range of topics and styles from the historical and religious to the surreal. Eventually, Paz made the logical paradox one of the most defining characteristics of his poetics. Considered one of the most important writers of the twentieth century, Paz has received the Premio Miguel de Cervantes (Madrid, 1981), El Premio Nacional de Letras (Mexico, 1977), and the Nobel Prize in Literature (Stockholm, 1990). PRINCIPAL WORKS: *Piedra de sol* (1957), *Blanco* (1967), *Ladera este* (1962–1968)

Excerpt from **Sunstone / Piedra de sol**

Eliot Weinberger, trans.

a crystal willow, a poplar of water,
a tall fountain the wind arches over,
a tree deep-rooted yet dancing still,
a course of a river that turns, moves on,
doubles back, and comes full circle,
forever arriving:
                          the calm course
of the stars or an unhurried spring,
water with eyes closed welling over
with oracles all night long,
a single presence in a surge of waves,
wave after wave till it covers all,
a reign of green that knows no decline,
like the flash of wings unfolding in the sky,

a path through the wilderness of days to come,
and the gloomy splendor of misery like a bird
whose song can turn a forest to stone,
and the imminent joys on branches that vanish,
the hours of light pecked away by the birds,
and the omens that slip past the hand,

a sudden presence like a burst of song,
like the wind singing in a burning building,
a glance that holds the world and all
its seas and mountains dangling in the air,
body of light filtered through an agate,
thighs of light, belly of light, the bays,
the solar rock, cloud-colored body,
color of a brisk and leaping day,
the hour sparkles and has a body,
the world is visible through your body,
transparent through your transparency,

I travel my way through galleries of sound,
I flow among echoing presences,
I cross transparencies as though I were blind,
a reflection erases me, I'm born in another,
oh forest of pillars that are enchanted,
through arches of light I travel into
the corridors of a diaphanous fall,

I travel your body, like the world,
your belly is a plaza full of sun,
your breasts two churches where blood
performs its own, parallel rites,
my glances cover you like ivy,
you are a city the sea assaults,
a stretch of ramparts split by the light
in two halves the color of peaches,
a domain of salt, rocks, and birds,
under the rule of oblivious noon,

dressed in the color of my desires,
you go your way naked as my thoughts,
I travel your eyes, like the sea,
tigers drink their dreams in those eyes,
the hummingbird burns in those flames,
I travel your forehead, like the moon,
like the cloud that passes through your thoughts,
I travel your belly, like your dreams,

your skirt of corn ripples and sings,
your skirt of crystal, your skirt of water,
your lips, your hair, your glances rain
all through the night, and all day long
you open my chest with your fingers of water,
you close my eyes with your mouth of water,
you rain on my bones, a tree of liquid
sending roots of water into my chest,

I travel your length, like a river,
I travel your body, like a forest,
like a mountain path that ends at a cliff
I travel along the edge of your thoughts,
and my shadow falls from your white forehead,
my shadow shatters, and I gather the pieces
and go on with no body, groping my way,

the endless corridors of memory, the doors
that open into an empty room
where all the summers have come to rot,
jewels of thirst burn at its depths,
the face that vanishes upon recall,
the hand that crumbles at my touch,
the hair spun by a mob of spiders
over the smiles of years ago,

setting out from my forehead, I search,
I search without finding, search for a moment,
a face of storm and lightning-flashes
racing through the trees of night,
a face of rain in a darkened garden,
relentless water that flows by my side,

I search without finding, I write alone,
there's no one here, and the day falls,
the year falls, I fall with the moment,
I fall to the depths, invisible path
over mirrors repeating my shattered image,
I walk through the days, the trampled moments,
I walk through all the thoughts of my shadow,
I walk through my shadow in search of a moment,

un sauce de cristal, un chopo de agua,/ un alto surtidor que el viento arquea,/ un árbol bien plantado mas danzante,/ un caminar de río que se curva,/ avanza, retrocede, da un rodeo/ y llega siempre:/ un caminar tranquilo/ de estrella o primavera sin premura,/ agua que con los párpados cerrados/ mana toda la noche profecías,/ unánime presencia en oleaje,/ ola tras ola hasta cubrirlo todo,/ verde soberanía sin ocaso/ como el deslumbramiento de las alas/ cuando se abren en mitad del cielo,// un caminar entre las espesuras/ de los días futuros y el aciago/ fulgor de la desdicha como un ave/ petrificando el bosque con su canto/ y las felicidades inminentes/ entre las ramas que se desvanecen,/ horas de luz que pican ya los pájaros,/ presagios que se escapan de la mano,// una presencia como un canto súbito,/ como el viento cantando en el incendio,/ una mirada que sostiene en vilo/ al mundo con sus mares y sus montes,/ cuerpo de luz filtrada por un ágata,/ piernas de luz, vientre de luz, bahías,/ roca solar, cuerpo color de nube,/ color de día rápido que salta,/ la hora centellea y tiene cuerpo,/ el mundo ya es visible por tu cuerpo, / es transparente por tu transparencia,// voy entre galerías de sonidos,/ fluyo entre las presencias resonantes,/ voy por la transparencias como un ciego,/ un reflejo me borra, nazco en otro,/ oh bosque de pilares encantados,/ bajo los arcos de la luz penetro/ los corredores de un otoño diáfano,// voy por tu cuerpo como por el mundo,/ tu vientre es una plaza soleada,/ tus pechos dos iglesias donde oficia/ la sangre sus misterios paralelos,/ mis miradas te cubren como yedra,/ eres una ciudad que el mar asedia,/ una muralla que la luz divide/ en dos mitades de color durazno,/ un paraje de sal, rocas y pájaros/ bajo la ley del mediodía absorto,// vestida del color de mis deseos/ como mi pensamiento vas desnuda,/ voy por tus ojos como por el agua,/ los tigres beben sueño en esos ojos,/ el colibrí se quema en esas llamas,/ voy por tu frente como por la luna,/ como la nube por tu pensamiento,/ voy por tu vientre como por tus sueños,// tu falda de maíz ondula y canta,/ tu falda de cristal, tu falda de agua,/

tus labios, tus cabellos, tus miradas,/ toda la noche llueves, todo el día/ abres mi pecho con tus dedos de agua,/ cierras mis ojos con tu boca de agua,/ sobre mis huesos llueves, en mi pecho/ hunde raíces de agua un árbol líquido,// voy por tu talle por un río,/ voy por tu cuerpo como por un bosque,/ como por un sendero en la montaña/ que en un abismo brusco se termina,/ voy por tus pensamientos afilados/ y a la salida de tu blanca frente/ mi sombra despeñada se destroza,/ recojo mis fragmentos uno a uno/ y prosigo sin cuerpo, busco a tientas,// corredores sin fin de la memoria,/ puertas abiertas a un salón vacío/ donde se pudren todos los veranos,/ las joyas de la sed arden al fondo,/ rostro desvanecido al recordarlo,/ mano que se deshace si la toco,/ cabelleras de arañas en tumulto/ sobre sonrisas de hace muchos años,// a la salida de mi frente busco,/ busco sin encontrar, busco un instante,/ un rostro de relámpago y tormenta/ corriendo entre los árboles nocturnos,/ rostro de lluvia en un jardín a obscuras,/ agua tenaz que fluye a mi costado,// busco sin encontrar, escribo a solas,/ no hay nadie, cae el día, cae el año,/ caigo con el instante, caigo a fondo,/ invisible camino sobre espejos/ que repiten mi imagen destrozada,/ piso días, instantes caminados,/ piso los pensamientos de mi sombra,/ piso mi sombra en busca de un instante,

Here / Aquí

Charles Tomlinson, trans.

My steps along this street
resound
        in another street
in which
        I hear my steps
passing along this street
in which

Only the mist is real

Mis pasos en esta calle/ Resuenan/ en otra calle/ donde/ oigo mis pasos/ pasar en esta calle/ donde// Sólo es real la niebla

Exclamation / La exclamación

Eliot Weinberger, trans.

Stillness
        not on the branch
in the air
        Not in the air
in the moment
        hummingbird

Quieto/ no en la rama/ en el aire/ No en el aire/ en el instante/ el colibrí

Altar / Custodia

Eliot Weinberger, trans.

A name
Its shadows
He   She
An i   An o
A mallet   A gong
A tower   A pool
A hand   A clock
A bone   A rose
A mist   A tomb
A spring   A flame
A brand   A night
A river   A city
A keel   An anchor
She male
He
Body of names
Your name in my name in your name my name
One to another one against the other one around another
One in the other
Unnamed

El nombre
Sus sombras
El hombre   La hembra
El mazo   El gong
La i   La o
La torre   El aljibe
El índice   La hora
El hueso   La rosa
El rocío   La huesa
El venero   La llama
El tizón   La noche
El río   La ciudad
La quilla   El ancla
El hembro   La hombra
El hombre
Su cuerpo de nombres

Tu nombre en mi nombre En tu nombre mi nombre
Uno frente al otro uno contra el otro uno en torno al otro
El uno en el otro
Sin nombres

Joaquín Pasos (1914–1947, Nicaragua)

Though he never left Nicaragua, Pasos was a champion of travel poetry. He is associated with the Vanguardia group and he wrote in the style of *poesía chinfónica*, a genre of comical rustic poetry. Influenced by World Wars I and II, his work is occupied with the destruction of the human consciousness and the devastation of war. His writings were published posthumously. PRINCIPAL WORK: *Poesías* (1960)

Excerpt from Warsong of the Things / Canto de guerra de las cosas
Steven F. White, trans.

When you reach old age, you will respect stone,
if indeed you reach old age,
if indeed there is any stone left.
Your children will love old copper,
faithful iron.
You will greet ancient metals in your homes,
you will treat noble lead with grace appropriate to its sweet character;
you will be reconciled with zinc, giving it a soft name;
with bronze, by considering it gold's brother,
because gold did not go to war for you.
Gold stayed, for you, playing the role of a spoiled child,
dressed in velvet, bundled up, protected by resentful steel . . .
When you reach old age, you will respect gold,
if indeed you reach old age,
if indeed there is any gold left.

Water is the sole eternity of blood.
Its strength, made blood. Its disquiet, made blood.
Its violent longing of wind and sky
made blood.
Tomorrow they will say blood became dust,
tomorrow the blood will be dry.
Neither sweat, nor tears, nor urine
will fill the hollow of the empty heart.

Tomorrow they will envy the hydraulic pump of a throbbing watercloset,
the living proof of a spigot,
the thick liquid.
The river will take charge of the ruined kidneys
and in the middle of the desert the crossed bones
will beg the water to return to the bodies of men in vain.

. . . .

Nature's husband is not with her.
The seeds of the crop haven't the strength to die,
and one hears their death like the little thread of blood that comes from the
    wounded man's mouth.
Single roses, flowers like those used in the festival of forgetfulness,
feeble odor of tombs, of grass that dies on inscribed marble.
Not a single cry. Not even the voice of a bird or a child
or the sound of a fierce assassin with his knife.
What you would give today to have your dress stained with blood!
What you would give to find some inhabited nest!
What you would give to have them plant a child in your flesh!

Finally, Lord of the Armies, here is the supreme pain.
Here, without pity, without subterfuge, without verses,
is the true pain.
At last, Lord, before us all is the pain stopped cold.
It is not pain felt for the wounded or the dead,
nor for the blood that was shed, nor for the earth filled with laments,
nor for the cities empty of houses, nor for the fields filled with orphans.
It is the whole pain.
There can be no tears, no sorrow,
no words, no memories.
Nothing fits now inside the chest.
All the noises of the world form one great silence.
All the men of the world form a single specter.
In the middle of this pain, soldier!, your post remains,
empty or filled.
The lives of those who are left have hollows—
complete voids—
as if they had taken mouthfuls of flesh from their bodies.
Look into this gap, the one I have here in my chest,
so you can see heavens and hells.
Look at my head. It has thousands of holes:
through it shines a white sun, through it a black star.
Touch my hand, this hand that yesterday bore steel:
you can pass your fingers through it in the air!

Here is the absence of man, the absence of flesh, fear,
days, things, souls, fire.
Everything remained in time. Everything burned over there, far away.

Cuando lleguéis a viejos, respetaréis la piedra,/ si es que llegáis a viejos,/
si es que entonces quedó alguna piedra./ Vuestros hijos amarán al viejo
cobre,/ al hierro fiel./ Recibiréis a los antiguos metales en el seno de vuestras
familias,/ trataréis al noble plomo con la decencia que corresponde a su
carácter dulce;/ os reconciliaréis con el zinc dándole un suave nombre;/ con
el bronce considerándolo como hermano del oro,/ porque el oro no fue a
la guerra por vosotros,/ el oro se quedó por vosotros, haciendo el papel de
niño mimado,/ vestido de terciopelo, arropado, protegido por el resentido
acero . . . / Cuando lleguéis a viejos, respetaréis al oro,/ si es que llegáis a
viejos,/ si es que entonces quedó algún oro.// El agua es la única eternidad
de la sangre./ Su fuerza, hecha sangre. Su inquietud, hecha sangre./ Su
violento anhelo de viento y cielo,/ hecho sangre./ Mañana dirán que la
sangre se hizo polvo,/ mañana estará seca la sangre./ Ni sudor, ni lágrimas,
ni orina/ podrán llenar el hueco del corazón vacío./ Mañana envidiarán
la bomba hidráulica de un inodoro palpitante,/ la constancia viva de un
grifo,/ el grueso líquido./ El río se encargará de los riñones destrozados/ y
en medio del desierto los huesos en cruz pedirán en vano que/ regrese el
agua a los cuerpos de los hombres.// . . . // La naturaleza tiene ausente a su
marido./ No tienen ni fuerzas suficientes para morir las semillas del cultivo/
y su muerte se oye como el hilito de sangre que sale de la boca del hombre
herido./ Rosas solteronas, flores que parecen usadas en la fiesta del olvido,/
débil olor de tumbas, de hierbas que mueren sobre mármoles inscritos./ Ni
un solo grito, Ni siquiera la voz de un pájaro o de un niño/ o el ruido de
un bravo asesino con su cuchillo./ ¡Qué dieras hoy por tener manchado
de sangre el vestido!/ ¡Qué dieras por encontrar habitado algún nido!/
¡Qué dieras porque sembraran en tu carne un hijo!// Por fin, Señor de los
Ejércitos, he aquí el dolor supremo,/ He aquí, sin lástimas, sin subterfugios,
sin versos,/ el dolor verdadero./ Por fin, Señor, he aquí frente a nosotros el
dolor parado en seco./ No es un dolor por los heridos ni por los muertos,/
ni por la sangre derramada ni por la tierra llena de lamentos/ ni por las
ciudades vacías de casas ni por los campos llenos de huérfanos./ Es el dolor
entero./ No pueden haber lágrimas ni duelo/ ni palabras ni recuerdos,/ pues
nada cabe ya dentro del pecho./ Todos los ruidos del mundo forman un
gran silencio./ Todos los hombres del mundo forman un solo espectro./ En
medio de este dolor, ¡soldado!, queda tu puesto/ vacío o lleno./ Las vidas
de los que quedan están con huecos,/ tienen vacíos completos,/ como si se
hubieran sacado bocados de carne de sus cuerpos./ Asómate a este boquete,
a éste que tengo en el pecho,/ para ver cielos e infiernos./ Mira mi cabeza
hendida por millares de agujeros:/ a través brilla un sol blanco, a través un

astro negro./ Toca mi mano, esta mano que ayer sostuvo un acero:/ puedes pasar en el aire, a través de ella, tus dedos!/ He aquí la ausencia del hombre, fuga de carne, de miedo,/ días, cosas, almas, fuego./ Todo se quedó en el tiempo. Todo se quemó allá lejos.

Nicanor Parra (1914–, Chile)

A poet/antipoet born in San Fabián de Alico, Chillán, Chile, Parra is one of nine siblings of the fabled folklorist, singer, and plastic artist Violeta Parra. The son of a schoolteacher, Nicanor Parra studied physics and mathematics at the University of Chile and continued his graduate work at Brown University in Rhode Island and at the University of Oxford, England. As he argued in the poem "Manifesto," a poet is not an alchemist but a man like all the others—like a bricklayer constructing a wall. Parra brought poetry down from its pedestal, perceiving it as necessity, not as luxury. Taking his cue from the vernacular popular poets, Parra changed and liberated Chilean poetry forever. Inspired by Taoism, Parra has been writing and drawing what he describes as "ecological" poems, convinced that the preservation of life on the planet is a universal matter beyond political partisanship. Recently, 10,000 people gathered to see his art and poetry exhibit at the Centro Cultural de la Moneda in Santiago. PRINCIPAL WORKS: *Poemas y antipoemas* (1954), *Versos de salón* (1962), *Artefactos* (1972), *Poesía política* (1983)

No President's Statue Escapes / De las infalibles palomas

Liz Werner, trans.

From those infallible pigeons
Clara Sandoval used to tell us:

Those pigeons know exactly what they're doing

No se libra la estatua de ningún presidente/ Nos decía la Clara Sandoval//
Las palomas saben múy bien lo que hacen

1973

Liz Werner, trans.

GREAT! . . . NOW
who's going to liberate us from our liberators?

U.S.A.

Edith Grossman, trans.

Where liberty
is a statue

If Fidel were fair about it
he'd believe in me
just as I believe in him:
History will absolve me

Third time this week
that a pigeon
shat on me
thank god
cows don't have wings

Given two women
you'd love the one that never existed

One out of every thousand Chileans
dies of sorrow.

Nobody's ever seen
a dead cop
on the street—
this means
that cops die in bed—
no one in his right mind
would say they're immortal

Donde la libertad/ es una estatua// Si fuera justo Fidel/ debiera creer en mí/
tal como yo creo en él:/ la historia me absolverá// Tercera vez/ en una
semana/ que me caga una paloma/ menos mal/ que las vacas no vuelan//
Entre dos novias/ se ama a la que nunca existió// Uno de cada mil chilenos/
se muere de pena// Nadie vió jamás/ un carabinero muerto/ en la calle/
de lo que se deduce/ que esos seres mueren en cama/ porque no vamos a
decir/ que son immortales . . .

The Individual's Soliloquy / Soliloquio del individuo
Allen Ginsberg and Lawrence Ferlingetti, trans.

I'm the individual.
First I lived by a rock
(I scratched some figures on it)
Then I looked for some place more suitable.
I'm the individual.
First I had to get myself food,
Hunt for fish, birds, hunt up wood
(I'd take care of the rest later)
Make a fire,
Wood, wood, where could I find any wood,
Some wood to start a little fire,
I'm the individual.
At the time I was asking myself,
Went to a canyon filled with air;
A voice answered me back:
I'm the individual.
So then I started moving to another rock,
I also scratched figures there,
Scratched out a river, buffaloes,
Scratched a serpent
I'm the individual.
But I got bored with what I was doing,
Fire annoyed me,
I wanted to see more,

I'm the individual.
Went down to a valley watered by a river,
There I found what I was looking for,
A bunch of savages,
A tribe,
I'm the individual.
I saw they made certain things,
Scratching figures on the rocks,
Making fire, also making fire!
I'm the individual.
They asked me where I came from.
I answered yes, that I had no definite plans,
I answered no, that from here on out.
O.K.
I then took a stone I found in the river
And began working on it,
Polishing it up,
I made it a part of my life.
But it's a long story.
I chopped some trees to sail on
Looking for fish,
Looking for lots of things
(I'm the individual),
Till I began getting bored again.
Storms get boring,
Thunder, lightning,
I'm the individual.
O.K.
I began thinking a little bit,
Stupid questions came into my head,
Doubletalk.
So then I began wandering through forests,
I came to a tree, then another tree,
I came to a spring,
A hole with a couple of rats in it;
So here I come, I said,
Anybody seen a tribe around here,
Savage people who make fire?
That's how I moved on westward,
Accompanied by others,
Or rather alone,
Believing is seeing, they told me,
I'm the individual.
I saw shapes in the darkness,

Clouds maybe,
Maybe I saw clouds, or sheet lightning,
Meanwhile several days had gone by,
I felt as if I were dying;
Invented some machines,
Constructed clocks,
Weapons, vehicles,
I'm the individual.
Hardly had time to bury my dead,
Hardly had time to sow,
I'm the individual.
Years later I conceived a few things,
A few forms,
Crossed frontiers,
And got stuck in a kind of niche,
In a bark that sailed forty days,
Forty nights,
I'm the individual.
Then came the droughts,
Then came the wars,
Colored guys entered the valley,
But I had to keep going,
Had to produce.
Produced science, immutable truths,
Produced Tanagras,
Hatched up thousand-page books.
My face got swollen,
Invented a phonograph,
The sewing machine,
The first automobiles began to appear,
I'm the individual.
Someone set up planets,
Trees got set up!
But I set up hardware,
Furniture, stationery,
I'm the individual.
Cities also got built,
Highways,
Religious institutions went out of fashion,
They looked for joy, they looked for happiness,
I'm the individual.
Afterward I devoted myself to travel,
Practicing, practicing languages
Languages,

I'm the individual.
I looked into a keyhole,
Sure, I looked, what am I saying, looked,
To get rid of all doubt looked,
Behind the curtains,
I'm the individual.
O.K.
Perhaps I better go back to that valley,
To that rock that was home,
And start scratching all over again,
Scratching out everything backward,
The world in reverse.
But life doesn't make sense.

Yo soy el Individuo/ Primero viví en una roca/ (Allí grabé algunas figuras)./ Luego busqué en lugar más apropiado./ Yo soy el Individuo./ Primero tuve que procurarme alimentos,/ Buscar peces, pájaros, buscar leña,/ (Ya me preocuparía de los demás asuntos)./ Hacer una fogata,/ Leña, leña, dónde encontrar un poco de leña,/ Algo de leña para hacer una fogata,/ Yo soy el Individuo./ Al mismo tiempo me pregunté,/ Fui a un abismo lleno de aire;/ Me respondió una voz:/ Yo soy el Individuo./ Después traté de cambiarme a otra roca,/ Allí también grabé figuras,/ Grabé un río, búfalos,/ Grabé una serpiente/ Yo soy el Individuo./ Pero no. Me aburrí de las cosas que hacía,/ El fuego me molestaba,/ Quería ver más,/ Yo soy el Individuo./ Bajé a un valle regado por un río,/ Allí encontré lo que necesitaba,/ Encontré un pueblo salvaje,/ Una tribu,/ Yo soy el Individuo./ Vi que allí se hacían algunas cosas,/ Figuras grababan en las rocas,/ Hacían fuego, ¡también hacían fuego!/ Yo soy el Individuo./ Me preguntaron que se dónde venía./ Contesté que sí, que no tenía planes determinados,/ Contesté que no, que de ahí en adelante./ Bien./ Tomé entonces un trozo de piedra que encontré en un río/ Y empecé a trabajar con ella,/ Empecé a pulirla,/ De ella hice una parte de mi propia vida./ Pero esto es demasiado largo./ Corté unos árboles para navegar,/ Buscaba peces,/ Buscaba diferentes cosas,/ (Yo soy el Individuo)./ Hasta que me empecé a aburrir nuevamente./ Las tempestades aburren,/ Los truenos, los relámpagos,/ Yo soy el Individuo./ Bien. Me puse a pensar un poco,/ Preguntas estúpidas se me venían a la cabeza,/ Falsos problemas./ Entonces empecé a vagar por unos bosques./ Llegué a un árbol y a otro árbol,/ Llegué a una fuente,/ A una fosa en que se veían algunas ratas:/ Aquí vengo yo, dije entonces,/ ¿Habéis visto por aquí una tribu,/ Un pueblo salvaje que hace fuego?/ De este modo me desplacé hacia el oeste/ Acompañado por otros seres, O más bien solo./ Para ver hay que creer, me decían,/ Yo soy el Individuo./ Formas veía en la obscuridad,/ Nubes tal vez,/ Tal vez veía nubes, veía relámpagos,/ A todo esto habían pasado ya varios días,/ Yo me sentía morir;/ Inventé unas máquinas,/ Construí relojes,/ Armas, vehículos,/ Yo soy el Individuo./ Apenas tenía tiempo para enterrar a mis muertos,/ Apenas tenía tiempo para sembrar, Yo soy el Individuo./ Años más tarde concebí unas cosas,/ Unas formas,/ Crucé las fronteras/ Y permanecí fijo en una especie de nicho,/ En una barca que navegó cuarenta días,/ Cuarenta noches,/ Yo soy el Individuo./ Luego vinieron unas sequías,/ Vinieron unas guerras,/ Tipos de color entraron al valle,/ Pero yo debía seguir adelante,/ Debía producir./ Produje ciencia, verdades inmutables,/ Produje tanagras,/ Dí a luz libros de miles de páginas,/ Se me hinchó la cara,/ Construí un fonógrado,/ La máquina de coser,/ Empezaron a aparecer los primeros automóviles,/ Yo soy el Individuo./ Alguien segregaba planetas,/ ¡Arboles segregaba!/ Pero yo segregaba herramientas,/ Muebles, útiles de escritorio,/ Yo soy el Individuo./ Se construyeron también ciudades,/ Rutas,/ Instituciones religiosas pasaron de moda,/ Buscaban dicha, buscaban felicidad,/ Yo soy el Individuo./ Después me dediqué mejor a viajar,/ A practicar, a practicar idiomas,/ Idiomas,/ Yo soy el Individuo./ Miré por una cerradura,/ Sí, miré, qué digo, miré,/ Para salir de la duda miré,/ Detrás de unas cortinas,/ Yo soy el Individuo./ Bien./ Mejor es tal vez que vuelva a ese valle,/ A esa roca que me sirvió de hogar,/ Y empiece a grabar de nuevo,/ De atrás para adelante grabar/ El mundo al revés./ Pero no: la vida no tiene sentido.

Violeta Parra (1917–1967, Chile)

Parra was a singer-songwriter, painter, burlap tapestry artist, and ceramist and was born in Malloa, Chile. She and her nine siblings worked from a young age due to the unemployment and early death of their father. Encouraged by her older brother, the poet Nicanor Parra, she rediscovered Chilean folklore and introduced her songs to the world in France, where her recordings first found recognition. She wrote "vulgar poetry" in a country that—like all of Latin America—showed disdain toward the oral culture peasants. Using folkloric forms, she composed modern tenths, legitimizing a language and a culture that had long been repressed and belittled under the label of "popular." She once told her brother, "Forgive me, Nicanor, for coming from the Louvre only to go to the Zanjón de la Aguada (a working-class neighborhood in Santiago), but it is in the latter where I draw my strength." To connect with the street she set up a circus tent in Santiago as her performance space. Ignored by Chileans, she committed suicide in that space. PRINCIPAL WORKS: *Poésie populaire des Andes* (1965), *Décimas: autobiografía en versos chilenos* (1970), *Cantos folklóricos chilenos* (1979)

Easy for Singing / Pa' cantar de un improviso

W. S. Merwin, trans.

If you're going to make up the singing
as you go you have to have some
talent, memory, understanding,
strength of a cock bred for fighting
you have to have the words performing
like hailstones with the storm breaking
you have to end up amazing
the devil himself so convincing
you are like what they were saying
when Peter and Paul were talking.

And beside ladies and gentlemen
you have to have strings to play on
a run of expression
an eloquent companion
a need to be number one
remembering all that went on.
I wish I remembered how one
sets down a challenge to someone
but I don't have any notion
that I'd come to glory in the long run.

For an instrument to play
the guitarrón is the one for me
its wire and its bass and the way
it resounds portentously
I tell it a five-part story
three of five two of three
from its pegboard to its feet
and its five curves on the way
its box should be singing away
four little devils inside it

And to do the best singing
you have to do your own playing
proud singer following
where the music is going
courting a flight of song
as long as the theme is flowing
to a fine chord coming
and with artful touch answering
I can see my head has nothing
that's needed for such a thing

So kind sirs who have been
lending me your attention
you can see how right I have been
to dodge this blade;
still I want nothing set down
against me by anyone
there is too much of it in
the papers already
I won't miss the moment
to sing like the canary.

Pa' cantar de un improviso/ se requiere buen talento,/ memoria y
entendimiento,/ fuerza de gallo castizo./ Cual vendaval de granizos/ han
de florear los vocablos,/ se ha de asombrar hast'el diablo/ con muchas
bellas razones,/ como en las conversaciones/ entre San Peiro y San Paulo.//
También, señores oyentes,/ se necesita estrumento,/ muchísimos elementos/
y compañero 'locuente;/ ha de ser güen contendiente;/ conoce'or de
l'historia,/ quesiera tener memoria/ pa' entablar un desafío,/ pero no me
da el senti'o/ pa' finalizar con gloria.// Al hablar del estrumento/ diríjome
al guitarrón/ con su alambre y su bordón/ su sonoro es un portento./ Cinc'
ordenanzas le cuento/ tres de a cinco, dos de a tres,/ del clavijero a sus pies/
l'entrasta'ura 'legante,/ cuatro diablitos cantantes/ debe su caja tener.// Y pa'
cantar a porfía/ habrá que ser toca'ora,/ arrogante la cantora/ para seguir
melodía,/ garantizar alegría/ mientras dure'l contrapunto,/ formar un bello
conjunto/ responder con gran destreza./ Yo veo que mi cabeza/ no es capaz
par' este asunto.// Por fin, señores amables,/ que me prestáis atención,/
me habéis hallado razón/ de hacerle quite a este sable;/ mas no quiero que
s'entable/ contra mí algún comentario,/ pa' cominillo en los diarios/ sobran
muchos condimentos./ No ha de faltarm'el momento/ que aprenda la del
canario.

Dumb, Sad, and Thoughtful / Muda, triste y pensativa

W. S. Merwin, trans.

Dumb, sad, and thoughtful my
brother left me yesterday
telling me about somebody
famous for his poetry
Big surprise to me when he
said to me Violeta
now you've got the way

of popular poetry
start telling me
your sad story in poetry.

God save me Nicanor
if I'm going to take it upon me
to go wandering door to door
digging up folklore
you don't know how sore
they make me what a pain they are
the verses I encounter
I don't have much in my pocket
and I've got four kids
I have to give something to eat

In the little time left me
between work and recording
I hang onto my guitarrón
or, say, the neck of my mare
and find in their company
a minute of peace for my nerves
since this proud world has set me
this job as my destiny
It's the profit that ruins you
the proverb says.

Like a flower garden
the whole countryside appears
to be blooming with fine verses
out of the heart of it
they sing of the sorrows
full of faith and hope
some of them beg for an end
to the bitter things we go through
ill-fated among the ill-fated
where they lead me I go.

So there my simple brother
you don't see how it is with me
you don't know that one lasso
is enough for one steer.
I'm too long in the tooth
to go around like an ostrich
with no light to show for it

no water to wash it down
for all the flags waving
whatever they wave for.

Muda, triste y pensativa/ ayer me dejó mi hermano/ cuando me habló de un
fulano/ muy famoso en poesía./ Fue grande sorpresa mía/ cuando me dijo:
Violeta,/ ya que conocís la treta/ de la versá popular,/ princípiame a relatar/
tus penurias "a lo pueta".// Válgame Dios, Nicanor,/ si tengo tanto trabajo,/
que ando de arriba p'abajo/ desentierrando folklor./ No sabís cuánto dolor,/
miseria y padecimiento/ me dan los versos qu'encuentro;/ muy pobre está
mi bolsillo/ y tengo cuatro chiquillos/ a quienes darl'el sustento.// En ratitos
que me quedan/ entre campo y grabación,/ agarro mi guitarrón,/ o bien, mi
cogot'e yegua;/ con ellos me siento en tregua/ pa'reposarme los nervios,/
ya que este mundo soberbio/ me ha destinado este oficio;/ y malhaya
el beneficio,/ como lo dice el proverbio.// Igual que jardín de flores/ se
ven los campos sembra'os,/ de versos tan delica'os/ que son perfeutos
primores;/ ellos cantan los dolores,/ llenos de fe y esperanzas;/ algotros
piden mudanzas/ de nuestros amargos males;/ fatal entre los fatales/ estoy
siguiendo estas andanzas.// Por fin, hermano sencillo,/ que no comprendís
mi caso;/ no sabís que un solo lazo/ lacea un solo novillo./ Pica'o tengo el
colmillo/ de andar como el avestruz,/ sin conseguir una luz/ ni una sed de
agua siquiera./ Mientras tanto, la bandera/ no dice ni chuz ni muz.

Goddamn the Empty Sky / Maldigo del alto cielo

John Felstiner, trans.

Goddamn the empty sky
and the stars at night
goddamn the ripply bright
stream as it goes by
goddamn the way stones lie
on dirt they're all the same
goddamn the oven's flame
because my heart is raw
goddamn the laws
of time in all their shame
my pain's as bad as that.

Goddamn the mountain chain
the coast range and the Andes
goddamnit Lord my land is
ten times as long as Spain
also crazy and sane

with candor and deceit
goddamn what smells so sweet
because my luck is out
goddamn what's not in doubt
what's messy and what's neat
my pain's as bad as that.

Goddamn the way the Spring
gets plants to blossom
and the colors of Autumn
goddamn the whole damn thing
clouds on the wing
goddamn them more and more
because I'm done for
goddamn Winter to bits
along with Summer's tricks
goddamn the saint the whore
my pain's as bad as that.

Goddamn getting on your feet
to watch the flag go by
damn every kind of lie
Venus and Main Street
and the canary's tweet
the planets and their motions
the earth with its erosions
because my heart is sore
goddamn the ports and shores
of the enormous oceans
my pain's as bad as that.

Goddamn the moon and weather
desert and riverbed
goddamn the dead the dead
and the living together
the bird with all its feathers
is such a goddamn mess
schools and places to confess
I'll tell you what I'm sick of
goddamn that one word love
with all its nastiness
my pain's as bad as that.

So goddamn the color white
the black and yellow too
bishops with all their crew

preachers and men of state
goddamn them it's too late
free man and prisoner
soft voice and quarreler
I damn them every week
in Spanish and in Greek
thanks to a two-timer
my pain's as bad as that.

Maldigo del alto cielo/ las estrellas con su reflejo/ maldigo los azulejos/
destellos del arroyuelo/ maldigo del bajo suelo/ la piedra con su contorno/
maldigo el fuego del horno/ porque mi alma está de luto/ maldigo los
estatutos/ del tiempo con sus bochornos/ cuánto será mi dolor.// Maldigo
la cordillera/ de los Andes y de la Costa/ maldigo Señor la angosta/ y larga
faja de tierra/ también la paz y la guerra/ lo franco y lo veleidoso/ maldigo
lo perfumoso/ porque mi anhelo está muerto/ maldigo todo lo cierto/
y lo falso con lo dudoso/ cuánto será mi dolor.// Maldigo la Primavera/
con sus jardines en flor/ y del Otoño el color/ yo lo maldigo de veras/ a la
nube pasajera/ la maldigo tanto y tanto/ porque me asiste un quebranto/
maldigo el Invierno entero/ con el Verano embustero/ maldigo profano y
Santo/ cuánto será mi dolor.// Maldigo a la solitaria/ figura de la bandera/
maldigo cualquier emblema/ la Venus y la araucaria/ el trino de la canaria/
el cosmo y sus planetas/ la tierra y todas sus grietas/ porque me aqueja un
pesar/ maldigo del ancho mar/ sus puertos y sus caletas/ cuánto será mi
dolor.// Maldigo luna y paisaje/ los valles y los desiertos/ maldigo muerto
por muerto/ y el vivo de rey a paje/ el ave con su plumaje/ y lo maldigo
a porfía/ las aulas y las sacristías/ porque me aflije un dolor/ maldigo el
vocablo amor/ con toda su porquería/ cuánto será mi dolor.// Maldigo por
fin lo blanco/ lo negro con lo amarillo/ obispos y monaguillos/ ministros y
predicandos/ yo los maldigo llorando/ lo libre y lo prisionero/ lo dulce y lo
pendenciero/ le pongo mi maldición/ en griego y en español/ por culpa de
un traicionero/ cuánto será mi dolor.

Gonzalo Rojas (1917–, Chile)

Born in Lebu, Chile, Rojas sings of love, freedom, and death. His father, a miner, died
when Rojas was four, leaving his mother to raise eight children. He went on to study
law and was a member of the surrealist group Mandrágora. He served as a diplomat
during the presidency of his friend Salvador Allende, but when Allende was over-
thrown, Rojas was targeted by the repressive military regime, which used its influence to block his access to sources of work. He then became a university professor in

Venezuela and the United States. He has earned many awards, including the Miguel de Cervantes Award. Rojas conceives of poetry as a call to a higher, critical awareness of reality, and his work—as Julio Cortázar pointed out—"gives back to poetry so many things that had been taken away from it." PRINCIPAL WORKS: *La miseria del hombre* (1948), *Oscuro* (1977), *El alumbrado y otros poemas* (1987)

You Shouldn't Copy Pound / No le copien a Pound

Elizabeth Macklin, trans.

You shouldn't copy Pound, no copying the marvellous
      flood of the copying
Ezra, let him write his Mass in Persian, in Cairene Aramaic, in Sanskrit,
with his half-learnt Chinese, his translucent Greek
straight from the dictionary, his leafstorm Latin, his freest
blurry Mediterranean, nonagenarian artifice
for making and remaking until gropingly reaching the great
      palimpsest of the One;
don't judge him for the diaspora: you'd need to amass
      atoms,
weave them up thusly, from visible to invisible, on the warp
      of what's fleeting
and the immovable threads; set him loose
with his blindness to see, to see again, for
      that is the verb: to see,
and that the Spirit, what's unfinished
and what's burning, what we truly love
and what loves us, if by chance we are Son of Man
and of Woman, numberless down at the bottom of the
      unnameable;
                no, new demigods
of language sans Logos, of hysteria, apprentices
of the original portent, you shouldn't steal his shadow
from the sun, consider the canticle
that opens as it closes like the act of germination,
      you should turn into air,
man-air like old Ez, who went along always
      in danger, leap fearlessly
from the vowels to the stars, taut drawn bow
of contradiction in all the velocities of the
      possible, air and more air
for today and forever, before
and after the purple
of the blowout
simultaneous, instantaneous

of rotation, because this blinking world
       will bleed,
jump off its mortal axis, and goodbye abundant
traditions of light and marble, and arrogance; you should laugh
       at Ezra
and his wrinkles, laugh starting now right up until then,
       but not plunder him: you should laugh, fickle
generations coming and going like dust,
       boiling
of scholars, laugh, laugh at Pound
with his Tower of Babel on his back like an advisory of the
       other
that came in his language:
                      canticle,
men of little faith, consider the canticle.

No le copien a Pound, no le copien al copión maravilloso/ de Ezra, déjenlo
que escriba su misa en persa, en/ cairo-arameo, en sánscrito,/ con su chino a
medio aprender, su griego translúcido/ de diccionario, su latín de hojarasca,
su libérrimo/ Mediterráneo borroso, nonagenario el artificio/ de hacer y
rehacer hasta llegar a tientas al gran palimpsesto de lo Uno;/ no lo juzguen
por la dispersión: había que juntar los átomos,/ tejerlos así, de lo visible a
lo invisible, en la urdiembre/ de lo fugaz/ y las cuerdas inmóviles; déjenlo
suelto/ con su ceguera para ver, para ver otra vez, porque el verbo es ése:
ver,/ y ése el Espiritu, lo inacabado/ y lo ardiente, lo que de veras amamos/
y nos ama, si es que somos Hijo de Hombre/ y de Mujer, lo innumerable al
fondo de lo innombrable;/ no, nuevos semidioses/ del lenguaje sin Logos, de
la histeria, aprendices/ del portento original, no le roben la sombra/ al sol,
piensen en el cántico/ que se abre cuando se cierra como la germinación,
háganse aire,/ aire-hombre como el viejo Ez, que anduvo siempre en el
peligro, salten intrépidos/ de las vocales a las estrellas, tenso el arco/ de la
contradicción en todas las velocidades de lo posible, aire y más aire/ para hoy
y para siempre, antes/ y después de lo purpúreo/ del estallido/ simultáneo,
instantáneo/ de la rotación, porque este mundo parpadeante sangrará,/
saltará de su eje mortal, y adiós ubérrimas/ tradiciones de luz y mármol, y
arrogancia: ríanse de Ezra/ y sus arrugas, ríanse desde ahora hasta entonces,
pero no lo saqueen; ríanse, livianas/ generaciones que van y vienen como el
polvo, pululación/ de letrados, ríanse, ríanse de Pound/ con su Torre de Babel
a cuestas como un aviso de lo otro/ que vino en su lengua;/ cántico,/ hombre
de poca fe, piensen en el cántico.

Qedeshím Qedeshóth

Elizabeth Macklin, trans.

Bad luck to go to bed with Phoenicians, I went to bed
with one in Cádiz, gorgeous
and I didn't hear about my horoscope until
long after when the Mediterranean began to demand

more and more wave surge from me; rowing
backwards I reached, near-dead of exhaustion,
the twelfth century: everything was white, the birds,
the ocean, the sunrise was white.

I belong to the Temple, she told me: I am a Temple. There is
no hooker, I thought, who won't speak words
to match the size of that complacency. 50 dollars
to go to the other World, I responded laughing; or nothing.
50, or nothing. She cried
great sobs against the mirror, painted
upon it in rouge and in tears a fish: Fish,
remember the fish.

She said lighting me up with her huge liquid eyes of
turquoise, and right there began to dance on the carpet the
entire ritual; first she placed in the air a Babylonian disc and
wound up the cot, doused the candles: the bed
was without a doubt a millenarian gramophone
to judge by the splendor of the music: doves, all
at once doves made their appearance.

All of this to be sure in the nakedest nakedness with
her reddish hair and those green shoes, high ones, that
sculpted her as if in cold marble and as sacred as
when they raffled her off in Tyre among the other she-wolves
of the port, or in Carthage
where she was a dancing girl with sheet privileges at
fifteen; all that.

But now, ay, to put it in prose one
may well gather that so much
angelic spectacle at a blow struck crisis into
my backbone, and lascivious and
seminal I violated her in her ecstasy as
if this were not a temple but a house of prostitution, I
kissed her rough, I did her
harm and she perhaps

kissed me in an excess of petals, we got
deliciously stained, burned in great flames
Cádiz far into the night aroar in an
oil of man and of woman that is written in no
Punic alphabet whatever, if the imagination's
imagination will suffice me.

Qedeshím qedeshóth, she-personage, theologianess
in madness, bronze, yowling
in bronze, not even Augustine
of Hippo who was also a fool and
a sinner in Africa would
for a single night have snatched his body from the
diaphanous Phoenician. I
a sinner confess before God.

Mala suerte acostarse con fenicias, yo me acosté/ con una en Cádiz
bellísima/ y no supe de mi horóscopo hasta/ mucho después cuando el
Mediterráneo me empezó a exigir/ más y más oleaje; remando/ hacia
atrás llegué casi exhausto a la/ duodécima centuria: todo era blanco, las
aves,/ el océano, el amanecer era blanco.// Pertenezco al Templo, me dijo:
soy Templo. No hay/ puta, pensé, que no diga palabras/ del tamaño de
esa complacencia. 50 dólares/ por ir al otro Mundo, le contesté riendo;
o nada,/ 50, o nada. Lloró/ convulsa contra el espejo, pintó/ encima con
rouge y lágrimas un pez: —Pez,/ acuérdate del pez.// Dijo alumbrándome
con sus grandes ojos liquidos de/ turquesa, y ahí mismo empezó a bailar
en la alfombra el/ rito completo; primero puso en el aire un disco de
Babilonia y/ le dio cuerda al catre, apagó las velas: el catre/ sin duda era
un gramófono milenario/ por el esplendor de la música; palomas, de/
repente aparecieron palomas.// Todo eso por cierto en la desnudez más
desnuda con/ su pelo rojizo y esos zapatos verdes, altos, que la/ esculpían
marmórea y sacra como/ cuando la rifaron en Tiro entre las otras lobas/
del puerto, o en Cartago/ donde fue bailarina con derecho a sábana a los/
quince; todo eso.// Pero ahora, ay, hablando en prosa se/ entenderá que
tanto/ espectáculo angélico hizo de golpe crisis en mi/ espinazo, y lascivo
y/ seminal la violé en su éxtasis como/ si eso no fuera un templo sino un
prostíbulo, la/ besé áspero, la/ lastimé y ella igual me/ besó en un exceso
de pétalos, nos/ manchamos gozosos, ardimos a grandes llamaradas/ Cádiz
adentro en la noche ronca en un/ aceite de hombre y de mujer que no está
escrito/ en alfabeto púnico alguno, si la imaginación de la/ imaginación me
alcanza.// Qedeshím qedeshóth, personaja, teóloga/ loca, bronce, aullido/
de bronce, ni Agustín/ de Hipona que también fue liviano y/ pecador en
Africa hubiera/ hurtado por una noche el cuerpo a la/ diáfana fenicia. Yo/
pecador me confieso a Dios.

César Dávila Andrade (1918–1967, Ecuador)

Almost all Ecuadorian students recognize a portrait of Dávila Andrade, the poet and narrator born in Cuenca, Ecuador. Called "the Fakir" because of his appearance and mystical leanings, he was the oldest of six children in a low-income family and dropped out of secondary school in order to support himself. He once wrote to his mother, "Tell me sincerely what you think about this son of yours. He is so strange." In Venezuela, he worked as a journalist and published much of his work until his suicide freed him from his torments. Juan Gustavo Cobo Borda once said that Dávila Andrade is "a peerless, unclassifiable figure . . . with an unmistakable voice within Latin American poetry" that touches on "the entire drama of Indian oppression, so real still in present-day Ecuador" while, "in a second focus of his poetry, he devotes himself to an alchemical search through enigmas that constitute a key to a deeper spiritual dimension." PRINCIPAL WORKS: *Espacio, me has vencido; Oda al arquitecto; Canción a Teresita* (1946), *Catedral salvaje* (1951), *Boletín y elegía de las mitas* (1957), *Materia real* (1970)

Excerpt from Bulletin and Elegy of Indian Enslavement / Boletín y elegía de las mitas

Molly Weigel, trans.

I am Juan Atampam, Blas Llaguarcos, Bernabé Ladna,
Andrés Chabla, Isidro Guamancela, Pablo Pumacuri,
Marcos Lema, Gaspar Tomayco, Sebastián Caxicondor.
I was born and suffered in Chorlavi, Chamanl, Tanlagua,
Niebli. Yes, I suffered unto death in Chisingue,
Naxiche, Guambayna, Paolo, Cotopilaló.
I sweated blood in Caxaji, in Quinchirana;
in Cicalpa, Licto, and Conrogal.
I endured the Christ of my people in Tixán, in Saucay,
in Molleturo, in Cojibambo, in Tovavela and Zhoray.
That's how I added more whiteness and pain to the Cross that my
      executioners brought.
To myself as well. To José Vacancela as well.
To Lucas Chaca as well. To Roque Caxicondor as well.
In Plaza de Pomasqui in a circle of other natives,
they sheared our heads till we felt the cold.
Oh, Pachacámac, Lord of the Universe,
your smile never felt more frigid to us,
and we went up on the high mountain plateau, heads bare,
to crown ourselves, weeping, with your Sun.

Melchor Pumaluisa, son of Guapulo:
they cut off his testicles in the middle of the hacienda's patio with a
      hog-butchering knife.

And, kicking him, they paraded him
in front of our tear-filled eyes.
He was spurting out great intermittent streams of blood.
He fell face down in the flower of his body.
Oh, Pachacámac, Lord of the Infinite,
You, who stain the Sun among the dead . . .

And your Lieutenant and Chief Justice,
José de Uribe: "I order you." And I,
with the other Indians, carried him wherever he ordered
from house to house, on his visits, in a hammock.
While our women, with our daughters, slaves,
were sweeping, carding, weaving, weeding,
spinning, licking mud dishes—of our making.
And laying with Viracochas,
our flowers with two thighs,
to bring forth the mestizo and future executioner.

Without pay, without corn, without a home,
without even hunger, from not eating anything,
only squash; weeping, old hail streaming down my cheeks,
I arrived carrying fruits from the valley
after four weeks of fasting.
They received me: My daughter split in two by Alférez Quintanilla.
Wife, his cohabitant. Two sons dead by the whip.
And I, by Life, oh Pachacámac. That's how I died.

And from such suffering, to seven skies,
by seventy suns, oh Pachacámac,
wife giving birth to my son, I wrenched his arms.
Still soft after so much disaster, she said:
"Break the baby's hands; I don't want
him to be Viracochas' slave." I broke.

And among the priests, too, there were some who seemed like
     devils, vultures.
No different. Worse than the other two-legged ones.
Others would say: "Son, Love, Christ."
Weaving inside the church, lamp oil,
wax of monuments, eggs of ash,
doctrine and blind teachers of doctrine.
Vihuela, Indian for the kitchen, girl for the house.
So they said. I obeyed.

And then: Sebastián, Manuel, Roque, Selva,
Miguel, Antonio, Matiyos, of grass, wood, charcoal,

straw, fish, stones, corn, women, daughters. Every service.
Of the llama-herders too, you ate
two thousand llama hearts in three months.
Of the woman you ate too,
near the ear of her husband and son,
night after night.

Arms led to evil.
Eyes to weeping and lament.
Men to the whistle of their whips.
Cheeks to the hardness of their boots.
Heart that they crushed, treading bodies of mothers, women, daughters
in front of the enslaved Indian.
Only we have suffered
the horrible world of their hearts.

In the workshop of cloth, tapestries, cloaks, ponchos,
I, the naked one, buried in dungeons, worked
a year and forty days,
with hardly a handful of corn for the effort
and was thinner than the thread I wove.
Shut up from dawn until the other brightness,
without eating, I wove, I wove.
I made the cloth in which the Masters dressed themselves,
who gave the solitude of whiteness to my skeleton,
and on Good Friday I dawned shut up,
face down, on the loom,
with vomited blood among the threads and shuttle.
Thus I dyed with my soul, nothing but ribs,
the cloth of those who stripped me.

Yo soy Juan Atampam, Blas Llaguarcos, Bernabé Ladña,/ Andrés Chabla,
Isidro Guamancela, Pablo Pumacuri,/ Marcos Lema, Gaspar Tomayco,
Sebastián Caxicondor./ Nací y agonicé en Chorlaví, Tanlagua,/ Niebla,
Guambayna, Paolo, Cotopilaló./ Sudor de sangre tuve en Caxaji,
Quinchirana,/ en Cicalpa, Licto y Conrogal./ Padecí todo el Cristo de
mi raza en Tixán, en Saucay,/ en Molleturo, en Cojibambo, en Tovavela
y Zhoray./ Añadí así más blancura y dolor a la Cruz que trajeron mis/
verdugos./ A mí, tam. A José Vacancela, tam./ A Lucas Chaca, tam. A Roque
Caxicondor, tam./ En Plaza de Pomasqui y en rueda de otros naturales,/ nos
trasquilaron hasta el frío la cabeza./ Oh, Pachacámac, Señor del Universo,/
nunca sentimos más helada tu sonrisa,/ y al páramo subimos desnudos de
cabeza,/ a coronarnos, llorando, con tu Sol.// A Melchor Pumaluisa, hijo
de Guapalo,/ en medio patio de hacienda, con cuchillo de abrir chanchos/

cortáronle testes./ y, pateándole, a caminar delante/ de nuestros ojos llenos
de lágrimas./ Echaba, a golpes, chorro en ristre de sangre./ Cayó de bruces en
la flor de su cuerpo./ Oh, Pachacámac, Señor del Infinito,/ Tú, que manchas
el Sol entre los muertos . . . // Y vuestro Teniente y Justicia Mayor,/ José de
Uribe: "Te ordeno." Y yo,/ con los otros indios, llevábamosle a todo pedir/
de casa en casa, para sus paseos, en hamaca./ Mientras mujeres nuestras,
con hijas, mitayas,/ a barrer, a carmenar, a tejer, a escardar,/ a hilar, a lamer
platos de barro—nuestra hechura—,/ Y a yacer con Viracochas/ nuestras
flores de dos muslos,/ para traer al mestizo y verdugo venidero.// Sin paga,
sin maíz, sin runa-mora,/ ya sin hambre, de puro no comer;/ sólo calavera,
llorando granizo viejo por mejillas,/ llegué trayendo frutos de la yunga/ a
cuatro semanas de ayuno./ Recibiéronme: Mi hija partida en dos por Alférez
Quintanilla./ Mujer, de conviviente de él. Dos hijos muertos a látigo./ Oh,
Pachacámac, y yo, a la Vida. Así morí.// Y de tanto dolor, a siete cielos,/
por setenta soles, oh, Pachacámac,/ mujer pariendo mi hijo, le torcí los
brazos./ Ella, dulce ya de tanto aborto, dijo:/ "Quiebra maqui de guagua;
no quiero/ que sirva de mitayo a Viracochas." Quebré.// Y entre curas, tam,
unos pareciendo diablos, buitres, había./ Iguales. Peores que los otros de
dos piernas./ Otros decían: "Hijo, Amor, Cristo."/ A tejer dentro de iglesia,
aceite para lámpara,/ cera de monumentos, huevos de ceniza,/ doctrina
y ciegos doctrineros./ Vihuela, india para la cocina, hija para la casa./ Así
dijeron. Obedecí.// Y después: Sebastián, Manuel, Roque, Selva,/ Miguel,
Antonio, Matiyos, a hierba, leña, carbón,/ paja, peces, piedras, maíz, mujeres,
hijas. Todo servicio./ A runa-llama tam, que en tres meses/ comiste dos mil
corazones de ellas./ A mujer que tam comiste/ cerca de oreja de marido y de
hijo,/ noche a noche.// Brazos llevaron al mal./ Ojos al llanto./ Hombres al
soplo de sus foetes./ Mejillas a lo duro de sus botas./ Corazón que estrujaron,
pisando ante mitayo,/ cuerpos de mamas, mujeres, hijas./ Sólo nosotros
hemos sufrido/ el mundo horrible de sus corazones.// En obraje de telas,
sargas, capisayos, ponchos,/ yo, el desnudo, hundido en calabozos, trabajé/
año cuarenta días,/ con apenas puñado de maíz para el pulso/ que era más
delgado que el hilo que tejía./ Encerrado desde aurora hasta el otro claror,/
sin comer, tejí, tejí./ Hice la tela con que vestían cuerpos los Señores/ que
dieron soledad de blancura a mi esqueleto,/ y Día Viernes Santo amanecí
encerrado,/ boca abajo, sobre telar,/ con vómito de sangre entre los hilos y
lanzadera./ Así, entinté con mi alma, llena de costado,/ la tela de los que me
desnudaron.

João Cabral do Melo Neto (1920–1999, Brazil)

Cabral made his career as a member of Brazil's diplomatic corps. As a young diplomat turned writer, Cabral incorporated the foreign literary styles he observed abroad with the native themes he learned while growing up on his family's sugarcane plantation in Pernambuco. Cousin to the poet Manuel Bandeira, Cabral was one of the most prominent members of Brazil's "Generation of '45." With his pragmatic and rigorous approach to poetry writing, he sought to achieve a perfect, seamless combination between form and content. PRINCIPAL WORKS: *O engenheiro* (1945), *A educação pela pedra* (1966), *Morte e vida Severina e outros poemas em voz alta* (1966)

Education by Stone / A educação pela pedra

James Wright, trans.

An education by stone: through lessons,
to learn from the stone: to go to it often,
to catch its level, impersonal voice
(by its choice of words it begins its classes).
The lesson in morals, the stone's cold resistance
to flow, to flowing, to being hammered:
the lesson in poetics, its concrete flesh:
in economics, how to grow dense compactly:
lessons from the stone (from without to within,
dumb primer), for the routine speller of spells.

Another education by stone: in the backlands
(from within to without and pre-didactic place).
In the backlands stone does not know how to lecture,
and, even if it did would teach nothing:
you don't learn the stone, there: there, the stone
born stone, penetrates the soul.

Uma educação pela pedra: por lições;/ para aprender da pedra, freqüentá-la;/ captar sua voz inenfática, impessoal/ (pela de dicção ela começa as aulas)./ A lição de moral, sua resistência fria/ ao que flui e a fluir, a ser maleada;/ a de poética, sua carnadura concreta;/ a de economia, seu adensar-se compacta:/ lições da pedra (de fora para dentro,/ cartilha muda), parra quem soletrá-la.// Outra educação pela pedra: no Sertão/ (de dentro para fora, e pré-didática)./ No Sertão a pedra não ensinaria nada;/ lá não se aprende a pedra: lá a pedra,/ uma pedra de nascença, entranha a alma.

Tale of an Architect / Fábula de um arquiteto

Richard Zenith, trans.

1.

Architecture: the art of building doors
to open up the building of openness;
building not to isolate and hem in
nor to shut up secrets, but building
every door an open door building
houses made only of doors and roofs.
Architect: the one who opens to man
(in open houses all would be cleansed)
doors-leading-to, never doors-against;
doors to freedom: air light sure reason.

2.

Until, intimidated by so many free men,
he stopped letting them live transparently.
Where there were openings he put in
opacities; instead of glass, plaster
resealing man in the chapel-uterus
with the old comforts, once more a fetus.

1./ A arquitetura como construir portas,/ de abrir; ou como construir o aberto;/ construir, não como ilhar e prender,/ nem construir como fechar secretos;/ construir portas abertas, em portas;/ casas exclusivamente portas e tecto./ O arquiteto: o que abre para o homem/ (tudo se sanearia desde casas abertas)/ portas por-onde, jamais portas-contra;/ por onde, livres: ar luz razão certa.// 2./ Até que, tantos livres o amedrontando,/ renegou dar a viver no claro e aberto./ Onde vãos de abrir, ele foi amurando/ opacos de fechar; onde vidro, concreto;/ até refechar o homem: na capela útero, com confortos de matriz, outra vez feto.

The Unconfessing Artist / O artista inconfessável

Richard Zenith, trans.

Doing this or that is futile.
Not doing anything is futile.
But between doing and not doing,
better the futility of doing.
But no, doing to forget
is what's futile never the forgetting.
But one can do what's futile knowing
it's futile, and although knowing

it's futile and that its sense
cannot in any way be sensed,
still do: for it is harder
than no doing, and hardly
will one be able to say
with more disdain, or say
more plainly to the reader Nobody
that what was done was for nobody.

Fazer o que seja é inútil./ Não fazer nada é inútil./ Mas entre fazer e não
fazer/ mais vale o inútil do fazer./ Mas não, fazer para esquecer/ que é
inútil: nunca o esquecer./ Mas fazer o inútil sabendo/ que ele é inútil, e
bem sabendo/ que é inútil e que seu sentido/ não será sequer pressentido,/
fazer: porque ele é mais difícil/ do que não fazer, e difícil-/ mente se poderá
dizer/ com mais desdém, ou então dizer/ mais direto ao leitor Ninguém/ que
o feito o foi para ninguém.

A Knife All Blade / Uma faca só lamina

Galway Kinnell, trans.

Like a bullet
buried in flash
weighting down one side
of the dead man,

like a bullet
made of a heavier lead
lodged in some muscle
making the man tip to one side,

like a bullet fired
from a living machine
a bullet which had
its own heartbeat,

like a clock's
beating deep down in the body
of a clock who once lived
and rebelled,

clock whose hands
had knife-edges
and all the pitilessness
of blued steel.

Yes, like a knife
without pocket or sheath
transformed into part
of your anatomy,

a most intimate knife
a knife for internal use
inhabiting the body
like the skeleton itself

of the man who would own it,
in pain, always in pain,
of the man who would wound himself
against his own bones.

Assim como uma bala/ enterrada no corpo,/ fazendo mais espêsso/ um
dos lados do morto;// assim como uma bala/ do chumbo mais pesado,/
no músculo de um homem/ pesando-o mais de um lado;// qual bala que
tivesse/ um vivo mecanismo,/ bala que possuísse/ um coração ativo// igual
ao de um relógio/ submerso em algum corpo,/ ao de um relógio vivo/ e
também revoltoso,// relógio que tivesse/ o gume de uma faca/ e tôda a
impiedade/ de lâmina azulada;// assim como uma faca/ que sem bôlso ou
bainha/ se transformasse em parte/ de vossa anatomia;// qual uma faca
íntima/ ou faca de uso interno, habitando num corpo/ como o próprio
esqueleto// de um homem que o tivesse,/ e sempre, doloroso,/ de homem
que se ferisse/ contra seus próprios ossos.

Olga Orozco (1920–1999, Argentina)

Orozco was born in Toay, Argentina, a town she kept close to her heart despite leaving for Bahía Blanca at the age of eight and traveling widely. After living and studying
in Buenos Aires, she joined a group of poets called the "Generación de '40." Infused
with nostalgia and hope, her writing addresses a variety of themes using different
techniques. The theme of the microcosm often appears in two forms: the human
body and the world as an image of a superior reality. Orozco spent a great deal of
her adult life traveling to Europe, to Africa, and throughout South America. She was
awarded numerous prizes, including the prize of the city of Buenos Aires in 1962 for
Los juegos peligrosos, the Grand Prize of Honor from the Fundación Argentina para la
Poesía. Togther with Enrique Molina and Alejandra Pizarnik, she is one of the most
successful surrealist poets of her generation. PRINCIPAL WORKS: *Desde lejos* (1946),
Los juegos peligrosos (1962), *La noche a la deriva* (1983)

Variations on Time / Variaciones sobre el tiempo

Mary Crow, trans.

Time:
you've dressed in the moth-eaten skin
    of the last prophet;
you've worn down your face to its last pallor;
you've put on a crown of shattered mirrors
    and tatters of rain;
and now you chant babble about the future
    with melodies dug up from the past,
while you wander in the shadows through your starving rubbish,
    like a mad king.

All your ravings of a fragmented ghost no longer
    matter to me,
you wretched host.
You can gnaw the bones of great promises
    on their rickety biers,
or relish the bitter brew that oozes from the beheaded.
And even then there won't be enough
until you swallow the last grinding in your Goyaesque elegance.

Our steps through those tangled labyrinths never
    kept pace together.
Not even in the beginning,
when you led me by the hand through the bewitched forest
and made me run breathless after that unattainable tower
or made me discover always the same almond
    with its dark taste of fear and innocence.
Ah, your blue plumage shining among the branches!
I could not embalm you or extract your heart
    like a golden apple.

Later you were the whip that goads,
too cruel,
the imperial coachman rolling me up between the feet
    of his horses.
Too slow,
you condemned me to be the unknown hostage,
victim buried up to my neck
    in centuries of sand.

Sometimes we've fought hand to hand.
We've struggled like wild beasts over each share of love,
over each pact signed with the ink you brew
    in some instantaneous eternity,

each face sculpted in the changing of fleeting clouds,
each house erected in the tide that never turns.
One by one you snatched from me
        the crumbled fragments of my temples.
Don't empty the purse.
Don't show off your trophies.
Don't tell me your deeds again like a shameful gladiator
        in the vast galleries of echo.

I never granted you a truce.
I broke your laws.
I forced your locks and climbed up to the storehouses
        called the future.
I made a single bonfire out of all your ages.
I turned you inside out like a broken spell
or mixed up your secret places as in an anagram whose letters
        change places and shift meaning.
I condensed you till you became a still bubble,
opaque, prisoner in my glass skies.
I stretched your dried skin over leagues of memory,
until, little by little, the pale holes of oblivion pierced it.
A toss of the dice made you pause above the immense
        void between two hours.

We've come a long way, rounding up our souls,
        in this atrocious game.
I know there'll be no rest,
and you can't tempt me, no, not with being invaded
        by the placid shade of age-old plants,
even though it does me no good to be on guard,
even though you stand there,
mercenary,
till the end of everything,
        receiving your wages,
mean bribe coined in your honor
        by the hoarse machinery of death.

And don't write "nevermore," then,
        on the white borders
with your ignorant hand,
as if you were some god of God's,
a guardian from the past, master of yourself
        in another you that fills up the darkness.
Perhaps you are only the most faithless shadow
        of one of his dogs.

Tiempo:/ te has vestido con la piel carcomida del último profeta;/ te has gastado la cara hasta la extrema palidez;/ te has puesto una corona hecha de espejos rotos y/ lluviosos jirones,/ y salmodias ahora el balbuceo del porvenir con las/ desenterradas melodías de antaño,/ mientras vagas en sombras por tu hambriento escorial,/ como los reyes locos.// No me importan ya nada todos tus desvaríos de/ fantasma inconcluso,/ miserable anfitrión,/ Puedes roer los huesos de las grandes promesas en/ sus desvencijados catafalcos/ o paladear el áspero brebaje que rezuman las/ decapitaciones./ Y aún no habrá bastante,/ hasta que no devores con tu corte goyesca la molienda/ final.// Nunca se acompasaron nuestros pasos en estos/ entrecruzados laberintos./ Ni siquiera al comienzo,/ cuando me conducías de la mano por el bosque/ embrujado/ y me obligabas a correr sin aliento detrás de aquella/ torre inalcanzable/ o a descubrir siempre la misma almendra con su oscuro/ sabor de miedo y de inocencia./ ¡Ah, tu plumaje azul brillando entre las ramas!/ No pude embalsamarte ni conseguí extraer tu corazón/ como una manzana de oro.// Demasiado apremiante,/ fuiste después el látigo que azuza,/ el cochero imperial arrollándome entre las patas de sus / bestias./ Demasiado moroso,/ me condenaste a ser el rehén ignorado,/ la víctima sepultada hasta los hombros entre siglos/ de arena.// Hemos luchado a veces cuerpo a cuerpo./ Nos hemos disputado como fieras cada porción de amor,/ cada pacto firmado con la tinta que fraguas en alguna/ instantánea eternidad,/ cada rostro esculpido en la inconstancia de las nubes/ viajeras,/ cada casa erigida en la corriente que no vuelve./ Lograste arrebatarme uno por esos desmenuzados/ fragmentos de mis templos./ No vacíes la bolsa./ No exhibas tus trofeos./ No relates de nuevo tus hazañas de vergonzoso gladiador/ en las desmesuradas galerías del eco.// Tampoco yo te concedí una tregua./ Violé tus estatutos./ Forcé tus cerraduras y subí a los graneros que denominan/ porvenir./ Hice una sola hoguera con todas tus edades./ Te volví del revés igual que a un maleficio que se quiebra,/ o mezclé tus recintos como en un anagrama cuyas letras/ truecan el orden y cambian el sentido./ Te condensé hasta el punto de una burbuja inmóvil,/ opaca, prisionera en mis vidriosos cielos./ Estiré tu piel seca en leguas de memoria,/ hasta que la horadaron poco a poco los pálidos agujeros/ del olvido./ Algún golpe de dados te hizo vacilar sobre el vacío/ inmenso entre dos horas.// Hemos llegado lejos en este juego atroz, acorralándonos/ el alma./ Sé que no habrá descanso,/ y no me tientas, no, con dejarme invadir por la plácida/ sombra de los vegetales centenarios,/ aunque de nada me valga estar en guardia,/ aunque al final de todo estés de pie, recibiendo tu paga,/ el mezquino soborno que acuñan en tu honor las roncas/ maquinarias de la muerte,/ mercenario.// Y no escribas entonces en las fronteras blancas "nunca/ más"/ con tu mano ignorante,/ como si fueras algún dios de Dios,/ un guardián anterior, el amo de ti mismo en otro tú que/ colma las tinieblas./ Tal vez seas apenas la sombra más infiel de alguno de/ sus perros.

The Obstacle / El obstáculo

Mary Crow, trans.

Strait is the gate
and maybe hungry black dogs watch over it
    or guard like dogs,
however much you see only winged space,
perhaps the blank sign of a dizzy gnashing of teeth.
It's narrow and uncertain and cuts off my road
    that makes promises with each welcome,
with each spark of annunciation.
I can't get through.
Let's leave for another time the great migrations,
the profuse baggage of insomnia, my bold escort
    of light in the darkness.
It's difficult to be born on the other side
even with all the tide in your favor.
Nor can I enter even though my retinue is reduced to
    silence,
to some few mysteries, to a memorial of love,
    to my worst stars.
Not even my shadow fits between each assault and the wall.
Useless to insist while I take my bundle of transparent
    possessions with me,
this insoluble fear, that gleam that was
    a garden beneath the frost.
There is no place for a folded soul, for a huddled body,
not even pressing their tangles to the most extreme darkening,
paring the clouds down to the size
    of some tiny dream lost in the attic.
I can't hide this beginning with the little that I am.
My hands are superfluous and my feet excessive
    for this slippery breach.
There's always one rib too many like an arm of the sea
    or the echo that's prolonged just because,
when it isn't blocked by a border like a dull, senseless ornament,
or when it surpasses, restless, the yearning of a wing.
I will never get to the other side.

Es angosta la puerta/ y acaso la custodien negros perros hambrientos y/
guardias como perros,/ por más que no se vea sino el espacio alado,/ tal
vez la muestra en blanco de una vertiginosa den-/ tellada./ Es estrecha e
incierta y me corta el camino que pro-/ mete con cada bienvenida,/ con
cada centelleo de la anunciación./ No consigo pasar./ Dejaremos para

otra vez las grandes migraciones,/ el profuso equipaje del insomnio, mi denodada escol-/ ta de luz en las tinieblas./ Es difícil nacer al otro lado con toda la marejada en/ su favor./ Tampoco logro entrar aunque reduzca mi séquito al silencio,/ a unos pocos misterios, a un memorial de amor, a mis/ peores estrellas./ No cabe ni mi sombra entre cada embestida y la pared./ Inútil insistir mientras lleve conmigo mi envoltorio de/ posesiones transparentes,/ este insoluble miedo, aquel fulgor que fue un jardín/ debajo de la escarcha./ No hay lugar para un alma replegada, para un cuerpo/ encogido,/ ni siquiera comprimiendo sus lazos hasta la más/ extrema ofuscación,/ recortando las nubes al tamaño de algún ínfimo sue-/ ño perdido en el desván./ No puedo trasponer esta abertura con lo poco que/ soy./ Son superfluas las manos y excesivos los pies para esta/ brecha esquiva./ Siempre sobra un costado como un brazo de mar o el/ eco que se prolonga porque sí,/ cuando no estorba un borde igual que no ornamento/ sin brillo y sin sentido,/ o sobresale, inquieta, la nostalgia de una ala./ No llegaré jamás al otro lado.

Idea Vilariño (1920–, Uruguay)

Born in Montevideo to artistic and intellectual parents, the Uruguayan poet, essayist, and translator exhibited a voracious appetite for literature at a young age. A member of the "Generation of '45," she was largely involved in the literary magazines *Clinamen* and *Número*. Vilariño traveled and lived abroad in Sweden, France, and Spain. She was the recipient of the Municipal Grand Prize in Literature in Uruguay. PRINCIPAL WORKS: *La suplicante* (1945), *Poemas de amor* (1962), *Pobre mundo* (1966)

Metamorphosis / La metamorfosis

Ruth Fainlight, trans.

Then I am the pines
I am the hot sand
I am a soft breeze
a mad bird raving through the air
or the sea thrashing at night
I am the night.
Then I am no one.

Entonces soy los pinos/ soy la arena caliente/ soy una brisa suave/ un pájaro liviano delirando en el aire/ o soy la mar golpeando de noche/ soy la noche// Entonces no soy nadie.

Poor World / Pobre mundo

Eliot Weinberger, trans.

They'll make it fall apart
it's going to fly to pieces
it will burst just like a bubble in the end
or wondrously explode
like a powder keg or just
suddenly be erased
as if a sponge
erased
its place
in space.
Maybe they won't do it
maybe they'll clean it up.
Life will fall like hair and spin around
like a sterile
mortal sphere
or slowly waste away
passing through the sky
like a whole
wide wound
or maybe just like death.

Lo van a deshacer/ va a volar en pedazos/ al fin reventará como una pompa/
o estallará glorioso/ como una santabárbara/ o más sencillamente/ será
borrado como/ si una esponja mojada/ borrara su lugar en el espacio./ Tal
vez no lo consigan/ tal vez van a limpiarlo./ Se le caerá la vida como una
cabellera/ y quedará rodando/ como una esfera pura/ estéril y mortal/ o
menos bellamente/ andará por los cielos/ pudriéndose despacio/ como una
llaga entera/ como un muerto.

A Guest / Un huésped

Andrew Graham-Yooll, trans.

You are not mine
you're not here
in my life
at my side
you do not eat at my table
do not laugh or sing
do not live for me.
We are distant
you

and me myself
and my house.
You are a stranger
a guest
who seeks nought wants nought
except a bed
sometimes.
What can I do
but let you have it.
But I live alone.

No sos mío/ no estás/ en mi vida/ a mi lado/ no comés en mi mesa/ ni reís
ni cantás/ ni vivís para mi. / Somos ajenos/ tú/ y yo misma/ y mi casa./ Sos
un extraño/ un huésped/ que no busca no quiere/ más que una cama/ a
veces./ Qué puedo hacer/ cedértela./ Pero yo vivo sola.

I Did Not Love You / No te amaba

Andrew Graham-Yooll, trans.

I did not love you
I do not
well do I know that I don't
no at all
it may be the light
the time
the summer afternoon
I know
but I love you
I love you this afternoon
today
as I loved you on others
desperately
with blind love
angrily
sadly rationally
beyond desire
or illusion
or waiting
awaiting still
waiting
seeing
that you came
at last

you arrived
briefly.

No te amaba/ no te amo/ bien sé que no/ que no/ que es la luz/ es la hora/
la tarde de verano/ lo sé/ pero te amo/ te amo esta tarde/ hoy/ como te amé
otras tardes/ desesperadamente/ con ciego amor/ con ira/ con tristísimo
ciencia/ más allá de deseos/ o ilusiones/ o esperas/ y esperando no obstante/
esperándote/ viendo/ que venías/ por fin/ que llegabas/ de paso.

Jaime Saenz (1921–1986, Bolivia)

Visionary poet and novelist Saenz was born in La Paz, Bolivia, and died of alcoholism
in the same city. Saenz is regarded as the greatest poet of Bolivia and a crucial member of the Latin American pantheon. His work mixes the mystical and the precise
observation of what is. Jerome Rothenberg has said, "The poetry is relentless and
the genius of the man who made it is inescapable." PRINCIPAL WORKS: *El escalpelo*
(1955), *Visitante profundo* (1964), *Vidas y muertes* (1986), *Immanent Visitor, Selected
Poems of Jaime Saenz* (2002), *The Night* (2007)

Excerpt from Anniversary of a Vision / Aniversario de una visión
Kent Johnson and Forrest Gander, trans.

I
The floating world is lost, and the whole of life catches in the spring light
   of your looking,
—and while you repeat yourself in the echo, horizon bound in smoke,
   I regard your departure,
clear substance and hope dehiscing in the distance:
you live on that sweetness when beauty, sorrowing, glances your way,
and you emerge in half-profile
to the iron ringing of nighttime instruments, golden and blue, a music
   shining and throbbing and taking wing
in the hollow of my heart.

I don't dare look at you lest I not be inside you, and I don't praise you lest
   joy steal away
—I'm content just to watch you, and you know this and pretend to not look at me
and you bounce around, exaggerating everything with divine insight,
as if you were riding a horse or a motorcycle
—your extravagance amazes me, enraptures me, it is my daily bread
—when it rains, at a turn of the head, shouts fly from your shoulders,

and you stroke your cheeks and your applause echoes in the water, in the
   wind, and in the fog
—it amazes me how much I love you!
I yearn for you the moment I hear you,
a sepulchral music vanishes and my death steps out of you,
beloved images become visible to the musicians
when it's you who is listening
—always, the musicians exult in silence
when it's you who is listening.

II

Your crossing the streets separates you from me, as the day and the streets
   are separate
—the whole city is a spider that hoards you from me,
and the light cuts you off; it isolates you and makes me see how well it
   cocoons you
—resplendent, your happiness on the street corners,
at grief's hour I ask myself if I will find the sublime, deep blue of
   your garments,
my nation,
the air of your voice when evening falls
—and I ask myself why I would joyously surrender to the joy you kindle in
   me.
Your likeness to me is not to be met in you, in me, nor in my likeness
   to you
but in a line randomly traced and made unforgettable by forgetfulness
—and in the scent rising from certain drawings that make us weep
and which at the same time enliven us,
because your stunning vision is a disquiet to the flavor of memories,
that gentle testimony left by youth of its leaving:
hidden image,
taste of youth waiting to blend with the hour of death which is your form
   walking in light and love through the days and the nights and the years
   only to gash my heart
—my death will have absconded with your gaze, because it reached inside
   you when you searched it out
though it is wrapped within you and remains there;
let me name for you its raiment,
youth will endure in you.

III

You exaggerate without exaggerating because you know that my
   exaggerations make you exaggerate,
and my exaggerations are invisible in order that your exaggerations may be
   visible, not only for this age,

and in such subtle manner I add my grain of sand to the discovery of a cure
   for love's malady
—still, I'm alone and bewildered, and need succor in the face of this spasm
   of exaggerations which announce a kind of chaotic glee
—and I don't know if it's you or the devil who bewilders me and makes me
   see what is not seen
and live a life that is neither life nor dream, but fear—a fear of dreaming
   what my soul doesn't know,
a miracle of tenderness and truth transformed into joke when at a butterfly's
   flight I burst into lament
and seeking life and meaning, my struggles and penuries ended
   up as farce
—because I didn't know we were supposed to impersonate others, being
   who we are,
and we are not what we are nor do we seem to be what we are,
rather you and I will be, and I will be you also and you will be me,
solely through the grace of imposture
—and, moreover, now I have come to find that love is nothing other than
   what is hidden in love;
and to find it, I will have to transgress what I believe myself to be, which is
   to say you, and come to be you, which is to say me
(in reality, you are because I think, and you are the true reality)
—and you will do the same,
yet don't sigh, don't go here and there,
but where the gaze is firm and sighs are real,
and where a wild bull charges at the mystery
which will unbaptize that it may baptize,
and which will truly name you—from the inside, and not from without.

IV

There being a miracle, there is none; and I call out for the word's
   effacement, the threading of kingdoms and communication through the
   eyes, the return to the soul—you will perish
and no one will have seen your soul except me;
and you, on the other hand, don't even see my face, although I recognize
   yours in the throng,
when you don't recognize me you believe I believe I'm a flea, and that
   I ignore that I know you and believe I believe as you;
but you should know that were I in fact a flea, even if you looked at me
   I wouldn't know at whom you looked, and I would look at you without
   feeling or understanding the wherefore
—and so, if I am as I was born, it is due to terror, whose son I am; because it
   would not have been out of the question to be born a flea—and of that
   there's no doubt, apparently;

and later, I can wail, as I can wail, and seek the cure to a malady that afflicts
    not me, but you,
someone who, in believing himself to be who he is not, looks at me, as
    though I were what he is, while still being me,
who looks at himself, but not at me, since in truth it is I who believe he
    looks at me,
when he doesn't look at me, because of my looking at him:
so to say, I am I and you are you, and I look at you and for that reason
    believe that you look at me, and you don't look at me but believe you do
    every time you look at me,
except that I don't look at myself but believe I do, looking at you,
which is to say, I am not I and you are not you but I;
in a word: there is and there is not communication; and you don't exist,
    and I cease to exist in concerning myself with you, since I leave myself so
    that you may exist
—in conclusion, I'm telling you that this is the tone to use to penetrate
    matters of love—a dark thing,
for whose explanation the tone will need to be dark, but not lucid;
and I say that common sense only serves to explain itself to itself
for in common sense's tone, you become entombed in your own common
    sense, believing you've managed to make sense of what you wanted;
dark, very dark the tone must be, if what is hidden in love is to be unleashed;
and the darkness of the tone in the illumination of my farewell from you
    shall be great indeed,
when I find myself as a body without a body and without you, an aerolite
    for lack of you,
without the silence of your eyes, without the vision your parting lips verged
    on revealing to me
and without the voyage and the arrival of dream and of light, which
    enfolded you already to bring you in fullness to me
—who knows with what gestures, with what somersaults I would have
    greeted your enchanted apparition!
—and while I wait years for you and keep myself from living
and wait for you a minute and live in a rush,
I would wish for the moon's eclipse just to see my last illusions of kissing
    you come true,
it wouldn't matter if half a kiss or no kiss at all and in the flash of darkness
    or of light
—and my hope, beneath your gaze,
would be the real life I see in the deepness of your eyes.

I/ Lo flotante se pierde, y toda la vida se queda en la luz de la primavera
que ha/ traído tu mirar/ —y mientras perduras en el eco yo contemplo tu
partida con el humo en pos del/ horizonte,/ y la esperanza y la substancia

transparente discurren a lo lejos:/ vives la dulzura cuando piensa la hermosura con tristeza tu presencia,/ y apareces de medio perfil/ al tañido de unos instrumentos nocturnos, azules y dorados, que relumbran, que/ palpitan y que vuelan/ en el hueco de mi corazón.// No me atrevo a mirarte por no quedarme dentro de ti, y no te alabo por que no/ pierdas la alegría/ —con tu contemplación me contento y tú lo sabes y finges no mirarme/ y sueles dar saltos exagerando con una divina profundidad,/ como si estuvieras a caballo o en motocicleta/ —tu extravagancia me asombra y me regocija, y es mi pan de cada día/ —cuando llueve, de tus hombros salen gritos al girar de la cabeza,/ y te acaricias las mejillas y das palmadas que resuenan en el agua en el viento y en/ la niebla/ —¡cómo te amo me asombra!,/ yo te echo de menos a tiempo de escucharte,/ una música sepulcral se pierde en el olvido y mi muerte sale de ti,/ a los músicos se les aparecen las imágenes amadas/ cuando escuchas tú/ —todo el tiempo, los músicos se alegran del silencio/ cuando escuchas tú.// II/ Tu recorrido en las calles te separa de mí, de igual manera que el día y las calles/ de por sí/ —la ciudad es toda entera una araña que te guarda de mí,/ y la luz te incomunica; te aparta, y me hace espiar lo bien que te vigila/ —brilla tu júbilo en las esquinas,/ a la hora de la desolación yo me pregunto si encontraré el alto azul profundo/ de tu vestimenta,/ mi país,/ el aire de tu voz al caer la tarde/ —y me pregunto por qué renunciaría jubilosamente al júbilo que tú me/ causas./ Tu parecido a mi no se encuentra en ti, ni en mí, ni tampoco en mi parecido a ti/ pero en alguna línea trazada al acaso y que el olvido hizo memorable/ —y en el olor que se desprende de ciertos dibujos que nos hacen llorar/ y que a la vez nos causan júbilo,/ por ser un miedo al sabor de las evocaciones tu visión conmovedora,/ aquel suave testimonio que la juventud dejó de su partida:/ imagen escondida,/ sabor de juventud a la espera de fundirse con la hora de la muerte que es tu/ forma que camina con luz y con amor a lo largo de los días y las noches y/ los años para lastimar mi corazón/ —mi muerte se habrá llevado tu mirar porque sentía dentro de ti cuando la buscabas,/ pues en ti se encubre y permanece;/ déjame nombrarte su ropaje,/ en ti se quedará la juventud.// III/ Tú exageras sin exagerar porque sabes que mis exageraciones hacen que exageres/ tú,/ y mis exageraciones son invisibles a fin de que tus exageraciones, no solamente/ por causa de la edad sean visibles;/ y de modo tan sutil, yo contribuyo mi grano de arena al descubrimiento de un/ remedio para el mal de amor/ —mas, estoy solo y deslumbrado, y necesito socorro frente a este paroxismo de/ exageraciones, las que anuncian algún júbilo caótico/ —y no sé si tú eres o si es el demonio quien me deslumbra y me hace ver lo que no se ve/ y vivir una vida que no es vida ni es sueño, pero miedo, un miedo de soñar en lo/ que mi alma no conoce,/ un milagro de dulzura y de verdad transformado en una broma cuando al vuelo/ de una mariposa prorrumpí en una queja/ y buscando vida y sentido mis esfuerzos y penurias resultaron siendo un chiste/ —pues yo no sabia que tuviésemos que fingir

ser otros por ser los mismos;/ y no somos como lo que somos ni tampoco
parecemos ser lo que somos,/ sino que tú y yo seremos, y también yo seré
tú y tú serás yo,/ tan solamente por medio del fingimiento/ —y además,
ahora he llegado a saber que el amor no es, sino lo que se oculta en/ el
amor;/ y para encontrarlo, yo tendré que traspasar lo que creo ser, o sea tú,
y llegar a ser/ tú, o sea yo (en realidad, tú eres porque yo pienso, y eres la
verdadera realidad)/ —y tú harás de la misma manera,/ mas, no suspires,
no vayas por acá ni por allá,/ pero adonde se mira con fijeza y se suspira
de verdad,/ y donde un toro iracundo embiste al milagro/ que desbautizará
para bautizar,/ y que de verdad te nombrará —por dentro, y no por fuera.//
IV/ De haber milagro, no hay tal; y yo clamo por el olvido de la palabra,
la unifica/ ción de los reinos y la comunicación por medio de los ojos, el
retorno al alma —/ tú perecerás,/ y nadie habrá visto tu alma, excepto yo;/
y en cambio tú, ni siquiera me ves la cara, y mientras yo reconozco la tuya/
entre muchedumbres,/ cuando no me reconoces crees tú que creo que soy
una mosca, y que ignoro/ que te conozco y creo que yo creo lo que tú;/
pero, has de saber que si yo fuese en verdad una mosca, aunque me mirases
yo no/ sabría a quién miras tú, y te miraría sin sentir ni comprender el por
qué/ —y por tanto, si soy como nací, eso se debe al terror, del cual soy hijo;
pues no/ era nada imposible nacer como mosca —y de ello no cabe duda,
según se ve;/ y luego, yo puedo clamar, como que clamo, y buscar remedio a
un mal que a mí/ no me aqueja, pero a ti,/ alguien que, al creer ser quien no
es, me mira, y de tal suerte, como si yo fuera lo/ que él siendo yo,/ se mira a
sí mismo, pero no a mí, desde que en realidad soy yo el que cree que él/ me
mira,/ cuando no me mira. por mirarlo yo:/ es decir yo soy yo y tú eres tú
y te miro y por eso creo que tú me miras, y tú no/ me miras pero crees que
lo haces toda vez que tú me miras,/ con la diferencia que yo no me miro a
mí sino que creo hacerlo por mirarte a ti,/o sea que yo soy yo, y tú no eres
tú sino yo;/ en una palabra: hay y no hay comunicación; y tú no existes, y
yo dejo de existir al/ ocuparme de ti, puesto que salgo de mí por que existas
tú/ —en conclusión, yo te digo que es éste el tono a emplearse cuando de
penetrar en/ las cuestiones de amor se trata —una cosa oscura,/ para cuya
explicación el tono apropiado tendrá que ser oscuro, pero no lúcido;/ y
yo digo que la sensatez tan solamente sirve para explicarse lo que es ella
misma,/ pues con el tono sensato, en realidad te has abismado en tu propia
sensatez cuando/ crees haber logrado aclarar lo que querías;/ oscuro, muy
oscuro deberá de ser el tono, si se quiere hacer desencadenar lo que/ el amor
oculta;/ y habrá de ser muy grande la oscuridad del tono en la iluminación
de mi/ despedida de ti,/ cuando me encuentre un cuerpo sin cuerpo y sin ti,
un aerolito por la falta de ti,/ sin el silencio de tus ojos, sin la fantasía que
iba a revelarme la forma de tus labios/ y sin el viaje y la llegada del sueño y
de la luz, que ya te envolvían para traerte/ por entero junto a mí/ —¡quién
sabe, con qué de gestos, con qué de volteretas yo hubiera saludado/ tu
aparición encantadora!/ —y mientras que te espero durante muchos años

y me contengo de vivir/ y te espero un minuto y vivo aprisa,/ yo quisiera un eclipse de luna para ver cumplirse las ilusiones que me/ quedan de besarte,/ no importaría con la mitad de un beso o sin un beso y en el trance de oscuri/ dad o de luz/ —y mis esperanzas, bajo tu mirar,/ se volverían la verdadera vida que yo miro en el fondo de tus ojos.

Juan Sánchez Peláez (1922–2003, Venezuela)

The initiator of contemporary Venezuelan poetry, Sánchez Peláez was born in Altagracia de Orituco, Guárico State, Venezuela. He was also a translator, diplomat, and teacher to new generations of writers. According to Stefan Baciu, when Sánchez Peláez settled for a while in Chile, "he changed the course of his own poetry and, to a large extent, also changed the course of the new Venezuelan poetry." His first book *Elena y los elementos* (Elena and the Elements), Baciu added, "inaugurated a new sound in his country's poetry." As a collaborator to the group Mandrágora, he worked with Huidobro and Rosamel Del Valle, and he debuted as a surrealist. After residing in Paris, his poetry became so refined that its clarity reflected a "reality" that kept a distance from the conventional order and in which dreams celebrated desire and tenderness and refused to negotiate with the powers that be. PRINCIPAL WORKS: *Elena y los elementos* (1951), *Animal de costumbre* (1959), *Por cuál causa o nostalgia* (1981)

Excerpt from From the Fleeting and Permanent / De lo huidizo y permanente

Naomi Lindstrom, trans.

1
The thing that leaves me out
The fleeting and permanent thing
Two bodies come together and the dawn is the leopard
My grief
Leaps up in the face of the singer of tales.
If you go in or out
A dense aureola
Disturbs the echo;
If you think,
The storm calls out every which way;
If you look,
The match flickers;
If I live,
I live in memory.

My legs lead out into the unlit alley.
I speak to who I was, already on my
way back.
I only touch myself through
with the back side to
the branching mass of flame.
Because of you, my absent one,
I hear the sea five paces
off from my heart,
And flesh is my heart
Whom my yesteryears brush by.
If you go in or out,
The confidence of love comes back to love.
Tell me
If I shatter with the years
a rainbow;
Tell me
If the years of maturity ripen in vain;
The woman shakes out a sack in the thin air
Goes down to the sand and runs in the ocean;
At dawn.
Because of you,
my absent one,
The rose-shaped chrysalis
A rose of pure water is the dark.

. . . .

10
O Thou, Sun God who haughtily restoreth to us the world. Up and
down the street or over by the royal palms, here we are in the
        virtual
flashing-out of our old age, wearing our best grimace, we're
        already
just barely visible, strange: We are to tramp the hard earth. O Thou,
virtually massless, bird of passage, masslessly I'm passing over into
sleep. Win, whiz along, smudge the tub and trample down
        the howl.

1/ Lo que no me tiene en cuenta/ Lo huidizo y permanente/ Se juntan dos
cuerpos y el alba es el leopardo./ Mi quebranto/ Salta a la faz del juglar;/
Si entras o sales/ Turba el eco/ Una aureola densa;/ Si piensas,/ Llama en
diversas direcciones la tempestad;/ Si miras,/ Tiembla el fósforo;/ Si vivo,/
Vivo en la memoria./ Mis piernas desembocan en el callejón sin luz./
Hablo al que fui, ya en mi/ regreso./ Sólo me toco al través/ con el revés/

del ramaje de fuego./ Por ti, mi ausente,/ Oigo el mar a cinco/ pasos de mi corazón,/ Y la carne es mi corazón/ a quien roza mi antaño./ Si entras o sales,/ Vuelve al amor la confidencia del amor./ Dime/ Si quiebro con los años/ un arco iris;/ Dime/ Si la edad madura es fruto vano;/ La mujer agita un saco en el aire enrarecido/ Baja a la arena y corre en el océano;/ Al amanecer,/ Por ti,/ mi ausente,/ La crisálida en forma de rosa/ Una rosa de agua pura es la tiniebla.// . . . // 10/ Oh Tú, Fetiche Solar que nos devuelves huraño el mundo. Casas/ abajo, bloques arriba, o cerca de la palmas reales, hemos aquí en el/ relámpago virtual de nuestra vejez con la mejor mueca, ya somos/ apenas visibles, extraño: Vamos a patear la dura tierra, Oh Tú, liviano/ de paso, ave de peso, sin peso paso a dormir. Ala, arre, y tizno la tinaja/ y estampo el aullido.

Dark Bond / Filiación oscura

Naomi Lindstrom, trans.

It's not the centuries old act of striking up fire from a stone.
> No.

To begin a true story, one must draw out in an ordered sequence of
ideas souls, purgatory, and hell.

Afterwards, human longing runs the known risk.
Afterwards, one knows what will come or doesn't know.

Afterwards, if the story is sad nostalgia sets in.
We speak of silent movies.

There's no before or after: no ageless act and no true story.

A stone with a name or with none. That is all.

One knows what comes next. If faking, it's serene. If doubting,
hesitant.

Most of the time, one knows nothing.

There are live men who spell out words, there are live men who
speak together familiarly
and there are dead men who speak to us familiarly,
but one knows nothing.

Most of the time, one knows nothing.

No es el acto secular de extraer candela frotando una piedra./ No.// Para comenzar una historia verídica es necesario atraer en sucesiva/ ordenación de las ánimas, el purgatorio y el infierno.// Después, el anhelo humano corre el señalado albur./ Después, uno sabe lo que ha de venir o lo ignora.// Después, si la historia es triste acaece la nostalgia./ Hablamos del cine mudo.// No hay antes ni después; ni acto secular ni historia verídica.// Una piedra con un nombre o ninguno. Eso es todo.// Uno sabe lo que sigue. Si finge es sereno. Si duda, caviloso.// En la mayoría de los casos, uno no sabe nada.// Hay vivos que deletrean, hay vivos que hablan tuteándose/ y hay muertos que nos tutean,/ pero uno no sabe nada.// En la mayoría de los casos, uno no sabe nada.

Jorge Eduardo Eielson (1924–2006, Peru)

Born in Lima, Peru, Eielson described his roots as "my four cultures: Spanish, Italian, Swedish, and Nazca"—by Nazca meaning the ancient pre-Hispanic civilization from the Peruvian coastal regions. His father passed away when he was seven years old. His mother encouraged his versatile precociousness. At age twenty-one, he received his country's National Poetry Award. He earned a scholarship that took him to Paris and later he moved to Italy where he lived until his death. As a plastic artist, his work is included in the Museum of Modern Art and the Nelson A. Rockefeller collections in New York City; he also took part in the Biennale of Venice numerous times. According to José Miguel Oviedo, he produced "a vast, experimental, and multifaceted work that covers practically all the literary genres and the most varied forms of visual art." His creation "equally expresses a fascination for the new and the permanence of the ancestral." In his ars poetica Eielson stated: *Nothing is clearer to me/ Than the mystery of death/ And nothing is darker/ Than sunlight itself.* PRINCIPAL WORKS: *Canción y muerte de Rolando* (1959), *El cuerpo de Giulia-no* (1971), *Primera muerte de María* (1988)

María's First Death / Primera muerte de María

Michelle Gil-Montero, trans.

In spite of her opaque tresses, her mysterious thinness,
her sadness golden and definitive like mine,
I adored my wife,
tall and silent as a column of smoke.

When I met her, María, in a poor neighborhood, covered by
dazzling planets on high, crisscrossed by whistles,
strange stenches, and starving dogs. Dampened
with María's tears, the whole neighborhood irredeemably sunk
in uncontainable dew.

María kissed the walls of the sidestreets and the whole city
trembled with a violent love for God.
María was ugly; her spit, sacred.

People, without admitting it, anxiously awaited the day
María, endowed with white wings or mounted on a divine
beast, would abandon the earth smiling for the first time at
the passersby.

But María's broken shoes, like two millennial-old nails,
stayed fixed in the earth.
While they waited, the restless throng spit on her
house, and on María's poverty and melancholy.

One night María was bumped by a blind man, as by
a tree brimming with flowers. María picked a flower and from its perfume
lived for years.

With that perfume, a milk bottle and a bony
dog—Isaías—María nourished her heart and body
and lived remotely in a wood cabin.

Until I appeared like a thirsty horse and took hold of
her breasts. The frightened virgin spilled her milk, and
a river of pearls trailed from her sadness.

Chased by a thousand pale veils, like a nuptial comet,
her innocent face appeared and disappeared in a grove of
flowering oranges.

Without her knowing it, in a flashing minute, the
virgin premiered her incorruptible, mortal
beauty: María became my wife.
But her happiness was as brief as her beauty.

Every night I broke a milk bottle in my room
while María bewept her lost innocence.
Little by little I managed to remove the ineffable perfume of the
blind man from her memory, and I killed Isaías with a blow to the stomach.

A few days later María fell to the ground enwrapped in flames.

My husband—she said—a child from your body devours my
body. My lord, I beg you: give me back my perfume, my milk
bottle, my miserable dog.

My poor wife, her thirsty body debating the flames,
asphyxiated by the live weight of my love!

The instant of beauty left in her transmuted into blood, tissue,
a flesh as live and painful as mine and hers.

I pushed her milk bottle toward her and made her drink a few redeeming
gulps. I opened the windows and returned her cherished

perfume. Almost instantly Isaías leaped into her arms,
hungry as usual, wagging his tail, smelling like
childhood, like loneliness, like the virgin who only he had
venerated.

Later a child with the purest of gazes opened his eyes before
me, while María closed hers, blinded by a golden
planet: happiness.

I held my crying son and fell to my knees before the saintly
body of my wife: devoured by an impossible fire, barely
a tuft remained of her black tresses, a gaze, a
cold hand over the hot head of my son.

María, María—I screamed—none of this is true, go back to your
poor neighborhood, to your melancholy, return to your cabin, my love,
to your dark sidestreets, to your incomprehensible daily crying!

But María didn't respond.
Isaías trembled solitary in a corner, as at the extreme
of a cone of divine light.
At the other extreme, the whole city, asked me for my son,
suddenly bursting with love for María.

I entrusted my son to the coat and protection of some oxen,
whose warm breath reminded me of María's tepid and impenetrable
purity.

A pesar de sus cabellos opacos, de su misteriosa delgadez,/ de su tristeza
áurea y definitiva como la mía,/ yo adoraba a mi esposa,/ alta y silenciosa
como una columna de humo.// Cuando la conocí, María en un barrio
pobre, cubierto de deslumbrantes y altísimos planetas, atravesado de
silbidos, de/ extrañas pestilencias y de perros hambrientos. Humedecido
por las lágrimas de María, todo el barrio se hundía irremediablemente
en un rocío incontenible.// María besaba los muros de las callejuelas y
toda la cuidad/ temblaba de un violento amor a Dios./ María era fea; su
saliva, sagrada.// Las gentes, sin confesarlo, esperaban ansiosas el día en
que/ María, provista de dos alas blancas o montada en un animal divino,
abandonara la tierra sonriendo por primera vez a los transeúntes.// Pero los
zapatos rotos de María, como dos clavos milenarios, continuaban fijos en
la tierra./ Durante la espera, la muchedumbre impaciente escupía la/ casa,
la pobreza y la melancolía de María.// Una noche María fue embestida por
un ciego, como por un árbol lleno de flores. María tomó una flor y de su
perfume vivió varios años.// Con tal perfume, una botella de leche y un
perro macilento—Isaías—María alimentaba su corazón y su cuerpo y vivía
apartada en una cabaña de madera.// Hasta que aparecí yo como un caballo

sediento y me apoderé de sus senos. La virgen espantada derramó su leche y un/ río de perlas sucedió a su tristeza.// Perseguida por mil velos pálidos, como un nupcial cometa, su rostro inocente aparecía y desaparecía entre un bosquecillo de naranjos en flor.// Sin que ella lo supiera, durante un minuto fulgurante, la virgen acababa de estrenar su incorruptible, mortal belleza: María se convirtió en mi esposa.// Pero su felicidad duró tan poco como su belleza./ Todas las noches yo rompía una botella de leche en mi habitación mientras María lloraba su inocencia perdida./ Poco a poco conseguí alejar de su memoria el inefable perfume del ciego y asesiné a Isaías de un golpe en el estómago.// Unos días más tarde María caía a tierra envuelta en una llamarada:// Esposo mío—me dijo—un hijo de tu cuerpo devora mi cuerpo. Te ruego, señor mío: devuélveme mi perfume, mi botella/ de leche, mi perro miserable.// ¡Pobre esposa mía, su cuerpo sediento se debatía entre las llamas, asfixiado por el peso viviente de mi amor!// El instante de belleza perduraba en ella convertido en sangre, en tejidos, en una carne viva y dolorosa como la mía/ y como la suya.// Yo le acerqué su botella de leche y le hice beber unos cuantos/ sorbos redentores. Abrí las ventanas y le devolví su perfume adorado. Casi simultáneamente Isaísas saltó a sus brazos, hambriento como siempre, moviéndole la cola, oliendo como la infancia, como la soledad, como la virgen que sólo él había/ venerado.// Luego una criatura de mirada purísima abrió sus ojos ante mí, mientras María cerraba los suyos, cegados por un planeta/ de oro: la felicidad.// Yo abracé a mi hijo llorando y caí de rodillas ante el cuerpo santo de mi esposa: devorado por un fuego imposible, apenas quedaba de él un hato de cabellos negros, una mirada, una/ mano fría sobre la cabeza caliente de mi hijo.// ¡ María, María—grité—nada de esto es verdad, regresa a tu barrio pobre, a tu melancolía, vuelve a tu cabaña, amor mío, a tus callejuelas oscuras, a tu incomprensible llanto de todos/ los días!// Pero María no respondía./ Isaías temblaba solitario en una esquina, como en el extremo de un cono de luz divina./ Toda la ciudad, en el otro extremo, me reclamaba a mi hijo, repentinamente henchida de amor a María.// Yo confié mi hijo al abrigo y la protección de algunos bueyes, cuyo aliento cálido me recordaba el cuerpo tibio y la impenetrable pureza de María.

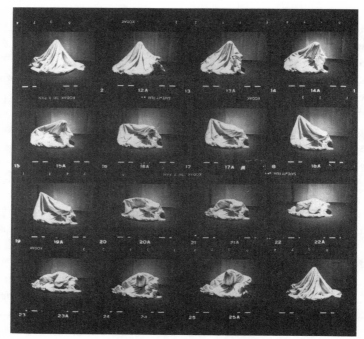

Paracas/Pyramid performance, Kunstakademie, Düsseldorf, 1974

Quipus 15 AZ-1, 1965

Carlos Martínez Rivas (1924–1998, Nicaragua)

Born in Chinandega, Nicaragua, the poet moved with his parents to Granada to study in a Jesuit school. At nineteen, Martínez Rivas published his first work, *El paraíso recobrado: Poema en tres escalas y un prólogo*. Noted for its precocious yet exact simplicity, it tells the story of two young lovers. In 1953, he published the more mature *La insurrección solitaria* and continued to publish in literary magazines, most notably *La prensa literaria*. In addition to his literary career, Martínez Rivas also served as cultural attaché to the Nicaraguan embassy in Madrid, as well as the director of the Library of the Ministry of Agrarian Reform under the Sandinista regime. PRINCIPAL WORKS: *El paraíso recobrado: poema en tres escalas y un prólogo* (1943), *La insurrección solitaria* (1953)

Excerpts from Two Murals: U.S.A. / Dos murales: U.S.A.

Steven F. White, trans.

I

The Upcoming Death
    (Diurnal Mural)

1

While prisoner of fire-
escapes
        courtyards like wells
                and nauseating
ice cream cones reached for by cherubs on tiptoe;
under the high   public   swinging cradle of light
           endlessly rocking;
through the flapping lamina of reflection and wind

        you step in:
on sandaled sole of celestial foot.
Big-handed as foot open like laughter.
      Loose.
rust-colored purple mane,
        mophead
concealing the century's negligence.
      Shark-woman, user of dyes
you sit down cross-bar as omen:
X   Sabres   Bolt: knitting needles in ball of yarn.

      You stoop
to whip the floor with wooden sole
to tie the stinking strap
that strangled the violetnail toe.

2

If arched back assumes curve
of the convex misfortune
legible heel hangs
and weighs over the center of the
Sphere.

At a prudent
distance your unknown captive
spies that
heel. The same
callus polished golden
elephant-ivory
brainmasher
that we already knew.

Nor do these chunks of rock
seem strange to me.
Such cliffs.
I recognize those reefs
flaming stifling leading me astray
calling me one from the other
—Charybdis from Scylla—
with tiny larynx
of firefly and puff of wind.

The rust the pied the itinerary
of silkworms in Indian file beneath
the leafy dampness
(Taumato
poea processionea)
To mine eyes
these freckles are not another's

the torrid desolation   the sand
at noon   the fly-befouled sun
of dead minnows in the basket
and the fishing line and net and string
of tiny eggs and the moldy canvas
and the fishy smell
(those reefs by heart!)

to summarize: I have seen the crags of women's backs
at my mercy
rolling down their stockings on the edge of a bed
where already I am waiting.

I/ La Muerte Entrante/ (Mural Diurno)// 1/ Mientras que prisionero de
las escalerillas/ de escape,/ los patios pozos/ y las asquerosas/ cremas en
pie de querubín;/ bajo la alta pública mecida cuna de luz/ en va y ven;/
por la batiente lámina de reflejo y ráfaga// entras:/ en sandalia la planta
pie celeste./ A mano grande como pie abierto como risa./ Suelta/ la crin
de púrpura y herrumbre,/ greñas/ amparando la negligencia del siglo,/
Tintorera/ te sientas cruzada a tranca y signo:/ X Sables Cerrojo agujas de
tejer en ovillo.// Te pliegas/ a azotar el suelo con la suela/ de palo a anudar la
hedionda correa/ que estranguló el pulgar uñavioleta.// 2/ Si arqueado lomo
asume curva/ de la convexa desventura/ talón legible pende/ y pesa sobre
el centro de la/ Esfera.// A prudente/ distancia tu cautivo/ incógnito espío
ese/ talón. El mismo/ callo pulido criso/ elefantino/ machacasesos/ que ya
supimos.// Tampoco me son extraños estos/ peñascos./ Tales acantilados./
Reconozco esos escollos/ llameando apagándose extraviándome/
llamándome uno desde el otro/ —Caribdis desde Escila—/ con laringilla/
de luciérnaga y soplo.// El sarro el motëado el itinerario/ de orugas en fila
india bajo/ la hojosa humedad/ (Taumato/ poea processionea)/ No me
son ajenas/ aquestas pecas// la tórrida desolación la arena/ del mediodía
el sol mosqueado/ de pepescas muertas en la cesta/ y el sedal y la red y la
ristra/ de huevecillos y la lona nacida// y el chiquije/ (¡de memoria esos
arrecifes!)// resumo: he visto esas escarpadas espaldas de mujer/ a merced/
mía soltándose las medias a la entrada de un lecho/ donde ya espero.

Gyula Kosice (1924–, Argentina)

Born Fernando Fallik, in Kosice, Czechoslovakia (now Slovakia), Kosice migrated to
Argentina with his parents when he was still a child. A multifaceted individual, he
is a poet, plastic artist, and theoretician. He studied drawing and modeling and
co-founded the magazine *Arturo* and the Movimiento Arte Madí (Madi Art Movement), both precursors of kinetic art and the viewer's active participation in the
work of art. Intent on moving further away from the figuration that was still present
in caligrams, he wrote poems that broke barriers by using—according to his own
Manifesto Madí (Madi Manifesto)—"concepts and images not translatable by means
other than language." He also elaborated a "Madi Dictionary," where all words and
definitions were invented by him. According to Gabriel Pérez-Barreiro, "In Kosice's
worldview the breaking of the frame is only a stage in the dissolution of all art forms
into a radical re-evaluation of art and its functions." PRINCIPAL WORKS: *Antología Madí*
(1955), *Arte Madí* (1982), *Obra poética* (1984)

Excerpts from Portable Madi Dictionary / Diccionario portátil Madí

Molly Weigel, trans.

F

Fetonia: Relaxation of the square trap. / Heart of the mesh.

Firstas: Equivalent of the weight of hinges. Measurement of squeaky reparation.

Fnax: Tech. Lowness in the form of a shallow platter, in the motors of infranavigation in deep space. / Disk.

Frogue: Captive word. / To cultivate symmetrical calligraphy.

Fu: Exclamation on catching sight of the corpulence of disaster. Used to refer to the nuisance that causes blind, heedless flight.

. . . .

W

Waquinate: Literal representation of the objective consulted from its base.

Weigalu: Prehemispheric region discovered by Anonymous. The hero exclaimed to his natality: "If I've ever had to figure as a pedestal, it's been with the sole aim of hiding myself from the most credulous."

Wior-Eil: Intuit the modification of a parasitic form. (The great nebula). / Roots of a new extension.

Wunhat: Imperfect visualization of proximity. / Equivocation. / Stumble.

Wura's: Preliminaries adopted in the course of meditation. / Circumstantially omitted clarification.

F// *Fetonia:* Descanso de la trampa cuadrada. Corazón de la malla./ *Firstas:* Equivalente al peso de los goznes. Medida de la reparación chirriante./ *Fnax:* Tec. Chatura en forma de plato playo, en los motores de infranavegación en la/ parte profunda del espacio. Disco./ *Frogue:* Palabra cautiva./ Cultivar la caligrafía simétrica./ *Fu:* Exclamación al avistar la corpulencia del desastre. Se dice del fastidio que causa un vuelo a ciegas.// . . . W// *Waquinate:* Representación literal del objetivo consultado desde su base./ *Weigalu:* Región pre-hemisférica descubierta por Anónimo. El héroe exclamó a su natalidad: "Si alguna vez he tenido que figurar como pedestal ha sido con el único fin de ocultarme a los más crédulos."/ *Wior-Eil:* Intuir la modificación de una forma parásita. (La gran nebulosa)./ Fundamentos de una nueva exención./ *Wunhat:* Visualización imperfecta de la cercanía./ Equívoco. Traspié./ *Wura's:* Preliminares adoptadas en el curso de la meditación./ Clarificación omitida circunstancialmente.

MADI

G. J. Racz, trans.

We Madists borrow unique elements from every art form to construct—
that is, we invent something REAL.

In so doing, we express nothing, depict nothing, forge symbols of
nothing. The thing we create is of pure presence and pure immanence.

The thing is in space and in time: it EXISTS.

This is a transcendental act and an act of wonder.

Ours is a human, profoundly human art, as it is the individual in all his
essence who CONSCIOUSLY creates, makes, constructs, and invents
IN REAL TERMS.

    Through the Madic invention
of objects in space
free of outside interference in their essential properties,
    MADI creates a new genre of plastic arts!

Photomontage by Grete Stern, Buenos Aires, 1947

Nosotros madistas, tomando los elementos propios de cada/ arte, construi-
mos; es decir, hacemos una invención REAL,/ Con eso no expresamos nada,
no representamos nada, no/ simbolizamos nada. Creamos la cosa en su sóla
presencia, en su/ sóla inmanencia,/ La cosa está en el espacio y está en el
tiempo: EXISTE./ Este es un acto trascendental, un acto maravilloso./ Nuestro arte es humano, profundamente humano, puesto que/ es la persona en
toda su esencia la que CONSCIENTEMENTE/ crea, hace, construye, inventa
realmente.// Por una invención mádica/ de objetos en el espacio/ sin inger-
encias extrañas a sus propiedades esenciales./ MADÍ crea un nuevo género
plástico!

Ernesto Cardenal (1925–, Nicaragua)

During his early twenties, Cardenal studied in Mexico, writing a thesis on new Nicaraguan poets, and in New York where he was profoundly influenced by Ezra Pound's
objectivism. In 1971, he experienced a religious conversion and decided to live in a
Trappist monastery in Kentucky. Thomas Merton became his spiritual advisor. When
he returned to Nicaragua, he founded a commune based on Liberation Theology on
the island of Solentiname and there lived with peasants and artists. He later became
minister of culture during the Sandinista administration. In particular, he attracted
attention for his use of nonliterary sources such as advertisements, newspapers,
magazine articles, and historical documents. PRINCIPAL WORKS: *Oración por Marilyn
Monroe y otros poemas* (1965), *El evangelio en Solentiname* (1975), *Los ovnis de oro
(poemas indios)* (1988)

Excerpt from Death of Thomas Merton / A la muerte de Merton
Robert Pring-Mill, trans.

Manrique said our lives were rivers
going down to the sea which is death
but the death they flow down to is life
And your death was more of a quirk, Merton
            (absurd as a zen koan?)
"Made by General Electric"
and your body flown to the States in an Army plane
        you'd have had a good laugh, given your sense of humour
you Merton bodiless and dying of laughter
likewise myself
The initiates of Dionysus used ivy leaves . . .
        I knew it not:
I tap out this word "death" with joy today

Dying isn't something like a car-smash
                 or a short-circuit
   we die throughout life
Contained in our lives—
         like the canker at the apple's core? No
not like the canker but
the ripeness !

Or like mangoes, here in Solentiname, in summer
going slowly yellow, waiting
for the golden orioles . . .
              the hors d'oeuvres
in restaurants were never as good
as in the advertisements
nor the poem as good as we hoped
nor the kiss.
We have always desired more than we lacked
We are Somoza seeking to own ever more haciendas
       More More More
nor yet just more, but something "different"
The coition of perfect will is the act
of dying.
       We move among things with the air
of having mislaid a most important
briefcase.
       Take escalators up and take them down.
Enter the supermarket or the store,
like anyone else, seeking the transcendental
product.
       We live as though waiting
for an infinite assignation. Or
                 to be called to the phone
by the Ineffable.
And are along
the grain that does not die, yet are alone.
We sit at ease on deck and dream
    contemplating sea the colour of daiquiri
waiting for someone to pass and smile at us and
say hello.

Not sleep but lucidity.
     Moving like sleepwalkers through the traffic
        past the traffic-lights
eye-open yet asleep
savour a Manhatten as though asleep.

Not sleep but
lucidity is the true image of death
            of its illumination, of the blinding
splendour of death.
Nor is it the Kingdom of Forgetfulness. Memory
        is secretary to forgetfulness.
                She keeps the past in filing cabinets.
But when there is no more future merely an instant present
all that has been lived relives no longer as memories
and reality reveals itself entire
in one flash.

Poetry was a parting too
like death. Full of the
sadness of departing trains or planes
                        the trains which pass in the night
                        through the station of Brenes
                        Cordobita below full of light
cante jondo in the depths of Granada . . .
In all beauty, a sadness
and a longing as in an alien land
                MAKE IT NEW
            ("a new heaven and a new earth")
but beyond this lucidity
the return to clichés, the return
to slogans.
It is only when we are not being practical
and concentrate on useless things that we
move out and find the world is opening out.
Dying is the act of being quite uninvolved
likewise: contemplation.

Love, love above all, as it were a foretaste
of death
            Kisses had the savour of death in them
                    being
                        involves being
                            in some other being
        we only are when we love
But in this life we love only by fits and starts
and weakly
        We only love and are when we cease being
when we die
            a nakedness of being that we may make love
                make love not war

going down to the love
which is life

the city come from heaven which is not Atlantic City—
    nor the hereafter an *American way of life*
                        Retirement in Florida
or one long limitless Weekend.
Death is a doorway opening
onto the universe
                    No sign which says NO EXIT
and into ourselves
                        (the journey
        into ourselves—
            not to Tokyo or Bangkok—
                            that is the *appeal*
        "air hostess wearing a kimono,
Continental cuisine"
the real *appeal* of those Japan Air Lines advertisements)
    A nuptial night, as Novalis put it
Not one of Boris Korloff's horror films
And natural, as is the fall of apples
subject to the law which draws the stars, or lovers
—There are no accidents
        just one more apple off the Tree
you're merely one more apple
Tom

Nuestras vidas son los ríos/ que van a dar a la muerte/ que es la vida/ Tu
muerte más bien divertida Merton/ (o absurda como un koan?)/ tu muerte
marca General Electric/ y el cadáver a USA en un avion del Army/ con el
humor tan tuyo te habras reido/ vos Merton ya sin cadáver muerto de risa/
también yo/ Los iniciados de Dionisos ponía hiedras . . . / (yo no
la conocia):/ Hoy tecleo con alegría esta palabra muerte / Morir no es
como el choque de un auto o/ como un corto-circuito/ nos hemos ido
muriendo toda la vida/ Contenida en nuestra vida/ ¿cómo el gusano en
la manzana? no/ como el gusano sino/ la madurez!// O como mangos en
este verano de Solentiname/ amarillando, esperando las/ oropéndolas . . . /
los hor d'oeuvres/ nunca fueron en los restaurantes/ como anunciados en
las revistas/ ni el verso fue tan bueno como quisimos/ o el beso./ Hemos
deseado siempre mas allá de lo deseado/ Somos Somoazas deseando
más y más haciendas/ More More More/ y no sólo más, también algo
"diferente"/ Las bodas del deseo/ el coito de la volición perfecta es
el acto/ de la muerte./ Andamos entre las cosas con el aire/ de haber
perdido un cartapacio/ muy importante./ Subimos los ascensores y

bajamos./ Entramos a los supermercados, a las tiendas/ como toda la gente, buscando un producto/ trascendente./ Vivimos como en espera de una cita/ infinita. O/ que nos llame al teléfono/ lo Inefable./ Y estamos solos/ trigos inmortales que nomueren, estamos solos./ Soñamos en perezosas sobre cubierta/ contemplando el mar color de daikirí/ esperando que alguien pase y nos sonría y/ diga Hello// No el sueño sino la lucidez./ Vamos en medio del tráfico como sonámbulos/ pasamos los semáforos/ con los ojos abiertos y dormidos/ paladeamos un manhattan como dormidos./ No el sueño/ la lucidez es imagen de la muerte/ de la iluminación, el resplandor/ enceguecedor de la muerte./ Y no es el reino del Olvido. La memoria/ es la secretaria del olvido./ Maneja en archivadoras el pasado./ Pero cuando no hay más futuro sino sólo un presente fijo/ todo lo vivido, revive, ya no como recuerdos/ y se revela la realidad toda entera/ en un flash.// La poesía también era un partir/ como la muerte. Tenía/ la tristeza de los trenes y los aviones que se van/ Est03ioncita de Brenes/ en Cordobita la Llana/ de noche pasan los trenes/ el cante jondo al fondo de Granada/ En toda belleza, una tristeza/ y añoranza como en un país extranos/ MAKE IT NEW/ (un nuevo cielo y una nueva tierra)/ pero después de esa lucidez/ volvés otra vez a los clichés, los/ slogans./ Sólo en los momentos en que no somos prácticos/ concentrados en lo Inútil, Idos/ se nos abre el mundo./ La muerte es el acto de la distracción total/ también: Contemplación.// El amor, el amor sobre todo, un anticipo/ de la muerte/ Había en los besos un sabor a muerte/ ser/ es ser/ en otro ser/ sólo somos al amar/ Pero en esta vida sólo amamos unos ratos/ y débilmente/ Sólo amamos o somos al dejar de ser/ al morir/ desnudez de todo el ser para nacer el amor/ make love not war/ que van a dar al amor/ que es la vida// la ciudad bajada del cielo que no es Atlantic City-/ Y el Más Allá no es un American Way of Life/ Jubilación en Flórida/ o como un Week-end sin fin./ La muerte es una puerta abierta/ al universo/ No hay letrero NO EXIT/ Y a nosotros mismos/ (viajar/ a nosotros mismos/ no a Tokio, Bangkok/ es el appeal/ stewardess en kimono, la cuisine/ Continental/ es el appeal de esos anuncios de Japan Air Lines)/ Una Noche Nupcial, decía Novalis/ No es una película de horror de Boris Karloff/ Y natural, como la caída de las manzanas/ por la ley que atrae a los astros y a los amantes/ —No hay accidentes/ una más caída del gran Árbol/ sos una manzana más/ Tom

Rosario Castellanos (1925–1974, Mexico)

The "Ambassador of Chiapas," the writer who—according to Saramago—"knew how to tell of the vicissitudes of the Indians and the outrages of the whites," Castellanos was a seeker of ways for women to be free. She was born in Mexico City, into a family of landowners. While growing up in Chiapas under the care of an Indian woman, she heard her mother protest that if one of her two children had to die—as predicted by a fortune teller—it had better not be the boy. She studied philosophy in Mexico and aesthetics in Madrid. In groundbreaking words, she dared to state that "the Mexican woman does not consider herself—nor is she considered by others—a realized woman if she has not borne any children and is not lit up by the aura of maternity." She died in Tel Aviv while heading her country's embassy. One of Mexico's most important literary voices, she was a poet, essayist, novelist, and playwright. Her bare words entitled her to a most ironic burial place in the Rotunda of Illustrious Men, in Mexico City. PRINCIPAL WORKS: *El rescate del mundo* (1952), *Balún-Canán* (1957), *Ciudad real* (1960), *Poesía no eres tú* (1972)

Livid Light / Lívida luz

Magda Bogin, trans.

I can only speak of what I know.

Like Thomas my hand is deep
inside a wound. And it burns both the other and myself.

Cold sweat of agony!
Convulsion of nausea!

No, I don't want comfort or oblivion or hope.

I want the courage to remain,
to not betray what is ours: this day
and the light that lets us see it whole.

No puedo hablar sino de lo que sé.// Como Tomás tengo la mano hundida/ en una llaga. Y duele en el otro y en mí.// ¡Ah, qué sudor helado de agonía!/ ¡Qué convulsión de asco!// No, no quiero consuelo, no olvido, no esperanza.// Quiero valor para permanecer,/ para no traicionar lo nuestro: el día/ presente y esta luz que se mira entero.

Silence around an Ancient Stone / Silencio cerca de una piedra antigua

Magda Bogin, trans.

I sit here with all my words intact,
as if with a basket of green fruit.

The fragments
of a thousand ancient toppled gods
seek each other in my blood, hold each other captive, eager
to repair the statue.
From their broken mouths
a song rises to my mouth,
smell of burnt resin, gesture
of hard-worked mysterious rock.
But I am oblivion, betrayal,
a shell that didn't even hold
an echo of the sea's least wave.
I don't look at the submerged temples;
I look only at the trees whose vast shade moves
above the ruins and whose acid teeth gnash
the wind as it streams by.
And the signs shut themselves beneath my eyes like
a flower in a blind man's clumsy grasp.
But I know: behind
my body crouches another,
and all around me many breaths
cross back and forth
furtive as jungle animals at night.
Somewhere, I know,
exactly like
a cactus in the desert,
a starry crown of thorns
awaits a man just as the cactus awaits rain.
But I know only certain words
in the language or stone
beneath which they buried my ancestor alive.

Estoy aquí, sentada, con todas mis palabras/ como con una cesta de fruta
verde, intactas.// Los fragmentos/ de mil dioses antiguos derribados/ se
buscan por mi sangre, se prisionan, queriendo/ recomponer su estatua./
De las bocas destruídas/ quiere subir hasta mi boca un canto,/ un olor de
resinas quemadas, algún gesto/ de misteriosa roca trabajada./ Pero soy el
olvido, la traición,/ el caracol que no guardó del mar/ ni el eco de la más
pequeña ola./ Y no miro los templos sumergidos;/ sólo miro los árboles
que encima de las ruinas/ mueven su vasta sombra, muerden con dientes

ácidos/ el viento cuando pasa./ Y los signos se cierran bajo mis ojos como/ la flor bajo los dedos torpísimos de un ciego./ Pero yo sé: detrás/ de mi cuerpo otro cuerpo se agazpa,/ y alrededor de mí muchas respiraciones/ cruzan furtivamente/ como los animales nocturnos en la selva./ Yo sé, en algún lugar,/ los mismo/ que en el desierto el cactus,/ un constelado corazón de espinas/ está aguardando un hombre como el cactus la lluvia./ Pero yo no conozco más que ciertas palabras/ en el idioma o lápida/ bajo el que sepultaron vivo a mi antepasado.

Malinche

Maureen Ahern, trans.

From the throne of command my mother said: "He is dead."

And threw herself
into the arms of another, usurper, stepfather
who didn't sustain her with the respect
a servant renders to the majesty of a queen
but groveled in their mutual shame
of lovers and accomplices.

From the Plaza of Exchange
my mother announced: "She is dead."

The scale
balanced for an instant
the chocolate bean lay motionless in the bin
the sun remained at mid-point in the sky
waiting the sign
which shot like an arrow
became the sharp wail of the mourners.

"The bloom of many petals was deflowered,
the perfume evaporated,
the torch flame burned out.

"A girl returns to scratch up the earth
in the place
where midwife buried her umbilicus.

"She returns to the Place of Those Who Once Lived.

"She recognizes her father assassinated,
ay, ay, ay, poison, a dagger,
a snare before his feet, a vine noose.

"They take each other by the hand and walk, walk,
disappearing into the fog."

Thus the wailings and the lamentations
over an anonymous body: a corpse
that was not mine because I, sold
to the merchants, was on my way as a slave,
a nobody, into exile.

Cast out, expelled
from the kingdom, from the palace, and from the warm belly
of the woman who bore me in legitimate marriage bed
who hated me because I was her equal
in stature and in rank
who saw herself in me and hating her image
dashed the mirror against the ground.

I advance toward destiny in chains
leaving behind all that I can still hear,
the funeral murmurs with which I am buried.

And the voice of my mother in tears—in tears!
she who decrees my death!

Desde el sillón del mando mi madre dijo: "Ha muerto."// Y se dejó caer, como abatida,/ en los brazos del otro, usurpador, padrasto/ que la sostuvo no con el respeto/ que el siervo da a la majestad de reina/ sino con ese abajamiento mutuo/ en que se humillan ambos, los amantes, los cómplices.// Desde la Plaza de los Intercambios/ mi madre anunció: "Ha muerto."// La balanza/ se sostuvo un instante sin moverse/ y el grano de cacao quedó quieto en el arca/ y el sol permanecía en la mitad del cielo/ como aguardando un signo/ que fue, cuando partió como una flecha,/ el ay agudo de las plañideras.// "Se deshojó la flor de muchos pétalos,/ se evaporó el perfume,/ se consumió la llama de la antorcha.// Una niña regresa, escarbando, al lugar/ en el que la partera depositó su ombligo.// Regresa al Sitio de los que Vivieron.// Reconoce a su padre asesinado,/ ay, ay, ay, con veneno, con puñal,/ con trampa ante sus pies, con lazo de horca.// Se toman de la mano y caminan, caminan/ perdiéndose en la niebla."// Tal era el llanto y las lamentaciones/ sobre algún cuerpo anónimo; un cadáver/ que no era el mío porque yo, vendida/ a mercaderes, iba como esclava,/ como nadie, al destierro.// Arrojada, expulsada/ del reino, del palacio y de la entraña tibia/ de la que me dio a luz en tálamo legítimo/ y que me aborreció porque yo era su igual/ en figura y en rango/ y se contempló en mí y odió su imagen/ y destrozó el espejo contra el suelo.// Yo avanzo hacia el destino entre cadenas/ y dejos atrás lo que todavía escucho:/ los fúnebres rumores con los que se me entierra.// Y la voz de mi madre con lágrimas ¡con lágrimas!/ que decreta mi muerte.

Apolônio Alves dos Santos (1926–, Brazil)

Born in Guarabira, Paraiba, Brazil, Alves dos Santos lived in Rio de Janeiro where he worked as a brickmaker while writing and selling *cordel* poetry. Author of "As bravuras de Ismael en defesa do amor," "A morte de Lampião ou a Vingança de Corisco," and other poems, his work was included in Sebastião Nunes Batista's *Antologia da literatura da Cordel* (1977). Literally, "literature on a string," literatura de cordel was a way for poor rural, and subsequently urban, Brazilian poets to showcase their writing. In a fashion similar to European pamphlet poetry, the Brazilian poets began to publish on small hand presses in the late nineteenth century. The poets would string the poems together and hang them between two posts in popular markets and streets. The cordel reached its zenith in the 1950s and was an important form of political and cultural commentary that is still practiced today. The pamphlets included an illustration made for each poem by a different artist, which became a signature inseparable from the whole, thus making the cordel yet another manifestation of visual poetry.

Antônio Conselheiro and the Canudos Rebellion / Antônio Conselheiro e a guerra de Canudos

Mark Lokensgard, trans.

Let me tell you the story
of Antônio Conselheiro
who in spite of being righteous
and fearful of our Lord
defended the town of Canudos
as a warrior most courageous.

In truth Conselheiro's name
was Antônio Maciel
he became a true repenter
of suffering most cruel
but in spite of his torment
he was a faithful soul.

I will tell you how it was
that he became converted
into a holy pilgrim
sad and most repented
of two horrendous crimes
that he in rage committed.

For Antônio was married
to an angel full of grace
as beautiful as a saint

on the altar of our Lord
and who was the hapless victim
of lies her name would taint.

For the mother of Antônio
would never call her 'daughter'
and never tired of saying
that Antônio should leave her
but in the face of all this slander
Antônio did not believe her.

And seeing that her son
would simply not believe
in his mother's denigrations
it was then that she resolved
to create the needed evidence
to prove her accusations.

The old woman said: My son
every time that you go out
to travel at the dawn
your wife her vows betrays
her lover comes and enters
at the hour you have gone.

If you wish to know the truth
heed me when I say
to tell your wife tomorrow
that you will be away
but then my words confirm
as hidden nearby you stay.

And then in the darkness
you will see a hooded man
steal around the back
to complete his shameful plan
and wait for the gate to open
and enter when he can.

And so Antônio did
he said to his dear spouse:
Today I will seek work
some distance from our house
I may return at night
or be back within the hour.

And so the evil crone
now had the trap prepared
and to make firm the plot
for the angel to be ensnared
dressed herself in men's clothing
to catch them unaware.

And at the usual hour
Antônio closed the door and left
and decided he would hide
at one corner of the fence
then he saw a hooded figure
approach with silent step.

Antônio was armed and ready
and sent bullet after bullet
at the figure from his revolver;
from inside, the sound of running
then his wife in shocked surprise
threw open wide the door.

Antônio seeing his wife
rained fire too upon her
the woman screamed for her life
a scream of one who suffers
and then, fatally wounded
fell back upon the floor.

Then Antônio Maciel
shaking with rage and fury
ran to see his rival's face
to pull back the figure's hood
and see if he would recognize
the man from some known place.

When Antônio then saw
the face of his own mother
he cried: In the name of Jesus
and Mary our protector.

Vamos ouvir a história/ de Antônio Conselheiro/ que apesar de beato/ temente a Deus verdadeiro/ em defesa de Canudos/ se tornou um guerrilheiro.// O seu nome verdadeiro/ era Antônio Maciel/ que se fez um penitente/ dum sofrimento cruel/ mas apesar de sofrido/ era uma alma fiel.// Vamos saber somo foi/ que ele foi convertido/ em beato peregrino/ triste e arrependido/ por doir monstruosos crimes/ ter ele então cometido.// Porque ele se casou/ com uma linda deidade/ bonita como um santa/ do altar da divindade/ a qual foi vítima inocente/ duma cruel falsidade.// Porque a mãe de Antônio/ com a nora não se dava/ para o filho abandoná-la/ sempre o aconselhava/ mas suas falsas calúnias/ ele não acreditava.// Mas ela vendo que o filho/ não queria acreditar/ em suas falsas calúnias/ resolveu a levanter/ um falso a sua nora/ e que pu desse provar.// A velha disse: Meu filho/ toda vez que você vai/ viajar de madrugada/ a sua esposa lhe trai/ o macho dela já sabe/ a hora que você sai.// Se quiser ter a certeza/ escute o que vou falar/ diga a sua mulher/ que hoje vai viajar/ e fique perto da casa/ para se certificar.// Verá um homem chegar/ aproveitando o escuro/ e ficar atrás da casa/ com o seu plano seguro/ esperando que ela venha/ abrir o portão do muro.// E assim Antônio fez/ disse pra sua senhora:/ Hoje eu vou viajar/ procurar trabalho fora/ não sei se voltarei logo/ ou tenha uma demora.// Então a velha maldita/ que estava prevenida/ para confirmar a trama/ com idéia pervertida/ trajou-se em roupa de homem/ e caminhou decidida.// De lá Antônio saiu/ no horário acostumado/ resolveu se ocultar/ num recanto do cercado/ nisto viu chegar um vulto/ em um capote embrulhado.// Antônio que estava armado/ com um revolver munido/ mandou pipoca no vulto/ ouviu-se grande estampido/ a mulher abriu a porta/ pra ver o que tinha sido.// Ele avistando a esposa/ também foi mandando brasa/ a mulher soltou um grito/ igual a quem se arrasa/ e mortalmente ferida/ caiu pra dentro de casa.// E Antônio Maciel/ bastante enfurecido/ correu para examinar/ aquele vulto caído/ para ver se conhecia/ quem ele havia abatido.// Quando ele descobriu/ o rosto da genitora/ gritou: Valha-me Jesus/ e Maria protetora.

Blanca Varela (1926–2009, Peru)

The daughter of composer Serafina Quinteros, Varela was born into a matriarchal family in Lima, Peru, where she studied arts and literature. She married painter Fernando de Szyszlo twice. While living with him in France, she befriended Octavio Paz, Julio Cortázar, Jean-Paul Sartre, and Simone de Beauvoir. Slowly but inexorably, and almost against her own wishes, she received international acclaim in the form of numerous awards and recognition by other poets and the general public. Her first book contains a praiseworthy prologue by Octavio Paz celebrating her "admirable rigor." With the passage of time, Varela's work—based on everyday experience, dry, devoid of metaphors and dramatics, and constantly antagonizing God—remains on guard. PRINCIPAL WORKS: *Ese puerto existe* (1950), *Canto villano* (1986), *El libro de barro* (1993)

I Bury My Hand in the Sand / Hundo la mano en la arena

Ruth Fainlight, trans.

I bury my hand in the sand and find the lost vertebra.
I lose it immediately. Bloodless shadow of ivory. My
father smiles. On this side of the sea the foam is dark.
It smells of beasts, my little friend says. The sea smells
of life and death, I reply. Let us suppose it is like that.

Health gripping the rock. Stone reactive to light.
The hunter lacks hands and feet. He is blind and desirous.
And his desire is the forest under the water, stocked
with flowering sexes or master flowers that pierce the silence
with their great slow red beaks.

Hundo la mano en la arena y encuentro la vertebra/ perdida. La extravío al
instante. Sombra de marfil,/ desangrada. Mi padre sonríe. De este lado del/ mar
la espuma es oscura. Huele a fiera me dice la/ pequeña amiga. El mar huele
a vida y a muerte le/ respondo. Supongamos que es así.// La salud aferrada a
la roca. Piedra sensible a la luz./ El cazador carece de manos y pies. Es ciego
y/ desea. Y su deseo es el bosque bajo el agua,/ poblado de sexos en flor o de
flores maestras que/ horadan el silencio con sus grandes picos rojos y/ lentos.

Exercises / Ejercicios

Ruth Fainlight, trans.

i
A poem
like a great battle
the poem flings me into
against no enemy except myself

I
and the great great wind of words

ii
the cloud lies
the light lies
the eyes
eternally deceived
never tire of so many lies

iii
obstinate blue
unaware of being in another iris
like god in the void

Blanca Varela   343

iv
I think of wings of music of fire
but no
that's not what I fear
only the grim justice of light

i/ Un poema/ como una gran batalla/ me arroja en esta arena/ sin más
enemigo que yo// yo/ y el gran gran aire de las palabras// ii/ miente la nube/
la luz miente/ los ojos/ los engañados de siempre/ no se cansan de tanta
fábula// iii/ terco azul/ ignorancia de estar en la ajena pupila/ como dios en
la nada// iv/ pienso en alas en fuego en música/ pero no/ no es eso lo que
temo/ sino el torvo juicio de la luz

Final Scene / Escena final

Ruth Fainlight, trans.

I have left the door ajar
I am an animal who won't accept it has to die

eternity is the dark hinge that yields
a small noise in the night of the flesh

I am the island that moves forward fed by death
or a city savagely besieged by life

or maybe I'm nothing
only insomnia
and the brilliant indifference of stars

desert destiny
inexorably the sun of the living rises
I acknowledge this door
there is no other

untimely spring ice
and a thorn of blood
in the rose's eye

he dejado la puerta entreabierta/ soy un animal que no se resigna a morir//
la eternidad es la oscura bisagra que cede/ un pequeño ruido en la noche
de la carne// soy la isla que avanza sostenida por la muerte// o una ciudad
ferozmente cercada por la vida// o tal vez no soy nada/ sólo el insomnio/
y la brillante indiferencia de los astros// desierto destino/ inexorable el
sol de los vivos se levanta/ reconozco esa puerta/ no hay otra// hielo
primaveral/ y una espina de sangre/ en el ojo de la rosa

Family Secret / Secreto de familia

Ruth Fainlight, trans.

I dreamed of a dog
of a flayed dog
its body sang its red body whined
I asked the other
the one who turns off the butcher's light
what has happened
why we are in darkness

it is a dream you are alone
there is no one else
light does not exist
you are the dog you are the barking flower
gently you sharpen your tongue
your lolling black four-legged tongue

human skin is parched by dreams
which waste and scorch
only the red canine pulp is clean
the true light lives in its gummy eyes
you are the dog
you are the flayed canine of every night
to dream of oneself is enough

soñé con un perro/ con un perro desollado/ cantaba su cuerpo su cuerpo
rojo silbaba/ pregunté al otro/ al que apaga la luz al carnicero/ qué ha
sucedido/ por qué estamos a oscuras// es un sueño estás sola/ no hay otro/
la luz no existe/ tú eres el perro tú eres la flor que ladra/ afila dulcemente
tu lengua/ tu dulce negra lengua de cuatro patas// la piel del hombre se
quema con el sueño/ arde desaparece la piel humana/ sólo la roja pulpa del
can es limpia/ la verdadera luz habita su legaña/ tú eres el perro/ tú eres el
desollado can de cada noche/ sueña contigo misma y basta

Currículum Vitae

Eliot Weinberger, trans.

let's say you won the race
and the prize
was another race
that you didn't drink the wine of victory
but your own salt sweat
that you didn't hear cheers
but the barking of dogs

and that your shadow
your own shadow
was your only
and disloyal competition

digamos que ganaste la carrera/ y que el premio/ era otra carrera/ que no
bebiste el vino de la victoria/ sino tu propia sal/ que jamás escuchaste
vítores/ sino ladridos de perros/ y que tu sombra/ tu propia sombra/ fue tu
única/ y desleal competidora

Décio Pignatari (1927–, Brazil)

A poet, graphic artist, and translator, Pignatari was born in São Paulo. In 1952,
he and Haroldo and Augusto de Campos founded the group Noigandres, and
in 1958, the three signed the "pilot plan for concrete poetry." Meanwhile in
Switzerland—unaware of what his Brazilian counterparts were doing—the Swiss
poet, Eugen Gomringer, born in Bolivia, was also discovering the unprecedented
potential of visual poetry. Pignatari and Gomringer met in Switzerland and
launched what became known internationally as the concrete poetry movement.
A new poetic language emerged—"a tension of things-words in Space-Time" as
defined by Augusto de Campos. Like an explosion, it sent shock waves around
the world. Their magazine *Invenção* (1962) became one of the most influential
sources of Vanguardist thought and literature. In one of his best-known poems,
Pignatari turned around the slogan "Enjoy Coca-Cola," revealing its hidden consequences. Today, Pignatari continues his vertiginous exploration of language
and considers himself a "language designer." PRINCIPAL WORKS: *Exercio exercício
findo* (1958), *Teoria da poesia concreta* (1965), *Poesia pois é poesia* (1977)

Hear the Earth / Ra terra ter

Drink Coca Cola / Beba Coca Cola

Carlos Germán Belli (1927–, Peru)

Born in Lima, Peru, Belli first read poetry from the notebooks of his mother, an avid reader who collected poetry by Rubén Darío and Giacomo Leopardi, among others. He graduated with a literature degree from the University of San Marcos, where he was later a professor. He was a civil servant in the Peruvian Parliament and a journalist for the newspaper *El comercio*. According to Vargas Llosa, Belli's work "has a dark narcissism; it's difficult, melodramatic, pervaded by a strange sense of humor, caustic, and highly cultured. It is made up of an inconceivable blend of Golden Age metrics and Lima's street jargon; injustice, the luxury of surrealism, and the squalor of middle-class life in a third-world society; nostalgia and the dream of abundance that shatters daily when it is contradicted by experience, stubbornly rebuilding itself by way of desire and imagination, only to shatter again at the first clash with the fateful reality principle." PRINCIPAL WORKS: *Dentro y fuera* (1960), *¡Oh hada cibernética!* (1962), *El pie sobre el cuello* (1964), *Por el monte abajo* (1967), *Sextinas y otros poemas* (1970), *En alabanza del bolo alimenticio* (1979)

Tortilla / La tortilla

Michelle Gil-Montero, trans.

If after the pains of choosing an egg,
and frying with it the tasty tortilla,
seasoned well with salt and pepper,
and oils deep from its soul and body,
so at last it might pass the gullet
and come to be the supreme bolus,
ever harbored in the human belly;
what a pain! if that tortilla
just seconds before being eaten,
suddenly suffered a turn
in the great skillet of the day's whim,
as if a sharp invisible fork pricked it
and seized its just fried surface,
the reverse falling face up,
not with glairs white nor yolks golden,
but a poultice of deadly hemlock.

Si luego de tanto escoger un huevo,/ y con él freir la rica tortilla,/ sazonada
bien con sal y pimienta,/ y del alma y cuerpo los profundos óleos,/ para
que por fin el garguero cruce/ y sea ya el sumo bolo alimenticio,/ albergado
nunca en humano vientre;/ ¡qué jeringa! si aquella tortilla/ segundos no
más de ser comida antes,/ repentinamente una vuelta sufra/ en la gran
sartén del azar del día,/ cual si un invisible tenedor filoso le pinche/ y le coja
su faz recién frita,/ el envés poniendo así boca arriba,/ no de blancas claras
ni de yemas áureas,/ mas un emplasto sí de mortal cicuta.

Sestina of Mea Culpa / Sextina del mea culpa

Michelle Gil-Montero, trans.

Forgive me, father, mother, for my wrong
was as the cradle of your otherly hurt,
ever since the first time my brain
interwove the meshes of my acts,
with twisted halters from arrears,
where captive I now lie until my death.

Just as a hot air balloon in death,
bloated with the bile of my wrongs,
my consience will resurface from arrears,
and dying so delimited by hurts,
will be the orb's most pitiable act,
that by luck is not of enlightened brain.

For these are things of a befuddled brain
not to be alert nor even in death
and in truth it is an intolerable act
that the soul stays clung to its wrong,
until submerged in raw hurts,
the body turns to dust in full arrears.

Of all my works and love, I'm in arrears,
by the exclusive schema of my brain,
I'm left like this by mortal hurts,
even at the threshold of my death,
as comes from forging all my wrongs
into the bulky ingots of my acts.

I, father, mother, your sweet acts
I've soured so by lying in arrears,
amiss within the thicket of my wrongs,
and you went running through my brain,
among gleeds of my blushes before death,
under the long deluge of my hurts.

Because my error engages my hurt,
by erring I hurt you in a vile act,
flinging you so freely into death,
while inert I lie forever in arrears,
at the whim my hoveled brain,
wherein are born the most mortal wrongs.

My brain now, father, mother, in arrears,
let it be my final act before my death
to pay for my hurts and expunge my wrongs.

Perdón, papá, mamá, porque mi yerro/ cual cuna fue de vuestro ajeno
daño,/ desde que por primera vez mi seso/ entretejió la malla de los hechos,/
con las torcidas sogas de la zaga,/ donde cautivo yazgo hasta la muerte.//
Como globo aerostático en la muerte,/ henchida por la bilis de los yerros,/
la conciencia saldrá desde la zaga,/ y morir cuán cercado por los daños,/
del orbe será el más lastimoso hecho,/ que suerte no es del ilustrado seso.//
Pues son cosas de un aturdido seso/ no ser despabilado ni en la muerte/ y
en verdad es un inaguantable hecho/ que adherida prosiga el alma al yerro,/
hasta cuando sumido en crudos daños,/ el cuerpo pase a polvo en plena
zaga.// De los oficios y el amor en zaga,/ por designio exclusivo de mi seso,/
me dejan así los mortales daños,/ aun en el umbral de la propia muerte,/
que tal sucede por labrar con yerros/ los espesos lingotes de los hechos.//
Yo, papá, mamá, vuestros dulces hechos/ cuánto agrié por yacer no más en
zaga,/ perdido en la floresta de los yerros,/ y corridos os fuisteis por mi seso,/
entre ascuas de rubores a la muerte,/ bajo el largo diluvio de los daños.//
Porque el error engrana con el daño,/ al errar yo os dañé como feo hecho,/
os lanzando cuán presto hacia la muerte,/ en tanto inmóvil yazgo siempre
en zaga,/ al arbitrario del antro de mi seso,/ donde nacen los más mortales
yerros.// Ya mi seso, papá, mamá, en la zaga,/ que postrer hecho sea ante la
muerte/ pagar los daños y lavar los yerros.

I Trust Now in Nothing / Yo en nada ya me fío

Michelle Gil-Montero, trans.

I trust now in nothing
not even on a timorous grain can I rest
of sand my slim foot,
as all the more brute usury
of the cruel not Inca male,
with fewer pinings I boast
and less leisure and less sweet love;
oh, craggiest orb! open for me
your pharmacy then,
so within the fog I might exalt
some troche,
that might free me, if briefly,
from this diver's helmet fast with a thousand fears
the brim of my skull despite my liking,
which distances me not only from the water
but from air and fire and everything.

Yo en nada ya me fío/ ni en un grano estribar medroso puedo/ de arena
mi pie flaco,/ pues a más fiera usura/ del no inga varón cruel,/ con menos
ansias cuento/ y menos ocio y menos dulce amor;/ ¡oh enriscado orbe!,
abridme/ vuestra farmacia entonces,/ para que entre la niebla pueda alzar/
algún trocisco yo,/ que me libere, bien que breve sea,/ desta escafandra de
mil miedos fija/ el ras del cráneo mío mal mi grado,/ que no sólo del agua
me distancia,/ sino del aire y del fuego y de todo.

Francisco Madariaga (1927–2000, Argentina)

Born in Buenos Aires, Madariaga is a poet who has become better known in the last couple of decades. His complete works, a ten-volume book called *El tren casi fluvial,* take place in the Argentine province of Corrientes and serve as a setting for the struggle and tension between rural and urban life. PRINCIPAL WORKS: *El pequeño patíbulo* (1954), *Resplandor de mis bárbaras* (1985), *El tren casi fluvial* (1987)

Black Colá Jara / Cambá Colá Jara

Molly Weigel, trans.

Were you pure, almost childlike, like the black adoring suns that
illuminated The Cabins of Life in a faraway Congo of yesteryear, very
yesteryear? . . . Certainly, back then, the serpent with lips the deceptive
green of death destroyed itself in your gaze, as beautiful as the yellowly
black shadow of African love.

My pal Colá, my godchild by the baptism of the date-laden forests and by
the hot water that flows from the mouth of the *Irupé*, that herb that
heals the waters, that round and natural barge for when the little yellow
monkey wants to leave the forest and sail out slowly on it through the
gleaming winter marsh.

My black gaucho, of the tilted silver-studded belt that came all the way
down to your toes. Your toes, the puma the colors of mud! You, the
resplendent Secretary of the Time of Day-Dreams, when the fiery
wine sang in the palm grove, or the moon was a white bleeding in the
guitar of your soul . . . White, like your mother, she who one day was
bewitched by the fresh black rider wearing the Brazilian silverplate, the
tall, gleaming chestnut hat, the polished boots, also tall and heeled with
spurs like golden silver dove's wings that flew up onto the horse-racing
cowboy of the Rio Grande, in the Correntino campaign of the fiesta . . .
His guitar and his coralline mandolin, with its chords of the skies of the
blind Ramirez Valley, enveloped the couple, taking them out of the fiesta,
out of the swell of spurs, of machetes and ponchos of sky-blue, red,
green . . . Then you were born, and you were a cattle-driver, and a rodeo
cowboy, but you also had your *coja* (garden) of *avatí* (corn), *manduví*
(corn), *yefi* (sweet potato), *cumandá* (bean), *mandi-ó* (manioc), *pefi-jhü*
(black tobacco) for *yeisu-ú* (chewing), the queen of your "vices." Black
ghost, and white, and unchanging, like me (me, without a political party
among Correntinos!; you, sky-blue) we'd walk *oro-pe*! (as if in a golden
state!) by the lakes, the marshes, the palm-groves, the country stores,
the performances, the roads, the vigils for the dead, crosses, or angels,
and wouldn't destroy anything or anyone, much less the splendor of the
enchanted creature, the spirit of the delicate wilderness, the live firefly

of the Corrientes cosmos . . . With you, I never whispered secret words
of love, as I had with your compatriot Teolindo Frutos, the only poet
in a state of nature I've ever known! I can still see his big hat, shading
him from the sun, and the enormous green shawl, crossed and reaching
almost to his hips! You and I, Colá, would speak very little, in Guaraní
or in something that you called "La Castilla," but we'd exchange looks
shining with sun-dappled adventures, in which esteem for beautiful,
creole legitimacy reigned . . . Did the two of us belong to the open
dream? To the hopeless hope? We two became allied with the white,
positive *porá* (spirit) of the *yatai* palm, and also with the other, with
that of water, she of whom one night at the vigil on the ranch of the
Primitive Medina, right next to Aguicha Franco's, Pelí Ramírez, a friend
of yours from the Paraje Estancia Caimán, said: "The *porá* of water keeps
her eye on the white horse, and usually steals it from its master when
they swim across any water." Pelí Ramírez, gaucho with the Malayan
face, of the prodigious memory! still living, but now by the shores of the
enormous, sacred, circular marsh *Trapiche-cué*! and surely he must still be
a hunter of women, the old man!

And do you remember that time in 1958 that wild horse, Llamarada, broken
in for barely one day, fell down with me on him while we were leaving a
fiesta for a saint, in the wee hours, in the company of Antonio Cardozo
and those friends who were visiting from Buenos Aires?

The fiesta was on the ranch of old Calí Ramírez and Kiyú Fernández, who
until his very recent death was a skilled and gentle cattle driver and
breaker . . . Oh stammering Kiyucito, horse whisperer of sorrels and
burning grasslands! Lover of the ardent, skinny mulatta Hilaronia, who
even now brings you in the graveyard, on All Soul's Day, offerings of
cakes and your ox-horn flask from the place where caimans dwell, heavy
with cane liquor and kept cool among the nocturnal *camalotes* of the
marsh.

How we flew in those small hours, with the horses calmed, through the
utterly white mist of the palm grove, and you, Colá, tried, from up
on your mount, to cinch yourself, grabbing by the bleeding bridle
the frantic horse of one of our companions . . . What a mess without
collisions in the beautifully sinister palm grove in the gradual
pre-dawn!

Oh Colá Jara, could you have loved another poncho that wasn't sky-
colored! Correntino by painful and ancient expansions of the river
Congo all the way to the coasts of Brazil (all the way to "the sugar of
the word Brazil," as Aimé Cesaire, the great black French Antillean
poet from Martinique, said) and then all the way to the abysmal
waters, bleeding, but of delicate and strong sustenance, of the Guaraní

marsh of Corrientes, today I feel that into my heart, always a little buffeted by the waters, the blade of your friendship enters, your stab of poetry—a beaten cloud—shrouding me with your celestial shawl.

Eras puro, casi infantil, ¿cómo los soles negros y adorantes que iluminaban Las Cabañas de la Vida, en un lejano Congo de antaño, muy de antaño? . . . Es claro que, por entonces, la serpiente de labios engañosamente verdes de la muerte se destruía en tu mirada, tan bella como la sombra amarillamente negra del amor africano.// Mi cumpa Colá, mi *ahijado* por bautismo de los montes adatilados y por el agua caliente que sale de la boca del Irupé, esa planta-curandera de las aguas, esa barcaza redonda y natural para cuando la pequeña mona amarilla quiera dejar el monte y sale a navegar lentita sobre ella por el estero resplandeciente del invierno.// Mi gaucho negro, de *tirador* ladeado, que te llegaba hasta los pies. ¡Tus pies, que eran la puma de los colores del barro! Tú, el resplandeciente Secretario del Tiempo de las Ensoñaciones, cuando cantaba el vino ardiente en el palmar, o la luna era una sangrarada blance en la guitarra de tu alma . . . Blanca, como tu madre, aquella que un día fuera la hechizada por el fresco jinete negro, de chapeado brasilero, de alto galerón retintado plateado, botines charolados, también altos y calzados con espuelas como alas de palomas de platas amarillas, que se erguían en caballero parejero de Río Grande, en la campaña correntina de la fiesta . . . ¡La guitarra y el *mandolín* coralino, con sus cuerditas de los cielos del ciego Valle Ramírez, envolvieron a la pareja y la fueron sacando de la fiesta, de entre la marejada de espuelas, de machetes y del poncherío de colores: celestes, colorados, verdes . . . Después, naciste tú, y fuiste tropero, y de rodeo, pero tenías también tu *coga* (chacra) de *avati* (maíz), de *manduví* (maíz), de *yefi* (batata), de *cumandá* (poroto), de *mandi-ó* (mandioca), de *pefi-jhü* (tabaco negro) para el *yeisu-ú* (la mascada), la reína de tus "vicios," Fantasma negro, y blanco, e intemporal, como yo (yo, ¡sin partido, entre correntinos!; tú, celeste) paseábamos ¡oro-pe! (¡cómo en estado de oro!) por las lagunas, los esteros, los palmares, las pulperías, las funciones, las carreras, los velorios de cuerpos, de cruces o de angelitos, y no destruíamos a nada ni a nadie, y menos aun al esplendor de la criatura encantada, del fantasma de la delicadeza salvaje, el animita viva del cosmos correntino . . . Contigo, yo no tuve "secretada para el trato en el amor," como la tuve con tu compadre Teolindo Frutos, ¡aquel único poeta en estado natural que yo he conocido!, ¡si aún veo casi sombrillar su gran sombrero, y el enorme pañuelo verde, cruzado, que le llegaba hasta las caderas! . . . Tú y yo, Colá, hablábamos muy poco, en guaraní o en alguna que otra palabra que pronunciabas en "la castilla," pero cruzábamos miradas resplandecientes para aventuras soleadas, en las que reinaba la estima de la bella y criolla legitimidad . . . ¿Los dos pertenecíamos al sueño abierto? ¿A la esperanza desesperanzada? Los dos nos aliábamos con la *pora* blanca y positiva de la palmera *yatai*, y también con la otra, con la del agua, aquella de la cual una noche en un velorio en el rancho de Primitiva Medina,

pegadito al de Aguicha Franco, decía Peli Ramírez, un compagno tuyo del
Paraje Estancia Caimán: "La *pora* del agua tiene mucha vista para el caballo
blanco, y se lo suele quitar al dueño cuando cruzan a nado alguna agua". Peli
Ramírez ¡gaucho de rostro malayo, el memorioso!, que aún vive, pero ahora
por las orillas del enorme, sagrado y circular estero *Trapiche-cué* ¡y es seguro
que debe seguir siendo *mariscador* de chinas el Caraí Tuyá!// ¿Y te acuerdas
de aquella rodada mía, de 1958, con aquel bagualito Llamarada, con apenas
un día de enfrenado, a la salida de una fiesta para un santo, de madrugada,
y acompañados por Antonio Cardozo y por aquellos amigos llegados de visita
desde Buenos Aires?// La fiesta era en el rancho del antiguo Cali Ramírez,
y de Kiyú Fernández, que fue tropero y domador suave hasta su muy reciente
muerte . . . ¡Oh Kiyucito tartamudo, cautivador de alazanes y de encendidos
pajonales! El amador de la ardiente y finita mulata Hilariona, que aún hoy te
lleva al camposanto, en el día de difuntos, ofrendas de pasteles y tu *chifle* de
cornamenta de buey del paraje camionero, cargado con "la caña" y refrescado
entre los camalotes nocturnos del estero.// Cómo volábamos aquella
madrugada, con los caballos aserenados, por entre la niebla totalmente blanca
del palmar, y tú, Colá, tratabas, desde arriba de tu montado, de asujetarte,
agarrándola por el sangrante freno, a la caballería desbandada de uno de
nuestros compañeros . . . ¡Qué entrevero sin choques en el palmarerío
bellamente siniestro de la pre-alba paulatina!// ¡Oh Colá Jara, que no adoraste
otro ponchillo que no fuera color cielo! Correntino por expansiones dolorosas
y antiguas del africano río Congo hasta las costas del Brasil (hasta "el azúcar
de la palabra Brasil," como dice el gran poeta negro antillano francés de la
Martinica, Aimé Cesaire) y luego hasta las aguas abismales, sangrantes, pero
de delicado y fuerte alimento, del estero guaraní correntino, hoy siento que
en mi corazón, siempre un poco vareado por las aguas, entre tu acero de
amistad, tu puñalada de poesía—una niebla bordoneada—me amortaja con tu
pañuelo celeste.

The Trivial Jungle / La selva liviana

Molly Weigel, trans.

1

The sound of a train that's drowned in the cataract of leaves.
Deep in the heart of the trivial jungle and the palm trees the level of lament
    goes under, the full weight of dreams.
Full weight of the sack of the perfume of grace, I'm in between the sword of
    scenery and the hot brick of landscape,
traveling with an ardor of jewel and blood.
Hearing the howl of my candor: my new fiesta.

2

Loads of whistles.

The train withdraws inside itself beside the nocturnal estuaries.
Its city dust is frightened of the great wetness of the earth,
of the air warmly electric,
of the swans of black night steam of the wound of the world.

3
The imagination burns wrapped in the wheels of a disoriented train.
Bananas and more bananas fall from the air.
In a temple a naked woman with a shotgun gnaws slowly on the ring of her
  heart.
Fruit-seller of misfortune, fruit-seller of destiny.

1/ El sonido de un tren que se ahoga en la/ catarate de las hojas./ Al fondo
de la selva liviana y los cocoteros/ se hunde el nivel de llanto,/ el peso
entero de los sueños./ Peso entero del saco de perfume de la gracia,/ estoy
entre la espada del país aje y el/ ladrillo caliente del olvido,/ viajando con
un ardor de joya y sangre./ Escuchando el aullido de mi candor: mi nueva/
fiesta.// 2/ A paladas silbatos./ El tren se encierra en sí al borde de los/
esteros nocturnos./ Su polvo ciudadano tiene miedo a la gran/ humedad
de la tierra,/ al aire cálidamente eléctrico,/ a los cisnes del negro vapor
nocturno de la/ herida del mundo.// 3/ La imaginación arde envuelta en
las ruedas/ de un tren desorientado./ Bananas y bananas caen al aire./ Una
mujer desnuda a una escopeta en un templo,/ roe lentamente en el anillo de
su corazón./ Frutera de la desgracia, frutera del destino.

Leónidas Lamborghini (1927–, Argentina)

Leónidas Lamborghini, brother of Osvaldo, was born in Buenos Aires. His exten-
sive and quite often political poetic works involve rewriting and parodying popular
songs and other poetic forms. He has written numerous poems and several novels,
including *Un amor como pocos* (1993) and *La experiencia de la vida* (1996). Lamborghini lived in exile in Mexico from 1977 to 1990. Since the early 1990s, he
lives in Buenos Aires, where his work has become a point of reference for younger
generations. PRINCIPAL WORKS: *Al público* (1957), *La canción de Buenos Aires* (1968),
Partitas (1972)

Excerpt from The Displaced Applicant / El solicitante descolocado
G. J. Racz, trans.

I stop myself a second
for a background check
try to solve pressing

problems of state;
oh my poetic soul, whisper to me contract
offer, combination
and auction.

Instead of that, this:
you've no voice of your own
no virtues
it said
and write only in order to
I tried telling it—that's a lie that's a lie
to purify myself

The dance floor is surrounded
by all species, all orders
and classes
but above all by the audience
the partner-less standing
in the front row.
As always some politician
some illustrious warrior, some
outstanding bureaucrat
kicks off the event
which is where I come in
right through the hoop.

Have a seat
no one should miss
a show like this
I let my dark laughter out
in the middle of the feature.

Here and again
up to my old tricks
in the land of the one-eyed
I am king.

Gluttonous, lazy, lascivious people
as economic curves
presently favor us
I beg you to set
a new consciousness in motion.

And if things become complicated
decentralize:
—Ready, here goes
to govern is to populate is to talk;

bending my ear
toward the demonstrating laborer:
it rattles.

Just then I recognize
manage to make out among some 200,000
my sweet old schoolteacher
holding up
a blue poster
with gold lettering.

—What kind of child were you?
—a, e, i, o, u
exceptionally bright and bighearted
before the sacrilege
she said to me, to my best student
—The earth slopes downward for those
who work it
—The revolution never ends.

She.
Moved by emotion she blows
my brains away
plucking its petals

he achieves he achieves not he achieves he achieves not he achieves he
    achieves not

—Your soul has a delicate
crystal neck
she says—sloping downward—
with a base of rustproof steel

Trying to reach
the stratosphere
I tendered my offer in an audible voice
—I am not worth a damn!

Nevertheless I invent
the economy without a shoestring
and catch in passing
"we are just fine here
hanging from the budget"

When the foreign investments arrived
ready to have an impact
and they asked

real wages, what
is your purchasing power?

(Ex)change
(Ex)change
(Ex)change
Where is
that simple money
legal tender
that plain old currency
the slightly innocent
copper
coin?

Yet before succumbing
the thinking economic interest
managed to babble about
oil, industry, agri-
culture.

It's going broke

With no bases
I set the latest
price.

Me detengo un momento/ por averiguación de antecedentes/ trato de
solucionar importantísimos/ problemas de estado;/ vena mía poética
susúrrame contracto/ planteo, combinación/ y remate.// En vez/ tú no tienes
voz propia/ ni virtud/ dijo/ y escribes sólo para/ yo quise decirle mentira
mentira/ para purificarme// La pista se rodea/ de todas las especies, de
todos los órdenes/ y clases/ sobre todo de público/ en la primera fila van/
los relegados.// Siempre algún gobernante/ algún guerrero ilustre, algún/
funcionario aventajado/ da el puntapié inicial/ entonces entro yo/ entrando
por el aro.// Tome asiento/ nadie debe perderse/ un espectáculo/ abro mi risa
negra/ a función continuada.// Y a la bartola/ haciendo de las mías/ en el
país del tuerto/ es rey.// Pueblo goloso perezoso lujurioso/ porque las curvas
económicas/ nos son favorables/ una nueva conciencia os pido/ en marcha.//
Y si las cosas se complican/ descentralizar:/ —Listo, vamos/ gobernar es poblar
es hablar;/ apoyando mi oído/ en el obreo concentrado:/ vibra.// Entonces
reconozco/ alcanzo a distinguir entre 200.000/ a mi buena maestrita/ llevaba/
un cartelón azul/ con letreros dorados.// —¿Qué clase de niño fuiste tú?/
—a, e, i, o, u/ inteligentísimo y de gran corazón/ antes del sacrilegio/ ella me
dijo a mi mejor discípulo/ —La tierra para quien la trabaja/ se inclina/ —La
revolución no se detiene nunca.// Ella./ Levanta emocionada/ la tapa de
mis sesos/ deshojando// cumple no cumple cumple no cumple cumple no/

cumple// —Tu alma tiene un delicado/ cuello de cristal/ —se inclina—/ su base
es de acero inoxidable// Tratando de llegar/ a las altas esferas/ hice mi oferta de
viva voz/ —¡No valgo un pito!// No obstante invento/ la economía sin un hilo/
y oigo al pasar / "aquí estamos muy bien/ colgados del presupuesto"// Cuando
llegaron las inversiones extranjeras/ dispuestas a radicarse/ y preguntaron/
salario real ¿cuál/ es tu poder adquisitivo?// Cambio/ Cambio/ Cambio//
¿Dónde está/ la moneda simple/ legal/ la moneda sencilla/ del menudo
candor/ la moneda de/ cobre?// Y antes de sucumbir/ el interés económico
pensante/ alcanzó a balucear/ petróleo, industrias, agro,/ pecuario.// Está
quebrando// Sin base/ cierro la última/ cotización.

Excerpt from Eva Perón at the Stake / Eva Perón en la hoguera

G. J. Racz, trans.

I

because of him
him
for him
the condor, him, if it weren't for him
him
blossomed from my innermost being. from me to him:
from my reason. my life.
what a condor is like, he unto me:
a sparrow in one immense.
unto me: I the most. a humble bird in the flock.
a sparrow and he taught me:
a condor, he, mid the heights. mid the peaks:
to fly.
if nearly nearby:
to fly
if nearly from:
to fly.
in one immense. a sparrow.
and he taught me:
if I see clearly. this is why:
if at times with my wings.
if I nearly touch nearly:
if I range mid the heights. if I see
if I nearly touch nearly
because of him
him:
all I possess:
from him.

all I feel:
from him.
all the love I have:
to him.
my all to his:
to him.

II

it's not by chance.
not all of a sudden
that I've been brought here:
this situation I'm in.
it's not and
suddenly
I'm a fanatic.
let me explain. the situation here.
not by chance:
a feeling.
a basic.
not all of a sudden
and suddenly
on to big things.
let me explain here.
a feeling that:
the Cause. let me explain:
the indignation.
a basic.
one in my heart.
a discovery that rules me
ever since:
to go back looking for, to return in time. pain there.
me here: before the.
every injustice I've: every memory.
this very day here
against some
against every
I stand on guard: ruling over me.
it's not and suddenly and I'm a fanatic
let me explain here: the Cause.
a basic.
one ruling me ever since.
one tearing me apart.
one in my heart
as if piercing me:
in my innermost.

revelation:
almost at once and I knew it:
the rich are like trees, the poor like grass.
wait, there's more
there's more
there's more: my only point. there's more, there's more:
a sadness.
the three Magi—no.
the camels—no: an impression truly.
almost at once
and I felt it.
a sadness:
wait, there's more
there's more: a sign. and I reacted. and truly.
I never managed to:
the poor—no. a sign. my words.
my actions truly.
an impression a sadness to the brim
truly.
wait, there's more
there's more and
I reacted: almost at once
to the brim truly: prayer or curse
I declare it: all this.
the poor like grass. revelation. a sadness
wait, there's more
there's more
the camels—no.
the three Magi—no.
the poor—no. like grass.
and I declare it
and I felt it:
all this will change.
prayer
or curse:
or both these things.

I/ por él./ a él./ para él./ al cóndor él si no fuese por él/ a él./ brotado ha de
lo más íntimo. de mí a él:/ de mi razón. de mi vida./ lo que es un cóndor él
hasta mí:/ un gorrión en una inmensa./ hasta mí: la más. una humilde en
la bandada./ un gorrión y me enseñó:/ un cóndor él entre las altas. entre las

cumbres:/ a volar./ si casi y cerca:/ a volar./ si casi de:/ a volar/ en una inmensa.
un gorrión./ y me enseñó:/ si veo claramente. por eso:/ si a veces con mis
alas./ si casi cerca de./ si ando entre las altas. si veo./si casi toco casi:/ por él/
a él:/ todo lo que tengo:/ de él./ todo lo que siento:/ de él./ todo el amor de
mí:/ a él./ mi todo a su todo:/ a él.// II/ no es el azar./ no es de buenas a/ que
me ha traído:/ el caso que me toca./ no es y/ de pronto/ yo fanática./ quiero
explicarme aquí. el caso./ no el azar:/ un sentimiento./ un fundamental./
no es de buenas a/ y de pronto/ a cosas grandes./ quiero explicarme aquí:/
un sentimiento que:/ la Causa. quiero explicarme aquí:/ la indignación./ un
fundamental./ un en mi corazón./ un hallado que domina/ desde:/ ir a buscar
atrás a remontarme. allí dolor./ allí he: frente a la./ cada injusticia he: cada
recuerdo./ hoy mismo aquí/ de alguna/ de cada/ guardo: que domina./ no es y
de pronto y yo fanática./ quiero explicarme aquí: la Causa./ un fundamental./
un que domina desde./ un desgarrándome./ un en mi corazón/ como si me
clavase:/ íntimamente.// III/ revelación:/ casi de golpe y que lo supe:/ los
ricos como árboles los pobres como pasto./ y hay más/ y hay más: mi tema
único. y hay más hay más:/ una tristeza./ los reyes magos no./ los camellos
no: una impresión muy./ casi de golpe/ y lo sentí./ una tristeza:/ y hay más/
y hay más: una marca. y reaccionaba. y muy./ yo nunca pude:/ los pobres no.
un marca. mis palabras./ mis actos muy./ una impresión una tristeza hasta el
borde/ muy./ y hay más/ hay más y/ reaccionaba: casi de golpe/ hasta el borde
muy: o ruego o maldición/ y lo declaro: todo esto./ los pobres como pasto.
revelación. una tristeza/ y hay más/ y hay más./ los camellos no./ los reyes
magos no./ los pobres no: como pasto./ y lo declaro/ y lo sentí:/ todo esto
cambiará./ o ruego/ o maldición:/ o las dos cosas.

amereida (c. 1965–, Chile)

amereida, a collective poem composed and published anonymously by a group of
poets and architects based at the School of Architecture of Universidad Católica
de Valparaíso, Chile, became the basis for a series of epic poetic journeys modeled
after the early practices of André Breton and the surrealists but carried out with the
expressed purpose of discovering the "interior sea," the largely unoccupied territory at the center of South America. The first "travesía," or poetic journey, took
place in 1965 and the practice still endures today. In each journey, readings and
performances are conducted outdoors and ephemeral art installations are created.
In 1970, the group created an "Open City" in the dunes of Ritoque, 25 km north of
Valparaíso, as a site for experimental poetry based on architecture. It is probably the
only site in the world where architecture is conceived as an outgrowth of poetry.

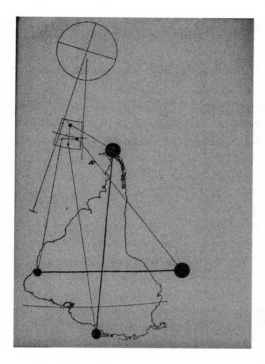

The Southern Cross laid over the
continent to guide the journey,
amereida, 1965

Excerpt from amereida

Simon Pettet and Cecilia Vicuña, trans.

Columbus
        never came to america
                he was looking for the indies

midway through his quest
            this land
                erupted as a gift

simply
      a gift
         arising
unintentional,
            thoughtless,
bringing
      its own offering,
            its own terms,
             its own borders,
                rending
    —open a wound as it simultaneously created—
unwanted adventures

. . . .

a continent discovered, yet unaccepted
                              did we not
dismiss it
              as an obstacle?

america we discovered then hid
                    wasn't that the plan?
to turn it into
              a trading post?

. . . .

what did we inherit
                    waking up on the perimeter?

what did we inherit when we presented ourselves
with this gift
              immigrants,
                        children of immigrants,
                              mestizos,
                              aborigines

all of us woke up, an "other"
                    via the offering

didn't we inherit
              a capacity for the unknown
                              or for the ocean
which empties us out to awe
                    and recognition?
we must clear the path—
and what may be spoken of
                    here
is a vast sea, a *mare magnum*

                    but hidden
                    because, though visible,

mostly ignored
the names —

colón/ nunca vino a américa/ buscaba las indias// en medio de su afán/ esta
tierra/ irrumpe en regalo// mero/ el regalo/ surge/ contrariando intentos/
ajeno a la esperanza/ trae consigo/ su donación/ sus términos/ sus bordes/
rasga/ —herida o abertura donde emerge—/ con/ una aventura involuntaria//
. . . // continente encontrado pero no aceptado/ ¿no se buscó más bien/
dejarlo de lado/ como un obstáculo?// américa encontrada y velada/ pues
aún/ apenas admitido su hallazgo/ ¿no fue la empresa/ volverla parte/ de un

centro distante?// . . . // ¿qué heredamos/ amanecidos en este borde?// ¿qué heredamos cuando nos sorprendemos/ en regalo/ immigrantes/ hijos de immigrantes/ mestizos/ o aborígenes// despertados otros/ en la donación?// ¿no heredamos/ esta capacidad de desconocido/ o mar/ que nos ahueca para la admiración/ y el reconocimiento?/ es menester abrir el camino—/ y lo que en esto se podría/ decir/ es un mare magno// e oculto/ porque aunque se ve// lo más dello se ynora/ los nombres —

Michel Deguy invoking fire, amereida journey, Patagonia, 1965

View from the sculpture, amereida journey, Patagonia, 1965

La Casa de Los Nombres (The House of Names), Open City, Ritoque, Chile, 1970s

Edgardo Antonio Vigo (1928–1997, Argentina)

The Argentine sculptor, artist, poet, and essayist was born in La Plata. In 1953, he traveled to Paris as a student where he first was exposed to the international art scene. In 1961, Vigo founded *Diagonal Cero*, a journal dedicated to visual poetry and based on the international mail correspondence that Vigo maintained with artists around the world. The practice of "mail-art" began as a form of communication between artists and grew into a new genre of art. Vigo developed a poetics based on the principles of concrete art, but independent from the Brazilian Noigandres group founded by Haroldo and Augusto de Campos and Décio Pignatari. PRINCIPAL WORK: His "mail-art" can be seen at Archivo Centro de Arte Experimental Vigo, La Plata, Argentina, www.eavigo.com.ar/

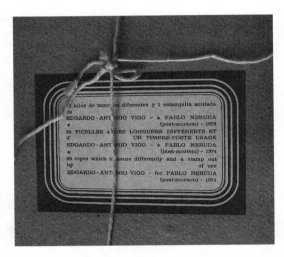

Twenty ropes that measure differently and a stamp out of use by EDGARDO ANTONIO VIGO—for Pablo Neruda (postmortem)—1974

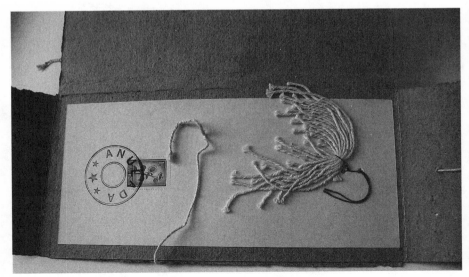

Enrique Lihn (1929–1988, Chile)

One of the key figures of Chilean literature, born in Santiago, Lihn was also a critic, narrator, and visual artist. Mario Campaña wrote that his incorruptible critical intelligence, his tireless belligerence, and his rhetorical richness allowed Lihn to try many modes of expression. For Lihn, writing was a contradictory enterprise. His intent was to return silence to words. "I distrust even my own ideology." PRINCIPAL WORKS: *Poesía de paso* (1966), *A partir de Manhattan* (1979), *El arte de la palabra* (1980), *Diario de muerte* (1989)

The Father's Monologue with His Infant Son / Monólogo del padre con su hijo de meses

Jonathan Cohen, trans.

You lose nothing by living, try it out;
here's a body just your size.
we have made it in darkness
out of love for the arts of the flesh
but also in earnest, thinking about your visit
as in a new game that's joyful and painful:
out of love for life, out of fear of death
and life, out of love of death
for you or for no one.

You are your body, take it, show us you like it
as we do this double gift
that we have made for you and that we have made for ourselves.
Sure, just a little
of that degrading first mud: the anguish
and pleasure in a shout of impotence.
From far away not a bird opening in the beauty
of the egg, in broad daylight, weightless and jubilant,
just a man: the
beast old from birth, defeated by flies,
drooling and panting.

But live and you will see
the monster that you are with kindness
to open an eye and another so wide,
to get the sky into your head,
to look at it all as though from within,
to ask things what their names are
to laugh with what laughs, cry with what cries,
to tyrannize cats and rabbits.

You lose nothing by living, we have
all the time in the time ahead
to become the emptiness that we are inside.
And childhood, listen:
there's no madman happier than a sane boy
nor a wise man so sure like a mad boy.
Everything we live we already lived
more intensely at the age of ten;
desires then
would fall asleep on each other.
Sleep came constantly, the sleep
that restores the perfect disorder in everything,
to free you from your body and soul;
there in that unreal castle
you were the king, queen, your henchmen,
the buffoon who laughs at himself,
the birds, the melodious beasts.
For lovemaking, your mother was there
and love was the kiss on the forehead from another world,
which comforts the sick,
a soft-spoken reading, the nostalgia
of no one and nothing that music gives us.

But over the years the years go by
and here you are an adolescent already.
You come down the mountain like Zarathustra
to fight for man against man:
a serious mission no one sends you on;
you inspire distrust among your family,
you talk about God in a sarcastic tone,
you come home a day later, dead.
They say that you are charming an old lady,
they have seen you doing somersaults in the air,
you prolong your studies with studies
which make your head swim.
There's no happiness that makes you so happy
as falling headlong into sadness
nor a grief that hurts you so deeply
as the pleasure of living for no reason.
A serious age, there are some who kill themselves
because they can't put up with death,
who give into an unjust cause
in their bloodthirsty desire for justice.
The bigger they are the harder they fall,

we lose track of the little ones.
All are betrayed in love:
love is the father of their evils.
If a woman feels tenderness for you
you'll force her to follow you to your grave,
to leave her family right away,
to move her business somewhere else.

But fatally the moment comes
in which your youth turns its back on you
and for the first time its unforgettable face runs away from
      you as much as you chase it
with a sidelong glance, not moving, seated in a black chair.
The moment to do something has come
it seems the whole world tells you
and you say yes, nodding your head.
At the height of metaphysical decadence
you now walk with a little address book in your hand,
impeccably dressed, with the modesty of a young man making
      his way in life
willing to do anything.
The plan you made takes on air and
sinks in the sky leaving things just as they were.
For some time now you move among them like a fish in water.
You live on what you get, you get what you deserve, you deserve
      what you live;
you are on the right path with your cross on your back.
Congratulations!
you are, finally, a man among men.

And so you reach old age
as someone who returns to his homeland
after a brief, endless trip
too short to be relived, too long to tell about
death waits for you inside you, your skeleton
with open arms, but you hold her back
for a moment, you want
to look at yourself long and hard
in the mirror that clouds up.
Helped along by distant travelers
you come and go dressed in black, at a trot, talking
to yourself shouting, like a bird.
There's no time to lose, you are the last
of your generation to put out the sun
and turn to dust.

There's no time to lose in this world
made more beautiful by its end so near.
You are seen everywhere spinning
around anything, as if in ecstasy.
Whenever you go out of the streets you come back
with your pockets stuffed with odd treasures:
pebbles, wild flowers.
Until one day you can no longer fight
to the death with death and you give in to her
to a sleep with no way out, paler each time
smiling, crying like a baby.

You lose nothing by living, try it out:
here's a body just your size,
we have made it in the dark
out of love for the arts of the flesh
but also in earnest, thinking of your visit
for you or for no one.

Nada se pierde con vivir, ensaya;/ aquí tienes un cuerpo a tu medida./
Lo hemos hecho en la sombra/ por amor a las artes de la carne/ pero
también en serio, pensando en tu visita/ como en un nuevo juego gozoso
y doloroso;/ por amor a la vida, por temor a la muerte/ y a la vida, por
amor a la muerte/ para ti o para nadie.// Eres tu cuerpo, tómalo haznos
ver que te gusta/ como a nosotros este doble regalo/ que te hemos hecho
y que nos hemos hecho./ Cierto, tan sólo un poco/ del vergonzante
barro original, la angustia/ y el placer en un grito de impotencia./ Ni de
lejos un pájaro que se abre en la belleza / del huevo, a plena luz, ligero
y jubiloso,/ sólo un hombre: la fiera/ vieja de nacimiento, vencida por
las moscas,/ babeante y resoplante.// Pero vive y verás/ el monstruo que
eres con benevolencia/ abrir un ojo y otro así de grandes,/ encasquetarse
el cielo,/ mirarlo todo como por adentro,/ preguntarle a las cosas por
sus nombres / reír con lo que ríe, llorar con los que llora,/ tiranizar a
gatos y conejos.// Nada se pierde con vivir, tenemos/ todo el tiempo del
tiempo por delante/ para ser el vacío que somos en el fondo./ Y la niñez,
escucha:/ no hay loco más feliz que un niño cuerdo/ ni acierta el sabio
como un niño loco./ Todo lo que vivimos lo vivimos/ ya a los diez años
más intensamente;/ los deseos entonces/ se dormían los unos en los
otros./ Venía el sueño a cada instante, el sueño/ que restablece en todo el
perfecto desorden/ a rescatarte de tu cuerpo y tu alma;/ allí en ese castillo
movedizo/ eras el rey, la reina, tus secuaces,/ el bufón que se ríe de sí
mismo,/ los pájaros, las fieras melodiosos./ Para hacer el amor, allí estaba
tu madre/ y el amor era el beso de otro mundo en la frente,/ con que se
reanima a los enfermos,/ una lectura a media voz, la nostalgia/ de nadie

y nada que nos da la música.// Pero pasan los años por los años/ y he aquí
que eres ya un adolescente./ Bajas del monte como Zaratustra/ a luchar por
el hombre contra el hombre:/ grave misión que nadie te encomienda;/ en
tu familia inspiras desconfianza,/ hablas de Dios en un tono sarcástico,/
llegas a casa al otro día, muerto./ Se dice que enamoras a una vieja,/ te han
visto dando saltos en el aire,/ prolongas tus estudios con estudios/ de los
que se resiente tu cabeza./ No hay alegría que te alegre tanto/ como caer
de golpe en la tristeza/ ni dolor que te duela tan a fondo/ como el placer
de vivir sin objeto./ Grave edad, hay algunos que se matan/ porque no
puedan soportar la muerte,/ quienes se entregan a una causa injusta/ en su
sed sanguinaria de justicia./ Los que más bajo caen son los grandes,/ a los
pequeños les perdemos el rumbo./ En el amor se traicionan todos:/ el amor
es el padre de sus vicios./ Si una mujer se enternece contigo/ le exigirás
te siga hasta la tumba,/ que abandone en el acto a sus parientes,/ que
instale en otra parte su negocio.// Pero llega el momento fatalmente/ en
que tu juventud te da la espalda/ y por primera vez su rostro inolvidable
en tanto huye de ti que/ la persigues/ a salto de ojo, inmóvil, en una
silla negra./ Ha llegado el momento de hacer algo/ parece que te dice
todo el mundo/ y tú dices que sí, con la cabeza./ En plena decadencia
metafísica/ caminas ahora con una libretita de direcciones en la mano,/
implacablemente vestido, con la modestia de un hombre joven que/ se
abre paso en la vida/ dispuesto a todo./ El esquema que te hiciste de las
cosa hace aire y se hunde en el/ cielo dejándolas a todas en su sitio./ De
un tiempo a esta parte te mueves entre ellas como un pez en/ el agua./
Vives de lo que ganas, ganas lo que mereces, mereces lo que vives;/ has
encontrado en vereda con tu cruz a la espalda./ Hay que felicitarte:/ eres,
por fin, un hombre entre los hombres.// Y así llegas a viejo/ como quien
vuelve a su país de origen/ después de un breve viaje interminable/ corto
de revivir, largo de relatar/ te espera en ti la muerte, tu esqueleto/ con los
brazos abiertos, pero tú la rechazas/ por un instante, quieres/ mirarte larga
y sucesivamente/ en el espejo que se pone opaco./ Apoyado en lejanos
transeúntes/ vas y vienes de negro, al trote, conversando/ contigo mismo
a gritos, como un pájaro./ No hay tiempo que perder, eres el último/ de tu
generación en apagar el sol/ y convertirte en polvo.// No hay tiempo que
perder en este mundo/ embellecido por su fin tan próximo./ Se te ve en
todas partes dando vueltas/ en torno a cualquier cosa como en éxtasis./ De
tus salidas a la calle vuelves/ con los bolsillos llenos de tesoros absurdos:/
guijarros, florecillas./ Hasta que un día ya no puedes luchar/ a muerte
con la muerte y te entregas a ella/ a un sueño sin salida, más blanco cada
vez/ sonriendo, sollozando como un niño de pecho.// Nada se pierde con
vivir, ensaya:/ aquí tienes un cuerpo a tu medida,/ lo hemos hecho en la
sombra/ por amor a las artes de la carne/ pero también en serio, pensando
en tu visita/ para ti o para nadie.

Those Who Are Going to Die Can't Wait / Los que van a morir pueden no esperar

Dave Oliphant, trans.

Those who are going to die can't wait
for the horror of history to end
The dying belong to the kingdom of doubt
despair and conviction
They don't believe the monster will give in
they lose hope in Ariadne's thread so unreal a trail
and in the reality of any such Theseus
They know that the labyrinth will fall of its own accord
on the head of an old minotaur incapable of supporting it
with his horns
his appetite gone for living meat

Those who are going to die suspect that other dreadful
        workers
will reconstruct the labyrinth a little farther on
for the consumers yet to come

Los que van a morir pueden no esperar/ que termine el horror de la historia/
De los moribundos es el reino de la duda/ la desesperanza y la convicción/
Dudan que el monstruo doble la cerviz/ desesperan del ovillo de Ariadna un
camino tan irreal/ y de la realidad del tal Teseo/ Saben que el laberinto se
desmoronara por sí solo/ sobre la cabeza de un viejo minotauro incapaz ya
de sostenerlo/ con sus cuernos/ inapetente ante la carne viva// Los que van a
morir sospechan que otros horrible trabajadores/ reconstruyen el laberinto
un poco más allá/ para los devoradores que vienen

Haroldo de Campos (1929–2003, Brazil)

Born in São Paulo in 1929, Campos is best known as one of the creators of Brazilian
concrete poetry. His early works employed the rich, magical language of the myth-
poem, varied in composition and lyrically dense. He became deeply involved in
experimental poetry during the 1950s and 1960s, when he began to play with the
disintegration of space and word structure. His wide-ranging works and translations
demonstrate his deep knowledge of multiple poetic traditions and his appreciation
of baroque poetry. He, his brother Augusto, and Décio Pignatari founded the group
Noigandres, which revolutionized the practice of poetry. PRINCIPAL WORKS: *Xadrez
de entrelas: Percurso textual* (1949–1974), *Galáxias* (1984), *Crisantempo* (1998)

The Ear's Pavilion / O pavilhão da orelha

Translated by the author

the ear's   pavilion   edging
   eager   pavilion
   aureola
   aura

      in cornucopia   ear
        snail miles
        teat of
        air
        win
        dy tower
        tur
        gid

               manages in maze
               sound fili
               sound
                    from palps
                    from nothing
                       ness nipples

o pavilhão da orelha ourela/ o ávido pavilhão/ auréola/ aura/ em cornu
cópia/ caramujo do ouvido/ munge a teta/ do ar/ a tur/ gida torre/ de vento/
labora em labirinto/ o som o filisom/ do palpos dos nenh'/ ures ubres

Born and Dies / Se nasce morre nasce

Translated by the author

      se
      nasce
      morre nasce
      morre nasce morre
           renasce remorre renasce
               remorre renasce
                   remorre
      re   re
    desnasce
  desmorre desnasce
desmorre desnasce desmorre
       nascemorrenasce
       morrenasce
       morre
       se

se = if
$nasce$ = (a human being) is born
$morre$ = (a human being) dies
re = again
$denasce$ = (a human being) is unborn
$desmorre$ = (a human being) undies

"Hans Arp once made the following comparison between the poetry of the painter-poet Kandinsky and the poetry of Goethe: 'A poem by Goethe teaches the reader, in a poetical way, that death and transformation are the inclusive condition of man. Kandinsky, on the contrary, places the reader before an image of dying and transforming words, before a series of dying and transforming words. . . . ' This poem wants to be an exact *presentification* of that proposition. The vital cycle (or the Joycean 'vicocycle')."

Excerpt from Galáxias: Flower Blower / Circuladô de fulô
Odile Cisneros with Suzanne Jill Levine, trans.

flower-border flower-blow godevil give to devil will may god guide you for i can
not guide no more and long live who gave to me flower-blower flower-flow and even he
who hasn't yet singing like a shamizen wrought with wire tensed
just a stick and a worn tin can at feastfriday's end noon sun high on high but for
others no more music for it could not be 'cause it could not be popular
music if it's not sung it's not popular it's out of tune out of tinkle out of
chink tarantine and then strummed the tripe of pain the tensed tripe of a
furious physical pain and hurting hurting like a pike on the palm of the hand a
rusty blind pike impaling the hand an open naked heart like a nerve
tense retensed a black blind pike upon the palm pulp of the hand under the sun
while for meager cruzeiros they sell those gourds where a good shape is
the fine thin line of miserly matter shape of famine half-baked clay in the spoils
of repulse till others vomit their plastic plates with embroidered borders
in empire style for a measly misery 'cause this is what's popular for the
patrons of the people but the people invent the people create and the people reflect
the people are the tonguetricksters the masters of malice with wily ways
and vice to improvise probing the passage while oiling the sun's axle
for the lackeys lacking servitude almost pure metaphor the people il miglior fabbro
with their rhymed martelo galopado on the sieve of the impossible in the lives
     of the unviable
in the crucible of the incredible of their rhymed galope martelado and oil and axle of sun
but that string that string that bladestring that irksome moaning molar like
a demented string tolling its tuneless wailing widowed ring like a pale fire
famished flower-border flower-blow flower-border flower-blow flower-border flower-blo'

because i cannot guide no more see this book this consumable commodity this godevil
give to devil book that i array and disarray then put together and take apart waggage
of a wanderer in the world's swirl may god will may devil guide you because i
cannot guide cannot glide cannot ride cannot stride cannot stray cannot trade but in my
meager things my cents my rings in my ten in my fewer than in my
nothings in my pains my antennas in the radios in those things so trivial
immaterial we call trifles viewing vervaine sugars or amaryllis or
petty circumstance all of that i know is worthless is cheerless i don't
know but listen how it sings praise how it tells taste how it moves and don't ask
me to guide you unask me to guide you unguide me to ask you a promise
to trust you and let you forget me and leave you forgive me unbid me in the bitter
end i'll be right in the end i'll go back in the end i'll make right and for the end
keep me right and you'll see that i'm right and we'll see what is done who has ways
for through bent i went straight weaving one he weaved all and if i don't
guide i don't regret for the master who taught me no longer gives instruction a baggage
of worldvision in a split-second illusion going back i went straight deftly turned
the evil ways i don't guide 'cause i don't guide 'cause i can't guide and please don't ask
for remembrance but dwell in my moments disobey my command
   and don't trust but defy
nor confide or bestride that through yes or through no for myself i'll take no
in the if of the yes put the no in the e of the me put the no and the no will be your mot

circuladô de fulô ao deus ao demodará que deus te guie porque eu não/
posso guiá eviva quem já me deu circuladô de fulô e ainda quem falta
me/ dá soando como um shamisen e feito apenas com um arame tenso
um cabo e/ uma lata velha num fim de festafeira no pino do sol a pino
mas para/ outros não existia aquela música não podia porque não podia
popular/ aquela música se não canta não é popular se não afina não
tintina não/ tarantina e no entanto puxada na tripa da miséria na tripa
tensa da mais/ megera miséria física e doendo doendo como um prego
na palma da mão um/ ferrugem prego cego na palma espalma da mão
coração exposto como um nervo/ tenso retenso um renegro prego cego
durando na palma polpa da mão ao sol/ enquanto vendem por magros
cruzeiros aquelas cuias onde a boa forma é/ magreza fina da matéria
mofina forma de fome o barro malcozido no choco/ do desgôsto até que
os outros vomitem os seus pratos plásticos de bordados/ rebordes estilo
império para a megera miséria pois isto é popular para/ os patronos do
povo mas o povo cria mas o povo engenha mas o povo cavila/ o povo
é o inventalínguas na malícia da mestria no matreiro da maravilha/ no
visgo do improviso tenteando a travessia azeitava o eixo do sol/ pois
não tinha serventia metáfora pura ou quase o povo é o melhor artífice/
no seu martelo galopado no crivo do impossível no vivo do inviável/
no crisol do incrível do seu galope martelado e azeite e eixo do sol/ mas
aquele fio aquele fio aquele gumefio azucrinado dentedoendo como/ um
fio demente plangendo seu viúvo desacorde num ruivo brasa de uivo/
esfaima circuladô de fulô circuladô de fulô circuladô de fulôôô/ porque

eu não posso guiá veja este livro material de consumo este aodeus/
aodemodarálivro que eu arrumo e desarrumo que eu uno e desuno
vagagem/ de vagamundo na virada do mundo que deus que demo te guie
então porque eu/ não posso não ouso não pouso não troço não toco não
troco senão nos meus/ miúdos nos meus réis nos meus anéis nos meus
dez nos meus menos nos meus/ nadas nas minhas penas nas antenas
nas galenas nessas ninhas mais pequenas/ chamadas de ninharias como
veremos verbenas açúcares açucenas ou/ circunstâncias somenas tudo isso
eu sei não conta tudo isso desponta não/ sei mas ouça como canta louve
como conta prove como dança e não peça que/ eu te guie no peça despeça
que eu te guie desguie que eu te peça promessa/ que eu te fie me deixe
me esqueça me largue me desamargue que no fim eu/ acerto que no fim
eu reverto que no fim eu conserto e para o fim me reservo/ e se verá que
estou certo e se verá que tem jeito e se verá que está feito/ que pelo torto
fiz directo que quem faz cesto faz cento se não guio/ não lamento pois o
mestre que me ensinou já não dá ensinamento bagagem de/ miramundo
na miragem do segundo que pelo avesso fui destro sendo avesso/ pelo
sestro não guio porque não guio porque não posso guiá e não me peça/
memento mas more no meu momento desmande meu mandamento e
não fie desafie/ e não confie desfie que pelo sim pelo não para mim prefiro
o não/ no senão do sim ponha o não no im de mim ponha o não o não
será tua demão

Excerpt from Galáxias: **Reza calla y trabaja**
Odile Cisneros with Suzanne Jill Levine, trans.

reza calla y trabaja on a wall in granada work in silence and pray
and silence and work and pray in granada a wall at the mauresque casa del chapiz no
lazy bum will go to heaven seeing from above an inner wall la educación
is the work of all ave maria in granada see him en su granada and that
day the deserted casa del chapiz no arabist for the arabesques
a woman looking after a child behind a low door and praying
working in silence knowing nothing and working unable to tell
us anything y reza and later plazuela san nicolás the white on white
on white and silence in the white on white on white whitewash swarming white
on white swarming whitewash round cobblestones on the street and a white within
a white arch whispering whitewash and white works a white wall
and beyond in the distance beyond the generalife's and alhambra's crimson contour
the white plaza contains itself containing itself like a scream of limestone and the
generalife and the alhambra crimson amid black cypresses mudéjar face
of granada and now priestley's garden cars stopping the guardias civiles
the british ambassador touring the place amid caudillo's gala

and from priestley's garden priestly emerges or it could be to receive him
an array of carriages scandalize the silent lime her british majesty's
ambassador visits a nobleman in granada kids scurrying
fleeing through the hollows of doors the violated white the marrow of white
wounded the wrath of whiteness flowing over plazuela
san nicolás is not what it used to be two minutes ago once broken
the secrecy of white wild waterless white of whitewash that whispers
and works y estamos sentados sobre un volcán a volcano the driver said on the
patio of the chartreuse the palm sitting on the patio of the alhambra christened by
the crimson afternoon waiting for them to rip a volcano open heart beating in
granada and that's why on the wall reza and work and silence san bernardo religión
y patria and again the albaicín with its gardens cármenes and glorietas
   albaicín hanging
gardens from a cliff with hundreds of minute miradores overlooking the alhambra
and the red generalife outlined in black scarlet turning gold
the bold moorish sun and the mauresque murals of granada but the silence in
plazuela or placeta san nicolás broken for a mere minute forever never
but whispers and whitewash quiet whisper of the first moment the first
white leaning out and hurling us catapulting us into white
overwhelming white mass of whiteness flinging us most pale rubber of
utter whiteness hurling us against the blackcrimson horizon landing of
another horizon the alwaysgrayhaired shimmery snow of the sierra nevada now
i write now the vision is paper and ink on paper the white is paper
autauric stuccos and mozarab masses of paper do not return but the cuticle
of time the lunule of the nail of time and that's why i write and that's why
i'm a scribe on the nail of time gnawing down to the root of the nail root of the tail
the juice of the junk i don't revoke the patina of paper the peel of paper the core
of paper the paper cork that covers the crimson carnal heart of granada where a
   volcano sitting above
explodes and that's why it whispers y por eso trabaja and that's why por eso

reza calla y trabaja em um muro de granada trabaja y calla y reza y/
calla y trabaja y reza em granada um muro da casa del chapiz ningún/
holgazán ganará el cielo olhando para baixo um muro interno la
educación/ es obra de todos ave maria em granada mirad en su granada e
aquele/ dia a casa del chapiz deserta nenhum arabista para os arabescos/
uma mulher cuidando de uma criança por trás de uma porta baixa y
reza/ y trabaja y calla não sabia de nada y trabaja não podia informar
sobre/ nada y reza e depois a plazuela san nicolás o branco do branco
do branco y calla no branco no branco no branco a cal um enxame de
branco/ o branco um enxame de cal pedras redondas do calçamento e o
arco branco/ contendo o branco a cal calla e o branco trabalha um muro
de alvura/ e adiante no longe lálonge o perfil vermelho do generalife e
a alhambra/ a plazuela branca contendo-se contendo-se como um grito

de cal e o/ generalife e a alambra vermelhos entre ciprestes negros cariz
mudéjar/ de granada e agora o cármene de priestley carros parando los
guardias/ civiles o embaixador inglês fazendo turismo entre as galas
do caudillo/ e do cármene de priestley sai preistley ou poderia ser para
recebê-lo/ aparato de viaturas escandalizando a cal calada o embaixador
de sua/ majestade britânica visita um patrício em granada crianças
correndo/ fugindo para os vãos das portas e o branco violado a medula
do branco/ ferida a fúria a alvúria do branco refluída sobre si mesma
plazuela/ san nicolás já não mais o que fora o que era há dois minutos
já rompido/ o sigilo do branco arisco árido do cálcio branco da cal que
calla/ y trabaja y estamos sentados sobre un volcán dissera o chofer no
pátio/ da cartuja sentados no pátio da alambra bautizada sob o sol da
tarde/ esperando que abrissem um vulcão coração batendo em granada e
por isso/ no muro reza trabaja y calla san bernardo religión y patria e de/
novo o albaicín com seus cármenes y glorietas o albaicín despencando/
de centenas de miradouros minúsculos sobre a vista da alhambra e do/
generalife vermelho recortado de negro escarlate cambiando em ouro
o sol mouro os muros mauros de granada mas o silêncio na plazuela
ou/ plazeta san nicolás rompido para sempre um minuto para sempre
nunca/ mais a calma cal a calma cal calada do primeiro momento do
primeiro/ branco assomado e assomando nos lançando catapulta de
alvura alba-/ candidíssima mola de brancura nos jogando branquíssima
elástico de/ candura nos alvíssimo atirando contra o hoizonte rojonegro
patamar de/ outro horizonte o semprencanecido esfumadonevado
da sierra nevada agora/ escrevo agora a visão é papel e tinta sobre o
papel o branco é papel/ yeserías atauriques y mozárabes de papel não
devolvem senão a cutícula/ do tempo a lúnula da unha do tempo e por
isso escrevo e por isso/ escravo rôo a unha do tempo até o sabugo até
o refugo até o sugo e/ não revogo a pátina de papel a pevide de papel a
cáscara de papel a/ cortiça de papel que envolve o coração carnado de
granada onde um vulcão/ sentados sobre explode e por isso calla y por
eso trabaja y por eso

Excerpt from Galáxias: Inscribedcorpse / Cadavescrito

Odile Cisneros with Suzanne Jill Levine, trans.

inscribedcorpse you are the dream of a dream writing in bittertongue to
survive dead buriedtongue vagamonde carrying your magicbaggage
zaubermappe to carry out the defense and illustration of this dead tongue
this ill-starred luck this hand that cuts the umbilicord that stuck me to the
door the diffuse degustibus non est and in one thousandpages there will be no
one none of nothings one night the nultimate in noctober or nonvember
or perhaps dismember through a never nihiliad of januarian vessels
newmoons worldend finisterre in your port and hence don't depart or transport
partition report disentangle this macarroniad eviltongue before the
portogallian gibber-jabber esperantoes the brasilisk and this brothelbabeloire
boils over hodgepodgepapers easily your plot is simple
the simplest subplot but still someone could mention didascalias
a word that rhymes with alias but certainly not distinguishing between
motif or theme or appealing to mythemes fabulemes or novelemes or
losing oneself in pursuit of the best translation for récit or the distinguishment
between nouvelle and novella nor is it useful to know whether fable or fairy tale
is the fair term for the russian skaz let silkworms worry themselves
sick with their threads and humps are so from the womb only set straight
in the tomb this is no matter of equivalegends but elusive edge ends dig and ye
shall find only the writing hand that digs simplicitude's simplicity
simplicissimo in sancta simplicitas put aside litter-ature leave the
belles-letters to the belle-latrines and note in this language
thread there's a thread of language like a rose is a rose like a
prose is a prose there's a voyage thread there's a message heard and
in this marginal margin there's at least marginalia stop already these
boring stories tattling tales babble rabble and disbelieve histrionic
histories of stories and keep this loss at last at best the rest we'll
see a bottle in the sea can be the clue wine bottle of bad brews
of live divas gift bottle the future foresees through dark via
delle botteghe oscure and when the tide is high you'll be coming by
morning in the sky you begin coming be and when night
is dead you'll be full of laugh for it's lovely and light write and read
this minussong of yours minusstory of yours without meanness or paltry pomp this
chant now turned a stubborn romp not done for less but who's broke can't
come if my train is no gain if the boat's full of leaks it's the future
that speaks die of old age for sure but i fight in the night by the skin
of my shin by the spin of my fin did so much died so much is my fate
for i know what i pay not to see two but three if i play i play all on the three
and i still have a say once upon this tale is a simple one it's a story
to surprise i don't tell because i can't tell because i don't want to tell
telling the told sun tallying the tallied sea tilling told a tale a tall tale of
earth sun sea and air my chant won't tell my tale just chants a tune

cadavescrito você é o sonho de um sonho escrever em linguamarga para/
sobreviver a linguamorta vagamundo carregando a tua malamágica/
zaubermappe para fazer a defesa e a ilustração de esta língua morta/
esta moura torta esta mão que corta um umbilifio que me prega à porta/
a difusa e a degustação de e em milumapáginas não haverá ninguém
algum/ nenhum de nenhúrias que numa noite núltima em noutubro
ou em nãovembro/ ou talvez em deslembro por alguma nunca nihilíada
de januárias naves/ noviluas finisterre em teu porto por isso não parta
por isso não porte/ reparta reporte destrince esta macarroníada em
malalíngua antes que/ o portogalo algaraviando-se esperante o brasilisco
e este babelório/ todo desbordele em sarrapapel muito fácil teu entrecho
é simples e/ os subentrechos mais simples ainda alguém poderá falar em
didascália/ uma palavra que termina em álea mas o certo é não diferençar
entre/ motivo ou tema nem apelar para mitemas fabulemas ou novelemas
ou se/ perder no encalço da melhor tradução para récit ou do distingo
entre/ novel e novela nem é útil saber se fábula ou conto-de-fadas é o/
termo que equivale ao russo skaz bichos-da-seda se obsedam até a/ morte
com seu fio e o corcunda só se corrige na cova não se trata/ aqui de uma
equivalenda mas de uma delenda esquiva escava e só/ encontrarás a
mão que escreve que escava a simplitude do simples/ simplicíssimo em
sancta simplicitas põe de lato a literordura deixa/ as belas letras para os
bel'letristas e repara que neste fio de/ linguagem há um fio de linguagem
que uma rosa é uma rosa como uma/ prosa é uma prosa há um fio de
viagem há uma vis de mensagem/ e nesta margem da margem há pelo
menos margem desliga então as/ cantilenas as cantilendas as cantiamenas
descrê das histórias das/ stórias das estórias e fica ao menos com este
menos o resto veremos/ uma garrafa ao mar pode ser a solução botelheiro
de más botelhas/ da vida diva dádiva botelha que o futuro futura pela
escura via/ delle botteghe oscure e quando a maré for subindo você virá
vindo/ e quando a manhã for saindo você virá sendo e enquanto a noite
for/ sumindo você estará rindo pois é lindo e ledo e lido e lendo este
teu/ cantomenos este teu conto a menos sem somenos nem comenos
este canto/ mesmo que já agora é teima e não se faz por menos mas nem
vem que/ não tem se não te serve o meu trem se a canoa tem furo por aí
é/ o futuro morre velho o seguro mas eu combato no escuro e pelo triz/
pelo traz pelo truz pelo trez tanto faz tanto fez minha sina eu que/ sei eu
que pago pra ver se no dois não acerto jogo tudo no três/ e ainda tenho
uma vez esta história é muito simples é uma história/ de espantar não
conto porque não conto porque não quero contar/ cantando cantava o sol
contando contava o mar contava um conto cantado/ de terra sol mar e ar
meu canto não conta um conto só canta como cantar

Juan Gelman (1930–, Argentina)

Born in Buenos Aires to immigrant Ukrainians, Gelman has spent his creative life in the fields of poetry, journalism, and translation. Former editor in chief of the daily *Noticias* and editor of the cultural supplement of *La opinion*, Gelman's left-leaning political tendencies were formed at a young age. As a result of his political militancy, he was exiled from Argentina from 1975 to 1988 and suffered the loss of both his son and daughter-in-law at the hands of the military dictatorship that seized power in 1976. His work is one of the most successful fusions of colloquialism and formal experimentation. PRINCIPAL WORKS: *Poemas* (1969), *Obra poética* (1975), *Poesía* (1985)

CDLVI

Andrew Graham-Yooll, trans.

where do they go those disgraceful swindling
Christians robbing everybody?
to Vietnam the Indies my home
wearing doublet sack combs trinkets and crockery

there are great pastures and good estates for breeding
in these countries to live in prosperous manner
and the city to be peopled will turn out a good seat
for blond killers good people of peace

ha! short of favor and long of vests they wear
and ancient hatreds as good as old
wine are worn by Indians around here
in many a valley and small village

from Peru Tucumán Chile Córdoba Vietnam
in huts of reeds of great beauty
and tame rhea which we raise at home
where we no longer cloth our loins

and they eat out of their own plate
and eat more than us then sleep with us
in beds of their own and later
do not let us sleep

do not let us live
those disgraces do not let us live
neither be good nor tame
nor let rhea grass grow

women still cover up with small rugs
and still need of men to cover more
but scream
in toncote indama zanavirona and lule they scream

idolaters idolaters!
they will buy them with French baubles and cloth
but one will remain
to light the flame and the rancor

with a small white sundial
one will remain

¿adónde van ladrones desuella-caras malos/ cristianos robando todo el
mundo?/ ¿van a Vietnam a las Indias a mi casa/ con jubones talegas penetes
vidrios e loza?// hay grandes pastos y muy buenos asientos para criar/ en
estos países para vivir prósperamente/ y terná buen asiento la ciudad que
se poblare/ con asesinos rubios buena gente y de paz// ¡ha! flaquísimo
favor y camisetas largas visten/ y odios añejos como buen/ vino visten los
indios de por acá/ en muchos valles y pueblos pequeños// del Pirú Tucumán
Chile Córdoba Vietnam/ con cabañas de yerba muy hermosas/ y mansos
avestruces que criamos en casa/ donde ya no tapamos nuestras vergüenzas//
y ella comen en propio plato/ y comen más que nosotros y se acuestan con
nosotros/ en propia cama y después/ no nos dejan dormir// no nos dejan
vivir/ esas vergüenzas no nos dejan vivir/ ni ser buenos o mansos/ no dejan
crecer pasto avestruces// las mujeres se cubren todavía con manta pequeña/
y necesitan todavía de hombre para cubrirse más/ pero gritan/ en toncoté
indama zanavirona y lule gritan// ¡idólatras idólatras!/ las comprarán
con perpiñanes y paños/ pero una quedará/ para encender el rencor y las
brasas// con un relojito de sol de hueso blanco/ alguna quedará

CDLXXXI

Andrew Graham-Yooll, trans.

in a river five leagues at its narrowest
or by snake or reptile or serpent
there is the same danger of death
you never know in these Indies

never will it be known if the remedy was
to enter the woods like starving wolves
axe in hand
with hand gun and automatic

oh! overwhelming need bring the days
and more months and years of this mortal life
so kill reptile or snake if sighted
as being better than a feast for a King

hey compatriots? the blond King eats pheasant
and kingfish in his golden kingdom
but it does not matter really
as none of that matters really

what does is our poverty
three Amerindians of pain is not the same as two
many days we have been stalled with fire passion in the cards
just as animals in this land

oh Indies stuck in the South!
in your face you wore hard anxiety
as in iron and in other things and rescued
the sailing and the rowing for example and dying like animals

the vassals kiss the Royal feet
the free have not even feet to kiss
that is the sense of loss
of catfish monkeys tigers under the sun

but nobody complains
nobody complains
nobody complains in these Indies
a muddy slow yellow
clouded the sky the day before

oh tomorrow! tomorrow!

en río lo más angosto cinco leguas/ y en víbora o culebra o serpiente/ hay
el mismo peligro de morir/ nunca se sabe en estas Indias// nunca se sabe si
el remedio era/ como lobos hambrientos meternos por los bosques/ con el
hacha en la manos/ con el fusil la metra// ¡oh! hartas necesidades traen los
días/ y más los meses y los años de esta vida mortal/ de modo que haber cerca
culebra o víbora y matarla/ es mijor de comer quel Rey// ¿eh compatriotas?
el Rey rubio comer faisán/ y dorado en su reino de oro/ pero no importa en
realidad/ nada de eso importa en realidad// sino nuestra miseria/ tres onas
de dolor no es lo mismo que dos/ muchos días estuvimos parados con tan
fiera pasión en la baraja/ como animales de esta tierra// ¡ah Indias varadas en
el Sur!/ había en tu rostro tarta ansiedá/ así en hierros como en otras cosas y
rescates/ el bogar y el remar por ejemplo y el morir como bestias// los vasallos
besan los Reales pies del señor/ los libres ni pies tienen para besar/ así es la
condición desamparada/ de bagres monos tigres bajo el sol// pero nadie se

queja/ nadie se queja/ nadie se queja en esta Indias/ un silencio amarillo lento
de barro/ tapó el cielo antiyer.// ¡ah mañana! ¡mañana!

XDV

Andrew Graham-Yooll, trans.

he was seen by doctors and doctors
one prodded the kidney spleen source or heart
one the femur pure melancholy
the defeat the coccyx the stomach

some checked the throat and song the nose the demanding plexus
the foot part of the spine with the same fired pause
the arms that looked dry the collecting stomach
the shout the let's go the understanding

no corner or point or stretch or place
did science not visit to see fondle inspect sound violate
they even checked the teardrops
the regrets the sadness

and then?
did anyone find the grief sickness
no one found the sickness
no one found the grief sickness

he was released on a grey day as slow as God
who ambled among all the women
he suffered as they say the nation
no one found the sickness

among elms willows hydrangea damp with cold
he wandered aware at the same time
as he saw the lightning flash of animals
killed at the feet of his shots

lo vieron médicos y médicos/ quien le tocó el riñón esplendida fuente
o corazón/ quien el fémur melancólico puro/ la siquitrilla el coxis el
estómago// algunos le revisaron la garganta canora la nariz el plexo
pedigüeño/ el pie el pedazo la médula con estancias de fuego mesmamente/
los brazos como secos el vientre cobrador/ el grito el vamos el entiendo//
no hubo rincón o sitio o palmo o lugar/ que la ciencia dejara de visitar y ver
y palpar auscultar analizar vejar/ hasta le vieron la lluvita/ el pésame la
triste// ¿y de ahí?/ ¿acaso alguno le encontró la pena enfermedad?/ ninguno
le encontró la enfermedad/ ninguno le encontró la pena enfermedad// lo
dieron de alta un dia gris y lento como Dios/ que giraha entre todas las

mujeres/ sufrió como se dice del pais/ ninguno le encontró la enfermedad//
entre olmos sauces hortensias húmedas de frío/ vagaba al pairo de la vez/
que vio un relámpago de bestias/ muertos al pie de sus balazos

Augusto de Campos (1931–, Brazil)

Experimental throughout his literary development, de Campos employed a fragmented syntax and associated words, phrases, and syllables with specific colors.
Close work with Haroldo de Campos and Décio Pignatari led to his involvement
with concrete poetry around 1958, which gave way to "popcretos," tension-filled
rearrangements of newspaper and magazine cutouts. Campos's visual poetry contains anti-symbols, which are used to criticize the mundane aspects of individuals
and society. He continued working with visual images during the early 1970s, during
which he experimented with "object-poetry." The visual nature of his work allowed
it to be seen and understood in a different vein than his earlier poetry. PRINCIPAL
WORKS: *O rei menos o reino* (1951), *Poemobilies* (1968–1974), *Viva vaia* (1979)

Eggtangle / Ovo novelo

Odile Cisneros, trans.

```
                e g g
            e n t a n g l e d
        new     in     the     old
        a   child   in   the   folds
        confined   in   the   knees
        an    infant    in    fount
        f e t u s   f a s h i o n e d
            in      the      hub
            of the heart


                n u-
            des    of    nothing
            e v e n   t h e   h u m
        an    a    mere    nu-
        mber         of         zero
        raw     child     ingrai
        ned    the    grain    of
            living   flesh   in
            end   nil
```

                              a
              p   o   i   n   t
          where   the   legend
          lies   even   before
          b e t w e e n   b e l l i e s
          when   chests   burn
          breasts   are   fingered
            buttons   in
                   turn

                   n o c -
              turnal   night
          entourage   of   murk
          darkness lacking contour
          death   black   knot   blind
          dream of a naked bat in
          s h a d o w s   e n t a n g l i n g
            him   black   letter
              t u r n i n g   i n t o
                   s u n

ovo/ novelo/ novo no velho/ o filho em folhos/ na jaula dos joelhos/ infante
em fonte/ feto feito/ dentro do/ centro// nu/ des do nada/ ate o hum/ ano
mero nu/ mero do zero/ crua criança incru/ stada no cerne da/ carne viva
en/ fim nada// o/ ponto/ onde se esconde/ lenda ainda antes/ entreventres/
quando queimando/ os seios são/ peitos nos/ dedos// no/ turna noite/ em
tôrno em treva/ turva sem contôrno/ morte negro nó cego/ sono do morcego
nu/ ma sombra que o pren/ dia preta letra que/ se torna/ sol

Eye for an Eye / Ôlho por ôlho

The original, a color collage from magazines, is 50 cm × 70 cm

Colocar a mascara / To Put On a Mask

Translated by Haroldo de Campos

colocaramas
caracolocar
amas**caracol**
oscaramas**car**
acolocarama
s**caracol**oca
ramas**caraco**
locaramas**ca**

```
racolocaram
ascaracoloc
aramascarac
olocaramasc
aracolocara
mascaracolo
caramascara
```

"The masking and unmasking of the poem's process. Like a snail slowly unfolding its going." (Haroldo de Campos, translator)

colocar a máscara = to put on the mask
mascara = mask, (it) masks
mas = but
cara = face
caracol = snail

Jaime Jaramillo Escobar (1932–, Colombia)

Born in Pueblorrico, Colombia, where he lived until the age of three, Jaramillo Escobar retains the memories of political and religious violence from his native town, violence that is still part of everyday life in Colombia. He learned about ver- sicle in the Bible, where he found—after discovering Whitman—"the great voice that I have always thought poetry should be." He read the poets of the world in old newspapers and magazines used to wrap groceries. He was a classmate and friend of Gonzalo Arango, the founder of Nadaism, an adventure he also embraced. At present, he lives scantily, teaching poetry workshops and writing naked, because— as he explains—he has nothing to hide. His is the joyful job of a wizard whose long versicles ooze—according to his countryman Cobo Borda—an "armed innocence" that uses irony and humor to rescue the black, peasant, and Indian voices of his homeland. PRINCIPAL WORKS: *Poemas de la ofensa* (1967), *Sombrero de ahogado* (1984), *Poemas de la tierra caliente* (1985)

The Leather Telegram / El telegrama de cuero

Elizabeth Macklin, trans.

It was my wedding night and I found myself lying already beside my wife
in our ample bed four yards wide before a vast window protected by an iron grille
crafted by the locksmiths of ten Spains, forged in ten Toledos,
and night had no desire at all to come down so the neighbors, out in the
    street, could contemplate our love.

The innkeeper's wife kept on bringing buckets of water and amassing them
in the front garden, not far from the sweet wisterias
and there were ever so many boys and girls perched in the grape arbor.
My naked wife smiled out from beneath my smile,
the bedlinens touched her before my hands did,
and the same with the curtains caught up at either end of the large window,
which flirted out in her direction.
The neighbors' laughter reached us through the grillework, mixed in with
stars and the hollering of the boys,
as is perfectly in keeping with the animated streets of the wedding night, in
front of the house of the new man and wife.
In our bedroom the small vials of essences remained as pure as ever, in front
of the mirrors,
and in actual fact the hubbub of the street, the neighbors' presence, didn't
bother us in the least.
Hurriedly everything and everyone erased itself from before my eyes and all
I had left in my hands was my wife,
whose thighs moved like two copper boa constrictors welded together
into whose joint mouths I ran my own rough fingers.
We occupied a violet kingdom of atmospherics specially prepared by our
friends and relations,
and the innkeeper's wife, ample and beaming, went on amassing buckets of
water in the front garden, opposite the sweet wisterias.
It was the bazaar of love and the young men in gypsy masks shook
tambourines and waved red neckerchiefs
in memory of a drop of blood.
Then we heard, coming out of the cross-street, a cart pulled by four horses
jingling with silver harness rings.
The innkeeper's wife came out to greet it, and exchanged a few brief words
with the new arrivals,
then turned and came to our window, making her way hurriedly through
the crowd with her two long, sturdy arms, not unlike the legs of my wife,
to bring us a telegram tooled in leather, large as a diploma, whose letters in
high relief were perfectly evident to the eyes of everyone present.

Era mi noche de bodas y me encontra-/ ba ya acostado con mi esposa/ en el
amplio lecho de cuatro metros de/ ancho frente a una enorme ventana
pro-/ tegida con rejas de hierro,/ hechas por los cerrajeros de diez Espa-/
ñas, forjadas en diez Toledos,/ y la noche no se quería oscurecer para/
que los vecinos, desde la calle, pudieran/ contemplar nuestro amor./ La
mesonera traía cubos de agua y los/ acumulaba en el antejardín, cerca
de las/ glicinas,/ y había tantos muchachos y muchachas/ que ocupaban
el emparrado./ Mi desnuda esposa sonreía debajo de/ mi sonrisa,/ los
velos del lecho la tocaban antes que/ mis manos,/ y lo mismo los velos

recogidos en los/ extremos del ventanal, que se agitaban/ hacia ella./ Las
risas de los vecinos nos llegaban a/ través de la reja mezcladas con estrellas/
y el grito de los muchachos,/ como corresponde a la animación de la/
calle en la noche de bodas, frente a la/ casa de los esposos./ En nuestra
habitación los frasquitos de/ esencias de conservaban puros frente a los/
espejos,/ y en realidad el rumor de la calle, la/ presencia de los vecinos,
no nos importu-/ naba./ Apresuradamente todo el mundo se me/ borró
y sólo me quedaba mi esposa entre/ las manos,/ cuyos flancos se movían
como dos boas/ de cobre soldadas autógenamente/ por cuyas juntas bocas
yo pasaba mis/ dedos ásperos./ Reinaba un ambiente violeta preparado/
especialmente por nuestros amigos y pa-/ rientes,/ y la señora mesonera,
amplia y sonrien-/ te, acumulaba cubos de agua en el ante-/ jardín, frente
a las glicinas./ Era el bazar del amor y los mozos dis-/ frazados de gitanos
agitaban panderetas y/ pañuelos rojos/ en memoria de una gota de sangre./
Entonces se oyó venir por la boca-calle/ un carro de cuatro caballos con
arandelas/ de plata sonando./ Fue recibido por la mesonera, quien/ habló
algunas breves palabras con los que/ venían/ y luego se dirigió a nuestra
ventana,/ abriéndos paso apresuradamente por en-/ tre la gente con sus dos
largos y robustos/ brazos, semejantes a las piernas de mi es-/ posa,/ para
entregarnos un telegrama labrado/ en cuero, grande como un diploma,
cuyas/ letras en relieve saltaban a la vista de to-/ dos.

Lorenzo Ramos (1960?–, Argentina, Mbyá Guarani)

Of Ramos, oral poet/singer and craftsman, we only know that Carlos Martínez
Gamba, the Argentine author, met him in the city of Puerto Rico (Misiones, Argentina) in 1976 in order to have Ramos dictate this and other poems to him, as sung
in the sacred tradition of the Mbyá. Extremely protective and secretive, the Mbyá,
who now live in Brazil, Paraguay, and the northeast of Argentina, kept their poetic
traditions hidden from missionaries until the twentieth century, when León Cado-
gan, Kurt Nimuendaju, and Pierre Clastres finally learned about them and made
them known to the world. Augusto Roa Bastos has said that they are without
parallel in the Western world in their mystical vision and poetic language. Nevertheless, as this poem attests, the Mbyá of Misiones are rapidly losing their tropical
rainforest and are facing a silent extinction, even as they resist the worldview and
value system of the invaders. PRINCIPAL WORKS: As an oral poet, most of his works
were not recorded.

The Foreigners Lie about What They Want / Jurua kuéry oipota ri teĩa/ Los extranjeros desean engañosamente

W. S. Merwin, trans.

1

The foreigners lie about what they want.
We beg to know how they do it.
We are troubling you so that it will not go on like this,
True Father Namandú, First One.

2

They are angry about the way
the cherished men and the good *jeguakávas* live
they are very angry about the way
the cherished women and the good *jachukávas* live
because it is not the way they live themselves.
We do not have high houses.
We do not have books.
We do not know how to read in their wise papers.
We do not pray to the children of their gods.
We do not have little crosses, certainly.

3

We entrust our consciences to you alone,
True Father Namandú, First One.

4

Even though the foreigners want us to be like them
that is something you did not ordain
Our True Father Namandu, First One.

5

Even though it is like this
the *jeguakávas* who pray as they should
the *jachukávas* who pray as they should
even though they see
even though they hear
things that they cannot help disliking,
they are not overcome with dislike, instead,
they lift the fog of imperfection from around the houses
of those who hear divine words,
they raise up to you the bed onto which divinity descends,
even in the midst of every kind of trouble.

6

The foreigners now and then bring us
spoiled flour,

and moldy corn to eat.
Not even because of this,
because of the spoiled flour,
because of the moldy corn,
because of anything we have seen in your earthly dwelling,
nor anything we hear in your earthly dwelling,
not for any of these things
will we forget you even a little.

7
We come again and again to trouble you so that this will not happen,
True Father Namandú, First One.

8
They use our true words
trying to deceive us,
as when they tell us that the seed of the word-soul
is the guardian angel.

9
Therefore, although the christians are wrong
I listen to them without believing what they say.
That way Our First Fathers
will make many words come to me
to strengthen my spirit.

10
Because things are like this we ask you to hear
our crying once again
around your inaccessible dwelling.
We entrust our consciences to you,
we chant our hymns to you,
True Father Namandú, First One.

1/ Jurua kuéry iopota ri teĩma ojekuéry ñembo'épy/ año año ña ñembo'e./
Oguerojeapo eỹ aguáre romoangeko,/ Ñamandu Ru Ete Tenondegua!//
2/ Ogueropochy pa katuĩ jeguakáva jeayu porangue i reko,/ ogueropochy
pa katuĩ jachukáva jeayu porãngue i reko:/ guírami ojekuéry rami eỹ,/
ndoreropy yvatéi ramo,/ ndoreywyra kuatiái,/ kuatia arandu ndoroikuaái
ramo,/ ore kuruchu i eỹ ramo, je./ 3/ Nde ree meme rojerovia roãmy,/
Ñamandu Ru Ete Tenondegua!// 4/ Ojekuéry rami tamora'e ñande
rerekóramo,/ kova'e nde ere va'ekue ỹ,/ Ore Ru Ñamandu Ete Tenondegua!/
5/ A'e rami ramo jepe,/ jeguakáva oñembo'e porã i va'e,/ jachukáva
oñembo'e porã i va'e,/ oecha ramo jepe,/ oendu ramo jepe oguero katu eỹ
va'erã,/ ndo guero katu pyry eỹi jewy,/ ojapychaka mbaraete porã ty va'e
opy roku rupi,/ oguerojere tatachina reko achy,/ oupi ndéwy ijyvára jerojy

rupa/ opa marangua mbytépy.// 6/ Ywypo amboae i kuéry oguerovaẽ i
jepi/ u'ichĩ reko achy,/ avachi vai kue i roupi i ağua./ A'e raminguáre jepe,/
u'ichĩ reko achy,/ avachi vai kue i,/ mba'eve ko nde ywy reko achy áry
roechávare,/ mba'eve ko nde ywy reko achy áry roendúvare,/ kova'e re raga
ri ty ra'e/ nde egui ore resarái kỹrỹ i va'e rae ỹ ko.// 7/ Kova'e ñemoingo eỹ
ağuáre jewy jewy romoangeko,/ Ñamandu Ru Ete Tenondegua!// 8/ A'e
kuéry, oipuru ore ayvu ete i va'e/ ore mbotawy che wy,/ a'e wy aipo e'i
Ñe'ẽğy Mbyte i, je,/ a'e a Ñe'ẽ Rarõ a.// 9/ A'e rami ramo, jurua kuéry
ojeawy i ramo jepe,/ aendu vei pa i va'e./ A'e rami ramo ae, mbaraete ve
reko rã/ mba'e e'iuka ño eterei va'erã/ Ñande Ru Tenonde kuéry.// 10/ A'e
rami ramo ma, ne amba poata rei katu eỹ re/ rojaeo ñendu jewy va'erã./
Nde ree meme rojerovia ro'ãmy,/ nde guero chapukái,/ Ñamandu Ru Ete
Tenondegua!

1/ Los extranjeros desean engañosamente/ que oremos solamente como
lo hacen ellos./ Para que esto no consigan hacer es que te molesto,/ ¡Padre
Ñamandú Verdadero, el Primero!// 2/ Ellos se enojan muchísimo con la
vida que llevan/ los bienamados y buenos jeguakávas,/ ellos se enojan
muchísimo con la vida que llevan/ las bienamadas y buenas jachukávas:/
porque no es a la manera de ellos,/ no tenemos casas altas,/ no tenemos
libros,/ no sabemos leer en sus papeles sabios,/ no rezamos a los hijos
de sus dioses (santos),/ no tenemos crucecitas, ciertamente.// 3/ Sólo en
ti confiamos en nuestras conciencias,/ ¡Padre Ñamandú Verdadero, el
Primero!// 4/ Aunque los extranjeros quieren que seamos como ellos,/
esto es algo que tú no dispusiste,/ ¡Nuestro Padre Ñamandú Verdadero, el
Primero!// 5/ Aunque esto sea así,/ los jeguakávas que rezan buenamente,/
las jachukávas que rezan buenamente,/ aunque estén viendo,/ aunque
estén escuchando cosas que no pueden sino disgustarles,/ no se disgustan,
sin embargo,/ sino que en torno a las casas de los que escuchan palabras
divinas/ hacen pasear la neblina imperfecta,/ elevan hasta ti el lecho en que
desciende la divinidad/ por en medio de toda clase de males.// 6/ Los
extranjeros nos hacen llegar, de tanto en tanto,/ harina imperfecta,/ maíz
descompuesto, para comerlos./ Ni siquiera por todo esto,/ ni por la
harina imperfecta,/ ni por el maíz descompuesto,/ ni por nada de lo que
vemos sobre tu morada terrenal,/ ni por nada de lo que escuchemos
sobre tu morada terrenal,/ ni siquiera por estas cosas,/ de ti nos hemos
de olvidar aunque sea mínimamente.// 7/ Para que esto no ocurra es que
repetidamente te molesto,/ ¡Ñamandú Padre Verdadero, el Primero!//
8/ Ellos utilizan nuestras palabras verdaderas (ore ayvu ete i)/ porque desean
engañarnos,/ y es así cómo dicen que el germen de la palabra-alma (Ñe'ẽğỹ
Mbyte)/ es el ángel de la guarda (Ñe'ẽ rarõ a.)// 9/ Por consiguiente, aunque
los cristianos se equivoquen,/ les escucho sin hacerles caso./ De esta manera,
para mi gran fortalecimiento espiritual/ me harán decir numerosas palabras/
Nuestros Primeros Padres.// 10/ Por ser así es que a ti te haremos oir/

nuestros sollozos nuevamente/en torno a tu morada inaccesible./ En ti nos confiamos en nuestras conciencias, a ti te entonamos himnos,/ ¡Ñamandú Padre Verdadero, El Primero!

Antonio Martínez (1940?–, Argentina, Mbyá Guarani)

Of the poet Antonio Martínez, called "Pa'i Antonio" by Carlos Martínez Gamba, we know nothing except that his poem, recorded by students in September 1979, focuses on the deforestation and loss of biodiversity, which now, almost thirty years later, are bringing about the extinction of his people. Deprived of their traditional way of life, and pushed out of the rainforest by logging companies into the most miserable quarters of the cities, the Mbyá of Misiones are suffering a covert geno-cide. As the poet says, they were not made to sell the trees. Holding fast to their worldview and poetic vision, the Mbyá prepare for death. PRINCIPAL WORKS: As an oral poet, most of his works were not recorded.

The Words of Pa'i Antonio / Pa'i Antonio ñemoñe'ẽ, frakrãme a
Puraéi / Las palabras de Pa'i Antonio y algunos cánticos, en Fracran
                                                                W. S. Merwin, trans.

1
Now we are as poor as we can be.
Now we are as poor as we can be.
Meat costs too much.
We do not eat cow meat anymore.
And the forests,
the forests are not beautiful anymore.
Now the forests are ugly.
We do not have our forests anymore.
The animals we used to know are gone now.
The deer, the wild pigs, all the rest.
Even if they are still there we do not kill them.
I cannot find myself anymore.
I cannot find myself here anymore.
If the governor can do it,
if this is something he can do,
let him give me some place with many animals.
Even if they are not forests, even if they are not forests,
I do not want them to lend me anything else.
I do not need any more tools.

A place where there are a few more animals
is what I want the governor to give me, if he can.

2

Pa'i Antonio
makes this prayer to Captain Chikú
but from this same place.
He prays to achieve immortality.
He prays because he does not want to die.
It is not the body that is looking for paradise.
With my earthly life I am looking for paradise.

3

So it will be hard
to get us to join in,
we, we the poor inhabitants of the forests,
now, now and from now on,
they will not take our ways from us.
Because our own Lord
made us Guaranis,
to be the little dwellers of the forests.
And now we have no forests.
Unless we buy them, we will have no forests.
And Our Father, Our Father never sold them.
The forests were for the joy of everyone, without exception.

4

And even now, the compassionate lords,
those who have a little compassion,
all they can do is hand us a little money,
those who like us give us a little clothing they do not want.

5

And we were not sent here to be soldiers.
There is no flag for us.
Where is there a flag?
What kind of flag?
We know nothing of such things.

6

And we, we, we,
we poor men,
we Guaranis . . .
And they are rich:
they have plantations, paradise and more,
tea and more,

matte tea and pine groves.
We never had to plant these things.
We do not know how to sell these things.
We never had to sell them.
We were not made to sell trees . . .
And these lords fight among themselves
over a little green laurel tree.
It is true! It is true!
They are greedy about the most useless trees.
The maker of trees
the maker of the earth does not fight over it.
But under the sky
they fight for the earth now:
"It is for me," they say.

7
And now the representative of Our Father,
the representative who came from Our Lord,
if we ask the representative
he will have to give us the forest
even though he may not want to.
If he really is the representative
designated by Our Lord
if it is true that he knows about Our Lord,
and even the poorest among us knows
that what they call municipality
is the representative of Our Lord,
we must ask them for the land,
for a place where we can stay for a time.

8
I will go to the ruins of Santa María.
I will go to Brazil.
Nothing can keep me from going.
Nothing can keep me from going.
Not even good money,
not even gold money can keep me from going.
I used to say that money was nothing but paper
but now I am not afraid of money,
now I know it a little more.
I am afraid of pigs
I am afraid of cows
It can put a hole on me
It can put holes all over me.
Even though I can eat it I am afraid of it.

Even though I can drink cane liquor
we keep drinking the piss of pregnant bitches,
now we are used to drinking jaguar piss.
Nothing on earth makes me happy.

9

What we call the devil,
the devil's dances
they frighten me.
I am here now only for a little while.
I do not know how to plant matte tea.
All I know how to plant is cassava and melon,
squash with fingermarks, sweet potatoes,
that's all I know how to plant.

1/ Ñande ñande poriaupáma,/ ñande ñande poriaupáma./ Epýma cho'o;/
ndaja'uvéimai vaka ro'o./ Ha ka'awy,/ ka'awy naiporai,/ ivaieterei ka'awy:/
ñandéve guara ndaipóri ka'awy./ Vícho jaea, ndaipovéima:/ guachu, taitetu
i a'e ramingua./ Oikóramo jepe, ndajajukái./ Che ndawy'avéima,/ apýpy
ndawy'avéima./ Ikatúramo el goviérno,/ ikatúramo el governador,/ ome'ēne
chéve peteĩ vícho etamivea./ Nda'éiramo jepe ka'awy, nda'éiramo jepe/
toiporukave'ỹ chéve mba'eve:/ tembiporu che aipota rivéma avei/ a vícho
etamivea tomboliga ikatúramo/ chéve el goviérno.// 2/ Pa'i António,/ ha'e
oñembo'e Kapitã Chikúpe,/ péro siémpre ko'ápe./ Ha'e oñembo'e omano'ỹ
ag̃uáme;/ ha'e nomanoséiguinte oñembo'e./ He'ongue ndojekái yváre:/
che, che rekove arojeka./ 3// Ha upévare orekuéra,/ ore ka'awyguami,/
ko'ág̃a, ko'ág̃a, ag̃ýgui ae/ ñande mboje'apa hag̃ua hasy,/ ndoipe'aichéne
ñande sistema./ Ja guarani jepéma Ñandejára opoi ñandéwy,/ guarani
jepéma,/ ka'awýrupi g̃uarãmíma./ Ha na ñande ka'awyvéima;/
ndajajoguáiramo, na ñande ka'awymo'ãi./ Ñande Ru, Ñande Ru novendéi
araka'e;/ a'e javi jawy'a ag̃ua va'ekue ína ka'awy./ 4// Ha ko'ág̃a peve,/
imborayúva karaikuéra, imborajumíva,/ tupamba'e mante ojapo va'erã,/
ao vai kuemi ome'ēne ñande rayúva./ 5// Ha ñandekuéragui konkríto
rã ndoúi araka'e,/ ha ni vandéra ndoikói ñandéve,/ mamo vandéra oĩ,/
mba'eichagua vandérapa oĩ!/ ha upéva ndajaikuaái.// 6/ Ha ore, ñande,
ñande, ñande avami,/ ñande guarani . . . / Ha'ekuéry génte ríko:/ paraíso
umíva, te umíva,/ ka'a, okarivéra:/ umíva nañañotỹi va'erã va'ekue
ñande,/ nañavendekuái,/ ñavende va'erã va'ekue'ỹ./ Ywyra ñande ñavende
va'erãicha ndajaikói . . . / Ha karaikuéra katu peteĩ aju'y yky'íre/ ja
ñorãiróma . . . (aquí, risas femeninas y asentimientos: Añete, añete . . .)/
Ywyra ykýre akate'ỹ./ Ywyra apo hare,/ ywy ñono hare noñorãirõi
ywýre . . . / Ko yvawýpy maẽ ñorãirõma ywýre:/ "Che wýpe g̃uarã," po
e'i.// 7/ Ha rire ag̃y, enkargádo Ñande Ru,/ enkargádo Ñandejáragui ou
va'ekue,/ jepe nome'ẽ rivechéi ñandéwype,/ enkargádope jajeruréramo,/

ome'ẽne ka'awy . . . / Enkargádo Ñandejáragui guare niko,/ añetérmao
Ñandejáragui oikuaáramo,/ teko'achymi jepe jaikuaa munisipalida jaea,/
upéva la encargádo Ñandejárama ína,/ ichupekuére va'erã ywýre,/ mamópa
ñaimemíta.// 8/ Che aháta Sánta Mariáre,/ aháta Brasílre;/ ndaipóri che
joko va'erã,/ ndaipóri che joko va'erã,/ ndaipóri che joko va'erã ína,/
pláta porã,/ pláta de óro ndachejokói./ Che plátape kuatia rive, po ha'e
ragẽ aikowy;/ che pláta ag̃ýguima ndakyychevéi,/ aikuaavéma./ Kurégui
akyyche,/ vakágui akyyche:/ che kutupáne merami,/ che kutupa reegua
rei./ Ho'okue ha'ukuaáva ri akyyche juaeri./ Ag̃y ha'ukuaapáma káña,/
jagua ipuru'áva ty meme ja'u,/ aguara ty rive katuĩma ag̃y japokuaa.//
9/ Ha'ramingua nachembowy' avéimai;/Demóño jaea,/ demoño jeroky,/
che che mongyjéma./Ag̃y i rive ete aĩ./ Nañotỹkuaái ka'a;/ añotykuaa i
va'e manji'o a'e sanjáu año i mante,/ andai kuã rãpẽpẽ i,/ ha'e ramingua
i te ma añotỹ i . . . /(jety i, le advierte una voz femenina,/ y el orador dice
entonces): jety i ramingua i . . . /Jety . . . , batata (risas femeninas).

1/ Nosotros estamos ya completamente pobres,/ nosotros estamos ya
completamente pobres./ Está cara la carne;/ nosotros ya no comemos más
carne de vaca./ Y los bosques,/ los bosques no son hermosos,/ son muy
feos los bosques:/ porque para nosotros ya no hay más bosques./ Eso que
llamamos bichos, ya no existen más:/ venados, cerdos monteses y todos
los demás./ Y aunque existan, nosotros no los matamos./ Yo ya no me
hallo más,/ aquí yo ya no me hallo más./ Si el gobierno puede,/ si puede el
gobernador,/ me ha de dar un lugar en donde abunden los bichos./ Aunque
no sean bosques, aunque no sean,/ que no me presten más nada:/ yo ya no
necesito más herramientas./ Un lugar en que haya un poco más de bichos/
que me consiga, si puede, el gobierno.// 2/ El pa'i Antonio,/ él le reza a
Capitán Chikú,/ pero siempre aquí./ El reza para adquirir immortalidad;/ él
riza porque no quiere morir./ No es su cadáver el que busca el paraíso:/ con
mi vida terrenal yo busco el paraíso.// 3/ Y por eso a nosotros,/ a nosotros
los pobres habitantes de los bosques,/ ahora, ahora, de ahora en más,/ les
será difícil mezclarnos,/ no nos despojarán de nuestro sistema./ Porque
ya guaraníes Nuestro-dueño/ nos largó a nosotros,/ ya guaraníes,/ para ser
pequeños habitantes de los bosques./ Y ya no tenemos más bosques;/ si no
los compramos, ya no tendremos más bosques./ Y Nuestro Padre, Nuestro
Padre, no los vendió nunca;/ para alegría de todos, sin excepción, eran
los bosques.// 4/ Y hasta ahora, los señores compasivos,/ los que tienen
un poco de compasión,/ sólo podrán hacer limosnas,/ ropitas en desuso
nos darán quienes nos quieren.// 5/ Y nosotros no fuimos enviados para
conscriptos,/ ni existe bandera para nosotros,/ ¿donde hay bandera?/ ¿qué
clase de bandera hay?/ esas cosas nosotros las ignoramos.// 6/ Y nosotros,
nosotros, nosotros,/ nosotros, hombrecitos,/ nosotros, guaraníes . . . / Ellos
son gente rica:/ tienen plantaciones de paraíso y demás,/ de té y demás,/
yerbales, pinares:/ esas cosas nosotros no teníamos que plantarlas,/ no las

sabemos vender,/ no teníamos que venderlas./ Nosotros no fuimos hechos para vendedores de árboles . . . / Y los señores, sí que por un arbolito verde de laurel/ ya están peleando./ ¡Es verdad, es verdad!/ Mezquinan los árboles más inservibles./ Quien hizo los árboles,/ quien colocó la tierra, no pelea por la tierra . . . / Pero debajo del firmamento/ ya pelean por la tierra:/ "Es para mí," así dicen.// 7/ Y ahora, el encargado de Nuestro Padre,/ encargado que nos vino de Nuestro-dueño,/ aunque no nos lo quiera dar,/ si al encargado se lo pedimos/ nos ha de dar el bosque./ Si verdaderamente es el encargado/ por designio de Nuestro-dueño,/ si es verdad que él sabe de Nuestro-dueño,/ y hasta los más pobrecitos de entre nosostros/ saben que eso que llamamos municipalidad,/ ése es el encargado de Nuestro-dueño,/ a ellos les tenemos que pedir la tierra,/ el sitio en que habremos de estar brevemente.// 8/ Yo me iré a las ruinas de Santa María,/ me iré el Brasil;/ no hay nada que pueda detenerme,/ no hay nada que pueda detenerme,/ ni el buen dinero,/ ni el dinero en oro podrá detenerme./ Yo antes llamaba al dinero simple papel;/ ahora ya no le tengo miedo al dinero,/ ya lo conozco un poco más./ Tengo miedo del chancho,/ de la vaca tengo miedo:/ me ha de clavar,/ me ha de clavar todo./ Y aunque su carne sé comer, igual le temo./ Ahora yo ya sé tomar caña,/ tomamos constantemente orina de perra preñada,/ ahora ya estamos acostumbrados a beber orina de tigre./ Nada sobre la tierra me proporciona alegría.// 9/ Eso que llamamos demonio,/ los bailes del demonio,/ ya me dan miedo./ Ahora estoy aquí por muy poco tiempo./ No sé plantar yerba;/ sé plantar la mandioca y la sandía solamente,/ el zapallito cruzado de dedos, la batata,/ esas cosas solamente yo las sé plantar.

Aurelio Frez (1920s?–1970s? Chile)

As with most oral poets, little is known about Frez. He was an "alférez" (from the Arabic "rider," standard bearer) a poet/shaman representing his *cofradía*, the religious confraternity of the "baile de chinos," the dance of the servants of the divinity. This ancient ritual, and the structure of the flute that produces the chino sound, can be traced back to the Paracas culture of 600 B.C.E. in Peru, and to the Aconcagua culture of 900–1400 C.E. in Chile. The ritual procession of the chino dancers/flute players advances in two parallel lines, their alférez poet in the middle, singing only when the flutes fall silent. Today it is performed by peasants and fishermen in Spanish for Christian divinities, on sacred dates of the Christian calendar, in thanks to or to request concrete favors from the divine. The improvised verses, quatrains in ten-line stanzas, are a re-oralization of the Bible applied to their daily language and needs. The poem included here is a supplication to the mother of life, the Virgin Mary, to end a drought. PRINCIPAL WORKS: As an oral poet, most of his works were not recorded.

Baile de chinos dancing in La Quebrada, central Chile, May 2003

Mother, Here We Are / Madre, aquí hemos llegado

Peter W. Kendall, trans.

Mother, here we are
with my eternal flag,
honoring you is
the Baile of Petorquita

The Baile of Petorquita,
my heart says to you,
is now in your presence,
I come to ask you a favor

I come to ask you a favor
with great peace of mind,
that you water this sacred earth,
that you bring an end to the drought

That you bring an end to the drought,
I sing asking for your help,
little by little it's running out
the water of Aconcagua

The water of Aconcagua,
I sing by the star of Venus,

so, then, Virgin Mary
bring water soon to this land

Bring water soon to this land,
I ask by all my initials,
the land is drying up
and the wheat fields are too

And the wheat fields are too,
it is written down in history,
you are the all-powerful queen
water, then, this drought-stricken land

Water, then, this drought-stricken land
written so it is,
the grasses are thinning out,
without water what are we going to do

Without water what are we going to do,
wronged by the bottomless pit,
the creeks will all dry up
and the baptismal fountain

And the baptismal fountain,
so it is written,
without water we cannot go on,
no one will be baptized now

I ask you on behalf of this land,
as fast as I can sing,
without water we Christians
will all soon become moors

We ask you for your peace,
give us water without delay
give us, then, Divine Mother,
give us water in abundance

Give us water in abundance,
I sing by the star of Venus,
you have always been the queen
of every single Chilean

You have always protected us
from all kinds of traitors,
when during a time you were
defending the colors

Defending the colors,
my heart prays to you,
I leave the way in good shape now
for another fine *hermanación*.

Madre, aquí hemos llegado/ con mi bandera infinita,/ te ha estado
celebrando/ el Baile de Petorquita// El Baile de Petorquita,/ te dice mi
corazón,/que a tu presencia ha llegado,/ vengo a pedirte un favor// Vengo
a pedirte un favor/ con tanta serenidad,/ que riegues esta tierra santa,/ que
acabe la sequedad// Que acabe la sequedad,/ yo canto porque lo hagas,/ se
está acabando de a poco/ el agua del Aconcagua// El agua del Aconcagua,/
canto por la estrella de Venus/ así pues Virgen María,/ riega pronto este
terreno// Riega pronto este terrena,/ por todas mis iniciales,/ las tierras se
están secando/ y lo mismo los trigales// Y lo mismo los trigales,/ escrito
en la historia está,/ tú eres reina poderosa/ riega pues la sequedad// Riega
pues la sequedad,/ escriturado se ve,/ los pastos van raleando,/ sin agua qué
vamos a hacer// Sin agua qué vamos a hacer,/ injuriados del abismo,/ se
secarán los arroyos/ y la pila del bautismo// Y la pila del bautismo,/ como
así está escriturado,/ sin agua no podemos andar,/ nadie será bautizado// Te
pido por esta tierra,/ en el cantar no demoro,/ que sin agua los cristianos/
todo pues seremos moros// Le pedimos a usted la paz,/ danos agua sin
tardanzâ,/ danos pues Madre Divina, danos agua en abundancia/ Danos
agua en abundancia,/ canto por la estrella de Venus,/ tú siempre fuiste la
reina/ de toditos los chilenos// Tú siempre nos defendiste/ de diferentes
traidores,/ cuando en un tiempo estuviste/ defendiendo los colores//
Defendiendo los colores,/ te ruega mi corazón,/ yo dejo el camino sano/ a
otra linda hermanación.

Alfredo Silva Estrada (1933–, Venezuela)

Poet, translator of French, Portuguese, and Italian, coordinator of literary workshops, and host of cultural radio programs, Silva Estrada was born in Caracas, Venezuela, and studied at the Sorbonne University in Paris. A prophet in his own land
and abroad, he received the National Literary Award from Venezuela and the International Poetry Award from the Liège Biennale in Belgium. According to Eugenio
Montejo, his contemporaries and the younger generations "have always seen in him
a wholehearted dedication to poetry, both as a search for verbal discoveries and as a
sacred guideline for living." Silva Estrada asserts, "I offer readers the transformation
of my life experiences into language. . . . I wish to transform the anecdotal into a
poem, into potential experience." He collaborated with Gego, the great visual artist.

PRINCIPAL WORKS: *De la casa arraigada* (1953), *Los moradores* (1975), *Los quintetos del círculo* (1982)

Grape Harvests / Vendimias

Jen Hofer, trans.

It's the exile of memory
Though the vertebrae ache
It's the exile of memory

Absent memory for astounding things
For the space of things that sing with the blood

Blood singing full-voiced
In the throat which is absence

Absence in the blood crying
The distance of the dead gesture

Dead in the voice and in the astounding thing
Something clambering out of the silence

Silence of wine-drenched clots
Dark sibling singing in the arteries

Arteries in the vertex of an echo in our blood
Hidden apotheosis in absent memory

Absent something submerges memory
Overflowed in sobbing and darkness

Darkness magnetized dazzles
Something that inhabits absent memory

Es el destierro de la memoria/ Aunque duelan las vértebras/ Es el destierro de la memoria// Memoria ausente para las cosas inauditas/ Para el espacio de las cosas que cantan con la sangre// Sangre cantando a toda voz/ En la garganta que es ausencia// Ausencia en la sangre que llora/ La distancia del gesto muerto// Muerto en la voz y en la cosa inaudita/ Algo trepando del silencio// Silencio de coágulos vinosos/ Hermano negro cantando en las arterias// Arterias en el vértice de un eco en nuestra sangre/ Apoteosis oculta en la memoria ausente// Ausente algo hunde la memoria/ Derramada en el llanto y las tinieblas// Tinieblas imantadas deslumbrando/ Algo que habita la memoria ausente

Alfredo Silva Estrada   **403**

Excerpt from The Dwellers / Los moradores

Jen Hofer, trans.

2

In the city that weaves cruelty and sweetness
—Lines of silken mountains with ironclad smoke

In the weave of day in the in-between seasons
The dwellers create space

Space of shelter embodied in the body

They occasion it, they irradiate it
from illuminated repose or blazing watchfulness

They trust in chance's sudden shortcuts
And in paths slowly observed

They inhabit plush colors between gaps
propelling them along slopes of dreams

They capture the volumes of scents
Savoring clusters of new hours

Greedy for the sound forgetting transmutes
They smell symbols and embody silences

3

The dwellers know the calm of being
the exaltation of light

When they hush
They exist in the outstretching of hands

The dwellers wait
While the false exiles reject all hope

. . . .

6

The dwellers baptize chance
And give it names with sweet vowels

With virgin consonants

Bodies that speak themselves in this
labial and resonant light

7

The dwellers present faces fashioned of language

Faces, speech, rising up from the earth

They are not exalted
And yet they possess so much air

So many gusts, sleeping, tamed, freed

With exultant irises and meek fire
They maintain shelter and scare off terror

2/ En la ciudad que trama crueldad y dulzura/ —Líneas de lenes montes
con aherrojados humos—// En la trama del día en entretiempos/
Los moradores crean espacio// Espacio de resguardo incorporado al
cuerpo// Lo suscitan, lo irradian/ Desde el reposo iluminado o la vigilia
ardiente// Confían en los súbitos atajos del azar/ Y en las sendas oteadas
lentamente// Habitan entre brechas los colores mullidos/ Los impulsan
en vertientes de sueños// Apresan los volúmenes de aromas/ Saborean
los racimos de horas nuevas// Avidos del sonido que transmute el olvido/
Olfatean los símbolos y encarnan los silencios// 3/ Los moradores conocen
el reposo de ser/ La exaltación de la luz// Cuando callan/ Existen en
la extensión de la mano// Los moradores esperan/ Mientras los falsos
desterrados niegan toda esperanza// . . . // 6/ Los moradores bautizan el
azar/ Y le dan nombres de vocales dulces// De consonantes vírgenes//
Cuerpos que se dicen en esta luz/ Labial y resonante// 7/ Los moradores
asumen rostros labrados de lenguaje// Rostros, hablas que ascienden
de la tierra// No se subliman/ Y sin embargo tienen tanto aire// Tantas
ráfagas dormidas, domadas, sueltas// Con iris exultante y fuego manso/
Mantienen el albergue y espantan el terror

Gerardo Deniz (1934–, Spain/Mexico)

Born Juan Almela in Madrid, Spain, Deniz escaped the Spanish Civil War to settle in
Mexico, where he has lived most of his life. Today he is regarded as one of the great
poets of Mexico. Octavio Paz wrote, "The sarcasm of Deniz is the art of opening
one's eyes in the midst of collapse." Deniz is a chemist by profession and translator of several languages, including Sanskrit and Russian. PRINCIPAL WORKS: *Adrede*
(1970), *Gatuperio* (1978), *Enroque* (1986), *Alebrijes* (1992), *Poemas poems* (2000)

Meditate / Meditar

Mónica de la Torre, trans.

It should alarm no one that the horizon gathers up behind the leaves volutes
  and clouds as if in a painting by El Greco: such a baroque evening
  is nothing but a dress rehearsal.
(In any case, if we were at the seaport, anyone keen on nautical things
  would adeptly determine by simply glancing at the water's vast
  extension: it is not the time for ring-sails.)
This questionable evening, hanging by its thumbs between the dust and
  the rain
over the gilded ostracism of the immense park, at the edge of lakes covered
  by rotten duckweed (*Lemna minor*),
it will be better if solitude listens to the barrel-organ swollen by whews and
  sighs:
if Descartes walked into a café a timelier silence couldn't be made.
  Sing the oblong tenements, with the faces of ironing women and morons
  behind windows:
sing the libraries where El Nigromante would have spent evenings listening
  to the buzz of flies, or lifting his sharp eyes to the ceiling, plunging into
  the effectual Rorschach of leaks while distant trains dragged their chains;
sing the supreme iron-work of the museum—the tapeworm, the
  hippocampus—and in the brown calligraphy of labels, so many sins
  against the Holy Spirit.
Sing the texts thrown into wastepaper baskets, the fried offal, the amorous
  tactics infringing on the Geneva Convention. And for tomorrow and the
  day after
sing most of all shit, a nitrogenated and hurlable thing.

A nadie debe alarmar que el horizonte acumule detrás de los follajes volutas
y nubes como del Greco: una tarde tan barroca no pasa del ensayo general./
(En cualquier caso, si estuviéramos en el puerto, al atento a cosas náuticas le
bastaría recorrer de un vistazo la vasta extensión de las aguas para asegurar con
suficiencia: —No está el tiempo para baticulos.)/ Esta tarde discutible, colgada
de los pulgares entre el polvo y la lluvia/ sobre el dorado ostracismo del
parque inmenso, a la orilla de lagunas podridas cubiertas de lentejuelas *(Lemna
minor),*/ mejor será que la soledad escuche el organillo henchido de chiflos y
refollamientos:/ si entrase Descartes en un café no se haría un silencio más
propicio./ Cante el barrio cuadrilongo, con caras de planchadoras y anormales
en las ventanas:/ cante las bibliotecas donde el Nigromante hubiera podido
apurar las tardes oyendo zumbar moscas o, alzando al techo la mirada aguda,
abismarse en el Rorschach eficaz de las goteras, mientras lejos los tranvías
arrastraban sus cadenas;/ cante el herraje supremo del museo—la solitaria, el
hipogloso—, y en la caligrafía parda de las etiquetas tantos pecados contra/ el
Espíritu Santo./ Cante los textos al cesto, duelos y quebrantos, tácticas galantes

que violan convenios de Ginebra. Y para mañana o pasado/ cante sobre todo
la mierda, que es cosa nitrogenada y arrojadiza.

The Authoritarian School and How a Respectable Literary Genre Was Born. / La escuela autoritaria y cómo nació un respetable género de literatura.

Mónica de la Torre, trans.

The benches are hard, and the professor is not that bright either. Frequently
    one can tell that he's improvising. That he invents traditions, heroes,
    anatomies,
in order to get by. And in the corridors it is rumored—I've heard it—
that his role is difficult, that he should have been something else,
a Turkish corsair, for example, or a painter of saints in adulterous bedrooms.
    That's no excuse.
The walls of the classroom are left smeared (like Rúnika's portraits in their
    horizon of stations)
with glistening trails, and that platinum is drool squandered
    by the snail-horned mentor
during his inept molluscous fumbling. Lift your paw high, brother rabbit
(if it weren't for you, protein of childhood, I'd rather be silent);
don't let yourself be caught off guard. Let them be held responsible, given
    the case:
"My ears are long; my deeds exude, from wherever one chooses to sniff,
a pronounced vegetarian odor." Yet despite this you're not appreciated
and the teacher allows himself to come in with a rifle
as if he weren't teaching the humanities
but hunting or target shooting. You share our terror, sister marten,
animalesse of an even suit, so smooth that it could be made into the
    softest of paintbrushes,
and of all beings you're the most shot at in Eurasia's forests; you feel that
    the teacher is referring to you, and rightly so,
so you meow your typical excuse of going out for a moment to blow
    the shavings off your pencil sharpener,
you flee and wait nervously under the playground's willoughbies
until class ends and some classmate in love lends you his notebooks
with questionable spelling. (Yet you shouldn't mess around with love;
    careful.)
And you too, brother dromedary, suffer from this jackass professor
who gives you no time to take the air out of your bagpipe
through the melodious little hole, an act which requires concentration and
    space.
That's why all the pupils rose in rebellion. (There are those who practice
    prose or poetry for forty-something years
without ever using the verb to rise. Whoever reads, will understand.)

Gerardo Deniz   **407**

Duras son las bancas, y el profesor tampoco tan lúcido. Con frecuencia se
nota que improvisa. Que falsea tradiciones, héroes, anatomías,/ para salir
del paso. Y si se murmura en los corredores—lo he oído—/ que su papel
de difícil, pues que se hubiera dedicado a otra cosa,/ corsario turco, por
ejemplo, pintor de santos de alcoba adulterina. No es disculpa./ Quedan
los flancos del aula embadurnados (y a la salida los retratos de Rúnika en
su horizonte de estaciones)/ de rastros relucientes y ese platino es baba que
derrochó el cornudo mentor/ en su tentar incompetente de molusco. Alza
en alto la pata, hermano conejo/ (si de ti no se tratase, proteína de la niñez,
preferiría callar);/ no te agarren desprevenido. Que tengan la culpa, dado
el caso:/ "Son largas mis orejas; mi desempeño exhala, por donde oler se
quiera,/ un pronunciado tufo vegetariano." Y sin embargo no se te aprecia/
y el maestro se permite llegar trayendo al hombro una carabina/ como si
no viniese a impartir instrucción humanística/ sino de caza o francotiro.
Compartes el pavor, hermana marta,/ animalesa de homogéneo traje sastre,
suave al grado de que sirve para hacer suavísimos pinceles,/ y eres el ser
más fusilado en las florestas de Eurasia; te sientes aludida, con razón,/ y
maullando la sobada excusa de salir un momento a soplar el sacapuntas,/
huyes y esperas nerviosa bajo los indalecios del patio/ que, conclusa la
clase, algún compañero enamorado te preste sus cuadernos/ de ortografía
insegura. (Mas con el amor no se juega; ojo.)/ También tú, hermano
dromedario, padeces con este profesor pelotudo,/ sin darte tiempo a que
le saques el aire a tu gaita/ por un agujerito melodioso, lo cual requiere
concentración y espacio./ De ahí que los discípulos se sublevaran todos.
(Hay quien ejerce cuarenta y tantos años prosa o verso/ sin emplear ni una
vez el verbo sublevarse. Quien lea, entenderá.)

Threat / Amenaza

Mónica de la Torre, trans.

The only frightful felid is the jeopard,
quietly leaping on high bookcases
with an unequaled knowledge of those loathsome tomes covered in dust
placed on the top shelves so that they're never read.
From these the jeopard extracts its gall, its tricks, its rage;
from up there it surveys, jeopardizes, proceeds,
cautiously marching across the top rails of open doors;
the jeopard seems to recriminate, as Rúnika does
(yet who hasn't loved an ugly woman, and even repeatedly? —I'll usually
    respond.)
It only lunges at what's secure.
Danger, emergency, loosening of the retina are its favorite words
and all is at its mercy, all,

all at stake, in jeopardy, at risk of being bludgeoned over the nape
without knowing it, for never does anyone look where it lurks.
      Interesting trait: the jeopard is mute.

Persuaded by examples such as this one, Rúnika soon converted to
    Christianity,
on top of the chest where she keeps her tights she glued a clipping of
    Saint Olaf
and announced that, at least, she'd become a martyr.

Único félido feo es el jeopardo;/ salta en silencio entre los estantes de más
arriba,/ conoce como pocos esos códigos odiosos cubiertos de polvo/ que
son puestos en las tablas superiores para no leerlos nunca./ De ellos el
jeopardo extrae sus yeles, sus trucos, su saña;/ desde allí mira, jeopardiza,
procede/ marchando cauteloso por el canto de las puertas abiertas;/ pareciera
reprochar, como hace Rúnika/ (mas ¿quién no ha sido bagrero, y aun
repetidas veces?—suelo contestarle)./ Cuando se abalanza es sobre seguro./
Peligro, emergencia, desprendimiento de retina son palabras que prefiere/ y
todo está a su merced, todo,/ todo en jaque o jeopardía y riesgo de percusión
en la nuca/ sin saberlo, pues nadie mira hacia donde él acecha./ Rasgo
curioso: el jeopardo es mudo.// Persuadida por ejemplos como éste, Rúnika
se convirtió pronto al cristianismo,/ en la tapa del cofre de sus mallas pegó
un San Olaf recortado/ y anunció que iba a ser, siquiera, mártir.

Romulus Augustulus / Rómulo Augústulo

Mónica de la Torre, trans.

And after some more talk we agreed that the
wisdom of rats had been grossly overrated,
being in fact no greater than that of men.

I effaced my footprints so well
that they'll never know anything. The sixth century is well on its way,
facing the Propontis a fool married a whore;
these things happen. Once they finish mending my evening
and I return slowly among the shadows in Campania
(frayed, yes, like the skin of Plotinus, by subterranean lava, tainted
by the spite to which I stopped paying attention),
if someone starts pondering grandiosities about sovereigns and generals
with a glimmer of envy in his goat eyes,
I'll say, bearing my childhood in mind but without naming it,
that all the stupidity in the world will be required
to begin another era, enormous and delicate,
and that the powerful will not be different

from those who erect them, hang them, restore them.
This rock was not in the way last night.
Miss Kovalevskaya? She was a logician.

Borré tan bien mis huellas/ que nunca sabrán nada. Ya corre el siglo sexto,/
mirando a la Propóntide un necio casó con una puta;/ cosas que pasan.
Ahora que me acaben de zurcir la tarde/ y regrese despacio entre sombras
de la Campania/ (roída, sí, como piel de Plotino, por lava subterránea,
salpicada/ de enconos a los que ya no atiendo),/ si alguien se pone otra vez
a ponderar enormidades de soberanos y generales/ con un brillo de envidia
en los ojos de chivo,/ le diré, con mi infancia presente y sin nombrarla,/
que hará falta toda la estupidez de todos/ para abrir otra era, enorme y
delicada,/ y que los poderosos no van a ser distintos/ de quienes los erigen,
los cuelgan, los restauran./ Esta piedra no estaba anoche en el camino./ ¿La
Kovalévskaya? Era una lógica.

Sexologic / Sexológica

Mónica de la Torre, trans.

The shoe squeaks
when rubbed
excessively: it can't possibly shine more
—so it squeaks.
There was soap, oil, wax.
That old cartoon by Oski:
a shoeshine man makes smoke come out
of his flannel rag: "Like this, or would you prefer them toasted a bit more?"
The client's persistence is reasonable:
in the words of admirable Dr. Gregorio Marañón
he who wears well-polished shoes, fucks
a lot.
Not even Freud came up with something so sound.

Grita el zapato/ si recibe fricción/ y superflua: no le es posible brillar más/
—entonces grita./ Hubo enjabonadura, grasa, cera./ Aquella vieja caricatura
de Oski:/ un limpiabotas hacía brotar humo/ forzando el trapo: —¿Así o
más tostados?/ Es comprensible la insistencia del cliente:/ según nuestro
estupendo doctor Marañón,/ quien exhibe calzado bien pulido coje/
mucho./ Ni a Freud se le occurió algo tan consecuente.

Isabel Fraire (1934–, Mexico)

Born in Mexico City of an American mother and a Mexican father, she is a poet, essayist, and translator having studied philosophy and letters at the UNAM (National Autonomous University of Mexico) where she was later a professor. She has lived in London and New York City and was the recipient of the prestigious Xavier Villaurrutia Poetry Award. Bilingual since childhood, she has translated works by Pound and Eliot, among others, and has written lucid critical essays about Latin American art and literature. Though politically committed, she does not follow the idea that poets must focus exclusively on social change and has criticized the segregation of literature by race, gender, nationality, or politics. According to Octavio Paz, "Her poetry is a continuous flight of images that dissipate, reappear, and disappear once again—not images in the air, but images made of air. Its clarity is the translucence of the sky high above the ground." PRINCIPAL WORKS: *Poemas en el regazo de la muerte* (1977), *Puente colgante* (1997)

A Moment Captured by a Japanese Painter of the Eighteenth Century Seen in a Moment of the Twentieth Century in a London Gallery / Momento de un dia del siglo dieciocho inmovilizado por un pintor japones visto en un momento del siglo veinte en una galeria londinense

Thomas Hoeksema, trans.

a plump black
bird
not very attractive
headfeathers bristling
from cold
or wind
forcefully clings to
a nearly vertical branch

his posture tells us
that the branch
is being stirred by the wind

the bird
stares
with small black eyes
like seeds
or buttons
at something
outside the scene
we cannot see

un pájaro gordo/ negro/ no especialmente bello/ con las plumas de la cabeza
erizadas por el frío/ o por el viento/ se agarra con fuerza de una rama casi
vertical// por su postura se adivina/ que la rama es mecida por el viento//
el pájaro/ mira/ con sus pequeños ojos negros/ parecidos a semillas/ o
botones// algo/ que está fuera del cuadro/ y nosotros no vemos

Untitled / Sin título

Thomas Hoeksema, trans.

the minute the sun comes out

    everything is beside the point

        it is enough

            to open your eyes
          to stretch your limbs
           like a cat

and all the rest
    philosophical
      political

          systems
    deep moral and
      aesthetic
        disquisitions

are only
    a pleasant means of whiling away the time
beautiful baroque flourishes from which you must retreat
      to recover
        here in the sun
      the simple pleasure of your

            own

             skin

en cuanto sale el sol// todo sale sobrando// basta/ con abrir los ojos/
desperezarse/ como un gato// y todo lo demás/ los sistemas/ filosóficos/
políticos/ las profundas disquisiciones/ éticas/ estéticas// son sólo/ una
manera agradable de pasar el rato/ bellos garigoleos barrocos de los cuales hay
que regresar/ para recuperar aquí en el sol/ el goce simple de la propia piel

"Housing Complex" / "Complejo habitacional"

Thomas Hoeksema, trans.

I

morning rises slowly like a mist climbing
            and spreading though the air

a child crosses   squares of green grass
            running   jumping   running
                        carrying
                        a shopping bag in its hand

II

the apartment buildings
                        present flat rectangular   surfaces

            the windows are equipped with gray steel shutters
            that close   or open
                        like lids
                                    each room a box

the garden   of smooth green grass   like a new carpet
            is framed by regular rows of identical trees
                        that cast an oblong shadow
                        like a wall

III

no one speaks to each other here   a neighbor tells me
            breaking the rule
                        after a year
at predetermined hours
                        two or three old men and a child
                        take their respective dogs out for a walk
                  one of them is in the habit of
                                    letting the dog run loose
                  the others stop
                  each time
                                    the dog stops

IV

usually silence prevails
                        broken only by the noise of traffic
            that swells
                        at the hours when offices open or close

but occasionally
            through paper-thin walls   one overhears
                        a bitter violent   discussion

full of resentment
    for a ruined life
        melodramatic panting
            background music
        from the television set

V

a block away
        large bulldozers
        busily demolish a small grove
in order to erect a mass of buildings
        exactly like this one

I/ la mañana surge lentamente como un vapor que se eleva/ y se difunde
en el aire// cruza los cuadros de verde pasto/ saltando corriendo saltando/
un niño/ con una bolsa de mandado en la mano// II/ los edificios de
departamentos/ presentan superficies planas rectangulares// las ventanas
tienen contraventanas grises/ que se cierran o abren/ como tapas/ cada cuarto
una caja// el jardín de pasto liso y verde como alfombra recién comprada/
está encuadrado por filas regulares de árboles idénticos/ que arrojan una
sombra continua/ como la de un muro// III/ aquí nadie se habla me dice
una vecina/ que después de un año/ ha roto con la regla/ a horas previsibles/
dos o tres viejos y una niña/ sacan a pasear sus respectivos perros/ uno de
ellos acostumbra/ soltarle la cadena/ los otros se detienen/ cada vez/ que se
detiene el perro// IV/ en general reina el silencio/ sólo roto por el ruido del
tráfico/ que aumenta notoriamente/ a las horas de entrada y salida de las
oficinas// pero ocasionalmente/ se oye a través de las paredes/ una discusión
agria violenta/ cargada del resentimiento/ de una vida estropeada/ o la música
de fondo/ melodramática y jadeante/ de la televisión// V/ a una cuadra de
distancia/ grandes máquinas/ se ocupan de arrasar un bosquecillo// para
levantar un gran conjunto de edificios/ idénticos a éste

Sergio Mondragón (1935–, Mexico)

Born in Cuernavaca, state of Morelos, Mexico, he is a poet, cultural activist, translator, and journalist by profession. He was co-founder and editor of the legendary
magazine *El corno emplumado* (1962–1969). After the Night of Tlatelolco—the
massacre of students by the governement—he was forced to travel to the United
States (where he was a university professor) and to Japan (where he worked as
correspondent for the newspaper *Excélsior* and discovered Zen Buddhism, a practice he has incorporated into his life). Upon his return to Mexico, he recaptured

the indigenous world and warned that Indians "are a human reserve . . . they are waiting for us, though we haven't yet embraced their contribution. . . . I hope we won't destroy them and will still have a chance to recognize them within ourselves and without, and I hope we treat them as they deserve to be treated." A promoter of literary workshops and poetry readings among the Mexican working class, he launched large printings of books by one hundred renowned authors. According to Mondragón, "Modern poetry is a way to salvation, a therapy of words or, perhaps, of the image contained in just one word—the word that can reinvent the world and fuse our being with the true reality of things." PRINCIPAL WORKS: *Yo soy el otro* (1964), *Pasión por el oxígeno y la luna* (1982), *Las eras imaginarias* (1998)

Excerpt from Exodus of the Gods / Éxodo de los dioses
James O'Hern, trans.

I
Gods of our kingdoms,
we have left
   to cultivate other lands
      to serve other tables
         to wash other dishes.

With the weight of our myths, mounted on our beasts, with *huaraches* and *petates* strapped across our backs, with *gordas* and *chile martajado* as our only *itacate,* we have left this place.

Now we live over there, our skin darker in shiny new suits, impeccably clean, using always the two sides of our brain in unison, like our sister *Tonantzin* taught us:

        to survive
        we have taken the memories with us
        left behind the clay pots
        abandoned our mothers and our wives
        all our small children
        our palaces and our huts
        and all our dogs.

We have left with you, little brothers, that which was ours. And it was not the hunger, that we were already used to, but the sadness that drove us out of this land: to know that you are ashamed of us, that you would like to see us dead, that you abhor our blood, that is the same that flows happily through your veins . . . Blood that runs like in *acequias* of ancient times, cleanly, connecting the kingdoms, feeding the birds, the corn entwined with squash and beans, sustaining the many towns. We have left this place

because now you don't want us
you never wanted us
and are ashamed of our languages
which sound like bells in the towers and the altars
of our grandparents and mothers
who have also forgotten us.

II

When are we coming back? Skillful at being shameless, impeccable in
robbery, adept at lying coupled with sublime stupidity, our descendants
don't want us here. Why should we come back? Our lands, fertile before,
are now dead, eaten by the nitrates or taken over by landowners, and our
families wander the city streets like skeletal phantoms begging for charity:

> "... *rumor of bare feet over the dust* ..."
>
> El Cántaro Roto.
>
> O. Paz

dust of the pavement, dust of soot, sticky and mortal, enters the blood and
lungs of all the people in this land who walk about disoriented to the
point of not knowing who they are, nor from where they come from, nor
of their true heritage.

Perhaps we will return when our little brothers wake from their beloved
nightmares: in which our land looks like the land where we wash dishes,
and Mexicans look like our present bosses, having forgotten forever their
origins, denying we are their ancestral gods ...

III

The grievance: first they seized our land and decided we should die of
hunger. Then, they cornered us into the high crossroads or pushed
us to the bare mountains where stone explodes in the sun. There,
miraculously, we were able to survive but there is hardly any trace left of
our altars and our wonders.

. . . .

Since then, we Mexicans are here, all against each other, while the world
turns indifferent to our troubles, our needs, and destiny. Regarding us,
if at all, with curiosity while they (the world) speaks (demeaningly), in
perfect Texan English, of our proud Capital which used to be a mecca of
brilliance and vitality.

> "... *Mexico City is a place you want to leave as soon as you can* ..."

Because, besides the dirt, there are so many barbaric acts here ... Things,
being as they are, we have no choice but to emigrate and look for
jobs and more dignity over there. Because, despite the risks of exodus:
hatred, discrimination, and the Migra. Even though this may seem
incredible, we feel more highly considered there than in Mexico.

So, we leave you, with your Secretary of Agrarian Counter-reform, with your
protection rights in agriculture, planned for the purpose of stealing rights
while guaranteeing impunity. As it is with other laws designed to protect
the elegant delinquents and other shameless nationals, mostly politicians
who continue to make up the numbers of the so-called decent people of
Mexico. We leave you (little brothers) with your new "international look,"
the country converted into a garbage dump with your new democracy,
your piles of political business deals, your pyramids of legislators, judges
and privileged bureaucrats in a country that survives (only) in misery: we
leave you with your impeccable macroeconomy of horrific consequences:

> 20 million terminally hopeless;
> 50 million in extreme poverty;
> 20 million plain poor;
> 10 million with burnt asses;
> 5 million decent and proper ones; and
> 100 thousand top millionaires, very decent, with their
> 50 thousand bank accounts, millions of dollars each; this
> without counting accounts in Switzerland, the Cayman
> Islands, nor those in . . .

IV

So you disapprove of our version of things and find our account rhetoric
and our images pretentious and poetic? Then, stay with your privileged
bureaucracy and your world of finances and global businesses, with your
restaurants and "first world" developments as you like to call them,
with endless exclusive beaches, of which 99 percent of Mexicans cannot
enjoy, and where they are allowed access only as maids with a minimum
wage; and with your buildings, the tallest in Latin America, and your
self-appointed title of the Ninth World Economy, and with . . .

In the end it will be our ancestral powers, converted into pure human
energy for creativity and life, which will pull this country out of the
ruins it is now. With all of you, little brothers, trapped inside it, and only
with you now, because we don't live here anymore . . .

Huaraches: indian sandals
Petate: a woven sleeping mat
Gordas: colloquial for thick corn tortillas
Chile martajado: spicy sauce made with freshly ground chili
Itacate: traveling provisions for the journey
Tonantzin: an Aztec lunar mother goddess associated with the Virgin of Guadalupe
Migra: colloquial name for the U.S. (INS) Immigration and Naturalization Service

I// Dioses de nuestros reinos,/ nos hemos ido de aquí/ a cultivar otras
tierras/ a servir otras mesas/ a lavar otros platos.// Con nuestras cargas

de mitos, montados en nuestras bestias, con los huaraches y los petates enrollados y terciados, con gordas y chile martajado como único itacate, nos/ hemos ido de aquí.// Ahora vivimos allá, más morenos en nuestras nuevas vestiduras, relumbrando de limpios, utilizando como siempre los dos lados de nuestro cerebro al unísono, como nos enseñó nuestra hermana Tonantzin:// para sobrevivir/ hemos llevado con nosotros los recuerdos/ hemos dejado atrás los tepalcates/ hemos abandonado a nuestras madres y/ a nuestras esposas/ a todos nuestros hijitos/ nuestros palacios y nuestras chozas/ y a todos nuestros perros.// Les hemos dejado a ustedes, hermanitos, lo que era nuestro. Y no fue el hambre, a la que ya nos acostumbramos, sino la pena, lo que nos expulsó de esta tierra: saber que se avergüenzan de nosotros, que quisieran vernos muertos, que abominan de nuestra sangre, que es la misma que fluye alegre por sus venas . . . Sangre que corre como corrían antaño las acequias, limpiamente, conectando los reinos, alimentando a las aves, a las milpas entreveradas de calabazas y habas, llevando sustento a los muchísimos pueblos. Nos hemos ido de aquí// porque ya no nos quieren/ ni nunca nos han querido/ y se avergüenzan también de nuestras lenguas/ sonoras como campanas en las torres/ y en los altares/ de nuestros tatas y nuestras madrecitas/ que también se han olvidado de nosotros.// II/ ¿Que cuándo vamos a volver? Hábiles en las sinvergüenzadas, impecables en el despojo, únicos en la mentira que va pareja con una sublime estupidez, los descendientes no nos quieren aquí. ¿A qué vamos a volver? Nuestras tierras antes fértiles ahora están muertas, comidas por el salitre o en manos de los terratenientes, y nuestras familias recorren como fantasmas adelgazados las calles de las ciudades solicitando caridad:// " . . . *rumor de pies descalzos sobre el polvo* . . . " // el polvo del pavimento, un polvo de hollín, pegajoso y mortal, que se mete en la sangre y los pulmones de todos los habitantes de esta tierra, que andan desorientados hasta el punto de ya no estar seguros de quiénes son, ni de dónde han venido, ni cuál es su verdadera filiación.// Quizá volvamos cuando los hermanitos hayan despertado del más querido de sus sueños aterradores: que nuestra tierra se parezca a la tierra donde nosotros lavamos los platos, y que los mexicanos se parezcan a nuestros patrones actuales, olvidados para siempre de su origen, que somos nosotros, sus dioses ancestrales . . . // III/ El agravio: primero nos despojaron de la tierra y decidieron que nos muriéramos de hambre. Luego nos arrinconaron en las encrucijadas de la sierra o nos empujaron hacia los cerros pelones donde las piedras se revientan con el sol. Allí de milagro hemos podido resistir; pero de nuestros altares y nuestros prodigios, apenas si queda rastro.// . . . // Y allí nos tienen desde entonces a los mexicanos, todos contra todos, mientras el mundo rueda indiferente a nuestros problemas y a nuestras carencias, y a nuestro destino, mirándonos en todo caso con curiosidad, mientras dice (el mundo) en perfecto inglés tejano y refiriéndose a nuestra orgullosa Capital, otrora emporio de frescura y vitalidad:// " . . .

Mexico City is a place you want to leave as soon as you can . . . "// Porque además de la mugre, hay tantas otras barbaridades que enseñorean por aquí . . . Así las cosas, no nos ha quedado otra que emigrar a conseguir trabajo allá, y de paso vivir más dignamente allá, afrontando el riesgo del éxodo, y el odio, y la Migra, y la discriminación. Ya que a pesar de eso, y aunque parezca increíble, allá nos sentimos mejor considerados que en México.// Allí los dejamos pues con su Secretaría de la Contrareforma Agraria y con su derecho de amparo en materia agraria, que está pensado para consumar el despojo y garantizar la impunidad, al igual que sus muchas otras leyes, diseñadas para que los delincuentes elegantes y todos los otros grandes sinvergüenzas nacionales, políticos en su mayoría, sigan engrosando las filas de la gente decente de México, como la llaman ustedes. Los dejamos con su nuevo "look" internacional y con el basurero en que está convertido el país, y con su nueva democracia y su montón de negocios políticos, con sus pirámides de legisladores, jueces y burócratas privilegiados en un país que sobrevive en la miseria: los dejamos con su macroeconomía impecable, de consecuencias espeluznantes:// 20 millones de desahuciados;/ 50 millones en extrema pobreza;/ 20 millones de pobres a secas;/ 10 millones con el rabo chamuscado;/ 5 millones muy acá, y muy decentes, con sus 50 mil/ cuentas bancarias de millones de dólares cada una, eso sin contar las de Suiza, ni las de Islas Caimán, ni las de . . . // IV/ ¿Que no les gusta nuestra versión de los hechos y que son retóricas nuestras cuentas y nuestras imágenes pretendidamente poéticas? Quédense entonces con su burocracia privilegiada y con su mundo de finanzas y negocios globalizados, con sus restaurantes y desarrollos residenciales de "primer mundo" como ustedes mismos los nombran, con sus interminables playas exclusivas de las que el 99% de ustedes no puede disfrutar y a las que sólo se les permite el acceso para que oficien como sirvientes de salario mínimo; y con su edificio más alto de América Latina, y con su título auto-otorgado de Novena Economía Mundial, y con . . . // Serán al final nuestros poderes ancestrales convertidos en pura energía humana para la creatividad y la vida lo que saque a este país del marasmo en que se encuentra, con todos ustedes, hermanitos, atrapados en él, y sólo con ustedes por ahora, porque nosotros ya no vivimos aquí . . .

Susana Thénon (1935–1991, Argentina)

An Argentine poet, translator, and artistic photographer, Thénon embarked into a lonely investigation of the strangeness of language. Among her unpublished work at the time of her death are *Ensayo general* and *Papyrus*. Her work has been translated in many European and American literary journals. In her native city of Buenos Aires, she is highly regarded as an original, important member of the "Generation of the '60s." PRINCIPAL WORKS: *Edad sin tregua* (1958), *De lugares extraños* (1967), *Obra completa* (1987), *Distances* (1994)

Poem with Simultaneous Translation Spanish–Spanish / Poema con traducción simultánea Español–Español

Renata Treitel, trans.

Christopher
    (Christ bearer)
son of a humble wool carder
    (son of someone who looked for wool to card)
set sail from the port of Palos
    (club in claw he set off)
not before persuading Her Majesty Queen
Isabella the Catholic of the goodness of the enterprise
he had conceived
    (not before persuading Her Royal Highness
    die Königin Bessy of the Logistics to pawn
    her crown at the greasy joint of Blumenthal *con-verso*)
even if gallons and gallons of
genuine ancient blood, RH factor negative, would flow
    (even if it would cost blood sweat and antipodal
    tears)
they put to sea
    (they put on seals)
and after months and months of munching alone
oxymoron in search of the coy orb
    (and after days and days of chewing Yorkshire pudding
    and a penguin to boot on Sundays)
someone cried land
    (no one cried *thálassa)*
they stepped ashore
in 1492 A.D.
    (they pissed galore
    in 1982 A.D.)
chiefs were waiting
in the raw

genuflecting
>   (big shots were waiting
>   stark naked
>   on their knees)
Christopher cocked the missal
>   (Christopher fired the missile)
told his peers
>   (whispered to his thugs)
cunt
>   (fuck)
see here the new worlds
>   (see here the new dudes)
keep them
>   (loot them)
for God and Our Queen
>   (for God and Our Queen)
A M E N
>   (O M E N)

Cristóforo/ (el Portador de Cristo)/ hijo de un humilde cardador de lana/
(hijo de uno que iba por lana sin cardar)/ zarpó del puerto de Palos/ (palo
en zarpa dejó el puerto)/ no sin antes persuadir a Su Majestad la Reina/
Isabel la Católica de las bondades de la empresa/por él concebida/ (no sin
antes persuadir a Her Royal Highness/ die Konigin Chabela la Logística de
empeñar/la corona en el figón de Blumenthal con-verso)/ así se vertiesen
litros y litros de/ genuina sangre vieja factor RH negativo/ (así costase sangre
sudor y lágrimas/ antípodas)/ se hicieron a la mar/ (se hicieron alamares)/
y tras meses y meses de yantar solo/ oxímoron en busca de la esquiva
redondez/ (y tras días y días de mascar Yorkshire pudding/ y un pingüino
de añadidura los domingos)/ alguno exclamó tierra/ (ninguno exclamó
thálassa)/ desembarcaron/ en 1492 A.D./ (pisaron/ en 1982 A.D.)/ jefes
esperaban/ en pelota/ genuflexos/ (mandamases aguardaban/ desnudos/ de
rodillas)/ Cristóforo gatilló el misal/ (Christopher disparó el misil)/ dijo a sus
pares/ (murmuró a sus secuaces)/ coño/ (fuck)/ ved aquí nuevos mundos/
(ved aquí estos inmundos)/ quedáoslos/ (saqueadlos)/ por Dios y Nuestra
Reina/ (por Dios y Nuestra Reina)/ AMÉN/ (OMEN)

Nuptial Song / Canto nupcial

Renata Treitel, trans.

i got married
i got married to myself
i said yes
a yes that took years to arrive
years of unspeakable suffering
crying with the rain
locking myself up in my room
because i—the great love of my existence—
was not calling myself up
was not writing to myself
was not visiting myself
and sometimes
when i dared call myself
to say: hello, am i OK?
i would deny myself

i even managed to write my name in a list of bores
i did not really want to join
because they babbled too much
because they'd not leave me alone
because they'd fence me in
because I could not stand them

at the end i did not even pretend
when I needed myself

i intimated to myself
nicely
that i was fed up

and once i stopped calling myself
and stopped calling myself

and so much time went by that I missed myself
so i said
how long has it been since my last call?
ages
must have been ages
and i called myself up and i answered and could not believe it
because even if it seems incredible
i had not healed
i had only shed blood

then i told myself: hello, is it me?
it's me, i told myself, and added:
such a long long time no see
me from myself myself from me

do i want to come home?

yes, i said

and we got together again
peacefully

i felt good together with myself
just like me
i felt good together with myself
and so
from one day to the next
i got married and i got married
and am together
and not even death can separate me

me he casado/ me he casado conmigo/ me he dado el sí/ un sí que tardó
años en llegar/ años de sufrimientos indecibles/ de llorar con la lluvia/ de
encerrarme en la pieza/ porque yo—el gran amor de mi existencia—/ no
me llamaba/ no me escribía/ no me visitaba/ y a veces/ cuando juntaba
yo el coraje de llamarme/ para decirme: hola, ¿estoy bien?/ yo me hacia
negar// llegué incluso a escribirme en una lista de clavos/ a los que no
quería conectarme/ porque daban la lata/ porque me perseguían/ porque
me acorralaban/ porque me reventaban// al final ni disimulaba yo/ cuando
yo me requería// me daba a entender/ finamente/ que me tenía podrida//
y una vez dejé de llamarme/ y dejé de llamarme// y pasó tanto tiempo que
me extrañé/ entonces dije/ ¿cuánto hace que no me llamo?/ añares/ debe
de hacer añares/ y me llamé y me atendí yo y no podia creerlo/ porque
aunque parezca mentira/ no había cicatrizado/ solo me había ido en sangre/
entonces me dije: hola, ¿soy yo?/ soy yo, me dije y añadí:/ hace muchísimo
que no sabemos nada/ yo de mí ni mí de yo// ¿quiero venir a casa?// sí,
dije yo// y volvimos a encontrarnos/ con paz// yo me sentía bien junto
conmigo/ igual que yo/ que me sentía bien junto conmigo/ y así/ de un
día para el otro/ me casé y me casé/ y estoy junto/ y ni la muerte puede
separarme

Roque Dalton (1935–1975, El Salvador)

Born in Quezaltepeque, El Salvador, the illegitimate child of an American bandit and a local nurse, Dalton joined the liberation movements of his country at an early age. He studied law and traveled extensively. A poet, essayist, and journalist, he addressed his brilliant, humorous irony equally to the political left and right. His openness and irreverence made him one of the most widely read poets of the 1960s, and his popularity was confirmed by the Casa de las Americas Prize for Poetry in 1967. He returned to El Salvador in the 1970s and was murdered by his own guerrilla companions. Since then he has become a mythical figure in Latin American letters. PRINCIPAL WORKS: *Mía junto a los pájaros* (1958), *El mar* (1961), *La ventana en el rostro* (1961), *El turno del ofendido* (1962), *Los testimonios* (1964), *Taberna y otros lugares* (1969), *Un libro levemente odioso* (1971), *Miguel Mármol* (1972), *Poemas clandestinos* (1973), *Historias prohibidas de pulgarcito* (1974), *Pobrecito poeta que era yo* (1976)

No, I Wasn't Always This Ugly / No, no siempre fui tan feo

James Graham, trans.

The truth is my nose got broken
by Lizano the Costa Rican who hit me with a brick
because I said it was obvious there was a penalty
and he yelled no and no and no
I'll never turn my back on a Costa Rican soccer player again
Father Achaerandio nearly died of fright
because when it was over there was more blood than on an Aztec altar
later Quique Soler hit me right in the eye
he threw his rock with the most perfect aim you can imagine
of course we were only trying to imitate the taking of Okinawa
but it shattered my retina
I had to spend one month lying absolutely still (at eleven years old!)
I went to Dr. Quevedo in Guatemala and also saw Dr.
Bickford who was wearing a red wig
that's why I sometimes squint
and coming out of a movie I look like a drug addict waiting for a fix
the other reason is that I was hit by a bottle of rum
María Elena's husband threw at me
really I wasn't trying to get fresh
but every husband is a trip
and if we take into account his thinking I was an Argentine diplomat
we'd have to thank God
the other time was in Prague and was never solved
four punks jumped me in a dark alley

two blocks from the Ministry of Defense
and four from the Police Headquarters
it was the night before the Party Congress started
so someone said it was a protest against the Convention
(in the hospital I met two other delegates
who'd gotten out of the respective assaults
with more broken bones than ever)
someone else said that the CIA wanted to make me pay for my jailbreak
others that it was really a show of anti–Latin American racism
and a few more that it was simply the universal desire to steal
Comrade Soboloff dropped by to ask me
if it wasn't because I'd touched the ass of a woman walking with someone else
and then he went off to the Interior Ministry to protest
on behalf of the Soviets
in the end nothing turned up
and giving thanks to God once again
I kept on as plaintiff right up to the end
in a criminal investigation in Kafka's homeland
in any case (and that's why I keep going on about it now)
I ended up with my Inferior Maxiliar smashed to bits
a severe cerebral concussion
a month and a half in the hospital and
another two months washing down my meals even the beefsteak was purée
the last time I was in Cuba
I was coming down a hillside in the rain
with an M-52 in my hands
all of a sudden a bull came charging out of nowhere
my legs got tangled up in the underbrush and I started to fall
the bull went right by me but as he was a big lazy brute
he didn't bother to come back to finish me off
it wasn't necessary in any case because
as I've been telling you I fell on top of the rifle
and it didn't know any better than to bounce back, like a revolution in Africa
it broke my zygomatic arch into three pieces
(very important for the aesthetic resolution of the cheeks)
That explains at least part of my problem.

Lo que pasa es que tengo una fractura en la nariz/ que me causó el tico
Lizano con un ladrillo/ proque yo decía que evidentemente era penalty/ y
él que no y que no y que no/ nunca en mi vida le volveré a dar la espalda a
un fubolista tico/ el padre Achaerandio por poco se muere del susto/ ya que
al final había más sangre que en un altar azteca/ y luego fue Quique Soler
que me dió en el ojo derecho/ la pedrada más exacta que cabe imaginarse/

claro que se trataba de reproducir la toma de Okinawa/ pero a mí me tocó ruptura de la retina/ un mes de inmovilización absoluta (ia los once años!)/ visita al doctor Quevedo en Guatemala y al doctor/ Bidford que usaba una peluca colorada/ por eso es que en ocasiones bizqueo/ y que al salir del cine parezco un drogadicto desvelado/ la otra razón fue un botellazo de ron/ que me lanzó el marido de María Elena/ en realidad yo no tenía ninguna mala intención/ pero cada marido es un mundo/ y si pensamos que él creía que yo era un diplomático argentino/ hay que dar gracias a Dios/ la otra vez fue en Praga nunca se supo/ me patearon cuatro delincuentes en un callejón oscuro/ a dos cuadras del Ministerio de Defensa/ a cuatro cuadras de las oficinas de la Seguridad/ era víspera de la apertura del Congresso del Partido/ por lo que alguien dijo que era una demonstración contra el Congreso/ (en el Hospital me encontré con otros dos delegados/ que habían salido de sus respectivos asaltos/ con más huesos rotos que nunca)/ otro opinó que fue un asunto de la CIA para cobrarse mi escapatoria de la cárcel/ otros más que una muestra de racismo anti-latinoamericano/ y algunos que simplemente las universales ganas de robar/ el camarada Sóbolev vino a preguntarme/ si no era que yo le había tocado el culo a alguna señora acompañada/ antes de protestar en el Ministerio del Interior/ en nombre del Partido Soviético/ finalmente no apareció ninguna pista/ y hay que dar gracias a Dios nuevamente/ por haber continuado como ofendido hasta el final/ en una investigación en la tierra de Kafka/ en todo caso (y para lo que me interesa sustentar aquí)/ los resultados fueron/ doble fractura del maxilar inferior/ conmoción cerebral grave/ un mes y medio de hospital y/ dos meses más engullendo licuado hasta los bistecs/ y la última vez fue en Cuba/ fue cuando bajaba una ladera bajo la lluvia/ con un hierro M-52 entre manos/ en una de esas salió de no sé dónde un toro/ yo me enredé las canillas en la maleza y comencé a caer/ el toro pasó de largo pero como era un gran huevón/ no quiso volver para ensartarme/ pero de todos modos no fue necesario porque/ como les iba contando yo caí encima del hierro/ que no supo hacer otra cosa que rebotar como un revolución en Africa/ y me partió en tres pedazos el arco cigomático/ (muy importante para la resolución estética de los pómulos)/ Eso explica por lo menos en parte mi problema.

The Country—Sir Thomas / El país—Sir Thomas

James Graham, trans.

In this sunlight
I look like the raw belly of a fetus:
As skinny as the horizon on bare hills,
down on my knees reaching out for a cloud,

full of its color dampened by someone else's spit.

This country is a steel thorn.
I don't think it exists except in my drunken mind,
certainly no one in England has ever heard of it.

Ah whirlwind full of poisonous snakes,
noontime that lasts a century!

To get to the solemn nighttime alive
with a permanent halo,
to be stabbed in the heart
by twelve drunken peasants,
to go down into a countryside of wild beasts
just to prepare one cup of coffee,
all that is absolutely natural around here!

If only a man could hold on to his religion!

Parezco bajo este sol/ la barriga colorada de un feto:/ flaco como el
horizonte de cerros pelados,/ arrodillado en procurra de una nube/ y lleno
de su color mojado por extraña saliva.// Este país es una espina de acero./
Supongo que no existe sino en mi borrachera,/ pues en Inglaterra nadie
sabe de él.// Oh torbellino de víboras,/melodía del tamaño de un siglo!//
Llegar vivo a la solemne noche/ con un halo indeleble,/ ser apuñalado en
el corazón/ por doce peones borrachos,/ bajar al territorio de las fieras/ para
prepararse una taza de café,/ todo es aquí absolutamente natural!// Si solo
conservara uno la fe!

Toadstools VIII / Los hongos VIII

Hardie St. Martin, trans.

In my last jail I prayed on two different occasions. Inconsistent, I know,
  in a middle-aged Communist but true all the same. What will go on
  puzzling me for the rest of my life is not that personal concession to fear
  but something I'd call the chance happening of extraordinary things.
  The first, everybody knows, was when the earthquake split open the
  wall of my cell. The second was when I was told they'd kill me the next
  day and smear the red ghost with all the shit allowed within the limits
  of the law.
A guard let me have a Bible for a quarter of an hour: I opened it
at random, venturing on a kind of painful game: and the first thing
I read was this: "He was led like a sheep
to the slaughter; and like a lamb dumb before his shearer,

so opened he not his mouth. In his humiliation
his judgement was taken away: and who shall declare his generation?
For his life is taken away from the earth."

As a miracle, let it pass, Father, but you can't deny
that this was really a dirty trick.

En mi última cárcel recé en dos ocasiones. Impropio, lo sé, para el caso de
un comunista de mediana edad, pero no menos cierto. Lo que me seguirá
intrigando el resto de mi vida no es aquella concesión íntima al miedo, sino
lo que yo llamaría la concurrencia de lo extraordinario. La primera, todo
el mundo lo sabe, fue cuando el terremoto rompió la pared de la celda. La
segunda fue cuando me dijeron que me matarían al día siguiente y que me
difamarían el fantasma rojo con toda la mierda/ de la ley./ Un policía me
prestó una Biblia por un cuarto de hora: la abrí al azar, proponiéndome
una especie de juego amargo: y lo primero/ que leí fue lo siguiente: "como
oveja/ a la muerte fue llevado, y como cordero mudo delante del que lo
trasquila,/ así no abrió su boca. En su humillación/ su juico fue quitado,
mas, su generación ¿quién la contará?/ Porque es quitada de la tierra su
vida."// Como milagro que pase, padre, pero no me negará Ud. que ello es
una verdadera cabronada.

Alejandra Pizarnik (1936–1972, Argentina)

One of the most widely read Argentine poets, her work has an international readership; since her untimely death she has become a mythical figure. She was born in
Buenos Aires to Russian Jewish immigrants, and she learned as a child to read and
write in Yiddish. She studied philosophy and literature. In 1961 she moved to Paris
and befriended Octavio Paz, Julio Cortázar, Italo Calvino, André Pieyre de Mandi-
argues, and Roger Caillois. Back in Buenos Aires, she published three of her main
poetry books. Paz said she achieved a verbal crystallization by fusing insomnia and
lucidity. She wrote, "When words don't protect you anymore, I speak." She died
from an overdose of barbiturates. Her themes were depression, alienation, and the
difficulty of communication. PRINCIPAL WORKS: *La última inocencia* (1956), *Arbol
de Diana* (1962), *Los trabajos y las noches* (1965), *Extracción de la piedra de locura*
(1968), *El infierno musical* (1971)

Nocturnal Singer / Cantora nocturna

María Rosa Fort and Frank Graziano, trans.

She who has died of her blue dress sings. Imbued with death she sings to
the sun of her drunkenness. Inside her song there is a blue dress, there
is a white horse, there is a green heart tattooed with echoes of her dead
heart's beat. Exposed to all perditions she sings beside the lost girl she is:
her charm of good luck. And despite the green mist on her lips, despite
the gray coldness in her eyes her voice eats away the distance stretching
between thirst and the hand that feels for the glass. She sings.

La que murió de su vestido azul está cantando. Canta imbuida de muerte
al sol de su ebriedad. Adentro de su canción hay un vestido azul, hay un
caballo blanco, hay un corazón verde tatuado con los ecos de los latidos de
su corazón muerto. Expuesta a todas las perdiciones, ella canta junto a una
niña extraviada que es ella: su amuleto de la buena suerte. Y a pesar de la
niebla verde en los labios y del frío gris en los ojos, su voz corroe la distancia
que se abre entre la sed y la mano que busca el vaso. Ella canta.

From the Other Side / Del otro lado

Lynne Alvarez, trans.

    Like sand in an hourglass
music falls over music.
    I am sad on this wolf-fanged
night.

    Music falls over music
as my voice over my voices.

Como un reloj de arena cae la/ música en la música.// Estoy triste en la
noche de colmi-/ llos de lobo.// Cae la música en la música como/ mi voz en
mis voces.

From a Copy of "Les Chants de Maldoror" / En un ejemplar de "Les chants de maldoror"

Lynne Alvarez, trans.

    Beneath my dress a field of flowers,
bright as midnight children, burned.

    The breath of light in my bones when I write the
word earth. Word or presence followed by perfumed
animals; sad as herself, lovely as suicide; and which
hovers over me like a dynasty of suns.

Debajo de mi vestido ardía un campo con flores/ alegres como los niños de la medianoche.// El soplo de la luz en mis huesos cuando escribo la palabra tierra. Palabra o presencia seguida por animales perfumados; triste como sí misma, hermosa como el suicidio; y que me sobrevuela como una dinastía de soles.

Fiesta

Susan Bassnett, trans.

I unfurled my homelessness
across the table, like a map.
I traced my journey as far
as my place in the wind.
The ones that get there never meet me.
The ones I wait for don't exist.

And I drank wild spirits,
to change faces into
angels, into empty cups.

He desplegado mi orfandad/ sobre la mesa, como un mapa./ Dibujé el itinerario/ hacia mi lugar al viento./ Los que llegan no me encuentran./ Los que espero no existen.// Y he bebido licores furiosos/ para transmutar los rostros/ en un angel, en vasos vacíos.

Useless Frontiers / Fronteras inútiles

Susan Bassnett, trans.

a place
I don't mean a space
I'm talking
          about
I'm talking about what is not
I'm talking about what I know

not time
just all those instants
not love
no
          yes
no

a place of absence
a thread of hopeless unity

un lugar/ no digo un espacio/ hablo de/ qué/ hablo de lo que no es/ hablo
de lo que conozco// no el tiempo/ sólo todos los instantes no el amor/ no/
sí/ no// un lugar de ausencia/ un hilo de miserable unión

Óscar Hahn (1938–, Chile)

Born in Iquique, in the north of Chile, Hahn was part of the so-called Dispersed
or Decimated Generation. His book *Mal de amor* (Lovesickness [1981]), uninvolved
with politics, was the only book of poems banned during the military dictatorship
in Chile. He was arrested on September 11, 1973, during Pinochet's military coup.
After his release from prison he moved to the United States where he has been a professor at the University of Iowa. Hahn's poetry holds love as a shield, in strictly formal, contradictory, unsettling compositions, that make us find ourselves in our own
irrevocably personal time. In 2006 the Casa de America of Spain awarded him the
poetry prize "for his commitment to the interpretation of the contemporary world."
In the words of Chilean novelist and essayist Jorge Edwards, "Hahn's language is one
of the most. . .original of our time." PRINCIPAL WORKS: *Arte de morir* (1977), *Versos
robados* (1995), *Apariciones profanas* (2002), *En un abrir y cerrar de ojos* (2006)

Restriction of Nocturnal Movements / Restricción de los desplazamientos nocturnos

James Hoggard, trans.

Or the super-little animal whose body increases or decreases
from left to right:

or the hunter moving toward the little beast
from right to left:

or the line that's erased or drawn on the blackboard
from left to right:

or the eraser gliding toward the white point
from right to left:

or the hunter or the eraser as sole survivors
on this page:
or this page I wad up and toss in the wastebasket:

or this thing noiselessly moving through the room toward me

upward: downward:
left to right or right to left:

wadding me up, tossing me in the wastebasket

O el animal super-chico cuyo cuerpo crece o decrece/ de izquierda a
derecha:// o el cazador moviéndose hacia la bestezuela/ de derecha
a izquierda:// o la línea que se borra o se marca en el pizarrón/ de izquierda
a derecha:// o el borrador deslizándose hacia el punto blanco/ de derecha
a izquierda:// o el cazador o el borrador como únicos sobrevivientes/ en
esta hoja:/ o esta hoja que arrugo o que tiro en el papelero:// o ese algo que
avanza hacia mí por el cuarto sin ruido// de abajo arriba: de arriba abajo:/ de
izquierda a derecha o de derecha a izquierda:// y me arruga y me tira en el
papelero.

Conjurer's Tract / Tractatus de sortilegiis

James Hoggard, trans.

In the garden were some very curious magnolias, listen
some really rare roses, oh,
and an awful smell of incest and blustery violets,
and semen flowing from hummingbird to hummingbird.
Then the girls came in the garden,
rain-soaked and full of white cockroaches,
and mayonnaise curdled in the kitchen
and their dolls began menstruating.
We caught you right in the act scrubbing pollen
off your shirt, nectar off your breasts, see?
Someone comes tip-toeing, a murmur of birds
being trampled, a skeleton being born in organza,
someone drew near in the middle of jokes and strawberries
and his grey hair waved green in the pool.
Tell me, you the one dead from laughter,
where you're taking the honeycomb of libidinous bees.
And carnations began blooming gloriously,
and gardenias ejaculating delightedly, die,
with their harshness and softness and paws
and yellow blood, ah!
Don't stand, don't sit, don't speak
with your mouth full
of blood:
let the blood dream of dahlias
and the dahlias begin bleeding
and the doves abort ravens

and pregnant carnations
and some very curious magnolias, hear,
some really rare roses, oh.

En el jardín había unas magnolias curiosísimas, oye/ unas rosas re-raras,
oh,/ y había un tremendo olor a incesto, a violetas macho,/ y un semen
volando de picaflor en picaflor./ Entonces entraron las niñas en el jardín,/
llenas de lluvia, de cucarachas blancas,/ y la mayonesa se cortó en la
cocina/ y sus muñecas empezaron a menstruar./ Te pillamos in fraganti
limpiándote el polen/ de la enagua, el néctar de los senos, ves tú?/ Alguien
viene en puntas de pie, un rumor de pájaros/ pisoteados, un esqueleto
naciendo entre organzas,/ alguien se acercaba en medio de burlas y fresas/
y sus cabellos ondearon en el charco/ llenos de canas verdes./ Dime, muerta
de risa, a dónde llevas/ ese panal de abejas libidinosas./ Y los claveles
comenzaron a madurar brilloso/ y las gardenias a eyacular coquetamente,
muérete,/ con sus durezas y blanduras y patas/ y sangre amarilla, aj!/ No
se pare, no se siente, no hable/ con la boca llena/ de sangre:/ que la sangre
sueña con dalias,/ y las dalias empiezan a sangrar/ y las palomas abortan
cuervos/ y claveles encinta/ y unas magnolias curiosísimas, oye,/ una rosas
re-raras, oh.

Vision of Hiroshima / Visión de Hiroshima

James Hoggard, trans.

Eyeshock: the bomb itself spraying eyes
from under the living mushroom:
eyes kaleidoscoping with blind humanity's brilliance.

The elders, decapitated by the fire, scattered,
the angels, decapitated by the fire,
rammed against sulfuric horns,
the virgins, haloed radioactively, were stopped,
decapitated by the fire.
All the children dispersed decapitated through the sky.
It wasn't maimed eye or paralyzed skin
or blood over melted street that we saw:
but coupling lovers astonished,
petrified by the inferno's magnesium,
the lovers fixed on the public road,
and Lot's wife
turned into a uranic column.
The hot hospital goes through the drains,
your gelid heart goes through latrines,
they go under the beds, like cats,
green and inflamed, they go on all fours,

cinders meowing.
The waters' vibration turns the raven white
and now you can't forget that skin stuck on the walls
because you'll drink in collapse, milk in riprap.
We saw domes phosphorescing, slow rivers
turned orange, bulging bridges
giving birth in the middle of silence.
The harsh color tore out
the heart of its own objects:
red blood, rosy leukemia, festering sore,
driven mad by the fission.
Oil ripped the toes from our feet,
chairs smashed against windows
tossed on the eyes' stormy currents,
liquified buildings came gushing
past headless treetrunks,
and among husks and milky ways,
suns or luminous pigs
paddling in celestial pools.

Footsteps climb the radioactive stairs,
broken ridges rise through the funeral air.
And what will we do with so many ashes?

Ojo con el ojo numeroso de la bomba/ que se desata bajo el hongo vivo./
Con el fulgor del hombre no vidente, ojo y ojo.// Los ancianos huían
decapitados por el fuego,/ encallaban los ángeles en cuernos sulfúricos/
decapitados por el fuego,/ se varaban las vírgenes de aureola radiactiva/
decapitadas por el fuego./ Todos los niños emigraban decapitados por
el cielo./ No el ojo manco, no la piel tullida, no sangre/ sobre la calle
derretida vimos:/ los amantes sorprendidos en la cópula,/ petrificados por
el magnesium del infierno,/ los amantes inmóviles en la vía pública,/ y la
mujer de Lot/ convertida en columna de uranio.// El hospital caliente se va
por los desagües,/ se va por las letrinas tu corazón helado,/ se van a gatas
por debajo de las camas,/ se van a gatas verdes e incendiadas/ que maúllan
cenizas./ La vibración de las aguas hace blanquear al cuervo/ y ya no puedes
olvidar esa piel adherida a los muros/ porque derrumbamiento beberás,
leche en escombros./ Vimos las cúpulas fosforescer, los ríos/ anaranjados
pastar, los puentes preñados/ parir en medio del silencio./ El color estridente
desgarraba/ el corazón de sus propios objetos:/ el rojo sangre, el rosado
leucemia,/ el lacre llaga, enloquecidos por la fisión./ El aceite nos arrancaba
los dedos de los pies,/ las sillas golpeaban las ventanas/ flotando en
marejadas de ojos,/ los edificios licuados se veían chorrear/ por troncos de
árboles sin cabeza,/ y entre las vías lácteas y las cáscaras,/ soles o cerdos

luminosos/ chapotear en las charcas celestes.// Por los peldaños radiactivos suben los pasos,/ suben los peces quebrados por el aire fúnebre./ ¿Y qué haremos con tanta ceniza?

Eugenio Montejo (1938–, Venezuela)

Born in Caracas, Venezuela, Montejo earned a law degree and also studied sociology of art in France. Montejo belonged to the Venezuelan poetic generation of 1958. He directed the Monte Avila publishing house and was a diplomat at the Venezuelan embassy in Portugal. In 1998 he received his country's National Literary Award, and in 2005 he obtained the acclaimed Octavio Paz International Prize for poetry. He created an imaginary place called Manoa and disguised himself under the heteronyms Sergio Sandoval and Tomás Linden. His lean texts are charged with inner tension, tirelessly weaving the eternal themes of love, time, and the miracle of existence. PRINCIPAL WORKS: *Algunas palabras* (1976), *Terredad* (1978), *Guitarra del horizonte* (1991)

The World's Practice / Práctica del mundo

Jen Hofer, trans.

Write clearly, God has no glasses.
Don't translate your deepest music
into numbers and codes,
words are born by touch.
The ocean you see runs in front of its waves,
why must you reach to catch it?
Listen to it in the chorus of palms.
What is visible in flowers, in women,
rests in the invisible,
what revolves in the stars wishes to stop.
Favor your silence and let yourself roam,
the stone's theory is the most practical.
Recount the dream of your life
with the clouds' slow vowels
that come and go tracing the world
without adding even a line of shadow
to its natural mystery.

Escribe claro, Dios no tiene anteojos./ No traduzcas tu música profunda/ a números y claves,/ las palabras nacen por el tacto./ El mar que ves corre delante de sus olas,/ ¿para qué has de alcanzarlo?/ Escúchalo en el coro de

las palmas./ Lo que es visible en la flor, en la mujer,/ reposa en lo invisible,/
lo que gira en los astros quiere detenerse./ Prefiere tu silencio y déjate rodar,/
la teoría de la piedra es la más práctica./ Relata el sueño de tu vida/ con
las lentas vocales de las nubes/ que van y vienen dibujando el mundo/ sin
añadir ni una línea más de sombra/ a su misterio natural.

A Bird's Earthness / La terredad de un pájaro

Jen Hofer, trans.

A bird's earthness is its song,
in its chest what returns to the world
with echoes of an invisible chorus
from a forest long dead.
Its earthness is its dream of finding itself
in those who are absent,
repeating a melody until the end
while the airs cross open
their wings transient;
though it may not know to whom it sings
nor why,
nor whether it might hear itself in others someday
as each minute it desired to be:
—more innocent.
Since birth nothing will separate it
from its earthly duty;
it works in the sun, procreates, seeks out its crumbs
and what it defends is solely its voice,
because in time it is not a bird
but a ray in the night of its species,
a pursuit of life without respite
so song might endure.

La terredad de un pájaro es su canto,/ lo que en su pecho vuelve al mundo/
con los ecos de un coro invisible/ desde un bosque ya muerto./ Su terredad
es el sueño de encontrarse/ en los ausentes,/ de repetir hasta el final la
melodía/ mientras crucen abiertas los aires/ sus alas pasajeras;/ aunque no
sepa a quién le canta/ ni por qué/ ni si podrá escucharse en otros algún día/
como cada minuto quiso ser:/ —más inocente./ Desde que nace nada ya lo
aparta/ de su deber terrestre;/ trabaja al sol, procrea, busca sus migas/ y es
sólo su voz lo que defiende,/ porque en el tiempo no es un pájaro/ sino un
rayo en la noche de su especie,/ una persecución sin tregua de la vida/ para
que el canto permanezca.

Good-Bye to the Twentieth Century / Adiós al siglo XX

Jen Hofer, trans.

I cross Marx Street, Freud Street;
I move along one edge of this century,
slow, insomniac, suspicious,
spy ad honorem of some gothic kingdom,
collecting fallen vowels, small round pebbles
tattooed with infinite murmurs.
Mondrian's line before my eyes
cuts the night into upright shadows
now that no further solitude fits
within the glass walls.
I cross Mao Street, Stalin Street;
I watch the instant when a millennium dies
and another's earthly domain begins to dawn.
My vertical century, full of theories . . .
My century with its wars, its postwars
and Hitler's drumbeat out there far away,
between blood and abyss.
I proceed through the stones of the old suburbs
toward a drink, toward a little jazz,
contemplating the gods who sleep dissolute
in the sawdust of bars,
while I decipher their names as I pass
and continue on my way.

Cruzo la calle Marx, la calle Freud;/ ando por una orilla de este siglo,/
despacio, insomne, caviloso,/ espía ad honorem de algún reino gótico,/
recogiendo vocales caídas, pequeños guijarros/ tatuados de rumor infinito./
La línea de Mondrian frente a mis ojos/ va cortando la noche en sombras
rectas/ ahora que ya no cabe más soledad/ en las paredes de vidrio./ Cruzo la
calle Mao, la calle Stalin;/ miro el instante donde muere un milenio/ y otro
despunta su terrestre dominio. Mi siglo vertical y lleno de teorías . . . /
Mi siglo con sus guerras, sus posguerras/ y su tambor de Hitler allá lejos,/
entre sangre y abismo./ Prosigo entre las piedras de los viejos suburbios/
por un trago, por un poco de jazz,/ contemplando los dioses que duermen
disueltos/ en el serrín de los bares,/ mientras descifro sus nombres al paso/
y sigo mi camino.

Osvaldo Lamborghini (1940–1985, Argentina)

Lamborghini created an inventive form of writing that challenged every existing Argentine literary form. His works are not in the traditional narrative form but, rather, purposely undermine traditional expectations, successfully intertwining violent language and sexual and political references as a unique and ultimately shocking form of social criticism. His pioneering writing style was adopted by other poets after his death in Barcelona. PRINCIPAL WORK: *El fiord* (1969)

Excerpt from **The Most Amusing Song of the Devil (A Prose Work Half in Verse, No Joke . . .) / La divertidísima cancion del diantre (obra en prosa y medio en verso, sin chanza . . .)**

G. J. Racz, trans.

Hamlet, that Creole pip,
And the Ghost of his dead Father:
I've been forced to make a slip.
Revenge . . . !

Oh chilly Song of the Garnett
On his Cross each variant word
And one and Soup and Sam
Still forward
              a!
b be nd me ov er
r re am me rov er
very deserted
be nd me ov er
I'll sing it ov er and ov er

it's the truth
though strongly asserted!

And forward!
Devil!
Oh Devils!
Song of the Devil!
The Amusing

IT'S MY LIFE!

Song of the Devil!

THE DEVIL YOU S

AY

???!!!

don't be so gutu

                    —I'll write you up in my book—

if you're here

                    —and not in the nook—

Unforgivable
the word sun glow
the word sunk low
unforgivable
but the silence is binding

                    —attention: the Aga Muffin is speaking—

AND SPACE
(why the capitals?)
devil on top of devil
and ass and devil and patience
(slow the pace)
and the sun glow sunk low
and before before in front of all
with clearsightedness

                    OF THE COLD
                    BIRTH OF TERROR

and still before

                    before!
                    before!
                    before!

I despise
Mia
Moa my own price!
like the tele tells you tele the vision
I remember all too well!
crazy alarming clock!
with its tick-tock!

                    the devil!

I suffer amnesia in no wise
but did I pay my own price?
Moa Mia
Where to go? A ir France?
be frantic and go wing it?
and should I

should I sing it?
fine!
the devil take it!

: OH MOST AMUSING
SONG OF THE DEVIL

Argentina is done,
The Old Dead Mare!
They knock quickly my beloved
fatherland Moa
Mia
on our doors over here

Moa Mia please!
it's the police!
it's the police!
it's the police!

Oh friolenta Canción del Garnett/ En su Cruz cada variante/ Y una y Sopa
y Sam/ Más adelant e/ ¡a!/ e éncu léme/ a ángu léme/ muy desierto/ en
cu le mé/ yo can ta ré/ *¡es verdad!*/ *¡es cierto!*/ ¡y adelante!/ ¡Diantre!/ ¡Oh
Diantres!/ ¡Canción de Diantre!/ La Divertida/ *¡ES MI VIDA!*/ Canción del
Diantre!/ ¡¡¡¡¡DIANTR/ EH/ ?????/ no seas tan gutu/ —que yo te ficho—/
si estás aquí/ —y no en el nicho—/ Sin perdón/ la palabra un día/ la
palabra hundía/ sin perdón/ pero el silencio ata/ —atención: habla el Atha
Philtrafa—/ Y ESPACIO/ (¿por qué mayúsculas?)/ diantre sobre diantre/ y
culo y diantre y paciencia/ (más despacio)/ y un día hundía/ y antes y antes
y delante/ y en videncia/ DEL FRIO/ PARTO DEL TERROR/ y todavía antes/
¡antes!/ *¡antes!*/ *¡antes!*/ ¡desprecio/ Mia/ Moa mi precio!/ como tele te lo
dice el tele el vizor/ ¡bien que me acuerdo!/ ¡loco y reloj!/ ¡despertador!/
¡diantre!/ no me amnesio/ ¿pero pagué mi precio?/ Moa Mia/ ¿Adónde ir? ¿A
ir France?/ ¿pero del ir ante?/ ¿y que yo/ *yo la cante?*/ *¡bueno!*/ *¡diantre:* OH
DIVERTIDISIMA/ CANCION DEL DIANTRE/ ¡Argentina!/ ¡Yegua Muerta!/
Rápido querida/ patria Moa/ Mia/ llaman a la puerta/ ¡Moa Mia!/ ¡es la
policía!/ ¡es la policía!/ ¡es la policía!

José Kozer (1940–, Cuba)

The son of Polish and Czech immigrants, Kozer was born in Havana and educated in the United States at New York University. Regarded as one of the most prominent and prolific figures of Latin American neo-baroque poetry, Kozer has published over thirty books of poetry and verse. Together with Néstor Perlongher and Severo Sarduy, Kozer's engaging but difficult poetics is widely respected. Kozer retired from his position of professor at Queens College in 1997. PRINCIPAL WORKS: *Bajo este cien* (1983), *No buscan reflejarse* (2002), *Stet* (2006)

A Meeting at Cho-Fu-Sa / Encuentro en Cho-Fu-Sa

Mark Weiss, trans.

Listen, Guadalupe; indirectly I write for you this imitation of Pound
    imitating Li Po, honoring by imitation now that my
    energy (which now sustains all things) begins to flag:
    we three are old already; some more than others,
    all three, contemporaries: three old pyramids, three
    ships pissing in the night; a river; Rapallo; a neigh-
    borhood in Havana eaten ounce by ounce by the
    worm called time, time's clock-chime bounces, here,
    in China, and from China to here, Pound Pound,
    pendulum and stroke the beat of time: the pen lacks
    ink, the pencil lead, Guadalupe, to call forth from
    the womb your form, long-since emptied but filled
    with fronds, with refuge, José's living ear: listen to
    Li Po listen to Pound hear them shifting parallel
    words, perfection passing beyond time: become its
    equal. What do I say to you (come to await me) they
    put it aside they continue, they already crown: they
    crowned it, and here they recount the moments like
    the merchant's young wife lamenting her lover's
    absence (you who conceive, Guadalupe, can you
    conceive of such nectar?) she was a girl, she grew to
    marriageable age, imagining lebanons, flagons of
    milk (she had to learn the matters of love from the
    books of others, matters, we say, well fit for the
    imagination of sensitive damsels seduced in all their
    senses by a calming hand) remember: they played
    together, accustomed (the poets tell us) since
    childhood to offering corollas clusters and splendors
    of yellow that the Emperor in his isolation didn't
    know, both, after the beloved's sixteenth year (and
    you, at eighteen), themselves become a splendor of

yellow, all of nature for that moment reduced
(remember) to four legs entwining, love's tendrils,
solace beyond interpretation, not called for; something intervened. He left, she waited (and you will
wait) and in the somnolence of waiting whispered
to Li Po some words gathered by Pound (and here
transcribed): in them, Guadalupe, he suggests to you
the hope for a reunion; and José from his own
geography (in the future) writes these words to you:
take, for example, La Belle Dame Sans Merci between your hands, take as well She Walks in Beauty (and fair is fair) hold between your hands Marlowe (The Passionate Shepherd to His Love): arise
and go, fear not, you are guided: an island, greenery
(understand) blues and unutterable umbers (for you,
who have loved more than anyone the word umbers,
I utter this) (sanctified; sanctified) plunge in; cross
thresholds; darkness is light, and puts aside that
science of air that Elifaz would have pronounced
while guiding Job, Job's Virgil, Job's Teresa or Juan
or the boy Keats; for a moment let's call Lezama to
the service of Julián, that other poet: all will serve
you, they are guides, all call out, and I myself will
cease my clamoring. Come to me. Time was not
hidden from Shaddai; out of time's irreversible
splendor (look) the flower of the plumtree (it's in
the poem: in Pound, in Li Po): the trace of his shadow
follows his passage, you will arrive at a height (the
bereft prairies scarcely symbolic), she calls to mind:
a city; a young man of twenty-six, perhaps a marriageable
merchant, will climb through deltas and counter-
currents toward foreign towns to negotiate the end;
less business of dailiness (dying): now this young
man this maker of wands (he's sixteen, we are you); his
skin caked with stains capillaries branches and hard-
enings is the flesh of the right hand of a Perfect Being:
look at it. Only look at it. Enter, a breath. To comfort,
Guadalupe, is your nature. Impart it to whoever you
await between two shores between two puffs of air,
a little form a little breath, impart a little of your
right side (your nature) tell him so as to hear it, speak
to him so as to listen, and from him (José) will come
again (Pound) the rain (Li Po): you and I we aren't
separate. It's here; here: this place has a name like

an unnameable name that has your nature: here we
will call it a dirge (what difference does it make);
we know that to escape this pass you must follow
my pace, that it rains lightly (rains well) and that
the flowery meadows of the word have swollen.

Escucha, Guadalupe; escribo para ti de soslayo esta imitación tomada/
de Pound de Li Po tomada, venerando al imitar, dado/ que mis fuerzas
(gracias a lo cual, ahora, todo se/ sostiene) flaquean: ya estamos viejos;
unos más que/ otros, los tres, concomitantes: tres pirámides viejas,/ tres
barcas en la noche a orinar; un río; Rapallo; un/ reparto habanero roído
por onzas de carcoma llamadas/ tiempo, las onzas relojeras del tiempo,
aquí, allá en la China, y entre la China y aquí, Pound Pound, péndulo
y martillazos la contera del tiempo: hace/ falta el punto de la tinta o de la
mina del lápiz,/ Guadalupe, para clamar a tu figura vaciada desde/ hace
años de matriz pero llena de frondas, de receptáculo, oído vivo de José:
oye a Li Po a Pound/ óyelos traquetear palabras coordinadas, perfección/
por encima del tiempo: ellos lo igualan. Qué te digo/ (ven a esperarme)
ellos lo deponen y continúan, ya/ coronan: coronaron, y aquí se cuenta
cómo la joven/ esposa de un mercader lamenta la ausencia del/ amado
(¿concibes, Guadalupe, tú que concibes, tales/ aguamieles?): era una
niña, se hizo casadera, conoció/ líbanos, cántaros de leche (ella tuvo que
imaginar/ tras el conocimiento de amor cosas de libros ajenos,/ cosas
muy verdaderas a la imaginación, digamos,/ de sensibles doncellas de
pronto seducidas, a todos/ los efectos, por la palma de una mano que
tranquiliza)/ recuerda: jugueteaban, y acostumbrados/ desde niños (según
nos cuentan los poetas) a ofrecerse/ corolas ramilletes y esplendores
amarillos que/ el Emperador en su aislamiento desconcoce, a partir/
de los dieciséis años de la amada (tú, a los dieciocho)/ fueron ambos
esplendor amarillo, viva naturaleza/ reducida a un momento de cuatro
piernas entrecruzadas/ (recuerda) en tijereta de amor, y fueron/ solaz sin
interpretación posible: innecesaria; otra/ cosa mediaba. El marchó, ella
quedó a la espera (tú,/ esperarás) y en la somnolencia de la espera dijo al/
oído de Li Po unas palabras recogidas por Pound/ (aquí transcritas): en
ellas, Guadalupe, se te menciona/ a la espera de un reencuentro; y de su
particular/ geografía (porvenir) te escribe José estas palabras:/ toma entre
tus manos, por ejemplo, La Belle Dame/ Sans Merci, toma asimismo She
Walks in Beauty y/ (fair is fair) coge entre tus manos a Marlowe (The/
Passionate Shepherd to His Love): échate a andar,/ nada temas, estás
guiada: una isla, verdor (hazte idea)/ azules y carmelitas inenarrables
(esto lo digo/ por ti, ya que amaste más que nadie a la palabra/ carmelita)
(santificada; santificada) adéntrate; atraviesa umbrales; la oscuridad es
luz, y deja a un/ lado esa ciencia de aire que dijera Elifaz guiando a/ Job,

Virgilio a Job, Teresa o Juan o Keats el jovencísimo/ a Job; llamemos por
un instante a Lezama al/ servicio de otro poeta llamado Julián: todos
te/ servirán, guían todos, todos llaman, dejaré yo/ entonces de clamar:
allégate. A shaddai no le han/ sido ocultados los tiempos; del esplendor
irreversible/ del tiempo (mira) flor de ciruelo (está en el/ poema: Pound,
Li Po): sigue al paso el trazado de/ su sombra, llegarás a una cima (las
pobres tierras/ llanas apenas simbolizan): contempla; una ciudad;/ un
joven de veintiséis años, posible mercader/ casadero subirá por deltas
y contracorrientes rumbo/ a poblaciones extrañas a negociar el asunto
interminable/ de todos los días (morir): ahora está varado/ el joven (tiene
dieciséis años, somos tú); su piel/ cuajada de manchas arteriolas las
ramificaciones y/ endurecimientos es carne a la diestra de una Perfección:/
mírala. Sólo, mírala. Adéntrate, hálito. En/ ti, Guadalupe, reconfortar es
natural. Imprímele a/ quien esperas entre dos orillas dos soplos, un poco/
de figura y hálito, imprímele otro poco de tu diestra/ figura (naturaleza)
nárrale para oírlo, háblale para/ escucharlo, y de él (José) vendrá otra vez
(Pound)/ la lluvia (Li Po): no estamos tú y yo dispersos. Es/ aquí; aquí:
el sitio tiene nombre como nombre/ innombrable tiene tu naturaleza:
le pondremos/ endecha (qué más da); bien sabemos que es para/ salir
del paso, sal a mi paso, que llueve fino (llueve/ bien) y las florestas de la
palabra se han hinchado.

Kafka Reborn / Rebrote de Franz Kafka

Mark Weiss, trans.

It's a modest two-story house not far from the river on a narrow
       street in Prague. In the early morning
between the 11th
and 12th of November he awoke with a start and descended the stairs
       to the small kitchen with its round table and linden-
       wood chair, its portable stove and methyl-blue
       flame. He lit

the burner
and the fire became at once (three) flames reflected in the window's
       three panes: smell of sulfur. He wished

to go
to the dining nook to drink a medicinal tea of honey and boldo leaves,
       he moved the chair and settled in before a sienna-
       colored clay bowl which he had placed, he'd forgot-
       ten when, on the six-colored wicker tray,

Felicia's
gift; and once again
Felicia appeared her hair in braids and the radiance of candles
reflected on the white oval of that face greedy for consecrated loaves and cakes, that face
three times
a burst of flames in the window pane: she appeared and was again
three times the child of her dead, a few chamber
players

responded to the stroke
of a triangle and the stroke of a bell (at three) in the high belfry not
far from the river: they took their ease, ten

cups, ten
chairs in the immense country house with its mansard roofs, the
house in which bay windows and glass doors (barns
and sheds) were open day and night, the water

and the sponges
shone. Yes: it was another time, and a chorus of girls tended the tea
pots (boiling) the eucalyptus (boiling), the marjoram
and a digestive water (mint leaves) respiratory

waters: at peace
at peace (at last), he climbed the stairs and saw himself stretched out
in the window pane (at last) no crowd of birds

in the window.

Es una casa pequeña a dos niveles no muy lejos del río en un callejón/ de
Praga. En la madrugada/ del once al doce noviembre tuvo un sobresalto,
bajó a la cocinilla con la mesa/ redonda y la silla de tilo, el anafe y la llama
azul/ de metileno. Prendió// la hornilla/ y el fuego verdeció a la vez (tres)
llamas en los tres cristales de la/ ventana: olía a azufre. Quiso// pasar/ a
la salita comedor a beber una tisana de boldo y miel, corrió la silla/ y se
acomodó delante de una taza de barro siena/ que había colocado no se
sabe hace cuánto sobre el/ portavasos de mimbre a seis colores, obsequio/
de Felicia: y una vez más/ apareció Felicia con la raya al medio, las dos
trenzas y un resplandor/ de velas en el óvalo blanco de aquel rostro ávido
de/ harinas y panes de la consagración, rostro// tres veces/ una llamarada
en el cristal de la ventana: apareció. Y era una vez/ más la niña tres veces
de sus muertos, acudían// al golpe/ del triángulo unos músicos de cámara
y al golpe de la esquila (las tres)/ en el alto campanario no muy lejos
del río: se arrellanaron, diez// tazas, diez/ sillas en la inmensa casona de
las mansardas, la casa en que los/ miradores y las cristaleras (establos y

galpones) se/ abrían día y noche, el agua// y las esponjas/ relucían. Pues,
sí: era otra época y un coro de muchachas vigilaba las/ teteras (bullir)
los eucaliptos (bullir) la mejorana y/ un agua digestiva (mentas) aguas//
de la respiración: todo/ tranquilo (por fin) todo tranquilo, subió los
escalones y vio que se/ tendía en el cristal de la ventana (por fin) sin una/
aglomeración de pájaros// en la ventana.

Rodolfo Hinostroza (1941–, Peru)

A multifaceted creator born in Lima, Peru, Hinostroza is a poet, playwright, narrator, translator, journalist, and astrologer. He lived in Cuba for two years, where he
befriended the Peruvian poet Javier Heraud and was witness to the missile crisis of
1962, documented in his poem "La noche" (The Night). The events of May 1968
found him at the French capital, from where he started a long journey around the
world. Since 1991, he lives in Peru. He is the author of the best-seller, *El sistema
astrológico* (The Astrological System), published in Spain. According to the Peruvian
critic and poet Julio Ortega, "Hinostroza is the enlightened chronicler of the City
of the Latin American Character, an undertaking imagined from a place that lies
between a wounded subjectivity and an alert vigor, between a history of loss and
liberating wonderings. His is an art of redemptions, where the redeemed word prevails against the struggling powers. His work is motivated by the immensity of the
task and crystallizes as unique and inimitable." PRINCIPAL WORKS: *Consejero del lobo*
(1965), *Contra natura* (1971), *Aprendizaje de la limpieza* (1978), *Poemas reunidos*
(1986), *Fata Morgana* (1995)

Excerpt from Contra natura

William Rowe, trans.

I

Leggierissima
        all eyes you entered my tent
        covered in flowers / olfactory animal /
thus the colour that attracts small beasts
                thus the peacock's headpiece
and I remembered: kinetic desire
            stasis in the contemplation of a body
millenarian repetition thus the butterfly and the coleopteran
& in your sex / the sea / trimethylamide
& coloured fauns played in your breast
          fish's eyes: I saw you and knew it
un coup de cheveux and I'm thrown to the ground
& before, I had entered you and seen: a liquid universe

tides within you
our bodies imitating the movement of the sea
The Fish and The Moon
above, a sky rotten jusqu'au bout
                              but the stars
man that wanders
                    Adieu
                    helm / anchor / astrolabe
& beyond even further back in the no man's land of orgasm
                                        the fish dreams

thus:

          liquid undifferentiated amoeboid form
implacable attraction
                        in suo esse perseverare conatur
Spinoza dixit
              not sex not the metallic smell of lust
                                        but
abominable love beautiful hate
                  Swim, my gamete! Go back up the liquid river
to the origin
The calcarea and the salamander
                        :so that I may open my tent
and a surge of thighs retrieve a whole life lost.

                              II
& they sent you to my tent
                    & I a goatherd
equally cankered by violence
                        ánima sola
& I watched the stars in silence /stupefied
and I saw you come thus: not the female that kills the male not the breeder
    of dogs
not l'heritage of the spider nor the senseless protest of the prey
                                                  but
complicity of blood
                  thus you played touching your body
                                        thus
dark eyes/aromas of millenia: myrrh and sodomy/cunnilingum
I was able to say: I'm the loneliest of animals
                                  but
un coup de cheveux and I am thrown to the ground.

I/ Leggierissima/ toda ojos entraste a mi tienda/ cubierta de flores/ oh
animal/ olfativo/ así el color que atrae a las pequeñas bestias/ así casco
de pavorreal/ y recordé: deseo cinético/ stasis en la comtemplación de un
cuerpo/ milenaria repetición así la mariposa y el coleóptero/ & en tu sexo/
el mar/ thrimetilamida/ & en tu pecho jugaban cervatillos de colores/ ojos
de pez: te vi y lo supe/ un coup de cheveux y ruedo por tierra/ & antes había
entrado en ti y vi: un universo líquido/ mareas dentro tuyo/ nuestros cuerpos
imitando el movimiento del mar/ El Pez y La Luna/ arriba un cielo podrido
jusqu'au bout/ pero las estrellas/ hombre errante/ Adieu/ gobernalle/ancla/
astrolabio/ & más allá aún más atrás in the no man's land del/ orgasmo/ el
pez sueña/ así:/ amiboide forma líquida indiferenciada/ atracción implacable/
in suo esse perseverare conatur/ Spinoza dixit/ no sexo no el olor metálico
del celo/ but/ amor abominable odio hermoso/ Nada, gameto mío! Remonta
el río líquido/ hasta el origen/ La calcárida y la salamandra/ :para que yo abra
mi tienda/ y un oleaje de muslos rescate toda una vida perdida.// II/ & te
enviaron a mi tienda/ & yo era un pastor de cabras/ podrido por la violencia
igualmente/ ánima sola/ & miraba las estrellas en silencio/ entorpecido/
y así te vi venir:/ no hembra que mata al macho no la que cría perros/ no
l'heritage de la araña no la disputa nonsense de la/ presa/ pero/ complicidad
de sangre/ así jugabas tocándote tu cuerpo/ así/ ojos oscuros/ aromas de
milenios: mirra y sodomía/cunilingum/ pude decir: soy el más solo de los
animales/ but/ un coup de cheveux y ruedo por tierra.

Antonio Cisneros (1942–, Peru)

Poet, university professor, and radio and television journalist, Cisneros was born in
Lima, Peru. As he has stated, he took his first steps "among piles of books," because
his father "was an avid reader, though he wasn't exactly an intellectual." He earned
a doctorate in literature and has been a translator of Portuguese and English into
Spanish. His continental recognition came with the Casa de las Americas Poetry
Award from Cuba in 1968. Cisneros was part of the Generation of the '60s that
renewed Peruvian poetry by undertaking a new reading of Anglo-Saxon poetry
and adopting colloquialism as a means of expression. Tactile and visual, Cisneros's
work is—according to Peruvian critic Ignacio Rodríguez A.—"a long, methodical,
and corrosive dissection of reality." PRINCIPAL WORKS: *Comentarios reales* (1964),
Canto ceremonial contra un oso hormiguero (1968), *El libro de dios y de los húnga-
ros* (1978), *Crónicas del niño Jesús de Chuca* (1981), *Drácula de Bram Stoker y otros
poemas* (1991)

The Dead Conquerors / Los conquistadores muertos

William Rowe, trans.

I

They came by water
these men with blue flesh
who trailed beards
& never slept
in order to rob each other blind.
Dealers in crosses
& brandy, who
founded their cities
with a temple.

II

During that summer in 1526
the rain tumbled down
on their daily work, & heads
& no one repaired
the rusty old armour.
Black fig trees grew
between the pews & altars,
while on the rooftiles
sparrows broke their beaks
silencing the bells.
Afterwards in Peru
no one, though master
in his own house,
could move around
without treading upon the dead,
nor sleep next to white chairs
or swamps
without sharing his bed
with some cancerous relative.
Shit upon by scorpions & spiders
few survived their horses.

I/ Por el agua aparecieron/ los hombres de carne azul,/ que arrastraban
su barba/ y no dormían/ para robarse el pellejo./ Negociantes de cruces/
y aguardiente,/ comenzaron las ciudades/ con un templo.// II/ Durante
este verano de 1526,/ derrumbóse la lluvia/ sobre sus diarios trajines y
cabezas,/ cuando ninguno había remendado/ las viejas armaduras oxidadas./
Crecieron también, negras higueras/ entre bancas y altares./ En los tejados/
unos gorriones le cerraban el pico/ a las campanas./ Después en el Perú,
nadie fue dueño/ de mover sus zapatos por la casa/ sin pisar a los muertos/

ni acostarse junto a las blancas sillas/ o pantanos,/ sin compartir el lecho
con algunos/ parientes cancerosos./ Cagados por arañas y alacranes,/ pocos
sobrevivieron a sus caballos.

Poem on Jonah and the Disalienated / Poema sobre Jonás y los desalienados

William Rowe, trans.

If men live in a whale's belly
they can only feel cold & talk
about the periodical shoals of fish & dark
walls like an open mouth & periodical
shoals of fish & dark
walls like an open mouth & feel very cold.
But if men don't always want to be talking about the same things
they'll try to build a periscope so as to know
how the islands & the sea & the other whales
fall into chaos—if it's true that all this exists.
And the apparatus must be put together from things
we have at hand & then the trouble
begins, e.g.
if we pull out a rib from our house
we'll lose its friendship for good
& if we take the liver or the beard it's capable of killing us.
And I'm inclined to believe that I live in the belly of some whale
with my wife & Diego & all my grandparents.

Si los hombres viven en la barriga de una ballena/ sólo pueden sentir frío y
hablar/ de la manadas periódicas de peces y de murallas/ oscuras como una
boca abierta y de manadas/ periódicas de peces y de murallas/ oscuras como
una boca abierta y sentir mucho frío./ Pero si los hombres no quieren hablar
siempre de lo/ mismo/ tratarán de construir un periscopio para saber/ cómo
se desordenan las islas y el mar/ y las demás ballenas—si es que existe todo
eso./ Y el aparato ha de fabricarse con las cosas/ que tenemos a la mano
y entonces se producen/ las molestias, por ejemplo/ si a nuestra casa le
arrancamos una costilla/ perderemos para siempre su amistad/ y si el hígado
o las barbas es capaz de matarnos./ Y estoy por creer que vivo en la barriga
de alguna/ ballena/ con mi mujer y Diego y todos mis abuelos.

Appendix to the Poem on Jonah and the Disalienated / Apéndice del poema sobre Jonás y los desalienados

William Rowe, trans.

And finding myself in such difficult times I decided to feed
the whale that was housing me:
there were days when I worked for well over twelve hours
& my dreams were strict assignments, my weariness
grew fat like the whale's belly:
what a job to hunt the toughest animals
strip off all the scales, open them
a rip out the gall & the backbone
                                    & my house grew fat.

(That was the last time I was tough: I insulted the whale,
grabbed my few belongings to go & look for
some home in other waters, & was just getting ready
to build a periscope
when there in the roof I saw swell up like two suns its lungs
—just like ours
only spread out over the horizon—its shoulder blades
were rowing against all the winds,
                                 & myself alone
with my sea-blue shirt in a big field
where they could shoot at me from any window: I the rabbit,
& the swift dogs behind, & not one hole.)

And finding myself in such difficult times
I settled into the softest & most pestilent regions of the whale.

Y hallándome en días tan difíciles decidí alimentar/ a la ballena que
entonces me albergaba:/ tuve jornadas que excedían en mucho a las doce
horas/ y mis sueños fueron oficios rigurosos, mi fatiga/ engordaba como el
vientre de la ballena:/ qué trabajo dar caza a los animales más robustos,/
desplumarlos de todas sus escamas y una vez abiertos/ arrancarles la hiel
y el espinazo,/ y mi casa engordaba.// (Fue la última vez que estuve duro:/
insulté a la ballena,/ recogí mis escasas pertenencias para buscar/ alguna
habitación en otras aguas, y ya me aprestaba/ a construir un periscopio/
cuando en el techo vi hincharse como dos soles sus/ pulmones/ —iguales a
los nuestros/ pero estirados sobre el horizonte—, sus omóplatos/ remaban
contra todos los vientos,/ y yo solo,/ con mi camisa azul marino en una
gran pradera/ donde podían abalearme desde cualquier ventana: yo el/
conejo,/ y los perros veloces atrás, y ningún agujero.)// Y hallándome en
días tan difíciles/ me acomodé entre las zonas más blandas y apestosas de/ la
ballena.

Juan Luis Martínez (1942–1993, Chile)

"The best-kept secret of Chilean poetry"—according to almost all present-day critics—Juan Luis Martínez was born in Valparaíso, a seaport city located in central Chile, where he also died. Self-taught and of poor health, he was marginalized and called "the madman" in his own city. His object-books—a blend of plastic art and literary work—place him among the most disruptive contemporary Latin American poets. Although not well understood by the critics of his time, today, however, he is regarded as a cult poet and an example of ethical standing. "His poetry has the effect that Goethe demanded, namely, the ability to make one shudder. It's been said that his writing was irrational, but . . . I think that, on the contrary, his poetry is strictly lucid, rigorous, even somewhat scientific," stated the critic Volodia Teitelboim. PRINCIPAL WORKS: *La nueva novela* (1977), *La poesía chilena* (1978), *Poemas del otro* (2003)

Remarks Concerning the Exuberant Activity of "Phonetic Confabulation" or "The Language of Birds" in Works by Jean-Pierre Brisset, Raymond Roussel, Marcel Duchamp, and Others / Observaciones relacionadas con la exuberante actividad de la "confabulación fonética" o "lenguaje de los pájaros" en las obras de J-P. Brisset, R. Roussel, M. Duchamp y otros

Roberto Tejada, trans.

a. By singing birds convey
   the communiqué that
   tells of their not telling

b. The language of birds is
   a language of transparent signs
   in search of a meaning's disbanded clarity

c. Birds encircle the meaning of their own song
   cast in the net of a voided language;
   a netting at the same time transparent and indestructible.

d. Even silence rendered in the interlude of each song
   is a link, too, in the netting, a sign, a flicker
   in the message nature tells herself.

e. It's not birdsong to nature
   nor its counterpart, human speech, but silence
   shaped into a message whose object
   is to so establish, cut short, or prolong communication
   as to determine whether the circuit's in order
   and whether back and forth the birds in fact communicate
   by way of humans ears
   that listen unsuspecting.

Note:
Even as we hear it in Spanish
birds sing in the avian vernacular.
(Spanish is an opaque language
containing countless ghost words;
theirs, an idiom transparent and speechless.)

a. A través de su canto los pájaros/ comunican una comunicación/ en la
que dicen que no dicen nada.// b. El lenguaje de los pájaros/ es un lenguaje
de signos transparentes/ en busca de la transparencia dispersa de algún
significado.// c. Los pájaros encierran el significado de su propio canto/
en la malla de un lenguaje vacío;/ malla que es a un tiempo transparente
e irrompible.// d. Incluso el silencio que se produce entre cada canto/ es
también un eslabón de esa malla, un signo, un momento/ del mensaje que
la naturaleza se dice a sí misma.// e. Para la naturaleza no es el canto de
los pájaros/ ni su equivalente, la palabra humana, sino el silencio,/ el que
convertido en mensaje tiene por objeto/ establecer, prolongar o interrumpir
la comunicación/ para verificar si el circuito funciona/ y si realmente los
pájaros se comunican entre ellos/ a través de los oídos de los hombres/ y sin
que estos se den cuenta.// NOTA:// Los pájaros cantan en pajarístico,/ pero
los escuchamos en español./ (El español es una lengua opaca,/ con un gran
número de palabras fantasmas;/ el pajarístico es una lengua transparente y
sin palabras.)

**Breathing House, Almost the (Author's) Little House / La casa del
aliento, casi la pequeña casa del (autor)**

Robert Tejada, trans.

(Interrogate the windows
about the absolute transparency
of the missing windows)

a. The house we build tomorrow is
    already in the past and it doesn't exist.

b. In that house we've yet to visit
    a window we forgot to shut stays open.

c. In the very same house, behind the very same
    window the curtains we pulled continue flapping.

"Maybe a house in the country
where the past is about to take place
and the future happened long ago."
(by T. S. Eliot, almost)

(Interrogar a las ventanas/sobre la absoluta transparencia/de los vidrios que faltan).// a. La casa que construiremos mañana/ ya está en el pasado y no existe.// b. En esa casa que aún no conocemos/ sigue abierta la ventana que olvidamos cerrar.// c. En esa misma casa, detrás de esa misma ventana/ se baten todavía las cortinas que ya descolgamos.// '"Quizás una casita en las afueras/donde el pasado tiene aún que acontecer/ y el futuro hace tiempo que pasó." (De T. S. Eliot, casi).

Ear (Study for a Conversation Piece) / El oído

Roberto Tejada, trans.

1. The ear is an organ in reverse; it listens only to silence.

2. If the ear was other than an organ in reverse, namely an organ meant for listening to silence, we'd hear only the deafening noise that galaxies, nebulas, planets, and all heavenly bodies release as they travel through vast outer space.

3. Sounds, noises, and words, as with all else our ears entrap, are ripples of silence that journey from a transmitting source to the ear's organ of silent reception.

1. El oído es un órgano al revés; sólo escucha el silencio.// 2. Si el oído no fuera un órgano al revés, es decir, un órgano hecho para escuchar/ el silencio, sólo oiríamos el ruido ensordecedor que producen las galaxias, ne/ bulosas, planetas y demás cuerpos celestes en sus desplazamientos a través de/ los enormes espacios interestelares.// 3. Los sonidos, ruidos, palabras, etc., que capta nuestra oído, son realmente/ burbujas de silencio que viajan desde la fuente emisora que las produce has/ ta el órgano receptor de silencio que es el oído.

The New Novel: The Poet as Superman / La nueva novela: El poeta como Superman

G. J. Racz, trans.

> Club-foot and hunchback love each other
> passionately, and therefore in their reciprocal
> relation offer the best guarantee for a
> harmonious "effect of the second order."
> —F. Engels

SUPERMAN has become extraordinarily popular thanks to his dual, perhaps three-part, identity. Hailing from a planet obliterated by catastrophe, wielding powers and abilities far beyond those of mortal men, he has taken up residence on earth, first in the guise of a newspaperman, then as a photographer, and finally behind the sundry masks of a disturbing young Chilean poet who renounces ownership of his very name so that he can appear at one and the same time shy and aggressive, elusive and anonymous. (The latter a humiliating disguise for a hero whose powers are literally and literarily unlimited.)

In essence, the myth of SUPERMAN satisfies the secret yearnings of modern man who knows he is weak and limited but dreams nonetheless of rebelling one day as a "person of exception," a "superhero" whose suffering is called upon to move the markers of being in the world.

LA NUEVA NOVELA: **EL POETA COMO SUPERMAN**

"El patizambo y la chepadita se aman apasionadamente y ofrecen, por tanto, en su doble aspecto, la mejor garantía para un "efecto armónico" de segundo orden".

F. Engels

SUPERMAN se hizo extraordinariamente popular gracias a su doble y quizás triple identidad: descendiente de un planeta desaparecido a raíz de una catástrofe, y dotado de poderes prodigiosos, habita en la Tierra: primero bajo la apariencia de un periodista, luego de un fotógrafo y por último, tras las múltiples máscaras de un inquietante y joven poeta chileno, que renuncia incluso a la propiedad de su nombre, para mostrarse como un ser a la vez tímido y agresivo, borroso y anónimo. (Este último es un humillante disfraz para un héroe cuyos poderes son literal y literariamente ilimitados).

En esencia, el mito de SUPERMAN satisface las secretas nostalgias del hombre moderno, que aunque se sabe débil y limitado, sueña rebelarse un día como un "personaje excepcional", como un "héroe" cuyos sufrimientos están llamados a cambiar las pautas ontológicas del mundo.

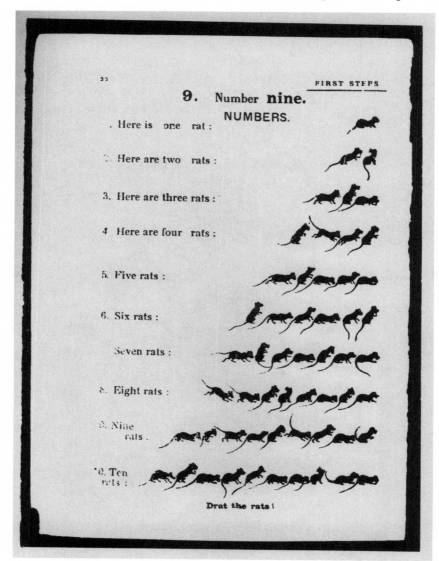

Gloria Gervitz (1943–, Mexico)

Of Eastern European Jewish descent, Gervitz was born in Mexico City and received a university degree in history. She has translated Anna Akhmatova, Marguerite Yource-nar, and Clarice Lispector and is presently considered one of the most important Mexican poets. Her poetry has an opulence that falls between the tradition of Sor Juana Inés de la Cruz and the broadest of feminist standpoints. Her lengthy poem-book, *Migraciones* (Migrations), is an epic that has been spun for twenty-six years and includes rewritten collections of poems previously published, containing stories that are Mexican yet universal in essence, stories about the Jewish uprooting, the sabbati-cal candles her grandmother lights from the side of death, the bougainvilleas, the pas-sage of time, the defeats, the oracle that always comes true in the end, and the dream called life. PRINCIPAL WORKS: *Shajarit* (1979), *Migraciones* (1991), *Pytia* (1993)

Excerpt from Migrations / Migraciones

Mark Schafer, trans.

The heart
       Crater
Witness
     Answer
          Answer me
The pale voice
       Falls
The bottomless words
         Fall
Inscriptions
      Dates
Deaths and what is born of them
              Don't explain
Lost in you
     You
          Don't explain
Every year
     Yizkor

. . . .

We landed one day at noon at the port of Veracruz.
We were wearing thick leather coats. In Havana I ate my first mango
To whom can I tell this?

. . . .

     And all those people, where are they now?

Nothing you tell me nothing

You who listen to me
The time of pain is over

Nothing nothing is left
You who listen to me
Do you still recognize the woman I was?

Tedium of waiting
the diagram of the rain   the movement of dreams
the lawn covered with leaves

And I was ashamed of my accent
and the ways of my house

Perhaps we are the same darkness the same words the same cries
You will never know   The dead   don't   understand
the living

And if I'd come within reach of your open jaws
And if I'd come within reach of remorse
You who no longer listen to me
You who no longer hear me cry
Offer me forgiveness   shelter me in your indifference

The earth has undone you
You don't know I'm here

The rain grows heavier   Parts like the waters of the River Styx
There is nothing to fear   We are complicit
I owe you nothing   grant me your
oblivion

Where is you death now?

And that smell of wet wood. That damp, brackish smell
Under the light the withered women (many in wigs) murmur newly learned
words in that foreign tongue, repeat them as if they were a litany

the stars unfasten themselves from the night   continue on their way
I follow them blindly from here

I still hear the sirens' song through a thick wrap of fog
I still know nothing of forgetting. Or of forgiveness

. . . .

can you still hear me?

Consciousness like a medusa
sears this dark obedient body
these words

poor exposed slumberous thing
that will end up covered by grass

or am I the one who lost myself?

Supplicant with no restraint
hostess with empty hands

barren mother

the light falls
insidious
gadfly

I am not allowed to understand

So many years to reach this morning
that is like any other

to reach this day
that is like all the rest

and receive it
as an offering

El corazón/ Cráter/ Testigo/ Contesta/ Contéstame/ La voz pálida/ Cae/ Las
palabras desfondadas/ Caen/ Inscripciones/ Fechas/ Las muertes y lo que de
ellas nace/ No expliques/ Perdida en ti/ Tú/ No expliques/ Cada año/ Yizkor//
. . . // Desembarcamos un mediodía en el puerto de Veracruz/ Traíamos abrigos
gruesos de piel. En La Habana comí mango por primera vez/ ¿A quién contarle
esto?// . . . // ¿Y toda esa gente, dónde está ahora?// Nada no me dices nada/
Tú que me escuchas/ La hora del dolor ha pasado// Nada no queda nada/ Tú
que me escuchas/ ¿Todavía reconoces a la que fui?// El tedio de la espera/ el
diagrama de la lluvia el movimineto de los sueños/ el pasto cubierto de hojas
secas// Y me avergonzaba de mi acento de extranjera/ Y de las costumbres de
mi casa// Acaso somos la misma oscuridad las mismas palabras los mismos
gritos/ Nunca lo sabrás Los muertos no entienden a los vivos// Y si fuera hasta
tus fauces/ Y si fuera hasta el remordimiento/ Tú que ya no me escuchas/ Tú
que ya no me oyes llorar/ Ábreme el perdón acógeme en tu indiferencia// La
tierra te ha deshecho/ No sabes que estoy aquí// La lluvia arrecia Se parte como
las aguas de la Estigia/ Nada que temer Somos cómplices/ no te debo nada
concédeme tu olvido// ¿Dónde está tu muerte ahora?// Y ese olor a madera
mojada. Ese olor húmedo y salobre/ Las mujeres exangües bajo la luz (muchas
usan peluca) murmuran palabras recién/ aprendidas en aquella lengua
extranjera, las repiten como si fueran una letanía// Las estrellas se desprenden
de la noche siguen su propia ruta/ Yo desde aquí las sigo a ciegas// Todavía oigo
envuelto entre la niebla el canto de las sirenas/ Todavía no conozco el olvido.
Tampoco conozco el perdón// . . . // ¿me oyes todavía?// Como una medusa la

conciencia/ quema este cuerpo oscuro y obediente/ estas palabras// pobre cosa
inerme y sonámbula/ que acabará cubriéndose de hierba// ¿o soy yo la que me
he perdido?// Suplicante en su desmesura/ anfitriona con las manos vacías//
en su resequedad de madre// la luz desciende/ insidiosa/ tábano// nada me es
dado saber// Tantos años para llegar a esta mañana/ igual a cualquier otra//
para llegar a este día/ igual a todos los días// y recibirlo/ en ofrenda

Soledad Fariña (1943–, Chile)

Born in Antofagasta, northern Chile, Fariña grew up in Santiago from the age of
two. During the 1960s, her experiences as a worker and a political science student
at the University of Chile paved the way for her political commitment and the Latin
Americanist views she has held until the present time. She participated in Allende's
government, got married, had two children, and then went into exile in Sweden,
where she started her studies in literature. Back in Chile in the 1980s, while opposing the dictatorship, she also devoted herself to defending women's rights. She
participates in feminist media projects and is presently a university professor in Santiago. Her writing incorporates two elements that have been silenced by Western
culture, namely, pre-Columbian thought and women's views. From this perspective,
she wrote *El primer libro* (The First Book). PRINCIPAL WORKS: *El primer libro* (1985),
Albricia (1988), *En amarillo oscuro* (1994), *Otro cuento de pájaros* (1999), *Narciso
y los árboles* (2001), *Donde comienza el aire* (2006)

Everything Calm, Immobile / Todo tranquilo, inmóvil

Jen Hofer, trans.

Had to paint the first book but which to paint
which first   to use all the ochres   also
the earth's dark yellow
layers one on top of another: clay terra-cotta ochre
to scratch at it a bit   lick fingers to form
that alloyed paste
to smear the fingers   arms   you're open now
white open pages   no beaten track
to try to cleave the fingers

—Why so sad   why are they like that   these colors,
   they say, they ask, the green-winged *choroyes*
   passing by in flocks
—Why that darkness, they shout
—There's a black that casts a shadow   covers us

They move away but can't see the red I discover
beneath my armpit

—No clarity, no clarity, they caw
—A grey cloud has fallen over my flight: they were hailstorms
    it was ice that snapped my wings

And there along the barbed wire, their flight suspended
they begin to murmur

everything calm   immobile   placid

Había que pintar el primer libro pero cuál pintar/ cuál primer tomar todos
los ocres también/ el amarillo oscuro de la tierra/ capas unas sobre otras:
arcilla terracota ocre/ arañar un poco lamer los dedos para formar/ esa
pasta ligosa/ untar los dedos los brazos ya estás abierto/ páginas blancas
abiertas no hay recorrido previo/ tratar de hendir los dedos// —Por qué
tan tristes por qué así estos colores,/ dicen, preguntan los choroyes de alas
verdes/ que pasan en bandadas/ —Por qué esa oscuridad, gritan/ —Hay un
negro que sombrea que nos cubre// Se alejan pero no alcanzan a ver el rojo
que descubro / Debajo de mi axila.// —No hay claridad, no hay claridad,
graznan/ —Ha caído la nube gris sobre mi vuelo: eran granizos/ era hielo el
que quebró mis alas// Y ahí en las alambradas, suspendido su vuelo/ se dan
a murmurar// todo tranquilo inmóvil apacible

Which to Paint Which First / Cual pintar cual primer

Jen Hofer, trans.

The black wings buzz
attentive the ear detects the wingbeat
deep fissure runs through the layers, clay-heavy
black lightning ray crosses the layers, yellow
strikes them down
violates the golden soft fine dust
the ear attentive detects the black wingbeat
of black wings
supporting the air that bears them
everything calm   immobile   placid

Zumban las alas negras/ atento el oído atisba el aleteo/ grieta profunda
atraviesa las capas arcillosas/ cruza rayo negro las capas amarillas/ las
fulmina/ transgrede la suavidad dorada del polvillo/ atisba el oído atento
el aleteo negro/ de alas negras/ que sostienen el aire que lo aguantan/ todo
tranquilo inmóvil apacible

Not Time Yet / Aún no es tiempo

Jen Hofer, trans.

The earth roars the ochre the terra-cotta the grey the black
to open the armpit, an immense wound there   volcano
restraining its howls:
to hush it

—Not yet, not yet time for the pruning of the creeping vines
     the *choroyes* mutter,
—Not yet time for the pruning of the creeping vines

To watch the hollow then—poor humors, grey
and sullen—to stop the impulse, to fling oneself into the hole:
there's a red that bellows to explode
—Not time yet,   not time yet

Muge la tierra el ocre el terracota el gris el negro/ abrir la axila, hay una herida
inmensa volcán/ reteniendo sus aullidos:/ acallarlo// —Aún no, aún no es
el tiempo de la poda de las/ guías rastreras,/ mascullan los choroyes,/ —Aún
no es el tiempo de la poda de las guías/ rastreras// Mirar el hueco entonces—
pobres humores grises/ y taimados-, detener el impulso, volcarse al agujero:/
hay un rojo que brama por estallar/ —Aún no es tiempo, aún no es tiempo

Where the Yellow / Donde el amarillo

Jen Hofer, trans.

To scatter the gaze
where the yellow   where
dark omen the joints black
rigid postpone   clarify   subside
the tempest subsides   subsides the morning
the green subsides
sweep away nocturnal sack the joints
and the yellow where
the hands scrape curves
dazed the circular fools fan out
(the cheeks) in radiant spiral
black poultice traverses the gazes submerged
in the forehead, deep bonds

—They're five, five, the *choroyes* note
—Five profound furrows   drilled

(the uneasy eye observes, noiseless the grimace
observes)

Esparcir la mirada/ dónde el amarillo dónde/ presagio oscuro las comisuras
negras/ rígidas postergan aclaran amainan/ el temporal amaina amaina
la mañana/ el verde amaina/ arrastran saco nocturno las comisuras/ y el
amarillo dónde/ escarban las manos curvas/ atolondradas aventan las necias
circulares/ (las mejillas) en radiante espiral/ recorre emplasto negro las
miradas hundidas/ en la frente, ataduras profundas// —Cinco son, cinco,
apuntan los choroyes/ —Cinco los surcos hondos taladrados// (observa el
ojo inquieto, silenciosa la mueca/ observa)

Paulo Leminski (1944–1989, Brazil)

Born in Curitiba, Paraná, in Brazil, Leminski is a noted poet, writer, musician, and
translator. His mixed African and Polish background was a source of pride and influence in much of his work. Leminski preferred brief poems and often wrote haikus. He published his first poems in the 1960s in the Brazilian magazine *Invenção*.
Although he never finished college, he spoke Japanese, French, and English. He used
these skills to translate many writers' and artists' works into Portuguese, such as
James Joyce, John Lennon, Samuel Beckett, Yukio Mishima, and John Fante. PRINCI-
PAL WORKS: *Caprichos e relaxos* (1983), *La vie en close* (1991)

Excerpt from Catatau

Odile Cisneros, trans.

The same. A monster phenomenon penetrated the folds of the land and
concentrated on the obvious. Time goes by, the monster does not show
itself, what a delay for a demonstration. They wanted to put me there.
I want to stay here, respect my wish. I assume a variety of forms, or
resume a variety of cases. I fell in myself and in those who mistake
me for someone else, find another me because I can't be the same. He
himself having acknowledged that, was put into effect. That's not good
enough, we need to show examples. Get used to this. To us, to us, here's
Occam. Who you can now see how it turned out. Without effort, he
deserves the gossip. The verb lights a fire, the subject comes over to get
warm, that's me, what's that? From here you can see the object clearly,
beyond—the no man's land of silence. It's cold here, I apologize for it
being so cold, it's been so long I'm cold that I don't even feel the cold,
I don't even know if that's cold anymore. The Toupinambaoults from
so much sniffing marofa turned into farofa. That's not fair. I stayed the
same, I'm even fine here redoing the knots you undid and reundid:
there's no one left who can undo a knot after the king of Gordium
invaded Persia. Occam ocultus, Occam vultus, Occam, the magician.

Occam twisted the signs. Occam disguised the reversals. Where's he going in such a hurry? I'm going to all of Persia, he's in a hurry. Occam sees the obvious. Leave the obvious where it is. Think of a sentence and the obvious disappears. Occam doesn't think anything, he nullifies himself and is missing. Analysis begins at home, word. To clean tears, a tomb. A stranger went by here. That's how you do it, you see. Show up on time. Do it this way, this way it's done. It's not viable for you to see me. At all. It's proven, no; it's precise. The obvious lives here. He lives in Kingsway, what delay—for a going-away. The obvious is alive. He got away and leapt that way. Came out there, stayed there, off to there. There it's big, big there. Here and there, something ended up being, I know what that is: it's the obvious. Once upon a time, he was going. Once upon a time, I was saying. Once upon a light, one day. I saw, it was a sound in my life, hearing me. I propose a witness, a test. This is my witness witnessing right and left. My name is Looked For, many have looked for me, few have found me. I will be to your right, making the sign. I am the torch that draws all eyes into the darkness of phrases. I create creatures. The obvious, unable to stop being, pontificated. We are appalled. We disappeared for a length of time, for a beat of space, the collapse was more than a scratch. May the obvious be fulfilled. The provident evident hid from the clairvoyant, music, due to a chance occurrence, a strange occurrence, caused this synopsis. Produced this delay, reflected this flux, affected the question. The solution is useless to overcome the problem. The evident has just been seen. Between twi-monster and light-monster, between the colossus and the sphinx, Occam remains the same. Remains the way he'll remain, remains with whom has ceased. The extravagant advances vaguely and stands in front: it is the obvious, and that's not fair. I'm aware how it should. It so happens that all that I say happens, therefore it happens. That, for instance, has been being for a long time. Later I'll say everything, don't say that I didn't warn you.

O próprio. Uma manifestação monstro adentrou-se nas dobras do terreno e concentrou-se no óbvio. Passa o tempo, o monstro não se mostra, que demora para uma demonstração! Queriam colocar-me aí. Quero ficar aqui, me respeitem. Eu assumo várias formas, ou arrumo vários casos. Caí em mim e nos que me equivocam, arranjem um outro eu mesmo que eu não dou mais para ser o próprio. Ele mesmo reconhecendo isso, foi levado a efeito. Isso não serve, temos que apresentar exemplos. Acostume-se com isto. Conosco, conosco, eis Occam. O qual já vem aí ver no que deu. Sem se esforçar, faz-se jus á voz corrente. O verbo acende um fogo, o sujeito vem se aquecer, esse sou eu, como é? Daqui dá para ver o objeto muito bem, além a terra de ninguém do silêncio. Aqui faz frio, peço desculpas por fazer tão frio, faz tanto tempo que sinto frio que já nem sinto frio, já nem sei se isso é frio. O Toupinambaoults de tanto farejar marofa virou farofa. Assim não vale. Fiquei idêntico, mesmo eu estou bem aquí refazendo os nós que desatastes e adesatastes: não há mais quem consiga desatar um nó, depois que o rei de Górdio invadiu a Pérsia. Occam ocultus, Occam vultus, Occam, o bruxo. Occam torceu a sinalização. Occam disfarçou as peripécias. Aonde vai com tanta pressa? Vou a toda Pérsia, vai depressa. Occam vê o óbvio. Deixa o óbvio ali. Pensa uma oração e o obvio desaparece. Occam não pensa nada, se nadifica e falta. A análise começa em casa, palavra. Para limpar lágrimas, uma lápide. Passou por aquí um desconhecido. Assim é que se faz, viu? Aparece na hora. Faz assim, assim se faça. Não é viável que você esteja me vendo. Absolutamente. Consta, não; é exato. O óbvio vive aqui. É aqui-del-reí que ele mora, quanta demora para um botafora. O óbvio está vivo. Escapou e saltou até lá. Lá saiu, lá ficou, lá vai ele. Lá é grande, grande lá. Ali e lá, algo vem sendo, eu sei o que é isso: é o óbvio. Era uma vez, ele ia. Era uma vez, eu dizia. Era uma luz, um dia. Eu via, era um som na minha vida, me ouvindo. Proponho uma testemunha, um teste. Esta é minha testemunha, dando testemunho para todos os lados. Eu me chamo Procurado, muitos me têm procurado, poucos têm me achado. Eu estarei á sua direita, fazendo sinal. Sou o facho que atrai todos os olhares na escuridão das frases. Eu crío seres. O óbvio, como não podia deixar de ser, pontificou. Estamos estarrecidos. Ficamos desaparecidos por um pedaço de tempo, por um compasso de espaço, o colapso passou de raspão. Cumpra-se o óbvio. O evidente previdente escondeu-se do vidente, a música, por um acinte do acaso, por um acidente esquisito, ocasionou esta sinopse. Originou esta deponga, refletiu este fluxo, repercutiu na pergunta. A solução é ineficaz para debelar o problema. O evidente acaba de ser visto. Entre monstrolusco e monstrofusco, entre o colosso e a esfinge, Occam fica como está. Fica como ficará, fica com quem cessou. O extravagante dá um passo avante devagar e fica perante: é o óbvio, e assim não vale. Estou ciente como se deve. Acontece que tudo que eu digo, acontece por tanto. Isso, por exemplo, já está havendo há muito tempo. Depois eu vou dizer tudo, não digam que eu não avisei.

Excerpt from Metamorphosis / Metaformose

Odile Cisneros, trans.

Like when a story has two endings, like when a story has several beginnings, like when a story tells a different story: fleeing Minos and the labyrinth, Dedalus, the unmatched craftsman, the crafty crafter, ended up on the shores of Sicily, on the beaches of King Cocalus. For Cocalus, the unmatched craftsman fashioned a throne hall where he could see without being seen, hear without being heard, and be present while absent. Minos, the lord of the sea, arrived to claim back his prisoner. In fear, Cocalus threw Dedalus into an oven, where he burned to death. How can we reconcile this ending with the flight of Dedalus and Icarus from the labyrinth and into freedom? Did Dedalus die after the fall of Icarus? Was the swan that possessed Leda simply a metaphor for a ship with white sails, a ship, a bird? Is the image of Narcissus the face of an odd passerby? Every spring is a beautiful girl who was loved by a god, who said no to a river, who fled from a satyr, nothing is real, nothing is simply that, all is transformation, all the patterns of constellations are parts of the sketch of an earthly play, all vibrates with so much meaning. What is a sphinx, a chimera, a medusa, a gorgon, compared with a father who kills his children and serves up their flesh to the King of the Gods? Final waters, this spring is what was left after the great flood. Facts are not explained with other facts, they are explained with fables. The fable is the budding structure, the archetype in bloom. Some are transformed into flowers, others are transformed into stone, still others are transformed into stars and constellations. Nothing is satisfied with its being and form. All transformation demands an explanation. Being itself remains unexplained. Some are transformed into beasts of prey; others become wolves, birds, pigeons, a tree, a spring. Only the nymph Echo was transformed into her own voice. What language should one speak with an echo? One one voice voice remembers remembers a legend a legend, Narcissus, Narcissus, Narcissus. What is a Cyclops compared to the story of a prince who killed his father and married his own mother? What is the creature that walks on four legs in the morning, two legs in the afternoon, and three legs in the evening? Ask the Sybil, listen to the pythoness, read the signs in the sky, the movement of the waters, Narcissus. Tyresias, the soothsayer, had told Laius, King of Thebes, I see horrors, I see darkness, you shall have a son who will kill you and will marry the queen, his mother. What horror can mirror this horror? Tyresias, a blind old man, a victim and vassal of Apollo, the god of light who grants the gift of divination, lord of the three ages, the god that sees everything, notices everything, knows everything. Laius puts the baby Oedipus into a box and casts it into the currents of the Nile. The box with the child washes ashore on a beach where a she-wolf finds it. Others say shepherds. Oedipus, the hidden prince, ignorant of his origins, grows up hardy among the shepherds. One day, he decides to visit Thebes, the great city, the city where the great king lives. Oedipus begins to fulfill his destiny, the wishes of the Moira, of fate, of fortune, of the blind powers of chance who govern everything on earth and heaven, in the lives of gods and in the lives of men, reflecting the supreme order. King Laius traveled incognito on the road from Thebes. He meets the shepherd, has an argument, they fight, Oedipus's youth prevails. Oedipus abandons to the vultures the body of his father, his slit throat oozing blood. The news arrives soon in the city, queen Jocasta is now a widow. Traveling incognito, the king was killed by a stranger. The city has been cursed. On the road from Thebes, the Sphinx, a monster with a female head and breasts, bird wings, a lion's body and legs, subjects all passers-by to a question, a riddle, *decipher me or I will devour you*. Hundreds of Thebans have been devoured, nobody dares leave the city. Oedipus decides to face the Sphinx, the interrogating monster, the monster-question, the proponent, the first philosopher, the question-being.

. . . .

What is an echo if not the transformation of a voice into stone, into what is eternally identical to itself, like the letters of the alphabet invented by Cadmus, the son of Agenor, King of Phoenicia, and of Queen Telephasse? Cadmus, the protégé of Athena, the hero who came from the Orient to meet his sister, Europa, abducted by Zeus in the shape of a bull, and to kill the dragon? Inspired by the goddess, he tears out the dragon's teeth and sows them. From the teeth sprout furious warriors who attack the hero. Cadmus manages to make them kill each other. Letters of the alphabet, dragon's teeth, arriving from Asia, the aleph, the beit, the gamma, delta, zaleth, seeds, sound bits of dust, loose atoms, epsilon, zed, yod, omega. What would the Seven Sages say about the Twelve Labors of Hercules? Each has a specific meaning, like the head of Medusa in the darkness of the goddess Athena. *Omnia mecum porto,* I carry with me all that is mine. No one lives who sees my face, says the Lord, says Medusa. Why were we fashioned from clay by the Titan Prometheus? Why did he steal the fire of Zeus for us? Yesterday, I was trying to interpret the war of Troy, the meaning of Ulysses, of Agamemnon, the abduction of Helen, the wrath of Achilles, the madness of Ajax, the wooden horse, what do these stories mean, in the Gordian knots of what's remembered and what's forgotten? It frightens one to think they are not stories, they do not carry a secret meaning. Only the most fantastic things never happened. Everything happened. All that happened. By the one hundred eyes of Argos all of that. Zeus loved the daughter of Inachus, a king and a river, Io, the priestess of Hera, Io, transformed into a heifer, guarded by Argos with one hundred eyes, fifty were open, while the other fifty slept. Who could make them all close, except the crafty god, Hermes, lord of stratagems and trickery? Argos, one hundred eyes, O, Argos, one hundred eyes, O, o, o, Argos, O, O, O, eyes. What do fables mean, other than the pleasure of fabulation? Love is what is left even after you say, I don't love you anymore. I dreamt in a dream that I lived everything inside a mirror. If the mirror exists, being does not exist. This spring is a cesspool, a cesspit, a gutter of myths. Dead myths stink, the stench of dead kings, of dead gods, of rivers strangled by Hercules. This myth is dead and upon this myth I shall build a new myth. Dea, idea. Err once. To last, the greatest miracle.

Como quando uma história tem dois finais, como quando uma história tem vários começos, como quando uma história conta uma outra história: fugindo de Minos e do labirinto, Dédalo, o artesão incomparável, o inventor dos inventores, foi das às costas da Sicília, nas praias do rei Cócalo. Para Cócalo, o incomparável artesão arquitetou uma sala do trono onde se podia ver sem ser visto, ouvir sem ser ouvido e estar quando ausente. Minos, senhor do mar, veio reclamar seu prisioneiro. Temeroso, Cócalo lançou Dédalo num forno, onde morreu assado. Como conciliar este final com o vôo de Dédalo e Ícaro, do labirinto para a liberdade? Ou Dédalo teria sido morto depois da queda de Ícaro? Ou o cisne que possuiu Leda era apenas uma nave de velas brancas, uma nave, uma ave? Ou a imagem de Narciso é o rosto de um transeunte estranho? Toda fonte é uma moça bonita que foi amada por um deus, que disse não a um rio, que fugiu de um sátiro, nada é real, nada é apenas isso, tudo é transformação, todo traçado de constelação é o pedaço de esboço de um drama terrestre, tudo vibra de tanto significar. Que é uma esfinge, uma quimera, uma medusa, uma górgona, comparada com um pai que mata os filhos e serve sua carne ao Pai dos Deuses? Última água, esta fonte é tudo que restou do dilúvio. Fatos não se explicam com fatos, fatos se explicam com fábulas. A fábula é o desabrochar da estrutura, arquétipo em flor. Uns são transformados em flores, outros são transformados em pedra, outros ainda, se transformam em estrelas e constelações. Nada com seu ser se conforma. Toda transformação exige uma explicação. O ser, sim, é inexplicável. Uns se transformam em feras, outros são mudados em lobos, em aves, em pombos, em árvore, em fonte. Só a ninfa Eco se transformou em sua própria voz. Em que língua falar com um eco? Uma uma língua língua lembra lembra uma uma lenda lenda, Narciso, Narciso, Narciso. Que é um ciclope comparado com a história de um príncipe que matou o pai e casou com a própria mãe? Qual é o animal que de manhã anda de quatro patas, à tarde anda com duas e à noite anda com três? Consultem a Sibila, ouçam a pitonisa, leiam sinais nos céus, no movimento das águas, Narciso. O adivinho Tirésias tinha dito a Laio, rei de Tebas, vejo horrores, vejo trevas, terás um filho que vai te matar e casar com a rainha, sua mãe. Que horror a este horror se compara? Velho Tirésias cego, vítima e servidor de Apolo, deus luminoso, que dá o dom de adivinhação, senhor dos três tempos, deus que tudo vê, tudo acompanha, tudo sabe. Laio põe o menino Édipo dentro de uma caixa e a solta na correnteza do Nilo. A caixa com o menino vai dar numa praia, onde a encontra uma loba. Outros dizem pastores. Édipo o príncipe oculto, ignorante de sua origem, cresce, robusto, entre pastores. Um dia, decide ir a Tebas, a grande cidade, a cidade onde mora o grande rei. Édipo começa a realizar seu destino, o desejo da Moira, do fado, da fortuna, das potências cegas do acaso que tudo regem na terra e nos céus, na vida dos deuses e na vida dos homens, reflexo da ordem suprema. O rei Laio viajava incógnito pela estrada que sai de Tebas. Cruza com o pastor, desentende-se com ele, lutam, a juventude de Édipo prevalece, Édipo deixa para os abutres o cadáver do pai, a garganta aberta, por onde escorre sangue. A notícia chega rápido à cidade, a rainha Jocasta está viúva. Viajando incógnito, o rei foi morto por um desconhecido. A cidade está amaldiçoada. Na estrada que sai da cidade, um monstro, a Esfinge, cabeça e peitos de mulher, asas de pássaro, corpo e patas de leão, submete todos os passantes a uma pergunta, um decifra-me ou te devoro. Centenas de tebanos tinha devorado, ninguém mais se atrevia a sair da cidade. Édipo resolve enfrentar a Esfinge, o monstro interrogador, o monstro-pergunta, o proponente, o primeiro filósofo, o ser questionário// . . . // Que é um eco senão a transformação de uma voz em pedra, no eternamente idêntico a si mesmo, como fazem as letras do alfabeto, inventadas por aquele Cadmo, filho de Agenor, rei da Fenícia, e da rainha Telefasse? Cadmo, o protegido de Palas Atena, o herói que vem do Oriente para encontrar a irmã, Europa, raptada por Zeus sob a forma de um touro e matar o dragão? Inspiração da deusa, arranca os dentes do dragão e os semeia. Dos dentes, brotam guerreiros furiosos que atacam o herói. Cadmo consegue que se destruam entre si. Letras do alfabeto, dentes do dragão, vindas da Ásia, o aleph, o beit, o gama, delta, zaleth, sementes, poeiras de sons, átomos soltos, épsilon, dzeta, yod, ômega. Que diriam os Sete Sábios dos Doze Trabalhos de Hércules? Cada um tem significado preciso, como a cabeça da Medusa no escuro da deusa Atena. Omnia mecum porto, tudo o que é meu carrego comigo. Ninguém vê meu rosto e continua vivo, diz o Senhor, diz a Medusa. Por que nos moldou do barro o Titã Prometeu? Por que roubou para nós o fogo de Zeus? Ontem, estava tentando interpretar a guerra de Tróia, o significado de Ulisses, de Agamenon, o rapto de Helena, a ira de Aquiles, a loucura de Ajax, o cavalo de madeira, que coisa querem dizer essas histórias, nós górdios do lembrado e do esquecido? Aterra pensar que não são histórias, não são portadoras de um sentido recôndito. Só o mais fantástico jamais aconteceu. Tudo aconteceu. Tudo aquilo aconteceu. Pelos cem olhos de Argos tudo aquilo. Zeus quis a filha de Ínaco, rei e rio, Io, sacerdotisa de Hera, Io a transformada em novilha, guardada por Argos de cem olhos, cinqüenta abertos, enquanto os outros cinqüenta dormiam. Quem para fazê-los todos fechar senão o deus astuto, Hermes, senhor das estratégias e falcatruas? Argos, cem olhos, O, Argos, cem olhos, O, o, o, Argos, O, O, O, olhos. Que significam fábulas, além do prazer de fabular? Amor é aquilo que subsiste mesmo depois de você dizer, não te amo mais. num sonho, sonhei, viver tudo em espelho. Se espelho existe, ser não existe. Esta fonte é uma fossa, esgoto, lixo, cloaca de mitos. Mitos mortos fedem, o cheiro dos reis mortos, deuses mortos, rios estrangulados por Hércules. Este mito está morto e sobre este mito morto construirei o novo mito. Déia, idéia. Erra uma vez. Durar, o maior dos milagres.

María Mercedes Carranza (1945–2003, Colombia)

The daughter of a poet and one of the most representative voices of contemporary Colombian poetry, Carranza was born in Bogotá, Colombia, where she also took her own life, haunted by "country pain"—the torrent of violence and death of the undeclared civil war of her country. Accompanying her father in his diplomatic functions, she lived in Spain, where she frequently sat at the table with his friends Dámaso Alonso and Pablo Neruda, among others. Back in Colombia, she studied philosophy and literature. She published *Vainas y otros poemas* (A Pain in the Ass and Other Poems), and directed the *Casa de poesía Silva* (Silva's House of Poetry) for sixteen years, where she decided to prove, as she said, "that words can replace bullets" and that "poetry helps one live." In 1991, she participated in her country's reform to the constitution, from her post at the National Constituent Assembly. Her life, her Colombia—a "non-country," as she referred to it in one of her last writings—was to her like a house where "we are all buried alive." PRINCIPAL WORKS: *Vainas y otros poemas* (1972), *Hola, soledad* (1987), *El canto de las moscas* (1998)

Homeland / La patria

Michelle Gil-Montero, trans.

This house with its thick colonial walls
and nineteenth-century patio with azaleas
has been collapsing for centuries.
As if it were nothing people come and go
through rooms in ruin,
make love, dance, write letters.
Often bullets whistle or perhaps it's the wind
whistling through the busted roof.
In this house the living sleep with the dead,
mimic their habits, repeat their gestures,
and when they sing, they sing their failures.
All is ruin in this house,
the embrace and music are in ruin,
fate, every morning, laughter are ruins;
tears, silence, dreams.
The windows reveal ravished landscapes,
flesh and ash conflate in the faces,
in the mouths words shuffle with fear.
In this house we are all buried alive.

Esta casa de espesas paredes coloniales/ y un patio de azaleas muy
decimonónico/ hace varios siglos que se viene abajo./ Como si nada las
personas van y vienen/ por las habitaciones en ruina,/ hacen el amor,
bailan, escriben cartas./ A menudo silban balas o es tal vez el viento/ que

silba a través del techo desfondado./ En esta casa los vivos duermen con los muertos,/ imitan sus costumbres, repiten sus gestos/ y cuando cantan, cantan sus fracasos./ Todo es ruina en esta casa,/ están en ruina el abrazo y la música,/ el destino, cada mañana, la risa son ruina;/ las lágrimas, el silencio, los sueños./ Las ventanas muestran paisajes destruidos,/ carne y ceniza se confunden en las caras,/ en las bocas las palabras se revuelven con miedo./ En esta casa todos estamos enterrados vivos.

Heels over Head with Life / Patas arriba con la vida

Mary Crow, trans.

"I know I'm going to die because I no longer love anything."—Manuel Machado

I will die mortal,
that is to say having passed
through this world
without breaking or staining it,
I didn't invent a single vice,
but I tasted all the virtues:
I leased my soul
to hypocrisy: I have trafficked
with words,
with signs, with silence;
I surrendered to the lie:
I have hoped for hope,
I have loved love,
and one day I even pronounced
the words My Country;
I accepted the hoax:
I have been mother, citizen,
daughter, friend,
companion, lover;
I believed in the truth:
two and two are four,
María Mercedes ought to be born,
ought to grow, reproduce herself and die
and that's what I'm doing.
I am the sampler of the twentieth century.
And when fear arrives
I go to watch television
in order to dialogue with my lies.

"Sé que voy a morir porque no amo ya nada."—Manuel Machado// Moriré mortal,/ es decir habiendo pasado/ por este mundo/ sin romperlo ni

María Mercedes Carranza   **471**

mancharlo./ No inventé ningún vicio,/ pero gocé de todas las virtudes:/ arrendé mi alma/ a la hipocresía: he traficado/ con las palabras,/ con los gestos, con el silencio;/ cedí a la mentira:/ he esperado la esperanza,/ he amado el amor,/ y hasta algún día pronuncié/ la palabra Patria;/ acepté el engaño:/ he sido madre, ciudadana,/ hija de familia, amiga,/ compañera, amante./ Creí en la verdad:/ dos y dos son cuatro,/ María Mercedes debe nacer,/ crecer, reproducirse y morir/ y en esas estoy./ Soy un dechado del siglo XX./ Y cuando el miedo llega/ me voy a ver televisión/ para dialogar con mis mentiras.

I'm Afraid / Tengo miedo

Michelle Gil-Montero, trans.

Look at me: fear inhabits me.
Behind these sober eyes, in this body that loves: fear.
Fear at dawn because the sun will inevitably come out and I'll have to see it,
at dusk because it might not come out tomorrow.
I heed the mysterious noises in this foundering house,
ghosts, shadows close in on me and I'm afraid.
I make sure to sleep with the lights on
and take up what I can of spears, armor, delusions.
But a stain on the tablecloth is perhaps enough
for the fright to take hold of me again.
Nothing calms or quells me;
not this useless word, nor the passion of love,
nor the mirror where I see my dead face.
Hear me, I scream it: I'm afraid.

Miradme: en mí habita el miedo./ Tras estos ojos serenos, en este cuerpo que ama: el miedo./ El miedo al amanecer porque inevitable el sol saldrá y he de verlo,/ cuando atardece porque puede no salir mañana./ Vigilo los ruidos misteriosos de esta casa que se derrumba,/ ya los fantasmas, las sombras me cercan y tengo miedo./ Procuro dormir con la luz encendida/ y me hago como puedo a lanzas, corazas, ilusiones./ Pero basta quizás sólo una mancha en el mantel/ para que de nuevo se adueñe de mí el espanto./ Nada me calma ni sosiega:/ ni esta palabra inútil, ni esta pasión de amor,/ ni el espejo donde veo ya mi rostro muerto./ Oídme bien, lo digo a gritos: tengo miedo.

Canto 17: Cumbal

Michelle Gil-Montero, trans.

In bluejeans
And with a made-up face
Death came
To Cumbal.
Florid War
With a machete edge.

En bluyines/ Y con la cara pintada/ Llegó la muerte/ A Cumbal./ Guerra
Florida/ A filo de machete.

Canto 18: Soacha

Michelle Gil-Montero, trans.

A black
Bird scents
The remnants of
Life.
It could be God
Or the killer:
It's all the same.

Un pájaro/ Negro husmea/ Las sobras de/ La vida./ Puede ser Dios/ O el
asesino:/ Da lo mismo ya.

Canto 3: Dabeiba

Michelle Gil-Montero, trans.

The river is sweet here
In Dabeiba
And brings red roses
Dispersed in the waters.
They aren't roses,
It's blood
Taking other routes.

El río es dulce aquí/ En Dabeiba/ Y lleva rosas rojas/ Esparcidas en las aguas./
No son rosas,/ Es la sangre/ Que toma otros caminos.

Arturo Carrera (1948–, Argentina)

Born in Coronel Pringles in the province of Buenos Aires, Carrera has had a long and prestigious literary career. In addition to his many publications, his writing workshops have granted him a direct access to younger generations. His current work explores the minutiae of everyday life in relation to a transcendentalism inspired by the rural landscapes of his native countryside. Carrera's many books involve a vast trajectory that moves from early visual practice to a more subjective poetics. He has been the recipient of multiple awards, such as a Guggenheim Fellowship and the Premio Konex. PRINCIPAL WORKS: *Escrito con un nictógrafo* (1972), *La partera canta* (1982), *El vespertillo de la parcas* (1997)

Excerpt from It Wasn't in Sicily, It Wasn't Here / No fue en Sicilia, no fue aquí

G. J. Racz, trans.

I
The men were sleeping, the boys
nodding off.
The young girls chatted, their laughter
floating toward the wondrous breeze
off the lagoon.

. . . it wasn't here, it wasn't in Sicily.

The footprint of a boy
out "walking" with his mother before she went to bed
was lapped by the sea froth
just at its edges . . .

The dogs raged near nightfall,
biting one another.

Now that same breeze lifts that same footprint,
the plaintive venation of reminiscence,
faint like a footstep in our dreams.
Two little girls in the sand by the sea
are mounting their own one-ring circus, out there
where a plunder of primers and catastrophes
appear close to confessing: "We are this plunder
of primers and catastrophes."

It isn't in Sicily, it isn't here.

In varying degrees of light, summer's persistence
pays visit to a dark-colored rainbow dissipating tenuously
in the sky.

The women under the still sure shelter of night
recount most likely true stories of love.

Ignoble appearance neither concerns
nor excludes them
but protects.

II
I'll leave this lagoon in front of you,

a lagoon that knows nothing about us yet
surrounds us still, bringing us together for the first time,
ever closer together.

And so we dare feel how these many forms
stick fast to one another, taking hold of a body no longer ours.

. . . .

seagulls in their nests continue grousing
as if they recognized us

(it isn't here, it isn't in Sicily . . .)

this lagoon knows nothing about us yet
surrounds us still
without cutting us off.

I'm inspired to listen for the stealth
with which space and sounds like laughter and shouting
stick fast to one another, taking hold of a body

(so far ahead of us,
that is).

III
may the earth swallow me whole.
may nature swallow me whole as well.

there go the bandurrias flying off to the lagoon

at dusk again, instruments without the routine
of flight,

passing by enveloped in a halo like the moon's,
like some predictable corona,
like a veil.

walks, walks,

a walk of tiny Fates around the lagoon,

not in Sicily, not here, but
on that unknown continent where the immigrants
who loved me emigrate with me now once again,
gathering with ease like animals on an ark
at the old call,

at the old sound of life on the lagoon

a life without history, geography or Columbus,
without the call of the family coat of arms
which Mandelstam termed
"the cup of boiled water."

On Monte Hermoso, just steps from the sea,
beneath the sea.

I/ Los Hombres dormían. Los niños/ caveceaban./ Las jóvenes muchachas
conversaban y sus risas/ iban a la brisa única/ de la laguna.// . . . no fue
aquí, no fue en Sicilia.// La huella del pie de un niño/ que "paseó" con su
madre antes que ella durmiera,/ fue lamida apenas por la espuma/ de los
bordes . . . // Los perros del anochecer, furiosos,/ se mordían/ La misma brisa
alza ahora la misma huella,/ la nervadura quejumbrosa de la reminiscencia/
como un paso en los sueños.// Dos niñas en la arena del mar/ construyen
su propio circo mínimo, allá,/ donde un botín de alfabetos y catástrofes/
parecen delatar: "Nosotros somos ese botín/ de alfabetos y catástrofes".//
No es en Sicilia, no es aquí.// En grados-luz la insistencia del verano/ visita
un arco iris oscuro que tenuemente/ se disipa.// La mujeres con su fábrica
de noche todavía cierta/ cuentan sus probables verdades de amor.// La
innoble apariencia no las toca;/ no las excluye y/ las protege.// II/ Dejo esta
laguna frente a ti,// esta laguna que nos ignora y sin embargo/ nos circunda,
nos une por primera vez, / nos va reuniendo.// Nos atrevemos a sentir
cómo tantas formas/ se adhieren y se apoderan de un cuerpo que ya no es
nuestro.// . . . // hay gaviotas en sus nidos todavía quejándose/ como si nos
reconocieran// (no es aquí, no es en Sicilia . . .)// esta laguna nos ignora
y sin embargo/ nos circunda,/ no nos aísla.// Me animo a escuchar con qué
sigilo/ el espacio y tantos sonidos como risas, voces,/ se adhieren y se
apoderan de un cuerpo// (pero tan adelante/ de nosotros).// III/ que esta
tierra me trague./ que esta naturaleza me trague.// allá van las bandurrias
volando hacia la laguna,// otra vez al atardecer, pero sin la rutina/ del
vuelo./ pasan envueltas en un halo parecido al de la luna,/ como una
corona anticipada,/ como un velo.// paseos, paseos,// paseo de las pequeñas
parcas alrededor de la laguna,// no en Sicilia, no aquí, sino/ en ese ignoto
continente donde los inmigrantes/ que me amaron ahora vuelven conmigo
a emigrar,/ se unen fácilmente, como animales de un arca/ al antiguo
reclamo,// al antiguo rumor a vida de la laguna// vida sin historia, sin

geografía, sin Colón,/ sin el reclamo del escudo familiar/ que Mandelstam llamó/ "el vaso de agua hervida".// En Monte Hermoso, a pocos pasos del mar,/ debajo del mar.

Cecilia Vicuña (1948–, Chile)

A poet and visual artist of indigenous and Basque lineage, Vicuña was born in Santiago, Chile, to a family of artists and intellectuals. Her work began in the mid-1960s with "The quipu that remembers nothing," an empty cord in space, and "arte precario," installations in nature and city streets, created as a way of "listening to an ancient silence longing to be heard." Forrest Gander said that hers "is a radical imagination, as her poetry moved out of the page, and into the world." In her multilingual oral performances she weaves people into an incantatory communal song, destabilizing the traditional boundaries between audience and performer. In her book *Instan* the poem migrates to dwell in the common roots of English and Spanish as seen from the indigenous perspective. Since 1980 she has divided her time between Chile and New York. PRINCIPAL WORKS: *SABORAMI* (1973), *Precario/ Precarious* (1983), *PALABRARmás* (1984), *Unravelling Words & The Weaving of Water* (1992), *QUIPOem/The Precarious, The Art and Poetry of Cecilia Vicuña* (1997), *CloudNet* (1999), *Instan* (2002)

Physical Portrait / Retrato físico

Rosa Alcalá, trans.

My skull is shaped like a hazelnut
and my buttocks feisty
over two ticklish melon-thighs.
With my heliotrope knees
and ankles of pumice stone
a neck of African birch
none of me is white
apart from my teeth,
not even the whites of my eyes,
which are of an indefinable color.
I have twenty fingers
I'm not very sure I can keep—
they are always on the verge of falling off
even though I love them.

The earth listening to us, Con cón, Chile, 1966

London khipu, 1966

After that, I end. The rest
I keep at the edge of the ocean.
I am not shameless enough
to tell the truth
and every time there is a ditch
I fall in
because I'm neither cautious
nor wary.

Tengo el cráneo en forma de avellana/ y unas nalgas festivas a la orilla/ de
unos muslos cosquillosos de melón./ Tengo rodillas de heliotropo/ y tobillos
de piedra pómez/cuello de abedul africano/porque aparte de los dientes/
no tengo nada blanco/ ni la esclerótida de color indefinible./ Tengo veinte
dedos/ y no estoy muy segura/de poder conservarlos/siempre están a punto
de caerse/ aunque los quiero mucho./ Después me termino y lo demás/
lo guardo a la orilla del mar./ No soy muy desvergonzada/ a decir verdad/
siempre que hay un hoyo/ me caigo dentro/ porque no soy precavida/ ni
sospechosa.

Excerpt from Instan

alba saliva
el instan

time bending
tongue

entwine
the betwixt

double
thread

madre
del habla

imán
del gen

palabra
estrella

mother
of time

el sign
      o
no es
si no
insi
nua t
    ción

de la nube
en la nave
ga t
    ción

the nuance
of words

the mist
to go through

. . . .

corazón
del aquí

why are
we here?

luz del
portal

mei
del migrar

changed
heart

the in me
grant
            ing
me
life

un creer
en el core

changing
the heart
of the ear
            th

latus del
llevo llevo

mi sed
de un

futur
        o
re late

gramma
ticar

de un
recipro
cate

carry back
el re   late

la justicia
de la relación

de volver
el juguito
vital

¿adónde
la leche
de una
teta
común?

a com mon
teat?

milk
del trans
late?

las venas
fulgentes
de un hilo
de luz?

a suckling
of musical
ink?

la her
mandad
de los rhythm

        s

virtu

    e

       del
cog
   nate?

Wilson Bueno (1949–, Brazil)

A poet and narrator born in Jaguapitá, Brazil, Bueno grew up in poverty but by age fourteen was already a professional feature writer. He founded the magazine *Nico-lau*, which was celebrated by Octavio Paz and became a magnificent venture that gathered the most prominent figures of Brazilian culture. During the intrepid and unruly 1960s and 1970s, he made Rio de Janeiro his home. There he wrote about "unmentionable, crazy deeds" and experienced "everything that can be imagined," from two existential breakdowns to opposing the dictatorship, Gal Costa, the Leblon beach, and "sex, drugs, and rock-and-roll." A devout reader of Clarice Lispector, he confesses that her works are like "prayers" to him. Describing himself as a "rewriter," he combined in his poetry Portuguese, Spanish, and Guarani with Portunhol (a border mix). Bueno aims at erasing the boundaries between these languages, embracing their territories and inflections in the text itself. PRINCIPAL WORKS: *Bolero's Bar* (1986), *Manual de zoofilia* (1991), *Ojos de agua* (1991), *Mar paraguayo* (1992)

Excerpt from Mar paraguayo

Erin Moure, trans.

: today le boy put me to hearing murmures of the lunaire storm in the
swelter of siesta, I knew sudden and à bout de breath he'd come: shadow
et dessin: foufounes so avid: nipples: hard thighs riding mounted: son
contour sharp: the chestnut silkfloss of his cheveux: I bite, remorse-
bitten: takwa'ahson: takwa'ahson tehota'a:ronte: the needle urges in:
crochet: escargot: curve: the corde: araignée: takwa'ahson: le boy so in
tune with me: already my peau and hair raise their hackles in a shudder:
c'est moi the enigme and such sphinx endowing: I've got to devour
him ever imprévisible: stroking in the g-string his brazen sex: but above
all his eyes vertes in a face of laugh and sun: such thorax in the lash
of wind et lament: to danse in siesta: rêve: j'suis his araignée: algebra:
ready boa constrictor: partout his adept tongue me caresse: I anoint him
totally with saliva and drool: humours: sweats: the miasmes: les spasmes:
the siesta sets my deep uterus ablaze: the boy: suddenly takwa'ahson:
if he'd just stick his tongue out lentement and run it over me: de mes
pieds jusqu'au ciel in mourning where I glimpse the murmurs of the
lunar storm: lip contre lip: spider and sprout: la danse de sa bouche:
takwa'ahson: the harpoon of the needle crosses the line weaving lineal:
before nudité the wantonness of piss: takwa'ahson tehota'a:ronte:
I force his tête upon my mouth: erase the baton from him: the eraser:
erase la ligne: the siesta: my crie: never to forget the boy's soupire
before all et tout se transforment: toile d'araignée, brume et nuage in
the murmurs of the lunar storm: in a single mortal sigh: mine and
his: the fiery couteau of his lance: fired: point final: nude: lancée: nu:
launched: period: nitakwa'ahsona:'a: takwa'ahson: the toile goes slack:
the lights se perdent in the growing nocturnal bleu: toile d'araignée:
takwa'ahson: the boy peut returner tomorrow: it could just be encore
and newly no more than the oblique projection of the hustler bringing
grief: takwa'ahson: look there: this boy who walks on pavement stones
sans even knowing j'existe above him: out there là in the dusk: rêve de
sleep qui a fait the ruby capitulation of the sole entité that can see him:
he who walks so imperiously: toward the mer: his taste of conch and
salt: I spin and spin et tisse the web: nitakwa'ahsona:'a: surrender: all

surrendered: had rendered imagination fébrile: figue-tree hour: iguane:
takwa'ahson tehota'a:ronte: in siesta: today in these stifling tuesdays:
massed mercredis: après-midi: the faun: I had le boy tooth and nail:
I had him couched in my belly's entrails: takwa'ahson: toile d'araignée:
nitakwa'ahsona:'a: only he doesn't know it: and the sea still has his taste
and semen: even son sexe ne peut couvrir ces traces: vanishable he came:
nitakwa'ahsona:'a transparence et lumières: takwa'ahson: takwa'ahson
tehota'a:ronte:

. . . .

La fatigue des métals, l'oeuf de l'oegg du scorpion, the vigil, the tacit meat
made a yoke, inheritance d'adulthood, what's spent, les years, moitié
ville, moitié vie, the scorched alley, rivière ébulliante de cinquante
winteres, the dark face of exhausted blood, kidneys already failing, la
pression artérial, nettle and paprika, the point, the sea, le cap, la mer,
the facte and the cape of good hope, those lost in the brambles, the fact,
the arc du sinistre, les pallid ones, dusk, our chambre, notre maison, all
khe'kenhren'stha', the humblest lamp, our bed, the amputated sexe that
still itches. And I choke it, the flaccid, le flou, the hollow of the hollowe
of the middle, it's all in half-light. And there's worse: demain il faut que
je me chante a new zany chanson, and maybe I will feel complete as are
toutes the stations of the Hour of Disgraces. Aquidauana, Dorados, Puerto
Soledad, cities of rivières and dust, of bones languid at exactement two in
the afternoon, sieste et feu, it dumbfounds us febrile in an imponderable
viscosité, it all goes sweaty and sucks, it all blanches emolient in a death
shudder of innards éclatés and more, the post-colic collapse made of
rips and vomit, the tree ne move pas tout seule, the taste of sex on the
tongue, la langue, le sexe in idiomes multiples, owen:na', almost like a
deflowered rose, death and sex don't talk but how splendide it feels—the
belly that lifts its hackles, resounding tremor of the skin touched par
desire and coma, the air, all the air as it was, choked, a thirst that can't
be slaked by water and fear prêt just as, after un peu, le dur soleil can
dry out les rues où reign only bordelles and bars de port—dead and vide
from this fatigue de personne et de no-one. Aquidauana. How tristes,
how mélancoliques sont les soirs qui s'attardent brûlants et encore
mutes, notre maison des femmes, a maindrag on the frontière, our
bedrooms suffocantes, sheet and sex and cette punishing chaleur. All of
it in ce temps-là, de forgetting, so it makes up a kind of destin—a way
of suffering less what God does not give only today to recognize cette
inclination de nous à martyrdom and jubilation. Deux couteaux et deux
blades. May thy great Hand ever save us so it doesn't sink in our souls,
the definitive cristal or his splendid shard, in the spume de blood et
grass. The seas tinged ruby. Kania:tare: onehshon. Kaniatara'ko:wa'.

: hoy el niño me pôs a ouvrir los rumores de la tempestade lunar: en
el mormaço de la siesta, pressenti nítido y casi arfante que el chegaria:
sombra y dibujo: ávida nádega: mamilos: duros muslos a cavalo: su
contorno preciso: la paina castanha del pêlo: muerdo: remuerdome:
ñandu: ñanduti: la aguja trabaja: crochê: caracol: curva: la línea: la linha:
la araña: ñandu: todo el niño se acuerda en mi: y já me estremece un eriçar
de piel y pêlo: soy yo el enigma y lo alforje esfinge: hay que devorarlo a el
siempre imprevisto: dibujado en la tanga su sexo ostensivo: mas sobretodo
los ojos verdes contra la cara de risa y sol: lo tôrax en los embates del
viento y del lamiento: a bailar en la siesta: sueño: soy su araña: álgebra:
pronta jibóia: toda me enlambe su língua destra: todo lo unto de cuspo y
baba: humores: suores: los miasmas: espasmos: la siesta me pone abrasado
el útero profundo: el niño: súbita ñandu: puede que ponga su língua
a lenta y me percorra: de los pies al cielo en luto donde vislumbro los
rumores de la tempestade lunar: lábio premindo lábio: araña y grêlo: la
dança de su boca: ñando: el arpón de la guja avança sobre la linha en
trenzada línea: antes del nudo los caprichos de la meada: ñandurenimbó:
fuerzo su cabeça contra mi boca: borro-lhe batón: el borrador: borrar
la linha: la siesta: mi grito: nunca olvidar el gemido que tuvo en niño
antes de que todo y tudo se transformasse: telaraña, neblina y nuvem en
los rumores de la tempestade lunar: de uno solo gemido mortal: mio y
dele: la faca en fuego de su lanza: lanzada: punto: nudo: laçada: nudo:
lanzada: punto: ñanduti: ñandu: la tela va aborrindo: las luces se pierden
en el azul más nocturno: telaraña: ñandu: el niño mañana puede que
retorne: puede que sea aún otra vez y nuevamente solo la projeción
oblíqua de la marafona que apena: ñandu: espreita: esto niño que marcha
por las piedras de la calçada sin sequer saber que sobrexisto: acá en el
entardecer: sueño de sueño hecho la rubra capitulación de uno ente que
solo puede verlo: a el que imponente marcha: dirección del mar: su gusto
de concha y sal: teço y teço y teço telaraña ñanduti: renda: rendados:
rendêra imaginación fabril: higuêra hora: iguana: ñandurenimbó: en la
siesta: hoy en estos martes sufocados: miércoles medrados: après-midi:
el fauno: tuvo a el niño a dentadas y mordidas: yo lo tuvo en mi ventre
entrañado: ñandu: teleraña: ñanduti: solo el no lo sabe: y sigue en el
mar su gusto y sêmen: ni el sexo há de tampar estos traçados: evaporable
véu: ñanduti: transparencia y luces: ñandu: ñandurenimbó:// . . . // La
fatiga de los metales, el huevo del huevo del escorpión, la espreita, la
carne tácita hecho un jugo, la herança de los mayores, lo que se gasta, los
anos, media ciudad, media edad, la calcinada travessia, el rio ferviente
de los cinquenta inviernos, la cara oscura de la sangre exausta, los rines
que ya no funcionan, la pressión arterial, la urtiga y la páprica, el cabo,

el mar, el cabo, el facto y el cabo de la buena esperanza, los pérdidos en
la rama, el facto, el arco del siniestro, los pálidos, el entardecer, nuestro
quarto, nuestra casa, ñemomirí, la lámpara humílima, nuestra cama, el
sexo amputado que todavia prossigue coçando. Y lo engasgo, todo el
flácido, lo flaco, el ueco del ueco del medio, es todo a media luz. E peor:
mañana yo terê de me cantar una nueva canción desatinada y, tal vez,
me sentirê completa como san completas todas las estaciones de la Hora
Aziaga.// Aquidauana, Dorados, Puerto Soledad, ciudades de rios y polvo,
de huessos moles a las duas en punto de la tarde, siesta y fuego, febril nos
assombra dentro una viscosidad imponderable, todo se suda y suga, todo
se emblanquiça emoliente en uno estertor de intestinos desatados y más
la derrota después de una colica toda hecha de esgar y vômito, el árbol
no se mueve de si, el gusto de sexo en la língua, la língua, el sexo en los
múltiplos idiomas, ayvu, casi asi como una rosa deflorada, la muerte y
el sexo nada hablan pero como esplendiente se siente—el ventre que se
eriça, el troar sonante de la piel tocada de deseo y coma, el aire, todo el
aire como se fuera, engasgos, una sede que no la sacia sequer la água y
el miedo pronto de que, más un poco, el duro sol pueda secar a las calles
donde imperam los prostíbulos ô los bares del cais—vacios y muertos desto
cansaço por nadie y ninguém. Aquidauana. Que tristes, que melancolicos
los demorados entardeceres encendiados y todavia mudos, nuestra casa
de mujeres, currutela en la frontera, nuestros quartos sufocados, lençol y
sexo y punitivo calor. Todo esto en neste tiempo, no olvido, se constituía
en una espécie asi de destino—una forma de sofrer menos que Dios no los
dá para solamente hoy compreender esta inclinación nuestra al martírio y
al júbilo. Dos facas y dos gumes. Salva-nos siempre Su gran mano para que
no nos afunde en la alma el definitivo cristal ô su caco eplêndido, en la
escuma de sangre y vidro. Tinge-se rubro el mar. Paraipieté. Pará.

Néstor Perlongher (1949–1992, Argentina)

Perlongher's body of poetry deals with the themes of sexuality and eroticism and is
strongly associated with the neo-baroque. Born and raised in Buenos Aires, he incorporated many elements of Argentine history into his writing. In 1982, he moved
to São Paulo to teach anthropology. His later works such as *Alambres* share with
Osvaldo Lamborghini's a poetics capable of addressing state and sexual politics as a
form of social criticism. In spite of dying only twelve years after he first started publishing, Perlongher's work—in addition to that of Kozer's—is considered to be one
of the most successful examples of Latin American neo-baroque poetics. PRINCIPAL
WORKS: *Austria-Hungaría* (1980), *Alambres* (1987), *Aguas aéreas* (1992)

Tuyú

Molly Weigel, trans.

History, is it a language?
Does this language have to do with the language of history
or with the history of language/
where it stuttered/
Does it have to do with this verse?
living tongues licking dead tongues
tongues rotting like socks
tongues, lingering, fungous
this language of history/which history?
if the long history of the tongue isn't taken as a story

They tell it
in a galley:

Miz Rudecinda
didn't the riding gear sprinkle the soul?
didn't the screamer bird scare itself?

(Melted gauchos, with their cow tongues, with their clubs
with their yokes and their silver coin belts
melted gaucho: he digs his spurs into the—melted—back
of the tongue, as if trapped in a rabbit warren)
A few kilometers from San Clemente, in the Tuyú
is the tomb of Santos Vega, where the orcas come in
and the surfers in their grass skirts, on the crystal waves
Broken crystal, ornery orcas of history: they go
to the harpooners with their hooks: they go
where the deck-clearings cleave: where, melted, the gaucho
takes out his jack-knife and disgraces himself:
it was history, that disgrace!
disgrace of lying in the Tuyú, of a widespread lying
The cannibals in that crystal harassed by rude waves;
and you, in that lethargy of rigor mortis, don't you take it lying down?
Take crystalline, plumed crests?

La historia, es un lenguaje?/ Tiene que ver este lenguaje con el lenguaje
de la historia/ o con la historia del lenguaje/ en donde balbuceó/ tiene
que ver con este verso?/ lenguas vivas lamiendo lenguas muertas/ lenguas
menguadas como medias/ lenguas, luengas, fungosas:/ este lenguaje de
la historia / cuál historia?/ si no se tiene por historia la larga historia de
la lengua// Cuentan/ en un fogón:// Ña-Rudecinda/ no roció el apero el
ánima?/ no se hizo jabón el chajá?// (Gauchos fundidos, con sus lenguas
de vaca, con sus trancas/ con sus coyundas y sus rastras/ Gaucho fundido:

él clava sus espuelas en el dorso—fundido-/ de la lengua, como atrapado
en una vizcachera)/ A unos kilómetros de San Clemente, en el Tuyú/ está
la tumba de Santos Vega, adonde acuden las toninas/ y los surfistas en sus
jabas, sobre las olas de cristal/ Roto cristal, tercas toninas de la historia: van/
donde los arponeros con sus garfios: van/ donde los zafarranchos cachan:
donde fundido el gaucho/ saca el facón y se disgracia:/ era la historia, esa
disgracia!/ disgracia de yacer en el Tuyú, de un yacer general/ Los caníbales
en ese cristal las rudas olas asaetan;/ y tú, en esa pereza de la yertez, no
jalas?/ Jalas de crestas cristalinas y empenachadas?

Mme. Schoklender

Molly Weigel, trans.

Decked out in prickly pears and gladioli: mother, how you whip
  those scenes
of candied bearcubs, those bitter honeys: how you flourish
the frothing featherduster: and the spiders: how
you scare the stunned brute with your acid strap: fasten, pound in, and
  crush:
crutches of a paraplegic mother: soiled pelvis, Turkish
  trousers: it's that mother who insinuates herself in the mirror offering
regalia of a night in Smyrna and baccarat: fasten and mark off: shed
the mother who offers herself changing into a befeathered lover,
  ruffle and ransacked: that plucking
of the mother who pulls down the gauzes of the whisky tumblers
  on the mouse
table: mother and runs: cuts off and hooking: and hiccups:
hanging from
the mother's neck a bracelet of blood, pubic blood, of bullets
and bad guys: blood weighted by those bills and those creams we
ate too much of on the little table of light in the shadow of our
easy anniversaries: that giant tassel: if you took my balls as fruits of an
intrepid and erect elixir: dingles from a glacé that sweetened you:
but killing you was going too far: sweetly: making myself eat
  from those
stiff small disgusts that crouch tender in the haughty castling of my
muscles, and that conch-er when you lick with your mother's mouth the
caverns of the rising, the waning: the caves:
and I, did I penetrate you? I could
hardly stop myself like a drunk male of hinges, shapeless, withered from
tequilas, from putting myself up in syrup, penetrating your blondnesses
  of a mother offering themselves,
like an altar, to the son—minor and mannered? adopting your fan

Néstor Perlongher   487

wires, the jewels you carelessly drop chiming onto the table,
amid the tumblers of gin, indecorously greased with that archaic
rouge of your lips?
                              like a wanton wolf cub, I could, rise up,
behind your petticoats and lick your breasts, as you'd lick my nipples
and leave dribbling on my tits—which seemed to titillate—
the purr:
                    of your murmuring saliva? the strap of your teeth?
could I mother?
                              like a gallant in ruins who surprises his sweetheart between
the crude flies of the longshoremen, on the docks, when
in the buttons, spawns loose, his protected perfidy? that secret
pubic place? how therefore I clutched that hand-hold, those tapirs
encrusted with orchid crutches, velvetly suspicious;
and supporting with my same member the cankerous spume of your sex,
to unload on your forehead? You'd smile tassled between the drops of
   semen of
the longshoremen who on the dock took you from behind, mildly:
I snatched you: what did you imagine?

Ataviada de pencas, de gladiolos: cómo fustigas, madre, esas escenas/ de
oseznos acaramelados, esas mieles amargas: cómo blandes/ el plumero de
espuma: y las arañas: cómo/ espantas con tu ácido bretel el fijo bruto: fija,
remacha y muele:/ muletillas de madre parapléxica: pelvis acochambrado,
bombachones/ de esmirna: es esa madre la que en el espejo se insinúa
ofreciendo/ las galas de una noche de esmirna y bacarat:
fija y demarca: muda/ la madre que se ofrece mudándose en amantes al
plumereo, despiole y despilfarro: ese desplume/ de la madre que corre las
gasas de los vasos de whisky en la mesa/ ratona: madre y corre: cercena y
garabato: y gorgotea:/ pende del/ cuello de la madre una ajorca de sangre,
sangre púbica, de plomos/ y pillastres: sangre pesada por esas facturas y
esas cremas que/ comimos de más en la mesita de luz en la penumbra
de nuestras/ muelles bodas: ese borlazgo: si tomabas mis bolas como
frutas de un/ elixir enhiesto y denodado: pendorchos de un glacé que te
endulzaba:/ pero era demasiado matarte: dulcemente: haciéndome comer
de esos/ pelillos tiesos que tiernos se agazapan en el enroque altivo de
mis/ muslos, y que se encaracolan cuando lames con tu boca de madre las/
cavernas del orto, del ocaso: las cuevas;/ y yo, te penetraba? pude/ acaso
pararme como un macho ebrio de goznes, de tequilas mustio,/ informe,
almibararme, penetrar tus blonduras de madre que se ofrece,/ como un altar,
al hijo—menor y amanerado? adoptar tus alambres de/ abanico, tus joyas
que al descuido dejabas tintinear sobre la mesa,/ entre los vasos de ginebra,
indecorosamente pringados de ese rouge/ arcaico de tus labias?/ cual
lobezno lascivo, pude, alzarme,/ tras tus enaguas, y lamer tus senos, como

tú me lamías los pezones/ y dejabas babeante en las tetillas—que parecían
titilar—el/ ronroneo:/ de tu saliva rumorosa? el bretel de tus dientes?/
pude madre?/ como un galán en ruinas que sorprende a su novia entre/ las
toscas braguetas de los estibadores, en los muelles, cuando/ laxa desova,
en los botones, la perfidia a él guardada? ese lugar/ secreto y púbico? cómo
entonces tomé esa agarradera, esos tapires/ incrustados con mangos de
magnolia, aterciopeladamente sospechosos;/ y sosteniendo con mi mismo
miembro la espuma escancorosa de tu sexo,/ descargar en tu testa? Sonreías
borlada entre las gotas de semen de/ los estibadores que en el muelle te
tomaban de atrás y muellemente:/ te agarré: qué creías?

Daisy Zamora (1950–, Nicaragua)

A poet and essayist born in Managua, Nicaragua, Zamora grew up under the protection of her upper-class family. She obtained a degree in psychology and participated in the insurrection that overthrew the dictatorship of Anastasio Somoza.
During the underground period preceding the victory of the Sandinista revolution,
she was in charge of programming for the FSLN (the Sandinista National Liberation Front) radio. Later she served as Vice Minister of Culture for that government.
At present, Zamora lives in the United States. In the words of American poet Sonia
Sanchez, her poems "resound with life. Commitment. Struggle. Love. She has been
a fighter for liberation and women's rights all of her life. Her poems say Woman.
Soldier. Woman. Mother. Woman. Poet. Woman. Lover. Woman. Woman. Woman."
PRINCIPAL WORKS: *La violenta espuma* (1981), *En limpio se escribe la vida* (1988), *La
mujer nicaragüense en la poesía* (1992), *A cada quien la vida* (1994)

Excerpt from Radio Sandino

Margaret Randall and Elinor Randall, trans.

—THIS IS Radio Sandino /
    Voice of Nicaragua's liberation
Official voice of the FSLN
    transmitting by short wave
        on the International
        41 meter band
from somewhere in Nicaragua
throughout the country until 11 P.M.

    My great aunt must be glued to her radio.
My mother and brothers in Honduras
glued to our voice
        our voices

this voice that comes in clandestinely
    every night
            broadcasting 'til dawn.
Reaching perhaps as far as a building in Mexico City,
to those who wait in exile:
            the dial's amber light
glancing off expectant worried faces.
One more voice in the family group
attentive to this voice, this hope
that filters through cracks in windows,
            in doors,
crosses streets, bridges, rushing water.
This voice unleashing torrential rains to the last report,
the last voices, until the rainstorm ends
and only the humidity remains,
the patter of drops until dawn.

—Radio Sandino
        PRESENTS
        its news report
        "Guerrilla Drum"

**Battle Communique from the High Command
of the "Rigoberto López Pérez" Western Front.**

1. The High Command of the "Rigoberto López Pérez"
Western Front reports that at 10:30 A.M. the general barracks of
Somoza's National Guard in the city of León were definitively
occupied. All the city's church bells are ringing madly, and the
people are in the streets, celebrating its total liberation.

2. Our forces recovered all weaponry and ammunition
belonging to the genocidal Guard. Their commander, General
Ariel Argüello, was shot down while trying to escape shielded
by a defenseless woman who was rescued by our troops.

3. Our Commander Guadalupe Moreno (Abel) fell heroically
at one o'clock yesterday afternoon, as he directed the attack on
the command post. Commander "Abel" took part in the
occupation of the same post in September of 1978.

. . . .

ESTELI, WITH YOUR NAME
WE WILL SIGN SOMOZA'S EPITAPH!

"There goes the General,
        through Estelí,

Homeland or Death
     sing the peasants of Wiwilí.

There goes the General,
        his decision made,
with his brave men and women
        ridding Nicaragua of the invader . . . "

. . . .

"Onward
     onward heroic guerrilla
     guerrilla forward march
     you are winning peace with your war
     with the weaponry of freedom.

Guerrilla /
     Guerrilla /
          Guerrilla ever onward
with the fire of peace in your gun
from mountains to plains ever onward
          Guerrilla, onward to win or to die."

("Verónica" was Flor de María Antuñez.
Iván Montenegro was called "Ernesto.")
Only in death will we regain our names
our given names and the nicknames
we learn to love as we grow
and recognize ourselves in them.
Our real name, the name
death gives us back.

—ESTA ES Radio Sandino/ Voz de la Liberación de Nicaragua/ Voz
Oficial del Frente Sandinista/ que transmite en la Onda Corta/ Banda
Internacional/ de los 41 metros/ desde algún lugar de Nicaragua/ hasta
las 11 de la noche de toda Nicaragua.// Mi tía-abuela debe de estar pegada
al aparato./ Mi mamá y mis hermanos en Honduras,/ pegados a nuestra
voz,/ a nuestras voces/ a esta voz entrando a escondidas/ cada noche/
esparciéndose hasta la madrugada./ Subiendo quizá hasta algún edificio de
México,/ acercándose a los exiliados:/ la luz amarilla del dial/ rebotando
en rostros expectantes y penumbrosos;/ Otra voz entre las voces del grupo
familiar/ atentos a la voz, a esta esperanza/ que se cuela por las rendijas
de las ventanas,/ de las puertas,/ que atraviesa calles, puentes, cauces.//
Esta voz que desata aguaceros hasta las últimas notas,/ hasta las últimas
voces,/ hasta que se apaga y sólo queda la humedad/ y el tic tic de las gotas
después de la lluvia./ al amanecer.// —Radio Sandino/ PRESENTA/ su espacio

informativo/ "El Atabal Guerrillero"// **Parte de guerra/ Del Estado Mayor Occidental/ "Rigoberto López Pérez".**// 1. —El Estado Mayor del Frenté Occidental "Rigoberto López/ Pérez" comunica que a las 10:30 A.M. fue tomado/ definitivamente el cuartel general de la guardia somocista en la/ cuidad de León. Todas las campanas de las iglesias están/ tocando a rebato y la población entera se ha volcado a las/ calles celebrando la liberación total de la cuidad.// 2. —Nuestras fuerzas recuperaron todas las armas y/ municiones de la guardia genocida. El jefe de la plaza,/ general Ariel Argüello, fue abatido cuando intentaba huir/ escudado en una indefensa mujer, quien fue rescatada por/ nuestros combatientes.// 3. —Nuestro Comandante Guadalupe Moreno (Abel) cayó/ heroicamente a la una de la tarde de ayer, dirigiendo el/ ataque al comando. El Comandante "Abel," participó en el/ asedio al mismo Comando en Septiembre de 1978.// . . .// ¡ESTELI, CON TU NOMBRE RUBRICAREMOS/ EL EPITAFIO DEL SOMOCISMO!// "Y allá va el General/ bajando Estelí/ Patria o muerte repiten/ los campesinos de Wiwilí.// Y allá va el General/ con su decisión/ con sus hombres valientes/ a limpiar Nicaragua del invasor . . . "// . . . // "Adelante/ adelante la heroica guerrilla/ guerrillero adelante marchar/ vas haciendo la paz con la guerra/ con las armas de la libertad.// Guerrillero/ Guerrillero/ Guerrillero adelante adelante/ con el fuego de paz del fusil/ de la sierra hasta el llano adelante/ Guerrillero vencer o morir."// ("Verónica" era Flor de María Antúñez,/ Iván Montenegro se llamaba "Ernesto")./ Sólo con la muerte recobraremos nuestros nombres./ El nombre familiar y sus variantes cariñosas/ que desde la cuna aprendimos a querer/ y a reconocernos en él./ Nuestro nombre verdadero, nuestro propio nombre/ que la muerte nos devuelve.

Raúl Zurita (1951–, Chile)

Born in Santiago, Chile, Zurita features his country in many of his controversial and expressive works. He started his professional life in the 1970s as part of the CADA collective, a group that staged avant-garde events for the public that were meant to raise questions. During one such event, he disfigured his cheek by throwing acid on himself, an act that later became part of one of his major works, *Purgatorio* (Purgatory). His work includes aerial photographs of huge messages written on the ground. His book *Inri* refers to the desaparecidos, the disappeared prisoners whose bodies were thrown into the sea during the military dictatorship in Chile. PRINCIPAL WORKS: *Purgatorio* (1979), *Anteparaíso* (1982), *La vida nueva* (1993), *Inri* (2003)

Excerpt from Inri: The Sea / El mar

William Rowe, trans.

Strange baits rain from the sky. Surprising bait falls
upon the sea. Down below the ocean, up above
unusual clouds on a clear day. Surprising baits rain on
the sea. There was a love raining, there was a clear
day that's raining now on the sea.

They are shadows, bait for fishes. A clear day is
raining, a love that was never said. Love, ah yes,
love, amazing baits are raining from the sky on the
shadow of fishes in the sea.

Clear days fall. Some strange baits with clear days
stuck to them, with loves that were never said.

The sea, it says the sea. It says baits that rain and clear days stuck to them, it says
unfinished loves, clear and unfinished days that rain for the fish in the sea.

. . . .

You can hear whole days sinking, strange sunny mornings, unfinished loves,
goodbyes cut short that sink into the sea. You can hear surprising baits
that rain with sunny days stuck to them, loves cut short, goodbyes that
not any more. Baits are told of, that rain for the fish in the sea.

The blue brilliant sea. You can hear shoals of fish
devouring baits stuck with words that not, days and
news that not, loves that not any more.

It is told of shoals of fish that leap, of whole
whirlwinds of fish that leap.

You can hear the sky. It is told that amazing baits rain down with pieces of
sky stuck to them upon the sea.

. . . .

I heard a sea and a sky hallucinated, I heard suns exploding with love fall like
fruits, I heard whirlwinds of fish devouring the pink flesh of surprising baits.

I heard millions of fish which are tombs with pieces of sky inside, with
hundreds of words that were never said, with hundreds of flowers of red
flesh and pieces of sky in the eyes. I heard hundreds of loves that were
stopped on a sunny day. Baits rained from the sky.

Viviana cries. Viviana heard whirlwinds of fishes rise up in the air fighting
for mouthfuls of a goodbye cut short, of a prayer not heard, of a love not
said. Viviana is on the beach. Viviana today is Chile.

The long fish that is Chile rises up through the air devouring the sun baits
of its dead.

. . . .

Tremendous plains rain down for the fishes: days that will now never be,
eyes stuck to a final sky, loves that were not said. It says tremendous
plains made of arms that couldn't embrace, of hands that didn't touch.
It says strange fruits that the fish devour, that the silver tombs which are
the fish devour. I heard extraordinary plains raining on the sea.

Extraordinary skies, days, dreams sinking into the silver whirlpools of
waves, I heard the silver mouths of fish devouring unfinished goodbyes.
I heard immense plains of love saying that no more. Angels, musical
scores of love saying no more.

Universes, cosmoses, unfinished winds raining down in thousands of pink
baits onto the carnivorous sea of Chile. I heard plains of love never said,
infinite skies of love sinking into the carnivorous tombs of the fish.

Sorprendentes carnadas llueven del cielo./ Sorprendentes carnadas sobre
el mar. Abajo el/ océano, arriba las inusitadas nubes de un día claro./
Sorprendentes carnadas llueven sobre el mar. Hubo/ un amor que llueve, hubo
un día claro que llueve/ ahora sobre el mar.// Son sombras, carnadas para
peces. Llueve un día/ claro, un amor que no alcanzó a decirse. El amor,/
ah sí el amor, llueven desde el cielo asombrosas/ carnadas sobre la sombra de los
peces en el mar.// Caen días claros. Extrañas carnadas pegadas de días/ claros,
de amores que no alcanzaron a decirles.// El mar, se dice del mar. Se dice de
carnadas que/ llueven y de días claros pegados a ellas, se dice de/ amores
inconclusos, de días claros e inconclusos/ que llueven para los peces en el
mar.// . . . // Se oyen días enteros hundiéndose, se oyen extrañas/ mañanas
soleadas, amores inconclusos, despedidas/ truncas que se hunden en el mar. Se
oyen/ sorprendentes carnadas que llueven pegadas de días/ de sol, de amores
truncos, de despedidas que ya/ no. Se dice de carnadas que llueven para los
peces/ en el mar.// El mar azul y brillante. Se oyen cardúmenes de/ peces
devorando carnadas pegadas de palabras que/ no, de noticias y días que no, de
amores que ya no.// Se dice de cardúmenes de peces que saltan, de/ torbellinos
de peces que saltan.// Se oye el cielo. Se dice que llueven asombrosas/ carnadas
adheridas de pedazos de cielo sobre el mar.// . . . // Oí un cielo y un mar
alucinantes, oí soles/ estallados de amor cayendo como frutos, oí/ torbellinos
de peces devorando las carnes rosa de/ sorprendentes carnadas.// Oí millones
de peces que son tumbas con pedazos/ de cielo adentro, con cientos de
palabras que no/ alcanzaron a decirse, con cientos de flores de carne/ roja y

Ni pena ni miedo (Neither Fear Nor Sadness), Atacama desert, Chile, 1993

pedazos de cielo en los ojos. Oí cientos de/ amores que quedaron fijos en un día soleado./ Llovieron carnadas desde el cielo.// Viviana llora. Viviana oyó torbellinos de peces/ elevarse por el aire disputándose los bocados de/ una despedida trunca, de un rezo no oído, de un/ amor no dicho. Viviana está en la playa. Viviana es/ hoy Chile.// El pez largo de Chile que se eleva por los aires/ devorando las carnadas de sol de sus difuntos.// . . . // Impresionantes llanuras llueven para los peces: días/ que ya nunca serán, ojos pegados a un último cielo,/ amores que no fueron dichos. Se dice de/ impresionantes llanuras hechas de brazos que no/ lograron abrazarse, de manos que no se alcanzaron a/ tocar. Se dice de raros frutos/ que los peces devoran/ que las

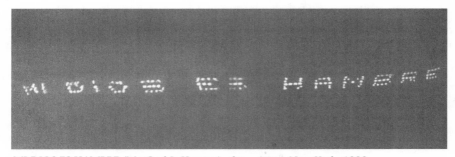

MI DIOS ES HAMBRE (My God Is Hunger), sky writing, New York, 1982

tumbas plateadas de los peces devoran. Oí/ impresionantes llanuras
lloviendo sobre el mar.// Impresionantes cielos, dias, sueños hundiéndose
en/ los torbellinos plateados de olas, oí las bocas/ plateadas de los peces
devorando despedidas/ truncas. Oí inmensas llanuras de amor diciendo
que/ ya no. Ángeles, partituras de amor diciendo que ya no.// Universos,
cosmos, inacabados vientos lloviendo en/ miles de carnadas rosas sobre
el mar carnívoro de/ Chile. Oí llanuras de amor nunca dichas, cielos/
infinitos de amor hundiéndose en las carnívoras/ tumbas de los peces.

Coral Bracho (1951–, Mexico)

Born in Mexico City, Bracho is a leading representative of contemporary Latin
American neo-baroque literature. She started publishing in 1977 with her book of
poetry *Peces de piel fugaz* and was awarded the Xavier Villaurrutia Prize in 2003
for *Ese espacio, ese jardín*. Forrest Gander says, "Her diction spills out along cease-
lessly shifting beds of sound . . . [her] poems make sense first as music, and music
propels them." Bracho is a professor of language and literature at the Universidad
Nacional Autónoma de México. PRINCIPAL WORKS: *El ser que va a morir* (1981), *Tierra
de entraña ardiente* (1992), *Ese espacio, ese jardín* (2003), *Firefly under the Tongue*
(2007)

Water's Lubricious Edges / Agua de bordes lúbricos

Forrest Gander, trans.

WATER of jellyfish,
lacteal, sinuous water,
water of lubricious borders; glassy thickness—Deliquescence
in delectable contours. Water—sumptuous water
of involution, of languor

in placid densities. Water,
water silken and plumbeous in opacity, in weight —Mercurial;
    water in suspense, slow water. The algal bloom
brilliant—In the paps of pleasure. The algae,
    the bracing vapor of its peak;

—across the arched silence, across the isthmuses
of basalt; the algae, its habitual rub,
its slippage. Light water, fish water; the aura, the agate,
its luminous border-breakings; Fire trailing the fleeing

elk—Around the ceiba tree, around the shoal of fish; flame
pulsing;
lynx water, sargo water (The sudden jasper). Luminescence
of jellyfish.
—Edge open, lipped; aura of lubricious borders,
its smoothness rocking, its nesting efflorescence; amphibious,
labile—Water, water silken
with voltaic charge; expectant. Water in suspense, slow water—The
    lascivious luminescence

in its oily crossing,
over faulted basalt. —The slither of opal through the sheen,
through the interior flame. —Water

of jellyfish.
Soft, lustrous water;
water traceless; dense,
mercurial
        its steely whiteness, its dissolution in graphite surges,
in burnished gloss; furtive, smooth. —Living water

upwelling ventral over dorsal, capsized bronze sun enfolding
—crystalline zinc, spouting water. Water of jellyfish, tactile water
fusing itself
to the unctuous indigo blue, to its reverberant honeycomb. Amianthus, ulva
    water
The catfish in its silt
—sucking; in the nutritious essence, in its delicate nectar; the aureous
reservoir, a limbo, transparentizes it. Light water, aura within amber
—graceful, anointed luminance; the tiger, its high tide
below the brittle shadow. Boundary water, eel water licking its profile,
its nocturnal migration
—In silk matrices; in the sage. —Water

between grey-finned hake. Gravid water (—The calm pleasure
tepid; its iridescence) —Water
its borders

—Its shifting smoothness, its enchantment
with what is nubile,
cadenced. Water,
silky water of involution, of languor
in placid densities. Water, water;   Its caress
—Otter water, fish water. Water

of jellyfish,
lacteal, sinuous water; Water,

Agua de medusas,/ agua láctea, sinuosa,/ agua de bordes lúbricos; espesura
vidriante—Delicuescencia/ entre contornos deleitosos. Agua—agua
suntuosa/ de involución, de languidez// en densidades plácidas. Agua,/
agua sedosa y plúmbea en opacidad, en peso —Mercurial;/ agua en vilo,
agua lenta. El alga/ acuática de los brillos —En las ubres del gozo. El alga,
el/ hálito de su cima;// —sobre el silencio arqueante, sobre los istmos/ del
basalto; el alga, el hábito de su roce,/ su deslizarse. Agua luz, agua pez; el
aura, el ágata,/ sus desbordes luminosos; Fuego rastreante el alce// huidizo
—Entre la ceiba, entre el cardumen; llama/ pulsante;/ agua lince, agua
sargo (El jaspe súbito). Lumbre/ entre medusas./ —Orla abierta, labiada;
aura de bordes lúbricos,/ su lisura acunante, su eflorescerse al anidar;
anfibia,/ lábil —Agua, agua sedosa/ en imantación; en ristre. Agua en
vilo, agua lenta—El/ alumbrar lascivo// en lo vadeante oleoso,/ sobre los
vuelcos de basalto. —Reptar del ópalo entre la/ luz,/ entre la llama interna.
—Agua/ de medusas./ Agua blanda, lustrosa;/ agua sin huella; densa,/
mercurial/ su blancura acerada, su dilución en alzamientos de grafito,/
en despuntar de lisa; hurtante, suave. —Agua viva// su vientre sobre el
testuz, volcado sol de bronce envolviendo/ —agua blanda, brotante. Agua
de medusas, agua táctil/ fundiéndose/ en lo añil untuoso, en su panal
reverberante. Agua amianto, ulva/ El bagre en lo mullido/ —libando; en
el humor nutricio, entre su néctar delicado; el áureo/ embalse, el limbo,
lo transluce. Agua leve, aura adentro el ámbar/ —el luminar ungido,
esbelto; el tigre, su pleamar/ bajo la sombra vidriada. Agua linde, agua
anguila lamiendo/ su perfil,/ su transmigrar nocturno/ —Entre las sedas
matriciales; entre la salvia. —Agua// entre merluzas. Agua grávida (—El
calmo goce/ tibio; su irisable) —Agua/ sus bordes// —Su lisura mutante,
su embeleñarse/ entre lo núbil/ cadencioso. Agua,/ agua sedosa de
involución, de languidez/ en densidades plácidas. Agua, agua; Su roce/
—Agua nutria, agua pez. Agua// de medusas,/ agua láctea, sinuosa; Agua,

Its Dark Force Curving / Su oscura fuerza curvando

Forrest Gander, trans.

A subtle gesture and its expansive threshold;
a caress and its outcropped cosmos;
a drop
and its center;
only love offers us the dimension of the real;
its dark force
curving; its delicate and ebullient breath;
its ardor,
the surround opening
its silences, its ocean

of shadow under the lintel of the real,
in its little, short-lived fruits.

Around the orange tree leaf,
interlaced,
a conflagration;   only its light,

its dense, occult magnetism lathing the time,
threshing and reopening time
its furtive universes;
its flame bending,
its graze,

the sense of the real.—Orb
of symmetries, of equivalencies, its arcane drag
and its sheltering
expansion; igneous seed;
irradiated thickness and its infinity
in the brilliance of this drop, the real

rendering itself.   Rainy orchard
and the sun
in its outburst of mirrors.

Un gesto suave y su umbral de vastedad;/ una caricia y su aflorado cosmos;/
una gota/ y su centro;/ sólo el amor nos da la dimensión de lo real;/ oscura
fuerza/ curvando. Su delicado y festivo soplo,/ su ardor;/ entorno abriendo/
sus silencios, su mar/ de sombra en el dintel de lo real,/ en sus pequeños
y breves frutos.// Sobre la hoja del naranjo,/ entreverado,/ un incendio; sólo
su luz,// su denso, oculto magnetismo torneando el tiempo,/ desmadejando
y reabriendo el tiempo/ de sus furtivos universos;/ su llama arqueando,/ su
roce,// la noción de lo real. —Orbe/ de simetrías, de equivalencias, su arcano
arrastre/ y su expansión/ acogiendo, ígnea semilla;/ irradiada espesura y su
infinito/ en el brillo de esta gota, lo real// cediéndose. Llovido huerto/ y el
sol/ en su efusión de espejos.

Give Me, Earth, Your Night / Dame, tierra, tu noche

Forrest Gander, trans.

In your fathomless waters,
in their jade
quietude, welcome me, spectral earth.
Earth of silences
and scintillations,
of dreams quick as constellations,

like filaments of sun
in a tiger's eye. Give me your dark face,
your clear time to cover me,
your soft voice. I would speak
in the softest tones.
With quartz sand I'd draw out this murmuring,
this spring bordered by crystals.
Give me your night;
the igneous expression of your night
so I might begin to see.
Give me your abyss and your black mirror.
The depths open up
like star fruit, like universes
of amethyst under the light. Give me their ardor,
give me their ephemeral sky,
their occult green: some path
will clear for me, some trace
through the coastal waters.
Among your tenebrous forests,
earth, give me silence and intoxication;
give me a wafer of time; the flickering
and flaking ember of time; its exultant
core; its fire, the echo
under the deepened labyrinth. Give me
your solitude.
And in it,
beneath your obsidian fervor,
from your walls, and before the breaking day,
give me, in a crevice, the threshold
and its furtive flamboyance.

En tus aguas profundas/ en su quietud/ de jade, acógeme, tierra espectral./ Tierra
de silencios/ y brillos,/ de sueños breves como constelaciones,/ como vetas de
sol/ en un ojo de tigre. Dame tu oscuro rostro,/ tu tiempo terso para cubrirme,/
tu suave voz. Con trazos finos/ hablaría./ Con arenas de cuarzo trazaría este
rumor,/ este venero entre cristales./ Dame tu noche;/ el ígneo gesto de tu noche/
para entrever./ Dame tu abismo y tu negro espejo./ Hondos parajes se abren/
como fruto estelar, como universos/ de amatista bajo la luz. Dame su ardor,/
dame su cielo efímero,/ su verde oculto: algún sendero/ se abrirá para mi, algún
matiz/ entre sus costas de agua./ Entre tus bosques de tiniebla,/ tierra, dame el
silencio y la ebriedad;/ dame la oblea del tiempo; la brasa tenue/ y azorada del
tiempo; su exultante/ raíz; su fuego, el eco/ bajo el ahondado laberinto. Dame/
tu soledad./ Y en ella,/ bajo tu celo de obsidiana,/ desde tus muros, y antes del
nuevo día,/ dame en una grieta el umbral/ y su esplendor furtivo.

Elvira Hernández (1951–, Chile)

Born Teresa Adriasola, Hernández was raised in Lebu, south-central Chile, and started writing poetry during the 1980s—a harsh decade for Chileans because of the dictatorship. In 1981, after being arrested, she wrote *La bandera de Chile* (The Chilean Flag), a long poem that was passed around from hand to hand until it became a banner, a cult book in xerox form. Hernández refuses to be placed inside the box of "so-called feminine poetry" because—she asserts—"poetry cannot be divided or classified according to the gender of its author." Her interest is to write from the underground, attending to the submerged spaces to "pick up that which is being erased . . . that which doesn't want to leave traces." In her book *Santiago waria* she gives back to the city its erased mestizo identity. PRINCIPAL WORKS: *Carta de viaje* (1989), *La bandera de Chile* (1991), *El orden de los días* (1991), *Santiago waria* (1992)

Excerpt from The Flag of Chile / La bandera de Chile

Daniel Shapiro, trans.

No one has said a word about the Flag of Chile
about its nobility its cloth
about all its rectangular desert
They haven't proclaimed
the Flag of Chile
missing

The Flag of Chile says nothing about itself
it reads itself in a round pocket mirror
it gleams delayed in time like an echo
there's a lot of broken glass
smashed like the lines in an open hand
it reads itself
seeking stones for its desire

. . . .

They order the Flag of Chile to its mast-tip

and because of this its fabric undulates and moves

and because of this they respect it

. . . .

The Flag of Chile is measured in square meters
its smell measured by twitches of the nose
it's measured by eyes blind to its facets of light and shadow
by patience for its diarrheas
the construction of a malnourished trust

The Flag of Chile is hung between two buildings
its banner inflated like an ulcerated belly
      —it falls like an old teat—
      like a circus tent
legs in the air, slit up the middle
      a little snatch for the open air
a little hole for the ashes of General O'Higgins
or an eye for the Avenue of General Bulnes

The Flag of Chile lies on its side
        forgotten

. . . .

The Flag of Chile doesn't sell itself
      they may cut off its lights they may leave it without
      water
      they may crush its ribs with sharp kicks
The flag is something like a decoy that resists
      they're worthless, the judges' sentences
      the calloused ropes that hoist it up
The Flag of Chile is end to end

. . . .

        hoist lower
        hoist lower
        hoist lower
        hoist lower
        hoist lower
        hoist lower
        hoist lower
        hoist lower
        hoist lower
        hoist lower
        hoist lower
        hoist lower
        hoist lower
        hoist lower
        hoist lower
        hoist lower
        hoist lower
        hoist lower
        hoist lower
        hoist lower

in the routine the Flag of Chile loses heart
and surrenders

Nadie ha dicho una palabra sobre la Bandera de Chile/ en el porte en la
tela/ en todo su desierto cuadrilongo/ no lo han nombrado/ La Bandera de
Chile/ ausente// La Bandera de Chile no dice nada sobre sí misma/ se lee en
su espejo de bolsillo redondo/ espejea retardada en el tiempo como un eco/
hay muchos vidrios rotos/ trizados como las líneas de una mano abierta/
se lee/ en busca de piedras para sus ganas// . . . // A la Bandera de Chile la
mandan a la punta de su mástil

y por eso ondea y mueve su tela

y por eso se la respeta

//. . . // En metros cuadrados se mide la Bandera de Chile/ su olor en
respingos de nariz/ en ojos que no ven sus aristas de luz y sombra/ en
paciencia sus diarreas/ las construcciones de desnutrida confianza// La
Bandera de Chile está tendida entre 2 edificios/ se infla su tela como una
barriga ulcerada/ —cae como teta vieja–/ como una carpa de circo/ con las
piernas al aire tiene una rajita al medio/ una chuchita para el aire/ un hoyito
para las cenizas del General O'Higgins/ un para ojo la Avenida General
Bulnes// La Bandera de Chile está a un costado/olvidada.// . . . // La Bandera
de Chile no se vende/ le corten la luz dejen sin agua/ le machuquen los
costados a patadas/ La Bandera tiene algo de señuelo que resiste/ no valen
las sentencias de los jueces/ no valen las drizas de hilo curado/ La Bandera de
Chile al tope// . . . // izar arriar/ izar arriar/ izar arriar/ izar arriar/ izar arriar/
izar arriar/ izar arriar/ izar arriar/ izar arriar/ izar arriar/ izar arriar/ izar arriar/
izar arriar/ izar arriar/ izar arriar/ izar arriar/ izar arriar/ izar arriar/ izar arriar/
izar arriar// en la rutina la Bandera de Chile pierde su corazón/ y se rinde

Reina María Rodríguez (1952–, Cuba)

Born in Havana, Rodríguez uses her writing to examine the ever-changing state of
her native Cuba. Early poetry portrayed Cuba's revolution in an optimistic light, but
later it turned cynical as Cuba's revolutionary fervor gave way to reality. Her poetry
also transformed from direct to more metaphorical language. Acclaimed worldwide,
she has won two Casa de las Americas literary prizes. Also known for hosting *La*

azotea (The Terrace) literary gatherings at her home in Havana during the 1990s, she founded a literary magazine by the same name, *Azoteas*. PRINCIPAL WORKS: *La gente de mi barrio* (1976), *Para un cordero blanco* (1984), *La foto del invernadero* (1998)

Twilight's Idol / Idolo del crepúsculo

Kristin Dykstra and Nancy Gates-Madsen, trans.

my desire in the imprint of my fear . . . my desire is the imprint of my
fear, in front of the mirror, a mature woman's serious face observes me
(scarcity of soft pubic hair, once very black). thighs together, apart;
together, apart, breasts (apart) with dark balls on the nipples like Aunt
Adelfa's. my hand upon me. sagging buttocks, pathetic, flabby? a deity
lurks behind my ear and something that doesn't come forward, isn't
seen, moves me into the species, my mate, what more can I offer? my
perfect foot which has not aged, so soft. I come together and separate
strangely. I like my lyricism because it generates an I (an other) in my
body who sinks down on the bed behind the glass, slowly, and I open the
windows so that the day's only low cloud enters with the glare. I undress,
I undress and there's no me. I open and close my legs (expansion and
contraction of the universe), it disappears around me, I pull myself
together and I do nothing. any gesture would be all-powerful in the
face of my expectations. lubricated, across from the mirror, I've just
discovered my body and rejected it because sometimes it tries to possess
a space, an obliqueness that distracts me from what is continuous, from
the interruption of the landscape (intimacy contained in a small flower-
pot with lilies). I am more than my body. my slenderness, its arrhythmia,
oblation. the weekend, small and without ceremonies, how does one
subvert the dark side of the self against those limits? I refuse to imagine
myself again in those lines or silences culminating in yellow behind
a shape and its emptiness (dark stain under the right buttock). poor
crater. my self is not this. something more committed than acceptance
or rejection; something lower and warmer than a surface (proud of
controlling myself inside one self and not in another that splits me into
two). this war has begun: when the flabbiness sprouts, it's mental. do you
like my flabbiness? it is clear. are you obsessed with my poverty and the
green excrement on the bottom of the pink cup? it's you, a broad body
to break my intimacy, but I am not two: not living, not living involves
life (life that is lived perishes and escapes) not loving, not loving involves
love . . . not thinking, not thinking involves thought. she, with her robe
threadbare at the elbows, in the afternoon she would rub her pubis with
pieces of dry ice, she would rub and rub herself in front of the window,
between the glare and the day's only low cloud. he would see her, a
virginity for the northern ice (open lips for the burning cold of the dead
ice). afterwards, she would wake up against the small hedge with the

pain of her images. the cloud had disappeared. it would be, then, a false
cloud born of her contact with the ice, a challenge to the landscape. each
afternoon a suicide and the lost memory of the previous fall (because
a suicide should be obsessive within itself), orgasmic leap, orgon. run
and take her, she too is me (the figure of my mother getting out of the
old bathtub with her green eyes fixed on a girl's pubis), how awful not
to be her anymore. you ask me to be indiscreet and whisper things in
your ear. I get very close, but in vain. I don't have words, or songs, or
other scenes opposite that leafy tree and the scent of those spiny weeds;
they get tangled up in your fingers, just to be doing something. nothing
that accepts me. I am my open, empty trap in its perfect transparency.
with the metallic teeth underwater in the glass resisting an old age that
overcomes my conscience, or a slice in time—open, still cutting—that
makes me go down, pushing me to be, again, twilight's idol. there will be
no more form, no body yielding in it curves, discordances, sinuousities:
transitory odors that remain when I open the window and my legs
and I ask forgiveness in the mud, just blood, dung curdling with blood
(patience and meekness that slip on any mud), and the corner of the
mouth smiles at me, obeying a strange purity by looking at me—the self
already some other—not accepting her eternal return either (the object
of the fantasy is evasive too). Narcissus, or man's love as impossible love
(the play of the spirit will consist of turning objects into the creation
of the subject, of taking reality as a ghost created by the author). the
obsession with discovering her while she's falling over the dark hedge—
nobody had warned me—to be simply a story that goes on repeating
itself, consuming itself, slowly against the cloudbreaker.

mi deseo en la huella de mi miedo . . . mi deseo es la huella de mi miedo.
frente al espejo, un rostro serio de mujer madura me observa (escasez de
los vellos del pubis, antes muy negros). muslos unidos, separados; unidos,
separados, senos con bolas oscuras en las puntas (separados) como los de
tía Adelfa. mi mano sobre mí. nalgas bajas, demasiado tristes, fláccidas? una
divinidad acecha tras mi oreja y algo que no se presenta, no se ve, me adentra
en las especie, pareja de mí, qué más puedo ofrecer? mi pie perfecto que no
ha envejecido, dulcísimo. me acerco y me separo raramente. me gusta mi
lirismo porque engendra en el cuerpo un yo (otro) que detrás del cristal,
lentamente, se hunde sobre la cama y abro las ventanas para que entre con el
resplandor, la única nube baja del día. me desnudo, me desnudo y no hay mí.
abro y cierro las piernas (expansión y contracción del universo) se difumina
alrededor, me integro y no hago nada. cualquier gesto sería todopoderoso
frente a mi espera. lubricada, frente al espejo, acabo de conocer mi cuerpo y
de rechazarlo porque él a veces pretende poseer un espacio, una oblicuidad
que me distrae de lo continuo, de la interrupción del paisaje (intimidad

contenida en un pequeño pote y azucenas). soy más que él. mi delgadez,
su arritmia, la oblación. fin de semana, pequeño y sin ceremonias, cómo
subvertir el lado oscuro del ser contra esos límites? me niego a representarme
otra vez en esas líneas o silencios que culminan en amarillo tras una forma y
su vaciedad (mancha oscura bajo la nalga derecha). pobre cráter. mi ser no es
esto. algo más comprometedor que la aceptación o el rechazo; algo más bajo
y tibio que una superficie (orgullo de poseerme en mí y no en otro que me
contiene doblemente). ha empezado esta guerra: la flaccidez cuando germina
es mental. te gusta mi flaccidez? es lúcida. te obsesiona mi pobretud y el
excremento verde sobre el fondo de la taza rosada? eres tú, un cuerpo ancho
para romper mi intimidad, pero no soy dos: no vivir, no vivir entraña la vida
(la vida que se vive perece y escapa) no amar, no amar entraña el amor . . .
no pensar, no pensar, entraña un pensamiento. ella con su bata raída en los
codos, en las tardes se frotaba el pubis con pedazos de hielo seco, se frotaba
y se frotaba frente a la ventana, entre el resplandor y la única nube baja del
día. él la veia. una virginidad para el hielo boreal (labios abiertos por el frío
quemante del hielo muerto) después, se despertaba contra el pequeño seto
con el dolor de sus imágenes. la nube había desparecido. era entonces una
falsa nube nacida de su contacto con el hielo, un desafio al paisaje. cada
tarde un suicidio y el olvido de la caída anterior (porque un suicidio debe ser
obsesivo en sí mismo) salto orgásmico, orgón. corre y tómala, esa también
soy yo (figura de mi madre saliendo de la bañera antigua con sus ojos veres
atrapados en un pubis de niña) qué horror no ser ya ella. tú me pides que sea
indiscreta y te cuente cosas al oído. yo me acerco muchísimo, pero en vano.
no tengo palabras, ni canciones, ni otras escenas frente a este árbol frondoso
y el aroma de esas yerbas espinosas que se enredan en los dedos, por hacer
algo. nada que me acepte. mi trampa abierta en su perfecta transparencia y
vacía soy yo. con los dientes metálicos bajo el agua del vaso resistiendo una
ancianidad que sobrepasa mi conciencia, o una tajada en el tiempo—abierta,
todavía cortante—que me haga descender empujándome a ser otra vez
idolo del crepúsculo. no habrá más forma, cuerpo doblegado en sus curvas,
inarmonías, sinuosidades: olores transitorios que se han quedado cuando
abro la ventana y las piernas y pido perdón sobre el fango, sólo sangre,
estiércol y sangre coagulándose (paciencia y mansedumbre que resbala en
cualquier lodo) y la comisura me sonríe obedeciendo a una extraña pureza de
mirarme—el ser ya alguna otra—inconforme también de su eterno retorno (el
objeto de la fantasía es también huidizo). Narciso, o el amor del hombre como
amor imposible (la jugada del espiritu consistirá en el hacer de los objetos
una creación del sujeto, en tomar la realidad por un fantasma creado por el
autor). obsesión de descubrirla cayendo sobre el seto oscuro—nadie me había
prevenido—ser simplemente una historia que se va repitiendo, consumiendo,
lentamente contra el rompenubes.

Emeterrio Cerro (1952–1996, Argentina)

Born in Balcarce, Buenos Aires, Cerro was trained as regisseur of opera at the Higher Institute of Arts of the Colón Theater. From 1986 to his death, he resided in Paris. Cerro's poetics was always closely associated with performance and the musicality of language. His prolific work constitutes one of the most intense explorations of nonsense and phonic poetry found in South America. He also founded a theater company, La Barrosa, in 1983, which is the title of one of his best-known poems. Cerro has contributed to numerous literary magazines, among them *Ultimo reino, El porteño,* and *XUL.* PRINCIPAL WORKS: *La barrosa* (1982), *El bochicho* (1983), *Las guaranís* (1996)

Excerpt from Miss Murkiness / La barrosa

Kathryn A. Kopple, trans.

missMurkiness		swoops	was
who		the branch	betrothed
cutting thirst	Devil		was
pours	bites		Rome
rider			
who	Devil	screeching	
tonsured	space	mountain	gates
hand		frightens	round
uncurls		the plaza	marked
pollen	Devil		deflated
who			
buttons	grain		cried
knives		cinnamon	
row thorn		turkey	
ay!	Devil	tobacco	
tear	peak	afraid	fangs
archangel			furious
wounded			spurs
push soar		looks	southerners
ay	Devil	throws	
rosy	wave	craw	turkey
dagger	Devil		beloved
nibble	pricks		slips
of the		cinnamon	countrywomen
Devil Hound		turkey	chickens
ay!	the		crowds of indians
ay!		history	

laBarrosa abate fue/ quien la rama novia/ hirientes sed Diablo fue/
vierte muerde Roma/ cabalgante/ quien Diablo gritona/ tonsurada
espacio montaña tranqueras/ mano espantas redondas/ desrizan la plaza

marcaron/ polen Diablo mordida/ quien/ abotonadas granito lloraba/
cuchillas canela/ boga espina el pavo/ ay! Diabla tabaca/ desgarra pico
asustado colmillos/ arcángela furiosos/ herida espuelas/ puja vuelo
mira sureñas/ ay Diablo tira/ sonrosada onda buche el pavo/ puñal
Diablo amado/ mordisco punza resbala/ del canela paisanas/ Diablo
Lebrel el pavo gallinas/ ay! la indiada/ ay! historia

Jorge Santiago Perednik (1952–, Argentina)

Born in Buenos Aires, Perednik founded the influential journal *XUL* in 1980,
which published its first issue during Argentina's military dictatorship. *XUL*'s defi-
ant gesture against censorship made it possible to create a more open forum for
experimental poetics. Perednik's own poetics are defined by the fusion of formal
experimentation and sociopolitical criticism. Also a very active translator, he has
translated Robert L. Stevenson, e.e. cummings, and Charles Olson, among others. PRINCIPAL WORKS: *El shock de los lenders* (1985), *El gran derrapador* (2002), *La
querella de los gustos* (2006)

Excerpt from Shock of the Lenders / El shock de los lenders
Molly Weigel, trans.

The most beautiful word of the language is stranger
Barbaric or Barbara
All men are mortal the shock lender is also
The most beautiful concept of the mother tongue
Sabotage?
We used to lend
I tell you, not them
"Look for a new almost because the old one is dis "

Cards thrown down simulating an Order
Protean tense: the lapse
Preterite tense: the cosmos
  ultrapreterite: the lapse
        present: the preteriduction machine
    such brief ᶦᵘᵐᵉ̶ᵗˣˣˢ
Something's stopp

Beauty is the order of sabotage. No
The order of beauty is an effect of sabotage. No
Beauty is a . . . from the order of sabotaging the order of . . . No?

The day is too clear to see what's happening
: a link in the chain has been broke
: crystals colors solstice equinox have been broke
Too clear to see
The fear   what's hidden under   always
Hell? concentric circles Why not Paradise?
"'Don't believe him it's all a   circumferences dis
setups of our police who I call dialing 666
and others call   oligice
                  oligarchy
                  oligophrenia
                  oligoclase hematite mineraloligopoly(ce)
etc etc'"

decentered circumferences crossing such that
each point is the intersection of multiple discs such that
each point constitutes an existence   (note: you for example)

(nothingness—neeche— (the only—stirner—
bah—the story you tell is just too pat
in your guilt I smell a rat slither bite infect squeal
turn around, I'll make a note of that turn around so he can steal you
or better: Truth is tails Beauty heads
both faces the being—duplicity—coin of this cosmos
the man who relates the eye and the finger
the name that relates flash and bang
what's more important, thunder or lightning?
Great balls of fire, I thought you'd never say it!

weapons, instruments of
The providers, etc
The commotion, etc etc
The corollaries that some call History
1. not to put up any more with the paternal hoop of the self or the law
2. to penetr (pay a price) assassin (shoot a) ate it
3. to be (nomen atque omen) the social lenders of the cause of
   maximum shock
Ego non baptizo te in nomine Diaboli et
Filii et Spiritus non Sancti—sed in nomine
Patris—madness is only definable negatively
amniotic fluid on the bodies
with her sister reason useless extremes one and the same rain from above
—not the (black) art of the deceivers but rather ascetic magic
Casing the city of god in the name of economy
Looking for special deals with Intelligence or Power or Angel
Bribing: Pull the trigger! Kill! (I'm waiting)

discovering a new kind of weapon: that has no one to aim at
that has nothing to fire at
real weapons

CHORUS (intellectuals if possible)
The electrical charges called shocks
can be caused when the wires corrode
their mothers would like back their cocks
to get back some of what they are owed
Their crest illustrates as it mocks
two red lions attached to her nodes
as they try to get into her box

My good and merciful god, you know that I don't approve of this
That I don't approve of anything that offends you
Yet you will approve it: habit and greed
But lord, the heart of an upright man . . . I mean, the abominations . . .
Leviticus VIII . . .
Better sleep and dream

La palabra más bella del idioma es extranjera/ Bárbara o Barbara/ Todos
los hombres son mortales también el shock lender es/ El concepto más
bello de la lengua/ Sabotaje?/ *Prestá—bamos*/ Se lo digo a Usted, no a
ellos/ "Búsquense una nueva casi porque la vieja se está des"// Barajas
que van saliendo y simulando un Orden/ Tiempo ᵽᵳᵉᵗéᵗᵉᵗᵒ: el lapsus/
Tiempo protérico el cosmos/ ultrapretérito: el lapsus/ pre sente: la máquina
pretéritoductora/ brevísimos/ Algo se ha deteni// La belleza es el orden de
los sabotajes. No El orden de la belleza es un efecto de los sabotajes. No/ La
belleza es un . . . de la orden de sabotear el orden de . . . ¿No?// El día está
demasiado claro para ver lo que sucede/ :se ha rompido un eslabón de la
cadena/ :se han rompido los cristales los colores el solsticio el equinoccio/
Demasiado claro para ver/ El miedo lo que se oculta bajo siempre/
¿Infierno? círculos concéntricos ¿Por qué no Paraíso?/ " "no le crea es todo
circunferencias desc/ trampas de nuestra policía que yo llamo discando el
666/ y otros llaman oligocía/ oligarquía/ oligofrenia/ oligistio hematites
mineraloligopoli/ etc etc" "/ circunferencias descentradas atravesándose
de modo que/ cada punto es la intersección de múltiples discos de modo
que/ cada punto configura una existencia (apunto: verbigracia vos)// (la
nada—nische— (el único estirner/ bah lo que usted dice está mal dicho/
en tu culpa hay un bicho galopa muerde contagia/ date vuelta que te ficho
date vuelta que te plagia/ o mejor: la Verdad es la ceca la Belleza el escudo/
ambas caras el ser la falsía la moneda de este cosmos/ el hombre que asocia
el ojo y el dedo/ el nombre que asocia fogonazo y estampido/ ¿cuál es más
importante, el trueno o el relámpago?/ ¡rayos, pensé que nunca lo dirías!//

armas, instrumentos de/ Los prestatarios, etc/ La conmoción, etc etc/ Los corolarios que algunos llaman Historia/ 1. —no soportar por más tiempo la argolla paterna del ser o de la ley/ 2. —penetr(pagar un precio) asesin (pegar un arla)/ 3. —ser (nomen atque omen) los lender sociales de la causa de máximo shock/ Ego non baptizo in nomine Diaboli et/ Filii et spiritus non sancti—sed in nomine/ Patris—la locura es definible solo negativa mentete/ líquido anneótico sobre los cuerpos con su hermana razón extremos inútiles de una la misma lluvia de arriba/ —no el arte (negro) de los embaucadores sino ascética magia/ En aras de economía recorrer la villa de dios/ Buscar tratos especiales con Inteligencia o Poder o Angel/ Sobornar a ¡Gatillen!¡Maten! (los espero)/ descubrir armas de un nuevo tipo: que no haya a quien apuntar/ que no haya que disparar/ verdaderas armas// CORO (en lo posible intelectuales)/ En otros tiempos llamaban/ a los shock eles chocones/ por venir esos varones/ de mujeres que deseaban/ que les rindan sus cojones/ Los emblemas lo ilustraban/ dos rubicundos leones/ prendidos de los pezones/ de una madre que horadaban// Mi buen y misericordioso dios, tú sabes que yo no apruebo esto/ Que no apruebo nada que te ofenda/ Ya lo aprobarás: costumbre y avaricia/ Pero señor, el corazón de un hombre recto . . . quiero decir, las abominaciones . . . Levítico VIII . . . / Mejor duérmete y sueña

Humberto Ak'abal (1952–, Guatemala)

Perhaps the best known of the contemporary indigenous authors, Ak'abal was born in Momostenango, Totonicapan, Guatemala, and grew up in extreme poverty. He dropped out of school at age twelve and educated himself by reading the books he could find, while working as a street vendor or factory worker. It was only after 1992 that his work began to enjoy widespread attention, especially in Europe, where he received the Blaise Cendrars Award. He writes in Maya K'iche and translates his work into Spanish. As a young man he witnessed the horrors of the war against the indigenous people in his country and has said "I belong to the culture of horror"; "We are invisible to those who do not speak our language." In his work, time and space are transformed in keeping with the Maya worldview and perceptions are exchanged as he speaks of the world as seen from the perspectives of animals and plants. In his performances, he re-creates the sonic communications of birds, the *xirixitem chikop,* or "bird noises," as he calls them. PRINCIPAL WORKS: *Ajyuq/El animalero* (1990), *El guardián de la caída del agua* (1993), *Ajkem tzij/Tejedor de palabras* (1996), *Poems I Brought Down from the Mountain* (1999), *Aqajtzij/Palabramiel* (2001)

Stones / Ri ab' aj / Piedras

Sylvia and Earl Shorris, trans.

It is not that the stones are mute:
they are only keeping silent.

Ri ab' aj man e mem taj:/ xa kakik'lo ri kich' awem.

No es que las piedras sean mudas:/ solo guardan silencio.

Advice / Ni'j / Consejo

Sylvia and Earl Shorris, trans.

Speak with anyone
so that you will not be taken for a mute,
my grandfather said to me.

And be careful that they
don't turn you into someone else.

Chat'tzijon ruk' japachinoq/ man kachomaj taj che at mem/ xub'ij
ri.numan chuwe.// Xa kachajij awib':/ rech man kak' ex taj awäch.

Hablá con cualquiera/ no vayan a pensar que sos mudo/ me dijo el abuelo.//
Eso sí: tené cuidado/ que no te vuelvan otro.

Effort / Chuq'ab' / Esfuerzo

Sylvia and Earl Shorris, trans.

The effort to forget
is also poetry.

Ri chuq'ab' ri kaqakoj che ri usachik sataq/ xuquje xik'ali./

El esfuerzo de olvidar/ también es poesía./

Navel / Umuxux / Ombligo

Sylvia and Earl Shorris, trans.

The sun
is the navel of the day.

The moon,
that of the night.

Ri q'ij/ are ri', ri umuxux paq'ij,// ri ik'/ are ri', ri umuxux ch'aq'ab'

El sol/ es el ombligo del día.// La luna,/ el de la noche.

Fireflies / Richupil q' aq' / Luciérnagas

Sylvia and Earl Shorris, trans.

The fireflies are stars
that come down from the sky,
and the stars are fireflies
that could not descend.

They turn their torches off and on
so that they will last the night.

Ri taq chupil q' aq'/ are ri', ri ch'umil/ ri xe'qha uloq cho ri kha,/ are k'u ri
ch'umil are ri', ri chupil q' aq'/ ri man xekwintha xe'qakij uloq.// Kakichup
kakit'iq ri kichäj / rumal k'u ri' kuq'i'jun ikeaqab' chike.

Las luciérnagas/ son estrellas que bajaron del cielo,/ y las estrellas son
luciérnagas / que no pudieron bajar.// Apagan y encienden sus ocotíos/ para
que les duren toda la noche.

Walker / Ajb' inel b'e / Caminante

Sylvia and Earl Shorris, trans.

I walked all night
in search of my shadow.

It had become confused
in the darkness.

Utiwwwwww . . .
a coyote.

I walked on.

Tu tu tukuuuuuuurrr . . .
an owl.

I continued walking.

Sotz', sotz', sotz' . . .
a bat chewing the ear
of a little pig.

Until the break of dawn.

My shadow was so long
that it hid the road.

Ximb'in jun aq'ab'/ xa rumal kintzukuj ri nunonoch'.// Ri nunbonoch'
xuyuj rib'/ ruk' ri q'eq'umal.// Utiwwwwww . . . / jun tukur.// Xink'am wanim
che ri b 'inem.// Sotz', sotz', sotz' . . . / jun sotz' kuwach' ri 'uxikin/ ri jun
alaj aq'.// Xsaqirisanik.// Sib'alaj nim ri nunonoch'/ su kuch' uq' ri nub'e.//

Caminé toda la noche/ buscando mi sombra.// Se había revuelto/ con
la oscuridad.// Utiwwwwww . . . / un coyote.// Yo caminaba.// Tu tu
tukuuuuuurr . . . / un tecolote.// Yo seguía caminando.// Sotz', sotz', sotz' . . . /
un murciélago mascándole/ la oreja a algún cochino.// Hasta que
amaneció.// Mi sombra era tan larga/ que tapaba el camino.

Learning / Ajetamanel / Aprendiz

Sylvia and Earl Shorris, trans.

In these "spurts"
the urge to write comes upon me,
not because I know something, but
because doing and undoing
is how I learn this craft,
and in the end
something stays with me.

The knolls,
the hills,
the canyons,
the old villages
have bewitching secrets
and I wish to extract these
to transfer them
to sheets of paper.

I must treat this beautiful craft
like an avocation although it pains me,
because I cannot give it as much time as I would like.
(I must work at something else in order to survive.)
My verses are as wet as rain,
or the tears of the evening dew,
and it could not be otherwise,
because they have been taken from the mountain.

Are chi' xaq jampa'/ kape ri jun rayinik che tz'ib'anik'/ man xata rumal
wetam,/ xa jewa wa' kinwetamaj/ kinchap jub'iq ucholaj wa jun chak ri'.//

Ri le'anik,/ ri juyub',/ ri siwan,/ ri ojer taq tinimit/ k'o ki je'lalaj keta'm ri
man kakib'ij taj/ rumal ri', kinrayij/ kinwesaj ul'oq pa ri wa'katem,/ pas
taq ri usaq wuj.// Wa jun je'lik chak ri',/ kinchakuj puwi' k'isb'al taq q'ij',/
xa ta ne' k'ex kinna'o/ ax man jamalik ta nuwech pa ri q'ij./ (Rajawaxik
kinchakun che ri uch'akik ri nu wa).// Ri nutz'ib e ch'aqalik rumal ri jäb/
rumal ri rex ja'/ xa rumal ri', k'amon uloq pa taw ri juyub'.

En esos "de repentes"/ se me viene la gana de escribir,/ no porque sepa sino/
porque haciéndolo y deshaciéndolo/ es como aprendo este officio y al final/
algo me va quedando.// Las lomas,/ los cerros,/ los barrancos,/ los pueblos
viejos/ tienen secretos encantadores/ y de ahí mi deseo de sacarlos a pasear/
en hojas de papel.// Este bello oficio tengo que tratarlo/ como sobretarea
aunque me duela,/ porque no cuento con el tiempo que quisiera./ (Debo
trabajar en otra cosa para sobrevivir.)// Mis versos tienen la humedad de la
lluvia,/ o las lágrimas del sereno, y no pueden ser/ sino así porque han sido
traídos de la montaña.

Buzzard / K'uch*

Dennis Tedlock, trans.

Buzzard:
box for the dead,
grave on the wing,
but you're not burdened
with the names of the dead.

K'uch :/ kaxa re kaminaq,/ muqub'al karapapik/ xawi karaj kaweqaj/ ri ub' ri
kaminaq

[* The title refers to the U.S. helicopters used by the Guatemalan governments against
the Maya of Guatemala.]

Elikura Chihuailaf (1955–, Chile)

Chihuailaf describes himself as an indigenous poet and "oralitor"—"one who is a
writer but stays close to orality, respecting, in addition, the way of thinking that
sustains him, which is also the way of thinking of his own people." He was born
in Temuco, a city in southern Chile that is also the center of the Mapuche culture.
He has been a university professor, a translator of Neruda into his language, and
an ardent representative of "the beautiful dark skin" in his country, which he says

must not be "erased or hidden under the rug of the hegemonic (whitewashing) identity." Creator of an original, elaborate bilingual (Spanish and Mapudungun) poetic architecture, Chihuailaf has been able to communicate and support his people's spirit and cosmogony and provide continuity to their dreams. PRINCIPAL WORKS: *El invierno y su imagen* (1977), *En el país de la memoria* (1988), *De sueños azules y contrasueños* (2000)

I Still Want to Dream in This Valley / Petu kvpa pewmalen tvfachi mapu mew / Aún deseo soñar en este valle

John Bierhorst, trans.

Rains tighten the strings of the wind
and a chorus above gives out the
        sounds of fruitfulness
There were many animals, it is saying
mountains, lakes, birds, good words
I move forward with closed eyes:
I see inside me the old one
waiting for the butterflies to return
living the days of his childhood
Don't ask my age, he says
        and I am content
why mention what doesn't exist?
Through the power of memory the land lives
also the blood of the ancestors
Can you see, can you see why,
he asks
I still want to dream in this valley?

Mawvn nvtrvgkvnutufi pvchi kvrvf ñi trarin/ ka, wenu, ti fvtra vl tripay zugun fillem/ ñi feypiley ñi neal choyvn/ Mvlewma fentren kulliñ— pilerpuy/ mawizantu, pvchike lafken, vñvm, kvme/ /zugu/ Umerkvlen amun:/ iñche ñi powimu, kvñe fvhca/ kizu vgvm ñi wiñomeal tipu llampvzkeñ/ ñi pvchike gemun tremkvlen antv mew/ Ramtukenueli tuntentripantv ñi mien, pienew/ feymu ayvwkvlean/ Chumael tukulpageafuy ti genolu?/ Ñi newen tukulpan mew mogeley ta mapu/ ka feymu mvley taiñ kuyfikeche tañi mollfvñ/ Kimaymi, kimaymi, chumgelu— feypi/ petu kvpa pewmalefun tvfachi mapu mew?

Las lluvias tensan las cuerdas de su brisa/ y, arriba, es el coro que lanza el sonido/ de la fertilidad/ Muchos animales hubo—va diciendo/ montes— lagos, aves, buenas palabras/ Avanzo con los ojos cerrados:/ Veo, en mí, al anciano/ que esperando el regreso de las mariposas/ habita los días de su infancia/ No me preguntes la edad—me dice/ y estaré contento/ ¿para qué pronunciar lo que no existe?/ En la energía de la memoria la tierra vive/ y en ella la sangre de los antepasados/ ¿Comprenderás, comprenderás, por qué/ —dice/ aún deseo soñar en este valle?

For I Am the Power of the Nameless / Nienolu vy tañi newen ta iñche / Porque soy la fuerza de lo innombrado

John Bierhorst, trans.

I have dreamed of the crescent moon,
    it says,
and I have worked the fields
Before there were words
before there were flowers, I existed
(and farther away)
For my daughters I build
the house of silver
as I ride my horse above the rainbow
hair streaming in the wind
I am the running water
The ocean goes to sleep inside me
The mountain awakes
For I am the power of the nameless,
    it says,
the light around the sun: your song.

Pewman ta we kvyen mew, pi/ ka kvzaw ke fiñ ta lelfvn/ Petu ñi zugu genon/ ka rayen rume genon femvn/ (welu zoy alv kamapu)/ Tvfawla ñi pu ñawe zeumalkefiñ/ lien ruka/ ka kvrvf negvmvñ ma meke enew/ ñi lonko/ pvrakawellkvlen wente relmu/ Witrunko ta iñche/ Umawtulen amuley lafken iñche mew/ ka nepey ta mawizantu/ Nienolu vy tañi newen ta iñche, pi/ tuwaymane chi antv: Tami vl.

He soñado en la luna creciente/ dice/ y he trabajado los campos/ Antes que las palabras/ y que las flores fui/ (y más lejos)/ Para mis hijas construyo/ la casa de plata/ mientras con el cabello al/ viento/ cabalgo sobre el arco iris/ Soy el agua que corre/ Dormido va el mar en mí/ y despierta la montaña/ Porque soy la fuerza de lo/ innombrado, dice/ corona del sol: tu canto.

Myriam Moscona (1955–, Mexico)

Born in Mexico City of Bulgarian Sephardim parents, Moscona is a poet, translator, and journalist. Recipient of a grant from the Guggenheim Foundation, she has translated an anthology by Kenneth Rexroth and obtained the National Translators Award in Mexico for her version of the poetry of William Carlos Williams. Nine of the biographical sketches of Mexican poets she collected in a book were adapted to Mexican television. She conducted a cultural news program that earned her network a distinction by UNESCO in 1999 as the world's best cultural channel. In an effort to widen the scope of poetry, she published *Negro marfil* (Black Ivory), a visual set of poems in which verbal plasticity reaches its maximum expression by establishing— according to Moscona's own description—"a superimposed dialogue" between the word and the graphic image. PRINCIPAL WORKS: *Las visitantes* (1989), *Vísperas* (1996), *Negro marfil* (2000), *El que nada* (2006)

Excerpt from Black Ivory / Negro marfil

Jen Hofer, trans.

I was sleeping when a small animal came into my room: its surface was damp and stained like a stone covered with moss. It approached the edge of my bed making the same noise jaws make as they chew a bone. I closed my eyes and saw it within me. I heard the second heart.

. . . .

I sing
      (I say)
Black deserts
      (I say)
Streaked things of dappled color
The background frayed
The fracture tarnished to evenness
Engraving garnet in garlands
      To God
The work of sound is consecrated

. . . .

Is covered the fabric the body is covered the water
In the rosy   Submerged steam
Beneath the organs of the chest
      A mother

(milk)   Bleeds in whites

Let's fragment the body into its parts   Leonardo did it
From right to left   Is written

Moment of purification   The vanes of all that's invisible
             Spin
The heart the size of a fist and of the joining of sole and nape at the apex of
    the chest and along the line Water water in
                         Agnus Dei

. . . .

Ink slid going and coming the thing and its opposite in two folds black-
    white

Intention spins   Traces
Beneath the loose string of the harps
On the paper   Bound to the axis
Without air   (The throat)
Aims at asphyxiation

. . . .

The Yellow river   Crosses the paper
Sewn in canvases   Two signs
Like birds   Made of rain
In the sky   Furrowed

Swallows   Below
The swamp   The birds shake
The cross   As they land
Come near   To eat
Worms   Trace
With monosyllables   chirping
In folds   Of writing
They cross   Worlds
Beneath the cold
Desert
In the sands   To turn round
The Night   To get confused
            Within
To drill through   Fog
From grey to   Grey
Alone   The swallow
From other   Times
          Arrives
To furrow   The *ritornelle*
       Stammerings
With a tonal   Vowel
Now   Mute
In India   Ink

The white (its impurity) at two extremes. To the left is the tongue. The
fly links the right side toward an order Chaos borders on two broken
snakes Why are they so slow to die? Warm half in the form of a lotus
flower.

Overdose of ivory black
Contrabass
One octave further in
side

        Throat
Sound with no figure
Knits meshworks   skeins nets
To the right (incisions, leaves, aqueducts)
Vena cava

                Runs aground
Where?
Is oiled   Is anointed
Is rotated   Toward the left:
        Cure

Dormía cuando entró a mi cuarto un animal pequeño: tenía la superficie húmeda y/
manchada como una piedra cubierta en musgo. Se acercó a la orilla de la cama con
el/ mismo ruido que hacen las mandíbulas al triturar un hueso. Cerré los ojos y lo
vi por/ dentro. Oí al segundo corazón// . . . *//* Canto// (digo)/ Desiertos negros/
(digo)/ Veteantes cosas de color mezclado/ Raído el fondo/ Se aja al ras la
quebradura/ Grabando guindas en la espalda / A Dios/ La obra del sonido
se consagra// . . . // Se cubre la tela el cuerpo se cubre el agua / En lo rosáceo
Vapor hundido/ Bajo los órganos del pecho // Una madre// (leche) Sangra
en blancos// Fragmentemos el cuerpo en sus partes Lo hizo Leonardo/ De
derecha a izquierda Se escribe/ Momento de purificación Las aspas de todo lo
invisible/ Soplan entorno/ El corazón del tamaño de un puño y de la juntura
de la planta a la cerviz en la sumidad/ del pecho y en la línea Agua agua en/
Agnus Dei// . . . // Tinta escurrida en ida y vuelta la cosa y su contrario en
dos rediles negro-blanco// Gira la intención Traza/ Bajo la cuerda floja de las
arpas/ Sobre el papel Amarrado al eje/ Sin aire (La garganta)/ Apunta hacia
la asfixia// . . . // El río Amarillo Atraviesa el papel/ Cosido en lienzos Dos
signos/ Como pájaros De lluvia/ En el cielo Surcado// Golondrinas Abajo / El
pantano Las aves sacuden/ La cruz De aterrizar/ Se acercan A comer/ Gusanos
Trazan/ Con monosílabos Piantes/ En pliegos De escritura/ Cruzan Mundos/
Bajo el frío/ Desierto/ En las arenas Versar/ La Noche Confundirse/ Dentro/
Horadar la Niebla/ De gris en Gris/ A solas La golondrina/ De otros Tiempos/
Llega/ Para surcar El *ritornelo*/ Balbuceos// Con vocal Tonal/ Ahora Muda/ En
tinta China// El blanco (su impureza) en dos extremos. En el izquierdo está
la lengua La mosca enlaza/ el derecho hacia un orden El caos linda en dos

culebras rotas ¿Por qué son lentas en /morir? Calurosa mitad en flor de loto.//
Sobredosis de negro-marfil/ Contrabajo/ Una octava más ade/ ntro/ Garganta/
El sonido sin figura/ Teje mallas tramas redes/ Al derecho (cisuras, hojas,
acueductos)/ Vena cava cala en su estar/ Encalla/ ¿Dónde?/ Se acepta Se unge/
Se rota Hacia el izquierdo:/ Curación

Josely Vianna Baptista (1957–, Brazil)

Born in Curitiba, Brazil, Baptista is the author of the books *Ar, Corpografia, On the
Shining Screen of Eyelids* (2003), and *Concha das mil coisas maravilhosas do Velho
Caramujo* (2001), which was the recipient of the VI Premio Internacional del Libro
Ilustrado Infantil y Juvenil. She has translated more than fifty books, including poems
by J. L. Borges (*Completed Works*, Globo) for which she was awarded the prestigious
Prêmio Jabuti award (1999). PRINCIPAL WORKS: *Ar* (1991), *Corpografia* (1992), *Los
poros floridos* (2002), *Musa paradisiaca* (2003)

A Sound of Ancient, Faded Flows / Um som de antigas águas apagadas
Michael Palmer, trans.

> . . . the rhyme is a mirage, fable of nothingness,
>   the flaws of speech deterritorialized,
> hermaphroditic speech, splinters magnetized,
> voice through transparency, buildings of sand.

> But your gaze the same, an iris-diaphragm,
>   photograms missing from the published book,
> the sun and dream plot and insular deliriums,
>   your transparent gaze, the image
> water's edge, and the fables of speech,
> the flaws of such nothingness—a surface of whitness

>   or arid scribblings.

> At page's border,
> marginalia of slopes.

. . . miragem a rima, a fábula do nada,/ as falhas dessa fala em desgeografia,/
a fala hermafrodita, imantação de astilhas,/ a voz na transparência, edifícios
de areia.// Mas teu olhar o mesmo, em íris-diafragma,/ fotogramas a menos
na edição do livro,/e o enredo sonho e sol, delírios insulares,/ teu olhar
transparente, a imagem/ margem d'água, e as fábulas da fala,/ as falhas desse

nada—superfície de alvura// ou árida escritura.// Na moldura da página,/
marginália de escarpas.

Traces / Riscos

t r a c e s ,   h i e r o g l y p h s
i n s c r i b e d   o n   t h e
c r e v i c e s   o f   a   c o n c h ,
p o e m   c h i s e l e d   o n
b a r n a c l e s ,   s h e l l –
m u r m u r s ,
h e r m a p h r o d i t e s
e n c r u s t e d   o n   c o a r s e
c a r a p a c e s   a r t e r i e s
o f   s t o n e   t h a t   t i m e
e n c o d e s ,   b r a i l l e
s h a v i n g s   s h a p e d   b y
t h e   w i n d   l i k e
i n d i c e s   —
s o o t h s a y e r ' s
i n c i s i o n s — i n t o
a n i m a l   e n t r a i l s ,
n o r t h   o f   o t h e r
a m e r i c a s   o r   l u c k y   i n
l o v e ,   o r   t r a c e s   o f
y o u r   b o d y
l a m i n a t i n g   m e m o r y
(m u s k   a n d
m o l l u s k) e m e r g i n g ,
m e t e o r - l i k e ,   t h e
p a i n   o f   s o m e
p a r a d i s e ,   m y   c r a c k e d
l i p s   o n   y o u r
b r a c k i s h   l i p s ,
m u r i c e s   a n d   m o r a y s
i n   a n   e c s t a s y   o f
h a n d s ,   s h e l l f i s h ,
c o r a l - b r a i n s ,   a c u m e n
l a u g h i n g   s a l i n e   m u d

riscos, hieroglifos/ inscritos nas frinc/ has de uma concha, p/ oema
cinzelado nas/ cracas, búzio—murmú/ rios, hermafroditos/ incrustados
nas car/ apaças ásperas: art/ érias calcárias que/ o tempo cifra, rasur/ a em

braile que o ve/ nto molda como indí/ cios—incisura de ar/ úspice—nas
víscera/ s de um bicho, norte/ de outras américas/ ou sorte amorosa, n/
o rastro de teu cor/ po laminando a memó/ ria (almíscar e mari/ sco) que
aflora, met/ eórica, a dor de um/ paraíso, os meus lá/ bios rachados em t/ eus
lábios salgado/ s, múrices e moréi/ as no êxtase das m/ ãos, moluscos, cora/
is—cérebro, lágrim/ a de alegria—o gume/ um riso de salsugem

The Grail / Graal

Odile Cisneros, trans.

```
g  r  a  i  l        i  n           v  i  l  a        v  e  l  h  a
o  r        o  n                 t  h  e              p  o  n  t  e
v  e  c  c  h  i  o  ,           i  t  s           s  t  o  n  e
s  l  a  b  s              p  o  l  i  s  h  e  d                 b  y
t  h  e              s  a  n  d  ,              o  n              t  h  e
s  t  r  i  p  e  d                          s  t  r  e  a  k
b  e  t  w  e  e  n           s  t  o  n  e                 a  n  d
m  o  s  s  ,              s  p  i  k  e  s                 o  f
j  a  d  e  ,              c  r  e  s  t  s                 o  f
g  r  a  n  i  t  e  ,           o  n        i  s  l  a  n  d  s
o  f        m  i  n  e  s  ,           n  e  b  u  l  o  u  s
h  a  z  e  ,           o  n        t  h  e        q  u  i  e  t
s  h  o  r  e  s           t  h  a  t        h  a  i  l  s
c  h  o  p  s  ,        a        t  r  e  m  b  l  i  n  g
o  f        l  i  p  s  ,        a        r  a  t  t  l  i  n  g
o  f        t  e  e  t  h  ,        i  n        y  o  u  r
j  o  y        o  r        i  n     t  h  e        s  e  n  s  e
o  f        s  l  i  p  p  i  n  g              a  n  d
s  l  i  d  i  n  g                          e  y  e  s
d  i  s  c  o  v  e  r  i  n  g              o  c  e  l  l  i
o  n        t  h  e              s  t  r  i  a  t  e  d
w  i  n  g  s        o  f        a        t  i  n  y
i  n  s  e  c  t
```

graal em vila velha/ ou na ponte vecchio,/ nas lajes limadas p/ elos grãos de
areia/, na listra riscada/ entre pedra e líque/ n, arestas de jade, c/ ristas de
granito, e/ m ilhas de minas, ne/ bulosidades, nas mar/ gens tranqüilas qu/
e o granizo frisa, n/ um fremir de lábios, / retinir de dentes, / na tua alegria
ou no/ senso em deslize do/ s olhos em falso de/ scobrindo ocelos n/ as asas
estriadas d/ e um pequeno inseto

Xunka' Utz'utz' Ni' (DOB unknown, Mexico, Tzoltzil Maya)

Xunka' Utz'utz' Ni is a fireworks maker and mother of nine children. She lives near San Andrés Larrainzar where she grows bamboo to form the structures for the exploding "castles" and "bulls" that are set off in celebrations. Utz'utz' Ni' mixes gunpowder, braids fuses, and, with the leftovers, weaves baskets. Her husband is an illegal immigrant who works in a slaughterhouse in Tennessee. PRINCIPAL WORKS: As an oral poet, most of her works were not recorded.

Prayer So My Man Won't Have to Cross the Line / K'u cha'al mu sa' abtel ta nom ti smalale / Encanto para no tener que ir al otro lado

Ámbar Past, trans.

Take into account, *Kajval,**
that I am speaking to you.

I bring you smoke.
I offer you flowers.

Take into account, *Kajval,*
what you are going to give me.

The others have horses.
They have sheep.

They have hens.
Trucks.

Take into account, *Kajval,*
how much you are going to give me.

I don't want to work on a plantation.
I don't want to go to someone else's house.
I don't want to work far away.

I don't want to go to Los Angeles.
I don't want work in Florida.

[* *Kajval:* My Lord, My Lady, used for addressing the gods.]

K'u yepal tana, Kajval,/ chajta ta k'oponel, chajta ta ti'inel.// Tzakbo ti jbej yo xch'ail./ Tzakbo ti jbej yo xnichime.// Vo'ot xanopbe atuk tana un./ Vo'ot xat'ujbe atuk tana un, Kajval.// Ti k'usi xavak'be une, ti k'usi xak'elanbe un./ A li yan avalabe, a li yan anich'nabe, Kajval:// Oy k'usi oy yu'un. Oy ska'ik, oy xchijik./ Oy yalak'ik, oy skamyonik.// K'u yepal tana, Kajval,/ k'usi xavak'bun, k'usi xak'elanbun.// Ja' ti mu xu' ti nom abtele./ Ja'

ti mu xu' ti pinkae./ Ja' ti mu xu' ti asyentae, Kajval.// Ja' mu jk'an xbat ta
Los Anjeles./ Ja'mu jk'an xbat ta Florida.//

Toma en cuenta, *Kajval*,/ que te estoy hablando.// Te traigo humo./ Aquí te
doy tus flores.// Toma en cuenta, *Kajval*,/ qué tanto me vas a dar.// Los otros
tienen caballos./ Tienen borregos.// Tienen gallinas./ Y camiones.// Toma en
cuenta, *Kajval*,/ qué me vas a dar.// No quiero trabajar en ninguna finca./ No
quiero ir a otra casa./ No quiero ningún trabajo lejos.// No quiero ir a Los
Ángeles./ No quiero ir a La Florida.

Loxa Jiménes Lópes (DOB unknown, Mexico, Tzoltzil Maya)

Loxa Jiménes Lópes is a weaver and seer from Epal Ch'en, "Many Caves." Lópes raises
sheep, spins wool, plants corn, and keeps a tiny store where she sells candy and soft
drinks. PRINCIPAL WORKS: As an oral poet, most of her works were not recorded.

Pexi Kola Magic / Sk'op jchon resku' / Conjuro para la Pexi Cola
Ámbar Past, trans.

Remind people to buy from me, *Kajval*.
Not from the other store.

Send me customers, *Kajval*.
With lots of cash, *Kajval*.

I want to sell my cigarettes one by one,
crackers, candy, salt.

Make them drink soda pop:
if it stays too long in the cooler,
the bottle caps rust.

Don't let your dew turn sour;
don't let your *Panta* rot, the *Pexi* go bad.

Make soda pop support me
like a son who works to feed his mom.

Vulesbo tal ta sjol tanich'nab une, Kajval./ Ak'o me taluk ti yajval une, Tot.//
Te to me sjoy pati komel yan tavalab une./ Te to me sjoy pati komel yan
tanich'nab une, Kajval.// Ti k'usi ta jchone, ti k'usi ta xkake';/ Ti jun resku'e,
ti jun sik'olale,/ Ti jun kayetae, ti jun lursee, ti jb'ej avatz'am, Kajval.// Mu
me jeche'uk li' sikub ta resku' une, Kajval./ Mu me jeche'uk li' xkuxin une,

Kajval.// Mu me jeche'uk li' xpajub une ta atz'ujulal une./ Mu me jeche'uk li' xpajub une ta *Panta*, ta *Pexi* une, Kajval.// Xchi'uk taresku' une Jtot, xchi'uk taresku' une, Kajval./ Resku' ti jmotone, resku' ti kaboltael une, Kajval.

Recuerda a la gente que me tienen que comprar./ Que no vayan a ir a la otra tienda.// Mándame clientes, *Kajval*./ Con harta paga, *Kajval*.// Quiero vender mis cigarros uno por uno,/ las galletas, los dulces, la sal.// Que tomen los refrescos;/ que no estén aquí enfriándose nada más/ porque se oxidan las corcholatas.// Que no se vaya a agriar tu rocío;/ que no se vaya a podrir el *Panta*, la *Pexi*.// Que me mantenga el Refresco como un hijo/ que trabaja para dar de comer a su madre.

María Ernándes Kokov (DOB unknown, Mexico, Tzoltzil Maya)

María Ernándes Kokov calls herself the "Defender of Angels" and has a "talking box," a commercialized version of an ancient Mayan oracle from which a saint speaks to her. The text of a speech from the box was taped in 1996 during an eclipse of the moon seen from her house on Huitepec Mountain, near the antennas of Televisión Azteca and a traditional animistic shrine. The saint, named Pagresito, "Little Daddy," spoke to her in a falsetto voice. Kokov takes care of the saint, intercedes with Pagresito, pleading for the interests of those who consult her, and performs cures. PRINCIPAL WORKS: As an oral poet, most of her works were not recorded.

The Talking Box Speaks / Xk'opoj jtotik ta kaxa / La caja que habla
Ámbar Past, trans.

"Are you there?
I'm from the Universe.
I want bread
and half a crate of soda pop.

Are you there, Sons of Man?
Same as always?
Got a question?
OK, I'm on my way.
Just a minute.
Don't worry.

Rin-Ran-Rin! I'm back.
What was lost can be found.

I'm going to look for it near Venus
and punish the guilty one.
Tipín, tipín, tipín! you'll hear my whip.
Ay, ay, ay! the thief will cry out.
Nothing to be done.
That's destiny.

That'll be fifty pesos
and a kilo of incense.

See you later,
Sons of Women.
Goodbye, Defender of the Angels."

"¿Mi li'ote?/ Likemun tal ta Banumil, ta vinajel./ Ta jk'an kaxlan vaj./ Ta jk'an olol reja resku'.// ¿Mi te oyoxuk, kalab nichnab?/ ¿Mi jech o'nox?/ ¿Mi oy k'usi xajak'?/ Ta xik'ot te./ Malaun jlikeluk./ Mu xavat avo'onton.// ¡Rin Ran Rin! Li'sut tal./ Ti k'usi ch'ayeme, ta sut tal.// A li k'usi mu xich' taele, ta xtal./ Ta jtam ta muk'ta k'analetik./ Xakak'utik stoj smul buch'u yich' pak'tael./ Ti xtimtun jnukul./ Ja yu'n ti j'eleke./ Mu'yuk xa xpoxil./ Mu'yuk xa spojel o.// Ak'bun lajuneb oxvinik pexu/ xchi'uk jun kilo pom.// Chabanuk komel, kalab jnich'nab./ Ta me xibat, Jchabivanej Ojovetik."

"Buenas noches./ Vengo del universo./ Quiero pan/ y media caja de refrescos.// ¿Están allí, Hijos de Hombre?/ ¿Igual que siempre?/ ¿Qué dices, mujer, una pregunta?/ Bueno, voy a llegar./ Espérenme un ratito./ No se preocupen.// ¡Rin-Ran-Rin! Ya volví ya./ Lo que se ha perdido va a regresar./ Lo que no se encuentra va a volver.// Lo voy a pepenar entre los planetas/ Y castigar al culpable./ ¡*Tipín, tipín, tipín!* van a oír mi látigo./ ¡*Ay, ay, ay!* Va a gritar el ladrón./ No tiene más remedio./ Esto es su destino.// Son cincuenta pesos./ Y un kilo de copal.// Saludos, Hijos de Mujer./ Adiós, Defensora de los Ángeles."

Tonik Nibak (DOB unknown, Mexico, Tzoltzil Maya)

Tonik Nibak was an exceptional woman from Zinacantán who had a great way with words. Robert M. Laughlin remembers her as the best storyteller he has ever known. Tonik worked as a servant in San Cristóbal from age seven, then became a weaver. Her last years were dedicated to making life impossible for her sons-in-law and selling roses door to door in San Cristóbal de Las Casas, Chiapas. PRINCIPAL WORKS: As an oral poet, most of her works were not recorded.

Dance of the Perfumed Woman / X'ak'otaj jxinulan/ Baile de la mujer perfumada

Ámbar Past, trans.

God willing, María!
God willing, Luchita!

Ojalá, Maruquita!
Ojalá, Chinita!

María is dancing.
Rosario is dancing.

I am a woman, I am a woman, I am a real woman.
I am a girl, I am a girl, I am a real girl.

The women are dancing.
The girls are dancing.

Pick off, pick off your lice, women.
Comb, comb your hair, niñas.

I am a perfumed woman.
I am a perfumed girl.

I am a bought woman.
I am a paid girl.

I am a puta woman.
I am a puta girl.

The Sun is dancing
The Moon is dancing.

¡Ojalá, María!/ ¡Ojalá, Luchita!// ¡Ojalá, Marukita!/ ¡Ojalá, Chinita!//
X'ak'otaj María./ X'ak'otaj Rosario.// Antzon ti antzon bi./ Tzebon ti tzebon
bi.// K'elo me, k'elo me avuch', antzetik./ Tuso me, tuso me ajol, tzebetick.//
X'ak'otaj antzetik./ X'ak'otaj tzebetik.// Jxinulan antzon, bi./ Jxinulan
tzebon, bi.// Manbil antzon, bi./ Manbil tzebon, bi.// K'a' antzon, bi./ K'a'
tzebon, bi.// X'ak'otaj Jtotik o./ X'ak'otaj Jme'tik o.

¡Ojalá, María!/ ¡Ojalá, Luchita!// ¡Ojalá, Marukita!/ ¡Ojalá, Chinita!//
María está bailando./ Rosario está bailando.// Soy mujer, soy mujer, soy
mujer de verdad./ Soy niña, soy niña, soy niña de verdad.// Las mujeres
están bailando./ Las niñas están bailando.// Espulguen, espulguen sus
piojos, mujeres./ Péinense, péinense sus cabellos, niñas.// Soy una mujer
perfumada./ Soy una niña perfumada.// Soy una mujer comprada./ Soy
una niña comprada.// Soy una mujer puta./ Soy una niña puta.// El Sol está
bailando./ La Luna está bailando.

Cristina Rivera-Garza (1964–, Mexico)

A poet and prose writer, Rivera-Garza was born in Matamoros, in Mexico's north-eastern border region. A historian by profession, she has taught at several American universities. At an early age, and with her family's encouragement, she became an avid reader and decided that she wanted to be a writer. Her work breaks down the boundaries between genres and has received enthusiastic recognition from, among others, Carlos Fuentes: "We are witnessing one of the most prominent works of fiction, not only in Mexican literature but in literature written in Spanish during this turn of the century. . . . I am a great admirer of her work and have just read what I consider a revelation: the novel by Cristina Rivera-Garza, *Nadie me verá llorar* (No One Will See Me Cry), is one of the most wonderful and disturbing novels ever written in Mexico." PRINCIPAL WORKS: *La guerra no importa* (1991), *La más mía* (1998), *Nadie me verá llorar* (1999), *La cresta de Ilión* (2002), *La muerte meda* (2008)

Excerpt from Third World / Tercer mundo

Jen Hofer, trans.

I.

It was at the far edge of the far edge
    about to exist and about not to exist like faith
a shack surrounded by miserable islets of corn and half-starved turkeys.
The Third World was a roofless house.

The *Terzo.*

There maniacs brought their treadmill-needy eyes, their plain index fingers
    which traced a countenance on the left side of chaos.
There little girls practiced that proclivity for proclivity
while men extolled the cawing of imaginary birds.

From above an ozone sky fell and the odor of used city seeped through the
    cracks.

Prewar cripples arrived at the *Terzo* prostrate and thirsty
    voracious black heralds with voices of pandemic and killing hands.
There far-out, far-gone lunatics broke down the mechanisms of language
    among the meditative vapors of alcohol and matches
        vowels were helium balloons filled with fireflies
        sentences dragged themselves along, sinuous with their long
        reptile tails.
Trippers and druggies and those forever mute spoke with the fervor of the
    converted.

There good-for-nothings were highly useful beings.

The dead crept through the *Terzo* with the somnolent little eyes of the
          resuscitated and they lived and they choked on smoke and they died
          again inside the box of their bodies.
There pariahs levitated with austere saints' faces and indifferent hands.
There the suicidal positioned themselves in their seats at unpredictable
          angles.
There the denizens of the underground came out of their lairs and spread
          their plunder across their laps — pocket watches, car parts, and
          wilted flowers.
And the hybrid daybreak advanced with the clumsy gait of certain black
          birds pecking at their sexes with a metal meekness
          showing its aching teeth, its cheap trophies, its karmic victories.
Beneath the cruel monotony of the summer deluge everyone spoke
          spitting words and maps and prophecies and prayers.

Let's go to the Terzo, they murmured, with the determination of those who
          place bombs or go
          Down towards the eternal primeval *towards*
          and never get there.

There shoes sank in the mud and to be buried was to be a tree and fruit of a
          tree
          immaculate flesh   mouth with sharp edges.

Outside, on the other side of the far edge, the biggest city in the world
          lied.

II.
A world not yet of men, not yet of women licked their moccasins with its
          iodine tongues
and the creatures with blue faces advanced upon the afternoon with no
          knowledge of necessity.

Those with winged sexes cut their hair military style and forgot the homes
          they came from.
Those trained to dominate sank for the first time into a fleeting weakness
          strident potions fed the slow unformed corners of their mouths
          their corners spread open as they fall in seven reelings disproportionate
          reeling arms of helicopteric light
          slice of night and slice of solar crust.

On the way to the *Terzo* they tore off the straitjackets of old names
and emerged from their pasts with fine, fine hides and bones with no
          history.
They were The She-Devil, The Giga-Dog, The Frog, Little Lulu, Red Rooster
          Ed, The Queen Beast.

Those destined to be men harbored, from time to time, the absurd shrieking
of lonely women in their teeth.
Those destined to give birth hid beneath the virile darkness of the upright.
Everyone changed places in the biblical days of the *Terzo*:
the last were always the first and those who laughed last always
laughed best.
Bifids sexually and in everything else unresolved
they smoked cigarettes categorically.
The strands of their bodies slid without difficulty through the needle's
tiny eye which was the gateway to eternity.

It was the left side of the sky where all games are games of chance.
It was a puddle of piss.
It was a prehistoric quagmire.

And when they headed out, dizzy, for The City, they took the *Terzo* with
them, hanging from their shoulders
proud of their shapelessness.

I. Estaba en una orilla de la orilla a punto de existir y a punto de no
existir como la fe un tendajo rodeado de isletas miserables de maíz y
guajolotes hambrientos. El Tercer Mundo era una casa sin techos. El
Terzo. Ahí llevaban los orates sus ojos necesitados de noria y el escueto
dedo índice que/ dibujaba un semblante en el lado izquierdo del caos.
Ahí las niñas ensayaban esa proclividad por la proclividad mientras los
hombres alababan el graznido de pájaros imaginarios. De arriba caía un
cielo de ozono y el olor a ciudad usada se colaba por las rendijas. Los
lisiados de preguerra llegaban al Terzo postrados y sedientos avorazados
heraldos negros con voz de pandemia y manos de matar. Ahí los locos
de remate descomponían el mecanismo del lenguaje entre el vaho/
meditabundo del alcohol y los cerillos las vocales eran globos de helio
rellenos de luciérnagas las oraciones se arrastraban sinuosas con su
larga cola de reptil. Los pirados y los/ drogos y los mudos para siempre
hablaban con el fervor de los conversos. Ahí los pránganas eran seres
utilísimos. Los muertos reptaban en el Terzo con los ojillos somnolientos
del resucitado y vivían y se atragantaban de humo y morían otra vez
dentro de la caja de sus/ cuerpos. Ahí los parias levitaban con adustos
rostros de santo y manos indiferentes. Ahí los suicidas se acomodaban
en ángulos impredecibles sobre los asientos. Ahí los subterráneos salían
de sus agujeros y desparramaban sobre los regazos su botín de/ relojes
de bolsillo, partes de auto y flores desmayadas. Y la madrugada híbrida
avanzaba con el torpe caminar de ciertas aves negras picoteaba los sexos
con mansedumbre de metal enseñaba sus dientes doloridos, sus trofeos
baratos, sus victorias kármicas. Bajo la cruel monotonía del diluvio estival

todos hablaban escupían palabras y mapas y profecías y rezos. *Vamos al Terzo*, murmuraban, con la determinación de los que colocan bombas o van Abajo hacia el eterno *hacia* primigenio sin llegar.// Ahí los zapatos se hundían en el lodo y enterrarse era ser árbol y fruto de árbol carne inmaculada boca con filos.// Afuera, del otro lado de la orilla, la ciudad más grande del mundo mentía. II. Un mundo que todavía no era de hombres o de mujeres lamía los mocasines con sus/ lengüetas de yodo y las criaturas de azules rostros avanzaban sobre la tarde sin conocer la necesidad. Las de sexo alado se cortaban los cabellos militarmente y olvidaban su casa. Los adiestrados en el dominio se hundían por primera vez en una fugaz debilidad estridentes pócimas nutrían sus lentas comisuras informes sus comisuras desdobladas al caer en siete aspavientos desmedidos aspas de luz helicoptérica/ tajada de noche y tajada de mendrugo solar. De camino al Terzo se arrancaban las camisas de fuerza de los nombres viejos y emergían de sus pasados en cueros finísimos y huesos sin historia. Eran La Diabla, el Perrote, la Rana, la Pequeña Lulú, el Lalo Gallo, la Bestia. Los destinados a ser hombres albergaban a ratos el chillar absurdo de las mujeres solas en los dientes. Las destinadas a dar a luz se escondían bajo la oscuridad viril de los enhiestos. Todos cambiaban de lugar en los días bíblicos del Terzo: los últimos eran siempre los primeros y los que reían al final siempre reían mejor. Bífidos en el sexo e irresueltos en todo lo demás fumaban cigarrillos categóricamente. Las hebras de sus cuerpos se deslizaban sin dificultad por el pequeñísimo ojo de la aguja/ que era la puerta de la eternidad. Era el lado izquierdo del cielo donde todo juego es un juego de azar. Era un charco de orines. Era un prehistórico lodazal. Y cuando partían mareados hacia La Ciudad, se llevaban al Terzo colgando de los/ hombros orgullosos de su informidad.

Juan Gregorio Regino (1962–, Mexico)

Regino was born in Nuevo Paso Nazareno, Chichicazapa, San Miguel de Soyalte-pec, in Oaxaca, Mexico, one of the new towns created after the ancient traditional lowlands of the Mazatec were flooded by hydroelectric dams. Educated first in his community and then in Mexico City, he became a schoolteacher and a linguist, authoring the *Alfabeto mazateco* (Mazatec Alphabet) now used in the bilingual edu-cation of his people. Currently he is the Director of Development of Indigenous Cultures for Mexico and is devoted to "recovering the historic, aesthetic and artis-tic memory of the indigenous people." His first book of poems, written in Span-ish and Mazatec, received national and international attention as it was the first to step out of the oral tradition that had produced masters such as María Sabina, into alphabetic writing. PRINCIPAL WORKS: *Tastjejin nga kjaboya/No es eterna la muerte* (1994), *Ngata'ara stsee/Que siga lloviendo* (1999)

Cantares / Nijmi en nima / Cantares

Eliot Weinberger, trans.

I

Four hundred zontles away,
Four hundred leagues to the endless,
Light, darkness, images.
The voice of the wise one comes from there,
The singer, the soother of woe.
Among the images of the divine,
Among the images of the earth,
His soft voice is heard,
His song of the divine,
His godly prayer.
He crosses over on the path of life,
He travels to the nest of perfect images,
To talk there,
To haggle there,
To plead there
With the gods who rule the fate of the world.
The small wind lulls him,
The sleeping lightning waits for him,
His godly voice echoes like thunder
In the center of the universe.

II

Say lord of the hills.
Say lord of the caves.
Say spirits of the canyons.
Say father of the storm.

Say goddess of fertility.
Say mother of orphans.
Say whore.
Say mistress of fire.

Say macaw feathers.
Say *aguardiente*.
Say fragrant flowers.
Say tobacco dust.

Say rains from the east.
Say center of the world.

Say fertile land.
Say hanging bridges.

Say doors to the sky.
Say greater forces.
Say west and east.
Say place of the images.

III
This is how the day reaches over,
This is how the image reaches over,
Seven leagues away,
Seven zontles to the endless.
From there my voice is heard,
From there my spirit reaches over.
House of the first beings,
I am the one who makes them appear,
I am the wise man, the prophet, the guide,
For I have the permit,
For I have the license
To enter the holy space
Where the wise books are found.
Blessed are you
Who dwell in the immaculate house.
We are thankful for the light that lights us.
We are thankful for the night that comes.
From there my footsteps travel,
From there I come,
To this house that offers shade,
To this house that refreshes.

IV
I am the wise singing man,
I am the wise soothing man,
I am the one who drags the captive spirits
From the darkness.
Where is this spirit?
What was it that happened?
I will drag him out,
I will free him,
I will lift him,
Even if he's underwater,
Even if he's under the rock.
From the images of the sky,
From the images of the earth,

I will set him free.
What was it that happened?
Where is the mistake?
Where is the error?
I've come to bring order,
I've come to do justice,
For it is part of my flesh,
For it is part of my blood,
For I am an honest lawyer,
For I am an explorer on the road.
From there my footsteps travel,
From there my words travel.
The soul is reaching across.
Time is reaching across.

I/ Nijun uchan yibua nga kjín./ Nijun ucha legua k' ajmí,/ ndi' í, jñú, isien./ Kiatjien fuchó nda chjinie,/ chjinie xi sié nga tsakí./ Nguijín isien k' a./ Nguijín isien nguindié./ Nday' a anda anda ndaá,/ só tsjatsoó,/ ndi nijmí ndasen./ Kuíxi fuatjún ndiyaá ngasandié,/ ndanga fuchó ndabua isien./ Kía chjianijmí,/ kiá futí,/ kia tsab' uxie' á/ nguijín Néná xi nchibutixamá ngasandié./ Tjo ch' an b'itiyá,/ chi'un kjifé ts'akunda,/ bikjín nday'aní nda,/ njuijín inima ngasandié.// II/ Xi tsi' e naxi, tsó./ Xi tsi' e tixa naxi, tsó./ Xi tsi' e xungaá, tsó./ Na'mí tjo 'ñú, tsó.// Xi ts'atsjáná nno, tsó./ Naan xta nima, tsó./ Tjian xtjien, tsó./ Xi tsi'e ndi'i, tsó.// Tsjá nisié iní, tsó./ Ya naxo xan, tsó./ Naxó sijen, tsó./ Ndsakuan tsjiun, tsó.// Stse ñanga b' utje ts'uí, tsó./ Ngamasien ngasandié, tsó./ Nangui nda, tsó./ Nchan ndié nday'a, tsó.// Ngatjua ngasandié, tsó./ Nga'ñú xi k'a ngase, tsó./ Nga ndibua nga utjé ts'uí, tsó./ Ngayá isien, tsó.// III/ Buats'en tjien nixtjín./ Buats' entjien isien,/ yito yibua ndojó,/ yito legua nga kjín./ Kiatjien fuchó ndaná./ Kiatjien fuchó isiená,/ ndiy' a xuta xi ncha tjún./ An xik'e kju'á'an,/ xi chjinie'an, xi ndiya'an, xi kjit' usu'an./ Ngat'e jé katsaéná kjuá./ Ngat'e jé tjiná kjuakití/ nga kus'iean ngayá isien/ ñanga kjiyijó libro ndikun./ Néná ngats'en chikunie taíjnu,/ nga ndiy'a tsjie tinchujun./ Ndakuchjíni tsien nga ndibuá ngajñú./ K'etsitjien fu'á ndsok'o'an./ K'etsitjien fu'á isien nixtjíná./ Kuí ndiy'a tjik'ien./ Kuí ndiy' a ch'an.// IV/ 'An xi chjinie sié'an./ 'An xi chjinie tsaki' an./ 'An xi b'uxiejí'an nga jnú/ isien nixtjín xi tjindo 'ñú./ ¿Ñá tikún isien nixtjín?/ ¿Kó jki'í ni xi kamá?/ 'An xi k'uxiéjí'an./ 'An xi kustjiéná./ Ndatsa nguindie nda./ Ndatsa nguindie ndijo./ Nguijín isien nixtjín k'a./ Nguijín isien nixtjín nangui./ 'An xi kutjojíná./ ¿Kó jki'í ni xi kamá?/ ¿Ñání nga kistinguí?/ ¿Ñání nga kistiyá?/ 'An xi k'uinda'an./ 'An xi kjuxi'a'an./ Ngat'e ti yijónaní./ Ngat' e ti jínání./ Ngat'e chijinie ndá'an./ Ngat'e máná minchisé ndiya./ K'etjien ja'a ndsok'o'an./ K'etjien ja'a nijmíná./ Kjijñá isiená./ Kjijñá nixtjíná.

I/ Cuatrocientos zontles de distancia./ Cuatrocientas leguas al infinito,/ luz, obscuridad, imágenes./ Hasta allí llega la voz del sabio,/ el cantor sobador de dolores./ Entre las imágenes divinas./ Entre las imágenes terrenales./ Se escucha su voz suave,/ su cantar divino,/ su plegaria piadosa./ El cruza la senda de la vida,/ llega hasta el *ndabua isien*./ Allá platica,/ allá discute,/ allá aboga/ con los dioses que rigen el destino del mundo./ La brisa lo arrulla,/ el rayo dormido lo acecha,/ retumba su voz piadosa/ en el centro del universo.// II/ Señor de los cerros, dice./ Señor de las cuevas, dice./ Señor de los cerros, dice./ Señor de las cuevas, dice./ Duendes del arroyo, dice./ Padre de la tempestad, dice.// Diosa de la fertilidad, dice./ Madre de los huérfanos, dice./ Mujer arrastradora, dice./ Dueña del fuego, dice.// Plumas de guacamaya, dice,/ carrizos de aguardiente, dice,/ flores perfumadas, dice,/ polvo de tabaco, dice.// Lluvias del oriente, dice./ Cerro del mundo, dice,/ Tierra fértil, dice./ Puentes colgantes, dice.// Puertas del cielo, dice./ Fuerzas superiores, dice./ Poniente y oriente, dice./ Lugar de imágenes, dice.// III/ Así es como está tendido el día./ Así es como está tendida la imagen,/ siete leguas de distancia,/ siete zontles al infinito./ Hasta aquí se escucha mi voz./ Hasta aquí se tiende mi espíritu,/ casa de seres principales./ Soy yo quien hace su presencia,/ el sabio, el guía, el adivinador./ Porque yo tengo el permiso./ Porque yo tengo la licencia/ de entrar al lugar sagrado/ donde yacen los libros sabios./ Benditos sean ustedes/ por vivir en la casa limpia./ Gracias por la luz que alumbra./ Gracias por la noche que llega./ Hasta aquí llegan mis pasos./ Hasta aquí llega mi presencia./ En esta casa que da sombra./ En esta casa que refresca.// IV/ Yo soy el sabio cantor./ Yo soy el sabio sobador./ Yo soy quien extrae de la oscuridad/ a los espíritus cautivos./ ¿En dónde está su espíritu?/ ¿Qué fue lo que sucedió?/ Yo lograré arrancarlo./ Yo lograré liberarlo./ Yo lograré levantarlo./ Aunque sea debajo del agua./ Aunque sea debajo de la piedra./ Entre las imágenes del cielo./ Entre las imágenes de la tierra./ Yo lo libraré./ ¿Qué fue lo que sucedió?/ ¿En dónde está su falta?/ ¿En dónde está su error?/ Yo vengo a poner orden./ Yo vengo a hacer justicia./ Porque es parte de mi carne./ Porque es parte de mi sangre./ Porque soy abogado justo./ Porque soy explorador de caminos./ Hasta aquí llegan mis pasos./ Hasta aquí llegan mis palabras./ Está tendida el alma./ Está tendido el tiempo.

Maureen Ahern is Professor in the Department of Spanish and Portuguese at Ohio State University. Her research interests include indigenous and colonial cultures and literatures of Mexico and Peru, translation theory, and Latin American women writers. She has translated and edited a number of contemporary Mexican and Peruvian literary texts, including *A Rosario Castellanos Reader* and *Five Quechua Poets*.

Rosa Alcalá has translated the work of Lourdes Vázquez, Cecilia Vicuña, and Lila Zemborain, among others. Her own poems appear in *The Wind Shifts: New Latino Poetry* and elsewhere. She teaches creative writing at the University of Texas, El Paso.

Regina Alfarano has worked as a translator and interpreter for more than twenty-four years and teaches online translation courses at New York University.

Esther Allen's translation of *José Martí: Selected Writings* was selected by the Los Angeles Times Book Review as one of the most important books of 2002. She teaches at Baruch College, City University of New York.

Lynne Alvarez is an award-winning poet and playwright whose work has been performed and published since the 1980s. She has also translated the work of Fernando Arrabal, Tirso de Molina, and Felipe Santander, among others.

Susan Bassnett is Professor of Comparative Literature at the University of Warwick. She is well known as a founding figure in the whole field of translation studies. Her collection of poems and translations of Alejandra Pizarnik, *Exchanging Lives*, appeared in 2002.

Samuel Beckett, Irish writer, poet, and playwright, translated numerous works into English, including his own work from French and that of several Mexican poets from Spanish.

Rachel Benson translated the work of many poets, including Carlos Pellicer, Luis Palés Matos, Xavier Villaurrutia, and Alfonsina Storni. She published *Nine Latin American Poets* in 1968.

Charles Bernstein is the author of forty books, ranging from large-scale collections of poetry and essays to pamphlets, libretti, translations, and collaborations. Recent full-length works of poetry include *Girly Man* and *With Strings*. He is currently Donald T. Regan Professor of English and Comparative Literature at University of Pennsylvania.

John Bierhorst is the author/translator of more than thirty books on American Indian literature. Specializing in Aztec poetry, he is the author of *A Nahuatl-English Dictionary* and the translator of *Cantares Mexicanos: Songs of the Aztecs* and the forthcoming *Ballads of the Lords of New Spain*.

Elizabeth Bishop, U.S. poet and writer from Massachusetts, served as U.S. Poet Laureate in 1949 and won the 1956 Pulitzer Prize for Poetry for *Poetry—North and South*. She traveled to Brazil in 1951, planning to stay for two weeks, but ended up staying for fifteen years, during which she translated into English the work of several Brazilian poets and writers.

Robert Bly, poet, editor, translator, and author of more than thirty books, brought the works of many European and South American poets to Americans. His own *The Light around the Body* won the National Book Award. Among his many books of translations are *Lorca and Jiminez: Selected Poems* and *Neruda and Vallejo: Selected Poems*.

Magda Bogin, novelist, translator, and journalist, has taught at Columbia, Princeton, and City College and, most recently, in Mexico. She has published numerous translations, including Isabel Allende's *House of the Spirits*. Fluent in Spanish, English, and French, she is the founder and director of Under the Volcano International.

Daniel Borzutzky is the author of *The Ecstasy of Capitulation* and *Arbitrary Tales*. He is the translator of Jaime Luis Huenún's *Port Trakl*, and he has translated works by Chilean writers Juan Emar and Manuel Silva Acevedo. Borzutzky lives in Chicago.

Mary Ann Caws is Distinguished Professor of English, French, and Comparative Literature in the Graduate School of City University of New York. She has held Guggenheim, Rockefeller, N.E.H., and Getty Foundation fellowships and is the author of many works, including *Picasso's Weeping Woman: The Life and Art of Dora Maar; Marcel Proust;* and *Virginia Woolf*.

Odile Cisneros is a poetry scholar and translator. She received a Ph.D. in Spanish and Portuguese languages and literatures from New York University in 2003 and currently teaches at the University of Alberta in Canada.

Jonathan Cohen is the author of prize-winning translations of Latin American poetry. He has translated the work of Ernesto Cardenal, Enrique Lihn,

Pedro Mir, and Roque Dalton, among others. In 2004, he published the first biography of Muna Lee, the premier translator of Latin American poetry during the early twentieth century.

Mary Crow is Emeritus Professor of English at Colorado State University. Her books of poetry include *I Have Tasted the Apple* and *Borders*.

Mónica de la Torre's books include *Talk Shows, Acúfenos,* and *Appendices, Illustrations and Notes*. She translated Gerardo Deniz's selected poems and co-edited *Reversible Monuments: Contemporary Mexican Poetry*. She is an editor at *The Brooklyn Rail*.

Kristin Dykstra has translated *Something of the Sacred* by Omar Pérez and *Time's Arrest* by Reina María Rodríguez. With Nancy Gates-Madsen, she co-translated *Violet Island and Other Poems*. Dykstra is co-editor of *Mandorla: New Writing from the Americas*.

Clayton Eshleman has published five collections of his translations, five collections of his poetry, and two collections of essays in the past decade, including *An Alchemist with One Eye on Fire, Reciprocal Distillations*, and *Archaic Design*. He is Professor Emeritus at Eastern Michigan University.

Ruth Fainlight has published thirteen collections of poems, translated two books of Sophia de Mello Breyner's poems, and work by Cesar Vallejo, Elsa Cross, and Victor Manuel Mendiola. Her translation of Sophocles' Theban Plays is due next year.

John Felstiner published *Translating Neruda: The Way to Macchu Picchu* (Commonwealth Club Gold Medal), *Paul Celan: Poet, Survivor, Jew* (Truman Capote Award), *Selected Poems and Prose of Paul Celan* (PEN, MLA, ATA prizes), and co-edited Norton's *Jewish American Literature* anthology. Yale University Press is publishing *So Much Depends: Can Poetry Save the Earth?*

Lawrence Ferlinghetti, author of more than thirty books of poetry (including *Americus, Book I* and *A Coney Island of the Mind*), co-founded in 1953 *City Lights* magazine and City Lights Book Shop in San Francisco, which became known as the heart of the "Beat" movement. He has translated the work of a number of poets, including Nicanor Parra, Jacques Prévert, and Pier Paolo Pasolini.

María Rosa Fort

Forrest Gander's books include *Eye against Eye* and *A Faithful Existence*. Besides editing anthologies of Mexican poetry, he has translated books by

Pura López Colomé, Coral Bracho, and (with Kent Johnson) Jaime Saenz. He teaches at Brown University.

Nancy Gates-Madsen is Assistant Professor of Spanish at Luther College, where she specializes in contemporary Latin American literature. She is co-translator of *Violet Island and Other Poems*, a bilingual anthology of Reina María Rodríguez's poetry. Other critical essays appear in *The Art of Truth-Telling after Authoritarian Rule* and *Letras Femeninas*.

Michelle Gil-Montero received her M.F.A. in poetry from the Iowa Writers' Workshop in 2007. She received an Academy of American Poets' Prize in 2006 and has recent work in *Colorado Review, Hayden's Ferry Review, Jacket, CipherJournal*, and *Zoland Poetry*.

Allen Ginsberg's *Howl and Other Poems* was published and banned in 1956, but "Howl" became one of the most widely read poems of the twentieth century. As the leading icon of the Beats, Ginsberg received the Chevalier des Arts et des Lettres and co-founded the Jack Kerouac School of Disembodied Poetics at the Naropa Institute in Colorado. He died in 1997.

James Graham has translated Roque Dalton, Pedro Juan Gutierrez, and many others. His *Delirium Tremens New York* was published in France in 2004.

Andrew Graham-Yooll is a journalist and writer. He is the editor of Argentina's only English-language daily, the *Buenos Aires Herald,* and has published more than twenty books, including *The Forgotten Colony*, *A State of Fear*, and *Se habla spanglés*. He has translated into Spanish the work of Blake Morrison, Harold Pinter, Siegfried Sassoon, Sylvia Plath, Robert Pinsky, and Tennessee Williams.

Frank Graziano is the John D. MacArthur Professor of Hispanic Studies at Connecticut College. His most recent book is *Cultures of Devotion: Folk Saints of Spanish America*.

Edith Grossman is the distinguished translator of major works by leading contemporary Hispanic writers, including Gabriel García Márquez, Mario Vargas Llosa, Álvaro Mutis, and Mayra Montero. She is the recipient of the 2006 PEN American Center Ralph Manheim Medal.

Gabriel Gudding is the author of two books of poetry, *A Defense of Poetry* and the long poem *Rhode Island Notebook*, a book he wrote in his car. His work appears in such anthologies as *Great American Prose Poems: From Poe to the Present* and as translator in such anthologies as *Poems for the Millennium* and *The Whole Island: Six Decades of Cuban Poetry*. He holds graduate degrees from Cornell and Purdue universities.

David Guss is a Professor of Anthropology at Tufts University researching cultural performance, myth, and ritual, among other subjects. He is editor and translator of several books, including *The Selected Poems of Vincente Huidobro*, *Five Meters of Poems* by Carlos Oquendo de Amat, and *Watunna: An Orinoco Creation Cycle* by Marc de Civrieux.

Thomas Hoeksema is the translator of several books from the works of Mexican poets, including *Poems in the Lap of Death* by Isabel Fraire, *Selected Poems* by José Emilio Pacheco, and *The Fertile Rhythms: Contemporary Women Poets of Mexico*. He was a Professor of English at New Mexico State University before he died in 1991.

Jen Hofer is a poet and translator. Her latest book is *lip wolf*, originally *lobo de labio* by Laura Solórzano. Forthcoming are translations of *Septiembre* and *sexoPUROsexoVELOZ* by Dolores Dorantes, *The Route* with Patrick Durgin, *Laws*, and *one*.

James Hoggard has translated numerous poems and stories by Oscar Hahn, Tino Villanueva, and other Spanish-speaking writers. An award-winning poet, short story writer, novelist, essayist, and translator, he is the Perkins-Prothro Distinguished Professor of English at Midwestern State University in Wichita Falls, Texas.

James Irby taught the first Latin American literature courses ever to be given at Princeton University and is a founding member of its Program in Latin American Studies. Co-editor and translator of Jorge Luis Borges's *Labyrinths: Stories and Other Writings*, he has published articles on Borges, Onetti, Cortazar, Lezama Lima, and other Latin American writers.

Maria Jacketti is Creative Writing Programs' Director for Warnborough College, online. She has published six books of translations of the work of Nobel Laureates Pablo Neruda and Gabriela Mistral. For more than two decades, hundreds of her poems have appeared in journals and magazines. She is a 1982 recipient of a poetry fellowship from the Pennsylvania Council on the Arts.

Kent Johnson teaches at Highland Community College. Editor and translator of many books, he worked with Forrest Gander on *Immanent Visitor: Selected Poems of Jaime Saenz*, which was a PEN Award for Poetry in Translation selection, and a second book of Saenz's work, *The Night*.

Lysander Kemp was a writer, professor, translator, and head editor of the University of Texas Press from 1966 to 1975. During his tenure at the press, he collaborated with Octavio Paz on numerous translations and oversaw the publication of two collections of Paz's essays and criticism.

Peter W. Kendall

Galway Kinnell has published several volumes of poetry, including *Strong Is Your Hold*, *A New Selected Poems*, a finalist for the National Book Award, and *Selected Poems*, for which he received both the Pulitzer Prize and the National Book Award. He has also published translations of works by Yves Bonnefroy, Yvanne Goll, François Villon, and Rainer Maria Rilke.

Kathryn A. Kopple is a specialist in Latin American Literature (Ph.D., New York University). She has published translations and articles in literary reviews and journals in the United States and England.

Kenneth Krabbenhoft is Professor of Spanish and Portuguese at New York University. He studied at Yale and at New York University. He has published translations of Pablo Neruda, St. John of the Cross, Borges, and Eugenio Trías, among others. His latest book is *Fernando Pessoa e as doenças do fim de século*, on Pessoa's theory of genius.

Charles Maxwell Lancaster was Professor of Languages at Vanderbilt University.

Frances LeFevre

Ursula K. Le Guin writes both poetry and prose, and in various modes, including realistic fiction, science fiction, fantasy, screenplays, and essays. An award-winning writer, she has produced more than seven books of poetry, twenty-two novels, more than one hundred short stories, four collections of essays, twelve books for children, and four volumes of translation.

Suzanne Jill Levine's most recent books are a translation (in collaboration with Carol Maier) of Severo Sarduy's last novella/prose poem *Beach Birds* and *Manuel Puig and the Spider Woman: His Life and Fictions*. She is a professor at the University of California, Santa Barbara, and her translations include the works of Guillermo Cabrera Infante, Alejandra Pizarnik, Adolfo Bioy Casares, Jorge Luis Borges, Julio Cortazar, Jose Donoso, and others.

Naomi Lindstrom is Professor of Spanish and Portuguese at the University of Texas at Austin. Her recent books are *Early Spanish American Narrative* and *The Social Conscience of Latin American Writing*. She is manager of the Web site and list-serv of the Latin American Jewish Studies Association (LAJSA).

Mark A. Lokensgard is Chair of the Languages Department at St. Mary's University in San Antonio. He has published on Luso-Brazilian culture in the United States, the United Kingdom, and Brazil, and he appeared on the MLA radio show "What's the Word?" to discuss Brazilian cinema.

Jean R. Longland is former Librarian at the Hispanic Society of America. Specializing in Portuguese and Brazilian contemporary literature, she has translated more than one hundred of Ana Hatherly's *Tisanas,* as well as numerous other works.

Elizabeth Macklin is the author of *You've Just Been Told* and *A Woman Kneeling in the Big City* and, most recently, is the translator of *Meanwhile Take My Hand,* by the Basque poet Kirmen Uribe. She is currently at work on a third collection of poems.

Paul Thomas Manchester was Professor of Languages at Vanderbilt University.

Roberto Márquez is a professor at Mount Holyoke College and editor-translator of more than three editions of the poetry of Nicolás Guillén, including *Patria o Muerte: The Great Zoo and Other Poems, Man-Making Words: Selected Poems* (with D. A. McMurray), and *My Last Name.* He is also translator-editor of the bilingual anthology *Latin American Revolution Poetry* and, most recently, *Puerto Rican Poetry: An Anthology from Aboriginal to Contemporary Times.*

Julio Marzán has published two books of poetry, *Translations without Originals* and *Puerta de tierra,* as well as *The Spanish American Roots of William Carlos Williams.* He has taught at Nassau Community College in New York and Harvard University.

Alejandro Merizalde was born in Quito, Ecuador, in 1979. He completed his studies in fine arts at the local state university. He is an artist and translator residing with his wife in New York City. He recently co-translated a large selection of the work of Mexican poet Jaime Sabines.

James Merrill founded the Ingram Merrill Foundation in 1956, which has since awarded grants to hundreds of artists and writers. Among numerous accolades, his *Nights and Days* won the National Book Award in Poetry in 1966, and *Divine Comedies* won the Pulitzer Prize in 1976. In 1995, Merrill died of a heart attack. His last book is *A Scattering of Salts.*

W. S. Merwin is the acclaimed author of more than fifteen books of poetry, including *Migration,* which won the 2005 National Book Award, and translator of nearly twenty books. In 1999, he was named Poetry Consultant to the Library of Congress, and in 2006, he received the Ambassador Book Award for Poetry. He lives in Hawaii.

Erín Moure is a poet and translator from French, Spanish, Galician, and Portuguese to English. Her recent work includes *O cadoiro* and *Little Theatres*. She has also translated Andrés Ajens, Chus Pato, and, with Robert Majzels, Nicole Brossard.

Henry Munn, poet and writer, has made numerous contributions to the field of linguistic ethnography. He has studied the use of hallucinogenic plants by the Conibo Indians of Eastern Peru and also the Mazatec Indians of the mountains of Oaxaca.

James O'Hern grew up in Laredo, Texas, where, as a boy, he was mentored and profoundly influenced by a Mexican mestizo who introduced him to the world of myth and Indian lore. His poems have appeared in *Spillway*, *OnTheBus*, and *Rattle*.

Dave Oliphant, a Texas writer and translator of Chilean poetry, retired from the University of Texas at Austin in 2006. *Figures of Speech*, his translations of poetry by Enrique Lihn, appeared in 1999. His translation of Nicanor Parra's *After-Dinner Discourses* was published in 2008.

Salvador Ortiz-Carboneres is a Principal Language Tutor and teaches Spanish language and Latin American poetry at the University of Warwick. Among his published translations are *Platero and I* by Juan Ramón Jiménez; Martin Carter's *Selected Poems*; Nicolás Guillén, *Yoruba from Cuba*; and Juan Ramón Jiménez, *Selected Poems*.

Michael Palmer is author or translator of numerous books of poetry, including *Company of Moths* and *The Promises of Glass*. His work has garnered two grants from the National Endowment for the Arts, a Guggenheim Foundation fellowship, and the Shelley Memorial Prize from the Poetry Society of America.

Ámbar Past was born in the United States in 1949. At the age of twenty-three, she immigrated to Mexico and became a Mexican citizen. She lives among the Tzotzil Maya in the state of Chiapas, where poetry is considered to be important in daily life and ritual.

Simon Pettet is an English-born poet and has resided for three decades in New York City. Most recently, he is the author of the collection *More Winnowed Fragments*.

Robert Pring-Mill, who died in 2005, brought Latin America to generations of students and poetry readers. His numerous translations and publications, infused with an ardent commitment to revolutionary literature and popular culture, did much to establish the international reputations of writers such as Pablo Neruda and Ernesto Cardenal.

G. J. Racz is Associate Professor of Foreign Languages and Literature at Long Island University, Brooklyn. His recent translations include works by the playwrights Lope de Vega, Calderón de la Barca, and Jaime Salom, as well as the poet and novelist José Lezama Lima.

Elinor Randall devoted the last half century of her life to translating the work of José Martí. Some of those translations were published in Cuba, others by Monthly Review Press in New York City. She was born in New York in 1910 and died in Albuquerque in 2006.

Margaret Randall, born in New York in 1936, is a writer and photographer who has also done a number of literary translations. In 1962, out of Mexico City, she founded and co-edited the bilingual journal *El Corno Emplumado / The Plumed Horn*. She has published more than 120 books of poetry, essays, oral history, and photography.

Justin Read is Assistant Professor of Spanish and Portuguese in the Department of Romance Languages and Literatures at the University at Buffalo (SUNY).

Alastair Reid, poet, translator, essayist, and writer of children's books, has served as staff writer at the *New Yorker* and has lectured on Latin American studies and literature throughout the United States and England. In 2004, he published *On the Blue Shore of Silence*, a selection of his translations of Pablo Neruda's sea poems.

Jerome Rothenberg is an internationally known poet with more than seventy books of poetry and several assemblages of traditional and contemporary poetry such as *Technicians of the Sacred* and *Poems for the Millennium*. *Triptych*, his twelfth book of poems from New Directions, appeared in 2007, and a nineteenth-century prequel to *Poems for the Millennium* was published in 2009.

William Rowe has translated a variety of Latin American poets. His *Poets of Contemporary Latin America* was published by Oxford University Press in 2000, and his translation of Raúl Zurita's *INRI* is forthcoming. He is Anniversary Professor of Poetics at Birkbeck College.

Ralph L. Roys was a Maya ethnohistorian and author of the seminal work, *Political Geography of the Yucatan Maya*, as well as *Indian Background to*

Colonial Yucatan and *Conquest Sites and the Subsequent Destruction of Maya Architecture*.

Mark Schafer has translated the works of many authors, including Alberto Ruy Sánchez, Virgilo Piñera, Jesús Gardea, and Eduardo Galeano. He translated Gloria Gervitz's epic poem, *Migrations/Migraciones* and in 2005, he received an NEA Translation Fellowship to complete translation of poetry by David Huerta. *Before Saying Any of the Great Words: Selected Poems* was published in 2009.

James Scully, poet, playwright, and essayist, was born in Connecticut and now lives in San Francisco. He is founding editor of the ART ON THE LINE series and author of several books of poetry, including *Donatello's Version* and *Santiago Poems*.

Daniel Shapiro's poems and translations have appeared in *American Poetry Review*, *BOMB*, and *Grand Street*. He received an NEA fellowship to translate Tomás Harris's *Cipango*. He is the editor of *Review: Literature and Arts of the Americas* at the Americas Society.

Sylvia and Earl Shorris have translated Mesoamerican literature for *In the Language of Kings*, *Words without Borders*, and other publications. Earl Shorris received the National Humanities Medal in 2000 from President Bill Clinton and the Order of the Aztec Eagle from Mexican President Vicente Fox.

David R. Slavitt is a poet, novelist, essayist, and translator, mostly from Greek, Latin, Hebrew, French, and Italian. This is his first venture into Portuguese. He lives in Cambridge, Massachusetts, with his wife and two cats.

Hardie St. Martin has translated work by Vincente Aleixandre, Roque Dalton, Enrique Lihn, Nicanor Parra, and Luisa Valenzuela, among others. He is the recipient of a number of fellowships and awards, including a John Simon Guggenheim fellowship in 1965 and a P.E.N. International Translation Award.

Jan Szeminski is a Polish historian. He teaches at the Hebrew University in Jerusalem. His work is considered one of the best efforts at reconstructing the indigenous perspective.

Dennis Tedlock is McNulty Chair in the Poetics Program and Research Professor of Anthropology at State University of New York, Buffalo. His research interests center on the indigenous languages, verbal arts, writing systems, and religions of the Western Hemisphere. The award-winning translator and editor of the *Popul Vuh* and *Rabinal Achi*, he is working on a book entitled *2000 Years of Maya Literature*.

Roberto Tejada received a 2006 NEA award for his translations of mid-century modernist José Lezama Lima. His own poetry has appeared in the United States and Latin America, including *Vuelta, The Best American Poetry 1996*, and *99 Poets / 1999: An International Poetics Symposium*. He is Associate Professor in the Visual Arts Department at the University of California, San Diego.

Jack E. Tomlins was responsible for the only English translation of Mário de Andrade's second book of poetry, *Paulicéia desvariada*.

Charles Tomlinson is the author of many poetry collections, of which the latest is *Cracks in the Universe*. He is the editor of *The Oxford Book of Verse in English Translation* and has translated the work of many poets, including Attilio Bertolucci and Octavio Paz.

Renata Treitel is an independent translator. She has worked on Susana Thénon's *distancias/distances*; Rosita Copioli's *Splendida lumina solis/The Blazing Lights of the Sun*; Amelia Biagioni's *Las cacerías/The Hunts*; and a second manuscript by Rosita Copioli, *Furore delle rose/Wrath of the Roses*, is in search of a publisher.

Alan S. Trueblood was Professor Emeritus of Hispanic Studies and Comparative Literature at Brown University and is the author of *Experience and Artistic Expression in Lope de Vega, A Sor Juana Anthology*, and *Antonio Machado: Selected Poems*.

Molly Weigel has published translations of the Argentine XUL group in *The XUL Reader, American Poetry Review*, and *boundary 2*. She translated Josefina Ludmer's *The Gaucho Genre* and received a 2008 translation fellowship from the National Endowment of the Arts for her translation of Oliverio Girondo's *En la masmédula*.

Eliot Weinberger was born in New York City, where he still lives. His edition of Jorge Luis Borges's *Selected Non-Fictions* received the National Book Critics Circle prize for criticism. In 1992, he was given PEN's first Gregory Kolovakos Award for his work in promoting Hispanic literature in the United States, and in 2000 he was awarded the Order of the Aztec Eagle by the government of Mexico.

Mark Weiss is the author of six books of poetry. Among his translations are Javier Manríquez, *The San Antonio Notebook*; and José Kozer, *Stet: Selected*

Poems. He edited *The Whole Island: Six Decades of Cuban Poetry* and, with Harry Polkinhorn, *Across the Line / Al otro lado: The Poetry of Baja California*.

Liz Werner, a native New Yorker, translator, poet, and playwright, has lived and studied in Chile, where she worked closely with Nicanor Parra in preparing these translations.

Steven F. White is co-translator with Greg Simon of *The Angel of Rain* by Cuban poet Gastón Baquero and *Seven Trees against the Dying Light* by Pablo Antonio Cuadra from Nicaragua. His most recent book of poems is *Escanciador de pócimas*. He currently teaches at St. Lawrence University in Canton, New York.

Brian Whitener divides time between New York, San Francisco, and Mexico City. His poetry can be seen in *Chain, Moria,* and *Chickenscratch*.

Christopher Winks teaches comparative literature at Queens College of the City University of New York. His essays, reviews, and translations have appeared in numerous journals and anthologies.

James Wright, whose poetry has been characterized as deliberately vulnerable, "confessional," and concerned with social justice, was elected a fellow of the Academy of American Poets in 1971, and the following year his *Collected Poems* received the Pulitzer Prize in poetry. He died in New York City in 1980.

Richard Zenith's translations include works by António Lobo Antunes and Fernando Pessoa. His new version of Pessoa's *The Book of Disquiet* was awarded the 2002 Calouste Gulbenkian Translation Prize. He lives in Lisbon where he is editor of the Portuguese Web site poetryinternational.org.

Adán, Martín, "Aloysius Acker Is Coming into the World" from *Obra poética en prosa y verso*, published by Pontificia Universidad Católica del Perú, 2006. "Without Time Signature, Hurrying Ad Lib/Played Freely, Etc." from Martín Adán, *Obra poética*, edited by Ricardo Silva-Santisteban, published by Fundación del Banco Continental para el Fomento de la Educación y la Cultura, Ediciones Edubanco, 1980.

Agustini, Delmira, "To Eros," "The Ineffable," "The Intruder" from *El libro blanco (Frágil)*, published by DM Bertani, 1907.

Ak'abal, Humberto, all poems reprinted by permission of Humberto Ak'abal. "Stones," "Advice," "Effort", "Navel," "Fireflies," "Walker," "Learning" translations from *In the Language of Kings*, published by W. W. Norton & Company, 2001. "Buzzard" translation reprinted by permission of Dennis Tedlock.

Alves dos Santos, Apolônio, "Antônio Conselheiro and the Canudos Rebellion" from *O cordel: Testemunha da história do Brasil*, edited by Olga de Jesus Santos, published by Fundação Casa de Rui Barbosa, 1987.

amereida, "amereida" from *amereida, poesía y arquitectura*, published by Ediciones ARQ de la Escuela de Arquitectura de la Pontificia Universidad Católica de Chile, 1992. Translation reprinted by permission of Ann Pendleton-Jullian.

de Andrade, Mário, "Inspiration," "Nocturne," "A Very Interesting Preface" from *Paulicéia desvairada*, published by Casa Mayença, 1922. Translations from *Hallucinated City*, published by Vanderbilt University Press, 1968. Reprinted by permission of Vanderbilt University Press.

de Andrade, Oswald, "Brazilwood," "Cannibal Manifesto" from *Pau Brasil: Obras completas de Oswald de Andrade*, 2nd edition published by Editora Globo, 1990. *Translations from Xul Reader*, Copyright © by XUL/Ernesto Livon-Grosman, 1997.

dos Anjos, Augusto, "A Philosopher's Agony," "Modern Buddhism" from *Eu e outros poesias*, published by L&PM Editores, 1998.

Anonymous, "And All Was Destroyed" from *La literatura de los Aztecas*, translated by Angel M. Garibay K, published by J. Moritz, 1964. Translation from *Panjandrum IV, Talking Leaves Issue*, June 1975. Reprinted by permission of David Guss.

Anonymous, "Atahualpa Death Prayer" Quechua version from *Apu Inca Atawallpaman: Elegía Quechua Anónima*, edited by J. M. Farfán, published by Ediciones Juan Mejia Baca, 1955. Spanish translation is part of an ongoing research project, copyright © 2007 by Odi Gonzales, courtesy of the translator. The English translation is reprinted by permission of James Scully.

Anonymous, "The Book of Chilam Balam of Chumayel" from *Chilam Balam [manuscript] artículos y fragmentos de manuscritos antiguos en lengua maya*, edited by D. Juan Pio Perez. Courtesy of University of Pennsylvania. Translation from *The Book of Chilam Balam of Chumayel*, edited by Ralph L. Roys, published by The Carnegie Institution, 1933.

Anonymous, "The Book of Chilam Balam of Mani" from *El Chilam Balam de Mani ó códice Pérez*, edición cuidadosamente revisada con un prólogo de Juan Martínez Hernández, published by Colegio San José de Artes y Oficios, 1909. Courtesy of the Berendt Collection, University of Pennsylvania. Translation by permission of John Bierhorst.

Anonymous, "Codex Cantares Mexicanos" from *Cantares Mexicanos: Songs of the Aztecs*, edited by John Bierhorst, published by Stanford University Press, 1985. Copyright © 1985 by the Board of Trustees of the Leland Stanford Jr. University.

Anonymous, "The Florentine Codex" from *The Florentine Codex: Book 12, The Conquest of Mexico* by Bernardino de Sahagún, translated by Arthur J. O. Anderson and Charles E. Dibble, published by The University of Utah, 1975. Courtesy of the University of Utah.

Anonymous, "Grant Don Juan V Life," "Eight-Line Acrostic" from *Xul Reader*. Copyright © by XUL/Ernesto Livon-Grosman, 2005.

Anonymous, "Inca Quipu." Private collection, New York.

Anonymous, "Maya Codex" detail and rollout photograph copyright © by Justin Kerr, K1196. "Lady scribe" courtesy of Dennis Tedlock.

Anonymous, "Popol Vuh" from *Popul Vuh: The Definitive Edition of the Mayan Book of the Dawn of Life and the Glories of Gods and Kings*, published by Simon and Schuster. Copyright © 1985, 1996 by Dennis Tedlock. Reprinted by permission of Dennis Tedlock.

Araneda, Rosa, "Cueca of the Lady Conductors" from *Aunque no soy literaria*, edited by Micaela Navarrete, 1998. Reprinted by permission of Biblioteca Nacional, Santiago de Chile.

Arturo, Aurelio, "Climate," "Lullaby" from *Cántico*, Año II, 1945, N°7, edited by Jaime Ibáñez, published by Extensión Cultural de la Universidad Nacional.

Arvelo Larriva, Enriqueta, "Emotion and Advantage of Proven Depth," "All Morning the Wind Has Spoken" from *Voz aislada*, published by Editorial Elite, 1939.

Ascasubi, Hilario, "The Slippery One" from *Paulino Lucero: Aniceto el Gallo*, edited by Jorge Luis Borges, published by Ediciones de Eudeba, 1960.

de Azevedo, Manuel Antonio Álvares, "Intimate Ideas" from *Lira dos vinte años,* published by Editora Escala, 2006.

Bandeira, Manuel, all poems in original Spanish from *Poesia completa y prosa,* edited by Sergio Buarque de Holanda, published by Aguilar, 1967. "Anthology," "Green-Black" translations from *The Selected Poems of Manuel Bandeira,* translated by David R. Slavitt, published by Sheep Meadow Press, 2002. Reprinted by permission of David R. Slavitt. "My Last Poem" from *The Complete Poems, 1927–1979,* by Elizabeth Bishop. Copyright © 1979, 1983 by Alice Helen Methfessel. Reprinted by permission of Farrar, Straus and Giroux, LLC.

Belli, Carlos Germán, "Tortilla," "I Trust Now in Nothing" from *El libro de unos sonidos,* published by Tsé-Tsé, 2005. "Sestina of Mea Culpa" from *Sextinas y otros poemas,* published by Editorial Universitaria, 1970. Reprinted by permission of Carlos Germán Belli.

Bilac, Olavo, "Portuguese Language" from *Poesias,* 1888. Published by Livraria Francisco Alves, 1944.

Bopp, Raúl, "Cobra Norato" from *Poesía completa de Raul Bopp,* published by Editora de Universidede de Sao Paolo, 1998.

Borges, Jorge Luis, all poems from *Borges: Obras completas,* published by Emecé Editores, 1974.

Bracho, Coral, all poems from *El ser que va a morir,* published by J. Mortiz, 1982.

Bueno, Wilson, "Mar paraguayo" from *Mar paraguayo,* published by Iluminares, 1992.

Cabral do Melo Neto, João, "Education by Stone" translation from *An Anthology of Twentieth-Century Brazilian Poetry,* edited by Elizabeth Bishop and Emanuel Brasil, Copyright © 1972 by Wesleyan University Press. Reprinted by permission of Wesleyan University Press. "Tale of an Architect," "The Unconfessing Artist" from *Education by Stone: Selected Poems* by João Cabral de Melo Neto, translated by Richard Zenith. English translation copyright © 2005 by Richard Zenith. Published by arrangement with Archipelago Books, www.archipelagobooks.org. "A Knife All Blade" from *Selected Poetry, 1937–1990* by João Cabral de Melo Neto, published by Wesleyan University Press, 1994. Reprinted by permission of Wesleyan University Press.

Cáceres, Omar, all poems from *Defensa del idolo,* edited by Pedro Lasta, published by Pequeña Venecia, 1997.

de Campos, Augusto, "Eggtangle" from *Antologia Noigandes* 5, 1962. "Eye for an Eye" from *Brazilian Poetry, 1950–1980,* edited by Emanuel Brasil and William Jay Smith, published by Wesleyan University Press, 1983. Reprinted by permission of Wesleyan University Press. "To Put On a Mask" from *Anthology of Concrete Poetry,* published by Something Else Press, 1967.

de Campos, Haroldo, all poems reprinted by permission of the Estate of Haroldo de Campos.

Cardenal, Ernesto, "Death of Thomas Merton" from *Nueva antologia poetica*, published by Siglo Veintiuno Editores, 2002.

Carranza, María Mercedes, "Homeland" from *Hola, soledad*, published by Editorial Oveja Negra, 1987. "Heels over Head with Life" from *Tengo miedo*, published by Editorial Áncora, 2003. Translation first appeared in *Grove* (Spring 1982) and was reprinted in *Woman Who Has Sprouted Wings: Poems by Contemporary Latin American Women Poets* (Latin American Literary Review Press, 1988). Reprinted by permission of Mary Crow. "I'm Afraid" from *Tengo Miedo: Poesía, 1976–1982*, published by La Oveja Negra, 1983. "Canto 17: Cumbal," "Canto 18: Soacha," "Canto 3: Dabeiba" from *Canto de las moscas*, published by Arango Editores, 1998.

Carrera, Arturo, "No fue en Sicilia, no fue aquí" from *El vespertillo de las parcas*, published by Tusquets Editores, 1997.

Castellanos, Rosario, "Livid Light," "Silence around an Ancient Stone" from *The Selected Poetry of Rosario Castellanos*, edited by Cecilia Vicuña and Magda Bogin, published by Graywolf Press, 1988. "Malinche" from *A Rosario Castellanos Reader* by Rosario Castellanos, edited by Maureen Ahern, translated by Maureen Ahern and others. Copyright © 1988. By permission of Maureen Ahern, Fondo de Cultura Económica, and the University of Texas Press.

de Castro Alves, Antonio, "The Slave Ship (Tragedy on the Sea)," 1880.

Cerro, Emeterrio, "Miss Murkiness" from *Xul Reader*. Copyright © by XUL/ Ernesto Livon-Grosman, 2005.

Chihuailaf, Elikura, "I Still Want to Dream in This Valley," "For I Am the Power of the Nameless" from *El invierno su imagen y otros poemas azules*, published by Ediciones Literatura Alternativa, 1991. Reprinted by permission of Elikura Chihuailaf. Translation from *UL: Four Mapuche Poets*, published by Americas Society, Latin American Review Press, 1998. Reprinted by permission of Cecilia Vicuña and John Bierhorst.

Churata, Gamaliel, "Khirkhilas" from *El pez de oro*, published by Editorial Canata, 1957.

Cisneros, Antonio, all poems reprinted by permission of Antonio Cisneros. Translations from *The Spider Hangs Too Far from the Ground* by Antonio Cisneros, published by Jonathan Cape. Reprinted by permission of the Random House Group, Ltd.

da Cruz e Sousa, João, "Lesbian," "Afra" from *Broquéis*, 1893. Courtesy of Fundação Biblioteca Nacional, Departamento Nacional do Livro, Brazil.

Cuadra, Pablo Antonio, all poems from *Pablo Antonio Cuadra: Poesía selecta*, edited by Jorge Eduardo Arellano, published by Fundación Biblioteca Ayacucho, 1991.

Dalton, Roque, all poems from *Small Hours of the Night: Selected Poems of Roque Dalton*, edited by Hardie St. Martin, Curbstone Press, 1996. Reprinted with permission of Curbstone Press. Distributed by Perseus/Consortium.

Darío, Rubén, all poems in original Spanish, from *Rubén Darío poesía*, edited by Ernesto Mejía Sánchez, published by Fundación Biblioteca Ayacucho, 1977. "Love Your Rhythm" translation from *El corno emplumado* #22, 1967. Reprinted by permission of Margaret Randall. "Nocturne" translation from *Selected Poems of Ruben Dario*, translated by Lysander Kemp. Copyright © 1965, renewed 1993. By permission of the University of Texas Press.

Dávila Andrade, César, "Bulletin and Elegy of Indian Enslavement" from *César Dávila Andrade: Poesía, narrativa, ensayo*, edited by Jorge Dávila Vázquez, published by Fundación Biblioteca Ayacucho, 1993.

Del Valle, Rosamel, "Canticle IX," "Magic Love" from *Poesía chilena contemporánea*, 2nd edition edited by Miguel Arteche, Juan Antonio Massone, Roque Esteban Scarpa, and published by Editorial Andrés Bello, 1984.

Deniz, Gerardo, all poems from *Gerardo Deniz: Poemas/poems*, edited by Monica de la Torre, published by Ditoria/Lost Roads Publishers, 2000.

Drummond de Andrade, Carlos, all poems from *Nova Reunião*, published by Livraria José Olympio Editora, 1983. Copyright © 1983 by Carlos Drummond de Andrade.

Eguren, José María, "The Lady i," "The Towers," "Favila" from *Obras completas*, edited by Ricardo Silva-Santisteban, published by Mosca Azul, 1974.

Eielson, Jorge Eduardo, "María's First Death" from *Primera muerte de María*, published by Fondo de Cultura Económica, 1988. "Paracas Pyramid Performance, 1974," "Khipu, 1965" from *Jorge Eielson*, edited by Alberto Boatto and Luca Massimo Barbero, published by Galleria d'Arte Niccoli, 2003.

de Ercilla y Zuñiga, Alonso, "The Araucaniad" from *La Araucana I*, edited by Marcos Augusto Morínigo and Isaías Lerner, published by Editorial Castalia, 1979. Translation from *The Araucaniad: A Version in English*, published by Vanderbilt University Press, 1945. Reprinted by permission of Vanderbilt University Press.

Fariña, Soledad, all poems from *El primer libro*, published by Amaranto Editores, 1985. Reprinted by permission of Soledad Farina.

de Figueroa, Francisco Acuña, "To the Most Holy Virgin Mary," "Multiform Salve," "Alphabetical-Numerical Prophecy" from *Obras completas*, edited by Manuel Bernández, published by Biblioteca Nacional, 1890.

Fraire, Isabel, all poems from *Puente colgante*, published by Universidad Autonoma Metropolitana, 1997. Translations from *Mouth to Mouth Poems by*

Twelve Contemporary Mexican Women, edited by Forrest Gander, published by Milkweed Editions, 1993.

Frez, Aurelio, "Mother, Here We Are" from *Con mi humilde devoción bailes chinos de Chile central,* edited by Claudio Mercado, Victor Rondón, Nicolás Piwonka, published by Museo Chileno de Arte Precolombino, 2003.

Garcilaso de la Vega, Inca, "Beautiful Maiden." Quechua, Latin, Spanish from *Comentarios reales de los Incas,* edited by Aurelio Miró Quesada, published by Fundación Biblioteca Ayacucho, 1976. Translation by Rose Alcala.

Gelman, Juan, "CDLVI," "CDLXXXI" from *Cólera buey,* published by Ediciones La Tertulia, 1965. "XDV" from *Oficio ardiente,* published by Ediciones Universidad de Salamanca, 2005. Copyright © 2005 by Juan Gelman.

Gervitz, Gloria, "Migrations" from *Migrations/migraciones.* Published by Junction Press, 2004. Reprinted by permission of Gloria Gervitz. Translation copyright © by Mark Schafer, 2004.

Girondo, Oliverio, all poems from *El las masmédula,* published by Editorial Losada, 1954.

Gonçalves Dias, Antonio, "Song of Exile" from *Primeiros cantos,* edited by Letícia Mallard, published by Autêntica Editora, 1998.

Gorostiza, José, "Death without End," "Elegy," "Pauses I" from *Muerte sin fin,* published by Fondo de Cultura Económica, 1964. Translation from *Nine South American Poets,* published by The Las Américas Publishing Co., 1968.

Guamán Poma de Ayala, Felipe, "Festival of the Inca," "Principal Accountant and Treasurer," "Priests Who Force the Indians to Weave Cloth" from *El primer nueva corónica y buen gobierno.* Images courtesy of the Royal Library, Copenhagen, Denmark, www.kb.dk/permalink/2006/poma/info/es/frontpage .htm. "Cachiuia" Spanish translation from *El primer nueva corónica y buen gobierno,* edited by John V. Murra y Rolena Adorno, translated from the Quechua by Jorge L. Urioste, published by Siglo Veintiuno, 1980.

Guillén, Nicolás, all poems from *Obra poética, 1920–1972,* edited by Ángel Augier, published by Editorial de Arte y Literatura, 1974. "Sensemayá," "Son Number 6" translations from *Yoruba from Cuba: Selected Poems of Nicolas Guillen,* published by Peepal Tree, 2005. "My Last Name I, a Family Elegy" translation from *Man-Making Words,* copyright © 1972 by Roberto Marquez and David Arthur McMurray and published by University of Massachusetts Press.

Hahn, Óscar, all poems reprinted by permission of Óscar Hahn. "Restriction of Nocturnal Movements" translation from *The Stolen Verses and Other Poems,* published by Northwestern University Press, 2000. "Conjurer's Tract," "Vision of Hiroshima" from *The Art of Dying,* published by Latin American Literary Review Press, 1987.

Hernández, Elvira, "The Flag of Chile" from *La bandera de Chile*, published by Libros de Tierra Firma, 1991. Translation from *Review: Latin American Literature and Arts*, no. 49, Fall 1994, published by the Americas Society.

Hernández, José, "Martín Fierro" from *Xul Reader*. Copyright © by XUL/Ernesto Livon-Grosman, 1997.

Herrera y Reissig, Julio, "Lunatic Tertulia" from *Poesía completa y prosa selecta*, edited by Alicia Migdal, published by Fundación Biblioteca Ayacucho, 1978.

Hidalgo, Bartolomé, "New Patriotic Dialogue" from *Poesía gauchesca*, edited by Jorge B. Rivera, published by Fundación Biblioteca Ayacucho, 1977.

Hinostroza, Rodolfo, "Contra Natura" from *Contra natura*, published by Barral Editores, 1971. Reprinted by permsission of Rodolfo Hinostroza.

Huidobro, Vicente, all works reprinted by permission of Fundación Vicente Huidobro. "Canto I" translations from *Altazor*, published by Wesleyan University Press, 2004. Reprinted by permission of Wesleyan University Press. "Non Serviam" translations reprinted by permission of Mary Ann Caws and Curtis Brown, Ltd.

Jaramillo Escobar, Jaime, "The Leather Telegram" from *Extracto de poesía*, published by Ediciones Colcultura, 1982.

Kilkerry, Pedro, "It's the Silence," "Mare Vitae" from *Re-visão de Kilkerry*, edited by Augusto de Campos, published by Fundo Estadual de Cultura, 1970.

Kosice, Gyula, "Portable Madi Dictionary," "MADI" from *Madigrafías y otros textos*, published by Nuevohacer Grupo Editor Latinoamericano, 2001. Copyright © 2001 by Gyula Kosice. Reprinted by permission of Gyula Kosice.

Kozer, José, "A Meeting at Cho-Fu-Sa," "Kafka Reborn" from *STET: Selected Poems*, published by Junction Press, 2006. Reprinted by permission of José Kozer and Mark Weiss.

Lamborghini, Leónidas, "The Displaced Applicant" from *El solicitante descolocado*, published by Ediciones de la Flor, 1971. "Eva Perón at the Stake" from *Partitas*, published by Ediciones Corregidor, 1972.

Lamborghini, Osvaldo, all poems from *Poemas, 1969–1985*, published by Editorial Sudamericana, 2004.

Leminski, Paulo, "Catatau" from *Catatau: Prosa experimental*, published by Editora do Autor, 1975. "Metamorphosis" from *Metaformose*, published by Iluminuras, 1998.

Lezama Lima, José, all poems from *Poesía completa*, published by Barral Editores, 1975. Translations from *José Lezama Lima: Selections*, edited by Ernesto Livon-Grosman, published by University of California Press, 2005. Copyright © 2005 by The Regents of the University of California.

Lihn, Enrique, "The Father's Monologue with His Infant Son" from *The Dark Room and Other Poems,* copyright © 1963, 1972 by Enrique Lihn, © by Enrique Lihn and Jonathan Cohen. Reprinted by permission of New Directions Publishing Corp. "Those Who Are Going to Die Can't Wait" from *Figures of Speech*, published by Host Publications, 1999.

Madariaga, Francisco, "Black Colá Jara," "The Trivial Jungle" from *Tsé-tsé* 12, May 2003.

Martí, José, "Waking Dream," "Love in the City" translations from *José Martí: Selected Writings* by José Martí, introduction by Roberto Gonzalez Echevarria, edited by Esther Allen, translated by Esther Allen. Copyright © 2002 by Esther Allen. Used by permission of Viking Penguin, a division of Penguin Group (USA) Inc.

Martínez, Antonio, "The Words of Pa'i Antonio" from *El canto resplandeciente/ Ayvu Rendy Vera, plegarias de los mbyá-guaraní de misiones*, published by Ediciones del Sol, 1984.

Martínez Rivas, Carlos, "Two Murals: U.S.A." from *Poets of Nicaragua: A Bilingual Anthology (1918–1979)*, selected and translated by Steven F. White, originally published by Unicorn Press, 1982. Translation reprinted with permission of Steven F. White.

Martínez, Juan Luis, all poems from *La nueva novela*. Published by Ediciones Archivo, 1985.

de Matos, Gregório, "Define Your City," "An Anatomy of the Ailments Suffered...," "To the City of Bahia...," "To the Palefaces of Bahia," "Upon Finding an Arm..." from *Poesía completa y prosa selecta*, edited by Margot Arce de Vázquez, published by Fundación Biblioteca Ayacucho, 1978.

Meireles, Cecilia, all poems from *Poesía completa: Cecília Meireles*, edited by Antonio Carlos Secchin, published by Editora Nova Fronteira, 2001. "Pyrargyrite Metal, 9," "Second Rose Motif" from *Anthology of Twentieth-Century Brazilian Poetry*, edited by Elizabeth Bishop and Emanuel Brasil, published by Wesleyan University Press, 1972, 1997. Courtesy of the James Ingram Merrill Papers, Washington University Libraries, Department of Special Collections.

Mistral, Gabriela, all poems in Spanish reprinted by permission of the Estate of Gabriela Mistral. "Drops of Gall" from *Gabriela Mistral: A Reader*, edited by Marjorie Agosin. Copyright © 1993, 1997 by Maria Giachetti. Reprinted with permission of White Pine Press, Buffalo, New York. "Airflower," "A Word," "The Other Woman" from *Selected Poems of Gabriela Mistral*, translated by Ursula K. Le Guin. Copyright © 2003 by University of New Mexico Press.

Molina, Enrique, all poems from *Obras poética*, published by Editorial Corregidor, 1984. "The Way It Must Be" translation from *Toward an Image of Latin American Poetry: A Bilingual Anthology*, edited by Octavio Armand, published by Logbridge-Rhodes, Inc., 1982.

Mondragón, Sergio, "Exodus of the Gods" from *Poesía reunida (1965–2005)*, published by Universidad Nacional Autónoma de México, 2006.

Montejo, Eugenio, all poems from *Antología de la poesía hispanoamericana, vol. II*, published by Monte Avila Editores, 1993.

Moro, César, "To Wait," "Trafalgar Square" translations from *Love Till Death*, published by the Vanishing Rotating Triangle Press, 1973.

Moscona, Myriam, "Black Ivory" from *Negro marfil*, published by Universidad Autónoma Metropolitana, Oak Editorial, 2000. Reprinted courtesy of Myriam Moscona.

Neruda, Pablo, "Melancholy Inside Families" translation from *Neruda and Vallejo*, edited by Robert Bly, published by Beacon Press, 1993; "Melancholy Inside Families" from *Residencia en la tierra II, Pablo Neruda*, published by Editorial Cruz del Sur, 1947; "Walking Around," "Right, Comrade..." from *Antologia fundamental Pablo Neruda*, published by Pehuen, 1988.

Orozco, Olga, "Variations on Time" from *Engravings Torn from Insomnia*. Copyright © 2002 by the Estate of Olga Orozco. Translation copyright © 2002 by Mary Crow. Reprinted with the permission of BOA Editions, Ltd., www. boaeditions.org. "The Obstacle" from *Olga Orozco: Obra poética*, edited by Manuel Ruano, published by Fundación Biblioteca Ayacucho, 2000. Translation from *Woman Who Has Sprouted Wings: Poems by Contemporary Latin American Women Poets*, published by Latin American Literary Review Press, 1988. Reprinted by permission of Mary Crow.

Ortiz, Juan L., "Village on the River," "Why?" from *La brisa profunda*, published by Editorial Este, 1954. Translation from *Poets of Contemporary Latin America: History and the Inner Life*, edited by William Rowe, published by Oxford University Press, 2000.

Palés Matos, Luis, "Prelude in Boricua," "Black Dance" from *Obras, 1914–1959*, published by Editorial de la Universidad de Puerto Rico, 1984. Translation from *Selected Poems by Luis Palés Matos*, translated by Julio Marzan, copyright © 2000 by Arte Público Press—University of Houston. Reprinted by permission of the publisher.

Parra, Nicanor, "No President's Statue Escapes," "1973" from *Antipoems: How to Look Better and Feel Great*, copyright © 1985, 2001, 2004 by Nicanor Parra, translation copyright © 2004 by Liz Werner. Reprinted by permission of New Directions Publishing Corp. "U.S.A.," "The Individual's Soliloquy" from *Antipoems: New and Selected*, copyright © 1985 by Nicanor Parra. Reprinted by permission of New Directions Publishing Corp.

Parra, Violeta, "Easy for Singing," "Dumb, Sad, and Thoughtful" translations printed by permission of W. S. Merwin. "Goddamn the Empty Sky" translation from *Woman Who Has Sprouted Wings: Poems by Contemporary Latin American Women*, edited by Mary Crow, published by Latin American Review Press, 1988. Reprinted by permission of John Felstiner.

Pasos, Joaquín, "Warsong of the Things" from *Poets of Nicaragua: A Bilingual Anthology (1918–1979)*, selected and translated by Steven F. White, originally published by Unicorn Press, 1982. Reprinted with permission of Steven F. White.

Paz, Octavio, "Here" from *Collected Poems, 1957–1987* by Octavio Paz, copyright © 1968 by Octavio Paz and Charles Tomlinson. Reprinted by permission of New Directions Publishing Corp. "Exclamation," "Sunstone," "Altar" from *Collected Poems, 1957–1987* by Octavio Paz, copyright © 1987 by Octavio Paz and Eliot Weinberger. Reprinted by permission of New Directions Publishing Corp.

Perednik, Jorge Santiago, "Shock of the Lenders" from *Xul Reader*. Copyright © by XUL/Ernesto Livon-Grosman, 2005.

Perlongher, Néstor, "Tuyú," "Mme. Schoklender" from *Poemas completos: 1980–1992,* published by Seix Barral, 1997. Translation from *Xul Reader.* Copyright © by XUL/Ernesto Livon-Grosman, 2005.

Pignatari, Décio, all poems from *Teoria da poesia concreta: Textos críticos e manifestos, 1950–1960,* by Augusto de Campos, Décio Pignatari, and Haroldo de Campos, published by Edições Invenção, 1965. Translations from *Review: Latin American Literature and Arts,* 64 (Spring 2002).

Pizarnik, Alejandra, all poems from *Obra completa,* published by Corregidor, 1993. "Nocturnal Singer" translation from *Alejandra Pizarnik: A Profile,* published by Logbridge-Rhodes, Inc., 1987. "From the Other Side," "From a Copy of 'Les Chants de Maldoror'" from *Woman Who Has Sprouted Wings: Poems by Contemporary Latin American Women Poets,* Latin American Literary Review Press, 1988. "Fiesta," "Useless Frontiers" from *Exchanging Lives: Poems and Translations,* published by Peepal Tree Press Ltd, 2002.

Ramos, Lorenzo, "The Foreigners Lie about What They Want" from *El canto resplandeciente/Ayvu Rendy Vera, plegarias de los mbyá-guaraní de misiones,* published by Ediciones del Sol, 1984.

Regino, Juan Gregorio, "Cantares" from *No es eterna la muerte,* published by Editorial Diana, 1994. Translation from *Reversible Monuments: Contemporary Mexican Poetry,* edited by Mónica de la Torre and Michael Weigers. Copyright © 2002 by Copper Canyon Press. Reprinted with the permission of Copper Canyon Press, www.coppercanyonpress.org.

Rivera-Garza, Cristina, "Third World" from *Sin Puertas Visibles: An Anthology of Contemporary Poetry by Mexican Women,* bilingual edition, edited and translated by Jen Hofer, copyright © 2003. Reprinted by permission of the University of Pittsburgh Press.

Rodríguez, Reina María, "Twilight's Idol" from *Páramos,* published by Ediciones Union, 1995. Printed by permission of Reina María Rodríguez. Translation from *Violet Island and Other Poems,* translated by Kristin Dykstra and Nancy Gates Madsen, published by Green Integer, 2004. Reprinted by permission of Doug Messerli.

Rodríguez, Simón, "Social Virtues and Illuminations" from *Sociedades americanas*, edited by Oscar Rodríguez Ortiz, published by Fundación Biblioteca Ayacucho, 1990.

Rojas, Gonzalo, "You Shouldn't Copy Pound," "Qedeshím Qedeshóth" from *Gonzalo Rojas: Obra selecta*, edited by Marcelo Coddou, published by Fundación Biblioteca Ayacucho, 1997.

de Rokha, Pablo, "Song of the Old Male" from *Pablo de Rohka en breve*, edited by Naín Nómez, published by Editorial Universidad de Santiago, 2001.

Rosas de Oquendo, Mateo, "The Mestizo's Ballade" from *Poesía colonial hispanoamericana*, edited by Horacio Jorge Becco, published by Fundación Biblioteca Ayacucho, 1990.

Sabina, María, "Life" from *Vida de María Sabina: La sabia de los hongos* by Álvaro Estrada, published by Siglo XXI Editores, 1977; and from the recording by R. Gordon Wasson of María Sabina's chants in the Mazatec language, recorded by Folkways Records, 1957. Translation from Mazatec into Spanish by Álvaro Estrada. Reprinted courtesy of Álvaro Estrada. Translation from *María Sabina, Selections*, published by University of California Press, 2003. Copyright © 2003 by The Regents of the University of California. Translation reprinted courtesy of Henry Munn.

Saenz, Jaime, "Anniversary of a Vision" from *Immanent Visitor: Selected Poems of Jaime Saenz. A Bilingual Edition*, by Jaime Saenz, translated by Kent Johnson and Forest Gander, published by the University of California Press, 2002. Copyright © 2002 by The Regents of the University of California.

Sánchez Peláez, Juan, "From the Fleeting and Permanent," "Dark Bond" from *Toward an Image of Latin American Poetry, A Bilingual Anthology*, edited by Octavio Armand, published by Logbridge-Rhodes, Inc., 1982. Translation reprinted by permission of Naomi Lindstrom.

Silva, José Asunción, "Ars" from *El libro de los versos*, 1923. Courtesy of Fundación Editorial Epígrafe.

Silva Estrada, Alfredo, "Grape Harvests," "The Dwellers" from *Los moradores*, published by Monte Avila Editores, 1975.

Solar, Xul, "This Hades Is Fluid..." from *Xul Reader*. Copyright © by XUL/Ernesto Livon-Grosman, 1997.

Sor Juana Inés de la Cruz, "First Dream," "This Coloured Counterfeit That Thou Beholdest," "Tarry, Shadow of My Scornful Treasure," "Diuternal Infirmity of Hope" from *Mexican Poetry: An Anthology*. Copyright © 1989 by Octavio Paz and Samuel Beckett and published by Indiana University Press. "Villancico VIII" from *Obras completas*, Vols. 1–4, edited by Alfonso Méndez Plancarte (vols. 1–3) and Alberto G. Salceda (vol. 4), published by Fondo Cultura Económica, 1995.

Sousândrade, "The Wall Street Inferno" from *Sousândrade: Poesia*, edited by Augusto de Campos, published by Agir, 1966.

Storni, Alfonsina, "World of Seven Wells," "An Ear" from *Obras completas*, published by Editorial Losada, S.A., 2002.

Tablada, José Juan, "Three Haikus," "Ideogram Lantern," "Havana Impressions" from *Tres libros: Un día... (poemas sintéticos), Li-Po y otros poemas, el jarro de flores (disociaciones líricas)*, edited by Juan Velasco, published by Hiperión, 2000.

Thénon, Susana, "Poem with Simultaneous Translation Spanish–Spanish," "Nuptial Song" from *Ova completa*, published by Editorial Sudamericana, 1987.

Torres García, Joaquín, "América Invertida," "City with No Name" courtesy of the Museo Torres García and Cecilia de Torres Ltd., New York.

Tzotzil poets: Xunka' Utz'utz' Ni', "Prayer So My Man Won't Have to Cross the Line"; Loxa Jiménes Lópes, "Pexi Kola Magic"; María Ernándes Kokov, "The Talking Box Speaks"; Tonik Nibak, "Dance of the Perfumed Woman." These poems were first published in Tzotzil in the book *Conjuros y ebriedades, cantos de mujeres mayas*, copyright © 1998 by Ámbar Past. The Tzotzil Mayan texts were recorded on a tape recorder by Ámbar Past, then transcribed in Tzotzil by Xalik BakBolom. The translations from Tzotzil to Spanish are by Ámbar Past, and they also appeared in the book *Conjuros y ebriedades, cantos de mujeres mayas*, copyright © 1998 by Ámbar Past. The translations from Tzotzil to English are also by Ámbar Past and appeared first in *Incantations by Mayan Women*, published by Taller Leñateros in 2005. Copyright © by Ámbar Past, 2005. They are also included in the U.S. trade edition of *Incantations by Mayan Women*, published by Cinco Puntos Press, www.cincopuntos.com, in 2008.

Vallejo, César, all poems and translations from *The Complete Poetry: A Bilingual Edition* by César Vallejo, edited and translated by Clayton Eshleman, published by the University of California Press, 2007. Copyright © 2007 by The Regents of the University of California.

Varela, Blanca, all poems from *Canto villano: Poesía reunida, 1949–1983*, published by Fondo Cultura de Económica, 1996. "Currículum Vitae" translation from *American Poetry Review*, March/April 1987, Vol. 26, No. 2. Reprinted by permission of Eliot Weinberger.

Vianna Baptista, Josely, "A Sound of Ancient, Faded Flows" from *Nothing the Sun Could Not Explain: 20 Contemporary Brazilian Poets*, published by Sun and Moon Press, 1997. "Traces," "The Grail" from *Corpografia*, published by Iluminuras, 1992.

Vicuña, Cecilia, all poems reprinted by permission of Cecilia Vicuña.

Vigo, Edgardo Antonio, "Object-Poems" courtesy of Ernesto Livon-Grosman.

Vilariño, Idea, all poems from *Poesía completa*, published by Cal y Canto, 2006. "Poor World" translation from *Borzoi Anthology of Latin American Literature*,

Volume II, edited by Emir Rodriguez Monegal, published by Alfred A. Knopf, 1977. Reprinted by permission of Eliot Weinberger.

Villaurrutia, Xavier, "L.A. Nocturne: The Angels," "Nocturne: Fear" from *Nostalgia for Death*, copyright © 1953 by Fondo de Cultura Económica. Translation copyright © 1993 by Eliot Weinberger. Reprinted by permission of Copper Canyon Press, www.coppercanyonpress.org.

Zamora, Daisy, "Radio Sandino" from *Clean Slate: New & Selected Poems*, 1993. Translation reprinted by permission of Margaret Randall.

Zurita, Raúl, "Inri" reprinted by permission of Raúl Zurita. Translation reprinted by permission of William Rowe. "Desert Writing" from *La vida nueva*, published by Editorial Universitaria, Santiago, 1994. Courtesy of Raúl Zurita. "Sky Writing" from *Anteparaíso*, published by Editores Asociados, Santiago, 1982. Courtesy of Ana María Lopez.

Every effort has been made to trace and contact copyright holders. The publisher will be pleased to correct any mistakes or omissions in future editions.